# A HISTORY OF
# THE ROUMANIANS

PLATE I

TUDOR VLADIMIRESCU

# A HISTORY OF
# THE ROUMANIANS

## FROM ROMAN TIMES TO THE
## COMPLETION OF UNITY

by

## R. W. SETON-WATSON

ARCHON BOOKS
1963

*First published 1934*
*Reprinted by permission of the*
*Cambridge University Press*

*Library of Congress Catalog Card Number: 63-16553*
*Printed in the United States of America*

AMICIS

ULTRA SILVAM HABITANTIBUS

AC PRAECIPUE

NAPORENSIUM

URBI STUDIOQUE

CIVIS ET DOCTOR

# PREFACE

In 1920 I delivered courses of lectures on Roumanian history at King's College in the University of London, and portions of these were afterwards published in *History* and in the *Slavonic Review*. The lectures were then re-drafted and twice delivered in a new form—the last time in 1931. They gave the first impulse to the present volume, but it has been expanded and rewritten out of all recognition.

It is symptomatic of growing interest in a long neglected subject, that since 1918 no less than four admirable monographs on special aspects of Roumanian history have appeared in English—the diplomatic studies of Mr W. G. East and Professor T. E. Riker, Mr Ifor L. Evans's *The Agrarian Revolution in Roumania* and Dr D. Mitrany's *The Land and the Peasant in Roumania* (for the Carnegie Foundation)—to all of which I am in various ways indebted. None the less my own book may fairly claim to be the first attempt by any British writer to give a complete survey of Roumanian history from its obscure origins down to the achievement of national unity in our own day. But I cannot go farther without acknowledging my vast debt, and the abiding debt of every serious student for generations to come, to Professor Nicholas Iorga, of Bucarest University, to whose amazing vitality and industry we owe a whole library of general histories, monographs and collections of documents, ranging over the whole field of Near Eastern, Byzantine and Turkish history.

For many centuries Roumanian development was retarded and distorted by the interference of powerful neighbours to the south, north and west: and stress has therefore been laid upon the relations of the two Principalities with Turkey, the Empire, Hungary and Russia, and in modern times, upon Roumania's place in the Eastern Question. Above all, the Transylvanian problem, which provides the key to a right understanding of the Roumanian problem as a whole, has received very special attention: and within this framework will be found the first full account in English of the sad but highly interesting and instructive history of the Roumanian Orthodox and Uniate Churches. The concluding chapters deal with Roumania's rôle in the Balkan Wars, her neutrality, intervention and defeat in the World War, the final and dramatic achievement of national unity and the conclusion of peace with Hungary in 1920.

I have tried to produce a plain narrative, treating of high and contentious matters without fear or favour. To some, Roumanian history may seem obscure and often inglorious: but there is a certain dynamic force in its vicissitudes, and Europe cannot show any more striking example of the corroding effects of foreign rule, of the failure of a policy of systematic assimilation and of the gradual triumph of national sentiment over unfavourable circumstances.

I owe a very special debt of gratitude to the Roumanian Academy, from whose rich collection of historical portraits the illustrations of this volume have been reproduced, and to Professor George Oprescu, of the Stelian Museum in Bucarest, for invaluable help in their selection and preparation. I am also indebted for constant advice during the preparation of the book to my friends Mr D. N. Ciotori, of the Roumanian Legation in London, Mr E. D. Madge, Mr Allen Leeper and Sir Bernard Pares, and not least of all to my wife. But needless to say, none of them are in any way responsible either for my facts or for my opinions.

R. W. SETON-WATSON

21 *May*, 1934

# CONTENTS

# LIST OF ILLUSTRATIONS

# CHAPTER I

# ROUMANIAN ORIGINS

"That which thou sowest is not quickened, except it die."

Roumanian territory was originally inhabited by Scythians, Cimmerians and Getae, probably akin to the ancient Illyrians in the West, and so to all the earliest strata of Balkan peoples. These races, writes Professor Pârvan, the foremost Roumanian archaeologist, "drove back Iranian invaders eastwards and Celts to the west, and founded the greatest barbarian empire ever known in this part of Europe. The Getic kingdom of Burebista included Bohemia and Western Hungary, as well as Bessarabia and Bulgaria, but the Transylvanian Carpathians remained the basis of its power. Even the Roman conquests beyond the Eastern Alps and the Adriatic were not complete until Dacia had submitted".[1] The history of the Daco-Roman people, he points out, begins as early as the third century before Christ. Already under Burebista, the great king who was at the height of his power about 50 B.C., there was a steady infiltration of Roman citizens and traders, finding their way across the Julian Alps and down the Save and Danube valleys, but also through the heart of the Balkan peninsula—as is suggested by the fact that numerous coins of Apollonia and Dyrrachium have been discovered in Moldavia. Burebista was strong enough to threaten the Roman organisation of Thrace, and Caesar not long before his death appears to have contemplated an expedition to the Lower Danube. The civil wars that followed Caesar's death postponed all danger to Dacia from without, but the loosely-knit realm of Burebista soon fell a prey to internal dissensions, as a consequence of which the victorious Octavius was able to expel the Dacians from Thracian soil and even to send a punitive force across the Danube.

During the first century of our era the Romans consolidated their rule in Thrace and Moesia and left the Dacians unmolested on the northern bank of the river. It was not till the reign of Titus that serious hostilities broke out between them, and by this time Dacia again had a ruler of exceptional merit, Decebalus, "a worthy opponent of the Roman

[1] V. Pârvan, *Dacia*, p. 2.

power". After two Roman generals had suffered serious reverses, a
third, Julianus, forced his way to the Dacian capital, won a victory at
Tapae (in the east of the Banat), and forced him to sue Domitian for
peace. That emperor's defeat by the Marcomanni prevented him from
following up this success, and not merely did he leave Decebalus to all
intents and purposes independent, but in the end purchased immunity
from Dacian raids by the payment of an annual tribute. Meanwhile the
influx of Roman settlers steadily increased: the Dacian king welcomed
skilled workers, engineers and craftsmen of various kinds and constructed fortresses according to Roman technique. Even apart from
these newcomers, there were already "a sufficient number of natives
who understood the language, for letters to be written in Latin".[1]

With the accession of Trajan the humiliation of a tribute was speedily
rejected by the Romans. In A.D. 101 war broke out between Decebalus
and Trajan, who massed his army at Viminacium (in North-east Serbia),
crossed the Danube into the modern Banat and after a stubborn resistance dictated peace in the Dacian capital, Sarmizegethusa. Decebalus retained his crown, but had to accept a Roman garrison and a
civil adviser, corresponding perhaps to the first Resident appointed to
an Indian native state. To secure his communication with the newly
conquered province Trajan built his celebrated bridge across the Danube
—the work of the architect Apollodorus of Damascus, but the strategic
point which he chose for it was no longer Viminacium, but a point below
the cataracts of the Iron Gates, near the pleasant modern town of Turnu
Severin, from whence there was easy access to the heart of Oltenia, and
to Sarmizegethusa up the valley of the Cerna. In 105–6 war broke out
a second time, Decebalus made desperate efforts to shake off the yoke,
and Trajan, warned of the danger by special messengers, embarked at
Ancona and hastened back to the Danube, equally determined to crush
all resistance finally. Forcing his way through the Carpathian passes,
he took the capital by storm after a prolonged siege. Decebalus escaped
in disguise, organised a fierce guerilla warfare, but was at last made
prisoner and saved himself by suicide from the fate of gracing a Roman
triumph. This triumph, when it came, was to be immortalised beyond
all others by the Column of Trajan in Rome and its long series of reliefs
of Dacian captives and victorious legionaries.[2] In modern times these

[1] V. Pârvan, *Dacia*, p. 159.
[2] Another monument of victory is the great circular ruin of the "Tropaeum
Traiani" at Adam Klisi, in the Dobrogea.

memories have fired the imagination of the Roumanian race and are treasured as a kind of ancestral charter, in which the rival claims of Roman and of Dacian origin are blended and confused.

The Dacians had not been a mere collection of barbarous tribes, but had a rudimentary culture of their own, and "a well-marked social and economic structure".[1] They did not therefore accept Roman rule willingly, and many of their warriors withdrew to the free north and coalesced with the still migrant German tribes. For this reason Trajan organised the new province of Dacia on very special lines, bringing large numbers of colonists from every part of the Empire, and technicians to develop the rich gold, silver and salt mines of the future Transylvania. The inscriptions which survive show that some came from Greece and Asia Minor, some from Spain, some perhaps from Persia and Egypt, for there are altars to Celtic divinities, while on the other hand the cults of Mithras and Isis are represented. Trajan's main object seems to have been to erect a strong barrier against the wild tribes already stirring in the steppes of what is now Southern Russia. Dacia, then, was above all a mountain *massif*, a fortress intended to dominate the Wallachian plain in one direction and the valley of the Theiss in the other: but these were neglected and only thinly populated. A wall was built from the Carpathians to the mouth of the Dniester, near the modern Cetatea Alba (Akkerman): and the inhabitants of all that lay between it and the river Olt were merely in a loose tributary relation to the Romans. The capital town, Sarmizegethusa, on the south-west fringe of the great sickle-shaped Carpathian range, was rechristened Ulpia Traiana: Apulum (Alba Julia), Napoca (Cluj), and Porolissum (near Gherla) were also towns of some importance. Under Hadrian Dacia was divided into an Upper and Lower province, and the name of "Dacia Felix" became current: under Marcus Aurelius it was even split into three sections, though a "concilium trium Daciarum" continued to meet at the common capital.

It is no part of my present purpose to sketch the process by which the provincials of Dacia extended the traditions and culture of Rome towards the north-east, building upon an essentially agricultural basis, and no less certainly intermingling from the very first with the native population. It must suffice to state that the latest results of archaeological, ethnographic and linguistic research show that the process of colonisation and penetration was much more gradual, more prolonged

[1] V. Pârvan, *Dacia*, p. 189.

and more effective than was supposed by earlier writers. A new and transformed nation was already in the making, when the Empire fell into decay and was driven on to the defensive. Unfavourable conditions arrested the process for many centuries, but the elements remained, and the emergence of the blade of wheat from the rich native soil of the Wallachian plain is the symbol of a mystery which we must accept by an act of faith, since we cannot hope to explain it by rational methods.

The middle of the third century witnessed those first mysterious migrations of the peoples which were gradually to transform the ancient world and lay the foundations of modern Europe: and it was but natural that the pressure should first become acute upon the Danubian frontier. It was no mere accident that the Empire in its hour of danger should have been saved by a succession of able soldiers and administrators whose native province was more immediately threatened. The Illyrian emperors, from Claudius II to Diocletian and Constantine, seemed to be transferring the Roman world's centre of gravity from Italy to the Eastern Adriatic and the Middle Danube. Carnuntum (near Vienna on the Danube), Emona (Laibach), Siscia (Sisak), Sirmium (Mitrovica), Aquincum (Buda), Singidunum (Belgrade) were not merely strategic outposts, but flourishing centres of trade and culture.

Maximin, writes Professor Iorga, illustrates in his own person "the incessant, imperceptible colonisation", in an inverse direction, of which Dacia was already the object by the end of the preceding century. "The parents of the future Caesar, a Goth and an Alan, come from 'Scythia', the land where one barbarian follows the other, to Roman Thrace, where they devoted themselves to a pastoral life: the 'Life of Claudius' shows that such incomers generally brought with them their numerous flocks of cattle, sheep and horses. The son, who has already acquired a fair mastery of Latin in these Roman or Romanised surroundings, attends to his father's herds. Eager for action and booty, he becomes a soldier, a centurion, and rises ever higher in the military career: after loyal service he leaves the army, and obtains a grant of land in the remote Thracian district where his childish years were spent."[1] And yet the whirlpool of great events was to suck him in and raise him to dispute, to rally, and to disaggregate an empire. To him and to several of his successors, whose careers were not altogether dissimilar, there can have been no hard and fast line between the half-assimilated hordes

[1] *Gesch. des rumänischen Volkes,* I, p. 48.

from the north and the rude provincials, to whom mixed marriages were an every day occurrence and whose minds must have been bewildered by a babel of rival religious creeds, all of them in obvious decay and scarcely enjoying even lip-service from the ruling class. Dacia was by now undergoing a process which was already scarcely less familiar in Gaul than in Moesia, at the two opposite ends of Europe.

As the Gothic menace grew, Decius, himself a native of Syrmia, rallied the forces of the Empire and won the title of "Restitutor Daciae" by defeating the invaders near Nicopolis on the Danube. But his triumph was short-lived: in 251 he and his son went down fighting in a great battle at Abritum, which has been roughly identified as in a swamp of the modern Dobrogea. The Goths on their side had suffered so severely as to lose for a time all powers of serious offensive: but a decade had not passed before civil disorder reduced the Empire to dire extremity and positively invited invasion. A last memorable rally was achieved by the Emperor Claudius, who won a decisive victory over the Goths at Naissus (Niš in Serbia) in 268, after they had penetrated into the very heart of Moesia Superior and seemed about to establish their strategic control over the entire peninsula. But Claudius, at once a great soldier and a just and constructive statesman, died prematurely after the briefest of reigns, and it became obvious that the situation could only be saved by a bold policy of cutting losses and a reorganisation of Empire strategy and defence. This was the task undertaken by Claudius's successor Aurelian, yet another successful and ambitious soldier of Syrmian peasant stock. In his brief reign of barely five years he took decisions which were to leave a permanent mark on history—checking the advance of the Alemanni and the secession of Gaul and Britain, destroying the short-lived empire of Palmyra, and giving to the city of Rome a circuit of walls more imposing and enduring than those of Servius Tullus. It was Aurelian, then, who also decided the future of the Roumanian race by his decision to evacuate Dacia in the year 271. He had come to the conclusion that the province formed too exposed a salient amid the waves of advancing barbarism, and that its strategic defence could not easily be combined with that of the wide Pannonian plain, in which the mighty Danube formed a natural boundary. The legions and officials were therefore withdrawn to the south of the river, and the name of Dacia was transferred to Upper Moesia (corresponding roughly to the central portions of modern Serbia). There is of course nothing that can be described as evidence regarding the extent of the abandonment. It is safe to assume that the wealthier settlers withdrew, but the great mass of the population remained behind. That the traces of Roman rule are scantier in the Roumanian lands than in other provinces is partly explained by the relative short-ness of full Roman occupation, but above all by the prolonged period of anarchy that followed.

Henceforth the territory which now forms Greater Roumania stood exposed to the shock of repeated invasions from the East. Beginning with the Goths and Gepids, almost all the many peoples who flooded into Southern Europe between the third and tenth centuries passed first over Roumanian soil. But it is to be noted that in every case the ob-jective of invasion lay beyond: the glittering plunder of Byzantium and of the rich Italian cities beckoned the barbarians onward. The Dacia of Trajan was a mere stage on the road, and nothing is more surprising than that the Goths in particular should have left virtually no trace throughout the territory in question. The absence of Gothic words in the Roumanian language has sometimes been used to prove the lack of continuity of the Roumanian race on the northern bank of the Danube: but to such arguments, admittedly resting upon mere conjecture, it may fairly be replied that if the Daco-Romans had in the fourth century already been concentrated south of the Danube, Gothic influences upon their language would have been quite inevitable, in view of the extent to which the Goths established themselves in what we now know as Bulgaria.

## THE BARBARIAN INVASIONS

As the Goths moved steadily onwards, their place was filled by the first Slavonic tribes, who permeated the whole Balkan peninsula and sub-merged more than one city of note, such as Philippi and Boroea. Follow-ing again upon their heels in the sixth century, the Avars settled in the Pannonian plain and penetrated to the Adriatic coast, only to be deci-mated and submerged in their turn by the advancing Croats and Serbs in the seventh century. In all this early period the fate of the native populations is quite obscure: conditions were of course rendered alto-gether fluid by constant invasion, yet it seems probable that the pro-vincials were already akin with the natives farther north, and constantly intermarrying with them. At the same time the towns rapidly decayed, the highways became unsafe and neglected, and rural life was primitive in the extreme. Many centuries were to elapse before the foundations of ordered government could be established. "The Slavs.", says Professor Iorga, "had to come in order to render possible the formation of a Roman people in the East."[1] In face of common dangers, the two peoples seem to have fraternised, abandoning the great plains for the remoter Carpathian valleys: and it may be supposed that the numerous Slav place-names in Roumanian territory date from this period.

Much more important than the Avar invasion was that of the Bulgars, a kindred Ural-Altaic tribe who swept across the plains of what we now call Moldavia in the second half of the seventh century and soon established themselves firmly between the Danube and the Balkan range, taking as their first capital Preslav—the already Slavised Marcianopolis. The Bulgarian empire reached its zenith in the ninth century under the savage Krum and that Eastern edition of Clovis the Frank, the politic and calculating Tsar Boris, who accepted Christianity at the hands of the Slav apostles, Cyril and Methodius. It is, however, to be noted that the Daco-Roman population, which was subjugated by the Bulgars as they passed through their territory, had already accepted Christianity before their arrival—though probably in the same imperfect and superficial manner as Scotland in the days of St Ninian.

In passing, it is interesting to note that most of the essential words relating to church observance are of Latin derivation. *Dumnezeu* (Dominus Deus), *pagan, crestin, biserica* and *tâmpla* for Church—which are thus dated to a period later than Constantine the Great, when basilicas and temples first acquired such use—*altar, cruce, mormânt, cimitir: preot, sânt* (*sînt* or *sfânt*) and *sânta scriptură* for Saint and Holy Scripture: *inger* (angelus) *martur, drac* (draco) for Devil: *eremit* and *eretic: Dumineca* (Sunday), *Florii* (Palm Sunday), *Rusalii* (Whitsun): *botez, cuminecare* and *ajun* for baptism, communion and fasting: *căsătorie* for marriage, and *cuninie*, the nuptial crown worn at the Orthodox marriage ceremony: *Tatal Nostru* and *Crez* for Our Father and the Creed. It is no less characteristic of the situation in those early times that most of the words for ecclesiastical dignities and for vestments should be Greek—*mitropolit, arhimandrit, arhipastor, episcop, energumen, eparhie, epitrafil, mineiu* (mass book), *octoih* (hymn book).

\*     \*     \*     \*

During the eighth and ninth centuries the Bulgars extended their sway, not merely over the future Roumanian principalities on the Lower Danube, but also over much of Moesia and of the central Pannonian

[1] *Gesch. des rumänischen Volkes*, I, p. 63.

plain. They thus became the neighbours of those ephemeral Slav states which preceded the Magyar conquest, and in particular of the Great Moravian empire, whose capital was at Nitra in Western Slovakia, but which at its height stretched far to the south and to the north also. This explains the close contact between the Bulgarian and Moravian courts at the time of the Slav Apostles—so puzzling to the modern reader who thinks in terms of twentieth-century geography and cannot conceive of Bulgaria and Moravia as contiguous. Here too lies the clue to the confusing habit, adopted by the pioneers of antiquarian and philo-logical studies a century ago, of using as convertible terms "Old Bul-garian", "Old Slovene", "Old Slavonic", to describe the language in which the two apostles composed the first Slav liturgy and for which they prepared the famous Cyrilline alphabet.

The first development of Slav Christianity lies beyond the purpose of this volume, but it is well to point out at the very outset that the Roumanians, though already Christianised in a somewhat superficial manner, owed to their early subjection to Bulgar rule the adoption of a Bulgaro-Slav rite which they did not shake off till the middle of the seventeenth century. We shall see that, as late as the middle of the nine-teenth, Roumanian liturgical books were still being printed in Slavonic characters. There is no evidence whatsoever as to the exact period at which the Bulgarian rite was adopted by the Roumanians, though it seems reasonable to suppose that it took place under Boris or Simeon. That it provided a strong rival influence to that of Byzantine hellenism, or in a certain sense a buffer between the two, cannot be doubted.

It is customary to claim that the long centuries of barbarian invasion destroyed the continuity of the original Roman element. But such an assertion rests upon dangerous theories of racial purity, long since aban-doned by all serious students of Roumanian origins. All that can be safely affirmed is that a population in which a strong pre-Roman native element was transfused and blended by Roman blood and influences, was submerged by a series of fresh invasions until the original admixture created under Roman rule found itself driven to the remoter mountain-ous regions. We are already in the domain of keen controversy, but whatever deductions may be drawn, nothing can obscure the essential fact of the racial and linguistic survival of something approaching a common stock in the bend of the Carpathians, in the Pindus and the remoter valleys of Epirus, and of minor fragments in Istria and Northern Dalmatia.

In the closing years of the ninth century (896 is the traditionally accepted, but somewhat arbitrary, date) the Magyars—another tribe of Ural-Altaic stock, akin to Hun, Gepid, Avar and Turk—crossed the Carpathians, broke to fragments the loosely knit Moravian state, and, by occupying the old paradise of the Huns, the great plains of the Danubian basin which they hold to this day, drove a permanent wedge between the Northern and Southern Slavs. At first retaining their nomadic habits, they seemed bent on following the track of earlier invaders into Italy and Germany. But Otto the Great's decisive victory near Augsburg in 955 checked their marauding raids and drove them to rest content with Pannonia as their home. Late in the ninth century they too had accepted Christianity, but this time definitely from Rome rather than Byzantium: and their Duke Stephen in 1000 accepted the kingly Apostolic Crown from Pope Sylvester and laid the foundations of the royal power on mainly feudal lines. Early in the eleventh century, as we shall see, the Magyars established their rule over Transylvania also, which till then had formed several isolated and loosely knit duchies, whose rulers were probably of Bulgarian blood. In 1102 they conquered Croatia, which then included the northern part of Dalmatia as far as the river Narenta, and which henceforth for just over eight centuries maintained a special autonomous position under the Holy Crown of St Stephen. It is not until the beginning of the thirteenth century that history breaks its long silence and reveals the existence of a "Vlach" or Roumanian nation.

The Magyars were the last of the conquering hordes to establish permanent settlements in Europe. Their successors, the Petchenegs, were no less formidable in their day, but their name has vanished as completely as that of the Avars and Gepids. They seem to have perished in internecine warfare, in strife with Byzantium, and in quarrels skilfully fomented by the empire with other neighbours. There remained yet another Asiatic tribe, the Cumans, who followed the Petchenegs across the Moldavian plains and were eventually welcomed as settlers in Hungary by King Béla III.

From this brief outline of known events—stripped so far as possible of controversial statements—it is only too obvious that the straw with which the historian is expected to construct his bricks is quite unusually scanty. The evidence is at best mainly circumstantial. With its aid two main theses have been constructed, which in their most extreme forms may be summarised as follows.

The Roumanians claim that they are the true descendants of Trajan's colonists, that Transylvania is the cradle of the race, and that historic continuity has never been lost. In their view the withdrawal during Aurelian's reign only affected the military and official classes; the bulk of the population remained behind, and though doubtless much reduced through long centuries of anarchy and modified by intermarriage with various invading tribes, managed to preserve its racial identity, withdrawing during periods of extreme stress into the remote fastnesses of the Carpathians.

The Magyars in their turn argue that continuity is a myth; that the abandonment of Dacia by the Roman element was complete; that in any case Romanisation of the provinces cannot really have struck very deep in so short a period as 163 years, and that of the colonists who originally crossed the Danube, the great mass were not of Roman blood at all. Arguing from the large admixture of Slav elements in the modern Roumanian language, they lay greater stress upon their Slavonic than upon their Latin origin. They point to the absence of any records showing them to have occupied their present territory during the Dark Ages, and proceed to argue that the Roumanians of to-day are descended from nomadic Balkan tribes who only crossed to the north bank of the Danube in the thirteenth century, and then gradually overflowed into Transylvania, in response to the welcome extended by the Hungarian kings to foreign settlers.

Into the controversy between Magyar and Roumanian certain Slav and German writers have intruded. In all four cases it is easy to detect an *arrière-pensée*. The Roumanian from obvious pride of race is anxious to prove his untarnished Roman descent, and hopes thereby to establish his claim as the earliest surviving owner of the soil. The Magyar, in his turn, claims to have arrived in Transylvania at least three centuries earlier than the Roumanians, and, engrossed as ever in his theories of historical right and tradition, jumps to the political conclusion *prior tempore, potior jure*, which is to justify his denial of political equality to the Roumanian helots on Hungarian soil. To strengthen his thesis still further, he sets out to prove that even in Wallachia they are merely thirteenth-century newcomers, which, if once established, would of course destroy for ever all idea of continuity in Transylvania. Led by this further theory, he is only too ready to exaggerate the rôle of the Roumanian element in the Asenid (or Bulgaro-Vlach) empire of the thirteenth century; and here he is at once met by the Slav, whose main desire is to minimise that rôle, to emphasise the essentially Bulgarian character of that empire, and even to throw doubt upon the Vlach origin of its dynasty. To the Slav, then, it is important to prove Roumanian continuity on the north bank; and, rendered confident by the generally admitted religious and linguistic influences of the Slavs upon the Roumanians, he has no reason to look askance at the idea of continuity in Transylvania. The German, again, infected by the Magyar theory of *prior tempore*, would feel happier if he could establish a priority on the part of the Saxon settlers in Transylvania, or even a more or less contemporaneous arrival.

Let us try for a moment to shake off these rival *arrière-pensées* and weigh the probabilities in the scales of historical fact and commonsense. In the first place, we may safely dismiss such arguments as are based upon the absence of early records. Much has been made by Magyar historians of the fact that the first charter containing any reference to Roumanian inhabitants of Transylvania dates from the year 1210. But here it is necessary to point out that the same profound obscurity surrounds the history of *all* the inhabitants of Transylvania till the beginning of the thirteenth century. The earliest document in existence only dates from 1165.[1]

The lack of records is due to a double cause—that throughout these south-eastern territories really ordered life can only be said to begin after the twelfth century, and that the terrible Mongol invasion which devastated Hungary in 1241 is responsible for a wholesale destruction of such records as existed.

Meanwhile it is obvious that the Roumanian claim of pure Roman blood is untenable: in 163 years the old Dacian element cannot have been wiped out, and must clearly form the lowest stratum of Roumanian nationality. At the same time it is impossible to travel very long in Roumania, and *especially* in Transylvania, without coming across strikingly Latin types among the peasantry; and the Roumanian language, for all its Slav admixture, is essentially Latin in texture.[2] That the new blood introduced by Trajan was very mixed, is less material to the argument; for our own day has shown the amazing and inexplicable capacity of a great modern nation not merely to assimilate, but

[1] With regard to the Maramureş district, only three documents exist dating from before 1241.

[2] It is worth noting, in passing, that almost all words relating to pastoral pursuits are Latin: *bou, vaca, vitel, taur, ariete, cal (cavallus), iapa (equa), porc, capra, oae (ovis), pecurar (pecorarius), pastor.*

even to evolve a new type out of alien elements. Anyone who has friends among the hyphenated Slavs or Latins of the United States will know what I mean, though the explanation seems to defy physiologists, psychologists and climatologists alike.

The Roumanians, it is safe to say, are Roumanised Dacians, infiltrated with Slav and to a very much lesser degree Tatar blood. The attempt to treat Roman and Roumanian as interchangeable terms was a not unnatural exaggeration from a period when criticism was in its cradle, and when past glories were conjured up to atone for an inglorious present of feudal oppression. The chroniclers of the eighteenth century, of whom we shall have to speak later, were gallant pioneers of patriotic revival, but lacked the first rudiments of historical criticism. We may safely endorse the phrase of Professor Xenopol, "the Roumanians are in the east Daco-Romans transformed by Slavs, just as the French are in the west Celto-Romans transformed by Germans".[1]

But what of the theory that they only reached their present home in the thirteenth century? Indirect arguments in its support may be found in two directions. The Magyar language, while full of words which it took over from the autochthonous Slavs of Hungary, has comparatively few traces of Roumanian—the inference being that there were not many Roumanians when the Magyars arrived. To this it may be replied that it was in Pannonia, not in Transylvania, where the Magyar language took definite shape, and that the Roumanians were able to avoid contact by retiring into their mountains, whereas the Slavs of Central Hungary had no mountains into which to retire. The Roumanians undoubtedly preserved their nomadic habits to a very late date, as is proved by the existence of Vlach colonies in Moravia (the so-called "Little Wallachia" —long since completely Slavised), in the county of Orava in Northern Slovakia, in Istria (where the last fragments of dialect make the district a paradise for philologists), and among the Morlachs (or Sea-Vlachs) of Northern Dalmatia. The primitive Vlach communities of the Pindus— shepherds who migrate every summer to the high mountains with their flocks—enable us to study the habits and customs of their nomadic ancestors in the Dark Ages.

It is curious to note in passing that all the chief place names of towns and rivers in Wallachia are Slav—Moldava, Bistriţa, Ialomiţa, Dumboviţa, Olteniţa, Craiova, Tîrgovişte, Zlatna, Ocna, Rîmnic, Trnava.

A document of 1426 prohibits the Hungarian nobles from intro-

[1] *Histoire des Roumains*, I, p. 130.

ducing "Walachos de partibus extraneis pro nutriendis animalibus et pecudibus". But this after all does not prove that *all* Roumanians were nomads, and indeed according to Simon Kéza, one of the earliest Magyar chroniclers (*circa* 1285) the Székels when they first arrived found an alphabet in use among the Roumanians.

But the weakness of the whole theory soon begins to emerge, if we ask its authors to explain what on their showing became of the Roumanians during the period of nine centuries which elapsed between their withdrawal by Aurelian and their reappearance as a budding state in the thirteenth century. It cannot be maintained that they continued to inhabit Northern Moesia after it was re-christened Dacia; for we know that province to have been submerged by Slav invasions and to have re-emerged long before the period in question as one of the most purely Slavonic states in Europe. There is probably no other Roman province in Europe where so many important towns so completely lost their former character and even name. Thus the very theorists who have banished the Roumanians from Transylvania for lack of records, are driven to admit an even more complete and far more perplexing lack of records regarding the Roumanians in their alleged Balkan home.

But quite apart from this, the theory involves six quite distinct stages of emigration—first, the settlement of Dacia by the Romans; second, complete withdrawal to the south of the Danube and eventually to the Pindus region; third, a re-settlement by the Roumanians in Moesia and other Slavised Balkan territories; fourth, a return of these populations to the north of the Danube through Wallachia into Transylvania, in the early thirteenth century; fifth, a re-emigration from Transylvania into Wallachia at the close of the same century; sixth, the gradual migration of Roumanians from the south into Transylvania ever since that time. This last process is the only one of the whole chain which is susceptible of complete historic proof.

Without desiring to dogmatise on a subject which has been rightly described as "an enigma of the Middle Ages", I venture to think that a much more *logical* and *simple* explanation is provided by the assumption that the modern Roumanians, who fall into two main groups—the so-called Daco-Romans and Macedo-Roumanians—owe their survival in each case to the shelter provided by high mountain ranges, inhospitable and difficult of access in early times—in the south the Pindus, in the north the Carpathians. Transylvania stands out as a mountainous island on the physical map of Europe, surrounded on three sides by great plains. What more natural than that it should serve as a refuge during the long centuries of invasion, and that the survivors should issue forth into the plains when at last the tide of invasion began to subside?

The theory that the Roumanians recrossed to the northern bank of the Danube in the thirteenth century rests upon the further theory that they were the dominant influence in the second Bulgarian empire, which certainly owed its origin to the revolt of Vlach shepherds in the Rhodope, led by the brothers Peter and John Asen, but which might not have crystallised or attained such importance, but for the almost simultaneous eclipse of Byzantine power by the Latin crusaders. The greater the rôle played by the Vlachs in the new state, the more inexplicable becomes their abandonment of it in favour of new settlements in the Wallachian plains, all the more so because these plains were still at least partially inhabited by pagan Cuman and Tatar tribes. Moreover, their emigration must have coincided more or less with the terrible Mongol invasion, from which Bulgaria was immune. Every motive points against their selecting such a moment to move up into the danger area. If the Magyar theory be accepted (and, incidentally, if the statement of the earliest Magyar chronicler, the "Anonymous Notary of King Béla", be rejected as mythical), an immense tract of country, comprising most of present-day Roumania, must have been for centuries without masters —a kind of No Man's Land. Hunfalvy, probably the ablest of the controversialists, has no better explanation to offer than that Transylvania, in particular, was a neutral territory, where Magyars and Petchenegs (a Mongol tribe which survived into the eleventh century) exercised hunting rights, but where the Bulgarians were excluded. This is hardly convincing.

But the decisive argument against re-immigration from the south of the Danube is to be found in the religious history of South-eastern Europe—which is not much less obscure than the political, but none the less offers certain concrete data. Far too little is known of the circumstances under which the Roumanians became Christian, for us to base any very definite arguments upon the specifically Latin form of ecclesiastical phraseology. But it is quite certain that one of the early Bulgarian tsars (probably Boris or Simeon) imposed the Slavonic rite used by the Christianised Bulgars upon the Roumanians, and that the Roumanians employed this rite until the seventeenth century. It is also certain that the Roumanians had no regular episcopate or distinct church organisation till the fourteenth century, but owned the ecclesiastical jurisdiction of the Bulgarian patriarchate. After the fall of the first Bulgarian state the victorious Eastern Emperor Basil reorganised the Bulgarian Church, establishing its centre at Ochrida, but hellenising the patriarchate and most of its suffragan sees (1018). There is documentary evidence to show that the Roumanians, as late as the second half of the fifteenth century, under Stephen the Great, still recognised the ecclesiastical jurisdiction of Ochrida.

Now the Asenid (or second Bulgarian) empire, in which we are asked to believe that the Roumanians predominated, did not recognise Ochrida, but re-established its own independent patriarchate, this time at Tirnovo. If, then, the founders of Wallachia had come from the territory of that empire, it is to be presumed that they would have recognised Tirnovo rather than Ochrida. And if, again, it be argued that the emigrants came from farther west in the peninsula than the jurisdiction of Tirnovo extended (and this of course involves their crossing Serbia, for which there is not a shadow of evidence), it is necessary to point out that throughout Macedonia and Thessaly the liturgy in universal use since 1018 was *Greek*, not *Slavonic*, and that the emigrants would therefore have brought a Greek, not a Slav, rite with them. In point of fact their liturgy remained Slav during the first three centuries of existence in national states. To my mind the jurisdiction of Ochrida deals the final blow to the theory of re-immigration, but it none the less remains a mystery, though an established fact. The only explanation forthcoming is that it rested on the rights exercised by the see of Prima Justiniana (i.e. Ochrida) over the left bank of the Danube, in accordance with a Bull of the Emperor Justinian himself (535). It seems now generally admitted that Prima Justiniana is not identical with Ochrida at all, but was somewhere near Skoplje[1]; but this does not affect the fact that its identity was universally accepted in the thirteenth century, and indeed till long after the period to which these arguments apply. The Bull itself is now regarded as a forgery, but of course only on the basis of modern critical objections, such as were unknown to earlier centuries: this is only one among many instances of an ecclesiastical claim resting upon forged charters whose genuine character remained unquestioned till quite modern times.

It will be seen that the methods inevitably adopted by the historian in his enquiry into Roumanian origins differ widely from those applicable to the early period in any other European country, even Russia or

[1] Xenopol, *Un Énigme du Moyen Âge*, p. 69.

the Balkans. We are dealing with perhaps the most obscure corner of all Western history. Even with the thirteenth century, when we at last begin to feel solid ground beneath our feet, it is by no means possible to provide a clear narrative of the foundation of the two principalities of Wallachia and Moldavia. The initial dates of 1290 and 1349, uncritically accepted by earlier historians, are now generally regarded as still more arbitrary than the dates of 678 and 896 ascribed to the Bulgarian and Magyar states. In both cases the impetus for their formation came from the north and west, and not from across the Danube, and the clues will therefore be found in a brief survey of Hungarian history and foreign policy in the thirteenth century.

Meanwhile, it may help the reader to visualise the unique obscurity of Roumanian history, if he is here reminded that we are reduced to the merest speculation and conjecture with regard to the contemporaries of Henry III of England and St Louis of France.

# CHAPTER II

# THE BEGINNINGS OF THE PRINCIPALITIES

"Völker verrauschen,
Namen verklingen,
Finstre Vergessenheit
Breitet die dunkelnachtenden Schwingen
Über ganzen Geschlechtern aus."

SCHILLER.

In order to obtain a clue to the process which led to the first state forma-
tions among the Roumanians, it is necessary to consider very briefly
the main lines of evolution in the Central Danubian basin. The history
of Pannonia was radically changed by the coming of the Magyars at the
close of the ninth century; the loosely knit Moravian state collapsed; a
wedge was driven in among the various Slav settlements of the great
plain, and the newcomers, altogether alien in race, customs and religion, entrenched themselves in a position of wonderful strategic
strength which was to ensure political predominance over their neighbours throughout the next thousand years.

For some generations after the conquest the Magyars remained
heathen and retained their nomadic habits, constantly raiding the
Alpine provinces and the Italian marches, and penetrating into Bohemia
and Southern Germany. The defeat inflicted upon them by Otto the
Great near Augsburg in 955 was a decisive check to the nomadic habit,
and the plains of the Middle Danube proved an ideal home for a nation
of born horsemen. By the close of the tenth century they were already
exposed to the same process of Christianisation which marks the early
history of the Goths, Franks and other invaders. Missionaries came
both from Germany and from Poland, one of whose princesses became
the wife of Géza: but the main credit rests with St. Adalbert, or Vojtěch,
of Bohemia, who finally won over the prince and baptised his only son
Stephen. The reign of Stephen (997–1038) gave a permanent directive
to Hungarian evolution for centuries to come. With him not merely
did Christianity triumph beyond the possibility of a relapse; but his
acceptance of a royal crown from Pope Sylvester in the year 1000 was
a check to Byzantine influence on the Middle Danube and identified the

dynasty with allegiance to the Roman See and zeal for Catholic interests in South-eastern Europe. The Holy Crown of St Stephen acquired with the passage of time a mystical meaning in the constitutional
theory of Hungary and became the symbol of national unity. At the
same time, Stephen, by his policy of welcoming foreign settlers and
according them special privileges within the framework of the state,
fixed a tradition of supranational tolerance which was to unite many
different races in a common loyalty, and was not seriously disturbed
until the nineteenth century, when for the first time an attempt was made
to identify the broader name of Hungarian with "the ruling Magyar
race". "Treat newcomers well", wrote the great king in a letter of
advice to his son, "and hold them in honour, for they bring fresh knowledge and arms into the country: they are an ornament and support of
the throne, for a country where only one language and one custom prevail, is weak and fragile" (Regnum unius linguae uniusque moris im-
becille et fragile est). Acting on this advice, his successors for many
generations did not hesitate to copy Slav and German institutions, to
rely upon German settlers for the growth of an urban middle class, and
to leave the defence of the southern frontier very largely in Roumanian
and Serbian hands.

After an interlude of civil dissension and German interference,
Hungary's consolidation made rapid strides towards the close of the
eleventh and in the opening decades of the twelfth centuries, notably
under her two great kings, St Ladislas and Koloman (1077–1095–1114).
The most durable achievement of the latter's reign was his acquisition
of Croatia by a judicious mixture of conquest, diplomacy and inheritance: and the crown of Zvonimir was henceforth to remain for eight
centuries united to that of St Stephen (1102–1918). Through this union
Hungary aspired to the control of the whole Dalmatian coast and so
became involved in a series of no less than twenty wars with the
Venetian republic.

It followed logically that she should have designs upon the still
embryonic states that were now forming in the interior of the peninsula,
and in particular upon Bosnia and Serbia, whose medieval names of
Rascia (Raška) and Rama figure among the titles of the Hungarian
crown. This, again, brought her into repeated conflict with Byzantium,
which had its last period of expansion northward during the second and
third quarters of the eleventh century.

Meanwhile Hungary was forced to look eastwards no less than southwards, owing to the constant menace of the nomadic Cumans and Petchenegs, two tribes which were as yet heathen and formidable, but like the Avars were in the end destined to be swallowed up by the surrounding populations. Considerable traces of the Cumans are still to be found in the plain of the Tisza, to the south-east of Budapest, and indeed the so-called districts of the Jazygians and Cumans, originally established by the deliberate policy of the Árpád dynasty, retained their separate privileges as late as 1848.

The anarchic and unsettled conditions which as yet prevailed along the whole lower course of the Danube, and the permanent danger of invasion which resulted, forced upon Hungary a forward policy in all those regions and in the first instance in Transylvania, to which geography has given a very distinct character and identity of its own, which makes it stand out boldly from any physical map of Europe. On the south and east its boundaries are the summits of the great Carpathian chain: on the north it ceases where the river Somes (Szamos) prepares to enter the great plain on its way to join the Tisza: on the west another high mountain barrier—from Bihar to Abrud—separates it from the Central Hungarian plain. Inside these limits Transylvania is an undulating country, fertile, well-watered, well supplied with mineral resources and full of natural beauty. Its very name is in some sense a programme: for "the land beyond the forest" implies or assumes that association with the lands lying to the west of it, which has lasted straight on to the twentieth century. It is, indeed, the projection of some medieval *Drang nach Osten*.

In the first years of the eleventh century the newly crowned King Stephen of Hungary reduced Transylvania to submission, its prince, Gelu or Gyula—variously claimed as Roumanian or Bulgarian by race —perishing in the struggle. For the next two centuries it was a common practice to nominate a prince of the Hungarian reigning family as duke or governor of Transylvania, as indeed in the case of Croatia also. The twelfth and last appears to have been the son of Béla IV in 1260, after which there grew up the office of Voivode, which was at least as much military as administrative.

During the eleventh and twelfth centuries Hungary strengthened her hold upon Transylvania, erected such key fortresses as Torda and Dej, established a bishopric between 1103 and 1113 at the former Alba Julia (Belgrad or Gyulafehérvár)[1] and introduced the religious orders,

---

[1] The "White city of Gyula".

notably the Cistercians at the famous monastery of Kercz (Carta) on the Olt, long since a ruin. By the end of this period a county administration appears to have been established on the same lines as in Hungary proper. But the country is scantily populated, and exposed to inroads from the wild semi-nomadic Cuman and Tatar tribes which inhabit Northern Moldavia and the boundless steppes beyond: and the policy of successive kings is to attract colonists from the West, who will at once protect the frontier and bring the deserted land under cultivation. Already Koloman and Stephen II in the first three decades of the twelfth century began to settle Magyar colonists—the so-called Székelys or Siculi[1]—whom an ancient but almost certainly erroneous tradition, lasting till our own day, regarded as descendants of Attila and his Huns. Not content with this, later kings invited numerous German settlers from the Rhine and even from Flanders, and assigned to them between 1143 and 1150 considerable lands in the valleys of the Mureş, Târnava and Olt. The motive which inspired this policy is revealed in the motto selected for the earliest charter granted to the newcomers—"ad retinendam coronam".[2] The generous promises made to the Germans from the very outset are well illustrated by the great lawsuit brought by the bishop of Transylvania in 1195 before the Roman Curia against the recently founded chapter (Propstei) of Hermannstadt, which was able to maintain its position as holding direct from the bishopric of Milcov—then the farthest outpost of Catholicism in Eastern Europe— and (after its destruction in 1336) from the primatial see of Hungary.

A fresh stage is reached in 1211, when Andrew II granted by charter to the Teutonic knights the care of the south-eastern border—the Burzenland (Ţara Bârsei), as the district round Kronstadt (Braşov) is called. But the far-reaching privileges granted to it inflamed the ambitions of the Grand Master, who induced the Pope to take the Burzenland under his direct and exclusive jurisdiction. In this, King Andrew, otherwise deplorably weak, acted promptly enough, and in 1225 drove the knights out of Hungary by force of arms: and it was only then that they turned to establish the little Baltic state which was to be the germ of modern Prussia.

Obviously what had encouraged Hermann in his enterprise had been the uprising of the Hungarian nobles against the kingly power, and

---

[1] *Szék* means "seat" or "dwelling", *el* "beyond": thus *Székel* is the Marchland and *Székelyek* frontiersmen. Hunfalvy, p. 45.

[2] G. D. Teutsch, *Gesch. der Siebenbürger Sachsen*, I, p. 12.

their extraction from him in 1222 of the famous Golden Bull, the Magna Charta of the Hungarian constitution. Undoubtedly also the straits in which the king found himself in face of the nobles led him to encourage a new middle class as a makeweight against them. This and the urgent necessities of frontier defence combine to explain the charter of 1224 (the "Goldene Freibrief") which he granted to the German immigrants. The name of "Hospites" or Guests, under which the charter refers to them, acquired a special and honourable significance in Hungarian history, serving as a reminder of the freedom and privileges of its bearers: but gradually the name of Saxon came into general use, and "Saxons" took the place of "hospites".

The essence of the charter was complete self-government for the Saxons under an elected count or comes, holding direct from the king; the right to elect their own judges and clergy without interference; the limitation of property in land to Saxons only, throughout the territories assigned to them; freedom from all tolls and dues for their merchants in all parts of the kingdom; and of course, on the other hand, military obligations to be fulfilled in peace and war. It contains the remarkable phrase that all the inhabitants of a certain territory, which it defines, are "One People", and thus prescribes a certain unity to the Saxon nation and their lands—the "Fundus Regius", or Königsboden, which was to retain its corporate existence virtually unimpaired from 1222 to 1868.

This charter is a decisive event which in a sense stereotypes the future and leads to constitutional development on highly original lines. During the next 200 years Transylvania falls into three distinct political groupings—finally crystallised by the events of 1437 into the three privileged nations, the Magyars, the Székels and the Saxons.

I. The Magyars were organised in seven counties[1] and administered on exactly the same lines as the counties of Hungary proper. The essential point to bear in mind is, that in medieval Hungary—that is, constitutionally speaking, in Hungary right up to the year 1848—there was an absolute hard and fast distinction between the nobles and people, between *populus* and *plebs*. All the political power, local and central, was concentrated in the hands of the populus, which was exempt from taxation, and only to certain military obligations, while the plebs not only had no political status whatsoever, but had the privilege of paying all the taxes.

[1] Alba, Hunyad, Küküllö, Doboka, Kolozs, Torda and Inner Szolnok.

II. The Székelys[1] formed a compact group in the south-east, in the bend of the Carpathians. They were organised in seven, afterwards eight, seats[2] or Sedes (Szék)—like the Saxons, under their own count, holding direct from the crown. Where they differed from their Magyar kinsmen of the first group is that the Székels were all "noble" in the technical sense, and therefore exempt from taxation, though the military service to which they were liable was of three different grades.[3] Another vital difference, doubtless a survival from the old tribal system, was that they held their land in common and so avoided the large feudal estates.

III. The Székels were thus in some ways the most democratic of the three groups. For the third, the Saxons, were from the first a comparatively small community, narrowly jealous of their privileges, and careful to exclude all newcomers from any share in them. That their fears were not unjustified is no doubt shown by the fate of Klausenburg (Kolozsvár), which, built as a German town, though not on the Königsboden, was then in the mid-fifteenth century administered equally by Magyars and Saxons, but already by 1568 had fallen under Magyar control, and in modern times became the chief centre of Magyarisation in its most intolerant form. Meanwhile the Saxon land consisted of nine Stühle (Sedes), the chief being Hermannstadt, and two districts, the Burgenland (with Kronstadt), and the Nösnerland (with Bistritz). The Saxons gave to their new home the name of "Siebenbürgen", generally derived from the seven castles which they built, but latterly sometimes from the "Sibin Burg", the castle of Sibin or Sibiu.[4]

Already in the earliest documents still extant there are traces of the presence of a Roumanian element in the population. In 1222 we find a "terra Blacorum" and a "terra Siculorum" side by side: the Saxon charter of 1224 refers to a "sylva Bissenorum et Blacorum" (the Bissenes being Petchenegs): and another document of 1231 refers more explicitly to lands situated "in terra Blachorum".[5] Throughout these thinly populated frontier districts—the phrase "desert and uninhabited" in contemporary sources is obviously not to be taken quite literally—there would seem to have been loosely organised Vlach communities,

---

[1] *Szekler* in German, *Siculi* in Latin.
[2] Maros, Udvarhely, Sepsi, Kézdi, Orbai, Csík, Gyergyö, then Aranyos. See Timon, *Ungarische Verfassungs- und Rechtsgeschichte*, p. 240. Benkö, *Transsilvania*, I, p. 299.
[3] *Primores, equites, pixiderii.* See Timon, *op. cit.* p. 241.
[4] *Urkundenbuch zur Geschichte Siebenbürgens*, ed. Teutsch and Firnhaber, I, no. xxviii.    [5] *Ibid.* no. xlix.

living the primitive life of peasants and shepherds, under "kenezen" of their own (the word is of Slav origin, identical with the Serbian *knez*, whose social value has fluctuated very greatly). These chiefs paid every fiftieth sheep or pig for the right of pasture and obtained hereditary privileges from the Hungarian crown: a century later, under Louis the Great, many of them were ennobled and gradually merged into the Hungarian nobility. In passing be it noted that Wallach—the name which soon attaches itself to the first organised independent principality of the Roumanians—is a foreign word derived from Vlach, the Slav word for Roumanian, which has passed into Latin as *Valachus*, into Magyar as *Oláh*, and into German as *Wallache*. The native tongue has always employed the words Românía, Român, Ţara Româneasca.

The first stage in this gradual expansion of Hungary towards the south-east was to seize and fortify the main strategic points, and to establish colonists whose loyalty and integrity was secured by special royal privileges and who would be capable of staving off invasion. It followed logically that Hungary should seek to extend her influence to the southern slopes of the Carpathians—especially Oltenia (the districts between the Iron Gates and the river Olt), where native Roumanian voivodes were establishing themselves. The castle of Severin, not far from Trajan's famous bridge over the Danube, was erected by Andrew II and made the centre of a Banat. Proselytising zeal went hand in hand with political and military ambitions, and in the Moldavian uplands he founded the short-lived Catholic bishopric of Milcov, which the Holy See favoured as an instrument for reclaiming the East from Orthodoxy, at a moment when a Latin emperor reigned in Byzantium and when the rulers of Bulgaria and Serbia were coquetting with Rome.[1]

Hungarian aggression, however, received a severe check in 1241, when the great Tatar invasion of Zenghis Khan, after displacing and crushing the nomad tribes on the Dniester and the Pruth, flooded over the Carpathians and for nearly a year wrought havoc in the Apostolic kingdom. Béla IV was crushingly defeated and took refuge in Dalmatia, till the tide slowly flowed back into Asia. Not the least direct effect of this disaster was to remove pressure from the Roumanians, and to leave them free to develop on their own lines. In 1247, it is true, King Béla assigned the banat of Severin and the lands evacuated by the Cumans

[1] In 1234 Prince Béla took oath, "falsos christianos de terris nostris pro viribus extirpare". Theiner, I, p. 124. Xenopol, *Histoire des Roumains*, I, p. 195.

to the French Knights Hospitallers, but at the same time specially exempted two voivodates on the Olt which "had hitherto been held by Roumanians".[1] In any case, for reasons which have not come down to us, the Order did not take advantage of the concessions offered to it. Moreover, Ladislas IV, so far from maintaining the Catholic zeal of his predecessors, became so infected by the habits and outlook of the Cuman refugees—who entered Hungary as heathens—as to have earned in history the title of "Ladislas the Cuman". For a generation to come Hungary was occupied in repairing the damage wrought by the Tatar hordes, whose thoroughness is well illustrated by the fact that virtually no documents have survived to us from an earlier period, the royal chancellory having apparently been destroyed and the local administration having for the most part shared its fate. It is this which makes it at once so easy to evolve, and so impossible to prove, rival theories of autochthony and immigration.

## THE FIRST PRINCES OF WALLACHIA

Little or nothing is known of the first Roumanian princes, beyond their names. In Oltenia in the second half of the thirteenth century, Litovoiu was sufficiently strong to refuse the tribute demanded by Hungary, but in the end was overthrown and killed in battle by Ladislas IV. His successor Ivancu, or Tihomir—a name suggesting that Slav and Roumanian were still intermixed among the leading families of the infant state—profited by the internecine troubles in Transylvania and Hungary in the last decade of the century, which continued after the extinction of the House of Árpád in 1301. A disputed succession between those foreign princes who could claim maternal descent from the national dynasty was a heaven-sent opportunity for the Roumanians to loosen the ties which bound them, and the fourteenth century witnessed their steady national consolidation, despite the parallel expansion of Hungary under the Angevins.

Early Roumanian chronicles assign the foundation of the Wallachian principality to the year 1290, and assert that a certain voivode of Făgăraş, named Negru-Vodă, crossed the mountains with many of his boiars and followers, established himself at Câmpulung in the southern foothills, and was recognised as "Domn" or Lord. This story was accepted by

---

[1] "Quam olachis relinquimus prout iidem hactenus tenuerunt".—Fejer, *Codex*, IV, i, p. 447. Xenopol, *op. cit.* I, p. 167.

Roumania's first great modern historian, A. D. Xenopol, but more recent research rejects it altogether and suggests a confusion with Radu Negru-Vodă who did actually rule in Wallachia a whole century later and was the father of Mircea the Old.

The most that can safely be affirmed is that the whole trend of Roumanian political life was in this early period from north to south, and that this was due at once to the growing hold of the Hungarian crown over Transylvania, the stiffening of the feudal regime, the advent of German and other settlers, and the renewed proselytising zeal of the Roman Church, of which the Apostolic king was as a rule the willing exponent, so long as his own rights were not unduly impinged upon. That there was a definite movement from the hills into the southern plains is shown by the title assumed by the first primate of the new state, and ever since borne by his successors—Metropolit al Ungro-Vlachiei și Exarh Plăiurilor (i.e. of the High Mountains), and yet again by the native names under which Wallachia and its people have always been known—Țara Munteneasca, Munteni (the mountain land, moun-taineers), though it is in the main a low, at most undulating, plain. Most significant of all is its choice of capitals—first Câmpulung, then Argeș, both in the mountain district, then Tîrgoviște by the foothills: only at a much later date the low-lying Bucarest. Thus we find a gradual tendency to move away from the shelter of the mountains and, as the state consolidated, to venture step by step further into the plain.

A further factor which contributed to the growth of an independent Roumanian state was the increasing importance of the trade routes from Poland and Northern Europe generally to the Black Sea—which at the same time explains the rise of the Saxon towns, notably Hermannstadt (Sibiu) and Kronstadt (Brașov). From the latter town the route passed to the Wallachian Cîmpulung, and there forked into two, straight south to the port of Giurgiu and eastwards to Brăila, which has ever since been one of the main centres of Danubian trade. The road from Hermann-stadt went through the Red Tower pass towards Argeș, and so to Cala-fat, at a point halfway between Vidin and Giurgiu. Meanwhile the great "Tatar" route, as it was called, passed through the future Moldavian state to Caffa, the famous Genoese emporium on the Black Sea, while another led to Chilia in the Danubian delta and Moncastro, also a Genoese colony, but better known under its later Roumanian and Russian names of Cetatea Alba and Akkerman. As the Roumanians themselves, in these early times and for centuries to come, were entirely agricultural, the trading class consisted almost exclusively of strangers, Germans and Poles, and Jews from the north, Greeks and Ragusans from the south, Genoese in the Black Sea ports, and Armenians, who gradually penetrated inland and formed settlements in such Transylvanian towns as Dej and Satu Mare. These foreign merchants used Hungarian, Byzantine and Polish money: among the natives most transactions were in kind, and land or luxuries were bartered for produce and livestock, and service rendered to the prince and his boiars in the same way.

The first consolidation of the Wallachian state may be said to date from the reign of Basarab (*circa* 1330–52), but there is not a single document or charter in existence from which we can supplement our scanty knowledge of him. Finding in Hungary the chief menace to his power, he naturally allied himself both by treaty and by marriage with his Bulgarian neighbours across the Danube. But Bulgaria was now in rapid decay and eclipsed by the rising star of the Serbian empire. Basarab found that he had backed the wrong horse: he came to the aid of his kinsman, Tsar Michael of Vidin, and shared his defeat at the hands of the Serbians at the disastrous battle of Velbužd in 1330. Michael fell fighting, and Bulgaria, weak and disunited, lingered on as little better than the vassal of Serbia, only to fall at last like a ripe fruit into the hands of the Turks.

Basarab's misadventure encouraged Charles Robert of Hungary to reassert Hungarian supremacy, and he invaded Wallachia with a large army, but at Posada suffered a severe reverse and barely escaped with his life by changing clothes with one of his retainers. As compensation for this failure he managed to recapture Severin, which now remained in Hungarian hands for most of the century.

## LOUIS THE GREAT AND WALLACHIA

In 1342 Charles Robert was succeeded by his young, brilliant and energetic son, known in history as Louis the Great, under whom Hungary may be said to have celebrated her golden age. Never was the net of Hungarian foreign policy thrown so widely and so successfully, but this very fact was the salvation of the Roumanians, for his major efforts were directed towards Venice, with whom he contested the Dalmatian coast, towards Italy, where his kinsmen of the Angevin house held the throne of Naples, and his brother Andrew became the consort and victim of the licentious Joanna; towards Serbia, under Tsar Dušan, with whom he was tempted to contest the supremacy of the Balkan peninsula and in particular the suzerainty of Bosnia; and above all, perhaps, towards Poland, whose throne he inherited by marriage in 1370 and in whose ambitions in the now decadent kingdom of Galicia and even in heathen Lithuania, he allowed himself to become involved. Speaking broadly, Hungary under the Angevins may be said to have had two main ambitions—to extend her domination at the expense of the still fluid Balkan world, to supplant the now obviously decaying power of Byzantium and prevent any of the young Slav states from usurping its place, and at the same time—and this was in full accord with the Guelf traditions of the new dynasty[1]—to spread the Catholic faith throughout South-eastern Europe at the expense of schismatic, heretic and infidel alike. The constant diversions which all this involved doubtless prompted him to evolve a special policy on his south-western frontiers, not altogether dissimilar from that adopted by the Frankish empire five centuries earlier towards the unsettled territories that lay to the east. In other words, he set himself to create a series of marches, that of Severin controlling the Iron Gates and the difficult country on either side of it; that of Vidin, farther down the Danube, as a point of vantage from which to extend his sway over North-western Bulgaria and take Serbia in the flank; that of Făgăraş, which he granted to Vlaicu, the grandson of Basarab, as "Ducatus Omlasii et de Fagaras", in the hope of bringing the "Transalpine" lands into the same sphere of influence as the Transylvanian; and, finally, the voivodate of Maramureş, in the mountainous and thinly populated districts that separated the north of Transylvania from the kingdom of Halicz or Galicia.

In the end the great king was prematurely aged and worn down by such varied and exacting ambitions. But though he attempted the impossible, in certain directions his policy was clearly defined and relatively successful, namely in his zeal for the interests of the Church and in his efforts to extend Hungarian influence to the south and south-east. He was in close and almost uninterrupted alliance with the Papacy, co-operating in many schemes for the extirpation of Balkan heresies and for the reunion of the Eastern Church with the Holy See, in return for help against Asiatic invaders. On one occasion the Emperor John VI

[1] Charles Robert was the grandson of Charles of Anjou, founder of the Kingdom of Naples, and champion of the Papacy against the last of the Hohenstaufen, Conradin and Manfred.

himself visited him at Buda and employed his good offices with the Pope. Louis, it should be added, showed from the first a clearer perception of the Turkish danger than many contemporaries. This is shown by his expedition to Vidin in 1365: for it was a prompt and energetic counter-move to the transference of the Turkish capital from Broussa to Adrianople in that year. Bulgaria was falling into two weak principalities, the more easterly of which had hastened to become the Sultan's vassal, and Louis was anxious to prevent Tsar Stracimir at Vidin from following this fatal example. His bold seizure of Vidin won him the ready support of Vlajko of Wallachia and led to the first direct encounter between Turk and Magyar. But Vidin was recovered by the Bulgarians in 1369, and Louis was absorbed in Polish affairs when the disastrous news of the Marica reached him in 1371. He was again swift to recognise the growing danger and ready to make war upon the Turks, but only on a grand scale or not at all: and in his negotiations with the Pope for this purpose, he imposed as his conditions that a crusade should be preached and that the Church should make special contributions. When Gregory XI boggled over such concessions and the other Powers with one accord found excuses for providing very inadequate assistance, he desisted from his plan and the Turks were left free to strengthen their stranglehold upon the Balkan peninsula. It is in Louis the Great's colonising policy on the north-east frontier of Hungary that we find the germ of a second Roumanian state. For about the year 1349 the Voivode Bogdan revolted against his strong overlord, and crossing to the eastern slopes of the Carpathians established himself in "Terra Moldavana" around the river Moldava, which rises in the modern Bukovina and eventually flows into the Siret at Roman. Here he was relatively safe from attack: and Hungary had no special incentive to push beyond the Carpathian watershed.

*    *    *    *

That Moldavia took shape somewhat later than the sister state was doubtless due to the fact that it had suffered far more from the great onslaught of the Mongols in 1241 and from the persistent inroads of Cuman and Tatar tribes both before and after that event. The new prince, on whom Wallachia looked askance without being able to hold him in check, adopted the oxhead and star as his coat of arms and circulated rude coins—stamped in the Polish mint—bearing the title "Bogdan Voevoda Moldaviensis". It is here that the title of Hospodar, which is simply the Slavonic "Gospodar" or Lord, first arises. Here too the centre of gravity is at first in the north—at Baia, at Cîmpulung,[1] Rădăuţi and Suceava: only in much later times was it transferred to the modern capital of Iaşi (Jassy), in the plains west of the river Pruth.

There can be no doubt that the withdrawal of powerful Roumanian nobles from Transylvania to the two young Principalities weakened the position of the Roumanian population which they left behind them. The remaining nobles were in process of time Magyarised, and their blood may still be traced in some of the great feudal families of Transylvania, such as Teleki, Mailáth and Jósika. Class interests proved stronger than blood, and from the fifteenth to the twentieth century the position of the Roumanians in that province was that of mere helots.

Conditions in both Wallachia and Moldavia remained extremely primitive for a long period after the first foundation. There were no real towns except a few market centres on the main north and south routes to which we have already alluded, and even they seem not to have been of sufficient importance to be walled. Very little money was in circulation, payments were mainly in kind. Both countries were completely isolated even from such general culture as then prevailed. Education was almost unknown. Even the Church was backward and unorganised, served mainly by Slav priests, using a Slav liturgy, and for a long time dependent on the Bulgarian bishops of Silistria and Vidin. This extreme weakness of the Orthodox Church in Roumanian lands was an incentive to Catholicism, powerfully fostered by the Hungarian kings as an instrument of policy: and for a time the Catholic bishopric of Milcov seemed likely to perform the function of Lübeck or Magdeburg in Baltic lands in earlier times. The Wallachian "Domn" Basarab and more than one of his family were influenced by Catholic doctrine, intermarriage playing its part, and Pope Urban V making special efforts to win them over. But the political danger turned the scale, and in 1359 the "Domn" appealed to Constantinople and obtained from it the nomination of a "Metropolitan of Ungro-Wallachia and Exarch of the Mountains".[2] The first metropolitan of Moldavia (or "Moldo-Vlachia" as it was at first called in Constantinople) was established at Suceava in 1374 and consecrated by the patriarch of Ochrida—a see originally Bulgarian, but hellenised by the Emperor Basil after his reconquest of Bulgaria. It soon became a tradition of the

---

[1] In what is now Bukovina—to be distinguished from the Wallachian Cîmpulung.

[2] Iorga, *Gesch. des rumänischen Volkes*, I, p. 276.

princes in both states to show great liberality in the endowment of monasteries—in which learning was virtually concentrated till quite modern times. But it was a long time before they could rival the noble example of the Serbian rulers of the thirteenth and fourteenth centuries, or of the great Rilo monastery in Bulgaria.

## EARLY ROUMANIAN INSTITUTIONS

The close personal connections between the nascent Roumanian court and those of Bulgaria and Serbia naturally enough led to the imitation of high dignities and administrative offices. The Logofet or Chancellor, the Vistiarnic or Treasurer, the Vornic,[1] who seems to have been at once Chamberlain and Supreme Judge, the Stolnic (Master of the Bedchamber), the Paharnic (Cupbearer), the Cluciare (Keeper of the Keys), are for the most part Slav titles, though of course the Slav States had in the first instance simply borrowed such functions from the elaborate ceremonial of Byzantium. The most important military office seems to have been that of Ban or Governor of Oltenia, who was responsible for defence against invasion.

It was a narrow oligarchic society in which the prince exercised virtually absolute power, and his council (or "Divan", as it came to be called in the Turkish days) was merely advisory. He alone could admit to the boiar or noble class, or make grants of land: and this he often seems to have done, not only at the expense of the subjected peasantry (dorobanţi), but even of the free peasants (călăraşi), when they failed to pay the contributions laid upon them.

The boiars were exempt from all direct taxation, exactly as the nobility in Hungary: but at the same time they were liable to dues on several of the most vital sources of agricultural wealth—sheep, cattle, wine, bees (always a great Roumanian industry), etc. They exacted from the subjected peasants one-tenth of their crop, corresponding to the feudal "robot" further west: but despite all the miseries of their lot, the peasants never entirely lost the right of property or the right of moving to a new home. The prince drew his revenue from these dues, and taxation only became really oppressive when under the Turks he was in continual need of squeezing more money from his subjects.[2] Meanwhile the prince owed his election to an Assembly of the Boiars

---

[1] From dvor or Court.
[2] Xenopol, *op. cit.* I, p. 233.

and higher clergy, and there was a recognised practice of submitting its decision, in a rough and ready way, to the acclamation of the crowd. But this practice, and the lack of any regular law of succession, gave rise to endless intrigues and rivalries and prevented internal consolidation. Election was open to every member of the reigning family, including illegitimate offspring, and the central fact of Roumanian history from the fourteenth to the seventeenth centuries is a recurrence of palace revolutions and the overthrow of one ruler after another by rival factions, only too often supported by foreign influence. There was of course the added complication of rivalry between the two thrones, which partly explains the arrogant titles assumed by the one to outbid the other, and at a later date offered constant temptation to intrigue and invasion.

In the period of three centuries between 1400 and 1700 the number of princes who occupied each of the two thrones was (according to the closely documented list of Professor Iorga)[1] about sixty-five. In other words, the average duration of a reign was barely seven years, and if we allow for the fact that at least a quarter of these rulers were driven out once, or even twice, the average will fall still lower. It is unnecessary to add that most of these flitting figures were mediocre and obscure to the last degree. Only a dozen of the more outstanding among them deserve to be rescued from oblivion: and it would be quite unprofitable, in a general survey such as the present volume, to dwell upon these complicated dynastic changes.

No clear theory, it may be added, has as yet been evolved by native historians to explain why the two original dynasties, which survived for nearly three centuries in circumstances such as rendered despotic rule inevitable, and which admittedly produced one or two men of very high ability, such as Mircea the Old, Vlad Ţepeş, Alexander the Good, Stephen the Great, Peter Rareş and Michael the Brave, should none the less have signally failed to establish the royal power on sure and lasting foundations. The lack of any worthy successor to two such notable princes as Stephen and Michael was, as we shall see later, a contributory factor of the first importance: and of course the geographical isolation of the two states, and their peculiar relations with Constantinople after the Turkish conquest, played a decisive part. But it would also seem as if some of the qualities essential to constructive political life had been lacking to the Roumanian ruling class in those early centuries and

[1] Iorga, *op. cit.* II, 529–39.

counteracted the amazing virility and persistence to type to which the Roumanian peasant owes his survival through centuries of oppression. The absence of a native middle class naturally left the nation more than usually dependent upon its nobility, and in this case they did not prove equal to the difficult task before them.

## THE TURKISH ADVANCE

Perhaps the answer to these speculations will suggest itself as we follow this brief thread further. Certainly as the fourteenth century closed, the two thrones were occupied by men of more than usual ability— Mircea the Old of Wallachia (1386–1418), and Alexander the Good of Moldavia (1401–31)—who were able to give a certain stability to their dominions at the very moment when Bulgaria and Serbia were on the point of extinction. Roumanian history can only be understood in its geographical setting, and it is essential to remember that the rise of the two principalities coincided with the decay of two powerful Slav states immediately to the south of the Danube and with the victorious advance of a new military power of the very first order, the Ottoman Turks. Bulgaria had already lost its powers of resistance since the defeat of Velbužd in 1330, and had fallen into three weak and loosely knit states, with their centres at Vidin and Trnovo and in the Dobrogea. Serbia, which had reached its zenith under Stephen Dušan (1332–56), "Tsar of the Greeks and Serbs", rapidly declined after his death: in 1371 even a combination of Serbs and Bulgars was crushingly defeated by the Turks, in a great battle on the Marica river: and henceforth the latter were faced, no longer by a strong and expanding Serbian empire, but by a whole series of ephemeral petty states, stretching from the Adriatic to the Danube and the Black Sea, badly organised and mutually suspicious.

In 1387 Sultan Murad I resumed his advance into the heart of the peninsula, and though defeated in that year, he won two years later the memorable victory of Kosovo, which is generally regarded, alike in poetic legend and in more sober history, as the deathblow to medieval Serbia. It has frequently been maintained that Mircea of Wallachia sent a contingent of troops to the help of the Serbs, and though there is no real evidence for this story, it is certainly a fact that the new Sultan Bayezid followed up the victory by invading Wallachia. Mircea was made prisoner, sent to Broussa and only released in return for an annual

PLATE II

MIRCEA THE OLD

From a fresco in the monastery of Cozia (XVI century)

tribute. Thus the year 1391 marks the first appearance of Wallachia on the register of vassals to the Sublime Porte.[1]

On his return Mircea sought new allies. In 1393 the last trace of Bulgarian independence was overthrown, and only the Danube now separated the Roumanians from the rapidly expanding Turkish empire. It was natural enough that Bayezid should next year direct his attack against Mircea, who more than held his own in a battle in the marshes of Rovine, on the Danube, and thus saved the country from actual conquest. It seems to have been on this occasion that King Marko, the hero of Serbian legend, met his death, ignominiously fighting in the Turkish ranks. But Mircea felt his situation to be desperate and in 1395 fled to Transylvania, where he concluded a treaty of alliance with the new king of Hungary, Sigismund of Luxemburg, the husband of Louis' daughter and heiress.

By this time Western Europe was acutely anxious as to the Turkish advance, though unhappily its desire to help the Christians of the East was tinged by political ambitions not dissimilar to those of the notorious Fourth Crusade, and by the proselytising designs of Rome against Orthodoxy.

In 1396, then, it came to a new crusade led by Sigismund himself, with many thousands of French, Burgundian and German knights. But all their gallantry and fine equipment could not avail against the foolhardy and arrogant tactics which had led an earlier generation to disaster at Crécy—the more so as they were measured against one of the most formidable military machines of the late Middle Ages. On the field of Nicopolis the Turks again won a crushing victory, the flower of French and Burgundian chivalry was wiped out or held to ransom, and Sigismund himself, after barely escaping with his life, was stripped of financial resources—a handicap which was to remain with him throughout life—involved in a disputed succession in Hungary and Croatia and irresistibly tempted to dabble in the politics of Bohemia, where his brother Wenceslas was rapidly making himself impossible. In a word, the prestige of Hungary, which under Louis the Great had stood very high in all the Danubian states, and which between Kosovo and Nicopolis had seemed to offer the main guarantee of salvation from the Turks, now fell under a sudden eclipse.

Small wonder then, if Mircea of Wallachia, deprived of active support from his northern ally, should have found the utmost difficulty in hold-

[1] Hammer-Purgstall, *Gesch. des osmanischen Reiches*, I, p. 187.

ing his own against the Turks, or that in their search for a substitute both he and Stephen, the voivode of Moldavia, should have turned to the more distant Poland, the latter even acknowledging it as his suzerain.

What secured to the Roumanians a much needed respite was the Mongol invasion of 1402, in which Sultan Bayezid was defeated and made prisoner by the redoubtable Tamerlane, his death in captivity being followed by a prolonged civil war between his sons. Unhappily it was merely a respite; there was no real possibility of a counter-offensive. For on the one hand Sigismund was absorbed in the struggle against a rival claimant in Hungary, his own cousin Ladislas of Naples, and also caught up in the first throes of religious and political unrest in his native Bohemia. Bulgaria was by now under the yoke and past helping, Serbia under the impotent successors of Lazar was already a liability rather than an asset to the Christian cause, while Bosnia was torn by religious dissensions. On the other side, Moldavia was in much closer connection with Poland than with Hungary: and Alexander the Good married as his third wife a kinswoman of King Wladislaw Jagiello, and even sent Roumanian troops to fight under the Polish flag at the great battle of Tannenberg in 1410. This did not prevent the two brothers-in-law, Wladislaw and Sigismund, from contracting a secret treaty which envisaged a possible partition of Moldavia.

Mircea's adroit speculations in the Turkish civil war ended in disaster; for his ally Musa was eventually overthrown by Mohammed I, who seized the three strong strategic points of Giurgiu, Nicopolis and Isaccea and very nearly captured the Genoese port of Moncastro also. Already the position of the Roumanians was precarious, but as yet the Turks were concentrating their efforts upon the main line of advance through the Morava valley to the Middle Danube, determined that first Serbia, then Hungary, should share the fate of Bulgaria. In 1417, then, Mircea found it necessary to acknowledge the suzerainty of the Porte, to pay a regular tribute of 3000 ducats, and to surrender all territory south of the Danube mouths (that is, the modern province of Dobrogea). A year later he died, after one of the few normally long reigns in Roumanian history.

For several decades after Mircea's death Wallachia was convulsed by the faction fighting of his sons and other rival claimants, and on Alexander's death in 1432 Moldavia fell into similar anarchy. It was doubtless this which forced Sigismund, who had so long been absorbed in the affairs of the West, to turn his attention once more to the Balkan peninsula. The brunt of the defence of Europe against the Turks thus came to be borne by Hungary, which now earned the proud title "propugnaculum christianitatis".

In the struggle between Sigismund and his cousin, Ladislas of Naples, Venice had played the *tertius gaudens*, laying the foundations of a rule of nearly four centuries along the Dalmatian coast. Sigismund had to accept the situation thus created, but all the more eager was he to assert Hungary's overlordship in Bosnia, whose last kings fatally alienated their subjects by their intolerant zeal against the prevailing Bogomil heresy. Meanwhile Stephen Lazarević and George Branković, the rulers of what remained of Serbia, sank to the level of Hungarian vassals, and Belgrade was garrisoned by Hungarian troops. Dan II of Wallachia also recognised Sigismund as his overlord, and it was his inability to maintain his throne against the rival Turkish candidate, that brought Sigismund himself to the Danube after an absence of almost thirty years. In 1427 he led an army through the Transylvanian passes, reinstated Dan and established a new fortress at Giurgiu. His plans were only very partially successful, and a year later he was badly beaten at Galambocz in an attempt to drive the Turks out of Serbia. More practical for the moment seemed his grant of Severin to the Teutonic Knights, in the hope of inducing them to organise the defences of the Lower Danube: and Klaus von Redwitz with a few comrades did actually settle there. Indeed it is interesting to note that towards the end of his reign Sigismund seriously urged the Order to transfer itself bodily to the Danube, on the ground that here lay the main danger which it had been founded to combat: his idea was that their Prussian lands might be partitioned among neighbouring princes![1] But nothing of course came of this: the Order had far too many commitments on the Baltic, and Sigismund was too full of German and Bohemian projects to pay more than sporadic attention to the south-east. Thus he failed in his designs for a Hungarian occupation of Vidin and Chilia. But he found a more serviceable tool than Dan in the latter's younger brother Vlad, commonly known as "Dracul" or "the Devil", who was once more allowed to hold the fief of Făgăraş and Amlaş. Vlad, however, was unable to stem the ever-recurring Turkish raids from the south of the river and was in the end carried into captivity: while Sigismund, so versatile and energetic, yet so unprincipled and fatally spendthrift, lacked alike the character, the resources and the free time, to persevere in what he

[1] See Aschbach, *Gesch. Kaiser Sigmunds*, IV, p. 291.

recognised as a permanent European interest, the erection of effective barriers against Turkish invasion.

On his death in 1437, Sigismund was succeeded by his son-in-law Albert of Habsburg, who won the allegiance of Hungary and with more difficulty, of Bohemia and was almost at once elected king of the Romans. He was young, able and energetic, of strong physique and good private morals, and in the words of a Bohemian chronicler, "though a German, bold and compassionate": and he now possessed the resources and vision which might have rendered possible a permanent and effective co-operation against the Turkish danger. He seems to have understood the need for defence far better than the factious nobles of his new Hungarian kingdom, and when in 1438 Murad II invaded Transylvania—this time with the aid of Dracul—he found that Magyar distrust of his German advisers was stronger than the flair for a neighbour's burning house, and had to look on impatiently while Semendria, George Branković's Danubian stronghold, fell before the Turks.

In October 1439 Albert died of dysentery on his way back to Vienna, at the early age of 42. This was an event no less disastrous for Danubian Europe than that of another Habsburg, Leopold II, three centuries and a half later. For the first time the three realms which a persistent marriage policy was afterwards to recover for the house of Austria, had been united under one head: but not for the first or last time had political and personal causes interfered with what some would call the natural processes of geography. The crown of Hungary was again separated from that of the empire, which fell to Albert's ineffective though persistent cousin Frederick of Styria, whose grandiose dreams of the future were to be fulfilled, but who during a long life was incapable of defending his own hereditary dominions, much less vindicating the imperial power, or holding the sultan at bay. Meanwhile Albert's posthumous son succeeded him in Bohemia and was crowned by one section of the Hungarian nobility. Frederick aimed at control of the child's person and an unified regency for all three countries, but the majority in Hungary not unnaturally viewed with alarm the prospect of a long minority while the Turk was hammering at their door, and elected King Wladislaw of Poland, in the hope that though even he was barely sixteen, he would become the symbol of union between the two most powerful kingdoms of that epoch and make a crushing offensive possible. The papal legate, Cardinal Cesarini, also strained every nerve to secure unity within and without and the death of the queen-mother left Wladislaw without a rival.

## JOHN HUNYADY

It is at this fateful moment that there appears the heroic figure of John Hunyady, who in modern times has formed a bone of contention between Magyar and Roumanian controversialists, instead of serving as a symbol of co-operation between two neighbouring races. All contemporary writers[1] are agreed in regarding him as Roumanian by race, but he was of course a signal example of that process by which men of many nationalities found entrance to the ranks of the Hungarian nobility and lost their identity in it. His father Voicu, or Vajk, was one of many such Roumanians, *not* of very ancient lineage, who had been ennobled by successive Hungarian kings and entrusted with the guardianship of the southern frontier: and the castle of Vajda Hunyad, his original estate, is one of the most picturesque feudal survivals of Hungary. John himself, after seeing some service in Bohemia and Italy, received fresh grants of land from Sigismund, with a view to raising further frontier forces. Entrusted by Albert with the organisation of the banat of Severin, he was the first to build a castle at Temesvár (Timişoara) and make it a strategic centre of defence against the Turks. Under Wladislaw he came rapidly to the front and was made Count of the Székels, voivode of Transylvania and Captain-General of the Hungarian forces. In 1441 he checked the Turks before Belgrade and in 1442, after an initial defeat, overthrew the invading Turks near Alba Iulia and killed their general Mesid Bey. He was therefore the right hand of young Wladislaw in the great Hungarian offensive of 1443, and it was he who won a resounding victory at Niš on 3 November, thereby bringing Hungarian prestige to its highest pitch throughout the peninsula and incidentally attaching Vlad of Wallachia more strongly to his cause. The events that followed can only be alluded to here, but they had effects equally momentous for Hungary and Roumania. The ten years' peace which Hunyady's victory led Sultan Murad to conclude and which restored Serbia and Hercegovina to Branković and recognised Hungarian suzerainty over Wallachia, was swiftly broken by the overconfident Wladislaw, spurred on by the fanatical Legate Cesarini,

---

[1] E.g. the Cilli Chronicle calls him "aus dem Landt Walachey pürtig", which is an overstatement, if taken too literally. Frederick III, when Matthias was elected king of Hungary, indignantly referred to him as "adolescentem peregrina gente, natum e patre valacho".

who, as he wrote to the emperor, could think day and night of nothing else than the final ruin of the Turks and urged the fatal doctrine that faith need not be kept with infidels. Wladislaw crossed the Danube, unduly late in the season and with altogether inadequate forces: Vlad Dracul told him roundly, "The Sultan when he goes hunting, has a larger suite than thy army". He reached the Black Sea coast, only to find himself suddenly confronted and outnumbered by the sultan (10 November 1444) and instead of waiting for reinforcements, flung himself into the fray and went down fighting. Cesarini paid for his perfidy with his life, and Hunyady retreated with a scanty remnant and found himself for some months in a prison of the treacherous Vlad, who doubtless thought it wise to curry favour with Murad, but eventually set his captive free.

The battle of Varna resounded through Europe, as well it might: for it seemed to proclaim the Turks as invincible, and it really sealed the fate of Byzantium, which received no further help from Europe and only held out nine years longer. It also ended the union of Hungary and Poland, and left the former but little choice save to accept the infant Ladislas as its ruler, even though he was in the hands of that none too satisfactory guardian the Emperor Frederick. Pending the boy's majority, the Hungarian parliament elected Hunyady as Gubernator and encouraged him to fresh action against the Turks. Hunyady's first step in the summer of 1446, was to invade Wallachia, to eject his personal enemy, the unreliable Vlad, and to establish the insignificant Vladislav, a son of Dan II, upon the throne: and at the same time he tried to terminate the internal feuds that were rending Moldavia and sapping its powers of resistance. In 1448 he was ready for a fresh invasion of Serbia and penetrated as far as the legendary plain of Kosovo, but here he suffered the greatest reverse of his whole career and on his flight northwards became the prisoner of yet another vassal princeling, George Branković—balanced so uneasily between the devil and the deep sea, and turning every time the balance shifted. On his return to Hungary, Hunyady had to contend against many powerful enemies: his flight was misrepresented both at home and abroad, and by no one more so than by Frederick's scholar-apologist Aeneas Sylvius, the future crusading Pope Pius II. His difficulties were only increased when Ladislas assumed nominal power in 1452, and though he really maintained his control of the administration, he had no surplus energies left for a forward foreign policy, and Hungary was rent by dissensions while Byzantium fell in

1453. Next year Mohammed the Conqueror, flushed by success, again invaded Serbia, and Despot George fled across the river. This time again it was Hunyady who saved Semendria from capture, defeated the Turks at Kruševac and advanced as far as Niš and Vidin. Hunyady's last, and still more famous, exploit was the successful defence of Belgrade against the Conqueror himself and the most formidable siege train that Europe had as yet seen: the sultan withdrew baffled, but in August 1456 the two chief Christian heroes, the monk Capistrano and Hunyady himself, died of the plague.

This was a fresh decisive blow for the Christian cause: and even Aeneas Sylvius wrote, "It is the death of all our hopes". Young Ladislas only survived him by a year, but within that period he found time to send Hunyady's eldest son to the scaffold. When he died without heirs in 1457, Bohemia and Hungary, again separating from Austria, each elected national kings of their own, George Podiebrad and the Governor's youngest son Matthias Corvinus[1]: and though both live in history as national heroes, it cannot be denied that the disintegration of the Christian forces due to their mutual rivalries and ambitions, did much to consolidate Turkish rule over the Balkan peninsula and even prepared the way for a further Turkish advance. Meanwhile the name of the great Governor passed into legend amid all the Christian races; and the Serbian, Bulgarian and Roumanian ballads of "Voivoda Janko" or "Jancu-Vodă" do but give added lustre to the fame of "Hunyady János".

Regarded from the purely national point of view, the reign of Matthias Corvinus will always remain as one of the most splendid and successful in the annals of Hungary, but in its wider European aspects, and especially in its bearings upon what may henceforth be called the Eastern Question, it contained the seeds of future decay. It is quite true that he held the river front of the Danube against all assaults from the south, that he welcomed many refugees from Serbia and Bosnia and organised them on a military basis for the defence of their new fatherland, that he showed no favour to one race rather than another, that his fame as an administrator has survived in the popular proverb; "King Matthias is dead, and with him Justice", and that his love and patronage

---

[1] The name of Corvinus was assumed by Matthias and is to be traced to the raven in the Hunyady arms. Bonfinius, a writer at his court, provided a bogus descent from "Corvinus Messala Valerius, the Conqueror of Pannonia" and through the Valerii to Hercules and Jupiter!

of art and literature gave the first real impetus to a national Hungarian culture. But on the other hand he allowed himself to exhaust the national resources in a series of wars of conquest against Austria and Bohemia, and viewing everything as he did from the standpoint of a great noble, he failed to foresee the disastrous effects which were bound to follow from the successful efforts of his caste to reduce the free peasantry to serfdom.

## VLAD THE IMPALER

One of Hunyady's last acts was to eject Prince Vladislav Dan from the Wallachian throne, in favour of his own nominee, Vlad IV, who took oath to the king of Hungary as his suzerain, on 7 September 1456: and no contrast could be greater than that between the heroic governor and the prince upon whom legend and history alike have branded the loathsome title of "the Impaler".[1] From the distinctly inadequate material at our disposal it is impossible to avoid the conclusion that Vlad was a man of diseased and abnormal tendencies, the victim of acute moral insanity. Without accepting all the tales of horror that are told of him by early chroniclers and have won acceptance in modern times, mainly through the medium of the historian von Engel, there none the less seems little ground for doubting that he inflicted wholesale tortures upon all and sundry, irrespective of sex, age, class or race, and took a devilish delight in watching the agony of his victims.[2] It seems equally certain that the suggestion that though cruel and barbarous to his enemies, he was just to the oppressed peasantry as opposed to the boiars, is a pure myth. The Greek historian Chalcocondylas recounts that a Roumanian prisoner told his Turkish captors that he feared death less than he feared Vlad and was executed rather than reveal any secrets, and that Sultan Mohammed made the terse comment, "A man who could inspire such fear in his subjects might have performed wonders at the head of a great army".[3]

The main incident of Vlad's short reign is his encounter with

[1] "Vlad Ţepeş" does not seem to have come into use till early in the sixteenth century—see Ioan Bogdan, *Vlad Ţepeş*, p. 61, which contains the most authoritative account of his career and hitherto unprinted material from German and Russian sources.

[2] Many of these stories are based on Bonfinius, a contemporary Italian writer at the court of Matthias Corvinus.

[3] Cit. Engel, *Gesch. der Walachey*, I, p. 176.

Mohammed the Conqueror. Vlad's consistently Hungarian policy had won the sultan's disapproval, and after the final conquest of Serbia in 1459 he was felt to be a hindrance and a strategic danger to a further Turkish advance. Moreover he had the spirit to refuse the Turkish demand for a tribute of 10,000 ducats and 500 youths. In 1461, then, Hamsa Pasha and a Greek intermediary named Catabolinos were sent to negotiate with Vlad, but with secret instructions to lure him into a trap and seize his person. The wily Vlad, however, was forewarned, forestalled their intentions by a surprise and proceeded to the wholesale impalement of his captives, honouring the Pasha with a stake higher than all the others and a ceremonial robe to cover his misery. Next year the furious Mohammed invaded Wallachia in person, and Vlad, after a bold but unsuccessful raid upon the Turkish camp, fled before him. Legend tells that even the ruthless Conqueror was moved to tears when he visited the scene of Vlad's hideous exploit and saw a whole valley desolate yet peopled with its thousands of stakes, on which still hung the mangled remains of impaled Turks and Bulgars. It was on this occasion that he is credited with the phrase already quoted from Chalcocondylas.

Vlad took refuge in Hungary, and for reasons which are not known to us, spent twelve years at Buda as the prisoner of Matthias. During this period he appears to have accepted Catholicism, and early in 1476 was reinstated by Matthias upon the Wallachian throne, but was dead within the year. But for the terror of his name, Vlad has no real title to fame: and with his fall Wallachian resistance to the Turk rapidly crumbled. Indeed the sultan at once filled the vacant throne with a subservient nominee of his own, Vlad's own brother Radu "the Handsome", who had grown up as a hostage at the Turkish court and owed advancement to the notorious vices of his master. For another generation the last hopes of Roumanian liberty lie with Moldavia and the really great ruler whom it now produced.

## STEPHEN THE GREAT

The career of Stephen the Great is certainly the least known among all the episodes of European defence: and yet he stands beside Hunyady, Sobieski and Eugene as one of the four great champions of Christendom against the Turk. Stephen was the grandson of Alexander the Good: his father Bogdan II, one of the many victims of dynastic intrigue and treachery, was murdered and supplanted by a younger brother, Peter Aron, who soon developed into an irresponsible and bloodthirsty tyrant. Thus Stephen owed his accession to a revolt of malcontent boiars and the military support of Vlad the Impaler, who with all his faults was genuinely concerned that the neighbouring throne should be held by one who gave precedence to the Turkish danger, and not to his own personal plans of revenge.

Stephen was confronted by new and momentous problems. The fall of Constantinople doubtless did not appear to him in the same perspective as to the modern historian: but it can have left him in no manner of doubt that in the place of an ancient, if slowly decaying, centre of civilisation, a new power had arisen, united under a ruler of equal military and administrative ability, inspired by religious fanaticism and full of explosive energy. At the same time he saw that it was useless to rely upon his more powerful neighbours—Matthias of Hungary, who was absorbed in soaring westward ambitions and when he turned eastwards showed himself scarcely less hostile to the Roumanians than to the Turks; Casimir of Poland, who was mainly interested in Baltic problems and the periodical disputes with Lithuania; Ivan of Moscow, who was still faced by a very real Tatar danger and could only occasionally turn his face westwards. The fall of Constantinople was instantly felt in the economic sphere, for it cut the trade route through the Straits and dealt a fatal blow to the Black Sea commerce of Genoa and Venice: and indeed the Turkish advance soon rendered trade down the Danube almost equally precarious and threatened to deprive the Roumanians of those contacts with the outer world to which her brief prosperity had been due. Their growing isolation was rendered still more acute during the first decade of Stephen's reign by the double success of Mohammed the Conqueror in reducing Serbia and Bosnia to complete vassalage (1459 and 1463).

Stephen, then, if he had shared the short views and craven or rancorous temperament which had disgraced so many recent holders of the two Roumanian thrones, would probably have paid the tribute demanded and sunk slowly into an ignominious servitude. But in him patriotism and religion were blended in resistance to an alien and repellent domination such as the Ottoman, and almost from the outset he devoted his whole energies to defending the liberties of his country. His first task was necessarily to organise his military resources and to build up an army which admirably reflected the social and political institutions of Moldavia.[1] The only real restriction upon his power came from the small class of landed boiars and from the royal pretenders whom the unsatisfactory right of succession encouraged to lurk beyond every frontier, in the hope of rallying some new faction on their behalf. But Stephen was too strong for the latter, and the boiars found their interest in supporting him. The real basis of his success, however, was the existence of a relatively free peasantry, whose rights to the soil rested upon military service. The total effective of his army has been estimated at 50–60,000 men—a proportion far superior to that which prevailed in Poland or Hungary. The Moldavian soldiery lacked elaborate defensive armour, and indeed relied mainly on home-made weapons and padded clothing: but this gave them the same military qualities as the Tatars and made them rely upon mobility, endurance on the march, efficient "intelligence" and the skilful choice of ground at moments of decision.

Moldavia had but few strong places, and Stephen felt it to be essential to secure strategic control of the main routes as they entered the country. In particular he looked anxiously to the Danube, which he, no less clearly than John Hunyady, regarded as the vital line of defence against the Turks. The fortress of Chilia in the delta, originally built by the Genoese, had been placed in the hands of Hunyady and fulfilled the same strategic function on the Lower as Belgrade on the Middle Danube. It is impossible to say what would have been the relations of Stephen and Hunyady: it is just possible that their common zeal for the overthrow of the Turks might have outweighed the Hungarian desire to keep the two Roumanian princes in a state of vassalage. But in any case with Matthias this latter motive proved stronger, and Stephen, who was bent upon complete independence, set his heart upon the recovery of Chilia, and after one unsuccessful attack in 1462, finally captured it in 1465. Naturally enough, this kindled Matthias's resentment, the more so as he had grounds for suspecting that the prince of Moldavia was encouraging a revolt in Transylvania: and so it came in 1467 to a war between the two states on which the defence against the Turkish danger most depended. That Matthias chose the month of November for his attack, suggests that he gravely underestimated his opponent. He was able to force the mountain pass of Oituz and advanced rapidly

[1] For a very clear sketch of Stephen's military achievements, see "Stephen the Great and the Turkish Invasion", by General R. Rosetti, in *Slavonic Review*, no. 16 (June 1927).

towards Bacău and Roman, ravaging as he went: but Stephen avoided battle, harassing the invader on all sides, and drawing him on as far as Baia, to the south of Suceava. Here, on 14 December 1467, Stephen fell upon him by night and cut his whole army to pieces: Matthias himself was wounded in the back and escaped, not without difficulty, through the forests into Transylvania. For the remainder of the century and of Stephen's long reign, Moldavia was immune from all Hungarian attack.

Stephen's next task was to strengthen his northern frontier against the danger of Tatar invasion, and he then found himself confronted by the much more thorny problem of Wallachia. Vlad Ţepeş had been followed on the throne by his brother Radu the Handsome, a name of equivocal meaning which he seems to have acquired in the sultan's harem during a prolonged detention as a hostage in the Turkish capital. Radu was definitely open to Turkish influence and disposed to prefer a vassalage, whose full dangers were not as yet apparent, to the rougher paths of resistance. Mohammed the Conqueror, on his side, saw in Wallachia a most favourable base of operations both against Moldavia and against Hungary through the Transylvanian passes, a fresh granary of supplies and perhaps even a recruiting ground: and his immediate aim was to secure bridge-heads and strong points to the north of the river and thus to guard his flank from attack, as his communications lengthened with the advance against Central Europe. The check which he had suffered before Belgrade in 1456 did not prevent him from completing the conquest of Serbia and Bosnia between 1459 and 1463, and by 1470 he seemed ready for a decisive assault upon Hungary.

In this position Radu became a convenience to the Turks but a grave danger to Stephen, who could not be indifferent to their acquiring a permanent foothold on the northern bank of the Danube. In 1471, therefore, he invaded Wallachia, routed Radu at Soci and placed on the throne his own nominee Basarab Lăiota, of the elder branch of the reigning family. In 1473 the challenge was taken up by the Turks, who advanced through Buzau but were decisively routed by Stephen at Rîmnic-Sărat.

Stephen's whole attitude was dominated by the awkward geographical plight of Moldavia, condemned more and more to play a triangular game between Turkey, Hungary and Poland. During more than one crisis the two latter were more concerned to impose their suzerainty on Moldavia than to give effective military aid against the common foe: and

PLATE III

STEPHEN THE GREAT

From a contemporary fresco in the monastery of Putna

on one occasion a sum of 100,000 ducats contributed by the Pope towards the Turkish wars was diverted to Matthias of Hungary, as claiming to be overlord of Moldavia. Thus Stephen often had to play a double game, sacrificing everything to the paramount need of securing further assistance from abroad.

The news of Stephen's victory at Rîmnic inevitably roused Mohammed to action, and in 1474 he sent an ultimatum demanding the surrender of Chilia and the payment of an annual tribute. But Stephen summoned a council of his boiars and with their full consent resolved not merely to refuse the Turkish terms, but if necessary, to lay waste their own country before the invader. In the summer of 1474, then, a powerful Turkish army was diverted from its operations in Albania and sent to reduce Moldavia to submission. Late in that year, the Grand Vizier Suleiman the Eunuch, with the help of the craven-hearted Basarab, crossed the frontier and advanced northwards. But the population was evacuated according to plan, all supplies were withdrawn or destroyed, the roads were impassable, and on 10 January 1475 Stephen fell upon the Turks at Racova, near Văslui, on the river Barlad, at a point known as "Podul Înnalt" or the High Bridge, and inflicted a crushing defeat. Four pashas were killed and 100 flags captured, some of which were sent as trophies to Casimir of Poland, Matthias of Hungary and the Pope. A simultaneous attack by sea upon Chilia and Cetatea Alba was also unsuccessful, though some months later the fall of Caffa sealed the fate of Genoese trade in the Levant.

Stephen knew that he was fighting for his life, but in his own rude way he felt himself to be the David or the Judas Maccabaeus of the Christian cause, chosen for the saving of the nations.[1] He had already made more than one appeal to the West—and especially to the Pope and the Venetians—for an alliance against the infidel: and he now addressed an urgent letter to the leading Christian princes, stressing the need for union, in order "to cut off the pagan's right hand". Sixtus IV, worldly and sensual though he was, had the cause genuinely at heart, foreseeing a possible Turkish menace even to Italy itself: and he now addressed a letter of warm greeting and encouragement to Stephen, to whom he applies the title of "Athleta Christi". In the monastery of Putna, founded by the munificence of Stephen, this document is still preserved, and with it a relic sent to him about the same time as a

[1] "Intendentes pro Christianitate totis nostris viribus debellare", he wrote to Sixtus IV in 1474—Hurmuzaki, *Documente*, II, Part II, no. 202.

talisman of victory, from one of the monasteries of Mount Athos. This relic—a carved ivory cross supposed to contain a fragment of the true Cross—had originally been presented to the monks by the Emperor Romanus I, who described it as having been jealously preserved in the imperial treasury since the days of Helena, the mother of Constantine the Great. Few relics can be found with a better authenticated pedigree.

Mohammed was now thoroughly roused and in 1476 took personal command of a fresh army of invasion. Stephen had sent urgent warnings to the Pope and to the king of Hungary, that he might be forced to make terms with the Turks, if no help were forthcoming. But so far from this, he found himself exposed to a simultaneous attack from the Tatars in the north. On 25 July he gave battle to the Turks, but was overwhelmed at the battle of Răsboieni, between Roman and Neamț, and had to fly to the Polish border. The Turkish ranks, however, were already ravaged by cholera, it was difficult to feed a large invading army in a country stripped of all supplies, with an armed and desperate peasantry hanging on its flanks: and at last a Hungarian army under Stephen Báthory crossed the Transylvanian frontier at a point which threatened the Turkish retreat. The sultan reluctantly ordered a withdrawal, and Stephen followed and inflicted severe losses upon the Turkish army as it recrossed the Danube.

Moldavia remained unmolested for the remainder of the Conqueror's reign: but in 1484 his successor Bayezid II, after concluding an armistice with King Matthias which Stephen appears to have regarded as applying to himself also, made a sudden surprise attack upon the two key-fortresses of Chilia and Cetatea Alba, which henceforth remained in Turkish hands. In his manifesto the sultan claimed that he had "won the key of the door to all Moldavia and Hungary, the whole region of the Danube, Poland, Russia and Tatary and the entire coast of the Black Sea". Though this was an obvious overstatement, there could be no doubt that their possession drove Moldavia on to the defensive and placed her at a growing disadvantage. A year later the Turks plundered and burned Suceava, the Moldavian capital: but once again Stephen rallied his forces and defeated the enemy at Catlabuga near the Danube, and again in 1486 at Scheia near Roman. For the rest of his reign he was unmolested from the south, but the old lion was definitely on the defensive, and there were no true cubs.

King Matthias died in 1490, and as he left no children, the throne of Hungary fell to Wladislaw of Bohemia, a brother of King John Albert of Poland: and now we find the unedifying spectacle of the two brothers, indifferent to the Turkish danger and planning a joint conquest of Moldavia, in favour of their third brother Sigismund. Already in 1484 Stephen had found it necessary to do public homage to King Casimir, the curtains of the tent being drawn aside at the very moment when he was on his knees! It was not till 1499, after a successful resistance to an invasion by John Albert, that he was able to conclude a treaty on equal terms, in which there is no word of suzerainty and a distinct pledge of Polish assistance in a new crusade against the infidel. Unhappily this pledge remained on paper, and Stephen's ever recurring efforts to organise a league of Christian sovereigns were undermined by the suspicion and distrust which separated the Roumanians from both Poland and Hungary, and the Poles from Lithuania and Moscow. In 1502 he told a Venetian envoy, "I am surrounded by enemies on all sides, and have fought 36 battles since I was lord of this country, and of these won 34 and lost two".[1] But his powers of resistance were failing, and on his deathbed he appears to have advised his son to make submission to the Turks: for after holding them at bay for half a century, he felt the hopelessness of an united Christian rally, the decay of all the neighbouring states and the essential weakness of his own nation. If, however, the Turks should insist upon more than an honourable suzerainty, leaving the framework of church and state untouched, "then it will be better for you all to die at the hand of the enemy than to look on at the dishonouring of your religion and the misery of your country. But the God of your fathers will be moved by the tears of his servants to raise up a man who shall help your descendants to their old power and freedom".[2]

Stephen was equally great as a warrior and as an administrator: and special mention should be made of his constant devotion to the Church, his generous grant of monastic lands and the encouragement which he gave to literature and art, then still in their infancy. He is known to have erected about forty stone churches in different parts of the country: and a special direction was thus given to Moldavian ecclesiastical architecture, which still survives in the churches of Baia, Dorohoiu, St Nicholas of Jassy and others. The bell-tower of Baia, erected in memory of the victory of 1467, has been admirably restored in recent times. Most famous of all Stephen's endowments is the mon-

[1] 7 December 1502—Hurmuzaki, *Documente*, VIII, no. 45.
[2] Cit. Engel. *op. cit.* I, p. 157.

astery of Putna, in the modern Bukovina, built as a thankoffering for
his defeat of the Tatars. Here many personal treasures, including some
embroidery by the ladies of his court, are still piously preserved.[1]

Unhappily Stephen was the last of the heroic breed, and none of his
successors proved even remotely worthy of him. On his death there
was marked and rapid decay, and we find ourselves in a new and inglorious epoch. His long and glorious reign, however, not unnaturally
gave a heightened national consciousness to his subjects, and this is
reflected in a phrase of the Hungarian chronicle of Oláh—"The Voivode of this province is less exposed to dangerous changes than the
Wallachian. The Moldavians hold themselves to be nobler and braver
than the Wallachians: their horses are better. They can put an army of
40,000 men into the field".[2]

The Venetian envoy Matteo Muriano, wrote home of Stephen as "a
man of great wisdom, worthy of high praise, much loved by his subjects for his clemency and justice, very vigilant and liberal, and well
preserved for his age if this illness (which had delayed his audience) had
not assailed him".[3] We may conclude with the estimate of Miron Costin,
the first serious Roumanian historian—"Stephen was not tall of stature:
he was irascible, cruel, prone to shed innocent blood, often at meals he
would order people to be put to death, without legal sentence. But he
was acute of judgment, sober, not proud, but a stubborn defender of
his rights, in war always on the spot, well versed in military science,
generally favoured by victory, never depressed by misfortune: ever
expecting a better turn to affairs. The Moldavians think of him in
political respects, with that veneration with which one holds a saint in
religious honour".[4]

In modern times there has been much barren controversy as to the
respective merits of the various Danubian and Balkan nations in saving
Europe from the Turkish yoke. The Magyars in particular are never
tired of putting forward an almost exclusive claim on their own behalf,
and indeed use it to justify certain modern ambitions at the expense of
their neighbours. In sober truth, it is quite impossible for any one

---

[1] The reader is referred to the richly illustrated monograph of Professors N. Iorga
and G. Balş, *L'Art Roumain*, especially pp. 311–40. Roumanian ecclesiastical and
domestic architecture deserves and will amply repay the study which the West
has not yet deigned to devote to it.

[2] *Hungaria*, CXIII—cit. Engel, *op. cit.* p. 151.

[3] Hurmuzaki, *Documente*, VIII, no. 45.

[4] Cit. Engel, p. 156.

nation to claim a monopoly, and in attempting a broad summary of their joint achievement, we may reasonably affirm that the brunt of the defence was borne by the Serbs in the second half of the fourteenth, by the Hungarians in the first half of the fifteenth and by the Roumanians in the second half of the same century, while the Albanians under Scanderbeg must never be forgotten; that with the progressive decay of all the Danubian states in the early sixteenth century, and especially after 1526, the task of organising that defence passed to the Imperialists under Habsburg leadership, and that in the slow recovery of the next two hundred years every nation played its part, as the history of the Croat, Serb, Hungarian and Roumanian frontier regiments amply testifies.

# CHAPTER III

# TURKISH VASSALAGE (1504–1714)

"The prince changes, and madmen rejoice"[1]—Roumanian proverb

With the death of Stephen the Great there is immediate and gross degeneration. His son Bogdan, known as the One-Eyed, had no grasp of the general situation and chased after the phantom of a Polish marriage, which the new king, Sigismund I, already hostile to Moldavia, was in no way disposed to accord to one whom he regarded as a barbarous and schismatic princeling. Bogdan had been ready to surrender the province of Pocutia in return for a princess's hand, but when this was finally refused to him, and when a marauding assault upon it failed, his hopes and ambitions were still concentrated northwards, and in 1517 he fell fighting against the Tatars. Meanwhile both he and his kinsman on the Wallachian throne—he eventually married a daughter of Mihnea the Bad (cel Rău)—seemed oblivious to the Turkish menace, or incapable of realising its immense potential dangers. While Radu paid a visit of personal homage to Constantinople, Bogdan, still trading on the reputation of his great father, concluded a treaty with the sultan which regularised a tribute of 4000 ducats, supplemented by 40 broodmares and 40 falcons for the sultan's own use. Bogdan may have salved his conscience by pointing to the clauses which insisted upon complete autonomy, respect for the Christian religion, and non-interference with the princely elections and placed a veto upon the erection of mosques or Turkish ownership of Moldavian land. But on the Turkish side the treaty was a mere "act of grace", to be more honoured in the breach than the observance. In effect it inaugurated the real period of vassalage, and the establishment of a permanent Moldavian envoy in Constantinople—the so-called Kapu-Kihaya—was really nothing else than the adoption of a system of hostages for good behaviour.

Between the death of Radu, misnamed the Great, in 1508 and the accession of Mircea the Shepherd (Ciobanul) in 1545, no fewer than eleven princes disputed the Wallachian throne among themselves, thus rendering any settled government impossible and undermining the

---

[1] Schimbarea Domnilor, bucuria nebunilor.

none too sure foundations of the state. Alone among them Neagoe Basarab deserves more than a passing mention, not for any political act, but solely as the founder of the church of Argeş, that earliest surviving gem of Roumanian ecclesiastical architecture, which serves to indicate what native talent might have achieved if Roumania could have developed on free and normal lines. He and his Serbian consort Despina spent all the revenues that they could spare, and even their personal jewels, on the endowment of the monastery of Argeş, at the dedication of which the Patriarch of Constantinople and many monks from Athos were present.

Meanwhile, the Turks, seeing the complete impotence of the Roumanians, were free to develop their plans against Hungary, which under the feeble rule of the Jagiello kings, was also by now in rapid decline. "We mean to elect a king," said the magnate Báthory, "whose hair we can keep a grip on", and they chose the feckless Pole, who was nicknamed "Dobrzy" because he said "Good" to every proposal. The union of the Bohemian and Hungarian crowns under Wladislaw II did not really make for strength: the two nobilities were excessively jealous of each other and bent above all upon hedging in the royal prerogative —no very difficult task towards so weak and sluggish a sovereign— and on extending their own privileges at the expense of the peasantry. This is not the place to dwell upon the internal situation in Hungary, still less Bohemia: but it is impossible to insist too strongly upon the deterioration in the status of the peasantry throughout all the Danubian countries as the fifteenth century closed, as one of the prime factors which gave the Turks their military predominance and hastened their victory. For while on the Turkish side were *élan*, discipline and religious enthusiasm, among the Christian nations most nearly menaced there was a deep-seated discontent which found expression in a series of wild *jacqueries*, ferociously repressed and used as an excuse for still greater extortions. Nowhere was the conflict more acute than in Hungary, where a peasant insurrection on a very large scale broke out in 1514, in consequence of the renewed Turkish war and the crusading appeals issued by the primate and the Pope. The masses found an able leader in George Dózsa, a Székely captain of some military prowess, and their fanaticism was fanned by some of the lower clergy. In the end the great nobles under John Zápolya reasserted their power and took a fearful vengeance: Dózsa was bound to a red-hot throne, crowned with a glowing crown of iron and torn with pincers, while some of his

4-2

followers were forced to eat the flesh from his still living body! While Zápolya was hailed as "Liberator of the Kingdom" by his fellow nobles, popular legend believed that he was struck with temporary blindness when he next presented himself at the altar, after deeds of such peculiar ferocity and treachery. But the name of the despised *kurucz* or crusader was to survive in Hungarian history and to give its sentimental inspiration to more than one movement of an ostensibly popular kind.

Far worse, however, than acts of repression when the foundations of the state were shaking, were the elaborate measures taken by the victorious nobility to reinforce the feudal regime by *robot* and *corvée* and payment in kind. The enslavement of the peasantry throughout Hungary and Transylvania—their "mera et perpetua servitus"—was now crystallised in the "Tripartitum", the famous legal code of Stephen Verböczi, which was to remain in full force for over three centuries, till the emancipation of 1848, and which provides the true key to the mentality of the Magyar ruling class from that day to this. A fatal gulf had been fixed between the *misera plebs contribuens* and the nobles, greater and lesser, who alone formed the *populus*, or political nation, and who in addition to all other privileges were eventually able to secure exemption from taxation also! Although the Roumanians played no such notable part in the events of 1514 as they had in the earlier rising of 1437, it was none the less for them too a parting of the ways: for the Roumanian noble class, with but few exceptions, henceforth almost inevitably came to identify itself more and more with the Hungarian nobility, leaving the Roumanian masses leaderless and depressed to a dead level of ignorance and serfdom.

These social evils, greatly aggravated by the desolation of the civil war, unquestionably weakened Hungary's powers of resistance to the Turkish danger: and this, it may be supposed, was fully known to the Turks and whetted their appetite for conquest in Central Europe. This time the fate of the Roumanians depended upon that of Hungary.

On Wladislaw's death in 1516 the royal power was still further diminished during the minority of his son Louis II: the magnates squandered their own and their country's resources by brawling and intrigue, instead of strengthening the southern frontier during the years of respite afforded by Sultan Selim's conquest of Egypt. When Selim died prematurely in 1520, his son the "Magnificent" Suleiman speedily showed his intentions by assailing the border fortresses along the Save. Belgrade still resisted, but Šabac fell before him in 1521. But even this grave warning and the final respite afforded by Suleiman's diversion against Rhodes, were disregarded by the warring factions into which the Hungarian nobility had fallen: while Europe's indifference was shown by its absorption in the conflict between Francis of Valois and Charles of Habsburg and the former's appeal for Turkish aid in a Christian quarrel. The young King Louis, who slept till midday, threw about his diminished revenues and was as indolent and ineffective as his father, made pathetic appeals to the sovereigns of the West, but none came to his aid save the Pope, who sent a contribution of 50,000 ducats. Ferdinand of Austria, who alone combined the good will and personal interest, was at this moment absorbed by a peasant revolt in his own dominions. When Suleiman opened his campaign on the Danube in April 1526 with a powerful army and a *corps d'élite* of Janissaries, Hungary was less prepared than ever, the treasury was empty, the taxes were in arrears, the fortresses in disorder, and the army lacked weapons and provisions. The Croats stood aloof and looked towards Vienna. The nobles continued to quarrel, and their factiousness and selfish rapacity form the constant theme of successive Venetian envoys, who had no motive whatsoever for hostility towards Hungary and every conceivable motive for co-operation with her. "If the Sultan really comes," wrote the Nuncio to the anxious Pope Clement in 1523, "I repeat what I have so often said: Your Holiness may regard this country as lost. There is boundless confusion. All that is needed for waging war is lacking. Among the Estates hatred and envy prevail: and the subjects would, if the Sultan gives them freedom, make a still more cruel rising than in the days of the Crusade" (i.e. of 1514).[1]

The poor young king was roused to action by the fall of Peterwardein in July: but he lacked the strength of mind to withdraw northwards and wait until further help could reach him. His advisers arrogantly underrated the value of the Turkish fighting machine, though well aware of its immense superiority in numbers. On 29 August 1526, then, King Louis gave battle to Suleiman at Mohács and was utterly routed. He himself, his two archbishops, five bishops and the flower of the Hungarian nobility fell at this Flodden of the East, and the whole kingdom was at the mercy of the conqueror, who entered Buda unopposed on 11 September.

Louis left no children, and for over a decade Hungary was disputed between his brother-in-law Ferdinand of Habsburg, who was also

[1] Cit. Pastor, *Gesch. der Päpste*, IV, ii, p. 442.

elected to the Bohemian and Croatian thrones, and John Zápolya, the ambitious opposition magnate who, though regarded by many as a mere upstart, had long aspired to follow Hunyady's example and found a new national dynasty. The sultan's ire was concentrated against the "King of Vienna", as Ferdinand and his successors to the third generation were contemptuously nick-named by the Turks: but the objective was not so much Ferdinand as his brother Charles, the "King of Spain", whose imperial position seemed the main obstacle to Ottoman conquest in the very heart of Europe. It suited Suleiman admirably to favour the ambitions of Zápolya and promote still further the deep divisions inside the Hungarian ruling class: and as time passed, discord was still further accentuated by the religious issue. The Reformation had been rapidly spreading in Hungary in the years preceding Mohács, and now a combination of religious and national motives led the main body of the Magyars to look towards Geneva, while the Saxons accepted the tenets of Wittenberg. Transylvania developed upon mainly Protestant lines and acquired a very natural distrust of the Habsburgs in proportion as they assumed the rôle of champions of the Catholic reaction.

At first sight it may seem that even this brief outline of Hungarian history lies outside the true scope of the present volume. But Mohács is a decisive turning point for the Roumanians no less than for the Magyars: and even a glance at the map will suffice to show the reason. Hitherto the Turks had followed the main line of strategic advance towards Central Europe, and this involved the complete subjection first of Bulgaria and then of Serbia, and as a corollary, the isolation of Bosnia on their left flank and of the Roumanian principalities on their right. They were now to control the great central plain of the Danube, to within a few days' march of Pressburg, Vienna and Graz and the whole lower course of the Drave, Save and Tisza. As a result, Wallachia and still more Moldavia were effectively cut off from their natural contacts with Europe, and driven in upon themselves: while Transylvania, its fertile valleys sheltered between the semicircular watershed of the Carpathians and the high Bihar range that dominates the plains of the Middle Tisza, of necessity extended the autonomy which it already possessed, into virtual independence. Henceforth, these three units— Wallachia, Moldavia, Transylvania—were more than ever interdependent: and though political distrust and racial jealousies made a barrier out of mountains through which numerous passes provided easy access, the history of four further centuries was to prove that the two Roumanian states must either be drawn into the orbit of a great Danubian empire or, in order to achieve a sure and permanent independence of their own, must attach Transylvania to themselves.

## PETER RAREŞ

The anarchy that followed Mohács brought to the front one of the most curious figures in Roumanian history—Peter Rareş, an illegitimate son of Stephen, who had already spent long years of exile at the Polish court. In 1527 he was raised by the boiars to the Moldavian throne, and at once found himself plunged into a complicated intrigue between Sultan Suleiman, now on the eve of his great expedition against Vienna, the sultan's agent the renegade Venetian Ludovico Gritti, Sigismund of Poland, with whom Peter had close personal relations, John Zápolya the puppet "king" of conquered Hungary and his rival Ferdinand of Austria, against whom Turkish fury was now rightly concentrated. A straightforward policy was indeed wellnigh impossible under the circumstances: Peter's only hope was to outbid his more powerful neighbours in suppleness and resource. While Ferdinand and Zápolya, with varying fortunes, were contesting such fragments of Eastern and Northern Hungary as still resisted the Turks, Peter clearly aspired to the possession of Transylvania for himself, and in 1529 he did actually secure not only the castles of Ciceu (Csicsó) and Cetatea de Balta (Küküllövár)— two important fiefs originally granted by Matthias to Stephen as possible places of refuge in case of disaster—but even a considerable portion of the Székely districts and not least of all, the silver mines of Rodna. A year later he set himself to capture Bistritz and launched barbaric threats against its Saxon inhabitants, that he would roast them alive if once he caught them. The town resisted for the moment, but made its submission before it was too late and paid tribute.

The next stage in his career, however, shows his restless and unstable character. Not content with consolidating his position westwards, he must needs revive the long dormant quarrel with Poland and attempt to recover from it the lost province of Pocutia. In 1531, after concluding treaties with Moscow and the Tatars, he became involved in war with King Sigismund, but the adventure ended abruptly in a crushing defeat at the battle of Obertyn, due largely to his own impatient tactics against trained troops. He was at least able to hold his own frontiers against Poland and turned back again with added zest to his Transylvanian dreams, in which he seems to have generally had the friendly support of the Székels. He must have known all the time that he was skating on the thinnest of ice, for in 1532, while Suleiman and Sigismund were engaged in not very sincere negotiations, he had to reckon with the scarcely concealed intention of the former to place the Roumanian lands under the rule of a pasha, and of the latter to reduce Moldavia to complete vassalage. "The Moldavian", wrote the sultan to the king of Poland, "is our servant and vassal, and therefore none may injure him" —an attitude which frightened Peter once more into the arms of Ferdinand.

The main reason for this lay in the secret design of Gritti, who now called himself "Protector Hungariae" and confident in his influence over the sultan, probably hoped to obtain Transylvania for his own son or some trustworthy nominee. In 1534 he came with full powers from Constantinople, and made a compact, on which he seems to have relied, with the treacherous Peter: but the folly and arrogance of his behaviour on reaching Transylvania, and especially his murder of Bishop Czibák, the envoy of Zápolya, alienated all parties from him. He had no choice but to surrender himself into the hands of the Moldavians, who "like ravenous wolves", ignoring the safe-conduct given by their own prince, handed him over to the incensed Hungarians. Stephen Mailáth was quite unimpressed by Gritti's claim to represent the person of Suleiman himself, and promptly ordered his execution: and his two sons, the younger only twelve years old, were sent off to the court of Jassy and there mercilessly beheaded by orders of Peter Rareş.

Peter knew that this meant war with the Turks and hastened to negotiate with Ferdinand, while the faithless Mailáth, hitherto the chief supporter of the Habsburg cause in Transylvania, made a sudden compact with Zápolya. The report of Reicherstorffer, Ferdinand's emissary to Moldavia, has survived and describes Peter as loud in his professions of zeal for "the salvation of all Christendom" and in exhortations to use the sultan's absorption in a Persian war, to recover Hungary and crush his rival, the "traitor" Zápolya. Ferdinand assigns to him the fortresses of Csicsó, Küküllö and Bálványos and the town of Bistritz and a yearly sum of 6000 ducats[1]: and Peter took a secret oath of homage to the king of the Romans, as the latter wrote to his sister. But the incredible shiftiness of the man now reveals itself more strikingly than ever. Beckoned

[1] March 1535—Hurmuzaki, Documente, II, (i), nos. 65 and 66.

onward by the absurd hope of driving the Poles from Pocutia, and well aware that Suleiman was returning to Europe after a successful Persian campaign, he enters upon new negotiations both with the Turks and with Zápolya, while his agents are still to and fro between Jassy and Vienna. Ferdinand's envoy is at Suceava, while the envoys of Suleiman and Zápolya meet at Jassy and join hands in the endeavour to win Peter against the Habsburgs: he shall be forgiven for his share in the murder of Gritti, he shall have what he wants from Poland, say the Turks, and as for Zápolya, he promises "seas and mountains" (maria et montes[1]).

Peter was near the end of his political legerdemain. It was obvious that he could not be trusted by anyone, and the great sultan decided to "crush him under the hoofs of the Ottoman cavalry". The last straw was provided when Zápolya intercepted the prince's correspondence with Ferdinand and sent it to Suleiman. In the summer of 1538, then, the sultan in person marshalled an army of some 200,000 men at Adrianople and, aided by an understanding with the curiously Turcophil Sigismund of Poland, speedily overran Moldavia, taking it almost in his stride, on the way to Buda. Peter fled across the mountains and spent a year in one of the vindictive Zápolya's prisons, while a nephew, whose name of Stephen was fitly parodied by the nickname of "the Locust" (Lăcusta), was placed by the sultan on the vacant throne. Suleiman, who in all this had the short-sighted approval and co-operation of Poland, definitely aimed at reducing the two Roumanian princes to complete subservience, as his nominees and vassals, and at establishing a series of key fortresses along the Danube and the Black Sea coast, such as would render all raids upon his long line of communications finally impossible. In pursuance of this policy he built a new fortress at Tighinea, henceforth to be known as Bender: and this, together with Cetatea Alba (Akkerman), dominated the whole lower course of the Dniester, served as a check upon Tatar or Cossack raids and held Moldavia firmly as in a pair of pincers.

The wretched "Locust", so called because of a symbolic plague of these insects during his brief reign, only maintained himself in Suceava by the aid of a strong bodyguard of Janissaries. But there still remained some boiars of spirit, who resenting his feeble tyranny, killed him and placed one of their own number on the throne. But Peter Rareş now

---

[1] Bánffy's report to Ferdinand—Fr. Schuller, *Urkundliche Beiträge zur Gesch. Siebenbürgens*, cit. Ursu, p. 133.

saw his opportunity, the more so as Zápolya also died in 1540, leaving his helpless widow Isabella of Poland with an infant in arms as successor to a disputed throne. Escaping from his Transylvanian prison, Peter therefore sent an abject message of submission to the sultan and appealed for permission to come and justify himself in person. This was granted, and in 1540 his powers of persuasion, his rich presents and political strategy won over the Porte to his side, and next year he was back upon the Moldavian throne, by the aid of a Turkish army. He had, however, to accept a bodyguard of 500 men, the tribute was raised from 4000 to 12,000 ducats, and his son was held as hostage in Stambul. That this was a wise precaution in face of such utter perfidy as that of Rareş, is sufficiently illustrated by the secret treaty which he concluded with the German armies then endeavouring to recover Buda. By it he was to betray the Turks at the crisis of the struggle, to hand over the sultan himself dead or alive and to receive in return a subsidy of 500,000 ducats.[1] It seems difficult to believe that this was seriously meant: certainly he never had an opportunity of acting. Meanwhile Suleiman with overwhelming forces was converting Central Hungary into a Turkish province, governed by a pasha in the key fortress of Buda, which fell finally into his hands in August 1541. The infant John Sigismund Zápolya was brought to his camp and recognised by him as "King of Hungary": but his mother and her astute counsellor "Brother George" —Cardinal Martinuzzi—were more and more restricted to Transylvania and the counties bordering upon it.

Much may be pardoned to the desperate straits in which Peter found himself, wedged in between at least four overbearing and unscrupulous foes: but it cannot be denied that the kaleidoscopic character of his perfidy is almost unique even in the annals of the sixteenth century. It is impossible to admit that he was in any way fitted for the rôle which a modern Roumanian historian has treated as feasible—namely that of rallying the Roumanian masses under the Habsburg banner and playing them off against the Hungarian nobility, which was using the dire anarchy of the times to strengthen its feudal power. The most that can be said for him is that he genuinely aimed at Moldavian independence, as achieved by his father in happier days, and also, if it might be, an extension of his power to the two neighbouring Principalities. Of

---

[1] Xenopol, *Hist. des Roumains*, I, p. 309. "Et quantum possibile ipsum Turcarum imperatorem suae illustrissimae dominationi ut supremo belli capitaneo vel vivum vel mortuum personaliter presentabimus."

PLATE IV

PETER RAREŞ

From a contemporary fresco

patriotism, as distinct from personal ambition and greed, there is but little trace in his story.[1]

## THE SUCCESSORS OF PETER

When Peter died in 1546, his shifty and unstable improvisations stood out as real statecraft, in contrast to the utter degradation of his successors. His eldest son, Ilie, was a mere creature of the sultan, and in the end not merely embraced Islam, but was content to serve as pasha of Silistria instead of prince of Moldavia: the younger son, Stephen, was a vile tyrant, who died of debauchery after a reign of eighteen months. He was succeeded by his cousin Alexander Lăpuşneanu, a red-eyed neurasthenic who maintained himself for a time by bribery and terror. The family tree of Stephen the Great offers us a sad study in princely degeneracy. The sons of Bogdan III, Ştefaniţa (1517–27) and Lăpuşneanu (1552–61 and 1564–8) were already evil enough, but the next two generations offer us the odious figures of John the Cruel (Ioan cel Cumplit, 1572–4), Aron the Tyrant (1591–5) and Peter the Cossack: and with the latter's nephew Alexander the Bad (cel Rău), who only reigned a few months, the race of Stephen the Great seems to have ended. The three sons of Peter Rareş were, as we saw, one more unworthy than the other, while Stephen's remaining son Alexander had no descendants save the miserable "Locust".

It remains to mention the sorry rôle of Peter Rareş's daughter Chiajna, who became the wife of Mircea of Wallachia. She won the support of the Porte for her husband and sons by herself visiting Constantinople with a treasure of 80,000 ducats and ingratiating herself with the reigning favourites of Suleiman's harem. At a later date she secured Moldavia for her son Peter by sheer bribery and outbid even Peter Cercel—"Peter of the Ear-rings", one of the most degenerate and unscrupulous princes even of this degraded period, who had, however, talent, a distinguished bearing and a knowledge of twelve languages. Indeed, for the death of Peter Cercel she went so far as to promise the grand vizier as much money as 600 horses could draw!

From the middle of the sixteenth century onwards the practice of nomination to the princely thrones is almost invariable. Each aspirant has to buy the consent of the Porte, and in view of the rapid spread of

[1] The fullest account of Peter's career is to be found in J. Ursu, *Die auswärtige Politik des Peter Rareş* (Vienna, 1908).

corruption at the fountain head of power, he has to consider not merely the great officers of state, but the sultan himself, the reigning sultana, the sultana-mother, the ladies of the harem, the eunuchs and mutes and "mussaips", and all the endless tribe of favourites and parasites that ministered to the sultan's whims or vices. All or many of these have to be converted to his claims by baksheesh applied with varying degrees of crudity or discretion. Moreover, the chaotic rules of succession to the two thrones, and the failure of any prince to establish a direct line from father to son, naturally strengthen still further the hold of the Porte. There are always a certain number of refugees in Constantinople, belonging to the rival princely and boiar families, and only waiting for a chance of supplanting the reigning prince of the moment.

As if all this were not enough, we find the most arrant adventurers gaining transient possession of the throne or aspiring to it with some hope of success. The most romantic instance is undoubtedly that of Jacob Basilic, known as Despota, who ruled in Moldavia from 1561 to 1563. He was a Greek by birth, who had travelled widely in Europe: at one time he had become the friend of Melancthon and a convert to Protestantism, at another he had served as a soldier of fortune in the imperial army both in Spain and Italy. This preposterous play actor, who wrote his name in purple ink and reeled off fantastic stories of his imperial Roman descent to the amazed and credulous boiars of his court, has about him faint reminiscences of Rienzi, though on an altogether lower and more vulgar plane. The manner in which he established himself in Moldavia and was finally betrayed and killed by the very boiars whose purposes he had at first served so well, is of no historical importance, save as a picture of society in an outlying Ottoman province. Then again there was Emanuel Aron, a baptised Jew, who bought the Moldavian throne in 1591, and again in 1592, for enormous sums[1] and recouped himself by new taxation, spreading his net so widely as to demand an ox from every family. Less than a generation later still, we find an obscure Italian, Gaspar Graziani, appointed prince of Moldavia in 1619, and other Italians, Cigalla of Messina, and Rosso, men of no standing or particular merit, making a determined bid for Wallachia.

Under such conditions the prestige of the two thrones had sunk to

[1] The debts which he contracted at Constantinople are given by Xenopol (*op. cit.* I, p. 427) as 1,000,000 ducats (25,000,000 pre-war francs).

zero, and the Turks treated its occupants with well-merited contempt. In Moldavia John the Cruel (Ioan cel Cumplit), in defiance of the terms under which he had surrendered, was sentenced by them in 1574 to be torn in pieces by camels. Mihnea II of Wallachia (1577–83) accepted Islam, in order to avoid imprisonment or death. Alexander the Bad, the last descendant of Stephen the Great—but reigning in Wallachia, not Moldavia—was in 1592 hanged in a public square at Stambul. Incidents of this kind are abundant proof that political independence was already a thing of the past. It must be confessed that the older Roumanian dynasties were, save for the rarest individual exceptions, quite unworthy of their national task, and that no adequate successor arose in the twilight period between vassalage and complete enslavement. But in common fairness it should be added that once the Turks were established at Buda, the position of the Roumanian Principalities was wellnigh untenable and grew even worse as the rivalry developed between Turk, Pole and Imperialist. Transylvania, left in mid-air after the triple partition of Hungary and eking out a precarious independence of its own, added a further complication to the international situation. The Roumanians thus found themselves taken in the rear: for the Turks could invade Transylvania from the west and north-west and at the same time overrun the plains of Oltenia and Moldavia and force the passes of the Carpathians. At the same time the Roumanians never succeeded in establishing relations of real mutual confidence with any of their other immediate neighbours, the Magyars, the Poles or even the Cossacks.

## MICHAEL THE BRAVE

At the turn of the century there is a brief but memorable interlude, whose immediate effects were very speedily effaced, but which may be compared to the firing of a gun in some Alpine valley, which sets an avalanche in motion. The achievement of Michael the Brave in uniting all the Roumanian lands under his rule, was an event far in advance of practical possibilities and indeed rested upon entirely false foundations. But it fired the imagination of the race, and, by showing what had actually been realised for a brief moment, it aroused aspirations which can scarcely be said to have existed before, but which were henceforth never to die out until they were realised under essentially different circumstances and in a much sounder form, in our own day.

It is natural enough that Michael the Brave should stand for the Roumanians as the last national hero before the shameful era of Turkish and Greek domination, and that four centuries later his statue in Bucarest should have become the rallying ground of irredentist demonstrators. But just as Marko Kraljević—the immortal hero of Serbian poetic legend—was in real life a petty enough vassal fighting in the Turkish ranks against his own kinsmen, so too in a certain sense the Michael whom that statue commemorates—the champion of Roumanian nationality—is a mere legendary figure, in whom the real Michael would have been puzzled to recognise himself. Michael was certainly national enough in feeling to resent the Turkish yoke, his own insecure tenure and the impossible financial strain imposed by tribute, bribery and exactions. But he was far more identified with the noble boiar class than with anything that could be described as a national movement. He was directly responsible for a marked deterioration in the lot of the Wallachian peasantry, while in Transylvania he deliberately threw himself into the arms of the Magyar nobility and helped them to suppress the Roumanian peasantry which had risen in the belief that he was coming to their aid. What gave him a force superior to his immediate predecessors, seems to have been the advent of a new class of landed gentry, who supplemented the greater boiars and were above all concerned to extend their own power at the expense of the yeomen and peasantry.

In 1572 John the Terrible, who ruled for three short years in Moldavia, had identified himself with the peasantry in an attempt to check the venality of the boiars, and thus, it may be affirmed—though it is perhaps dangerous to apply such modern phraseology to another world of ideas—to find a more popular basis of resistance to the Turks and a means of dispensing with arbitrary taxation. John put himself in the wrong by his cruelties: he was soon betrayed, overpowered and killed by the boiars, who henceforth took good care, in both Principalities, to prevent any fresh alliance between prince and people.

Michael the Brave acquired the Wallachian throne in 1593, and his comet-like career barely lasted eight years. He appears to have owed his success in no small measure to the influence of the English and Transylvanian envoys at the Porte, backed by the powerful Phanariot Andronicus Cantacuzene: but like so many other favoured candidates, he had to pay in hard cash, and seemed likely to be at the mercy of his overlord. Yet almost his first action was one of revolt against the Turkish creditors who were settling like locusts upon Wallachia, accompanied the tax collectors on their rounds and thus extorted all sorts of illegal contributions, in addition to the monstrous sum already extracted. These harpies made the mistake of thinking that he was at their mercy. Imprisoned by them in his own palace, he turned the tables upon them by an act of deep and sudden treachery typical of the period midway between Rizzio and Wallenstein: and setting a strong guard round the building in which they had assembled at his invitation, he burnt it ruthlessly to the ground. Knowing very well that this was equivalent to a declaration of war, he then struck at once: his troops, stiffened by a small corps of picked Cossacks, stormed the fortress of Giurgiu and Brăila, while the Moldavians seized Ismail. He then routed the first Turkish forces sent against him and even made a winter raid across the Danube as far south as Adrianople.

The Turks naturally resolved to crush the rebel, both in order to avenge their outraged dignity, and because the loss of Wallachia appears already to have affected the provisioning of Constantinople. The famous grand vizier, Sinan Pasha, himself led an army against Michael, who in his need for allies, concluded in May 1595 a treaty of the most stringent character with his Transylvanian neighbour, the worthless Sigismund Báthory. Under it, he not merely acknowledged Sigismund as his suzerain, but actually renounced the right of concluding separate treaties or even granting pardons within his own dominions: while taxation inside Wallachia itself was actually to be fixed by the Diet of Transylvania, augmented by twelve Wallachian boiars.

At first sight this might well seem to be worse servitude than that from which he was endeavouring to escape. But Professor Xenopol was undoubtedly right in concluding that Michael "accepted the nominal authority of a Prince who lacked the means to enforce it, in order to escape the very real authority exercised by the Turks over his country".[1] Even if Sigismund had been less vacillating and incompetent than history reveals him, he could still scarcely have hoped to secure much more than nominal obedience. He was doubtless led to underestimate Michael by his own close family connections with Poland and by his success in dethroning Aron of Moldavia and substituting a nominee of his own, a gallant boiar known to history as Stefan Vodă.

It would be absurd to deny that the agreement with Sigismund was

[1] *Op. cit.* I, p. 351.

merely one out of many acts of duplicity in Michael's career or to claim for him a high standard of public morality. It is, however, necessary to allow for the extraordinarily dangerous and equivocal position in which he now found himself—drawn into a vortex of intrigue between the three Great Powers of Eastern Europe in his day—Turkey, Poland and the Empire—the more distant Russians and Tatars and his unstable neighbours Moldavia and Transylvania. And indeed, if we compare his policy and methods with those of most contemporaries, not merely in Constantinople and Prague, but even in Rome, Paris and Madrid, we certainly shall not find him worse than the age and the milieu into which he was born.

For the moment Michael's opportunist policy was a success. For though he gained a remarkable victory over Sinan Pasha at Călugăreni on 23 August 1595—in which three pashas were killed and the Green Banner of the Prophet was captured—he could not save his country from being overrun and its two little capitals, Tîrgovişte and Bucarest, being stormed and plundered: and it was only the assistance brought by Sigismund of Transylvania and his Moldavian nominee—including some Florentines collected by the grand duke of Tuscany for a strangely belated crusade—that enabled Michael to rally his forces and compel the Turks to retire. He now enjoyed a respite, for in 1596 the Turks concentrated their forces against Hungary and routed the imperialists at the great battle of Mezökeresztés. This left the two Principalities again in the air, and Moldavia in particular at the mercy of Polish aggression: but fortunately for Michael, while Ştefan Vodă was captured and suffered death by impalement, it suited the convenience of the Turks to conclude a truce with him and postpone the day of reckoning. In 1597–8 there was a deadlock between the Turks and the imperialists, who took Raab but twice failed before Buda.

If the policy of Michael now became more tortuous than ever, the necessity for this was forced upon him by the action of Sigismund Báthory, in many ways the least satisfactory or reliable of all the native princes. Mediocre in intellect and character and brought up by Jesuit advisers in narrow and bigoted ideas, Sigismund never knew his own mind for long and at intervals threw up the sponge and renounced the government, then thinking better, or rather worse, of it, returned to complicate still further a situation already almost incapable of unravelment. The first of these fits of despair occurred in 1598, when he ceded his princely rights to the Emperor Rudolf II in return for two Silesian duchies, and then withdrew to his relatives in Poland.[1] Michael, as his vassal, genuinely tried to hold him back, having little fancy for merely replacing Turkish by German rule and fearing that this new turn of the wheel might compromise his ultimate aim of complete independence. Failing to restrain Báthory, he made cautious overtures to the Porte, both through his friend the English envoy and through the Patriarch: but finding that the Turks insisted upon a renewal of the tribute as an indispensable condition, and being determined to resist this at all costs, he at last accepted the inevitable and entered into relations with Vienna, or rather with Prague, which Rudolf had made his permanent residence. He took an oath of fealty to Rudolf as king of Hungary, but otherwise secured far more liberal terms than those exacted by Báthory three years earlier. Instead of a tribute, he was to receive a subsidy for his army, and the free right of election was guaranteed to the "Estates" of Wallachia in the event of Michael leaving no heirs. This allegiance was paid in June 1598, at the monastery of Dealu, before the tomb of Michael's father, and at the spot where only three years later his own murdered remains were to be buried.

The fickle Sigismund, however, soon changed his mind and in August 1598 returned unannounced to his abandoned throne, partly influenced by Polish jealousy of the Habsburgs and this time ready to advance his own selfish ends by an unholy alliance with the Turks against the Empire. Rudolf naturally enough resented Sigismund's treachery and looked upon Michael as a useful instrument of policy against him: but Michael on his side seems to have pleaded Sigismund's cause with Rudolf—being in his own exposed position less concerned to promote this or that political intrigue than by a united front to hold the Turkish danger at arms-length. The preposterous Sigismund could not, however, be relied upon for many months at a time. Though he sent two of his foremost dignitaries, Stephen Bocskay and Bishop Náprágy, to negotiate once more with Rudolf, he could not await the issue, but on 30 March 1599 again solemnly renounced the Transylvanian throne. This time it was in favour of his young cousin Cardinal Andrew Báthory, who enjoyed the full backing of the Polish crown and

---

[1] A contemporary report throws a curious sidelight upon Sigismund's "Wanderlust". He wanted apparently to visit England (*voluit ire in Angliam*), but was dissuaded by a certain "doctor quidam iuris Scotus natione, perspectus ipsius moribus vagabundis et levioribus"—Hurmuzaki, *Documente*, XII, no. 706. Cf. also nos. 762, 835.

thus found himself in the unnatural position of ally of the sultan against the emperor. Michael's position between hammer and anvil was all the more uncomfortable because Andrew was related to the Movilă family, which in 1595 had successfully ousted the heirs of Stephen from the Moldavian throne and was now known to have designs upon Wallachia also.[1] Michael, as heir of the old princely family of the Basarabs, may be assumed to have felt specially resentful on this point.

Andrew promptly sent envoys demanding a renewal of homage from Michael, who for the moment did not dare to refuse, but who can obviously have had no real intention of keeping his word. Andrew, however, showed equal duplicity, not merely by giving his backing to Michael's special enemies in Moldavia, but by using Michael's submission as a means of ingratiating himself with the Porte, whose suzerainty he promptly recognised for all three states—Transylvania, Moldavia and Wallachia. Michael was now desperate, surrounded on all sides by treacherous foes: Rudolf, himself an adept in tortuous diplomacy, seemed to be his only hope. Nothing, however, can avail to palliate the revolting treachery revealed in the secret correspondence between Rudolf and Michael, in which a scheme for the murder of Andrew is submitted to, and duly approved by, the emperor, and merely abandoned for reasons of expediency. We can only remember the barbarous standard of contemporary sultans and tsars, of Selim the Sot and Ivan the Terrible, the papal attitude towards murder plots against Elizabeth and William of Orange, the general atmosphere of treachery among the diplomatists of the Spanish and French Leaguers.

Michael certainly showed himself a past master at the game of deception. To cover his designs, he negotiated with the Turks, and by renewing the tribute secured their consent to the evacuation of the essential Danubian fortresses of Giurgiu and Brăila. Meanwhile—after delays due to the very different outlook of that masterly but unscrupulous imperialist general, George Basta—he secured Rudolf's authorisation for the invasion of Transylvania and all the time gave fair

---

[1] Jeremias Movilă reigned in Moldavia from 1595 till 1600 and again from 1601 to 1606, and his sons Constantine and Alexander from 1607 to 1611 and from 1615 to 1616. Jeremias' brother Simeon held Wallachia from 1601 to 1602 and Moldavia from 1606 to 1607, and the latter's three sons Michael, Moise and Gabriel also reigned for brief periods—the last from 1618 to 1620 in Moldavia. This constant shuffling between five kinsmen in a space of twenty-five years is characteristic of the chaotic and unprofitable character of Roumanian dynastic history, from which however we cannot entirely escape.

and specious messages to the envoys of Andrew. Then, when his secret military preparations were complete, and while the distant and star-stricken Rudolf was still urging delay, he made a sudden dash across the Carpathians, with an army of some 30–40,000 men—including not only his Moldavian levies, but Serb and Albanian mercenaries and his faithful Cossack guard, and a small Magyar contingent under the experienced Stephen Bocskay. With these he fell upon Andrew at Schellenberg near Hermannstadt and utterly routed him (28 October 1599). The young Magyar prince owed his defeat to arrogant contempt for the Wallach "herdsman" and "son of a whore" and had rejected the wise mediation of the Nuncio Malaspina.[1] He was killed by Székely shepherds as he fled from the battlefield and his head was brought to the victor. But Michael strongly disapproved, beheaded the murderer and gave his dead rival a magnificent funeral. Michael meanwhile had pressed on and entered Alba Iulia in triumph: a single blow had laid the whole Principality at his feet. He now assumed the elaborate title of "Voivode of Wallachia, Councillor of His Most Sacred Imperial Royal Majesty and his Lieutenant in Transylvania and its dependencies (Partes)". He thus won the support of the Saxons, always favourable to the Habsburg cause, which then and for two centuries still to come represented national safety for so remote and minute a racial island. It is interesting to note, in passing, that Clement VIII, who wisely disapproved of both the Báthorys, was by no means ill-disposed towards Michael and in April 1600 invited him to join the Roman Church.[2]

But all this was no sure basis upon which to hold Transylvania: it was necessary for him to display equal or even greater qualities of tact and persuasion towards at least one of the other two racial elements in the country. He was at the parting of the ways, and there was no time for hesitation. Was he to choose his own kinsmen, the Roumanians, who already formed the majority of the population, though held almost entirely in a position of serfdom and backward culture, and who, stirred by some dim consciousness of future destiny, had promptly risen in revolt against their masters, on the news that a "Domn" of their own race had crossed the mountains? Or was he to rely upon the Magyar nobles, in whose hands the administration, and the real political power rested, but who distrusted him almost equally as a foreigner, as a

---

[1] Hurmuzaki, *Documente*, III, i, pp. 511 sqq. Malaspina's report is followed by Huber, *Gesch. Oesterreichs*, IV, p. 421.

[2] Pastor, *Gesch. der Päpste*, XI, p. 229.

member of the despised "Wallach" race, and as, at least nominally, the exponent of Habsburg power? The question answers itself: for to pose it in such a form or to suppose that he could have chosen the former alternative, is only possible if we look at the sixteenth with the eyes of the twentieth century and are guilty of a gross anachronism. Given his environment and the social conditions of Eastern Europe in that age, Michael made the choice which it is easy enough for us, with our eyes on the culmination of the Roumanian drama in modern times, to describe as the wrong one, but which was the only conceivable one in such a situation.

The backbone of his power at home in Wallachia was the boiar class and the mercenaries whom he attracted to his standards. His policy of expansion cost money and was already involving him in heavy impositions upon the peasantry and in such concessions to the great landlords as led to frequent expropriations and the rapid extension of serfdom. Thus it seems obvious that even if he could have conceived an idea so alien to that age and milieu as a prince relying upon the democratic forces of a more than half submerged peasantry, he could hardly have won the support of the Roumanian masses in Transylvania without losing the confidence of his own class at home. His course therefore was clear. He took oath to the constitution of the Three Nations; he showered favours upon the Magyar nobility and higher clergy—except for a few open enemies, whose estates he confiscated—and tried to win their confidence by severe measures against the ringleaders of the peasant *jacquerie*. But the Magyars as a whole—even though such eminent men as Bishop Náprágy, Moses Székely and Gaspar Kornis took service with him—were not, and perhaps could not be, sincerely reconciled: they watched for any opportunity, and events speedily gave them their chance against him.

Ambition and safety alike drove Michael on: he could not stop half-way in his slippery career. Michael and Rudolf were almost equally insincere, the latter bent upon establishing a mainly German administration, the former upon extending his own power under cover of the imperial name and seeking to hold off the Poles by an understanding with their enemies farther east, Boris Godunov and the Cossacks. Moreover, Michael speedily found that he could not safely allow Moldavia to remain a hotbed of Polish and Magyar intrigue. In May 1600, with the same *élan*, resolution and dramatic suddenness as a year before, he achieved the conquest of Moldavia, driving headlong Movilă and his

Polish allies, exacting a prompt oath from the boiars and not troubling to wait for Rudolf's hesitating sanction. Nor did he await the imperial orders before assuming the fresh title of "Prince of all Ungro-Wallachia, of Transylvania and of Moldavia". For one brief moment, as by the stroke of a magician's wand, all the Roumanians found themselves under a single rule.

Rudolf, however, though he confirmed Michael as Imperial Lieutenant, was now seriously alarmed at his enterprising vassal's progress and set himself to undermine his position. Complicated triangular intrigues followed, which lie beyond the scope of any general narrative. Michael favoured the Magyar claim to unite some of the Hungarian border counties with Transylvania, both because it suited his ambition and seemed calculated to win him Magyar support: the emperor intrigued with the Magyar malcontents for Michael's overthrow, reckoning upon the armies of General Basta to reduce them to submission after the interloper was gone: and they in their turn made a silent calculation as to ridding themselves of the imperialists when once the hated Wallach was eliminated.

Rudolf sent special envoys from Prague to negotiate with Michael— in particular a certain Dr Pezzen, who already had considerable experience in negotiations with the Porte. The comedy was kept up for some time: though Rudolf had again nominated Michael as Imperial Lieutenant, Pezzen's main task, by flattery and veiled menace, was to induce him to abandon Transylvania of his own free will. When at last he saw that Michael would never consent, he secretly organised a conspiracy of the Magyar nobles, which burst into open revolt a month after his own departure from the country. It was now too late to throw himself into the arms of the Roumanians, who had been fatally alienated by his earlier concessions to the nobility, by his forced levies and by the conduct of his foreign mercenaries and soldiers of fortune.

In the summer of 1600 Basta advanced from the north to join the "loyal" rebels, with a small and compact imperialist army, and once again the fate of Transylvania was decided by a single blow. Not merely was Michael completely defeated on the field of Mirişlau (18 September 1600) and forced to fly across the Carpathians, but as an immediate result the Poles under Zamoyski rapidly overran Moldavia and replaced the puppet Movilă upon its throne. Even in his native Wallachia he found it difficult to hold his own, and suffered a serious reverse near Buzău at the hands of Movilă's brother Simon, who aspired to oust him finally even from his patrimony.

Even in this desperate situation, however, Michael soon recovered from his initial hesitation and took a step which might seem to be the most straightforward in his devious career. He addressed to Rudolf a very lengthy Latin *apologia* for his conduct[1] and having thus prepared the ground, made his way to Prague with only a few followers, confident that he could convince the Emperor of his loyalty towards him, or at least of their essential common interests. The fact that after his expulsion from Transylvania the Magyars lost no time in turning against Rudolf, allying themselves with Poland and recalling the worthless Sigismund for the third time, seemed to provide a plausible justification of Michael. He was well received by Rudolf, upon whose mercy he had thrown himself, and he was now entrusted, conjointly with Basta, with the task of recovering Transylvania for the Habsburgs. Basta, himself an arch-intriguer, seems to have been completely duped by his temporary Magyar allies, but perhaps for that very reason vented his resentment upon Michael and of course must have had real qualms lest Michael might altogether forestall him in the imperial favour. Incautious language of the voivode seems to have confirmed this impression.

This aim was in fact accomplished without much difficulty by their joint victory at Goroszló on 3 August 1601. But the treacherous Basta could not endure so dangerous a rival: the Moor had done his duty, the Moor could go. Within a few weeks of the battle Basta picked a quarrel with the voivode and sent some Walloon mercenaries to Torda to effect his arrest. In the scuffle that ensued Michael was made away with, on orders from the general (19 August). We have Basta's own cynical report to the Archduke Matthias, which announced that "the Wallach had begun to aspire to new things and to put a great part of the province to fire and sword" and to destroy churches (in reality the followers of Michael and Basta seem to have shared the honours for plunder and outrage). Having convinced himself, so Basta continues, that certain intercepted letters of Michael (letters which we now know to have been forged, though their actual origin remains obscure) were really authentic, "I was forced to try to secure his person, but he, being bent on defending himself, was killed, *I having given this order* to those who

[1] Hurmuzaki, *Documente*, IV, no. 195—17 January 1601—supplicatio humilima.

PLATE V

MICHAEL THE BRAVE

did the execution ".[1] Neither Matthias nor his brother Rudolf approved the murder, but the mischief was already done and the general seemed indispensable for the reduction of Transylvania.

The brief Roumanian dream of glory was at an end. Michael's son was too young to take his place and indeed made no mark in later life. Thus what the father had created died with him. But the imperialists did not profit by this perfidy. Only four years later Transylvania rose in insurrection and attained its Golden Age under Bocskai and Bethlen, as a bulwark of Protestantism in Europe, negotiating on almost equal terms with the Western Powers and reconciled to the Turks by a common hostility towards the Habsburgs.

The achievement of Michael the Brave, taken by itself, was little more than a brief episode, ending in complete failure. But it is the stuff of which great drama is made, and it may well be that some day a Roumanian poet will find in it the inspiration which Schiller found in the career of Wallenstein. Certainly it is from this angle that it deserves to be studied: for though its political results were almost instantly effaced, it fired the imagination of the Roumanian race and acquired a legendary, well-nigh mythological, significance which cannot be extracted from contemporary records, but which in modern times— doubtless under the impress of pseudo-nationalist doctrine—played a very real part in the evolution of the race towards cultural and political unity.

Moreover, though but a passing incident, it almost inevitably attracted the attention and emphasis of all subsequent writers, for the very simple reason that it is the last event in Roumanian history before the period of national revival, which can be quoted with any feelings save those of anger and humiliation: for we are now about to enter a long period of decline and paralysis. There are, however, two other aspects from which Michael's career may be profitably regarded. It illustrates most graphically the hopelessly unfavourable position in which all modern Roumanian rulers found themselves and the sorry shifts to which even the ablest among them were inevitably reduced, amid the ever moving sands of Ottoman and imperial diplomacy. But it also may be held to illustrate—though this is a much more contentious claim, and

[1] Hurmuzaki, *Documente*, IV, no. 224—23 August 1601 (in Italian). That the Walloon captain had orders to make "the Wallach" prisoner and kill him if he resisted, is confirmed both by the Nuncio Spinelli and the Venetian envoy at Vienna. See *ibid.* VIII, nos. 326, 327 (3 and 4 September 1601).

one which still meets with strong challenge—the essentially inter-dependent relations of all three Principalities. Just as the world-position of England was only assured after she had secured unity in her own island and was no longer menaced by the very much weaker but never negligible Scotland, with her powers of diversion by invasion and alliance, so no state on the Lower Danube could hope for anything like stability, so long as it had no control over the "natural fortress" of Transylvania. Thus in the fulness of time, as under Trajan so in our own age the Carpathians came to form the central vertebra, and no longer the periphery or outer crust, of a new and potentially powerful Dacian state.

\* \* \* \*

Michael was the last Roumanian prince for some centuries who was really able to direct events, instead of being their tool. After his death both Principalities soon sank back into incredible degradation—Moldavia between the Turkish hammer and the Polish anvil, and both at the mercy of warring factions and endless financial levies. When that all too rare bird, a prince who was eager to ease the position of his subjects, appeared, the usual result was that a reduction of taxes left him with less available cash and so enabled some rival to out-bribe him at the Porte and thereby eject him from power. From 1602 to 1611, it is true, Radu Şerban, an experienced boiar who through his mother was descended from Basarab Neagoe, held the Wallachian throne, and defended himself valiantly against all comers—Turks, Poles and Tatars, the latter of whom suffered a crushing defeat at his hands. Moreover he was twice able to repel direct Magyar attacks. Moses Székely, one of the leaders of the revolt against Michael, had himself secured the Transylvanian throne and now aspired to conquer Wallachia also. In his arrogance he boasted to his captains that they would soon see what "the fat Wallach will get from me".[1] But rashness and self-confidence were his undoing, and he was defeated and killed at Rosenau on 17 July 1603, by Radu Şerban acting in the emperor's name. But the new voivode, unlike Michael, made no effort to establish his own rule in Transylvania, and eight years later had to meet and overcome a similar attack near the same spot (1611)—this time from the tyrannous Gabriel Báthory.

In the end, however, Radu Şerban lost support and lacked the neces-

---

[1] Engel, *Gesch. der Walachey*, p. 273.

sary resources: and he ended his life in exile at Vienna, neglected by the emperor who had for a moment found him so useful a tool. His successor Stephen Tomşa proved himself a more than usually bloodthirsty tyrant, and the manner in which during his brief reign he decimated the boiar class had serious effects in the future. There was a barbaric scene in the prince's council chamber, when the gypsy executioner, in presence of the victims, openly addressed Stephen in the phrase, "My lord, the rams have grown fat".

There was already a vicious circle in the situation, for resistance to a prince did not necessarily help matters. It merely meant that his successor must raise fresh sums to win the Porte's consent or else must risk Turkish invasion and its attendant plagues. The princes themselves, demoralised by the methods by which alone they could reach, and retain possession of, the throne, were paralysed and rendered cynical by their utter uncertainty of tenure: while the Turks never learned the elementary lesson of politics, that a well-governed people is a surer source of revenue than a people which has every interest to vegetate and wait passively upon events. On the other hand, so great were the natural resources and fertility of the Roumanian lands, then as now, that it was always possible to extract a profit from the soil, even despite all the hazards of war and spoliation. Professor Xenopol calculated the normal revenue of the Roumanian lands at 600–800,000 ducats, and then allowing two-thirds for tribute and bribery on the grand scale, 60–80,000 for the pay of mercenary troops, and 20,000 for court expenses, considered that the prince might often hope for a balance of 100,000 (or the equivalent of 2,500,000 francs in pre-war French currency).[1]

From the reign of Michael onwards, the most momentous fact in Roumanian history, next to the Turkish suzerainty and its economic consequences, is the growth of serfdom and the decay of the free peasantry. This not merely augmented the power of the greater boiars, but had the further effect of undermining the old foundations of military resistance. For the Călăraşi, a sort of mounted yeomanry till then recruited from the free peasants, decayed as the numbers of the latter fell: while the infantry, which was composed of the lowest class of peasants, also fell into decay as serfdom tightened its hold, for military service involved removal from their domicile, whereas it was then the chief aim of the great lords in most countries to tie them irrevocably to the

[1] *Op. cit.* I, p. 431. The ducat varying from 1 to 1½ piastres.

soil. At the close of the sixteenth century there was, as we have seen, a certain recrudescence of warlike spirit among the ruling class, which only needed bold and efficient leadership to produce practical results. But by the third decade of the seventeenth century—in which Moldavia in particular was becoming a battleground between Turks, Poles and Cossacks—there was a very marked decline in military power, and when the change of regime came in the early eighteenth century, any serious resistance on the part of the Roumanians was wholly impracticable.

All through this period there was a steady diminution of small holdings and an extension of the larger estates: already under Michael the Buzeşci family owned 128 separate estates. In the course of time the princely domains were for the most part squandered or granted away, and the chief source of reward for the boiars was at an end. The next stages were that encroachment upon peasant rights to which allusion has just been made, and an ever increasing hunt for places. During the seventeenth century the boiars tended to become less warriors and more functionaries about the court, which affected a certain Byzantine magnificence atoning in some measure for the lack of security or ultimate power. This change is reflected in the unmartial flowing robes of the courtiers. There also grew up a new intermediate class between the boiars and the peasants, the so-called "Mazils" (or "dispossessed from office")—a lesser gentry of boiar origin, but hardly differing in culture from the surrounding peasantry.

## MATTHEW BASARAB AND BASIL THE WOLF

Gloomy as conditions in the Roumanian lands had become for the generation following upon Michael the Brave, there was a temporary recovery in both countries in the second quarter of the century. In 1632 Matthew Basarab, a last scion of the old reigning family—popularly known as Mateĭ Aga—rallied the boiars of Wallachia behind him and after going in person to obtain the consent of the Porte (which of course meant a discreet but wholesale distribution of baksheesh), managed to maintain himself on the throne for the most unusual period of twenty-two years. Two years later the Moldavian crown was acquired by Basil the Wolf (Vasile Lupu), a man of Albanian origin. Their accession to power was due to a certain rebound of national feeling: yet its effect was to stereotype the process, already beginning, of Greek penetration.

Speaking quite broadly, it may be said that throughout the seven-teenth century Turkish sovereignty and Greek culture were the two dominant factors, the latter steadily driving Slav influences backwards, while in the international field the two Roumanian states were caught up in the triangular conflict of Turkey, Poland and the Empire. In the eighteenth century Turkish sovereignty and Greek culture were as strong as ever, but were transfused and modified in ways that fall to be described later. But in the foreign field there was a complete redis-tribution of forces. Turkey's decline, despite occasional fits of recon-valescence, had become crassly apparent, and everything turned more and more round the rivalry of Austria and Russia, first for the Turkish, then for the Polish, then once more for the Turkish inheritance, while the other Powers, with their fitful cross-influences and intrigues, served alternately as irritants, deterrents or spoil-sports.

Both Matthew and Basil were brave soldiers, and skilful statesmen, though forced to maintain themselves by the usual periodic payments. Unhappily their personal jealousy and ambition led to continual quarrels, which undermined the remaining strength of both countries at a moment when Turkey showed evident signs of decay. The main blame lies with the inordinate and restless ambition of Basil, who coveted the wealthier throne of Wallachia. Already in 1637 and again in 1639 he led an army against Matthew, but in each case was decisively defeated. As a result of his intrigues and bribery at the Porte, the Turks were induced to invade Wallachia, but Matthew withdrew into a strong defensive position near Ploeşci and adopted Fabian tactics, which, combined with judicious bribery at the Porte and a close entente with George Rákóczy of Transylvania, checkmated Basil's plans. For the next ten years Basil turned his energies eastwards, being used by the Porte as intermediary both with Moscow and the Cossacks, and doing what he could to keep Poles and Russians quiet so long as the war with Venice lasted. The extent of his influence may be partly measured by the marriage of two of his daughters, to the Polish magnate Jan Radzi-will and to Timothy, son of the Cossack Hetman Chmielnicki.

In 1650 the Porte summoned both princes to pay personal homage to the sultan, which was simply a veiled way of demanding more money. Matthew's answer was humble but firm. He was an old and tired man, no longer fit for long journeys: he had always fulfilled his duties to the Porte. If it was now desired to displace him, he would gladly end his days in a cloister. But the only safe successor would be a suitable candidate from Constantinople itself: if an already ruling prince were sent—a direct hit at the ambitions of Basil—he could not answer for the consequences to Turkey.[1]

For a time he was again left in peace, but in 1652 Basil renewed his plotting, hoping to obtain Wallachia for himself and then to hand over Moldavia to his son. He and his Cossack son-in-law made a combined raid into Wallachia, but he was again decisively routed at the battle of Finta, on the Ialomiţa, and had to fly for his life. The veteran Matthew, who turned the scale by his personal prowess, captured Timothy and a rich booty, including a letter of the grand vizier inciting Basil to attack and depose the "traitor" Matthew.[2] This time Matthew was left triumphant and unassailable: for a conspiracy of Moldavian boiars overthrew Basil and forced him to take refuge with the Tatar Khan, and though the Turks looked upon him with favour—doubtless in the main because it suited them that the two hospodars should quarrel and not combine—he never recovered his throne.

In April 1654 Matthew himself died. As Engel remarks, "a long reign in Wallachia is of itself a panegyric to the Prince", and Matthew, though the circumstances of his day condemned him to questionable methods and occasional subservience, had the welfare of his subjects more at heart than most hospodars, did much for the arts and the liberal endowment of churches, and though as courageous and skilful a soldier as Michael the Brave, was essentially pacific in his policy, and it was no fault of his if he was constantly interrupted in the task of husbanding Wallachian resources. It is true that in his later years he fell under the influence of certain extortionate and oppressive boiars, but he was certainly the most enlightened Roumanian ruler since Stephen the Great.

## THE PHANARIOTS

It may fairly be argued that the Phanariot regime dates from the accession of these two princes, though there are doubtless two distinct stages—that of permeation (1634–1711) and that of direct domination (1711–1821). What assured the triumph of Greek influence was of course the position gradually acquired by the Greeks of the Turkish capital, who, with the Oecumenical Patriarch at their head, inhabited the Phanar or Lighthouse quarter of Stambul, and thus came in time

[1] Hurmuzaki, *Fragmente*, III, p. 154.
[2] *Ibid.* p. 181.

to be distinguished by the malodorous name of Phanariot. In the first flush of Turkish power after the fall of Byzantium, the Greeks, like other Christians, could only acquire influence by apostasy, and many Greeks rose to high office in this way. But before long the Greeks adapted themselves to the new circumstances and concentrated in two main directions—the Church, as the surest bulwark of nationality, and commerce as the source not only of riches, but of political exemptions and influence. Some of the leading Greek families became the sultan's men of affairs and bankers on a large scale and amassed huge fortunes. One of their most obvious functions was to arrange the payments— both cash and credit—for vacancies on the patriarchal or minor epis- copal thrones and on the thrones of Wallachia and Moldavia: and this brought them into close contact first with the princes when they visited the Porte for purposes of bribery or as fugitives seeking vengeance against a rival, and of course less directly with boiars of the rival parties and so with every phase of life in the two principalities. Some of them became interested in the growing trade in corn, agricultural produce and livestock in the rich Wallachian and Moldavian plains, on which Constantinople depended more and more for its supplies, in proportion as the prosperity of Asia Minor became utterly a thing of the past. Their influence even at the close of the sixteenth century is revealed by a clause in the treaty between Michael the Brave and Sigismund Báthory, stipulating that no Greek shall be included among the twelve boiars summoned to the Diet of Transylvania.

The Turks in their great days had preferred dictation to negotiation and had therefore employed only very subordinate persons in their dealings with foreign Powers. As necessity drove them off their high horse, they found themselves gravely handicapped by ignorance of foreign languages and methods of procedure. The Greeks, a maritime race, with a natural aptitude for commerce, a love of travel, a keen, versatile and pliable character and real linguistic gifts, proved most useful as interpreters and translators and as agents in every kind of transaction.

During the long siege of Candia one of these Greeks, Panayataki, a native of the island of Chios, had made himself indispensable at the Porte and was in 1669 appointed to the new office of grand dragoman or interpreter. It was in the first instance his business to examine and translate the documents supplied by foreign envoys, but he thus auto- matically became a focusing point of diplomatic negotiations. He was allowed to grow a beard, to wear the dress of high Turkish dignitaries (save for the turban), to ride on horseback followed by attendants: and other more concrete distinctions were added later. A Greek proverb of those days declares that it is as hard to find a green horse as a wise man in the island of Chios, and hence Panayataki, who was its living refutation, was ironically known as the Green Horse. Of his successor, Alexander Mavrocordato, we shall hear later.

Perhaps the most notable of all these families was that of Cantacuzene, which, without ever forgetting its imperial origin, became purveyors to the harem and extremely rich and influential. Its head, Michael Cantacuzene, after the great naval defeat of Lepanto (1571) presented the Porte with fifteen vessels built and equipped at his own expense, to make good the Turkish losses. But it was dangerous to be too rich in such a country as Turkey, and in 1578 Michael was hanged before the gate of his own palace on the Black Sea, the pretext being his alleged share in the removal of John the Terrible from the Moldavian throne and the complications which ensued. A generation later his five grandsons settled in Wallachia, bringing with them the remnants of the family fortune, and soon rose to high honours in the state. The youngest, Constantine, by his disinterested conduct, became extremely popular with all classes, and his execution in 1663 by the hospodar, at the instance of the Greek party, gave the Cantacuzene family the position of leaders of the national party. At last in 1679, Şerban Cantacuzene, a grandson of Michael, found it safer, instead of pushing a candidate who might afterwards turn against him, to mount the Wallachian throne himself: and though it cost him no less than 650,000 piastres, he at any rate contrived to retain his hold upon it for almost ten years, in an unusually critical period of foreign policy. Other Greek or hellenised families which rose to power at this same period and reigned in one or other principality were the Ducas, the Ghicas (really of Albanian origin) and the Rosettis.

## GREEK INFLUENCE IN ROUMANIA

Matthew and Basil had both owed their accession to power in some sense to a last flicker of national feeling against the slow infiltration of Greek influence—already noticeable in the late sixteenth century as the result of intermarriage with Greeks instead of Poles and Hungarians. But they themselves succumbed to this very influence, partly from the necessity of humouring the Phanariot clique which could otherwise compass their overthrow, partly from the desire of supplanting Slavonic by Greek in the Church, partly because their very generosity to the Church strengthened the hold of the Greeks over the monasteries and their broad lands. From this epoch dates the practice of "dedicating"[1] new monastic foundations to such famous centres of Orthodox faith as Athos, Sinai or Jerusalem, the result being that their control fell into Greek hands and their resources were drained away for alien purposes, until the changed situation in the nineteenth century rendered expropriation almost inevitable. Until the close of the century, then, it may be said that Greek influence was little more than on the surface, but it already controlled the choice of the princes, it dominated commercial life and permeated the Church, while Greek became the almost exclusive language of inner court circles.

Specially marked was their influence in the sphere of culture, in an age when culture meant merely a few rocks projecting above the vast morass of ignorance. Side by side with Greek merchants came the Greek clergy and Greek monks, who soon ejected Slav from the services and liturgy of the Church, and so, as a consequence, from its rather unnatural position as the official language. We have already seen that ever since the ninth century the liturgical language had remained Slav. Its knowledge had to be acquired by the clergy (to whom it was a foreign and eventually a dead tongue) in certain monastic schools. Roumanian texts were almost non-existent. As there was scarcely any education or schooling of any kind outside the control of the clergy, the position occupied by the Slav language in the Church acted as an absolute hindrance to Roumanian literary development, and hence its removal, as we can see to-day, was an absolute preliminary condition to any real national awakening.

With the coming of the Greeks, however, there was nothing to save the artificial position of Slavonic. Its prospects had very materially changed since the sixteenth century, when Slav was the *lingua franca* of the whole Balkan peninsula and even employed by sultans, grand viziers and janissaries. In the seventeenth century, on the other hand, a knowledge of Bulgarian had already died out among the Bulgarian clergy. A striking illustration of this is provided by the experience of Matthew Basarab, who was publishing certain books translated from the Slav and had to send to Bulgaria for a man whose literary attainments would

[1] See *infra*, pp. 215, 307.

enable him to control the texts. But it proved impossible to find anyone in the whole country for such a purpose, except a certain Croat priest named Raphael.

A quite unexpected result followed. Slavonic was abandoned by general consent: but the mass of the clergy knew even less of Greek than of Slav, and so it was found necessary to introduce the Roumanian vernacular as the language of the liturgy. Thus, by a strange paradox of history, Roumanian literature owes its first revival to an attempt at hellenisation. The first printed books in Roumania had been a Slav liturgy and Gospels, published in 1507 and 1512 in Wallachia: but, as we saw, zealous Saxon Protestants in Kronstadt printed the Gospels in Roumanian and also Lutheran sermons and catechisms suited for pro-selytising purposes. There can be little doubt that the main reason for the failure of this experiment, and of the Magyar Calvinist effort of a century later, was the monstrous system of combined social and re-ligious restraint imposed upon the Roumanian Orthodox population to the north of the Carpathians.[1]

In 1634 Matthew Basarab established a printing press at the monastery of Govora, which, after issuing Slav works which are now of extra-ordinary rarity, published in 1640 the first Roumanian book printed in the two Principalities. This was the *Pravila cea Mica*, or Small Code of ecclesiastical laws. Not the least notable feature of these reigns was this first serious attempt at codification, for a second collection—known as *Pravila cea Mare*, the Great Code—appeared at Govora in 1652, while Basil also had issued in 1646 a collection of laws, translated from the Greek. This latter came from the printing press established at the monastery of the Three Hierarchs at Jassy, from which vernacular books of sermons and theological polemics against the Protestants began to appear. Many of these, especially as organised by the Metro-politan Barlàam of Moldavia, were a direct rejoinder to the proselytising literature issued in Roumanian by the Transylvanian princes, of which we shall have to speak later.

Of special note were the publications of the Metropolitan Dositheus of Moldavia, who was strongly under Polish influence and in the end exposed himself so much in the cause of John Sobieski as a Christian champion, that he found it expedient to withdraw to Poland, where he died as bishop of Zolchiew. He is chiefly remembered by a highly original metrical version of the Psalms—extending to about 8600 lines

[1] See pp. 113, 123.

PLATE VI

Hostes terret, & ingenuos uel ipsa sola urget Imago;
Quid? si cogat eos, hos quoque respiciat.

Marcus Boschonus Venet. f.

MATTHEW BASARAB

and betraying the literary influence of Jan Kochanowski, the great poet of the Polish Renaissance: this was actually printed, not at home in Moldavia, but at Uniew, near Warsaw, in 1673.

Still more epoch-making was the Roumanian Bible of 1688, commonly known as "Şerban's Bible", because it was issued under the auspices of Şerban Cantacuzene, who appointed a special commission of bishops and learned boiars to supervise it. There has latterly been considerable controversy as to whether it was the work of the Spatar (or commander-in-chief) Nicholas Milescu, as Haşdeu and earlier scholars alleged, or merely a revised version adapted from already existing translations. Certainly Milescu was a man of remarkable culture in that age and milieu and capable of such a task: he had travelled widely in the west and north of Europe, had composed a treatise on Orthodox doctrine in Paris, had been the tutor of the Tsar's sons and was sent by him on missions to China and Siberia. Besides the modern languages acquired on his travels, he had a scholar's knowledge of Greek, Latin and Russian, though not of Hebrew. Needless to say, such figures were few and far between in the Roumania of his day.

There was to the last very strong opposition to the abandonment of the Slav liturgy. The common people were attached to it, even though they could not understand it: and professors of Slavonic were summoned from Kiev to Jassy in order to direct a school for its cultivation. But the facts of nature were too strong, and by degrees even this last stronghold came to teach only Roumanian or Greek.

## MATTHEW'S AND BASIL'S SUCCESSORS

The relative success with which Matthew humoured the Turks and held his own against the attacks of jealous neighbours, may account for the unusual fact that his successor Constantine Şerban was appointed by something approaching popular election. The metropolitan invited the assembled boiars to declare their wishes, and the new prince was then chosen by the joint acclamation of the boiars and the "crowd": he was at once anointed and robed, and accepted the homage of his subjects. It must, however, at once be added that before he could secure confirmation in office, he had to expend greater sums upon bribery than ever before, and that from this moment dates the malpractice of exacting an additional charge from a prince whose predecessor had died in office —a kind of oriental caricature of our modern death duties. Şerban's total accession expenses are estimated at 800,000 piastres (or 20,000,000 francs!), those of Şerban Cantacuzene in 1679 at 650,000.[1] The extent to which the tribute and the endless incidental charges of ever recurring elections clogged the whole economic progress of the two states, can hardly be exaggerated. Even when all legal dues had been met, there was a constant leakage of presents to every imaginable Turkish dignitary—valuable furs and horses or prize stock, while requisitions for the Turkish army, for which compensation was but rarely forthcoming, must have been a serious cause of impoverishment, especially in border districts. Moreover there was a tendency to impose special taxes on all the staple articles of trade, on sheep, cattle and every kind of agricultural produce. As time went on, the wretched peasantry were fleeced more and more systematically by the official tax collectors and by certain merchants to whom was assigned a special privilege of extortion.

\*　　　　　\*　　　　　\*

The marked ability and energy of Matthew and Basil and the unwonted length of their reigns offered a certain hope of stabilisation after the constant shiftings of fortune's wheel: but unhappily their acute personal rivalry marred the picture, and their disappearance from the scene was followed by a fresh relapse. Constantine Şerban and his Moldavian contemporary, George Ştefan, were men equally lacking in capacity and initiative and allowed themselves to be dragged in the trail of George Rákóczy II, in whom soaring ambition and rash initiative far outran his slender resources, and whose mad attempt to seize the crown of Poland in 1657 ended in well-merited disaster. Rákóczy dragged down the two hospodars in his fall and while he himself was replaced by Achaz Barcsay, the Porte sent to Moldavia George Ghica, the first of an Albanian family which was henceforth to play a notable rôle in Roumanian history, and to Wallachia that sorry adventurer, Mihnea III, claiming princely parentage, but thoroughly Greek in feeling, ready not merely to pay heavily for the throne, but to plunge the country into grave danger by an ill-conceived and treacherous conspiracy against his suzerain. On two occasions he massacred those boiars who hesitated to join him, throwing their bodies from the palace windows to the sound of music![2] Then he took flight into Transylvania amid general execration, leaving the unhappy Wallachians to bear the vengeance of the Turks (1659).

[1] Xenopol, *op. cit.* II, pp. 54, 72.
[2] Hurmuzaki, *Documente*, v, i, p. 61.

In the thirty-two years that followed the fall of Basil twelve phantom princes followed each other on the Moldavian throne, not one of whom really deserves to be rescued from oblivion. Few of them were of Roumanian blood, though Ghica, Rosetti and Duca were to become increasingly Roumanian and in later times to deserve well of their country. Basil's son Stephen was in no respect worthy of his father's name and was speedily discarded as useless, and the most Roumanian of them all, Iliache, a descendant of Peter Rareş, had been brought up at the Phanar and in his own Divan stood as much in need of an interpreter as any Greek. Little more can be said for their contemporaries in Wallachia. Şerban Cantacuzene alone showed the qualities of a statesman or can be said to have had his share in guiding events: the others drifted on the current and sank almost without leaving a ripple.

It is worthy of passing notice, that with Matthew Basarab there passed away the last worthy scion of the ancient Basarab dynasty, while the male line of Stephen the Great failed in 1668 with the fall of the insignificant Iliaş Alexander. This imparted added uncertainty to the succession, though we shall see that a few subsequent princes could trace descent in the female line from the original dynasties.

## THE PORTE AND THE EMPIRE

The degradation and utter uncertainty which beset the two Principalities under the successors of Matthew and Basil was above all due to a change in the external situation. The second half of the seventeenth century was marked by a revival of Ottoman power, of which the capture of Crete in 1669 and the conquest of Podolia and large tracts of the Ukraine at the expense of Poland (1672–8) were the most notable features. This great outburst of Turkish energy was in no sense a sign of healthy recuperation: for corruption in high places, harem intrigue and degeneracy in the imperial family itself had reached their culmination in Mohammed IV (1648–87), with his boundless mania for the chase and his methods of unrestrained terrorism and barbaric punishment. It was far rather a supreme exploitation of the martial qualities of the Turk and his many subject races, and was only rendered possible by the emergence of a brilliant series of Mayors of the Palace—Mohammed Küprüli (1656–61), his sons Ahmed (1661–78) and Mustafa (1689–91) and his cousin Hussein—who restored the army to something of its old renown as a fighting machine and by partial reforms checked for a time the dry rot in the central administration. Degenerate as they were, the sultans and those who ministered to their pleasure had sufficient intelligence to realise that without some such action they were lost and that to assume the offensive is in certain circumstances the best defence against a crowd of enemies.

The Turkish offensive had immediate and direct consequences for the Roumanian Principalities, and it is with these that we are specially concerned. The renewal of the Turkish threat to Transylvania in 1658 and the years following, had a double motive. It sought to deprive the emperor of an ally who had many motives, political, religious and personal, for playing a doubtful game of balance between the rival camps, but who none the less held a valuable strategic position along the whole eastern border of the great Turkish salient in Central Hungary. At the same time the complete subjection of Transylvania would have greatly facilitated Turkish military designs against Poland: and it was with Poland above all that the Turks had to deal in the sixties and seventies. It was inevitable that they should in these years have tightened their hold upon the fortresses along the Dniester and the Black Sea and relied more than ever for commissariat and other supplies upon the unfortunate districts which intervened between the Danube and the great debatable land of the Ukraine. For the most urgent military reasons, quite apart from their conqueror's mentality and the dividing arrogance of creed, they could not be expected to encourage any movement tending to loosen their stranglehold upon the two Principalities: and indeed they more than once seriously considered the question of reducing Moldavia to a status of a mere pashalik like Roumelia. Finally, there was always the motive of personal greed: the more frequent were the changes on the two thrones, the more baksheesh flowed into innumerable secret channels. Thus the Roumanians found themselves between two pincers in a struggle of the first magnitude: their territory offered several short cuts through the Carpathian passes, whenever the Turks chose to threaten Transylvania, while it was the first objective of every attack by Pole, Cossack, Tatar and eventually Russian. The struggle between Turkey and Poland reaches its height between 1672 and 1678, the initial conquests of the former, as embodied in the Treaty of Buczacz, being repudiated by John Sobieski, who twice won signal victories at Chotin on the Dniester and before Lemberg. But in the end he found it necessary to yield, and the Treaty of Zurawna in the latter year left Turkey in possession of the greater part of Podolia and Ukraine, though she renounced her claim to a Polish tribute and pledged herself to hold back her Cossack and Tatar vassals from raiding Polish territory.

In all this the rôle of the hospodars was humiliating in the extreme. They were as a rule forced to attend the sultan or the grand vizier during the campaign, to provide troops for the Turkish army or lines of communication and to submit to merciless requisitioning. Moldavia in particular bore the brunt of any invasion, whether from the side of Poles, Cossacks or Tatars, and its territory was again and again laid waste. Indeed, even in the rare intervals of peace the Tatars made frequent raids on a large scale, carried off the population of whole villages and thus replenished the slave markets. The princes were at the mercy of any whim of the pashas in whose hands military operations lay, and were continually being overthrown or superseded.

Ahmed Küprüli, perhaps the greatest of all the grand viziers, did not long survive the Peace of Zurawna, by which he had achieved for Turkey its greatest expansion: and his immediate successors, giving free rein to their arrogance and greed, plunged into impossible adventures. The triangular struggle between Turkey, Poland and Russia for the possession of the vast booty of the Ukraine, was soon to be resumed: but Poland is already in the third place. Russia, the mightiest of Turkey's enemies—now for the first time her immediate neighbour, as a result of her successes against Poland—allies herself with the Cossack Hetman Doroshenko and after four years of war concludes at Radzim in 1681 the first of a long series of treaties in which the Porte cedes territory to the tsar. Russia's hold upon Kiev and the major part of the Ukraine—already successfully asserted against Poland by the Treaty of Andrusovo in 1667—is now acknowledged by Turkey also and thus becomes definitive. Poland is almost spent as an aggressive Power, and her pretensions to Moldavia and the Danubian frontier, though upheld till the very close of the century, no longer correspond to realities.

In all this period of upheaval and terror along the Moldavian frontier —so vividly portrayed for modern readers in the prose epics of the Polish novelist Sienkiewicz—not the least surprising feature is the long acquiescence of the Emperor Leopold. Amid the many great names of the Habsburg dynasty Leopold reveals no spark of greatness and emphatically had achievement thrust upon him. His failure to make the most of Montecuccoli's brilliant victory at St Gotthard in 1664 remained as a permanent reproach among large sections of his subjects:

and the only excuse that can be put forward on his behalf is his persistent absorption in the affairs of Western Europe and in religious questions nearer home. During the seventies the Turkish danger seemed in Austrian eyes to have become entirely secondary, compared with the struggle against the Bourbons.

There came a sudden and rude awakening. The grand vizier, Kara Mustafa, a man of boundless ambition and ferocity, inflamed by an un-Turkish addiction to drunken excesses, saw himself set free by the conclusion of peace with Russia and turned his eyes once more towards Europe. He found encouragement in the hostility of Louis XIV to the Habsburgs and in the gathering storm of insurrection in Northern Hungary, under the restless and ambitious Magyar Protestant leader, Emerich Tököli. Early in 1683 Kara Mustafa and Sultan Mohammed in person led a powerful Turkish army northwards, in the hope of finally vanquishing the Habsburgs: and at the same time the treacherous Tököli, who had welcomed an imperial envoy at his recent marriage with Helen Zrinski, openly allied himself with the Porte and overran Slovakia. It was only reluctantly and with many a backward glance at Louis XIV, that Leopold manned himself for the struggle in the East: and it was soon only too obvious that the defences of Austria were altogether inadequate. Vienna was only saved by the heroic defence of Starhemberg and the tempestuous advance of a Polish army under John Sobieski, whom papal mediation had won to the emperor's side despite all the seductions of Louis.

While Tököli did not actually appear in the Turkish camp, the two hospodars, Şerban Cantacuzene and George Duca, were forced to attend with contingents of 4000 and 2000 men, to whom was assigned the task of building the bridges of boats on the Danube and maintaining communications. Şerban sent secret information to the defenders of Vienna, and according to the not very reliable Del Chiaro, loaded his cannon with balls stuffed with straw! Certainly his sympathies were revealed by the tall cross, with its Latin inscription, which he erected outside the city and left behind him on retreating.[1]

The relief of Vienna was quite definitely the turn of the tide in the long Turkish wars: it infected the Turkish armies with panic such as had never yet assailed them, and thanks not so much to the emperor as

---

[1] Engel (*Gesch. der Walachey*, p. 326) gives the full text, which begins as follows: "Crucis exaltatio est conservatio mundi, Crux decor Ecclesiae, Crux custodia Regum, Crux confirmatio fidelium, Crux gloria angelorum et vulnus daemonum".

to the duke of Lorraine and other imperialist generals of genius and initiative, there was an immediate pursuit, a fresh victory at Párkány and the capture of Esztergom (Gran), the seat of the Hungarian primate.

The effect of these victories was immediate in many directions. It reverberated through the Balkan peninsula and roused new hopes among the subject races, Serb, Roumanian, Greek, Bulgarian and Albanian alike. It was a severe blow to the hopes of Tököli, who was almost equally distrusted by Vienna and Stambul and by Michael Apafi, the reigning prince of Transylvania. It led to the fall of the defeated vizier, who was bowstrung at Belgrade in December 1683 by the retreating sultan's orders, and this in turn led to important changes in the diplomatic methods of the Porte, which were to affect very specially the fortune of the Roumanians. What was virtually a palace revolution placed increased influence and power in the hands of the grand dragoman and of the leading Phanariot families from which that office was henceforth recruited. For the next two decades in particular, an altogether exceptional position was acquired in the councils of the Porte by Alexander Mavrocordato "the Exaporite", a man of great erudition, self-restraint and diplomatic resource, who had studied law at Bologna and medecine at Padua, had published learned works in Italy and was thoroughly versed in those Western languages which it had been beneath the dignity of ruling Turks to acquire, but which amid Turkey's changing relations with the outer world were indispensable for purposes of negotiation. Already in 1673 he had succeeded in office the redoubtable "Green Horse of Chios" and had been opposed to a policy of adventure in Central Europe. For a moment he was dragged down in Kara Mustafa's fall and accused of responsibility for what he had condemned: but when his innocence stood revealed, he rose to higher influence than ever and retained it till his death.

The crowded events of the remainder of the century cannot be recounted here: but a bare outline is necessary for a right understanding of Roumanian history. The Turkish defeats and the conclusion of a twenty years' armistice with France encouraged the none too venturesome Leopold to conclude in March 1684 the Holy League with Poland, Venice and the Pope. In three successive campaigns Charles of Lorraine waged an offensive against the Turks, leading up to the recapture of Buda in September 1686, after more than five generations of subjection. A natural effect of this steady advance was to leave Tököli more and more in the air and to decrease his value as an ally to either side. Already in 1685, after the fall of Neuhäusel the Turks had offered to hand him over to the emperor, as the sole cause of Kara Mustafa's invasion, and soon after the pasha of Grosswardein (Oradea Mare) seized the Magyar leader and sent him in chains to Belgrade. But Vienna took the unexpectedly sagacious line of attaching little or no value to the head of "the Kurucz king": upon which he was released and temporarily abandoned as impotent, while most of his followers in the north made terms with the Habsburgs, despite their harsh repression of the Protestant faith. At this stage the Pope aired a project for making the duke of Lorraine prince of Transylvania, but Leopold by now hoped to recover it for himself and invited Michael Apafi to join the Holy League and recognise more fully the imperial suzerainty. Apafi on his side hesitated to break with the Porte until he saw the imperialists masters not merely of Buda, but of the (to him) still more vital fortresses of Eger (Erlau) Grosswardein and Temesvár (Timişoara). Meanwhile Leopold's hopes did not stop short at Transylvania, but extended to Wallachia and Moldavia also: and this at once aroused the jealousy of Poland, who had her own very concrete ambitions in the same quarter.

The imperialist advance was carried a stage further in 1687. This time it was the elector of Bavaria and the margrave of Baden who routed the Turks at the battle of Harsány and occupied the line of the Drave: while Charles of Lorraine, equally alive to strategic and political considerations, speedily occupied Transylvania, put garrisons in the twelve chief towns and induced the prince and Estates to return to the Habsburg allegiance and renounce the protection of the Porte, in return for a pledge of religious freedom (9 May 1688).

Meanwhile Leopold had sent the Jesuit Dunod on a confidential mission to Şerban Cantacuzene, inviting him to espouse openly the Christian cause, nominating him as an imperialist general and promising him a hereditary throne, the right to annex all the territory that Wallachia had ever possessed and lost, and a safe refuge at Hermannstadt in the event of disaster—all this in return for a tribute of 75,000 piastres and presumably an armed contingent and the opening of his frontiers to the imperialist armies. There was an undercurrent of flattery towards the scion of an ancient Byzantine reigning house, and indeed Şerban seems to have had daydreams of a restored imperial throne. But traditional caution made him chary of binding pledges, until Leopold's troops were at his side: yet, when in the summer of 1688 they took him at his word, his whole efforts were directed to securing their withdrawal and protesting against their drastic requisitioning. A fresh imperialist advance, crowned by the capture of Belgrade in September 1688, might well have roused Şerban at last to declare himself: and two of his brothers and his son-in-law Bălăceanu were sent to Vienna to negotiate further. But early in November Şerban died prematurely, and at the time it was widely believed, though without adequate proof, that the Habsburg party among the boiars had administered poison.

It is characteristic of the double game which all these princes were driven to pursue, that simultaneously Cantacuzene had feelers out towards the rising power of Russia. The Archimandrite Isaiah of Athos carried to Moscow messages both from Şerban and from the Greek and Serbian Patriarchs, appealing to Russia to free her Christian kinsmen from the yoke of the Turk, the emperor, Venice and the Roman Church. This truly comprehensive programme ended in the fantastic assurance that a Russian army on the Danube would be met by 300,000 Serbs and Bulgars in revolt. On his return from Russia—with the even more fantastic answer that the hospodar should first join the Russians on the Dnieper in crushing the Tatars, and then the time of liberation would be at hand—Isaiah was arrested in Transylvania by General Heissler, and the proofs of double-dealing were thus divulged, though their utter futility must also have been apparent.[1]

It was at this moment that peace negotiations were initiated, Alexander Mavrocordato and Zulficar Effendi being sent on a mission to Vienna and kept waiting for three months until it pleased Leopold to receive them. The discussions were entirely abortive: their interest lies in the fact that one of the main conditions put forward on the imperial side—whether in entire seriousness or not, may be disputed—was the cession of both Wallachia and Moldavia, as former fiefs of the Hungarian crown. This was an immediate source of disagreement between Leopold and Poland, who demanded from him as the price of continuing the war, a written recognition of her claim to Moldavia. In February 1691 the Poles went still further and claimed both Principalities, with the Danube as frontier, as their share of the Turkish booty. Leopold replied evasively, that Moldavia had always been part of Hungary and that he must consult the Hungarian Estates, but he of course never took any action in this sense.[2]

[1] See Zinkeisen, *Gesch. des osman. Reiches*, v, p. 147 and Uebersberger, *Russlands Orientpolitik*, p. 45.
[2] Hurmuzaki, *Fragmente*, III, pp. 337, 352.

Şerban Cantacuzene was succeeded on the throne by his nephew Constantine Brâncoveanu, who combined all the Phanariot influence of his kinsfolk with such prestige as still attached to the blood of the old Basarab dynasty from which his mother descended,[1] and who had the further advantage of an enormous private fortune and astonishing gifts of diplomatic finesse and dissimulation. That he maintained himself on the throne for twenty-six years, amid constant war and upheaval, was in itself no small achievement. His policy was one of perpetual, but cautious, oscillation between the Porte, the Empire, Poland and Russia, which we now see coming rapidly into the fore-ground.

Brâncoveanu owed the throne to the Turcophil and anti-Austrian party, though he took care to reinforce his claim by lavish presents to the grand vizier and his horde of subordinate officials. His loyalty was soon to be put to the test, for in April Michael Apafi died, and the Turks, with French approval, tried to establish Emerich Tököli upon the Transylvanian throne and demanded Wallachian aid. Brâncoveanu, though well aware that Tököli had designs of his own upon Wallachia and that he himself was distasteful to Tököli's French patrons, none the less consented to a joint campaign, and crossing the Carpathians, de-defeated and captured the imperialist General Heissler at the battle of Zerneşti (21 August 1690). It might seem that after this no accommo-dation with Vienna would ever be possible, yet only a year later he is known to have written a letter to Leopold—of which the text has un-fortunately perished—explaining away his hostile conduct. As the future neutrality of Wallachia was a matter of no small strategic im-portance, his overtures were not rejected by the Austrian court: but it is highly characteristic of his balancing methods that he promptly sent two of his most trusted boiars to Constantinople to distribute judicious bribes and dispel awkward suspicions. Meanwhile his neutral attitude unquestionably helped on the consolidation of Transylvania under direct Habsburg rule, after the death of Apafi and the brief incident of Zerneşti. This was work which Vienna had specially at heart: the court

---

[1] Şerban's mother was a sister of Constantine Basarab (1654–8 in Wallachia and 1659–61 in Moldavia), whose father Radu Şerban (Wallachia 1602–10) was through his mother a great-grandson of Basarab Neagoe, the founder of Argeş (1512–21). Neagoe was fourth in male descent from Mircea the Old (1386–1418) and eighth from the original Basarab (circa. 1330–52). Constantine Brâncoveanu was the son of Şerban's sister Stanca.

PLATE VII

CONSTANTINE BRÂNCOVEANU

fully endorsed Veterani's opinion that Transylvania was "the tiller of the whole machine".[1]

Meanwhile the Christian cause languished and suffered more than one set-back. The capture of Belgrade in 1688 had been followed a year later by a brilliant campaign of Louis of Baden into the very heart of Serbia. But in August 1690 Niš had to be once more abandoned, and in October even Belgrade itself was recovered by the grand vizier. The Serbian patriarch and many thousands of his compatriots who had responded to Leopold's manifesto to the Balkan Christians, now found it necessary to withdraw into Hungary with the retiring armies, and were settled in Syrmia and the rich plain of the Bačka. In the following year the Turkish rally was again checked, Louis of Baden overthrowing and killing the grand vizier Mustafa Küprüli at the battle of Szalánkemen (17 August 1691) and capturing the key fortress of Grosswardein in June 1692. But the strain of a great war on two fronts—for it is to be remembered that the emperor was now once more the ally of England and Holland in the struggle against Louis XIV—was wearing down his resources both in men and money, while the great generals of the first period were replaced by such mediocrities as Croy, Augustus of Saxony and Caprara. In 1693, then, a fresh attack upon Belgrade definitely failed: in 1694 the imperialists remained on the defensive: in 1695 a new Turkish offensive was launched for the recovery of Transylvania, and although this was prevented, General Veterani was defeated and killed at Lugoş and the Turkish line was again pushed forward to the north. In 1696 the elector of Saxony's designs on Temesvár were unsuccessful, and General Heissler was killed in an indecisive battle on the Bega. Poland had meanwhile become a doubtful ally: Sobieski, justly alienated by Leopold's cold ingratitude and influenced by many political and personal ties with the French, was playing a lone hand in the east, and in any case after his death in 1696 there was a rapid decline in Polish powers of offensive.

In such circumstances the situation of Constantine Brâncoveanu was highly precarious. He had to keep the emperor in play and save Wallachia from becoming a centre of operations, while at the same time he had to submit to Turkish requisitioning and to justify to the Porte the fact of his negotiations with Vienna, which he could not hope to conceal. As ever, bribery figured prominently in his tactics. In 1693 he

[1] "Timone di tutta la macchina", December 1691—Hurmuzaki, *Documente*, III, p. 366.

was in extreme danger, for the Turks were preparing to launch their next attack northwards through the Wallachian passes, and their ally the Tatar Khan might be relied upon to strip the Roumanian lands utterly bare, ere ever he reached enemy territory. Fortunately the new imperialist menace to Belgrade compelled the Turks to renounce their advance through Wallachia. Emerich Tököli—so long Constantine's most dangerous enemy, just because he was within the same camp— fell finally into disgrace with the Turks, and this affected the French attitude towards Wallachia: and almost at the same time another enemy, Constantine Cantemir, died, and his place on the Moldavian throne was filled for a time by Brâncoveanu's own son-in-law Constantine Duca. Above all, Brâncoveanu established a close and cordial understanding with the grand dragoman, Alexander Mavrocordato, whose influence was now at its height at the Porte: and this was sealed a little later by a marriage between a daughter of the hospodar and a son of the Exaporite.

The respite thus obtained seemed destined to expire when the sultan himself passed through the west of Wallachia after defeating Veterani at Lugoş. Brâncoveanu, in terror lest his secret correspondence with the fallen imperialist general might have become known to the Turks, none the less felt it expedient to wait upon the sultan at Vidin, and to accept the inevitable humiliations of holding his suzerain's bridle and kneeling prostrate before him as he passed. It is once more characteristic of his tortuous policy of reinsurance, that he at once sought to atone to Vienna for this act of submission by ransoming at his own expense a large number of German prisoners. Yet twist and turn as he might, he could not save Wallachia from being bled white between the contending parties: at best, he could claim to have given Wallachia a continuity of policy and a relative immunity from invasion which Moldavia in the same period did not know.

Moldavia, indeed, presents to us the reverse of the medal which immortalises Sobieski's relief of Vienna: for then and for years afterwards the wretched province was a prey to selfish Polish ambition and constant marauding raids, in which various worthless pretenders to the throne were backed by Pole, Russian, Cossack and Tatar. For a time the Poles had taken possession of the north-western districts of Moldavia, including Suceava, Cernauţi and Soroca: and the central authority in what was left of the province was so weak as to be often virtually in abeyance.

After years of seeming stalemate another decisive change occurred in the general situation in the year 1697. The elector of Saxony, none too competent as a general, now became candidate for the throne of Poland and with Leopold's backing acquired Sobieski' succession. His command was entrusted to the youthful Prince Eugene of Saxony, whose genius and energy immediately ended the deadlock. His crowning victory at Zenta (11 September 1697) in which the grand vizier and many Turkish notables fell, decided the fate of Hungary. This and the knowledge that the Peace of Ryswick would relieve the emperor from all danger from the side of France and enable him to concentrate his whole force upon the Danube front, assured the ascendancy of the peace party at the Porte. It saw itself faced by the alternative of a fresh war in Hungary, in which it risked the probable loss of Belgrade and Temesvár, the keys to Serbia and Wallachia, or of a concentration against Russia, to avert the impending loss of the Crimea to that rising Power. Sanity prevailed, and Alexander Mavrocordato was entrusted with the delicate task of making peace overtures to the Emperor Leopold, at first through the medium of Lord Paget and William III, but eventually direct. Long delays followed, owing to disunion among the members of the Holy League, and Tsar Peter, hastening in person to Vienna, attempted to delay the discussions still further, on the ground that the emperor was far too moderate in his demands. Russia, indeed, had every interest in postponing a decision, for Peter's second campaign in 1698 had resulted in the capitulation of Azov, and he was busily building ships at Voronezh, in the hope of extending his first foothold upon the Black Sea coast.

At last in July 1698 the real peace negotiations opened at Karlowitz, the small Danubian village near Peterwardein assigned by the Emperor Leopold as the place of refuge of the Serbian Patriarch Arsenius. From the outset the two chief figures were Lord Paget, as patient mediator between the Christian Powers, and Mavrocordato, as the supple advocate of Turkish claims, only too conscious that he had been driven on to the defensive. It has often been alleged that the decisive factor in the peace was a gigantic bribe of 100,000 gold ducats to Mavrocordato, and though no evidence of this can be adduced, it certainly seems probable that he feathered his own nest with presents, according to the universal Turkish practice.[1] He cannot, however,

[1] In Hurmuzaki, *Documente*, are several documents which throw partial light on this. On 17 October 1698 he writes to Count Kinsky, begging "ne ulla de me et

reasonably be represented as a traitor to the Turkish cause:[1] for indeed but for his stubborn insistence upon the principle of *uti possidetis* as the basis of peace, Turkey would have fared very much worse. Incidentally, it was he who, at a time when precedence and etiquette in the relations of states received such an exaggerated emphasis, devised the ingenious expedient of a circular pavilion, which each plenipotentiary entered simultaneously by a separate door and took his place at a huge round table where none could claim to be above his neighbour.

The Peace of Karlowitz, signed on 26 January 1699, opens a new era in the history of the Near East. The Habsburgs recovered all Hungary save the Banat of Temesvár, all Croatia-Slavonia to the river Una, and the whole of Transylvania. Poland, after first claiming the Danube frontier, consented to evacuate Moldavia, but retained the fortress of Kameniec (on which King Augustus set such store as to describe it as "the bulwark of Christendom")[2] and the Porte henceforth abandoned all claim to Podolia or Ukraine. Venice retained Morea, Zante and the Dalmatian hinterland. The Magyar Protestant leader Tököli was abandoned by all, and henceforth eked out a miserable existence, under constant surveillance, first in Constantinople, then in Asia Minor. The Russo-Turkish negotiations dragged on till the summer of 1702, when Azov was for the first time ceded to the tsar. The main effect of the settlement was to reveal Turkey to the world as a declining Power, to give precedence to the house of Austria in all further competition for

---

hac patria fiat mentio", because this would excite extreme suspicion at the Porte, and explaining this caution by the "instability, perfidy and other barbarous and cruel vices of the Turks" (vol. v, no. 341). There are letters from Alexander and Nicholas Mavrocordato, acknowledging rèceipt of "1000 leoni" and of 2125 thalers in respect of certain claims against the Transylvanians and citizens of Debreczen and a note from Lord Paget, in Italian, confirming this (*ibid.* VI, nos. 4 and 5). There is a very lengthy report of Count Oettingen, the imperial ambassador, who has brought with him to Constantinople the promised "donativ", but has held back payment till certain frontier differences were regulated. In this connection he uses the phrase "damit den speckh auf die fallen legen sollte". He quotes long talks with Mavrocordato, who finally refused his offer of cash, because if it became known "sie ums ihren kopff khommen wuerden": but the balance of the Debrezcen claim was finally paid off (24 October 1700—*ibid.* VI, no. 6).

[1] A. A. C. Sturdza in his *L'Èurope orientale et le rôle historique des Maurocordato*, p. 55, defends Alexander, not altogether convincingly, against the charge, on the ground that there is no trace in the *Calendar of State Papers*.

[2] In a letter to Leopold I—Hurmuzaki, *Documente*, III, p. 427.

the Ottoman inheritance, and to turn the eyes of the Balkan Christians more than ever towards Vienna.

Its influence upon the evolution of the Roumanian Principalities was also very great. That their status remained unaltered, was mainly due to the discord between Vienna and Warsaw. The Polish claim to one or both of them was now finally liquidated, and Austria had for the time being to postpone her designs upon them. But with the restoration of Habsburg rule in Transylvania, they too came increasingly under Austrian political and cultural influences. They were now the neighbours, no longer of a small state less backward but scarcely more powerful than themselves and occupying the same uncertain position of vassalage, but of a Power of the very first magnitude, at the height of its renewed military power, and having their absorption as one of the many aims of its complicated foreign policy. During the next century certain foundations were laid among the despised Roumanian masses in Transylvania, on which, as we shall see, the whole superstructure of Roumanian national unity was eventually to rest.

* * * *

The Peace of Karlowitz was followed by a lull in the eastern crisis, but Constantine Brâncoveanu's situation became if anything still more precarious. He lost the favour of the grand dragoman and found increasing difficulty in appeasing the rapacity of the high dignitaries at the Porte and buying off intrigues against his tenure of the throne. In 1703 he visited Constantinople in person and in return for an increased tribute obtained the promise that he should remain for life: but this exhausted his private resources and forced him to resort to increased taxation. Meanwhile he experienced extreme difficulty in holding aloof from the complications of the Rákóczy rebellion in Hungary, and by so doing drew down upon himself the renewed illwill of the French, to whom the Magyar *frondeur*, like Tököli before him, was a convenient pawn in the great European game between Bourbon and Habsburg. He continued, however, to maintain his connections with Vienna, fully conscious that he was playing with fire, but also that the Turks looked upon him as a convenient intermediary.

Brâncoveanu followed a natural and inevitable tendency when in the second half of his reign he turned more and more towards Russia. While the War of Spanish Succession absorbed the Western and maritime Powers, while Turkey was recovering from her wounds, Northern

Europe witnessed a triangular struggle between Poland, Russia and Sweden, in which the first, already fallen from her greatness under Sobieski, became an object of rivalry between Peter the Great and Charles XII. The northern war culminated in Peter's great victory at Poltava (27 June 1709) and the flight of the Swedish king and his Cossack ally Mazeppa to Moldavian territory. For five whole years Charles made his headquarters at Bender and the strange assortment of tents and improvised *baraques* nicknamed Carlopolis, and devoted himself to inciting Turkey against Russia. His Polish agent Poniatowski outmanœuvred his cruder Russian rival Tolstoy, who actually tried poison when wholesale bribery had failed: and in the winter of 1710, thanks very largely to Charles's intrigues, the sultan was induced to declare war upon the tsar. Peter took up the challenge all too confidently, and one of his first steps was to issue a manifesto against Turkish perfidy and disregard for treaties, and a summons to "the Greeks, Wallachs, Bulgars and Serbs groaning under the yoke of the barbarians". This was solemnly made public at a great service in the cathedral of Moscow, when the imperial guard received new flags and a cross bearing the legend "In hoc signo vinces". At the time and long after, this ceremony, like Peter's legendary "Testament", were regarded as proof of his ambition to reconstitute the Byzantine Empire under the dynasty of Romanov.

Immediately after Poltava Brâncoveanu had sent an envoy to the tsar, conveying not merely congratulations on the victory, but an appeal for help for the Christians: and this doubtless encouraged Peter in the belief that active help would be forthcoming. These soundings took place in an atmosphere of mutual intrigue and denunciation: for successive princes of Moldavia were also making tentative approaches to Russia. To give but a few examples, Michael Rakoviţa, originally one of Brâncoveanu's own nominees, was denounced by the latter to the Porte, to cover his own action, and at a later date, despite his Russophil leanings, made himself an instrument of the Porte in order to take vengeance upon Brâncoveanu: while Demeter Cantemir, whom the Turks deliberately placed on the Moldavian throne to work their will upon Brâncoveanu, speedily went farther than any of his predecessors on the road of treasonable relations with Russia. Cantemir had the Porte's instructions to seize the person of Constantine, and it was supposed that his personal connections (his wife was a daughter of Şerban Cantacuzene and therefore a cousin of Constantine Brâncoveanu) would make this easier. But once he was on the throne, he had no motive in seizing his rival, and the two princely intriguers soon discovered their common bond of secret negotiation with the tsar and cautiously drew together again. Cantemir, it must be added, was something much more than a mere political acrobat: he was a man of equal learning and flair, who had studied profoundly the origins of the Ottoman state and reached the conviction that Turkey was near her end, that Russia was the coming Power, that war was inevitable and that Moldavia would be inexorably involved, from all which it followed that he must ally himself with the winning side.

The different characters of the two men emerged when Peter entered Jassy with his army in July 1711. Cantemir, defying the grand vizier's renewed order to lay hands on Brâncoveanu, called in Russian troops and issued a public proclamation against the Turks: he had already signed a secret convention (13 April), by which the tsar guaranteed to Moldavia her independence, to Cantemir himself a hereditary crown, and pension and estates if after all he should be driven into exile. Brâncoveanu on his side, who had made almost identical promises to the tsar and on whom the Russian army depended for its supplies, sent the message that he was eager to keep his word, but could not move so long as the Turkish and Tatar forces were in such close proximity: and almost in the same breath he sent the grand vizier a large contribution in money and promised more.[1]

This attitude had the gravest possible effects. Peter had pushed forward far too hastily and suddenly found himself short of essential supplies and outnumbered almost five to one by the Turks. A sharp reverse at Stanileşti, on the Pruth, on 11 July, showed him to be surrounded: for a moment capitulation seemed inevitable, and the straits in which he stood are revealed by his instructions to the envoy whom

---

[1] Cantemir himself is frankness itself on all this. In his *History of the Othman Empire* (pp. 451–2) he writes that the sultan "sent him into Moldavia, with orders to seize Brâncoveanu under colour of friendship, alliance or any other pretence which he thought proper and send him alive or dead to Constantinople", and then to take possession of Wallachia. On arrival, however, he received exorbitant orders, and intolerable burdens were imposed upon him. "From these firstfruits Cantemir, perceiving how little faith was to be expected from the infidels, throws off his attachment to the Turkish interest, and esteeming it better to suffer with Christ than wait for the deceitful treasures of Egypt, sends a trusty messenger to the Czar, with an offer of himself and his Principality."

he sent to negotiate. He was even ready to surrender Livonia, in fact almost anything save the territory round his new capital of Petersburg! Providentially for Russia his envoy Shafirov was able to administer heavy bribes to the grand vizier and his chief officers, and by consenting to restore Azov, to raze his new fortresses against the Tatars and to renounce interference with Polish affairs, he secured a treaty of peace which enabled the tsar and his army to retire hastily beyond the Pruth and leave Moldavia to its fate (12 July 1711). Thus ended Russia's second territorial advance against Turkey, with a setback that was not to be made good for two generations.

Several members of the Cantacuzene family, including the commander of the Wallachian cavalry, had already gone over to the Russians: Demeter Cantemir and twenty-six of his leading boiars had no choice but to follow their example. Cantemir, who actually escaped swathed in the rugs of the empress's barouche, never returned from exile: he played a certain part in Russian society, was a moving spirit in the foundation of the Academy of Sciences at St Petersburg[1] and enjoyed a high reputation in the learned world of his day, being elected to the Prussian Academy and in correspondence with foreign scholars. As a pioneer of research, he has earned a place of his own in history. His Latin history of the Turks was the first serious work of its kind in any European language: his description of Moldavia is an unique source of information on his native country on the eve of Phanariot rule. His Roumanian chronicle and still more his essays on the reign of Brâncoveanu are full of inaccurate details and partisan conclusions, even though they are based upon much documentary research and in many directions show a real critical faculty ahead of his age. Their main interest will always lie in the fact that here for the first time is advanced the claim that the inhabitants of Moldavia, Wallachia and Transylvania alike are of pure Roman blood and have held the Dacian lands ever since the days of Trajan. And not content with stressing the unity of the modern race and their uninterrupted descent, he expounded, as confidently as any chauvinist pamphleteer of the closing nineteenth century, the impossible theory that nothing was left of the old Dacian blood and that Trajan's colonists were all authentic Romans, and not, as we now know, gathered from every province and race of the Empire. We are at the dawn of a revived national consciousness, of patriotism

---

[1] He has been inaccurately described as a member of the Academy, but he died in 1723, before it actually came into being.

PLATE VIII

DEMETER CANTEMIR

in its modern sense and of the extravaganzas to which it everywhere gives birth.

\* \* \* \*

The fugitive Cantemir was replaced on the Moldavian throne by Nicholas Mavrocordato, who had already held it from 1709 to 1710: and it is from his reign that the Phanariot era is generally reckoned. The new prince was the son of the famous dragoman and through his mother could claim descent in the female line from Stephen the Great, in much the same way as his enemy Brâncoveanu traced back to the Basarab princes. Like his father, he was a man of high culture, had been educated in Italy, spoke and wrote the languages of the West no less than Turkish, Arab and Persian, had great diplomatic experience and a large private fortune, the key to most Turkish doors. He was a genuine believer in the Turkish orientation, and in Moldavia his policy followed the double line of strengthening the Greek element and curbing the power of the boiars, even by the most drastic means. But in this he was in no way prompted by merely Greek sympathies, being inordinately proud of his Roumanian descent: his motive was compounded of family ambition and a genuine belief that Roumanian interests were bound up with the Porte. Ere long he began to covet the more important throne of Wallachia, and in this he had the backing of the French Embassy—consistently hostile to Brâncoveanu throughout his reign: of Charles XII and his clever agent Poniatowski, and of the influential Magyar exiles under Francis Rákóczy. In addition to this, Brâncoveanu, compromised by the capture of some correspondence with both Vienna and Moscow, had the misfortune to quarrel with the whole Cantacuzene connection, and the circle of his enemies was thus almost complete. His former protégé, Michael Rakoviţa, offered himself for the part of Judas: it was his duty to deliver the hospodar alive into the hands of the Porte.

At last, on 4 April 1714, a Turkish emissary, Aga Mustafa, with a small detachment of troops and written orders from the sultan, arrived in Bucarest and proceeding to the palace, flung a black handkerchief over Brâncoveanu's shoulder and pronounced him to be "Mazil" (deposed). The prince called desperately from the palace windows for aid, but neither his guards nor his boiars dared to lift a hand.[1] Two days later he and his family were sent away by road to Constantinople, the whole population following his carriage with sincere but impotent

[1] Cf. Kogălniceanu, *Hist. de la Valachie et de la Moldavie* (1839), pp. 365–6.

lamentation. On arrival the old man was thrown into the prison of the Seven Towers, and tortured in front of his children. He was invited to save himself by a forfeit of ten million piastres, but as this fantastic sum was far beyond even his utmost resources, he was executed, with his two sons and his son-in-law, in presence of the sultan himself, outside a summer kiosk on the Bosphorus. A French traveller gives a touching account of the execution. The younger son, a boy of sixteen, terrified at the sight of his relatives' death, offered to accept Islam in return for his life: "on which the father exhorting him to die 1000 times, if it were possible, rather than deny Jesus Christ, to live a few years longer on the earth, he said to the executioner 'I wish to die a Christian: strike', and at once the latter cut off his head, as he had done to the others. At the last he beheaded the father, on which their bodies were thrown into the sea and their heads exposed for three days above the great gate of the Seraglio".[1]

The longest reign in two centuries of Roumanian history thus ended, as it was bound to end, in disaster. Constantine Brâncoveanu had always tried to be on the side of the strongest, to balance between contending forces, to reinsure against every accident: but his lack of all principle or moral force left him in the end without friends. Professor Xenopol has aptly summed up the historical process of which this marks the close. "Stephen the Great, Michael the Brave, Constantine Brâncoveanu, each at the interval of a century, mark three stages traversed by the Roumanian people. It gradually descends from liberty to slavery, from the courage of the lion to the cunning of the fox, from an honourable to an abject life."[2]

[1] La Mottraye, *Voyage en Europe et Asie* (1717), II, p. 212.
[2] *Hist. des Roumains*, II, p. 135.

# CHAPTER IV

# TRANSYLVANIA UNDER NATIVE PRINCES

"Quamvis valachica natio in regno inter Status reputata non sit,
nihilominus tamen donec propter emolumentum regni tolerabuntur."
"Approbatae Constitutiones" of Transylvania,
Pars I, Tit. VIII, Art. I (1540).

We have already seen that Transylvania from early times developed an autonomous life of its own, under the three privileged groups of Magyars, Székelys and Saxons. In the fourteenth century, though remaining an integral part of the Hungarian crown, it tended more and more to transact local business in its own Diet—something between the central parliament (which its delegates continued to attend) and those county assemblies which have always formed the backbone of Hungarian political life, or the National Assemblies which replaced them among the Székels and Saxons. This Diet, or Congregatio Generalis, bore the title of "Universitas Nobilium (i.e. of the Magyars), Siculorum, Saxonum", and documentary evidence, though fragmentary, records at least ten of its meetings between 1322 and 1526.[1] The basis of representation differed in each of the three groups, the two latter sending delegates from their elected assembly, whereas originally all nobles were supposed to attend.

This latter date is the turning point of Hungarian history—the fatal battle of Mohács which led to the Turkish conquest of Central Hungary, the independence of Transylvania and the native Principalities, and the accession of the house of Habsburg in such fragments as remained in the west and north. But there are two other dates in the hundred years preceding the batttle which are not sufficiently stressed in the ordinary textbooks, but which really provide the clue to the whole subsequent development of Hungary, to the Transylvanian problem in its modern phase and to the relations of the Magyar and Roumanian races. These are the so-called Fraternal Union of 1437 and the Great Peasant Rising of 1514.

There can be no doubt that at this period the Roumanians already

[1] 1322, 1363, 1377, 1461, 1463, 1467, 1470, 1498, 1524, 1526. Kemény, *Arpadia*, III, p. 25. Bedeus v. Scharberg, *Die Verfassung Siebenbürgens*, p. 26.

formed a very important element in Transylvania, which King Sigismund, in a letter to the Pope in 1412, describes as a country "of mixed races and language" (promiscuarum gencium et linguarum). That they were still on a footing of equality is shown by such a document as that of 1291, by which Andrew III conferred "with all our Nobles, Saxons, Székels and Roumanians in the Transylvanian lands",[1] or that of a century later (1399), which has a reference to "Universis nobilibus tam Ungaris quam Vlachis"[2]—which incidentally illustrates the mixed origin of the Hungarian nobility.

By the fifteenth century the whole tendency was towards a strengthening of the feudal landed class at the expense of the masses. Class interests at this date were far stronger than race instincts, and the Roumanian boiar class gradually merged with the Hungarian nobility, in a joint encroachment upon yeoman and peasant rights. This community of interests is exemplified in John Hunyady, who, as we saw, was a Roumanian by race, but a Hungarian noble in rank and an ardent Catholic by religion.

In 1437 there was a formidable peasant rising in Transylvania, in which Magyar and Roumanian made common cause against their lords and which was only suppressed with the utmost difficulty. The result was the "Brotherly Union" concluded at Kápolna between the three nations—the Magyars, Székels and Saxons. Still gasping at the danger so narrowly averted, they pledged themselves to loyalty to the Holy Crown and mutual aid not merely against the Turks but above all against those "most wicked peasants" (nefandissimi rustici). A speed of three miles a day was specially prescribed to the relieving forces, and failure to fulfil the pledge was punishable by death. In a document of 1458, renewing the union still more closely, there occurs the significant phrase "regnum hoc totum Transilvaniense".[3] Even under King Matthias and still more under his weak successors, Transylvania is developing an autonomous position.

We thus see a constitution founded upon an oligarchic basis which it was never to lose. The three privileged nations defend themselves against all other aspirants. They are the three "united" or "Recognised"

[1] "Cum universis Nobilibus Saxonibus Siculis et Olachis in partibus Transilvaniae"—Teutsch and Firnhaber, Urkundenbuch zur Gesch. Siebenbürgens, p. 167.

[2] Kemény, op. cit. v, 173.

[3] Timon, Ungarische Verfassungs- und Rechtsgeschichte, p. 729. In a document of the year 1437 occurs the phrase "Universitas Hungarorum et Valachorum huius principatus Transylvanie". Teleki, x, p. 2.

Nations ("nationes unitae" or "receptae"): the others, including the Roumanians, are only "Tolerated" Nations,[1]—or, in the words or Benkö, the chief Magyar authority on Transylvania in the eighteenth century, "those who do not possess the right of citizenship and access to the political public honours of the Principality, but are held to be merely tolerated by grace".[2] We must be careful not to read the racial feuds of to-day back into the annals of the dying Middle Ages, but it is highly significant that a law passed in 1463 lays down that serfs left behind to defend the home territory during military operations against the Turks, *must be of Magyar blood*.[3] It does show that there was already the double barrier of blood and of social privilege. Whatever may have been the situation in the Dark Ages, there is no manner of doubt that from the beginning of the fresh era of colonisation—that is, from the eleventh century onwards—the mass of the population in Transylvania consists more and more of Roumanian stock, held more and more in bondage by masters of alien blood and religion, ruthlessly using the power conferred by feudal land tenure and social distinction.

King Matthias, great as was his authority among all sections of the nation, Serbs, Bulgarians and Roumanians no less than Magyars, could not check the growing power of the nobles and of the Church, and the consequent further encroachments upon the rights of the peasantry. The change after his death in 1490 is dramatically expressed in the popular proverb "King Matthias is dead and with him Justice". Under the Jagiellon kings the Hungarian crown rapidly lost all power and prestige: it failed, or was unable, to maintain the necessary forces upon which he had relied, and its revenues shrank and almost threatened to dry up altogether. The utter lawlessness of the nobility, often amounting to civil war, brought Hungary to the verge of dissolution long before the final crisis of foreign invasion: and it may indeed be assumed that its internal plight was not unknown to the Turks and served to whet their appetite.

In 1514 these desperate internal conditions caused a new Peasant

[1] The full list throws an interesting light upon racial stratification—"Valachi, Armeni, Graeci, Judaei, Moravi, Poloni, Russi, Bulgari, Servii, Sclavi et Zingari".

[2] Benkö, *Transsilvania*, I, p. 472. That they were regarded as useful, and indeed indispensable, is shown by a fuller phrase of Benkö, "*nec cavere Valachis sine irreparabili damno* nobiles Transilvani possent: eorum siquidem servitiis jobbagionalibus utantur potissimum". *Ibid.*

[3] Iorga, *Les Roumains de Transylvanie*, I, p. 137; Hurmuzaki, *Fragmente*, I, p. 147.

Rising, this time mainly among the Magyar population; and the strengthening of the feudal system following upon its suppression was, as has already been pointed out, one of the main reasons why Hungary offered so little resistance to the next great Turkish onslaught.[1]

The battle of Mohács led at once to a partition of Hungary, which was to last for 160 years. The Turks overran the great plains of Central Hungary, and in 1541 the fortress of Buda became the advance guard of Islam in Europe—as they themselves called it, "the pivot of the Holy War", ranking tenth among the cities of their empire. The fragments that remained were disputed between rival claimants to the throne: each of the two dominant factions in turn seized the crown jewels and crowned its candidate. Thus for twelve years, amid the yearly recurring menace of Turkish invasion, John Zápolya and Ferdinand of Habsburg continued the civil war. But while the latter became more and more the rallying point of Christian defence, Zápolya, in the very year that Suleiman the Magnificent besieged Vienna, did personal homage to him not far from the field of Mohács, swearing to succour him with all his worldly goods, even though only three or four Moslems were left beside him.

At last in 1538 Ferdinand and Zápolya signed a treaty leaving each in possession of what he actually held at the moment. Thus Zápolya retained Transylvania with certain additional counties (including Debreczen and Kaschau), while Ferdinand kept the rest of Slovakia, the districts west and north of Lake Balaton and most of Croatia. Zápolya was to retain the kingly title, but only for his lifetime. It is from this treaty that the separate existence of Transylvania as a state unit is generally, and quite reasonably, considered to date. That Zápolya had little idea of keeping faith is shown by the fact that he almost immediately married a daughter of the Polish king and strengthened his ties with the sultan. He himself died in 1540, only a few months after the birth of his son John Sigismund. Suleiman at once recognised the infant as king and renewed his efforts against Ferdinand, reducing further fortresses on the north and organising his conquests into regular vilayets, under the centralised control of the pasha of Buda. It of course suited him admirably to have Transylvania half suspended in the air, under the precarious rule of a woman and a child in arms. There was a long struggle between Ferdinand and Isabella for the possession of Transylvania: it centres round the romantic but dubious figure of Cardinal Martinuzzi (really a Croat friar named Utješinović, but gener-

[1] See *supra*, pp. 51–3.

ally known to history as "Frater George"). In the end the Turks turned the scale against the Habsburg cause—the sultan himself, during one of his many campaigns in Hungary, commanding the Estates to return to their allegiance to John Sigismund (1555).

Henceforth, with two short interruptions, Transylvania is ruled by native princes till the closing decade of the seventeenth century. Its position is almost unique: for it now owns two parallel allegiances. Habsburg Hungary had to hold the Turks in check with imperialist aid, and at the same time to defend the constitution against a foreign court in Vienna, with German and Spanish ideas: and then as the Reformation spread, it had to defend the reformed doctrines against the Catholic and Jesuit reaction. Meanwhile farther east Transylvania—in this respect like its two Roumanian neighbours across the Carpathians—is balanced uneasily between Vienna, Warsaw and Constantinople. In theory it always remains part of the Hungarian crown,[1] and the Tripartitum is the basis of its public law, exactly as in Habsburg Hungary—supplemented, but not replaced, by the "Approbatae Constitutiones", that is, the laws passed by the Transylvanian Diet. Thus the prince takes oath to the king of Hungary, though he is perpetually trying to filch from him further scraps of territory: yet owing his position largely to Turkish favour, he submits to investiture by the sultan and pays him an annual tribute. Subject to these two restrictions, there is no interference by the Porte. The Estates are free to elect their prince: there are only two or three instances of that imposition of a prince from without which was already becoming the normal practice in the two Roumanian principalities. Another very vital difference is that Turkish attempts to extort an increased tribute from Transylvania almost always failed, although her valuable sources of revenue—salt, gold, silver—made her a very coveted object. A good illustration of the dual allegiance is to be found in the action of the Saxons, who suffered specially from Gabriel Báthory, the only one of the Transylvanian princes who belongs to the same category of bloodthirsty tyrants as Ioan cel Cumplit or Stephen the Locust. In their distress in 1613 they directed simultaneous appeals to the emperor in Prague and to the sultan in Constantinople.

The princely power develops quite logically out of the old office of Transylvanian voevode. Already under Matthias the offices of voevode and of count of the Székels had been united, mainly for military reasons —the Transylvanians forming technically the left wing of the Hun-

[1] "*Membrum Sacrae Coronae.*"

garian army. When the central power collapsed after Mohács, the voe-vode was the real centre of gravity in Transylvania. While constitu-tional theory remains untouched, from 1542 there is in reality a new constitution due to stress of circumstances. Till that year the three Nations, though meeting in local Diets, had been represented in the Hungarian Parliament, and all laws passed there held good for Tran-sylvania also. But henceforth the local Diet became a real Parliament, being faced with the harsh necessity of levying new taxation. Thus the Union of the Three Nations undertakes to share the burdens of defence and administration in equal proportions. An important result of this was that the Székels lost their freedom from taxation, and also the special privileges which rendered them immune from confiscation of land. By 1562 a portion of them were reduced to serfdom, the "Ius Regium" was introduced, and on their territory lands were often granted on the same sort of tenure as in other Magyar districts.[1] The hold of the big feudal families on affairs grew stronger, the prince being invariably selected from their ranks. Of the twenty-three holders of the princely office—a list from which some must be excluded as doubtful—Michael of Wallachia was the only non-Magyar. Ten belonged to the families of Báthory and Rákóczy: of the others, Zápolya, Apafi and Bocskay, all three now extinct, were among the greatest families of their day, while Kemény and Bethlen are still among the foremost leaders of the Magyar oligarchy.

The title which they assumed varied according to the shifting cir-cumstances of the time. John Zápolya had been lawfully crowned king of Hungary, and his son continued to style himself "Electus Rex Hungariae". Most of their successors bore the title of "Princeps Tran-sylvaniae et Partium Hungariae" (i.e. of the border counties): but this was expanded by the ambitious if incompetent Sigismund Báthory into the grandiloquent style "Dei Gratiae Regnorum Transilvaniae Mol-daviae Valachiae Transalpinae et Sacri Romani Imperii Princeps, Partium Regni Hungariae Dominus et Siculorum Comes".[2]

It lies outside my present purpose to recount the intricate though romantic details of Transylvanian history, but rather to select those outstanding incidents which decided its evolution and which link it indissolubly with that of the two Roumanian principalities, until the great events of our own era at last welded all three into a single unit.

---

[1] Marczali, *Ungarische Verfassungsgeschichte*, p. 75.
[2] Schuler von Libloy, *Siebenbürgische Rechtsgeschichte*, I, 213–18, 307.

One of the outstanding features of the period of native princes (1540–1690) was the coming of the Reformation, which found a specially favourable field in the Saxon "Königsboden". Several reasons combined to explain this—first, the unusually wide ecclesiastical autonomy enjoyed by the chapters of Hermannstadt and Kronstadt in the south, and of Bistritz in the north—all holding direct from the primatial see of Esztergom and exempt from the jurisdiction of the bishop of Alba Iulia; secondly, the practice of free election of the priest by the commune, a privilege conferred by the royal charter of 1224; but above all, the intimate connections with Wittenberg and Leipzig, which resulted from the Eastern trade passing through a chain of German towns in Silesia, Moravia, Slovakia, Zips, down into Transylvania and on to the Danube. On the eve of Mohács king and Parliament united in an effort to check by force the rapid spread of Lutheran doctrines in Hungary. In 1524 a messenger from Wittenberg was burnt in Pest, and an enactment of the following year orders that "all Lutherans shall be extirpated, and wherever found, shall be seized, not only by the clergy but also by the laity and burnt". But these penalties remained mainly on paper, and after the great disaster repression became impossible, because the machinery for enforcing debatable measures had collapsed, or rather, had fallen into three fragments. Even Ferdinand, who remained a fervent Catholic, was powerless in face of the rapid spread of Protestant doctrines throughout his hereditary dominions and in Bohemia, much more therefore in the Hungarian lands where his authority was so much weaker.

In Transylvania the Reformation found a leader of real mark, who in less narrow surroundings might have acquired the same fame as Zwingli or Knox or Beza—Johannes Honterus, who returned to his home in Kronstadt in 1533. He was not only a religious reformer, but a real humanist, with wide mathematical and philosophical learning, admired as a poet, and possessed of a technical knowledge of printing and woodcutting. He had published a once famous Latin Grammar at Cracow, and he brought back with him equipment for a printing press at Kronstadt. With it he published Luther's catechism and the Augsburg confession, and his influence was tested when in 1536 the town priest Benckner resigned in impotent anger. In 1542 Honterus carried the day in Kronstadt. The new priest married, the Mass was abolished, his so-called "Reformations-büchlein" (comparable to Knox's *Book of Discipline*) was issued, and the town council adopted his school laws, for here, as in Scotland, reformation and education went hand in hand. In 1544 Honterus himself succeeded as the town parson (Stadtpfarrer) of Kronstadt, and a year later the two chapters of Hermannstadt and Kronstadt united all the Saxon clergy of the Transylvanian diocese to form a single "Spiritual University".[1] Finally, in 1550, unity was given to the new Church by the formal adoption of Honterus's book in the revised form of a "Kirchenordnung aller Deutschen in Siebenbürgen", and the Saxon university prescribed its uniform adoption in all Saxon towns. The result was an exact coincidence of the Saxon nationality and the Lutheran religion throughout the Königsboden.

Meanwhile Protestantism found a famous Magyar exponent in Matthias Biró, best known as Dévay—also a native of Transylvania. Appointed by the town council of Kaschau as Pfarrer in 1531, he was carried off to prison in Vienna, and only released owing to high personal influence. After years in Germany he returned to Pest, only to be driven out in 1541 by the Turks. This second exile was spent in Switzerland, and thus his final years at Debreczen gave a more Zwinglian turn to Magyar Protestant development. Protestantism among the Magyars met with more opposition than among the Saxons, developed more slowly and on more confused lines, and was not unaffected by national sentiments. No unity was possible while Ferdinand was straining every effort in his remaining territory to check and suppress heresy, and for a time the Magyar Protestants were more or less divided between the Lutheran and the Zwinglian or "Sacramentarian" tenets. But when the latter was swallowed up in Calvinism, Debreczen rapidly became a Calvinist stronghold, with its famous church, college, library and press. It gradually came to be known as the Geneva of Hungary, while a distinction was drawn between "a magyar hit" (the Magyar faith) and the "német hit", by which was meant the German or Lutheran creed.

During the middle of the century the Magyar nobility defected steadily to Protestantism, and increasingly to Calvinism. By the death of Maximilian II in 1576, it has been seriously asserted (though the statement is undoubtedly an exaggeration) that only three of the great families of Hungary were still Catholic.[2]

While in north Hungary "the Confession of the Four Towns", drawn up in 1549, laid the basis of Lutheranism among the Magyars

[1] In the medieval sense of the word *Universitas*.
[2] Fessler, *Geschichte Ungarns*, III, 656.

and Slovaks, Calvinism struck root in the great plains. In Transylvania John Sigismund Zápolya, the young prince and titular king, gradually moved to the left in a religious sense. The Diet in 1557 proclaimed mutual toleration: "every man", it laid down, "is at liberty to declare for the religion which pleases him: the use of the new or the old customs is left entirely to the free will of every man. But the adherents of the new faith are forbidden to cause each other offence". As a result, Calvinism was organised with its centre at Klausenburg (Kolozsvár, Cluj) under the court preacher David, and in 1563 adopted the Genevan Confession of Beza. In the following year the Diet recognised the right of every individual to opt freely for Klausenburg or Hermannstadt, that is for Reformed or Lutheran, and in effect (as it has remained ever since) for Magyar or German. But the instability of doctrinal views in that age is revealed by the next and final stage in the Transylvanian Reformation. In 1556 David, and the no less influential Blandrata, an Italian who was the prince's body-physician, seceded from the Calvinist faith, and, infected by the close intercourse with Poland and its then powerful Socinian colonies, founded at Klausenburg the most famous of the Unitarian Churches of the Continent.

At last, after several violent public disputations between the rival sects, the situation was definitely stabilised in 1571, when the Diet passed a law recognising "the four Received Religions" namely: "the Evangelical—Reformed or Calvinist, the Lutheran or that of the Augsburg Confession, the Roman Catholic, and the Unitarian or Antitrinitarian", and assuring their free exercise and equal status for all time".[1] So to the three Received Nations are added the four Received Religions, thus composing that sevenfold basis of privilege which the famous Magyar patriot Wesselényi described in a cynical manner as the "Seven Deadly Sins of Transylvania". Transylvania becomes perhaps the most interesting field of experiment for religious tolerance in the very epoch which history has branded as that of the Wars of Religion —an epoch when the young reformed Churches had everywhere developed the same deadly fanaticism which they condemned so bitterly in their Catholic persecutors. It is true that tolerance was always relative. Apart from the seizure of Church lands, for which at least a plausible case can be made out, the Catholic bishop of Transylvania was forced to leave the country, and it was not really till the eighteenth century that Catholicism was able seriously to revive its organisation

[1] G. D. Teutsch, *Geschichte der siebenbürgischen Sachsen*, I, p. 233.

in Transylvania—a complete contrast to Habsburg Hungary during the seventeenth century, where the Counter-Reformation recovered a great portion of the ground lost in the preceding century.

The order in which the four religions are named in the Act just quoted is significant of the predominant position attained by Protestantism. Even under the Báthory princes, who succeeded the semi-unitarian John Sigismund, and who were zealously Catholic and under Jesuit influence, it appears that Catholicism was forced entirely into the background, Stephen Báthory only hearing Mass or confessing in places remote from the public eye, or on hunting expeditions. It is true that after his accession to the Polish throne in 1579, he secured the return of the Jesuits to Transylvania and their control of the education of his young kinsman Sigismund Báthory, whose fickle and shifty character brought many troubles upon the country in the closing decade of the century, when sultan and emperor, Poland and Wallachia were all competing for its possession. But in the long run this only served as a fresh incentive to Protestantism: the imperialists with their Italian mercenaries and their Jesuit advisers, provoked a strong reaction of national and religious feeling. In 1605 Transylvania rose and shook itself free, and for the next generation under two such able princes as Stephen Bocskay and Gabriel Bethlen, acquired an European position as one of the Protestant powers, in constant treaty with Brandenburg, Saxony, Sweden, England and France.

There can be no doubt that, with all its imperfections, the Transylvanian religious settlement was far in advance of its age, and contrasts favourably with the conditions prevailing in any of the Western countries. But there was one fatal flaw which vitiated the whole system, and which is constantly slurred over in modern historical literature. The three privileged nations rigidly excluded from all political power the fourth and not less numerous (and indeed, with each succeeding century proportionately more numerous) Wallach or Roumanian nation: and in exactly the same way the equal rights assured to the four "received religions" were deliberately withheld from a Church which, at the most moderate estimate, had far more adherents than any one of the four—namely, the Orthodox or Eastern Church, to which all Roumanians save the Magyarised nobles adhered.

Social, political and religious circumstances alike were combining to widen the gulf between the Roumanian and Magyar races. The Roumanian noble class, so prominent in the earlier defence of the Hungarian frontiers against the Turks, was being steadily merged in the Hungarian and finding common interests against the serf class—those who escaped this process drifting across the Carpathians to the two neighbour Principalities. The periodical privileges granted by the crown to the Roumanians ceased under the native princes, and the fatal distinction between "received" and "tolerated" received growing emphasis. A statute of 1579 even made this status dependent upon "the goodwill of the Princes and citizens" (usque ad beneplacitum principum et regnicolarum) and bluntly declared that "though the Wallachian nation does not belong to the Estates in this land, nor its religion to the recognised religions, yet it is further tolerated *for the advantage of the kingdom* (propter regni emolumentum), subject to its priests observing certain conditions".[1]

The gulf was finally fixed when the status of the four Religions was regularised and the Orthodox Religion ("az oláh vallás"—the Wallach faith)[2] firmly excluded. That Protestantism made no conquests among the Roumanians is unquestionably due to the gulf already existing, racially and socially, between the privileged adherents of the new religion—the Magyars and Saxons—and the unhappy Roumanians who formed the substructure of the state—the underground cellars, as it were. An interesting parallel might be drawn between the submerged Orthodox of Transylvania under the Báthorys and Bethlens and the Catholics of Celtic Ireland under Elizabeth.

We now find two parallel tendencies—a certain proselytising zeal of the Saxon Protestants and a consistent Magyar effort to isolate the Roumanians from their co-religionists beyond the frontiers, and while keeping them as utter serfs in their own territory, to play them off against the Saxons on the Königsboden and so perhaps swamp or weaken the Saxon element.

The first of these currents was the natural expansive effort of adherents to a new faith, no sooner than their own position had been assured. Already in 1550—only five years after the Saxon towns had established uniformity—we find Wagner, the town Pfarrer of Kronstadt, translating the Lutheran catechism into Greek (still the liturgical and church language of the Roumanians) and in 1559 issuing a Greek Testa-

---

[1] Hintz, *Gesch. des Bisthums der griech.-nichtunirten Glaubensgenossen in Siebenbürgen*, p. 11.

[2] Religionem Orthodoxam, vulgo Vallachicam, is a phrase from a document of 1601, Schaguna, *Gesch. der griech.-orientalischen Kirche in Oesterreich*, p. 45.

ment. In the latter year another leading citizen, Benckner, published a Roumanian edition of the Catechism and in 1560 of the Gospels—both in the Cyrilline characters; then in 1562 a Slav Gospel, liturgy and hymn-book (Octoic).[1] Finally in 1580 Hirschner published more books in both types, and in 1582 a Roumanian translation of the Old Testament. The policy is almost identical with that pursued at the same time from Tübingen, through the medium of the Slovene language, for the conversion to Protestantism of the Balkan Slavs and thus indirectly of the Turks, among whom Slav was still widely spoken. But in the case of the Roumanians it failed utterly, despite the more than imperfect organisation of their hierarchy and the state of passivity to which they were thus reduced.

Much more important was the policy pursued by successive princes of forbidding intercourse with the hierarchy of Wallachia, and restricting or controlling such Orthodox clergy as entered from the Principalities. There was the clear aim of separating and keeping apart the Roumanians of the two sides of the mountains, and the shock of alarm produced by Michael's conquest strengthened this tendency. In 1564 the Orthodox Bishop Sabas was expelled from office, and a Calvinist superintendent, George de Szent György, was officially entrusted by the Diet with the task of preaching the true faith to the Roumanian villagers. Recalcitrants were liable to heavy penalties, bishops and priests to expulsion, as traitors to the state. In 1567 the same man was appointed "Bishop and Superintendent of the Roumanian Churches": the prince ordered the Orthodox clergy to submit, and also to substitute the "Roumanian for the Serbian language", as he called the Slavonic, then still in liturgical use. In 1569, on Szent György's death, another Magyar Calvinist, Tordassy, was appointed, who summoned a Synod and in it forced through the condemnation of the worship of the Saints, the prohibition of the Last Sacraments to those ignorant of the Creed and the Lord's Prayer (a grim side-light upon the ecclesiastical standards of that period) and ordered the ejection of such priests as still used the Slavonic rite. In this John Sigismund—who himself had made the round of all four recognised confessions, beginning as Catholic, passing through Lutheranism and Calvinism and dying as an Unitarian—had the political aim of getting the Roumanian masses directly under the princely control,

---

[1] Müller, *Beiträge zur Verfassungs- und Verwaltungsgeschichte der Deutschen in Ungarn*, p. 28 (in *Magazin für Geschichte und Literatur Siebenbürgens*, III, ed. J. Trausch (1852)).

as an *instrumentum regni*. His successor nominated a certain monk Euthymius as Orthodox Bishop, but Tordassy's activities continued, and the confusion was increased by the consecration of another bishop in 1578 by the metropolitan of Wallachia, claiming jurisdiction over all the Roumanians.[1] A year later the clergy were permitted to elect their own bishop, subject to the prince's consent—the motive again being obviously to wean them from "Transalpine" influence. The official attitude is shown by persistent references to the Orthodox clergy as "pastores Valachi", not "sacerdotes". This jurisdiction of the see of Tîrgovişte was formally recognised in the treaty concluded in 1594 between Michael the Brave and Sigismund Báthory.

The one practical thing which Michael did for his kinsmen in Transylvania during his very brief rule there was to erect a cloister at the historic site of Alba Iulia, where the city of "Karlsburg" now stands, and to take steps for co-ordinating church life on both sides of the Carpathians. But after his overthrow the Magyar nobility turned resentfully upon his followers and "ordered them to be killed where they could be found"[2] and there was an absolute prohibition upon crossing the Wallachian frontier or upon any priests coming from there. They were to be treated as "seditious and incendiary" and Roumanian monks, if caught, were to be publicly degraded. Attempts at proselytism continued to break down against the extraordinary powers of passive resistance of the Roumanian people. But the position was utterly deplorable, and the misery and lack of culture in which they were held is revealed by the legislation of the Transylvanian Diet. Till 1609, even the priests, if sons of serfs (as the great majority inevitably were), were bound to the soil and subject to all seignorial exactions. In that year they were freed from "plebeian burdens" and might move to some other place with their families, subject to their bishop's leave.[3] Yet even their married sons remained liable to the same obligations as the serfs around them. Section IX of "Approbatae Constitutiones" of 1653 contains the following phrase: "Though the Wallach nation has been admitted *propter bonum publicum* to this country, they have, forgetful of their low station, infringed on some of our brethren the nobles, by the demand that they should not work on their feast days: hence it is ordered that they shall not prescribe to the Magyar nation in this

---

[1] Cf. charters of 1609, 1659, 1663.
[2] Iorga, *Histoire des Roumains de Transylvanie*, p. 288.
[3] *Approbatae Constitutiones*, Tit. VIII, Art. III.

matter".[1] Again, an act of 1678 lays down that in future the Roumanian clergy "cannot be ennobled or possess property".[2]

*        *        *        *

The career of Michael the Brave and the dramatic manner in which he united all the Roumanians under a single rule have already been briefly described. As we have seen, it was, so far as contemporary history is concerned, the merest episode, the spiritual effects of which, distorted like a distant view in misty weather, still lay in the far future. In the history of Transylvania he was a bold intruder, who never won the confidence either of the ruling nations or of the submerged majority. His treacherous murder in 1601 left the country for the moment at the mercy of the imperialists. But Başta, with his mercenary troops and Jesuit advisers, soon drove the whole population to despair by their extortions and misrule. Rudolf's absolutist designs upon the constitution and his attempts to re-impose Catholicism by force in his dominions provided a double motive of resistance, civil and religious, and drove Transylvania back into the arms of the Turks.

On his orders, the chief towns of Northern Hungary, which had long been in Protestant hands, were forcibly transferred to the Catholics: and the town church of Klausenburg was assigned to the Jesuits. Measures of this kind united the Magyar nobility and the German townsmen. The "Ius Resistendi" (secured under the famous clause 31 of the Golden Bull) was formally invoked, and there was a general rising which led to the election, in April 1605, of Stephen Bocskay as "Prince of Hungary and Transylvania".[3] He was even invested as king by the Turks, on the famous electoral field of Rákos, near Pest, and accompanied the grand vizier after the capture of the primatial city of Esztergom. But he wisely did not insist upon the royal dignity, merely using his new position to bring Rudolf to reason: and the treaty of Vienna, which he concluded in 1606, is a landmark in Hungarian history because it secured for the first time a legal recognition of religious liberty, which was frequently violated during the coming century, but never utterly lost. It recognised Bocskay in Transylvania and the neighbouring

---

[1] A similar clause, phrased slightly less crudely, already occurs in *Approbatae Constitutiones*, Tit. IX, Art. 1 (1640).
[2] Benkö, *Transsilvania*, I, p. 473. "Graeci et popae Valachici nobilitari in posterum non possint nec bona possidere."
[3] Schuler von Libloy, *Siebenbürgische Verfassungsgeschichte*, I, p. 305.

counties, the so-called "Partes".[1] We need not concern ourselves with a definition of the frontiers between Transylvania and Habsburg Hungary: it will suffice to point out that they constantly varied according to the military fortunes of the Turks, at one time coinciding with the actual line of the principality proper, at other times including Grosswardein (Nagyvárad, Oradea Mare), Kaschau or even Debreczen itself.

The Peace of Zsitvatörök, concluded in the same year between the emperor and the Porte, is no less memorable in foreign policy: for it ends Vienna's tribute to Constantinople and places diplomatic negotiations on a footing of absolute equality between the two Powers (till then the sultan's arrogance towards the "King of Vienna", and that of his envoys, had known no bounds): and it is shortly followed by the concession of special consular and ecclesiastical privileges for Habsburg subjects on Ottoman soil.

For the next generation and a half (1606–58) Transylvanian independence is a reality, even though Bocskay dies prematurely and is succeeded by a particularly loathsome tyrant, Gabriel, the last of the Báthory family. Habsburg aggression is virtually impossible during this period, first owing to the disputes between Rudolf and Matthias and the religious troubles in Austria and Bohemia, and then, after Matthias's death, owing to the complications of the Thirty Years' War.

Gabriel's tyranny found special vent against the Saxons: he burnt and plundered part of Hermannstadt and tried to do the same with Kronstadt: and it was on this occasion that the Saxons appealed simultaneously to the emperor and sultan. At last one of the other great nobles, Gabriel Bethlen,[2] found his life threatened and fled to the Turks, who invested him as prince and sent troops to help him to overthrow Báthory. The tyrant was duly defeated and murdered, and the Estates of the Three Nations, meeting at Klausenburg, elected Bethlen as their prince. But they imposed certain preliminary conditions (recognition and restoration of existing privileges): and this practice continued for the remainder of the period of independence. Bethlen reigned from 1613 to 1629, and under him Transylvania celebrated its Golden Age. At home he restored peace and ordered government, based above all on the old charters and upon equal rights for the four

[1] Together with the district of Kövár.
[2] Better known as Bethlen Gábor, by those who do not realise the Hungarian practice of placing the Christian name *after* the surname.

Religions and the maintenance of their churches and schools. Abroad, of necessity, he adopted a cautious policy of balance, relying on the Turkish alliance for the defence of independence and constitutional rights, but showing quite clearly that he would prefer an alliance of the Christian Powers against the infidel and continually feeling his way towards such a result. But he had given the Porte a pledge of "devotion with heart and soul"[1] and he took care never to lose Turkish favour, never to withdraw the one foot until he had found foothold for the other.

The rock upon which all such projects were wrecked was the religious issue between Catholicism and Protestantism, and the attitude of the house of Habsburg towards it. The emperor Matthias was a man of half measures, and on the one hand not sufficiently fanatical himself and on the other too much hampered by the action of the Estates in his hereditary dominions and in Bohemia to be capable of aggression against Transylvania. But even in his reign the appointment of the redoubtable Jesuit Peter Pázmány as primate of Hungary (1616) seriously modified the situation. The tide of Counter-Reformation, already strong in Austria, began to flow strongly through Habsburg Hungary also: Pázmány's tireless energy, his social adroitness and above all his minute and brilliantly conceived educational policy, reclaimed a large section of the Hungarian nobility for Catholicism and divided the rest of the nation. His view was that Hungary "cannot remain entire between those two powerful Empires: either we must be swallowed up by the pagans, or else we must seek protection beneath the wings of the neighbouring Christian Power".[2] Thus his very patriotism allied itself with his religious convictions to accept Habsburg rule and often to submit to unconstitutional action on the part of the dynasty as a lesser evil.

With the accession of Ferdinand II in 1619 the religious conflict grew specially acute. His cause became openly identified with three aims—the forcible reimposition of Catholicism, the establishment of absolute power at the expense of the Constitution, and the centralisation and Germanisation of the administration. The Jesuit Stankovics prayed for "the glorious day when the whole of Hungary will speak but one language and will be united in the ancient faith":[3] and this sums up the

[1]  Cit. Teutsch, *Gesch. der sieb. Sachsen*, I, p. 379.
[2]  Cit. Andrássy, *Development of Hungarian Constitutional Liberty*, p. 461.
[3]  Cit. Knatchbull-Hugessen, *Political Evolution of the Hungarian Nation*, I, p. 150.

PLATE IX

GABRIEL BETHLEN

attitude of those who regarded the Turks and Protestants as equal dangers and gave the extermination of the latter precedence over war with the former. The attitude of their opponents is to be seen in a popular cry of the period—"Rather Allah than 'Wer da?'"

Bethlen became at one and the same time the champion of Hungary's constitutional liberties and of Hungarian Protestantism. In the opening Thirty Years' War he actively espoused the cause of Bohemia and did all he could by diplomatic means to unite the Calvinists and Lutherans of Germany for mutual defence. When Bohemia was in open revolt and chose the Elector Frederick as its king, Bethlen marched against the Habsburgs, overran the whole of Slovakia and was elected king of Hungary at a Diet held at Neusohl (Zvolen). But he, like Bocskay before him, wisely refrained from the irrevocable step of coronation, and when Bohemian independence collapsed at the battle of the White Mountain, he soon realised that he was too weak to stem the tide alone, and gradually entered into negotiations with the emperor which led in 1622 to the Treaty of Nikolsburg. By it he renounced the royal title, but remained prince of Transylvania and was created a prince of the empire, with Oppeln and Ratibor as hereditary duchies. Seven counties of North-east Hungary were left in his possession, though under the legal jurisdiction of the Palatine (the supreme mouthpiece of the crown in Habsburg Hungary), and sending delegates to the Hungarian Parliament. Ferdinand granted a full amnesty to the Estates and to the population generally in his part of Hungary, and confirmed all the constitutional rights of Hungary and the religious concessions of the Treaty of Vienna.

This treaty did not end the conflict or assure permanent peace, but it marked the establishment of a certain balance of forces. In effect it prolonged the partition of Hungary, but it also saved her from the national extinction to which the Habsburgs reduced Bohemia during the seventeenth century. By its close the high-water mark of religious intolerance and of princely absolutism had been passed, and in the eighteenth century both assumed milder forms, which no longer offered the same acute danger to Magyar nationality.

For the rest of his reign Gabriel Bethlen was a figure of international importance. He married Catherine of Brandenburg and so entered the intimate circles of North German Protestantism. He concluded an alliance in 1626 with Denmark, when Christian IV entered the Thirty Years' War as Protestant champion, and even with Holland and England; then, after the Danish failure, he again allied himself with Gustavus Adolphus his brother-in-law, and was preparing for a parallel campaign with him, when in 1629 he died. Meanwhile at home he improved administrative and judicial conditions, showed himself to be ahead of his age in matters of religious toleration, and did much for education—notably by the foundation of the Bethlen College and the encouragement of students at Heidelberg and other Protestant universities.

It is clear that his main interests lay towards the West and centred round the restoration of Hungary's broken unity, on firmly Protestant foundations: he certainly had a wider vision of Europe than any other prince who sat on the Transylvanian throne, and his attitude towards the Turks rested on very different conceptions from the self-seeking and hand-to-mouth expedients of the Roumanian Domns. It is curious, however, to watch the old expansive tendencies of Hungarian foreign policy breaking out in new forms. The times were not favourable to the reassertion of vanished claims to Serbia, Bosnia or Dalmatia: only a Power whose centre of gravity lay much further west could hope to oust the Turks from the western half of the peninsula, and the day was not yet. But south and east of the Carpathians there was an intermediate situation in which it was possible to dream of a reconstituted "Kingdom of Dacia".

Bethlen's widow Catherine soon proved herself incompetent to rule, and the first of the Rákóczy princes was elected to the throne. Under his moderate and distinctly more pacific rule (1630–40), Transylvania really enjoyed more relative prosperity than any of its contemporaries. Its curiously anomalous position continued—seemingly independent and free from Turkish interference save for the quite trifling tribute of 10,000 ducats, but in effect one in sentiment with Habsburg Hungary and in closest contact with it, all the more so because its own comparative immunity from religious strife increased its prestige and influence with all those who suffered from the continual illegalities of the Habsburgs both in the political and in the ecclesiastical field. But nothing throws greater light upon this situation than the attitude of Cardinal Pázmány himself, who, with all his zeal for the restoration of Catholicism, actually preferred that a Magyar prince, Protestant though he were, should continue to reign in Transylvania, as the best check upon German domination at the Habsburg court.[1] This may serve as a fresh reminder that in

[1] Cf. his opinions as expressed to Kemény: cit. Fessler, *Geschichte Ungarns*, IV, p. 220.

all this period Transylvania politically meant the three nations only, and that the Roumanian masses were in utter helotry.

George Rákóczy in 1633 concluded a treaty of mutual defence with Matthew Basarab, who sent him 6000 gulden a year as a kind of tax upon the annual visits of nomad Roumanian shepherds to the high Carpathians. A year later the treaty was extended triangularly to include Basil the Wolf also: but by 1637 this fortunate harmony was disturbed, and Rákóczy and Basil plotted together to drive Matthew from the Wallachian throne. In other words, the temporary revival of the two Principalities was marred by mutual discords and intrigues at the very moment when a united front might have enabled them to achieve greater internal stability: while the prince of Transylvania, instead of making common cause against the Turks, promoted these discords between his two neighbours, and himself entertained territorial ambitions altogether beyond his slender resources.

In the second half of his reign George Rákóczy was forced into fresh hostilities with Vienna on behalf of the oppressed Protestants of Northern Hungary, and allied himself for this purpose with France and Sweden (1643). But the Catholic party was by this time strong enough to hold him in check, and the Treaty of Linz in 1644, though it reaffirmed on paper all existing rights and the freedom of religion, could no longer stem back the Counter-Reformation. A sufficiently clear sign of the times is the single fact that when the dispossessed Protestants were to be reinstated in their churches, they only succeeded in actually recovering 90 out of 400.[1]

George Rákóczy II inherited his father's foreign alliances and ambitions, but lacked his caution. He had designs upon the Polish throne, and as the ally of the king of Sweden invaded Poland, occupying first Cracow and then Warsaw. But in this he over-calculated his strength in the most preposterous manner. The Swedes left him in the lurch, the Poles were not on his side, the Emperor Leopold naturally disapproved and helped his enemies. His armies were dispersed and a large war indemnity imposed, and as a final disaster he found himself exposed to the vindictive anger of the Turks, whose express prohibition he had defied in embarking upon the expedition. In 1657, at the threat of the Turkish envoys, Rákóczy was deposed by the Diet, who recognised openly that their "existence depended upon Turkish favour".[2] And

[1] Marczali, *Ungarische Verfassungsgeschichte*, p. 85.
[2] Teutsch, *op. cit.* 1, 388.

yet they soon had the folly to reinstate him, with the result that the grand vizier, Mohammed Küprüli, with an enormous Turkish and Tatar army, invaded and ravaged the south of Transylvania. The tribute was raised from 15,000 to 50,000 ducats, two successive princes were appointed by the Turks, and for a time it was intended to convert Transylvania into a mere pashalik. Leopold was appealed to for help, and the Turks and imperialists fought over the exhausted country.

The great victory of Montecuccoli at St Gotthard in 1664 marks the first real turn of the tide, though the peace which followed it did not secure to the Emperor Leopold the advantages which skilful negotiations might have earned. But Transylvania never recovered from the destruction and misery wrought in these years. The princely power decayed, and for the remainder of the period of independence was held by men of mediocre attainments. Of the Three Nations, the Székels had already tended to fall into the background for a century past, the Saxons could at best doggedly hold their ground: the real control was in the hands of the Magyar nobles, and they now split more and more into rival factions. Thus Transylvania, weak and distracted, lost its prestige and power of attraction for Northern Hungary, and was no longer able to champion the Protestant cause beyond its own border. Meanwhile the court at Vienna was encouraged, by this very fact and by its growing resources and military power since the Peace of Westphalia, to develop quite definite designs for the suppression of the Hungarian constitution, and simultaneously, of course, of Protestantism.

This period of Hungarian history, lasting roughly from 1660 to 1681, need not concern us here. But in the latter year, when Leopold at last made up his mind to summon the Hungarian Parliament, a rival meeting of the Estates was convoked at Kaschau, under Emerich Tököli, the leader of all the Magyar malcontents and the Protestant party, whom Leopold's intolerance had driven into closer and closer contact with the Turks. When, then, the latter made their supreme effort against Vienna in 1683, Tököli—like Zápolya and Bocskay before him—was closely leagued with the invader, though instead of obeying the grand vizier's summons to the army, he devoted himself to strengthening his hold over the northern provinces. But the tables were suddenly turned, and the failure of the Turkish siege was followed by the great imperialist advance which placed Leopold in possession not only of Tököli's own strongholds in the north-east (Kaschau, Késmark, etc.), but above all of Buda itself and the whole central plain. The whole situation was thus completely transformed, and a fresh Parliament, in recognition of these victories, proclaimed the Hungarian crown to be no longer elective, but hereditary in the house of Habsburg. Tököli's impassioned appeal in favour of the Turks and against the emperor fell absolutely flat; he himself had to take refuge with his allies, and his wife, after an heroic defence, was forced to surrender the fortress of Munkács.

In 1688 the way into Transylvania lay open for the imperialist armies. Negotiations followed, in which the ferocious General Caraffa intimidated the delegates of the Principality into signing a document expressing its unconditional return to the crown of Hungary, renouncing the Turkish allegiance, pledging all military support, and merely begging humbly for the emperor's confirmation of existing privileges and religious liberties. The prince and Diet were rushed into ratifying this act of submission, and merely sent in, as a kind of unbinding supplementary memorandum, the various points which they should have put forward as preliminary conditions to recognition. Leopold characteristically took note of the act of homage, but ignored the memorandum, though he had the wisdom to confirm publicly the liberties of the four Received Religions. In 1690 Michael Apafi died, and while Leopold refused the Diet's request that he should confirm the younger Apafi as prince, the sultan promptly nominated Tököli to the throne and made a determined effort to overrun Transylvania, with the aid of Tököli himself and of the prince of Wallachia, Constantine Brâncoveanu. But the tide was turning definitely against the Turks, and by December 1691 reunion was a final and accomplished fact.

The so-called "Leopoldine Diploma", issued in that month, is a detailed confirmation by the sovereign of all existing laws, rights and privileges, civil and religious, and at the same time a pledge to employ only native Transylvanians in offices of state. But though nominally united with Hungary, Transylvania still retained its separate identity under the Diet, composed as hitherto of the representatives of the Three Nations, and under two executive organs, namely (i) the Gubernium or Governor's office, first in Alba Iulia (Gyulafehérvár), but soon transferred to Klausenburg (Kolozsvár), and (ii) after 1694, a specially constituted Transylvanian Aulic Chancellory (Hofkanzlei) in Vienna, quite distinct from the Hungarian Chancellory. This new status was completed in 1696, when young Apafi renounced all claim to the princely throne, in return for a pension and a title, and in 1699, when Turkey renounced its suzerainty over Transylvania, as one of the main provisions of the Treaty of Karlowitz. Thus from 1691 right on till 1867 (with a brief interlude in 1848) Transylvania enjoyed complete autonomy under Vienna, forming *de jure* an integral part of the Hungarian crown, but *de facto* being linked by a mere personal union and really controlled by the emperor. In 1765 Maria Theresa stressed its separate character still further by assuming the title of "Great Prince". The seals and coins in use in Transylvania bore the imperial double eagle.

During the seventeenth century the status of the Roumanian peasantry in Transylvania sank still further: and it was a settled policy of the Protestant princes to prevent so far as possible all contact with their kinsmen across the Carpathians, and in particular any extension of the ecclesiastical jurisdiction of Tîrgovişte or the Moldavian sees. This explains such occasional concessions as Gabriel Bethlen's grant to the Roumanian clergy of Făgăraş, of immunity from tithe due to the prince and the feudal lord, which was rigidly retained everywhere else. In 1638, again, George Rákóczy I made a number of minor concessions to the Roumanian clergy, and again in 1659 Barcsay freed them throughout Transylvania from the tithe, as a reward for the services of their metropolitan, Sava Branković, on a mission to the Hetman of the Cossacks. In 1675 Apafi issued a special letter of protection in favour of the Orthodox clergy, but this did not meet with the favour of his nobles, still less of the Catholic clergy, and these various exemptions were only very imperfectly observed by the Three Nations.

Proselytism was the constant and avowed aim, and we need not stop to examine how far religious and national motives were blended and confused. That both were present is perhaps best illustrated by the simple fact that almost to the last man Saxons and Magyars respectively gravitated towards Lutheranism and Calvinism, whereas the Roumanians clung desperately to Orthodoxy. We shall see that the hybrid Uniate experiment of the closing century owed such success as it achieved to the national factor.

In 1643, then, the Metropolitan Elias Joresti—who had come five years earlier with a recommendation of Prince Matthew—was deposed at Rákóczy's instance, ostensibly for misconduct, but really because of his bold resistance to Calvinism. The inferior standing of the Roumanians is sufficiently revealed by the fact that the deposed prelate was actually whipped like some highway robber! The tendency towards crypto-Calvinism among a section of the Orthodox clergy was now encouraged still further, and the successor of Elias, Stephen Simonovici, was placed under the jurisdiction of the Calvinist Superintendent Gelei. Being a mere creature of his, he accepted an "Instruction" of fifteen points absolutely irreconcilable with Orthodoxy: they contained, for instance, undertakings to celebrate Communion *only* under both kinds, and only to adults, not to oppose or condemn those Roumanians who might adopt the Calvinist faith, and to refer disputes between bishop and clergy in the last instance to the Calvinist superintendent! There was, however, one other point which was to have memorable and unexpected results—namely the introduction of the Roumanian language in religious services and instruction. There is no little irony in noting that Rákóczy's aim was to loosen the Roumanian connection with Greek and Slav traditions and thus to undermine Orthodoxy in the Protestant interest, and that the innovation was keenly opposed by the Metropolitan Barlaam of Wallachia. The result was a certain competition in the publication of Roumanian books on the two sides of the Carpathians, George Rákóczy establishing a printing press at Alba Iulia, and issuing vernacular editions of the Psalms and New Testament and even translating the Calvinist Catechism into Roumanian. To this latter Barlaam issued a polemical answer from the press of Tîrgovişte. The ultimate effect of this conflict was to strengthen and stereotype the cause of Roumanian nationality, but at the time this was clearly foreseen by neither side.

The position of Sava Branković, who was metropolitan in Transylvania from 1656 to 1680, was for a time somewhat exceptional, and his valuable relations with Kiev and Moscow enabled him to retain the favour of the prince and to obtain occasional concessions for his downtrodden flock. But the Calvinist clergy worked ceaselessly to undermine his position, to assert their authority over him, to stop his salary, even to prevent ordinations by him: and at last in 1680 he was condemned on a trumped-up charge of immorality, deprived, stripped of all his property, and despite illness and advanced age thrown into prison. Pressure from Şerban Cantacuzene upon Michael Apafi secured his release, but he died the same year. His successor was consecrated in Bucarest and recognised the ecclesiastical jurisdiction of Wallachia, but he was none the less a complete nonentity, unable to hold his own against Calvinist pressure.

Such was the highly precarious situation at the close of the seventeenth century, when Transylvania passed under direct Habsburg rule. Calvinism speedily found itself driven on to the defensive: Catholicism—

now once more in the ascendant in the Slovak districts of Northern Hungary—set itself to recover its lost ground in the land beyond the Forest. What more natural than that the Jesuits, strong in the confidence of Leopold I and court circles in Vienna, should have turned their eyes to the Roumanians as a useful instrument of centralist and Catholicising tendencies? They, like everyone else at that period, regarded the masses as mere cannon-fodder in the spiritual war. They therefore bent their efforts upon the hierarchy and clergy, to whom they had many inducements to offer. Submission to the Holy See involved the acceptance of four essential points—the papal supremacy, unleavened bread, Purgatory and the Filioque clause in the Creed.[1] Otherwise the existing liturgy and canon law remained untouched, as also the marriage of the clergy, the wearing of beards, the internal arrangement of churches (with iconostasis, etc.) and similar points of external detail. What was really decisive, however, was that the archpriests had lost their freedom of election to the metropolitan see under Calvinist control, and welcomed the union as a means of shaking off the galling Calvinist jurisdiction; that the union secured to the clergy who accepted it equality of rights with the Roman clergy and therefore a very vital rise in social status, and exemption for them and their families from serfdom and feudal dues; and that it provided for proper endowment of the Uniate Church and its hierarchy. In the phrase of a witty Jesuit of that day, the Roumanian clergy was "not led by supernatural principles, but by temporary necessities".[2]

In February 1697 the union was proposed to the Orthodox synod by the Metropolitan Theophilus and unanimously accepted in principle, subject to a demand for proper endowments and equality for *laymen* of the new Church. The death of Theophilus during the summer caused delay and opened the door for disputes among the clergy, but his successor Athanasius lost no time in resuming negotiations, and the document of union was formally signed in October 1698. The final stage was reached at the synod of Alba Iulia, on 4 September 1700, when no less than 54 archpriests and 1563 priests followed their metropolitan's lead.

The union[3] was legalised by an imperial diploma of Leopold I, issued on 16 February 1699, announcing that the Uniates were to enjoy the same Christian freedom "as the members of the Latin rite", and en-

---

[1] I.e. the procession of the Holy Spirit "from the Father *and* the Son".
[2] S. Dragomir, *Ist. Desrobirei religioase a Românilor din Ardeal*, I, p. 5.
[3] Full accounts will be found in the works of Hintz and Schaguna, already quoted.

joining respect for the new privileges upon all officials and prelates of the principality. A further edict of 6 August was addressed to the Roumanians, assuring them that they were free to join any recognised religion or to retain their existing status. That the Magyar outlook was by no means identical with the imperial is shown by the grudging attitude of the Diet in its discussions on the change of status due to the union, and still more by the rescript issued on 26 September 1699 by the Gubernium. This laid down that two clergy should suffice for the largest Roumanian communes, and one for the smaller (an attempt to restrict to a minimum the number of persons exempted from serfdom); that the bishop should not be free to consecrate unworthy priests, but only such as passed an examination; that clergy without cures must live in cloisters until they obtained them; that "as the Wallachs have no good schools", their candidates for the priesthood are to be instructed "in the school of that religion with which he wishes to unite" and otherwise not to be ordained (a last attempt to leave the door open to Calvinist, as opposed to Roman, proselytism). [1] Nothing shows better the humiliating and subordinate position of the Roumanians, and yet another imperial decree of 12 December 1699, assuring the Roumanians that they were free to remain as hitherto or to unite with any one of the four Religions, [2] suggests that there was still some competition for the allegiance of the shepherdless Orthodox flock, and that Leopold's advisers did not all share his romanising zeal. His pious hope "that everyone should live peaceably in his religion" was merely a phrase intended to cover ulterior designs: and the angry remark that those who spoke of an attempt to force the Catholic faith upon the Wallachs were "disturbers of the public peace", shows clearly enough what was being said on all sides. Indeed, the alleged free choice was a hollow farce, for the material advantages of the union were irresistible, human nature being what it is, whereas the alternative of surrendering to the Calvinist Magyars was not really an alternative at all. Humiliating as the methods employed to achieve it may have been, the union proved to be one of the most memorable events in the rise of Roumanian nationality, of which we shall have to trace the effects in a later chapter.

[1] Schaguna, *op. cit.* pp. 86–90.
[2] Eam esse voluntatem nostram positivam ut Valachis liberum sit alterutram quatuor receptarum in Transilvania religionum amplecti eiusdemque privilegiis et immunitatibus gaudere: si vero animus sit iis suis in ritibus permanere quos hodiedum observant, id quoque liberum esto.

# CHAPTER V

# THE PHANARIOT REGIME (1714–1821)

*"Les Phanariotes étaient en quelque sorte un second État dans l'Empire Ottoman."*
M. P. ZALLONY.

The year 1714 may be said to mark yet another change for the worse in the political and social status of the two Principalities. The gradual Greek permeation of the preceding sixty years was now to be followed by a century of Greek domination, in its peculiar Phanariot garb. Till then there had been native princes on both thrones, drawn at first from the native dynasties, then from the higher boiars, and at least representative of the narrow ruling class. It is true that their tenure had already been most uncertain and that confirmation in office involved appalling sacrifices, and a constant drain upon the whole resources of the population. In the nature of things these princes had never been conspicuous for their loyalty to the Porte, and the Turks on their side, who regarded them with arrogant contempt, were doubtless satisfied so long as tribute and supplies were forthcoming and internal dissensions prevented the growth of any serious armed force. But by the opening decade of the eighteenth century Turkey was in obvious decline and defending herself desperately against the fast reviving powers of Austria and Russia: her statesmen were conscious of the danger and felt the urgent necessity of strengthening their strategic control of these outlying provinces, and especially the fortresses of the Danube and Dniester. The intrigues of such princes as Brâncoveanu and Cantemir with Vienna and Moscow had to be stopped at all costs, and complete subservience reimposed upon provinces which were acquiring such extreme importance as granaries of the Turkish capital.

After dispossessing the two princes, the Porte at first thought of reducing Wallachia and Moldavia to mere pashaliks: but on consideration it was felt that they would be safer in the hands of Phanariot Greeks, who had no ties with foreign Powers, whom interest and tradition rendered entirely dependent upon their Turkish masters, and who, being adepts at financial manipulation, might be expected to raise a maximum of revenue. By a curious paradox of history the Principalities were far more effectively controlled from Constantinople in

the eighteenth century, when Turkey was already in full decline and
her overthrow constantly prophesied, than in the sixteenth, when she
held all Europe in terror.

The Phanariofs continued as princes the diplomatic intrigue in which
they had already become past masters at Stambul. Their long habit
of abject servility seemed to render them suitable tools for the Porte's
new system of government, but it was short-sighted in the extreme, for
the new princes were almost always rapacious, often treacherous, and
thought only of their own material interests. They may be compared
to a farmer holding insecurely by a short lease, who tries to extract as
much as possible from the land, regardless of the laws of cropping and
rotation, and so very quickly exhausts and ruins it.

It is impossible to conceive a more disheartening task than that of
recording in detail the history of these hundred years in Wallachia and
Moldavia, and the western reader would only read it with impatience
and under protest. There are no really outstanding figures even among
the hospodars, the boiar class is degraded and subservient, there is
virtually no middle class at all, the masses are sunk in ignorance and
stupor. The chief landmarks are the periodical foreign invasions and
occupations: for the changes on the throne are far too numerous to
serve as landmarks. The incredible nature of the regime is perhaps
most eloquently expressed in a few bald statistics. Between 1714 and
1821 there were forty-one changes on the throne in Wallachia, between
1711 and 1821 thirty-six in Moldavia: in the one case there were twenty-
three, in the other twenty-four, princes, several being appointed more
than once, and as several passed from one throne to the other at different
times, the total number of reigning princes was not seventy-seven, but
thirty-three, and all of these were drawn from twelve families (eight of
them entirely Greek, two others, the Cantacuzenes and Mavrocordatos,
partially Roumanian on the distaff side, while the Racoviţas and Callimachis—really Calimaşi—were hellenised Roumanians). One alone,
Constantine Mavrocordato, reigned longer than twenty years, but this
total is only reached by adding together no less than six brief reigns in
Wallachia and three in Moldavia (though from 1731 to 1749 he reigned
consecutively in one or the other). These men were continually intriguing against each other, in particular the Moldavian princes in order
to obtain the richer prize of Wallachia, and they often paid for their
ambition with their heads, yet fear of punishment did not deter their
successors and intrigue was rife to the very end. We thus reach the

surprising result that the average duration of a reign in either Principality during a whole century was about two years and a half!

In a word, most of these princes deserve to be consigned to a merciful oblivion, and it would be subjecting the reader's patience to too severe a test to attempt any detailed chronological survey. But while the policy of individuals is of little more than local interest, it is by no means unprofitable to present a general picture of political conditions and of their deplorable social and economic consequences: for the plight of the two Roumanian Principalities under the Phanariot regime is not merely an important factor in what was now coming to be called "the Eastern Question", but also a really classic example of the effects of bad government under an alien conqueror, once mighty but now in full decline. From this point of view there is no instance even in the long and varied history of Turkish misrule that is more instructive than this.

Seldom has there been anything quite analogous to the position of these princes, living from day to day on the brink of disaster and consumed by fear of the morrow. Towards their subjects they were absolute despots, with little or no restraint upon them, while towards the sultan and his chief ministers they were abject slaves, with no redress against the whim of the master.[1]

On appointment they were invested by the sultan himself, with the same pomp as any pasha or vizier, and received with music and military honours: they then proceeded in solemn procession to the Church of the Patriarchate. On their journey to Bucarest or Jassy, which was by slow stages and took three or four weeks, they were as a rule accompanied by a bodyguard of two hundred Orthodox Albanians and a suite of several hundred others. On arrival they made a state entry, were blessed by the metropolitan at the cathedral, assumed the title of "God's Anointed" and convoked a meeting of the assembly, where the firman of appointment was read and followed by a speech of pious

---

[1] Compare the phrase of Count Hauterive in 1785 (*Voyage en Moldavie*, p. 368) —according to which the subjects of the hospodar "sont des esclaves d'un homme qui tremble devant les esclaves de la Porte". An acute English observer, Dr Macmichael (*Journey from Moscow to Constantinople*, p. 107), made a similar comment as late as 1817—"the extraordinary phenomenon of a pure despotism exercised by a Greek prince who is himself at the same time *an abject slave*....What adds to the curiosity of so unusual a sight is that this violent form of government is upheld without the aid of any military force: nowhere is there the least appearance of an army, the Hospodar has no troops, except about 20 Serb and Albanian guards...."

platitudes from the new prince.[1] But this assembly was the merest formality, for all appointments were entirely in the prince's hands. It is true that certain posts were reserved for native boiars, but all the key positions, such as home and foreign affairs, such few military posts as still survived, and that of Grand Intendant, were invariably given to Phanariots enjoying the newcomer's confidence or belonging to his own suite. Often enough the prince would secure to them the rank and privileges of boiars by arranging their marriage with the daughter of some native boiar. There was thus a steady infiltration of upstart Greeks in the ranks of the Roumanian nobility, and needless to say, many princes made a considerable revenue by selling such preferment to ambitious newcomers.

It is not sufficiently recognised that in the words of Professor Iorga, "the Phanariots formed a close caste, from which came dragomans, Grand Dragomans, diplomatic agents, spies, Bishops, Metropolitans, Patriarchs, high dignitaries of the 'Great Church' of Constantinople, Logothetes, Skeuophylaks and finally Princes of Wallachia and Moldavia....Intruders they did not tolerate, and if later on an Alexander Ypsilanti or a Kostaki Moruzi attained to the highest posts attainable by Christians, they had first of all had to ally themselves with wives of the blood of the Mavrocordatos".[2]

At court there was the greatest luxury. The prince and his family rarely received even boiars at their own table, and at the divan or council or at audiences the most humiliating ceremonies were observed. It was the function of high officials to support the prince under the shoulders, as he moved from room to room[3]: and he affected the motionless pose of Turkish dignitaries. Only a few of the highest boiars were allowed to seat themselves in his presence, most of them might not even kiss his hands, but were happy to kiss his foot or the hem of his garment. One of the first Austrian residents in the Principalities, writing in the eighties of the eighteenth century, tells us that he had often seen a boiar making the sign of the cross before he was received in audience. For there was virtually no check upon the prince's merest whim, and even a boiar had little remedy against disgrace or the seizure of his fortune.

[1] See Dem. Cantemir, *Beschreibung der Moldau*, pp. 138–64; W. Wilkinson, *Account of the Principalities*, p. 46; Zallony, *Essai sur les Fanariotes*, p. 42.

[2] *Gesch. des osman. Reiches*, IV, p. 368.

[3] This is described as late as 1817 by Dr Macmichael, in his *Journey from Moscow to Constantinople*, p. 93.

Rajčević relates that Constantine Rakoviţa (1753–6) on one occasion ordered the arrest of a German doctor who had offended him, and had him stripped and flogged before him night after night until he died.

While, then, the prince was so servile towards the representative of the sultan, that he would dismount and approach a pasha on foot and publicly kiss the hem of his robe, the same man was more arrogant towards his courtiers than the greatest sovereign of the West, and would force the boiars to carry him in their arms from one room to another inside the palace, and when gracious would allow them to kiss his hands or knees. This subservience had its obvious explanation, for every Turk who came to him might be a spy, and every pasha at Giurgiu or Brǎila or Bender, might one day be grand vizier and able to take signal vengeance for a slight. "What is remarkable about these despots", wrote Carra, "is that all their riches, money, jewels, hordes and furnishings, are always in trunks and travelling coffers, as if they had to leave at any moment."[1]

The boiars in their turn took toll for such humiliations from their inferiors. The external luxury which they displayed was very great—rich clothes, jewels, horses, carriages, furs. Their wives too wore the costliest furs and dresses, but were held in little esteem and occupied an inferior status. Count Vincent Batthyány, travelling to Constantinople in 1805, records that at dinner the men never even spoke to their womenfolk. The boiars lent themselves slavishly to the desires of the prince, and indeed without their support he would really have been helpless. They had in common with him a complete cynicism of aim, directed towards rapid enrichment: and this could only be attained at the expense of the peasants, who had no real means of redress and were mercilessly squeezed on all sides.

Rapid exploitation, then, was the beginning and end of all policy with princes who had no security of tenure and never knew when they might be superseded. Each prince arrived burdened with debt, owing to the sums which he had disbursed as highest bidder for the throne: and he had in the first instance to make good his losses as quickly as possible, and if fortunate enough to remain a little longer than usual in office, to amass fresh reserves out of which he might make a fresh bid for one or other throne. "The prince changes, and madmen rejoice", ran a contemporary proverb.

[1] Carra, *Hist. de la Moldavie et de la Valachie* (1781), p. 184.

Zallony,[1] himself a Greek, gives a graphic picture of the methods to which most princes resorted. Whenever a special levy was ordered from Constantinople, the prince would promptly double it or even raise it four or fivefold, and then of course pocket the balance or share it with the boiars. If the Porte ordered the construction or repair of a border fortress and fixed the number of workmen to be employed at, say 10,000, with so many carts and such and such wages, the prince would come to terms with some Greek contractor, and employ only 1500 men, but of course burden the revenue for the total number. He would prohibit the import of certain articles—for instance, the Transylvanian plums from which the famous plum brandy was made—and then he himself would organise the smuggling of that very article. He would juggle with the exchange of foreign currencies, reducing their value at the time when he was collecting revenue, but raising it again when he had to make his payments to Constantinople. There were even cases when he would depose a metropolitan and appropriate his large revenues during a prolonged vacancy. And of course if he felt his fall to be imminent—and "flair" in this respect was perhaps the most essential of all qualities for success—he would sell offices shamelessly, in order to augment his resources.

He always kept a resident envoy at Constantinople, known under the Turkish title of Bash-Kapukihaya, generally, though not always, a kinsman of his own: and this man was virtually master of the prince's fate, since so much depended upon his skill in negotiation, in humouring the Porte and distributing suitable *douceurs* among the grandees of Stambul, in watching and countering the intrigues of dispossessed princes, of whom there were generally two or three, or of ambitious aspirants. Sometimes, despite all the care exercised in filling the post, the Kapukihaya came to covet the throne for himself, and then the prince's downfall was likely to be catastrophic. For in that case there would be no previous warning, whereas as a rule not all the secrecy preserved at the Porte with regard to impending changes could prevent an agent whose very existence depended on minute intrigue and infinite powers of corruption, from gaining an inkling of the decision and sending a courier hot-haste across the Danube, so that the prince usually had time to cook his accounts and deplete the treasury before his successor could arrive. Occasionally the Kapukihaya was decidedly more powerful than the prince: for instance Stavraki, who in the middle of

[1] *Essai sur les Fanariotes*, Marseilles, 1824.

the century represented Moldavia at the Porte, but was able to impose his creatures upon both thrones and fleece all classes with a ruthless impartiality. It is true that he was finally strangled by order of the sultan in 1765, as a result of the disaster and unrest which his misdeeds provoked. Four years later another envoy, Nicholas Suţu, who for a time was dragoman and all-powerful in Roumanian affairs, was similarly executed. In a word, it may be said that the Porte, itself as venal as it was rapacious, relied upon constant change, and consequent fresh payments, and was only restrained by the restricted number of possible candidates.

A few rare princes such as Constantine Mavrocordato and Alexander Ypsilanti, attempted to reform and simplify taxation by suppressing indirect charges. But their reforms were for the most part annulled by their successors; and in any case the chief effect of simplification was to render still heavier the almost intolerable burden upon the peasantry. Even these two princes, relatively so enlightened, became cynical in later life and renounced all idea of making their own reforms effective. So rigorous were the exactions that a peasant would sometimes kill his cattle to escape the "văcărit" or cow-tax, or even destroy his house to avoid the "fumărit" or chimney-tax.

During the second half of the eighteenth century especially the whole system had steadily developed into a wondrously elaborate design for killing the goose that laid the golden eggs. It was undermining all incentive to work or improvement in a country more than usually endowed by nature. The Austrian consul Rajčević—an Italianised native of Ragusa, an acute if caustic observer—in the Italian treatise which he published in 1788, remarks, "All posts, from the highest to the lowest, not only bring in a good income, but carry with them the right to plunder the people".[1] But every traveller of the period had the same tale to tell of "organised brigandage" on the part of the prince and the horde of Greek officials who either executed his will or defied him on direct orders from the Porte and plundered on their own account. Rajčević again describes how every spring Greek merchants came with a firman of the Porte and drove off 5–600,000 sheep from the Principalities, bought at a price which they themselves had fixed. "No one dares resist", he writes, "for such a middleman is capable of going back and shouting upon the market of Constantinople, that the princes are

[1] *Bemerkungen über die Moldau und Wallachey* (from the Italian), Vienna, 1788, p. 78.

rebels, plotting with the Russians and the Germans and will not let them buy sheep to save the people of the Prophet from starvation".[1]

Trade remained entirely in the hands of foreigners—mainly Greeks, but also Macedonians, a few Transylvanian Roumanians, Armenians and Galician Jews, whose numbers now begin to grow. This "Peru of the Greeks", as it has aptly been called, was incredibly backward and neglected: education was almost non-existent, there was no real middle class, and indeed very few towns. In 1764 Lord Baltimore, returning from Constantinople to the West, "could not enter Jassy till daybreak, because of the deep mud which surrounds it" and found the streets laid with "deal boards, laid crossways," and the houses "on one storey, low and miserable and little better than in the scattered villages built of earth". Yet Wilkinson, one of the first British Consuls in Bucarest forty years later, considered the Moldavian capital to be far better built, though considerably smaller. By that time Bucarest and Jassy, according to his estimate, had 80,000 and 40,000 inhabitants, with 366 and 70 churches respectively—a proof of the munificent piety of generations of wealthy boiars.

By the turn of the century the economic conditions of the two Principalities were an even greater condemnation of the Ottoman regime and threw even harsher light upon its rapacity and incompetence than the grimmer incidents of massacre and oppression in Greece and Serbia. For by their systematic plunder of splendid natural resources and of a docile and industrious population, they defeated their own ends and dried up the fountain at its source. Yet the forced cession of the Crimea by Turkey to Russia in 1783 very greatly enhanced the importance of the Roumanian lands, which were more than ever the granary from whence Constantinople itself drew enormous quantities of corn, livestock, horses, butter, cheese, honey, wax and even wood for the arsenal. On most of these the Porte maintained a kind of special lien, making its purchases by forced bargain and not leaving the natives free to sell in the open market. Besides, export was altogether prohibited, and thereby of course the enrichment of the country artificially checked. It is true that despite this, about 20,000 horses were sent every year surreptitiously, or by bribing the customs officials, into Poland and Hungary, while a considerable number of cattle in the high pasturage of the Carpathians were also smuggled across the border.

The Principalities, wrote the Russian General Langeron, "are

[1] *Op. cit.* p. 51.

favoured by nature, but persecuted by fate". In other words, the mass of the Roumanian population, in spite of the natural fertility and riches of the soil, was plunged in utter misery, and its situation actually deteriorated from decade to decade, till at the turn of the century it was unquestionably worse even than that of the completely subjected Bulgarian or Serbian population. Indeed, districts which a century later were to produce some of the finest wheat in Europe were only used for stock breeding, and emigration across the Carpathians into Transylvania was constantly on the increase.

Throughout these hundred years the fiscal burden of Turkish rule grew beyond all conception. It has been calculated that towards the close of his reign Constantine Brâncoveanu had an annual revenue of 492,000 piastres and that of this only 132,000 were spent on home affairs, mercenaries, etc., while 360,000 went to the Turks—135,000 being the legal tribute and 225,000 being made up of every imaginable kind of illegal exaction, baksheesh, presents, blackmail, call it what we will. But the drain steadily increased right through the century, and as we shall see, actually reached its height between 1790 and 1810. There was naturally enough a decline in the number of families paying taxes, and there was steady emigration—mainly to Transylvania—and occasionally it came to a serious *émeute*. As a result of this, Gregory Ghica of Moldavia in 1766 reduced the number of days on which the peasants were liable to forced labour, but in 1775, during his second tenure of office, he found it necessary to revoke his concessions. The peasant sank into utter dependence upon the boiar class and its parasites, the Greek and Jewish usurers; and the more he was fleeced, the less incentive he had to prosper. Moreover, the periodical foreign occupations[1] of which we shall now have to speak—with their accompaniments of ill-discipline, pillage, wholesale requisitioning, plague and epidemics—added still further to the uncertainty and misery of the situation.

\*　　　\*　　　\*　　　\*

A Turkish proverb describes the hospodars of Wallachia and Moldavia as "the two eyes of the Porte, turned towards Europe": and it is sometimes contended that the Phanariot regime, bad as it was, averted the two still worse alternatives of direct Turkish rule or of conquest by one of the Great Powers. It is obvious that anything would have been preferable to the former, but it is at least open to argument that the

[1] In 1711, 1736–9, 1769–74, 1787–92, 1806–12.

extension of Austrian rule to the whole of the Principalities would have averted many evils from the whole of South-east Europe and actually promoted a healthy national evolution within the framework of a powerful supra-national state.

In actual fact, the two Principalities, thanks to their geographical situation even more than to political considerations, became a pawn in the diplomatic offensive of Europe against the decaying Ottoman Empire, and this was to last for over a century. Nor can it be denied that their parlous internal state was one of the incentives to aggressive action on the part of both Austria and Russia, one of the symptoms which made their statesmen, and others in Europe also, believe in the imminent collapse of Turkish power. The Phanariots on their side continued as hospodars the diplomatic intrigue which they had learned at the Porte and almost always played a double game. Indeed it is difficult to understand the boundless levity of the Turks in trusting such men— difficult even when we remember the extent to which corruption and venality had infected all classes of Turks.

The first of these princes, however, Nicholas Mavrocordato, who reigned in Moldavia from 1709 to 1710 and again from 1711 to 1716 and from 1716 till 1730 in Wallachia, does not deserve such sweeping condemnation. During his second reign he even found it possible to play upon the fears of the Turks, and by securing a certain respite from their exactions, to reduce for a time the burdens upon the clergy and people. It is true that he never won popularity, and seeing himself regarded as an alien found himself obliged to rely upon, and further, the Greek element. But it is possible to note under him the first faint glimmering of constitutional practice, when he referred to the boiars an account of state revenues.

His position in Wallachia after 1716 was affected by foreign complications. In 1714 the Turks had renewed the war against Venice, and after their conquest of Corinth and Nauplia Austria gradually became involved. A contemporary document in the Viennese archives sets out the reasons which seemed to make war inevitable. In the first place the very structure of the Turkish state, it contended, forced it into conflict with the Empire: "war is life to the Turks, peace is death". In the second place it was contrary to Austrian interests that any change should be made in the constitution of Moldavia and Wallachia, and great stress was laid upon the importance of Bender and Hotin. "If the King of France", it was argued, "builds a small tower on the Rhine, politicians

say it is the gate to universal domination. But if the Turk builds great
fortresses on the Christian borders, contrary to treaty, this is treated as
nothing." Formerly, the Empire might care little for the two Principalities, but now they bordered immediately upon Hungary, and fertile
as they were, they could easily maintain 60,000 Turkish troops ready
for instant attack through the Transylvanian passes. It was the Turkish
aim to uproot the Wallachians, settle Tatars in their place, and establish
pashas and military rule in both provinces.[1] In modern parlance, the
strategic position of Roumania was the decisive argument.

This able exponent of what may be called the Eastern, as opposed
to the Western, school of thought, seems to have convinced both
Charles VI and Prince Eugene. The great captain crowned perhaps
the greatest of all his campaigns by the battle of Peterwardein (5 August
1716) in which the grand vizier himself fell, and the conquest of Temesvár and the whole Banat followed in October. A further corollary was
the occupation of Bucarest, effected by a flying column of only 1200 men
—mostly Serbian volunteers—under the impress of greater victories:
Nicholas Mavrocordato was made prisoner and removed to Brașov, his
brother John being utilised as Imperial Statthalter in his place. A further
raid into Moldavia was less successful: Jassy was occupied, and then
abandoned, and Tatar hordes harassed the retreating imperialists.
Michael Rakovița, to prove his devotion to the Porte, tortured or
executed any boiars suspected of helping the enemy.

A year after Peterwardein Prince Eugene, "der edle Ritter",
stormed Belgrade and utterly routed the Turkish reinforcements. The
Porte would still have liked to continue the war and still played with
Francis Rákóczy and Magyar *émigrés*, but for the present the means
were lacking, and it contented itself with exacting the surrender of the
Morea by the exhausted Venetians. For Austria the Peace of Passarowitz (Požarevac), on 21 July 1718, represents the zenith of her Eastern
power and prestige. Not only did she recover the whole Banat, thus
ejecting the Turks from the last remnant of their Hungarian conquests,
but in addition she annexed Belgrade and the whole of Northern Serbia
(comprising the famous Šumadia district and corresponding in the
main with the first autonomous Serbian state of a century later), certain
districts in North-west Bosnia and above all the five Roumanian districts then commonly known as "Little Wallachia"—the whole territory lying between the Iron Gates, the Carpathians and the rivers Olt

[1] 1716 (undated), in Italian—Hurmuzaki, *Documente*, XX, no. 72.

and Danube. A commercial supplement secured to the imperialists free trading rights in the Turkish dominions. As a point of detail the voivode Nicholas Mavrocordato and his family were exchanged for two captured imperialist generals, while the Porte promised to keep the Magyar exiles under supervision, at a distance from the frontiers.

These substantial gains, obtained unaided, while Russia had been reduced to passivity even under her greatest of rulers, seemed to foreshadow Austria's speedy expansion throughout the Balkan peninsula, perhaps even the conquest of Byzantium and the reunion of the two imperial crowns. The final result was merely postponed: the Turk was assuredly doomed. Such indeed seems to have been the calculation of the Christian populations themselves. The contact between the Serbs of Turkey and their kinsmen of Southern Hungary and the now extended Military Frontiers was especially close: and under Austrian rule the ecclesiastical centre was transferred from Karlovci to Belgrade. But there was a similar, though weaker, movement of feeling among the Roumanians: and on the eve of the peace negotiations a deputation, led by Radu Golescu and Ştirbei, went to Vienna and begged the emperor to make George Cantacuzene their voivode and to call together and consult the Estates—by which was doubtless meant the boiars and clergy. If he could not secure their complete liberation from the Turkish yoke, he was asked to stipulate that henceforth only native Wallachians, and not Greeks or other foreigners, should be appointed as hospodars. It is interesting that at the same time a Wallach petition from Transylvania found its way to Prince Eugene.[1]

Unhappily the Austrian administration in Wallachia failed to justify expectations. On their arrival they found intolerable conditions. In addition to direct contributions the wretched population was subjected to a series of special taxes—upon bees, wine, pigs, tobacco, horned beasts, sheep, hay, smoked fish, cloth, chimneys: these were extracted by arbitrary methods, backed by flogging and even torture. No receipts were given, and it was thus often possible to collect the same tax twice. Everywhere was fraud, abuse and disorganisation. The peasants had every interest in appearing as poor as possible, and those who had livestock kept them so far as possible in remote mountain districts. None the less the natural riches of Oltenia were so great that according to an Austrian estimate of 1731 there were 50,000 cattle, 100,000 horses,

[1] Cit. A. Beer, *Die orientalische Politik Oesterreichs*, p. 7.

300,000 sheep, 300,000 pigs and 200,000 beehives in these five districts alone. The Austrians wisely reduced the number of taxes, but some of those which remained were increased, and one of the chief merits of the regime to modern eyes, its attempt to levy taxes equally from all classes, aroused great indignation among the boiars, who, like the corresponding class in Hungary, demanded complete exemption. To the peasant there came one real advantage—that they now had to pay fixed sums and knew how many days of forced labour they had to perform. But there appear to have been many abuses among the military transport officers, the troops were lacking in discipline, and road-building and mending were rigorously enforced. The officials evidently did not know how to apply the old Roumanian proverb of "plucking the hen without making it cluck". The depreciation of the currency caused general annoyance and dislocation.[1] The clergy, at this time rapacious and ignorant, contrived to extract many special concessions of exemption: but any gratitude which this might have secured was more than counterbalanced by the Austrian blunder of subordinating the bishopric of Rîmnic to the Serbian metropolitan see in Karlovci, and of setting up a Catholic bishop for the benefit of Bulgarian proselytes. It is but fair to add that the material for self-government—an idea quite alien to both the time and the place—was almost non-existent. If Austrian rule had endured, it may be supposed that the policy of colonisation, by which the Banat and Bačka were reclaimed for civilisation, would have been applied to Oltenia: but of course it would not have had the same justification in a well-peopled province as in the malarial desert to which the Turks had reduced the Banat, and any attempt to apply it would have led to further friction.

During this period of occupation Turkey, exhausted by her recent efforts, became involved in internal convulsions and a long quarrel with Persia and left all Western ambitions in abeyance, while Austria on her side found herself diverted from the Near East by German and Italian affairs. In 1726, however, she concluded an alliance with Catherine I of Russia, which was the forerunner of almost two centuries of Austro-Russian parallel action. By it she guaranteed Russia's European possessions and pledged herself to intervene if Russia should be

[1] Xenopol gives a clear summary of the Austrian period in his *Hist. des Roumains*, II, pp. 202–7, based mainly on the documents in Hurmuzaki, *Documente*, VI. The fullest account is obtained in Jacubenz, *Die cisleithanische Walachei unter kaiserlicher Verwaltung*, but this I have not been able to procure.

attacked by Turkey. When in 1736 this *casus belli* actually arose, Austria for nearly a year endeavoured to mediate between Russia and Turkey. This delay in fulfilling her treaty obligations was due to the difficulty of reconciling their rival claims to the Turkish inheritance. Neither was modest, for Russia demanded the Crimea and Kuban, the freedom of the Straits and the independence of Moldavia and Wallachia under her protectorate, while Austria wished to extend her frontiers not only in Bosnia and Serbia, but in Wallachia as far as the Dîmboviţa or even Brăila, and in Moldavia to the Pruth. No agreement was reached, for such vast changes could only be wrung from Turkey by overwhelming victory. The French envoy Bonneval was right when he wrote that "to take Austria as mediator, is like confessing to the fox".[1] In the end Austria joined the war against the Turks, and hoping to take them unawares made a hurried dash upon Niš and Vidin, and parallel raids upon Bucarest and Jassy. But the mantle of "the little Capuchin" had not fallen upon Seckendorf, Wallis and Neipperg, one general more incompetent than the other; none of these new conquests could be held, and the Turks, rallying to the surprise of all contemporaries, prepared for the recovery of Oltenia and even of Belgrade. Their vassal on the Wallachian throne, who had no cause to love Austria, issued a manifesto inviting the inhabitants of "Imperial Wallachia" to return to their allegiance: and it is significant of Austria's failure that both clergy and boiars responded with enthusiasm. Meanwhile Gregory Ghica in Moldavia had played a similar shifty game, warning the Turks of Russian military preparations and supplying the Turkish commissariat.

The war went badly for the Christian allies, and by 1739 Niš had fallen, Belgrade itself was in question, and Ali Pasha told the Austrian negotiator, Count Neipperg, to his face that he knew the road to Vienna and would leave a trail of fire and blood to its very gates. The Russians were more successful: one by one they reduced Azov, Ochakov and Hotin, and in August 1739 Marshal Münnich occupied Jassy and was welcomed by the population. But his arrogance soon alienated laity and clergy alike: ignoring Peter the Great's benevolent tactics, he treated Moldavia as a conquered province and imposed heavy burdens upon it—tactics all the more singular since he himself appears to have had serious pretensions to the Moldavian throne. His brief sway in Jassy and the excesses of the Cossack troops effected a noticeable cooling in the Russophil temper of Moldavia.

[1] Vandal, *Une Ambassade française*, p. 265.

The humiliating Peace of Belgrade (18 September 1739), in which the French Ambassador, M. de Villeneuve, played so notable a part by promoting Austro-Russian dissension, preventing a general Congress or Anglo-Dutch mediation[1] and stampeding the incompetent Neipperg into concessions,[2] was a grave setback to the Christian allies and gave the Turks a much-needed respite of twenty years. But it was especially serious for Austria, who after filling the entire stage in 1718 and acting as sole prospective candidate, had as it were allowed the joint claims of a rival and now saw herself in danger of being outstripped by that rival. In the years of peace that followed Belgrade Austria and Russia were already neck and neck, and the position of Russia as co-religionist of all the Orthodox Christians (the Russian being the only Orthodox Church not under infidel rule), and as blood relation of all the Slav races, served as a powerful handicap in her favour, which she was not slow to use. Thus in the eighteenth century, as a century earlier, there was again a long procession of bishops, archimandrites and lesser church dignitaries to Moscow and St Petersburg, begging for assistance, and "the rolling rouble" already became a familiar phrase among Russia's suspicious neighbours. None the less, peace was preserved in South-eastern Europe for almost thirty years—the longest known period since the first coming of the Turks to Europe! But this was due on the one hand to exhaustion and internal preoccupations and on the other to the absorption of Austria and Russia in the problems of Northern Europe—above all in the Habsburg succession under Maria Theresa, in Prussian territorial ambitions, and in the appetites whetted by the swift decline of Polish power.

During the forties the dearth of adequate candidates for the two thrones provided a certain limited opportunity for the only man of real eminence among all the Phanariot princes. Constantine Mavrocordato, son of the hospodar Nicholas, reigned no less than six times in Wallachia and four times in Moldavia, though their grand total only makes up twenty-two years. Under enormous difficulties, he, almost alone of his class, appears to have evolved definite theories of government and to have realised that the social pyramid cannot rest indefinitely upon its apex. In this perception he was assisted by the alarming growth of emigration, due to despair at the exactions of the tax-farmers and the

[1] Hurmuzaki, *Documente*, IX, no. 292, for Fleury's instructions to Villeneuve.
[2] See the brilliant study of M. Vandal, *Une Ambassade française en Orient sous Louis XV*.

PLATE X

CONSTANTINE MAVROCORDATO

landed class. According to the well-informed and accurate General von Bauer, a rough census of 1741 had revealed the presence of 147,000 peasant families in Wallachia, but during the next four years their number had fallen to one half, and by the end of his reign, incredible as this would seem, to one quarter. This exodus was mainly across the Danube into Turkish territory, where there was the same corruption as at home and the added drawback of alien and military rule, but where at least the landlord had less control over the labour of the peasantry. There was also emigration westwards into the Banat, where Count Mercy was pursuing his great work of colonisation on paternal, but enlightened, lines, and northwards into Transylvania: but this latter has been much exaggerated by Magyar propagandists, in the futile attempt to prove that the Roumanians are less prolific than the Magyars! It stands to reason that the extreme feudalism of Magyar rule would not attract any save the most desperate, and it is to be noted that at this very period large numbers of the former Serb immigrants into southern Hungary revolted against Magyar feudal oppression and that many of the survivors accepted an invitation from the Empress Elizabeth of Russia, and were settled by her on the rich soil of the Ukraine.

Faced by this crisis, Constantine Mavrocordato, between 1743 and 1746, attempted really drastic reforms. While abolishing the three taxes which weighed most heavily on the boiars[1] and exempting the clergy and monasteries, he set himself to arrest the process which for over a century past had been depressing the free peasant to the level of a mere serf, until "vecini" ("neighbours", villagers who had originally been prisoners of war, and were tied to the soil) and "rumâni" (the once free peasant proprietors) came to be almost identical terms. His first step was to divide the peasants into three classes—the fruntaşi, mijlocaşi and codaşi, or owners of twelve, eight and four oxen respectively, and to assure to them a minimum of land to cultivate, free pasturage for their beasts, and the right to cut wood for fuel. Moreover, every unfree peasant was given the right to buy his freedom for ten piastres: this was embodied in a formal document signed by the boiars and bishops, in favour of their "brothers in Christ, subjected by an evil system". These reforms, however, caused much effervescence among the boiars, who induced the Porte to transfer Constantine to Moldavia: but he persevered in his views and in 1749 decreed the emancipation of the vecini

[1] The văcărit (on cattle); vadrărit (on wine presses); pogonărit (on vineyards).

there also. The Assembly, in ratifying this, referred to "complaints that the word 'service' does not differ from 'slavery', that some land-lords have been in the habit of selling serfs (vecini) like slaves (robi), treating them like gypsies,...separating children from their parents and transferring them from one place to another".[1] As a corollary to his care for the peasantry, Constantine tried to raise the standards of the clergy, insisting that they must at the very least be literate! He pub-lished a new Roumanian Psalter and other ecclesiastical literature, and founded schools, mainly for the younger boiars, the best of whom he even sent on bursaries to a famous Greek school at Venice. But he had touched too many interests to be left unchallenged: and by the end of 1749 his fall was accomplished. He was exiled to Lemnos and had to pay 300 purses to the grand vizier to secure his release. He was twice restored to the Wallachian throne, in 1756 and 1761, but in 1763 he was again deposed by the Porte and thrown, in an almost penniless condition, into the celebrated prison of the Seven Towers.

In his later reigns he was unable to extend or even consolidate his reforms, and the taxes which he had remitted were gradually reimposed. In 1766 forced labour was extended in Moldavia by a reluctant decree of Gregory Ghica II, and the amount stipulated for as a day's service being twice or thrice in excess of what was possible, the door was opened for an indefinite extension of the number of days. None the less, right on to the end of the Phanariot regime the boiars were con-stantly pressing the hospodars for measures stiffening these servitudes: and we shall see that even in the days of the Règlement Organique the enlighted Kiselev had to combat a similar tendency.

The "urbarial" system inaugurated by Mavrocordato has been well described by Dr Mitrany as "a mixed regime, reducing serfdom with-out according complete freedom".[2] The process of utter subjection never went so far as in the feudal west and centre of Europe, and it is curious that it was arrested at a time when political liberty was at its very lowest ebb. None the less, "the weakening of the central authority and the growth of Austrian and Russian influence, reduced the Rou-manian provinces to a political no-man's-land, in which the boiars did as they pleased. Mr and Mrs Hammond wrote in their *Village Labourer* that 'in England the aristocracy had power and no privileges: in France the aristocracy had privileges and no power'. In the Roumanian pro-

---

[1] A. A. C. Sturdza, *La Terre et la Race Roumaine*, p. 190.
[2] *The Land and the Peasant in Roumania*, p. 16.

vinces the boiars had both power and privileges. Nominally high functionaries on behalf of the prince, they were in fact the keepers and uncontrolled defenders of their own interests as landlords. They had apportioned the land among themselves".[1] All the more credit to such a man as Constantine Mavrocordato, who amid the twilight of an iron age maintained moral standards and a rough conception of social justice. His name stands beside those of Vladimirescu, Cuza and Kogălniceanu as the pioneers of peasant liberty.

[1] *Ibid*, p. 23.

# CHAPTER VI

# AUSTRIA, RUSSIA AND THE ROUMANIAN PROBLEM

The two middle decades of the century are a period of constant change on both thrones—in twenty years eleven reigns in Wallachia and nine in Moldavia! This was due to the simple facts that by this time the Porte had a wider choice of candidates, and that there was a more than usual agile and arrogant Kapu-Kihaya in the person of the odious Stavraki, who carried bribery and extortion to their utmost limits. In the end it came to open revolt against the demands of his princely nominees, and when the alleged facts were laid before Sultan Mustafa, that poet-prince yielded to his natural avarice and solved the problem by hanging Stavraki before his own palace and seizing his vast ill-gotten fortune (1765). This incident was, however, a sign of increased Greek influence at the Porte, to whom the Phanariots had by now become indispensable despite their constant intrigues with France, Austria and other Powers.

What secured to the Principalities this period of ignominious calm was the great struggle of the Seven Years' War, whose most lasting and memorable results were outside Europe altogether, but which led to a complete reversal of the traditional alliances of the Continent and thereby set the Eastern Question once more in motion. The accession of Catherine the Great in 1762 gave a new direction to Russian policy. She saw in Frederick the Great her natural ally in any designs upon the liberty of Poland and rightly assumed his relative indifference to the fate of Turkey: and in view of these two facts the Austro-French alliance by which Maria Theresa and Kaunitz responded, seemed a minor evil. But the Porte viewed her designs with the utmost alarm and foresaw some of the dangers involved in her foisting her weak favourite Stanislas Poniatowski upon the throne of Poland. It was not, however, till September 1768 that, yielding to the steady incitement of a group of Polish exiles, and of Vergennes, the Minister of Louis XV, the Turks could bring themselves to declare war on Russia: they then had the double excuse of Russia's occupation of Cracow and a Cossack blood-bath in the Tatar town of Balta—on Turkish territory near the Bessarabian border. But they had thus assumed the rôle of aggressor, and Austria decided this time on neutrality, resisting on the one hand French promptings to a Turkish alliance and Russia's suggestion that the two allies of 1737 should attempt a final settlement of the Turkish question.

There were many delays before the two enemies really came to grips, but in September 1769 the Russians won a decisive victory at Hotin, and the two Principalities—the main objective of the campaign—were rapidly overrun and occupied. A manifesto of Catherine, promising liberation from the Turkish yoke, was publicly read out at Jassy amid much apparent enthusiasm. "The barbarous domination of the Turks", so runs one of its phrases, "seeks to fling back into the abyss of impiety the souls of the Christians who live in Moldavia, Wallachia, Bulgaria, Bosnia, Hercegovina, Macedonia and other provinces of the Ottoman Empire." Gregory Ghica, then hospodar of Wallachia, already known as a Russophil and fearing for himself the fate of Callimachi, allowed himself to be captured and removed with his family as prisoners to St Petersburg. But the veteran "Constantine Vodă", now on the Moldavian throne for the last time, was captured on his flight to the Turkish camp at Reni and made no concealment of his belief that the Turks would return on the morrow and drive out the Russians like dogs. An indignant Russian officer drew his sword and inflicted a head wound from which the old hospodar died miserably at Jassy some weeks later. Meanwhile the current was running strongly for Russia, and a deputation from both provinces, including the Metropolitan Gregory, several bishops and members of the Cantacuzene and Brâncoveanu families, visited St Petersburg and was received in solemn audience by the empress, slavishly kissing her knees and footprints. For the next four years Jassy and Bucarest were under Russian administration: and bogus treaties dating from the fourteenth and fifteenth centuries were unearthed in order to prove the contractual relations between the Roumanians and the Porte,[1] as a basis for reducing Turkish sovereignty to zero. A small clique of big boiars favoured Russian incorporation, in the selfish and probably accurate calculation that this would mean government by a narrow landed oligarchy and chances of speedy enrichment.[2] That all this was part of a still wider and more ambitious design was shown by the sensational despatch of a Russian fleet to the Mediterranean and its attempt to rouse the Greek population of Morea

---

[1] Iorga, *Gesch. des osman. Reiches*, IV, p. 501.
[2] Iorga, *Gesch. des rum. Volkes*, II, p. 181.

and the islands by similar promises of liberation. Unfortunately, despite the brilliant sea victory of Chesme (5 July 1770), Russia was unable to protect the Greeks from fierce Turkish reprisals, and meanwhile the land war began to languish, for political even more than for military reasons. It is true that during 1770 Russia completed her strategic hold over the Principalities by the successive capture of the key fortresses of Akerman, Chilia and Ismail. But though they remained the immediate booty upon which Catherine had set her heart, she was well aware that the Powers were watching her and might force her to renounce the prize within her grasp. Late in 1770 she communicated to Frederick the Great (soon after his meeting with Joseph II at Neustadt) what she regarded as the terms of a just peace: and he then warned her that one prominent item, the independence of Moldavia and Wallachia—which would obviously have been equivalent to a Russian protectorate, at a moment when even Poland, with its infinitely greater resources, could not stand up against the Muscovite power—must be abandoned if she wished to avoid war with Austria. Joseph indeed was already eager to reoccupy Oltenia, if the Russians should cross the Danube, and was probably held back from rash action mainly by the consideration that this would involve an Austro-Russian war and that Prussia would then at once become the arbiter not only in the Near East but in Germany itself.

The slackening of the Russian offensive is however to be explained by another still more fundamental factor. The initial steps were already being taken for a partition of Poland, and although we are not concerned with the complex secret negotiations of those years, it is necessary to point out the extent to which the fate of the Roumanians, now completely passive victims, was bound up with that memorable crime and its consequences. The year 1771 was filled with manœuvre and countermanœuvre by the rival Powers. Already in January Frederick had suggested that Catherine should renounce Moldavia and Wallachia and "take a province of Poland at her good pleasure (*à sa bienséance*)".[1] In July Austria concluded a secret treaty with the Porte against Russia, pocketing a fat subsidy in advance and a promise of the retrocession of Oltenia for her services. But this did not prevent her from conducting parallel discussions with Russia as to a fresh alliance for the ejection of the Turks from Europe. In one of the "combinations" then put forward Austria would have left the two Principalities as well as Con-

[1] Sorel, *La Question d'Orient*, p. 139.

stantinople and the Straits to Russia, and modestly contented herself
with Serbia, Bosnia, Albania and Macedonia: in another, the Russian
frontier would have been advanced to the Danube, while Austria took
Serbia, Bosnia and Oltenia, but the rest of the peninsula would have
formed a Russian vassal state, with Byzantium as its capital, while an
Austrian archduke reigned in Morea. By the turn of the year Catherine
was ripe for the renunciation of Moldavia and Wallachia, so long as she
could retain the border fortresses of Ochakov and Bender. Maria
Theresa and her less scrupulous son and Chancellor were faced by
embarrassing alternatives. At whose expense should she aggrandise
herself—at that of her new Turkish ally or her ancient Polish friend, or
in other words, was she to take Bosnia, or Moldavia and Wallachia, or
Cracow? Frederick meanwhile was far more interested in Poland than
in Turkey, for the very simple reason that geography would prevent
him from sharing in the spoils of the latter, which would go to increase
the bulk of his two imperial rivals, whereas he was confident that of
Poland he could secure the maximum obtainable. He therefore had
every interest in diverting both Russian and Austrian appetite from
Turkey to Poland, while using the continuance of the Turkish war to
keep those appetites within bounds. Above all, he had to make Austria
an accomplice in the Polish crime, and here he was helped by Joseph,
who was as greedy and cynical in foreign policy as he was high-minded
and idealistic in home affairs. Joseph bargained for the whole of Moldavia and Wallachia, if Austria was to have no share in Poland. His
wiser mother disliked the idea of taking provinces which were "unhealthy, devastated, open to Turks, Tatars and Russians, where many
millions and many men would be needed in order to maintain oneself"
and she felt that this "might lead to our ruin after robbing us of our
credit".[1] In the Polish affair also she was most reluctant, saying "on
voulait agir à la prussienne et l'on voulait en même temps retenir les
apparences de l'honnêteté"; but in the end, in Frederick's biting
phrase, "elle pleurait, et prenait toujours".

The First Partition of Poland, signed on 15 July 1772, assured to
Turkey yet another respite, and thereby at the same time averted the
transference of the Roumanians from infidel to Christian rule: the
question whether they thus gained more in the end than they undoubtedly lost at the beginning is one for the speculative historian
rather than for the plain narrator, and indeed can only be answered by

[1] Sorel, *op. cit.* pp. 199–202.

those who presume to interpret the purposes of Providence. Meanwhile in April a peace conference had been summoned on Roumanian soil at Focşani, but a deadlock was reached over the question of the independence of the Crimean Tatars. In 1773 a second congress at Bucarest also failed, because of Russia's Black Sea demands. But the Russian army, when it then resumed the offensive across the Danube, failed before Silistra, and only escaped from the same dangers as Peter the Great upon the Pruth thanks to the incompetent leadership of the grand vizier. There was thus a military deadlock, and the death of Sultan Mustafa and the Porte's disillusionment at Austria's demands prepared the way to peace.

The Treaty of Kütchük Kainardji (21 July 1774) is a landmark in the history of the Eastern Question, and to a lesser degree in the evolution of modern Roumania. Russia was far from obtaining all that she had at first hoped for, and indeed restored most of her conquests in Asia and in Europe, only retaining Azov and certain border fortresses. But she insisted on the independence of the Crimean Tatars—a last stage on the road to their absorption in the Russian Empire—and on the free navigation of the Black Sea and the Danube. For the first time Russia was to have permanent diplomatic representation at the Porte, and the right to appoint consuls where she judged necessary. But by far the most important clauses were those in which the religious and political imperceptibly blended. The right to erect a "Russo-Greek Church" in the suburb of Galata might at first seem insignificant, but it was the first concession of this nature since the Turks had established their rule over Christian subjects, and thus became, to Moslem and Christian alike, a symbol in stone of the rising power of Russia. The right of pilgrimage to the holy places assured to all Russian subjects had a similar sentimental value. But most important of all was the loosely worded Article VII, which pledged the Porte to protect the Christian religion, and allowed the Russian minister to make representations "en toute occasion" in favour of those serving the new Russian Church. The Porte was bound to receive his remarks as coming "from a neighbouring and sincerely friendly Power". From this clause dates that ill-defined protectorate over the Orthodox Christians of the East which Russia was constantly extending by the treaties of the next half century, and which, being blended of moral authority, true religious sentiment and naked imperialistic greed, was to survive in a new form even after the Powers had fought a war to end it. From the point of view of

Turkish prestige it may be regarded as the most fateful provision yet signed by any sultan.

It was, however, another article with which we are specially concerned, and which supplied Russia with a practical lever for undermining the Ottoman edifice still further. Not only Bessarabia, but Moldavia and Wallachia, were handed back to the Porte, but a whole series of conditions was imposed upon it. In addition to a general amnesty for all Roumanians, free exercise of the Christian religion and exemption from the tribute for the first two years after the peace, it was expressly laid down that the tribute itself should in future be fixed, and all the vast array of presents and baksheesh be swept away. Each prince was to have his own diplomatic agent at Constantinople, "who despite his slight importance shall be considered a person subject to international law and free from all violence". Finally, to Russia was conceded the right to speak in favour of the Principalities, the Porte promising here again "to listen with the consideration shown to friendly and respected Powers".

In other words, Russia, mainly for the sake of Austrian friendship, abandoned her original idea of annexing the Principalities, but substituted a virtual protectorate which might at any time enable her to apply the principle, *reculer pour mieux sauter*. But to the Roumanians, who were thus handed back to Turkish rule, the conditions attached to the surrender must have provided but scanty consolation at the time: and there was a tragic sequel to the treaty which they bitterly resented, though it eventually proved to have certain redeeming features. During a visit to Transylvania and Galicia in 1773 Joseph II had the idea that in order to improve communications between them through the Carpathians, and thus strengthen the frontier defences, it would be well to annex the northern districts of Moldavia as far as the river Sbrucz. "From the military and political standpoint," he held, "it was at least worth as much as western Wallachia." Kaunitz therefore instructed Thugut to intimate to the Porte that the cession of Bukovina would be a proper method of rewarding Austria for her good offices! As the Turks not unnaturally thought otherwise and played for time, orders were issued in Vienna in September 1774 for the occupation of the coveted territory. The Turks at first talked of "shameful plunder", but finding Russia complaisant and no other help forthcoming, they ended by formally ceding Bukovina to Austria (7 May 1775)—doubtless hoping that they were thereby diminishing the prospects of Austria joining some fresh conspiracy against them, and in any case needs must, when the devil drives. Still, they did things in style, and described the cession as "an unequivocal proof of friendship, affection and good neighbourliness".[1] On the other hand, the note of Thugut, disclaiming all hostility and adducing the triple motive of direct communications with Transylvania, the prevention of military desertion and a claim derived from northern Moldavia's former connection with Pocutia,[2] seemed to be adding insult to injury. But after all the Turks could afford to be indifferent to so remote a district of their Empire. The real losers were the Roumanians: for the ceded territory included the former capitals of Suceava and Rădăuţi, the scene of Stephen's greatest triumphs, and many of his most famous monastic endowments. We shall at least see that it was justly and mildly governed by the Austrians, and that the status of its Roumanian inhabitants differed very greatly from that of the Roumanians under Hungarian rule.

Russia looked with secret disfavour upon Austria's action, but contented herself with inciting Gregory Ghica, whose reappointment to the Moldavian throne she had secured from the Porte, to resist the cession. But he and his boiars were helpless without some external backing, and he eventually found it more politic to intrigue with Vienna and to assure Thugut that he had always worked for cession. Thugut, himself cynical and unscrupulous, was far too well informed to accept the assurances of "the perfidious and faithless Greek". But he does not seem to have been in any way concerned with the final tragedy. In October 1777 a certain Ahmed Bey was sent from the Porte to Jassy, with orders to bring Ghica, dead or alive, to Constantinople. On arrival he shammed illness and invited the prince to visit him at his lodging. Ghica was suspicious and first sent his own physician, but eventually came himself and found Ahmed lying on a sofa, breathing heavily. A brief conversation followed, and Ahmed clapped his hands for the usual refreshments. This was the signal for an attack by armed janissaries:

[1] Zinkeisen, *Gesch. des osman. Reiches*, VI, p. 114.

[2] We saw that in the sixteenth century Moldavia claimed Pocutia, and Poland periodically reduced Moldavia to vassalage. Austria now inverted the facts and claimed Moldavia as having formed part of Pocutia, which she had taken from Poland in 1772! A map with a fictitious frontier was also supplied to the Porte, but this attention was probably wasted upon officials who only a few years before had taken the Venetians seriously to task for letting the Russian fleet pass down the Adriatic on its way from the Baltic to the Aegean! Geography was not their strong point.

Ghica defended himself with his sword, but was cut down and killed. The hetman of the Albanian bodyguard was made Kaimakam, and the prince's widow, stripped of her fortune, was sent into distant exile. The exact motives of the murder will always remain obscure, and though his main crime was his Russophil outlook, the story that he died because of his resistance to any cession of national territory is a mere legend.

After Kütchük Kainardji there was again a lull of some years in the Eastern Question, though the Porte spared no pains to evade fulfilment and much friction resulted. Russia was preparing for the final absorbtion of the Crimea, while Maria Theresa in her closing years felt that Austria had already gone too far. "The partition of the Ottoman Empire", she wrote to her confidential adviser Count Mercy, "would be of all enterprises the most hazardous and dangerous, for the consequences it might evoke. What should we gain by pushing our conquests even to the gates of Constantinople? Unhealthy provinces, without culture, depopulated, or inhabited by perfidious and ill-intentioned Greeks, would be more apt to exhaust than to augment the resources of the Monarchy."[1]

Five years of Russo-Turkish haggling seemed to be leading to fresh war: but both sides hesitated at the last moment, and on 4 March 1779 concluded the Convention of Ainali Kavak, which recognised the Russian candidate as Khan of the Tatars (thereby really sealing the fate of the Crimea), and reaffirming the rights of Russian ships and traders. The clauses relating to the two Principalities were of special importance. The tribute was henceforth to be paid every two years and to be imposed "with moderation and humanity", without any extras. The princely agents to the Porte were to be of the Orthodox faith. Russia undertook not to use her "right of intercession" on behalf of Moldavia and Wallachia "except solely to conserve the conditions specified". It will be seen that this clause, while seeming to limit Russia's rights, in reality extended them, by inevitably leaving her the interpreter of what demanded "intercession". Moreover, from 1782 onwards, her growing influence was strengthened by the appointment of a Russian Consul at Bucarest. It is true that this was counteracted by the despatch of an Austrian "Agent", and that after the turn of the century, when French and British consuls were also installed both in Bucarest and Jassy, the two capitals became hotbeds of rival intrigue. But none the less it was

[1] *Correspondence du Comte Mercy-Argenteau*, II, no. 7, 31 July 1777.

the first sign of a European control upon the actions of decadent Turkey. The first Russian was a rough and arrogant Georgian who won but little love, the first Austrian, Ignaz Stephen Rajčević, was a cultured Ragusan in the imperial service, whose "Observations on Moldavia and Wallachia" are a permanent source for our knowledge of the period. He had a caustic pen, and many objects upon which to use it, but posterity will not quarrel with his general conclusion that "all the faults of the nation have their source in the more than despotic Government and in the most wretched education", and that there would be very rapid improvement under better rulers. The black pall of separation from the outer world was slowly being drawn aside, and during the next few decades a number of able foreign advisers make their appearance at the two courts—men like Rajčević, Hauterive, Lechevallier and later on Belleval, Mondeville, Recordon, Laurençon, Colson and Pertusier—and are not without influence upon the course of events.

Both provinces had suffered severely from the long Russo-Turkish war, but it was followed by a slight revival, and where good rulers were so rare it is necessary to insist upon any exception to the general rule. Alexander Ypsilanti, who reigned at Bucarest from 1774 to 1782, was responsible for a new civil code of justice, paid district judges and reorganised courts. He reduced the contributions of the clergy, made a serious attempt to simplify taxation, and devoted part of his efforts to the foundation of charitable institutions and the improvement of Bucarest itself. It should be added that a tradition of generous bequests to monasteries, hospitals and schools, and public foundations was already growing up among the wealthy boiar class, and has survived into modern times. None the less, Ypsilanti was but a "white raven" amid a clique of rapacious aspirants to the two thrones. He owed to marriage with the family of Moruzi his admission to the inner Phanariot ring, and the Moruzis, Callimachis and Suţus in their turn were descendants of the Mavrocordatos. During the eighties two other upstart families —Caragea and Mavrogheni—entered the competitive arena and, having no roots in the country, ruled more than ever as blind instruments of the Porte and for their own personal enrichment.

For most of the eighties peace was still preserved, but the renewed intimacy of Austria and Russia and the widespread belief of European diplomacy that Turkey was on the point of collapse pointed to a resumption of the struggle. Already in May 1780 Joseph and Catherine met at Mohilev, and a main subject of discussion was a project for the partition of Turkey between their two empires. This took clearer shape in the secret proposals of Catherine, dated 10 September 1782 and known in history as the "Greek Project". Her central idea was the creation of an independent "Kingdom of Dacia", consisting of Moldavia, Wallachia and Bessarabia, bordered by the Dniester and the Olt and governed by a Christian prince: this would form a buffer state between the two empires, who would be pledged to respect its independence. If, however, the allies should succeed in capturing Constantinople, she asked that Joseph should consent to the restoration of the Greek empire under her own grandson, who would then renounce all right to the Russian succession. The best proof that she was in earnest is that the Grand Duke Paul's younger son was christened Constantine: and that six Greek wet-nurses were brought from the Aegean islands, in order that the future emperor should imbibe at once Greek milk and hellenic sentiments. Unhappily the long journey interferred with this design, and the child had to fall back upon a supply from Russian cows! Joseph meanwhile, after obtaining Kaunitz's approval, answered Catherine that the proposed Greek empire would meet with no obstacle from his side, but took care to specify the territory which Austria would require for herself—Serbia, Bosnia-Hercegovina and the Dalmatian coast (which Venice might surrender in return for Morea, Crete and Cyprus), and further east Orsova, Vidin, Oltenia and the fortress of Hotin to guard the new Bukovinian frontier. Joseph also stipulated that the new Greek and Dacian empires must promise to his subjects commercial freedom on the Danube and through the Straits.[1]

At first no attempt was made to put this project into execution, but Catherine took advantage of the *rapprochement* with Austria in order to annex the Crimea: and the Turks, after indignant assurances that they would sooner be hacked in pieces than submit, realised that they were helpless, and on 8 January 1784 signed the formal treaty of cession. In the words of the Prussian envoy Diez, "Il faut traiter les Turcs à la turque".[2] The Turks, in their anxiety, made unwonted concessions to the Roumanians. A Hattisheriff was issued enacting that hospodars were henceforth not to be removed save for obvious insubordination, that they were not to be made to pay for confirmation or retention of office, and that the tribute was to be fixed at 619 and 135 purses for the

[1] *Joseph und Katharina: Briefwechsel*, pp. 153, 172.
[2] Zinkeisen, *op. cit.* VI, p. 524.

two Principalities and to be paid over direct by their agents at the Porte, in order to avoid leakages and baksheesh on the way. Needless to say, these promises were not kept, but the mere fact that they were made was a sign of rapidly changing times.

Frederick the Great in his latter days paid growing attention to the Eastern Question, not of course for its own sake, but as an important factor in the European Balance of Power: but his death in 1786 came as a relief to his two eastern neighbours. Next year Joseph paid a second visit to Catherine, this time amid the vanished splendours of the Crimean Khans, and it was tacitly agreed that the time had at last come for action, though he affected to regard the empress as "exaltée" and was alarmed by a triumphal arch with the inscription "On to Byzantium". The Prince de Ligne, who was present, tells us that the two sovereigns "sounded each other as to the poor devils of Turks. As a lover of antiquity I spoke of restoring the Greeks, Catherine of renewing Lycurgus and Solon. I spoke of Alcibiades, but Joseph, who was more for the future than the past and for the positive than the chimerical, said, 'What the devil are we to do with Constantinople?'" And indeed this embarrassing problem was left to be solved by events— as the issue proved, very wisely, for the poor devils still had a good deal to say. In August 1787 war opened between Russia and Turkey amid mutual accusations of treaty-breaking, and in February 1788 Joseph in his turn issued a war manifesto against the barbarians. Writing to the French court, he even assumed the posture of "avenger of mankind".[1] The Turks on their side acted on the principle, "Better die once than die daily".[2] They had ceded Bukovina to Austria and she claimed Bosnia, they had made over the Crimea to Russia, and she asked for the whole Caucasus: it was time, therefore, to die fighting.

Yet again the high hopes of Austria and Russia were disappointed and Turkey displayed altogether unsuspected powers of resistance: failure was eventually determined by momentous events in Western and Central Europe. This time it was Austria who occupied Jassy, but in the summer this was far more than countered by the Turkish offensive into the Banat, culminating in the victory of Lugoş, where Joseph was within an ace of being taken prisoner. The Russians too were strangely unprepared for their great enterprise, and made no progress

[1] Zinkeisen, op. cit. VI, p. 645.
[2] Sauveb&oelig;uf, Mémoires historiques, I, p. 84. Cit. Iorga, Gesch. des osman. Reiches, V, p. 54.

till Suvarov's storming of Ochakov in midwinter (17 December 1788).
There was not much quarter given on either side, and the explanation
is doubtless to be found in despatches of the British Minister to the
Porte, Mr Ainslie, to Lord Carmarthen, reporting the periodic arrival
in Constantinople of "bags of ears" belonging to Austrian wounded
or prisoners.[1] Throughout this war it was above all the Roumanians
who paid and suffered: two of the battles of 1789 were fought
on their soil—at Focşani and Martineşci — they were subjected
to merciless requisitioning on all sides and were a prey to utter
political uncertainty. To complete the irony, Nicholas Mavrogheni, the
brutal and theatrical, but courageous upstart who filled the Moldavian
throne, stood almost alone in his loyalty to the Turks, but having
alienated Greeks and Roumanians alike, and having lost his only powerful patron Yusuf Pasha, was sent in disgrace to Constantinople and
there executed. Meanwhile Bucarest was held by the Austrians under
the prince of Coburg, and Jassy by the Russians under Prince Potem-
kin, the empress's favourite, who dreamt of founding a dynasty of his
own in the future Dacian kingdom. Another, and for a brief moment
more serious, project of territorial readjustment was that propounded
by the Prussian Foreign Minister Hertzberg, who hoped to secure
Danzig, Thorn and Posen for his own sovereign at a fresh partition of
Poland, as compensation for Russian expansion on the Black Sea.
Austria's share of the booty was to be Wallachia and Moldavia, but
without Bessarabia. Hertzberg actually sounded his envoy Diez as to
whether the Porte might not consent to these cessions, if in return the
Powers would permanently guarantee the line of the Danube, Save and
Una as the Ottoman frontier. Needless to say, the Turks would not
look at such a scheme, and indeed quite apart from national pride they
would have been mad to do so, considering the utter worthlessness of
any guarantees in that ultra-cynical age. But in any case, by the winter
of 1789–90 there was a stalemate on every front.

The death of Joseph II in February 1790 really ended all possibility

[1] 15 April–1 May 1788—quoted in App. 49 and 50 of Blancard, *Les Mavroyéni*,
I, p. 677. A British report of the year 18— (F.O. 78/103: Wallachia) throws further
light on this question of "no quarter". "An Austrian soldier who sees a Turk deliberately cut off the head of his officer (who perhaps from his horse being shot under
him has the misfortune to be made a prisoner) loses his *sang froid*, his superiors that
*esprit de corps* and feeling of humanity which adorns the character of most European
and particularly English officers and often prompts them at the hasard of their own lives
to save that of a fallen foe. This war in Turkey is conducted on all sides with fury...."

of maintaining the offensive against the Turks. His successor Leopold II favoured peace, and well he might, for he was confronted at one and the same time by revolution in Belgium, a Hungary ready to burst into flame, a hostile Prussia massing troops upon his northern frontier, complications in Italy and Poland, and as a final portent the ominous news from Paris and the growing danger to his sister and her husband's throne. By the Peace of Sistov (4 August 1791) Austria restored Belgrade and all her other conquests to the Turks and was left with the solitary gain of Orsova, then a fortress commanding the Iron Gates. For a time Russia continued the war alone, but European complications forced her too to conclude peace. By the Treaty of Jassy (January 1792) all existing treaties were reaffirmed (including the cession of the Crimea), but the Principalities were again evacuated, the Dniester remained the boundary between the two empires, and Russia's gains were restricted to the one paltry fortress of Ochakov.

Turkey's successful resistance to the joint assaults of Austria and Russia in the war of 1787–92 came as a surprise both to those Powers and to the rest of Europe, which was already reckoning with the final dissolution of the Ottoman Empire. What forced them to accept defeat and gave the Turks a much needed respite was the outbreak of complications in the West, leading to the long wars against revolutionary and Napoleonic France. Incidentally of course it stimulated the decision of the Eastern Powers to complete the ruin of that other Sick Man of Europe, the Polish Republic.

\*        \*        \*        \*

It was at this time that the first faint signs of national feeling made themselves felt among the Roumanians. In August 1791, when peace, and consequently the revival of Ottoman rule, seemed imminent, an appeal for help was addressed to Austria and Russia by a group of Wallachian boiars. It is full of new ideas, of a kind which we are not accustomed to look for in the sordid annals of that age. It speaks of a "Wallachian nation", it protests against the idea of Wallachia and Moldavia being mere Turkish provinces. It ascribes their decay above all to Phanariot rule since the days of Nicholas Mavrocordato. It sees the main remedy in the return of native princes and the creation of a national army. For its authors declare that they would rather perish like Lisbon or Lima (a reference to the two great earthquakes of the eighteenth century—the equivalent of San Francisco and Messina in our own day) than return to the Moslem yoke. They therefore demand that the Danubian fortresses should be dismantled and that the election of the prince should be entrusted to "a small number of electors from the three Estates". The tribute should be paid as hitherto every two years, but it should be conveyed by special delegates to Constantinople and handed over through the Russian and Austrian Ambassadors as intermediaries, so that further baksheesh should be rendered unnecessary. At the same time they urged that the two Principalities should be declared neutral in all future wars, and should be allowed to form a national militia such as would render occupation by a Christian neighbour superfluous. Thus the framers of this appeal had devised an all too ingenious plan for standing well with both worlds. By playing off rival forces against each other they were to rid themselves both of Turkish exactions and of foreign occupation—to remain tributory vassals of the sultan, yet to enjoy the effective protection of the two imperial courts. Their action of course led to nothing and merely deserves to be recorded as a first symptom of the new age in which the general principles that were already fermenting throughout the west and centre of Europe were beginning to stir the dry bones even on the Lower Danube.

In a position of such isolation and of such political degradation, it is remarkable that Western, and especially French, influences should have penetrated so rapidly. In the case of the Greeks, a seafaring people, close to the highways of Mediterranean life and brought to new prosperity and fresh connections by the commercial developments of the long French wars, it is easy enough to understand: but in that of the Roumanians it will always require a certain effort of imagination to realise the process. The Phanariot princes, it is true, despite their low moral standards, had a certain general culture, and their French secretaries played at times a very notable part in the political and intellectual progress of the Principalities. There were also German doctors, as a rule finding their way from the northern side of the Carpathians; merchants and traders from the West, and a certain number of foreign officers, notably during the Russian and Austrian occupations, who brought with them fragments of encyclopaedic doctrine from the West. Nor should it be forgotten that the upper class of Russians of that period were permeated with French influence, and that a few powerful families, such as the Ypsilantis, Cantacuzenes and Cantemirs, had Russian connections.

Meanwhile, it may safely be maintained that the period of the revolutionary and Napoleonic wars, so far from bringing any improvement or alleviation to the Principalities, marks their lowest degradation. The Porte continued its exactions and ignored Kütchük Kainardji: and between 1792 and 1802 there were no less than six changes on the Wallachian and five on the Moldavian throne. The rival families of Moruzi, Suţu, Ypsilanti and Callimachi, intrigued against each other at the Porte, accusing each other of treachery with the Russians and extorting more than ever from their subjects to maintain themselves in power. Moreover, famine and pestilence followed the long wars, and as if this were not enough, the disintegration which was so marked a feature of Turkish administration in the last decade of the eighteenth and the two opening decades of the nineteenth century, exposed the Principalities to the plundering and exactions of neighbouring pashas. Notably Pasvan Oglu, the redoubtable pasha of Vidin, who played so decisive a part in the events leading to the first Serbian insurrection, plundered freely across the Danube in Wallachia, and the wretched hospodar had to send him vast supplies at demand and yet at the same time to contribute heavily towards the cost of the Turkish armies which unsuccessfully tried to reduce Vidin.

The princes of this period deserve nothing better from the historian than the pillory and the branding-iron. Worst of all perhaps was Constantine Hângerli, a Greek of the Archipelago, who in 1797 succeeded the relatively estimable Alexander Ypsilanti in Wallachia, and promptly doubled all the taxes, adding on his own behalf a văcărit or cattle tax which had been abolished sixty years earlier, in the reign of Constantine Mavrocordato, by a solemn oath of hospodar, metropolitan and boiars. The metropolitan of the day had spirit enough to refuse a dispensation for so monstrous a betrayal, whereupon Hângerli obtained what he required by sending a bribe of fifty purses to the patriarch in Constantinople. So exorbitant was this demand as virtually to amount to the confiscation of the herds of all Wallachia. The collectors were ordered to levy the increased tax within the brief space of ten days, and employed very severe measures, not stopping short of torture. When at last despairing protests were made before the palace—in itself a most unusual event—the prince appeared at a window and called out angrily, "Pay the taxes, and you won't be killed".

Two incidents[1] will serve to illustrate the depths of degradation

[1] See Xenopol, *op. cit.* II, pp. 256–7.

reached under the wretched Hângerli. In 1798 Hussein Pasha, who commanded the Turkish army at the siege of Vidin, suffered a severe reverse at the hands of Pasvan Oglu and made his way to Bucarest, where Hângerli received him with great servility and kissed his hand in public. Noting that the boiars, when they attended a reception in his honour, did not bring their wives with them, the pasha ordered them to appear at the palace at an early date. The boiars were shrewd enough to suspect a trap, but too subservient and cautious to disobey. They therefore dressed up a number of the prostitutes of Bucarest and presented them at the ceremony as their wives. At the end of the evening the pasha ordered that the best-looking among these women should be removed to his quarters and told his Agas that they might make their choice from those that were left!! Surely depravity on both sides could scarcely go further.

The treacherous Hângerli was meanwhile denouncing Hussein to the sultan as responsible for the disaster before Vidin: but he was not sufficiently versed in the secret scandal of Stambul to realise that Hussein's wife was the mistress of Selim III, and so this intervention brought disaster upon his head. An emissary was sent from the Porte to Bucarest, accompanied by a tall negro executioner. Forcing his way into the palace and into the very presence of the hospodar, he produced a firman of the sultan and ordered the negro to strangle the wretched Hângerli then and there, before the eyes of his terrified guards (1 March 1799). When some of the boiars rushed in, they found that the prince's head had already been hacked off, and the room was deluged with blood.[1] His naked body was then thrown out into the street and left there till evening![2] An admirable picture of Turkish culture in the dying century.

His successors Alexander Moruzi and Michael Suţu found themselves helpless in face of the increasing depredations of Pasvan Oglu, who laid waste large tracts of Oltenia, cutting off the noses and ears of those who dared to resist, and threatening Bucarest itself so seriously that the prince and his chief nobles fled to the Transylvanian frontier. Fortunately the pasha of Vidin was more quiescent in his latter years, partly because his accomplices, the Janissaries who held Serbia to ransom, became involved in conflict with the insurgents under Kara George: and the Roumanians enjoyed a respite from direct attack.

[1] Vinzent Batthyány, *Reise nach Constantinopel* (1810), p. 252.
[2] Engel, *op. cit.* IV, ii, p. 67.

In 1802 a fresh convention was concluded between Russia and Turkey which involved changes of very real importance for the Roumanian nation. For the highly ambiguous provision of 1779 regarding Russia's "right of intercession", there was now substituted a clause by which no hospodar might henceforth be dispossessed without the express consent of Russia, and appointments to the throne were to be for a period of seven years. All new taxation introduced since 1773 was to be revoked: all offices were to be given by preference to natives of the two Principalities, and the divan acquired the right to raise objections to levies in kind. Needless to say, these provisions were as yet more honoured in the breach than in the observance, but they were a clear sign that the old unlimited extortion was nearing its end.

It is not surprising that under these circumstances the two new princes, Constantine Ypsilanti and Alexander Moruzi, were more than ever subject to Russian influence. The former dared to refuse a Turkish requisition of sheep, acted as intermediary between the Serbs and St Petersburg and did what he could to embroil the French and the Porte—in this case without success, for General Sebastiani, Bonaparte's envoy, so far from being impressed by his splendid reception at Bucarest, at once denounced the two hospodars to the Porte as traitors and influenced its decision to dethrone them both without any previous consultation of Russia (August 1806). This clear violation of a recent treaty brought Russia and Britain closer together, in proportion as Napoleon coquetted with the Turks and revived his dreams of oriental adventure. Italinski and Arbuthnot demanded the reinstalment of the hospodars and became involved in angry discussions with the Divan, which was by now under the nervous spell exercised by Napoleon's victories. But almost at the very moment when the combined pressure of the two ministers had extracted the necessary firman from the sultan, the Russian Government grew tired of haggling and ordered the occupation of the two Principalities by its troops. This was met by a Turkish declaration of war (27 December).

The events which followed are closely interwoven with the history of Europe's long conflict with Napoleon, and lie outside the purpose of such a narrative as the present. But it is impossible to leave altogether unrecorded the strange manner in which the Principalities were drawn into the vortex of European policy and became pawns on Napoleon's chess-board of territorial redistribution. If the forcing of the Dardanelles by Admiral Duckworth's fleet, in sympathetic alliance with

Russia, had led to the fall of the Turkish capital instead of ending as a brief and isolated incident of romance, it is quite possible that the Russo-British alliance would have been a permanence, and the history of the later coalitions would have taken quite another turn. In that case the Dacian project would probably have descended from the clouds to solid earth. In actual fact, however, Russia and Britain all too soon fell apart, for the tsar, deprived of his northern ally by the downfall of Prussia at Jena, and himself beaten at Eylau and Friedland, found it advisable to come to terms with Napoleon. At the memorable interview between Napoleon and Alexander at Tilsit (June 1807), the Eastern Question was one of the decisive subjects of discussion, and in it the Principalities played a very vital part, as the lure for the Russian bird. Napoleon, it is well known, was once more dreaming of Eastern conquest, though Western complications and the loss of sea-power were to prove fatal obstacles. In the final treaty of alliance it was laid down that if the Porte refused French mediation, the two new allies would make common cause to "remove all the European provinces of the Ottoman Empire from the yoke and vexations of the Turks", save Constantinople itself and Roumelia (a somewhat indeterminate and elastic expression which probably meant what we now call Bulgaria and Thrace). It was on this occasion that Napoleon spoke of Constantinople as "the key of the world". But it is clear that Napoleon had not made up his mind as to the fate of Turkey and was bargaining in all directions: and indeed the first mention of partition at Tilsit seems to have been in a memorandum of the Prussian statesman Hardenberg.[1] In his instructions to Caulaincourt, whom he sent in the following winter to continue discussions with the tsar, Napoleon expressed a preference for leaving Moldavia and Wallachia in Turkish hands, but would be ready to cede them if that would definitely win over Russia, and in return for "just compensation in the Prussian provinces".[2] After his arrival Caulaincourt reported his belief that Alexander had made the alliance with France in the calculation of securing the Principalities and Finland for himself.[3] The haggling went on for months, Alexander trying to fob off Napoleon with Bosnia and Albania, and Napoleon (in whose mind an Illyrian experiment was already taking shape) doubtless assuming that these could be obtained without Russian help and therefore laying the main

[1] *Mémoires*, II, pp. 461–3. Vandal, *Napoléon et Alexandre I*, I, p. 71.
[2] Full text in Appendix to Vandal, *op. cit.* I, p. 511.
[3] S. Tatistcheff, *Alexandre I et Napoléon*, p. 267.

stress upon Silesia as the only possible compensation.[1] Caulaincourt urged upon the tsar that it would be no small thing to realise the project of Catherine and make the Danube his frontier.[2] But appetite comes with eating, and there was a lively competition in plans of partition. "Tell Alexander", wrote Napoleon, "I do not press the evacuation of Moldavia and Wallachia: let him not press the evacuation of Prussia. I am not far from planning an expedition to India and the partition of Turkey." He and the tsar would crush England, ignore Austria and Prussia, and virtually divide the world between them. But when the French pegged out a claim to Constantinople, Alexander took alarm, and Caulaincourt penetrated to the heart of the matter when he warned his master that Russia would not willingly agree to this, whereas in return for his own possession of Constantinople and the Straits Alexander could be won for anything in the way of dynastic or political upheaval.[3] After a series of conversations between the tsar and the ambassador[4]—fantastic, impudent, and in reality no more than lightning rapier thrusts, forgotten as soon as made—the two emperors came once more to grips at Erfurt in September 1808: and an important feature of their new treaty was that Napoleon recognised full Russian sovereignty over Wallachia and Moldavia, with the Danube as frontier, and even recognised their union with Russia as taking effect "from this moment".[5] But from this moment the more ambitious schemes of Turkish partition slowly recede into the background, and the deep-seated distrust which lay behind their mutual compliments was already preparing the eventual final rupture between them.

Meanwhile the Roumanian provinces lay utterly prostrate while the Powers fought and intrigued over their bodies. According to a confidential British report of September 1807, at Bucarest "the Russians and the French employ the one half of the town to spy upon the other: c'est une police d'enfer".[6] But though the Russo-Turkish war continued, the main forces of Russia were engaged in the direction of Poland and the Baltic, while the double revolution in Constantinople— by which the unruly Janissaries overthrew first Selim III and then the

---

[1] Champagny to Caulaincourt, 14 January 1808—Tatistcheff, *op. cit.* p. 267.

[2] Tatistcheff, *op. cit.* p. 291.

[3] 16 March 1808—Vandal, *op. cit.* I, p. 307; Tatistcheff, *op. cit.* p. 241.

[4] The full details are to be found in Vandal's brilliant book, and in Sorel, *L'Europe et la Révolution française.*

[5] Vandal, II, p. 479.

[6] F.O. 78/58 (Turkey)—Marco to Summerers, no. 2, 23 September 1807.

worthless Mustafa IV—paralysed Turkish military effort. Napoleon had used his passing ascendancy at Tilsit to force a rupture between St Petersburg and London, and this ended the Russo-British alliance on the Golden Horn. Britain made peace with the Turks in 1808, and that able diplomatist Sir Robert Adair was sent to concert measures with Austria and win the Porte by a system of subsidies: and London and Vienna joined hands in their dislike of Russia's Danubian ambitions.

During 1809 and 1810 the war upon the Danube languished. The Russian leadership was bad, and the tsar's eyes were perforce set upon Prussia and Poland, while Adair reported the Turks to be equally lacking in officers, munitions, supplies and money. It was of course his business, especially as Franco-Russian relations slowly deteriorated, to do all in his power to promote peace between Russia and the Porte: and it is interesting to find him, in one of his later reports, taking the line that Moldavia and Wallachia, whose population is *entirely Greek*, "ought rather to belong to Russia than the Porte".[1] Even the advent of the brilliant Kutusov as Russian commander did not avail to overcome the deadlock: during 1811 the campaign swayed around the fortresses of Rushchuk and Giurgiu, and the Turks, so long renowned for their powers of offensive, now proved, as at Silistra, Kars and Plevna later in the century, their tenacity and endurance in defensive positions. Meanwhile the plight of the Principalities was truly pitiable. The long occupation of six years contributed still further to loosening the ties that linked the Roumanians with Turkey. But the Russians on their side did nothing to reconcile, and everything to alienate, a Christian population which was already predisposed to look to them for liberation. The wholesale requisitioning and exaction of compulsory labour, enforced by very real threats of deportation to Siberia; the notorious corruption of the Russian civil and military administration, the ruthless debasement of the coinage and the favour shown to Greek ecclesiastics and merchants—all combined to instil that profound suspicion of Russia which the experience of the next hundred years was to deepen still further. Kutusov, brilliant but dissolute, devoted his spare time to his mistresses and amusements, showing himself completely indifferent to the poignant appeals of the population; and on one famous occasion he exclaimed, "Je ne leur laisserai que les yeux pour pleurer". The tsar,

[1] Adair, II, p. 6. Zinkeisen, *op. cit.* VII, p. 675. This is a classical example of the confusion caused by the use of the word "Greek" in the ecclesiastical sense of "Orthodox".

when one of the Roumanian petitions at last came before his eyes, indignantly declared that he could no longer tolerate such atrocities,[1] but Russian misgovernment remained chronic throughout the occupation. "The Russian army had so devoured this country", wrote a French agent, "that early in 1809 it offered the appearance of a desert", and food for the army had to be brought from the Ukraine. "Whole villages and towns were wasted and empty, everyone took what he found, wherever he found it."[2] High Russian officers threatened to hand over Ypsilanti to the Turks unless he paid them exorbitant sums, and when he had drained his own resources dry, he found it wiser to fly to Russia, renouncing the last sorry vestiges of civil control. It was calculated that the contributions of Moldavia under the Russian occupation had risen from 3 to 8 million piastres, while those of Wallachia increased fivefold![3]

In 1811 events moved towards a fresh crisis in Europe. Napoleon not so much offered, as imposed, his alliance upon Austria and Prussia, and prepared seriously for an attack upon Russia whose issue was to leave him supreme in Europe and in Asia. In these circumstances it was essential for Russia to clear her quarrel with the Porte out of the way, and by the early months of 1812 the psychological moment for peace negotiations had been reached. Adair had gone home in the summer of 1810, and chance afforded to his young and daring successor, Stratford Canning, the first decisive stroke of a long diplomatic career. He it was who established contact between sultan and tsar (despite the fact that Britain and Russia were still technically at war), and gradually overcame the rigid arrogance and ingrained suspicion of the Turkish ministers. He turned the scale by communicating to them a secret Austrian memorandum proposing to Napoleon a partition of Turkey "at the first convenient juncture".[4] The Porte might be excused for suspecting Canning's motives: the desire to see Russia free to concentrate all efforts against Napoleon was only too obvious. Towards the end Canning, losing all patience, told the Reis-Effendi that by acting for the Porte's service he only exposed his Government "to every sort of caprice and insult" and that the Porte would "learn her

---

[1] Zinkeisen, op. cit. VII, p. 712.        [2] Ibid. p. 711.
[3] Hurmuzaki, Documente, Supplement II, pp. 452, 621, 690–7; see also Xenopol, op. cit. pp. 272–4.
[4] Lane Poole, Life of Stratford de Redcliffe, I, p. 166. "This alarming and unprincipled paper I conveyed in the most impressive manner to the Reis-Effendi."

error when it is too late".[1] Fortunately the plenipotentiaries in the field, Galib Effendi and Demetrius Moruzi, had more sense of reality than the Reis-Effendi in the capital: the Turkish army on the Danube lacked resources and was in great distress, while Admiral Chichagov was eager to withdraw his troops for the defence of Russia (and indeed it was these very troops which afterwards turned the scale on the Borodino).

The Treaty of Bucarest (28 May 1812)—the first of the four which bear that name—may fairly be described as opening a new era in the history of the Balkan peninsula. In one sense it was an abandonment, for Russia handed back the two Principalities over which she had so recently assumed sovereignty, and also left Serbia to her fate, with the result that the first insurrection collapsed and Kara George had to flee the country. On the other hand it was a mere recoil to gain strength for a better jump: for Russia maintained all her existing treaty rights of interference and was soon to resume her defence of Roumanian self-government, while the name of "Serbia" made its first appearance in an international treaty, and the Turks gave their first partial recognition of Serbian autonomy, in however attenuated a form. Thus, though to the Roumanian and Serbian contemporaries it seemed a setback, it must be regarded by us, with the perspective of a crowded century and a quarter, as the modest, but firm, foundation on which future progress could rest.

There can be no doubt that the Porte was at the last extremity, and that a continuance of the war would have cost the sultan his throne: yet it is highly characteristic of Turkish arrogance that the two plenipotentiaries, Galib and Moruzi, instead of earning credit for a surprisingly favourable peace, should have been subjected to dire punishment. What angered the sultan was that while the Principalities were recovered and the Asiatic frontiers maintained, Russia had been allowed to retain in full sovereignty the district lying between the Dniester and the Pruth, which though it had an identity of its own under the name of Bessarabia, was none the less an integral part of Moldavia. It may be argued that Moruzi miscalculated in not holding out for the restoration of the whole Moldavian territory, or again that he had his own designs upon the Moldavian throne and tried in his tortuous way to conciliate Russia and the Porte simultaneously. In any case, Galib set himself to lay the whole blame upon his colleague, and in this he was aided by the

[1] Lane Poole, *op. cit.* 1, pp. 173 and 156.

agents of Napoleon, who represented Moruzi and his brother as bribed by the Russians. Warned not to return, but knowing that his family was in the power of the Porte and confident that he could justify himself, Moruzi set out for Constantinople: but as he reached Shumla he was set upon by Turkish soldiers outside the gates of the pasha's house and hacked to pieces by their sabres.[1] His head and that of his brother were placed according to custom above the gate of the seraglio. The treacherous Galib fell into disgrace, but saved his life.

We may view with equal indifference Russia's failure to enforce her claim and Turkey's annoyance at a further shrinkage of her empire. What really matters is that for the second time in the Phanariot period Turkey made terms with Europe by a sacrifice of vital Roumanian interests—in 1775 to Austria, in 1812 to Russia. The net result of the series of Russo-Turkish wars between 1769 and 1812 was the dismemberment of the Roumanian lands, and now for two generations still to come, as the decay of Turkey entered upon a fresh and more acute stage, what remained of them was exposed to constant danger from the territorial appetite of both Russia and Austria. Fortunately the Roumanians, though situated at a special point of danger and much coveted, were saved by the very conflict of interests which balanced and checkmated each other in the councils of Europe, and delayed any supreme decision until in the fullness of time they were ready to work out their own fortunes and take advantage of world constellations.

For Roumania, then, it is the treaty of 1812 that marks the end of an era, whereas the Congress of Vienna, which is the great landmark for Western and Central Europe after the long wars, has a merely formal interest, in that it confirms the territorial integrity of the Ottoman Empire. For the moment, indeed, there is no change in the relations between the Porte and the Phanariot princes, or in Russia's right of interference: but it is obvious, even to the most superficial observer, that the prevailing system is nearing its end and that now the least shock is likely to prove fatal to it.

## WALLACHIA AFTER THE PEACE

A very vivid description of the good and evil sides of the situation of those days is contained in an early British Consular report (F.O. 78/103), from which the following extract is quoted.

[1] Wilkinson, *Account of the Principalities of Wallachia and Moldavia*, p. 121.

" ... The so-called necessaries of life—meat, bread and wine—are in such abundance and consequently so cheap (from the exportation, except to Constantinople, and even *that* at a *maximum*, being prohibited), that this year and every year of peace many proprietors have found themselves reduced to the necessity of throwing away whole magazines of damaged corn, which they had preserved for some time in hopes of a war, or such an increase of price as would cover the expense of sending it to market.

"A labouring man would find difficulty in eating a farthing's worth of bread a day, good wine is sold at a halfpenny a bottle, meat in proportion, horses eat only barley and are allowed as much as they desire. The kilo (800 lbs.) of barley is sold in summer for about 2s. 6d. English, a wagon load of hay for a shilling, and delivered and stowed by the seller. This abundance produces upon the characters of the lower classes the necessary concomitants of gluttony, drunkenness, natural indolence and violent sensual appetites. But it renders them healthy, strong, bold, quick of apprehension and (in the intervals of positive corporal pain from the Zabtchis) [Zaptiehs, or Turkish collectors], proud, contented and courteous. A Wallachian peasant (the very poorest) eats regularly four times a day and no Prince in Christendom fares more luxuriously [this is obviously a ridiculous overstatement of his point]. He may consider the whole country at his disposition, he sows and mows hay where he pleases, merely leaving a tenth of the crop for the ground landlord, *whoever he may be*—a fact of which he does not always take the trouble of enquiring. His wife makes his clothes, and he has no other care (and consequently no other incitement to labour) than the repeated demands of the Zabtchi (collector of taxes, an officer of the Izpravnik or Governor of the Province). This functionary is always attended by Albanians, armed with pistols, musquets, sabres, daggers and particularly whips of an appalling consistency. The genuine Wallach scarcely ever pays a para without having previously submitted to as many blows as his posteriors can endure.

"He has as natural an antipathy against the payment of taxes as the Englishman, Scotchman or Irishman, but being unable to call meetings of his brethren, to appeal, remonstrate, menace or rebel, he seems to have listened to and adopted Mr Benjamin Constant's advice to Frenchmen, the doctrine of passive resistance, but invariably finishes as the French have done, by paying not only the original demand, but the Albanians for administering and the Zabtchi for superintending the punishment."

The remedies which the writer envisages for the parlous state of affairs were, first and foremost that the Prince should reign for life, and then (i) the reduction of fastdays and festivals (which he gives at 240 in the year!); (ii) reduction in "the immoderate number of priests and monks"; (iii) resumption of church lands for the use of the state; (iv) a law against "donations and legacies in mortmain"; (v) "free commerce upon payment of moderate duties, permission to export the immense (and actually useless and valueless) forests of timber, to Russia and the Crimea (where none is to be had), to export corn, hemp, flax, wine, horses, bullocks, sheep and swine into Germany or through the Bosphorus into the Mediterranean".

# CHAPTER VII

# TRANSYLVANIA UNDER HABSBURG RULE
## (1699—1792)

"Est natio Valachica omnium in Transylvania antiquissima.... Omnis moderna tristis Valachorum sors non legibus, sed injuriae temporum debetur."

"Supplex Libellus Valachorum" (1791).

While the two Roumanian Principalities were subjected to the humiliations of the Phanariot regime, the neighbouring Principality of Transylvania, whose destinies for a century and a half had been intimately interwoven with theirs, fell upon quieter times under Habsburg rule and remained as a peaceful political backwater till the middle of the nineteenth century.

Transylvania's retention of her autonomy was by no means due to scrupulous observance of pledges by the court of Vienna. Indeed, at the beginning, it was expressly planned as essential to the renewed designs of Leopold I at the turn of the century against the Hungarian constitution and in particular against the position of the Protestants in Hungary. In this he worked in close conjunction with the powerful Cardinal Kollonics of Esztergom, to whom has been attributed the much challenged phrase, "faciam Hungariam captivam, postea mendicam, deinde catholicam".[1] The acute discontent aroused by this policy —a practical example of which was the reoccupation of the Protestant churches in the north and the prohibition of Protestantism altogether in the districts recovered from the Turks—was increased by extremely heavy taxation and by the economic miseries resulting from the long wars. All this combined to produce the famous rebellion of Francis Rákóczy—the so-called "Kurucz Wars" of 1703–11. Aided by the complications of the general war in Europe, actively encouraged by Louis XIV and at one time by Peter the Great, Rákóczy convoked the Estates, was unanimously elected prince of Transylvania by them, and succeeded in overrunning the greater part of Slovakia. The high-water mark of his success was the Diet of Ónod, which in 1707 committed the

[1] Fessler, *Gesch. von Ungarn*, IV, p. 517—generally attributed to Emperor Ferdinand II.

tactical blunder of deposing the house of Habsburg, thus serving as a precedent for Kossuth in 1849 and for Károlyi in 1918. But as his foreign alliances snapped in his hand, his internal position correspondingly decayed, and the Peace of Szatmár in 1711, concluded by Joseph I just before his death and ratified by his successor Charles VI, restored Habsburg rule and steered the ship into calmer waters.

The eighteenth century, then, is for Transylvania a period of reconstruction and convalescence after centuries of storm, and relatively uneventful, since no enemy crosses its borders. It shares the extreme exhaustion felt by all Hungary; a pamphlet issued early in the century depicts her dying at the feet of the emperor, and this may fairly be taken to reflect contemporary feeling.[1] The constitutional position is stereotyped on paper, but in reality "the power of the Court had increased to such an extent that it commanded and had to be obeyed. Transylvania or the individual nation concerned learned of the most far-reaching measures only when they came to be carried out. A paper power had arisen against which they were powerless. A good part of the history of the century consists in law pleas and petitions, in memoranda to the Hofkanzlei and the Gubernium, in complaints addressed to the court. The sword had become blunted, and defence had to take other forms.... Not a general, but a statesman was required by the new epoch".[2] But the Three Nations still occupy the foreground, without a brief description of which the Roumanian background is incomprehensible.

The real control lay in Vienna. The Diet continued to meet, but was increasingly ineffective, doing little more than register the contributions demanded. Its revision and publication of the constitutional code of Transylvania in 1744 did not in the least check illegal interference from above. The "absolute kaiserliche Dominat" was almost unchallenged.[3] Its power of nomination was more and more asserted in open defiance of the right of election of officials, as constitutionally guaranteed. This went hand in hand with an aggressive campaign for the re-Catholicisation of Transylvania. The Catholics, though in so crushing a minority that a single episcopal see had hitherto sufficed for them, were assigned an absolute majority in the Gubernium. In 1716 their bishop was quite properly reinstalled at Alba Iulia (Gyulafehérvár)—now rechristened Karlsburg in honour of the new fortress constructed by Charles VI.[4]

---

[1] F. Teutsch, *Gesch. der sieb. Sachsen*, II, p. 49.
[2] *Ibid.* p. 33.      [3] *Ibid.* p. 131.
[4] Charles III of Hungary.

But at the same time numerous churches were forcibly seized from the Protestants and made over to almost non-existent groups of Catholics, in each case with the aid of the military command. The Jesuits were allowed to return, though expressly excluded by the Leopoldine Diploma, and became very active educationally. In 1731 an attempt was even made to induce the Diet to overthrow the equality of the four Religions[1] and to restore to Catholicism all buildings which it had held before Mohács. But though this aroused such opposition as to be abandoned, the aggressive policy persisted. In 1744 a Catholic convert was appointed to the post of Saxon Count, though the Saxons almost to the last man were Protestants—a double affront to religious sentiments and to the constitutional right of election. Secession from the Catholic Church was made punishable by a flogging of twenty-five strokes on the public square. All this time, side by side with far-reaching designs of Catholicising the Roumanian masses and thereby incidentally swamping both Magyar and Saxon Protestants, the authorities were seriously considering the dissolution of the Union of the Three Nations, the redistribution of Saxon territory and the transference of the Roumanians upon it to a kind of militarised frontier.[2] The Diet was treated with scant ceremony by the governor and the commanding general—twin organs of power—and allowed to feel its importance.

Meanwhile relations between the Magyars and Saxons slowly deteriorated. The noble attitude is well revealed in the words of the governor in the year 1727: "The Saxons must not think themselves the equals of the other nations: if there should be no difference between the noblemen and the townsmen, then I will send my son to Hermannstadt or Kronstadt and let him marry a tailor's daughter".[3] During the century there is a steady growth of the theory that the Saxons were mere "Kammerbauern", a sort of serfs of the crown, or indeed intruders who had usurped a position of equality.[4] At the root of this was not only caste arrogance and racial dislike, but also the meaner motive of envy. The Saxons were relatively the most prosperous of the three, and were looked upon as fair game for an unequal distribution of taxation. The Magyar nobility naturally held the same views on exemption from taxation as their fellows in Hungary proper. In 1762 an attempt was

---

[1] Hermann, *Das alte und neue Kronstadt*, II, p. 245.
[2] See J. Höchsmann, *Studien zur Gesch. Siebenbürgens* (in *Archiv des Ver. für sieb. Landeskunde*, XVI, 1880), pp. 31 sqq.
[3] Teutsch, *op. cit.* II, p. 109.   [4] *Ibid.* p. 53.

even made to extract almost sixty years' arrears of the so-called "Martinszins", from which Joseph I had dispensed them in 1705:[1] and there were constant efforts to undermine Saxon holdings in land, and especially to reduce the standing of those who had settled outside the territory of the "Fundus Regius".[2]

In general, it may be said that the lot of the peasants was made progressively intolerable by the lords, though this was pre-eminently so in the case of the Roumanians. The best that can be said is that Maria Theresa in her Urbarium—the Domesday Book of the Danubian basin in the eighteenth century—did a great deal to clarify the position of the serfs, and that she also placed some restriction upon the stringent punishments still in vogue, which ranged from prison to chains, flogging and often what was in effect torture.

After 1765 there was again an improvement in the position of the Saxons, due to the only Transylvanian of real mark in that drab century, Samuel von Brukenthal, whose name still lives in the museum and library of Hermannstadt. He managed to win the lasting confidence of Maria Theresa, and was at first Chancellor (1765), then Gubernator (1774) of Transylvania, and among other things reorganised the whole system of taxation. Nor was it a mere detail that in 1766 he secured to the Saxon nation the title of "inclyta" instead of "alma" as hitherto.[3] In a country whose whole structure rested on privilege, this was equal to the strengthening or confirmation of status. Meanwhile, it is necessary to note an unexpected decay of trade after the Treaty of Belgrade in 1739, due very largely to the wretched state of the Roumanian Principalities. Saxon commerce declines, and it is from this period that the rise of Greek and Armenian merchants in the Transylvanian towns dates. As a curious indication of the trade situation, in 1771 only twelve out of the thirty-two non-Greek firms in Kronstadt were Saxon, the remainder being Roumanian and Bulgarian.[4]

Joseph II visited Transylvania during his mother's lifetime, and is very severe in his criticisms alike of the efficiency of the executive, of prevailing standards of justice, of the attitude of the nobility to the serfs and of the utter distrust between Magyars and Saxons, who were only agreed upon a single point, namely the repression of the Roumanian element. These unfavourable impressions doubtless strengthened him in his centralist leanings, and were renewed during his second visit in

---

[1] In 1783 this was actually enforced, and was paid off finally in 1823—Teutsch, op. cit. II, p. 126.    [2] Ibid. p. 132.    [3] Ibid. p. 286.    [4] Ibid. p. 139.

1783. The Josephine era lies outside our present scope: it must suffice to say that he tried to bring Transylvania into line with his other dominions by the usual arbitrary, if idealistic and well-intentioned, methods. In 1784 the constitution was abolished by imperial decree, the three privileged nations were dissolved and the whole country was cut up into eleven new counties, on the lines of Hungary proper. The Edict of Tolerance, issued as early as 1781, represented great progress for Hungary and Austria, but it fell quite flat in Transylvania, where all it contained, and a great deal more, had already been enjoyed for two centuries—despite many infringements, and of course with the one ominous exception of the Roumanians. The new regime was resented by all equally, but hit the Saxons hardest, since the Magyar nobles, though hostile to Joseph, took advantage of the change to encroach upon the position both of the Saxon townsmen and peasants and of the Roumanian serfs. But even this advantage was soon swallowed up in the general discontent, and the solitary innovation pleasing to the Saxons, namely the establishment of German as the official language, did more than anything else to rouse Magyar national feeling. The opposition against his reforms swelled from year to year, until the crisis produced by an unsuccessful foreign war forced him, almost upon his death-bed, to issue the Edict of Restitution.

In Transylvania, in particular, the constitutional *status quo* was promptly restored: but the spirits which Joseph had evoked could not be brought to rest again. In the first place, the customs barrier which had till then existed between Transylvania and Hungary was not re-established. Above all, the national question had suddenly become a burning issue. The seat of the Gubernium was transferred from Hermannstadt to Klausenburg (Kolozsvár) and remained there henceforth, because it was Magyar, not German: and the Diet, when it opened in December 1791, at once demanded that minutes of the assembly should in future be kept in the Magyar language. Parallel with this went the Magyar movement for union between Transylvania and Hungary, which now began to be canvassed in both countries, though the time was not yet ripe for action. Its motive force was of course to strengthen the Magyar front against Vienna.

At the Diet of 1791 the constitutional position was completely re-affirmed, and commissions were appointed for the revision of local administration. But the events of the revolutionary and Napoleonic wars affected even Transylvania and absorbed all its surplus energies, and its political life may be said to have slumbered from 1791 till the thirties of last century, and indeed virtually till the great year of revolution, 1848.

It may be useful to give some idea of the Diet on the eve of modern times. It must be remembered that, as in Hungary proper, it was only the year 1848 that brought the first fundamental changes from the medieval system of government: the bureaucratic innovations of the eighteenth century had merely been superimposed upon the old structure: 1848 was the first attempt at a rebuilding. In 1791, then, the Diet had as many as 419 members, but of these 68 were officials, 232 Regalists (persons summoned by the crown), and only 119 elected. Of this total, 384 were nobles and Székels, only 35 were Saxons. Thus the Saxons, who paid 36 per cent. of the taxes, had only 8 per cent of the representation.[1] Till then this was not so serious, because voting was by nations, not by persons: but now the so-called "Kuriatvotum" was abolished, and the sole resource of the Saxons, henceforth hopelessly outnumbered, was an appeal to the distant court of Vienna, which was often hard of hearing. Compare this for one moment with the population figures, and the true situation will become clear. Already a generation earlier under the civil census of 1761, and under the religious census of 1766, the population of Transylvania was composed as follows: Roman Catholic 93,000; Reformed, 140,000; Lutheran, 130,000; Unitarian, 28,000. Thus, speaking very roughly, the Saxon formed little more than one quarter of the total Magyar and German population. But beside them already stood 547,243 Roumanians, who were not merely unrepresented, but on more than one occasion expressly excluded from all right to representation. It is to the history of these helots that we must now turn.[2]

*     *     *     *

The Union with Rome, as accomplished by the Imperial Patent of 1699, seemed to be the death-knell of Orthodoxy among the Rouman-

---

[1] Teutsch, *op. cit.* II, p. 338. Taxation was as follows: Magyar counties, 719,220 gulden; Székel districts, 136,431; Saxon districts, 489,320 or 35 per cent., as against 61 per cent. for Magyars and Székels combined.

[2] In 1733, out of 135,000 taxable families in Transylvania, 85,000 were Roumanian. See Fiedler, *Die Union der Walachen in Siebenbürgen*, p. 351; Müller, *Beiträge zur Verfassungs- und Verwaltungsgeschichte der Deutschen in Ungarn*, p. 16. In 1790 there were 86,630 Saxons and 65,570 Roumanians in the eleven Saxon districts—*ibid.* p. 28.

ians of Transylvania: and the very suspicion with which it was regarded by Magyar and Saxon alike is the best proof of the irresistible attraction which it exercised upon the rank and file of the clergy and through them upon their peasant kinsfolk. The motive force came from the Jesuits who surrounded Leopold I and thought of the Union as a two-edged instrument for simultaneous use against Orthodox and Protestant: Habsburg and Rome were to advance hand in hand towards Byzantium.

For more than half a century, then, the Orthodox Church found itself in a most precarious position, for it had lost the right to elect a bishop of its own, and its connections with Bucarest and Suceava were virtually severed. How slight was the contact between the two sides of the Carpathian watershed is shown by the incident of a certain Orthodox monk named Dositheus Ţirca, who came back claiming to have received episcopal consecration in Wallachia and proceeded to ordain village popes. This was very promptly forbidden by the authorities, and in the end he was induced to accept the union and became Uniate bishop at Munkács among the Ruthenes, the most backward and isolated of all Hungary's subject nationalities. Henceforth there were occasional visits of Orthodox monks, who sought to strengthen the faithful in their resistance, but it was not till 1759 that the Government forbade the endemic persecution of those who refused to enter the union and two years later placed the Roumanian Orthodox under the jurisdiction of the Serbian bishop of Pest.

For some decades the state of the new Church was almost as desolate. The Metropolitan Athanasius was weak and powerless, though he was received and decorated by the emperor and enthroned with considerable pomp. On his death in 1713 the head of the Jesuits in Klausenburg was entrusted with the general supervision of the Church, and there was even some idea of appointing a Hungarian as bishop. In the end the choice fell upon John Pataki, a scholar of fair distinction who had spent some years in Rome: but he remained the merest cipher. He was not allowed to reside at Alba Iulia, where the historic Roumanian Church erected by Michael the Brave was deliberately pulled down, to make way for the new fortress of Karlsburg, named after the Emperor Charles VI: and his residence was transferred to the more remote Făgăraş. This, it must at once be added, had two advantages: it was in the centre of one of the most strongly Roumanian districts, and the former castle and domain of the Apafi princes was placed at his disposal.

The religious schism seemed to have reduced the Roumanian nation to the very depths of helplessness and demoralisation: yet, by one of the very strangest turns of fortune's wheel, the despised Union—the work of alien clerics and political schemers, dependent for its effect upon a premium on apostasy—was to become the main instrument of kindling submerged national feeling, raising the standards of education, encouraging the growth of almost hereditary priestly families, introducing a first breath of Western culture and establishing that link with Rome which was to have so memorable a psychological effect upon the whole nation. How little this corresponded with the intentions of the court is seen from the appointment of an official adviser to the Uniate bishop —bearing the title of "causarum auditor generalis"—who performed a police function rather than a political one, and followed frankly centralising aims. The office was in the hands of the Jesuits and was designed to substitute an Ultramontane for a Calvinist influence among the Roumanian clergy.

When the ineffective Pataki died in 1729, there was an unexpected development. A young and altogether untried man was selected as his successor, almost straight from the seminary, on the assumption that he would be a mere pliant tool of the authorities. But John Innocent Micu—perhaps better known by his germanised name of Klein, especially after the new bishop was raised by Charles VI to the rank of Baron—soon proved to be of resolute will, courage and endurance, consumed by the burning desire to redress the woes of his oppressed nation. His first efforts were devoted to the material welfare of his diocese and clergy, who often lacked almost the bare necessities of life: but almost from the first he besieged the crown with complaints at the inequality from which the Roumanians suffered and the persistence with which the Three Nations withheld from them even the scanty concessions of the Leopoldine Diploma. Great was the annoyance of the Estates when Charles VI appointed a commission to investigate these grievances: and as Klein was from 1733 onwards a member of the Diet, he could not easily be reduced to silence. He also regarded himself as the representative not only of his own Church, but of the whole nation, and, not content with pointing out the many directions in which the Uniate charter still remained a dead letter, skilfully reminded the clericals of the Habsburg court that both Lutheran and Calvinist had the advantage over Catholic in Transylvania, and that the Roumanians, though excluded from the number of the Recognised Nations, far out-

PLATE XI

IOAN INOCENȚIU KLEIN

numbered all three combined, the census of 1733 having returned no less than 85,857 "Wallach" families.[1]

His claims were met with a point-blank refusal from the Diet, which drafted the indignant answer: "The Uniate Bishop and clergy demand things which no one has ever demanded from our ancestors and could not demand from our descendants, things in the highest degree contrary to the ancient privileges and exemptions acquired from our Kings and Princes..., things which do the utmost violence to that noble privilege of which we are the sole guard, which shake and disturb the whole system maintained hitherto in this country, alike in religious affairs and in the political and fiscal sphere—in short, things which it would never be fitting should belong to the Wallach clergy and plebs, in view of their well-known character".[2] The Wallachs in the body politic, it was said, fulfilled the same function as "moths in clothing".[3] Klein was treated by the Diet as "a ridiculous person"; his claims and protests and his bad Latin evoked shouts of laughter: and a competent modern writer could so far assimilate the mentality of those days as to ask, "How could the Jesuits put so incompetent a man in this high post? Nothing is more remarkable than the assurance with which he submitted to mockery and abuse". Nearly two centuries were to pass before the despised and misjudged bishop was to be vindicated by a distinguished cleric of his own faith.

The dispute assumed a more acute form in the Diet of 1737. When the bishop presented a memorial "in his own name, and in that of the whole nation of Wallach name in Transylvania",[4] this first public profession of faith roused storms of abuse on all sides and cries of "There is no Wallach nation, there is only a Wallach plebs".[5] Even the word "gens" was disallowed as applied to the Roumanians. But Klein this time refused to retract a single word. "Our nation", he uncompromisingly declared, "is not inferior to any in Transylvania, either in virtue, in knowledge or in judgment of affairs." He had indeed gone so far that

[1] Bunea, *Episcopul I. I. Klein*, p. 37.
[2] Bunea, *op. cit.* pp. 43–4. Hurmuzaki, *Documente*, xv, pp. 1655–6.
[3] "Das Ungeziffer der Motten in den Kleidern"—see Höchsmann, *Studien zur Gesch. Siebenbürgens*, p. 83.
[4] Suo ac totius nationis per Transilvaniam Valachicae nomine.
[5] The reader is once more reminded of the fundamental distinction in Hungarian constitutional history up to 1848, between the *populus*, or noble class which alone enjoyed political rights, and the *plebs*, which enjoyed the exclusive privilege of paying taxes from which the *populus* was exempt.

retreat was wellnigh impossible. In 1738 the Uniate headquarters were once more transferred, this time to the little market town of Blaj (Balázsfalva), half-way between Alba Iulia and Sibiu (Hermannstadt), which was henceforth to be perhaps the main centre of Roumanian culture in Hungary right on till the liberation. Here his clergy rallied round him in the claim for enforcement of their equality with those of the Latin rite, but at the same time in resistance to the latinising tendencies of their Jesuit advisers.

The accession of Maria Theresa led the bishop to take up the cudgels anew, keeping ever in the forefront of his argument the warning that the union was doomed to failure and collapse, unless the pledges solemnly granted were ere long made a reality. He insisted that the clergy of the Greek rite were entitled to full equality with their Latin fellow clergy; that proper houses and endowments must be provided for them; that they should be free to erect a church in every parish with an Uniate majority, even if a Roman Catholic church was already there; that the sons of the clergy must remain free from feudal obligations to the lord, and that Roumanian children must no longer be deliberately prevented from attending school. The last two points are especially significant and show how imperfectly applied the Imperial Diploma still was. But his memorial culminated in the claim that the Uniate Roumanians had a right to the status of a Received Religion, side by side with the other four[1] and should be represented in the Diet by three clergy and three laymen nominated by the bishop.

Maria Theresa was sympathetic, but could not, amid the conflict with Frederick the Great, afford to offend Magyar opinion. The question was again referred to a commission, and again nothing happened. After an interval the impatient Uniate clergy addressed an appeal to the throne, under the pathetic, if barbarously ungrammatical title, "Request, written in blood and humbly kneeling, of the Transylvanian Wallach clergy and nation as united with the true Roman Catholic Church, for most gracious consideration of the unannounced bloody request".[2] In it, and in a later "most humble supplication" of Bishop

---

[1]  See *supra*, p. 110.

[2]  "Blutfliessendes kniefälliges Bitten des mit der wahren römisch-katholischen Kirche vereinigten siebenbürgisch-wallachischen Cleri und Nationis um allergnä-digste Ansehung des invermeldten blutigen Bitten: an die allergnädigste Königin und Frau Frau"—1744—Hurmuzaki, *Fragmente*, II, p. 112.

Klein, Maria Theresa was besought to do for the Uniates what was done even for Jews and heathens, and to put an end to the deliberate policy—contrary alike to "the laws of Christianity, Catholicism, justice and reverence"—of "holding the clergy and nation of the Wallachs in Egyptian bondage under the bloody whip".[1] This was not without effect, and in June 1744 the crown submitted proposals to the Diet, such as would assure equality to the Uniates and at the same time remove all restrictions upon the Catholics of either rite and especially upon the Jesuits. The Uniate Church would thus be added as a fifth Received Religion.

The Diet doubly resented the proposal: for the majority, belonging to the two Protestant sects and to the Unitarians, had a well-grounded distrust of Jesuit activities, while they were firmly opposed to any curtailment of their feudal dues and tithes, even in favour of a limited number of clergy and their families. It therefore sent in a "Supplicatio" of its own "contra Valachos", and meanwhile altered the imperial draft in many respects. When the daring bishop protested on behalf of a people "wounded to the marrow" and accused the Diet of running counter to the wishes of the crown, he was challenged on all sides and forced to withdraw his words. There was a cry, "The Wallachs are mere vagabonds", to which Klein replied, "It cannot be otherwise, since they are bloodily oppressed". "They are only peasants and serfs", said another deputy, but the bishop pointed to the Roumanians of noble race in the district of Făgăraş, and the freemen on Saxon territory. Then came shouts of "They are brigands, they are lazy thieves", to which the bishop retorted, "You cannot wonder, for to the poor you leave nothing but their skins, on which to live. Do the Roumanians not work the salt and iron and gold mines for you, and some you actually dont despoil of their skins also?[2]" His plea that it was unfair to force the Roumanians to contribute to the support of the Protestant clergy while their own priests were in the direst straits, is unanswerable to-day: but to an audience mainly drawn from the landed nobility his arguments were as offensive and unconvincing as his tone. A joint petition of Roman and Greek Catholics, reminding the crown that the Uniates were far more deserving than "the stubborn Arians, Calvinists and Lutherans" and looked for help neither to the patriarch of Con-

[1] Hurmuzaki, *Fragmente*, II, p. 124.
[2] Bunea, *op. cit.* pp. 98–9: Dragomir, *Ist. Desrobirei relig. a Românilor din Ardeal*, p. 133.

stantinople, like the schismatics, nor to England, Holland and Prussia, as the Magyar Protestants notoriously had done in the past, but to Rome and to the imperial house[1]—such tactics only stiffened the Diet still further. The most that it would concede was that noble Roumanians might be allowed henceforth to attach themselves to one or other of the Three Nations (the obvious intention being that they should thus be absorbed): but those of non-noble rank, it laid down, could not be placed on the same footing as the Three Nations or even admitted to membership in one of them.

The bishop's keen sense of injustice outran his discretion: in a letter to the Aulic Chancellory he appears to have complained that they wished to treat him as a court jester (Hofnarr)![2] He was now summoned to Vienna, but not allowed to see the empress until he could prove his "innocence". In his isolation he appears to have feared that he was to be confined in a Graz asylum. Under pretext of a pilgrimage to Maria Zell, he escaped from Vienna, made his way to Rome and appealed to the Pope on behalf of his unhappy flock. But he thereby played straight into the hands of his enemies: for though the Curia was sympathetic, it could not quarrel with Vienna over the obscure Uniates. His memorial to the empress remained unanswered, and meanwhile the authorities ordered all his property to be sequestrated, thereby reducing him to destitution in Rome and forcing him to sell his pectoral cross. He continued to sustain the unequal struggle, and in 1746 issued from exile a ban against the Jesuit vicar-general, Father Balog, and when his own nephew and virtual deputy, Peter Aron, hesitated to act on such orders, he even suspended the latter from office. The Transylvanian Government ordered that Klein should henceforth be ignored by the faithful, and in 1751 there was nothing left but surrender. He abandoned his see and lived on in his Roman exile till 1768. He lived too in the hearts of his people, of both faiths, and for many a year the peasants would greet some preacher with sad cries of "Our Bishop, our Bishop!"[3]

It may seem that this unfamiliar story has been told at undue length: but the valiant bishop's first biographer, the late Canon Bunea, himself a valued worker in the same cause, was fully justified in pleading that it deserved the closest attention, as containing "the germ of a political,

[1] Hurmuzaki, *Fragmente*, III, p. 123.
[2] G. B. Duica, *Procesul Episc. Clain*, p. 9, cit. Bunea, p. 96.
[3] Iorga, *Gesch. des rum. Volkes*, II, p. 217.

religious, cultural and social movement still in process of fulfilment in the life of the Roumanian people".[1]

*     *     *     *

Klein's successor as bishop was his nephew Peter Paul Aron, less impetuous, some would say more time-serving, but a stern ascetic and, though never popular, a faithful and untiring worker in his day both for the Union and for Roumanian nationality. He obtained a papal bull condemning all attempts to promote secessions to the Latin rite: he won the favour of the civil authorities by the strange device of raising a squadron of 130 hussars during the Seven Years' War: he was able to endow the monasteries at Alba Iulia and Blaj, following the Basilian rule; he bought and set up a printing press, and in 1754 opened a seminary at Blaj, from which the best pupils were sent on to the Propaganda in Rome. But he had to face difficult times: for the interregnum before his appointment had produced a dangerous ferment throughout the Church. It was widely rumoured that Klein had left his diocese because he had become convinced that the Union was mistaken and untenable. There was a wave of secession from the Union: many Orthodox crossed into Wallachia, obtained ordination and returned surreptitiously as priests. The powers of the Jesuits caused wide alarm, and the Serbian Orthodox patriarch at Karlowitz, realising that his Church would probably be the next victim of successful proselytism, sent in 1744 the hermit Visarion on a mission of encouragement to the leaderless Orthodox of Transylvania.[2] He was speedily expelled, and an Imperial Patent of October 1746 enjoined on the civil authorities the "urgent duty" of spreading the Union, of watching the frontier to prevent the entry of Orthodox clergy or literature, to imprison those who had sought ordination south of the mountains and to punish any priest who reverted to Orthodoxy.

Despite all handicaps the devotion of the common people to the ancient faith was truly touching: and the latent demand for an Orthodox bishop and freedom of religion slowly became more vocal and was roused by the Uniate example. In 1759 a poor priest named Sofronie acquired a remarkable ascendancy among the peasantry along the south-

[1] Bunea, *op. cit.* p. 271. This book, of which I had failed to obtain a copy, was most kindly presented to me by Monsignor Suciu, Primate of the Roumanian Uniate Church, whose guest I was at Blaj in 1920.

[2] Dragomir, *Ist. Desrobirei*, pp. 137–50.

west frontier and brought many back to Orthodoxy. When arrested by the authorities, he was forcibly released and then guarded and kept in hiding by the peasantry employed in the royal mines of Abrud. For a time they were in virtual revolt and openly declared that "the power of the lords is at an end, it is we who are now the masters". Finally General Buccow was sent to pacify them and win them over to enlistment, and Sofronie was eventually captured by the aid of the soldiers. But it was long ere the repugnance of the Orthodox peasantry could be overcome. In 1763 a petition was addressed in these terms from the district of Bistritz to the Serbian bishop of Buda, Novaković, whom the Government had allowed to make a visit of enquiry—"We are being ruined body and soul, we die without confession or communion, like the beasts, and like sheep without a shepherd. If you will not take pity on us and bring us aid and consolation, we shall not turn back homewards, where arrest and punishment await us, but shall go to other lands, where we can hold peacefully to our religion: for we are firmly resolved to perish rather than accept the Union".[1]

That Vienna came to realise very clearly the dangerous ferment among the masses and the need for concessions, may be gathered—to take but a single instance—from a report addressed by the Chancellor Kaunitz to the empress in October 1758. In this he recognises the risk of "rebellions, emigrations and other evil effects" and at the same time the ingrained love of forcible measures and "the hatred towards all Illyrians" on the part of the Transylvanian authorities. None the less he held that the Orthodox (graeci non-uniti), who numbered several millions, were "a treasure and a true jewel of the august Arch-House", and if only they could be "preserved from oppression and injustice" and "led with discrimination, as a rough and warlike nation should be", would be of great use and value to the state. The appointment of an Orthodox bishop (episcopus exemptus) would promote "religion and the state", and so far from destroying the Union, might in the end promote its interests.[2] Eventually Bishop Novaković was allowed to hold a canonical visitation and to convoke the Orthodox clergy and laity to an assembly at Hermannstadt. An Imperial Patent of 6 November 1762[3] at last provided an organisation for the Orthodox community in Transylvania, though of course there was still no question of equality with

[1] Hurmuzaki, *Fragmente*, III, p. 180. Bunea, *Episcopii Aron şi Novacovici*, p. 210.
[2] Cit. Slavici, *Die Rumänen*, pp. 90–1.
[3] Text in Bunea, *op. cit.* pp. 244–7.

the Uniates, still less of inclusion among the "Received Religions". Thus a minimum of concessions had perforce been made to "this people so stubborn and refractory in religious matters", to use a phrase of Count Bethlen, the Transylvanian Chancellor.[1]

If in the first half of the century ecclesiastical questions played a dominant part in the evolution of the Roumanians of Hungary, in the second the weight lay with social problems. The Roumanians were the chief, though by no means the only, victims of a feudal system of extreme severity. All executive power being in the hands of the nobles, except on the Saxon Königsboden, there was nothing to tone down or moderate the system, or even to check its constant tendency to encroach upon the rights of the freeholders and yeomen, as had already happened among the Székels. On many estates the peasants were held to the Robot from the Monday to the Saturday: where only three days' service was the rule, rainy days were not counted, and other devices increased the burden exacted. The peasant, apart from the labour of his hands, had to pay in kind a tithe on the produce of his fields, and generally a sum in cash according to the acreage in cultivation, while his wife had to spin a certain amount of flax for the lord. He could not under any circumstances own land—"rusticus praeter mercedem laboris nihil plus habet", was the prevailing motto of authority. As he was not recognised as a juridical person, he could not plead in court and had no real redress for illtreatment. His own and his children's backs were always at the mercy of the lash, and lucky was he who escaped with the regulation "five and twenty". The higher nobles had the *ius gladii*, and the lower nobles were still only liable to a fine of 40 gulden for the death of a serf.[2]

The peasants were unarmed and helpless, but the discontent was acute and glimmered below the surface. Towards the middle of the century social and religious unrest combined to tempt many families to escape across the mountains to their kinsmen in Moldavia and Wallachia, carrying with them such livestock and scanty possessions as they could. When the exigencies of the Seven Years' War led the central authorities to recruit among them, there was trouble in more than one district: the situation was anxiously debated by the military authorities, and innovations were made which were to affect very materially the social status of the Roumanian masses.

[1] Hurmuzaki, *Fragmente*, III, p. 171.
[2] *Ibid.* p. 150.

The Military Frontiers, enjoying a peculiar form of military self-government, had been established by the Habsburgs in the sixteenth century for defence against the Turks, and as the imperialists gained ground, had been steadily extended along the Save and Danube. After the final recovery of the Banat three new frontier units, those of Slavonia, the Theiss and the Maros, were established, and now in 1763 Baron Buccow, the general in command of Transylvania, urged that a "Wallach frontier militia" should be organised from the Iron Gates eastwards along the Carpathian border. This was recommended to Vienna with the characteristic argument that the Wallachs, except for a few specially privileged boiars, are "merely tolerated in the country and hence the monarch enjoys unlimited power and prerogative over them".[1] Their enrolment should, however, be limited to the Uniates, as otherwise there might be an awkward exodus of "schismatics" from Saxon territory, to enjoy the benefits of enrolment. This throws an interesting sidelight on a problem which was to grow steadily more acute for a whole century to come. For even at this period the Roumanians were far more prolific than the Saxons, who were therefore bent at all costs on withholding from them equal rights in the mixed villages and sometimes resorted to such drastic measures as eviction or the burning of houses.[2]

At the same time two regiments of infantry and one of hussars were set up among the Székels, and nothing illustrates better the difference of status between Roumanian and Magyar than the different way in which the innovation was received by them. For while the Roumanians eagerly enrolled themselves, the Székels protested and it came to serious incidents, in which a large unarmed deputation of peasants was fired upon by the military, the village of Mádéfalva partially burnt down and various repressive measures adopted.

For nearly two decades after this the fire smouldered unnoticed by the ruling class, in whose vocabulary the word "progress" found no place: but it is not too much to say that while the condition of the peasantry everywhere was deplorable, it was nowhere more so than among the Roumanians of Transylvania (and to be more exact, worst in the Magyar counties, sufficiently bad in the Székel districts, and much less so, though still most unsatisfactory, on Saxon territory). This did not escape the piercing eye of Joseph II, who during his visit to the

---

[1] Friedenfels, *Bedeus von Scharberg*, I, pp. 360–73.
[2] Iorga, *Hist. des Roum. de Trans.* II, p. 169. Teutsch, *op. cit.* II, pp. 164–9.

Banat in 1768 was horrified at the backwardness of the Roumanian and Serbian population, and, learning that things were much worse in Transylvania, was anxious to see for himself. His visit in 1773, in which he received 19,000 petitions and listened to all and sundry on every conceivable point of detail, became almost legendary in the memory of the masses, and it soon became obvious that he leaned more to them than to the nobility. In reporting his impressions to Maria Theresa, he stressed the mutual hostility of Magyar and Saxon (both being almost equally to blame), and the fact that they only agreed on one point, the oppression of the Wallachs. His heart bled at the denial of justice to the poor. Already at this date he would have liked to see the old constitution drastically reformed, Transylvania united with the Eastern Hungarian counties and the Banat, and Grosswardein made the capital: national feuds would be ended by mixing the nations with one another! But his mother chose the milder alternative of appointing new and more efficient men, notably that able Saxon bureaucrat Baron Brukenthal as governor.

Joseph's accession to undivided power on his mother's death in 1780 marks a new era throughout his dominions: and nowhere did his reforming zeal produce so great a ferment as in the backward province of Transylvania. To the Roumanians in particular he was already a shadowy, all-powerful figure: during his royal progresses it was the usual practice to kneel as his carriage passed, and in common parlance the Imperial Majesty and the Deity were treated with equal respect. All that the down-trodden peasant could see in his far-reaching centralist reforms was their tendency to undermine ancient political privilege and the existing social order. His earliest action in Transylvania—the introduction of "Concivilität" or equality of citizenship for all inhabitants of the Königsboden (1791)—was in itself sufficiently exciting: till then the Roumanians there had not only had no citizenship, but were excluded from the guilds.[1] Another measure that closely affected the peasant was the abolition of torture or flogging to extract confession— in the teeth of the Gubernium's plea for its retention "so long as the inhabitants are not more cultivated and moral".[2]

Joseph's second visit to Transylvania in the summer of 1783 was a proof of abiding interest: and under its impression he issued a first

---

[1] Hunfalvy, *Die Rumänen und ihre Ansprüche*, p. 187. F. Teutsch, *op. cit.* II, p. 280.

[2] Schaser, *Denkwürdigkeiten aus d. Leben des Baron Brukenthal*, p. 58.

decree of emancipation (16 August) permitting every serf to marry, practise a trade or dispose of his property without the sanction of his lord, forbidding evictions without legal verdicts or the reimposition of burdens already abolished. This sufficiently illustrates the arbitrary regime with which he had to deal.

The ferment produced by this decree and the passive resistance of the landed class was intensified early in 1784 by Joseph's order for the introduction of military conscription. The belief spread that all who were enrolled would henceforth be free of serfdom and possess their own fields: and the peasants flocked to every garrison town for enrolment, to the anger and alarm of the nobility. For instance, a deputation of ten peasants waited on the commanding officer in Karlsburg to express their eagerness for military service. In August Brukenthal reported to Vienna a tumultuous movement in the villages, and the distribution of mysterious leaflets. In October there came an outburst of elemental fury on the part of the peasants, who found three leaders in Horia (Ion Ursu was his real name), Cloşca and Crişan, capable of voicing the grievances of their class. Horia had been one of those who appealed to Joseph during his recent journey, and in March 1784 had made his way to Vienna and in some still unexplained way obtained an audience with the emperor. A contemporary account, plausible though not fully authenticated, tells how Horia made an impassioned appeal for the emancipation of his nation, and meeting with what he took to be assent, fell at Joseph's feet in gratitude.[1] Whatever really happened, certain it is that Horia's imagination betrayed him, that he returned home convinced of "Imperial backing", and that his friend Cloşca, gathering the peasants at Brad on 28 October, claimed on his behalf to have the emperor's orders to arm, to assemble at Alba Iulia, and to attack all who resisted the abolition of serfdom. It was believed that Horia had received a gilt cross from Joseph's hands, though it does not seem to have materialised. Early in November, then, the movement got out of hand, and thousands of half-armed peasants spread through the Abrud district and along the Mureş valley, plundering and burning. The most dangerous moment was when Horia sent a kind of ultimatum to the fugitives in Déva: the sense of its incoherent Six Points was that there should be no more nobles, that they must give up their land and pay taxes, and that the land should be divided among the peasantry. But Déva held out till the military had control of the situation, and by the

[1] Densuşianu, *Revoluţiunea lŭi Horia*, p. 109.

end of the year the frenzy had died down and the marauders were in prison or back in their villages. There had never been a clear-cut plan or any chance of success: but 230 castles and manors had been sacked, and about 100 nobles murdered, while a few had saved their lives by enforced acceptance of the Orthodox faith. In one case a Magyar pastor was murdered in his own church.[1]

Joseph ordered sharp and speedy repression, but an amnesty for all save the leaders.[2] Horia and Cloşca were broken on the wheel and disembowelled alive in the presence of 2500 peasant delegates from many districts, and their limbs were then stuck on pikes and distributed (28 February 1785): Crişan escaped this fate by suicide. There is a striking difference in the attitude of the authorities towards the two ringleaders; Cloşca, whom they held most responsible for the excesses, receiving twenty blows, but Horia being given the *coup de grâce* at the second stroke.[3] Yet the official verdict distinctly credits him with claiming written authority from the emperor, and Count Kálnoky, high sheriff of an affected district, alleged that Horia "did not shrink from calling himself King of Dacia".[4] And indeed a medal was actually struck (though its origin is unknown) bearing a heart pierced by a dagger, a triple cross and the words "Horia Rex Daciae 1784", and on the reverse a crown with the legend "Nos pro Caesare".

Mystery will always surround the figure of Horia, for all we know of him comes through the medium of his highborn and hidebound enemies. The emperor towers above them all: in writing to Brukenthal to forbid summary executions, he concludes, from the reports that have reached him, that the county officials "have lost all control and see their safety in pike and wheel alone, against no matter whom and how many". To the commissary at the trial, Count Jankovics, he wrote that it concerned him "very closely" (unendlich nahe). "The Wallachs have been hardly treated for long years and could get no remedy for their grievances: the Magyars are highly incensed and believe that their lives and property can only be preserved by the severest treatment towards the whole Wallach nation". Jankovics is to do all in his power to dissuade the nobility from showing "an irreconcilable hatred and revenge" towards the Roumanians.[5] But long before these words became known

---

[1] *Kurze Geschichte der Rebellion in Siebenbürgen* (1785), p. 23.
[2] Densuşianu, *op. cit.* pp. 453, 466.　　　　[3] Schaser, *op. cit.* pp. 62, 83.
[4] F. Szilágyi, *A Hora Világ*, pp. 236, 238.
[5] 13 December 1785—Schaser, *op. cit.* pp. 90-2.

to the world, the name of Joseph had been enshrined in the hearts of the Roumanian peasantry as "our emperor" (Împĕrat), the first ruler since Matthias who had sought justice for the serf.

In the August following the rising Joseph issued a further decree of emancipation for Transylvania, abolishing the hated name of "Jobbagio", declaring the serf to be no longer tied to the soil or to menial positions and free to buy and sell, so long as he gave previous notice to his lord. But to the three ruling nations even this was dwarfed by his suspension of the whole Transylvanian constitution (by decree of 4 July 1784): and though this was enforced, there was deep dissatisfaction and passive resistance, and the emperor's third visit in 1786 did not avail to overcome its delays. With their tragic failure we are not concerned here. It must suffice to remind the reader that by 1790, thanks to the dangers of the home and foreign situation, the whole fabric of reform collapsed, the old feudalism was restored, and Joseph died a broken and disappointed man. Joseph had many faults: he lacked tact and patience, he forgot that Athena springing from the brain of Jove was not the normal process of nature, but he left behind him a legacy of idealism and effort which in other hands than his hidebound nephew's might have placed Austria permanently in the van of all progress in Europe.

None the less, the ideas of revolutionary Paris were now everywhere in the air, and penetrated even to remote Transylvania, kindling Hungary upon their way. It is important to bear in mind that though the Magyar national movement proved much the strongest—naturally enough, in view of its central strategic position, its control of the administration, and the traditional experience of the nobility as a governing class—the awakening came just as early among the non-Magyar races. The first Slovak newspaper was published as early as 1783 in Pressburg; the Serbian National Congress at Temesvár in 1790 was a landmark in the Serbian movement: the Croat delegates at the joint Parliament of 1791 were already putting forward linguistic demands. But all alike were soon out-distanced by the Magyars, who not only made full use of their virtual political monopoly, but also produced during the next generation and a half a rich crop of poetical literature which, owing to the limited appeal of the Magyar language, has never received from Europe the attention which it deserves.

Among the Roumanians also there was a great stirring of the dry bones, but this time the initiative came from above, not from below.

Alarmed at the proposals for the union of Transylvania with Hungary which were now put forward for the first time in the Diet early in 1791, though strongly discouraged by the crown, the two Roumanian bishops, the Orthodox Gerasim Adamovici and the Uniate Ioan Bob, assisted anonymously by Mehesi, a former secretary to the Hofkanzlei, composed a memorial to the crown, bearing the vague signature of "the clergy, nobility and laity of the whole Wallach nation in Transylvania" (clerus nobilitaris civicusque status universae nationis in Transylvania valachicae). In it the claim of the Roumanian nation to be autochthonous, and hence the most ancient inhabitants of Transylvania, to have formerly enjoyed political rights until unjustly dispossessed, and to form by this time the most numerous element in the population, led up logically to the demand for recognition as the fourth nation of the country, side by side with the nobles, Saxons and Székels. Many of its arguments were based on passages from early Magyar chroniclers such as the "Anonymous Notary of King Béla", whom his own compatriots now found it necessary to discredit. It argued that the technical Latin word "admissa" applied to the Roumanian nation was better suited to those other nations who were "admitted" at a much later date than the indigenous population, and it therefore demanded the abolition of such objectionable titles as "admissa", "tolerata", or "non-recepta". Its main claims were for a "restoration" of political and civil rights, equal rights for the clergy and laity of the two Roumanian faiths on the same footing as other nations, a proportionate share in official posts for Roumanians and a reversion to the use of Roumanian place-names in districts which were predominantly Roumanian. Finally it asked for a National Congress in which details could be discussed.

The petition, which lives in history as the "Supplex Libellus Valachorum", marks the adoption of new tactics in the national struggle. It might perhaps have been wiser to lay the main stress on the humanitarian tendencies of the age, the need for reforms and the right of all to their due share in them. But in the sultry atmosphere of those days historic right was the sole argument likely to weigh with the Estates: and so inevitably the Roumanians were driven along the path of proving their ancestral priority or continuity of tenure. Thus began the barren controversy between Magyar and Roumanian savants which was to embitter the relations of the two peoples for three generations.

Leopold II received the petition sympathetically and requested the

Diet to consider it carefully and devise means for helping the Roumanians, especially in the spheres of religious equality and education.
On 21 June it was read aloud amid a deathly silence—"great consternation on all faces", wrote one deputy in his diary.[1] Before the
reading was at an end the fire alarm was rung outside, and many deputies
rushed to the lobbies: but Baron Wesselényi, in a voice of thunder,
bade them stay in their places, "for here in the House is a far bigger fire
to be put out". After long delays the Diet discussed the question fully
on 5 August and in its answer to the crown devoted itself to refuting
point by point the weak historical foundations on which the petition
rested. In the end all that resulted was the passing of a law which conceded "the free exercise of its religion" to the Orthodox Church, *ad
instar reliquorum incolarum*. Even this was better than its original proposal that, as the Uniate Church was associated with the Catholic, so
the Orthodox Church should associate itself with one of the other
Received Religions—which would have meant in practice the reimposition of Protestant control over Orthodoxy, as it had prevailed in
the sixteenth and seventeenth centuries!

The admission of the Roumanians to equality with the Three Nations
or as a Church with the Four Religions was absolutely rejected: and the
argument by which their claims were repelled was that the constitution
rested not on nationality but on nobility[2], and that thus a German, Slav
or Roumanian noble must belong to and form part of the Hungarian
nobility. "The noble of Wallach origin", it was said, "enjoys the same
liberties and privileges as the Hungarian and Székel nobles: the freemen
have the same liberties and duties of taxation, whether they belong to
one nation or another, and in the same way the serfs are subject to the
same obligations and in no way to greater". Of course the fatal flaw
in this was that the vast majority of the Roumanians were in the third
category, and that only a few individuals were affected by concessions
to those of noble birth. Finally, in education the Estates admitted it
to be desirable that "the still rude and uncultured Wallachian nation
should acquire salutary principles regarding the duties of a citizen and
a Christian man and thus become more useful to the Fatherland". But
in their view such recent events as the Horia rising were largely due to
the ignorance and degradation of the clergy, who "are often themselves
authors of crimes". It followed that a scheme for the better education

[1] Zieglauer, *Die politische Reformbewegung in Siebenbürgen*, p. 537.
[2] See *supra*, pp. 21, 52.

of the clergy was greatly needed, but for this they were not prepared to pay, and so nothing more was done for over a generation!

The Diet was active right on into 1792: it even urged on the crown the desirability of acquiring Moldavia and Wallachia, as former Hungarian fiefs, and received a severe snub from Leopold when it asked for a special Transylvanian representative at the Peace of Sistova. But under Francis II the general crisis in Europe took precedence of internal reform, the committees appointed to work out the details slowly petered out for lack of encouragement, and Transylvania may be said to have stagnated from 1792 till 1834.

# CHAPTER VIII

# THE GROWTH OF ROUMANIAN NATIONALITY
## (1812–1848)

"My rigour relents: I pardon something to the spirit of liberty"
EDMUND BURKE.

We have already seen that Roumanian history presents several features which distinguish it from that of any other country in Europe. There is simply no parallel to the mysterious silence which shrouds the Roumanians for the thousand years following the withdrawal of Aurelian and his legions—a period in which there are neither chronicles nor charters nor architectural remains, and which therefore lacks the very basis for reconstructing even the barest outline of history. But even in the opening decades of the nineteenth century Roumanian history contains elements of surprise for which there is no parallel elsewhere. The ignominious Phanariot regime turned a Greek face to the outside world: and to the superficial observer (and how few observers did more than scratch the surface in those days) the two Principalities passed as Greek rather than Roumanian. To such an extent was this the case, that the Greeks themselves—not merely the Phanariot clique in Constantinople, and at Bucarest and Jassy, but also the Greek nationalist groups outside Turkey—nursed the strange illusion that the Principalities were destined to take first place in the coming Byzantine renaissance, and that Bucarest might become the capital of a new Hellenic state, firmly planted between the Danube and the Carpathians.

Thus the Greek Revolution of 1821 is inaugurated in Moldavia and Wallachia by the son of a former hospodar, but ends like one of those dissolving views that are thrown upon the screen. For a moment it is Greek, then the outlines fade and waver and vanish, and suddenly in the twinkling of an eye the Greek is gone and has been replaced at every point by the Roumanian. There are many cases, especially in the Balkans, of national movements passing almost unnoticed—scorned or ignored till the very eve of a decisive explosion: but there is no other example of the leaders of a national revolt so completely misconceiving the nature of their own problem as to address themselves in the first instance to a people which was not only alien in blood, but indifferent and even hostile to all their aims and outlooks.

* * * *

The decade following the Peace of Bucarest, then, is a period of relative calm before an impending change. The two princes who were appointed in 1812, Ion Caragea in Wallachia and Scarlat Callimachi in Moldavia, remain in office for the unusual period of seven years, but they pay the same constant attention to extortion as their predecessors. Caragea in particular is credited with the almost incredible feat of augmenting the taxation eightfold, by such measures as the erection of an *octroi* in every village and the creation of as many as 4000 new boiars. In the end, after squeezing over 90,000,000 piastres out of the unhappy country, he fled ignominiously to Italy, there to enjoy his ill-gotten hoards. Small wonder if a Roumanian proverb spoke of "stealing as in the days of Caragea", and if fifty years later there still survived that other expressive phrase, "the winter of Hângerli, the earthquake of Ypsilanti, the famine of Moruzi, the pestilence of Caragea".[1]

Both Caragea and his colleague on the Moldavian throne were strongly Greek in feeling. They were interested in education, and aspired to establish a university or academy, but it would have been entirely Greek, just as the schools which they founded were Greek and as the civil codes which they issued towards the close of their reigns were modelled on the Byzantine manual of Harmenopoulo and issued in the Greek language.[2] Certain prominent boiars of their courts also favoured close union, not to say fusion, between Greek and Roumanian, as a preparation for the vain dream of a restored Byzantine Empire.

With these sentiments, it is not surprising that Caragea stood in secret relations with the famous revolutionary society "Philike Hetairia". This organisation had its headquarters at Odessa, where many Greeks made their fortune during the French wars through the Black Sea grain trade. It deliberately aimed at "an armed union of all Christians of the Turkish Empire and the triumph of the Cross over the Crescent", and it had ramifications in every part of the peninsula: but its outlook and objectives were very definitely Greek. It was of course helped and encouraged by the growing Philhellene movement in Europe. Here, as elsewhere, local conditions and Western ideas acted and reacted upon

---

[1] P. Eliade, *De l'Influence française sur l'Esprit public en Roumanie*, p. 114.
[2] They were not translated into Roumanian till 1833.

each other: Rhigas, the forerunner of Hellenic liberty, was strongly influenced by French revolutionary literature and composed the national song of the Greeks on the direct model of the Marseillaise. Many prominent Greeks found their way into the Russian service, and looked to Russia as their liberator—notably the Corfiote Capodistrias, who became foreign minister to Tsar Alexander I, Rodofinikin, the first Russian diplomatic agent at Belgrade, and Alexander Ypsilanti, son of the hospodar Constantine, and an aide-de-camp and general enjoying the tsar's special favour.

The Porte appears to have been better informed as to Greek revolutionary activities on Russian soil than was the Russian police itself. In filling the vacant thrones in 1819, it showed a not unjustified nervousness and decided henceforth to restrict candidates both for them and for the post of Dragoman to four of the few Greek families whom it still regarded as reliable—Callimachi, Moruzi and the two branches of the Suţu. Alexander Suţu of Wallachia, feeling that the revolutionary movement was growing beneath his feet, aspired to make a speedy fortune for himself: but he was handicapped by the refusal of the Russian ambassador in Constantinople to sanction his application for leave to levy additional taxes. His suspicious opposition to the Hetairia led to an attempt upon his life in November 1820, and in the following January he was successfully poisoned,[1] only a month before the first outbreak. Meanwhile, by way of contrast, his cousin Michael Suţu, since 1819 hospodar of Moldavia, did all in his power to encourage the movement, which was now assuming a character not altogether dissimilar from that of the Carbonari in Italy. He subsidised it to the amount of 130,000 piastres, promised to keep a possible insurgent army in supplies, wrote to the tsar and to Capodistrias in favour of Greek emancipation and asked to be allowed asylum in Russia in the event of failure. Alexander Ypsilanti, who became head of the Hetairist organisation soon after Suţu's accession, enjoyed a double prestige, as the son of one of the very few reigning princes who was remembered without abhorrence, and as a soldier who was believed to enjoy the tsar's personal confidence and backing, and might therefore become the leader of a successful rising.

Ypsilanti was a man of romantic and unbalanced temperament. Unduly encouraged by the death of Alexander Suţu, and by the double game of Michael, he hoped to carry all before him: and his eventful

[1] Iorga, Gesch. d. rum. Volkes (II, p. 240), treats his death as natural.

passage of the Pruth on 20 February 1821 may quite fairly be regarded as the first act in the Greek revolutionary drama. Indeed, from this moment onwards for a whole century the problem of nationality in the Balkan peninsula was to figure prominently on the international stage, the glamour of the Hellenic tradition kindling a sentimental interest which the earlier Serbian rising could not hope to arouse.

Ypsilanti met with no opposition in Jassy, where his banner was blessed by the Metropolitan Benjamin at the Church of the Three Hierarchs: but he recognised that the real test would be the attitude of Bucarest. But the boiars were suspicious and held aloof, the peasantry was completely indifferent, the commercial class was frightened by a foolish massacre of eighty Turkish merchants perpetrated by the Hetairists at Galaţ. The most serious blow of all was the public disavowal issued by the Russian consul in the name of his Government. Tsar Alexander—that sentimental autocrat, ever vacillating between liberalism and reaction and infected by the vague ideas of Orthodox and Byzantine mysticism—had undoubtedly played with the Greek movement. But at this particular moment his hands were very definitely tied by reasons of high politics: he could not afford to offend his allies in the Holy Alliance, all the more so in view of Castlereagh's increasingly reserved attitude, and eventually at the Congress of Laibach in May 1821 he repudiated all sympathy with the Greeks, even in the Morea.

Ypsilanti's cause was already more than half lost when the tsar expelled him from the Russian army and ordered his consul in Jassy to communicate the patriarch's formal anathema against the rebels. In actual fact, this was made public by the metropolitan of Moldavia, the very prelate who had so recently blessed the invader's banner: and his next step was to head a deputation of boiars to request the hospodar, as an accomplice of the invaders, to leave the country. To this ignominious order Michael Suţu feebly submitted. Ypsilanti's prospects were still further injured by the ill-discipline and excesses of his followers, who were never numerous and were for the most part adventurers playing for their own hand. To-day it is easy enough to see what he does not seem himself to have ever grasped. What ruined him was that to the peasant the Greek was identified with rapine and extortion, while to the boiar he was an intruder and supplanter in the highest offices of state. Both had an additional reason for not attaching themselves to the Greek cause, when they saw that no military help was to be expected from Russia and that they would all too soon be left exposed to Turkish vengeance.

In Moldavia, then, the boiars were frankly hostile, and addressed themselves to the pashas commanding on the frontier for help against Ypsilanti and his "brigands". In Wallachia the movement of hostility to the Greeks was still more marked, and here it found a popular leader in Tudor Vladimirescu, a man of peasant origin but of minor boiar education, who had served as an officer in the Russian army and acquired there a certain amount of culture, but who had also seen something of Kara George during the first Serbian rising and had been infected by the rough notions of equality which prevailed among the Serbian chiefs. It should be added that he too had been connected with the Hetairia, and that in the first instance Iordache (Ypsilanti's chief lieutenant, a man of Albanian origin who had belonged to the princely bodyguard) expected Tudor to be one of his main supports.

From the first there was a certain popular, democratic note in Tudor's pronouncements. "Roumanians, the hour has come to shake off the yoke of the Ciocois[1] and of the Phanar: follow me, and I will put an end to their plundering and restore to you your rights and your national government. No laws can prevent you from returning evil for evil. If a serpent crosses your path, hit it and kill it, for it will probably endanger your life. But the dragons—our ecclesiastical and political chiefs—who have devoured our rights, how long shall we let them suck our blood, how long shall we remain their slaves?"[2] He very soon had Oltenia behind him, and appealed not only against the Greeks, but also against the oppressive rule of the boiars. But he was careful to avoid setting all authority against him: and his proclamations, while telling the people that they were free to pillage "the ill-gotten fortunes of the tyrant boiars", also insisted that there were many patriotic boiars who shared the ideas of the people and who must be spared. He therefore recognised the provisional Government which had been formed in Bucarest and adopted an entirely conciliatory attitude towards it. Indeed his movement, though really quite as much social as political, had the active support of many of the more enlightened boiars and was never confined to one class. His attitude towards the suzerain Power and to foreign Powers followed similar lines of compromise. He denied that his revolution was directed against the Ottoman Empire or the

[1] A hostile nickname for lesser boiar *parvenus*, of mixed Greco-Roumanian blood.
[2] Cit. Mitrany, *The Land and the Peasant*, p. 24.

sultan, but solely against the prevailing tyranny and for better administration: and through the pasha of Vidin he begged the sultan to deliver
the Roumanians from "these wolves". To the Russians he argued that
the movement was inevitable, because the people could no longer endure
the exactions of incompetent alien princes. To the reproaches of the
conservative boiar Nicholas Văcărescu, he replied with these indignant
words: "You pretend that we have risen against our country, and you
treat our action as a crime. But the country is surely the people and not
the horde of its despoilers. What step have I taken against the people?"
Unfortunately it must be added that there was a great lack of discipline
in his ranks, and he was joined by many whose sole aims were plunder
and personal advantage.

While the Turks hesitated to act until they saw how the boiars would
meet so unfamiliar a crisis, Vladimirescu marched on Bucarest and
occupied it without difficulty, the rival party flying across the snow.
The peasants rallied readily enough round the popular figure of
"Domnul Tudor" (or even "Tudor Vodă", as he was beginning to
be called): but he also found a large section of the boiars friendly to
him, notably such men as Constantine Golescu, who has been called
"the first modern Roumanian":[1] and an understanding was speedily
reached between him and the provisional Government. They sent a
memorial to the tsar, justifying his action as rendered necessary by the
exactions of alien rulers, and thus at once giving an anti-Greek turn to
the movement. In the same way they tried to convince the Porte that
their hostility was not directed against the *native* boiars or indeed
against the Porte itself, but only against the alien princes and their clique.

Only ten days after his arrival Ypsilanti and his Greeks also reached
Bucarest (25 March 1821). There was by now so open a conflict of aim
that a clash was inevitable. Ypsilanti wished to throw off the Turkish
yoke and identify the Principalities with the Greek cause, while Vladimirescu, like the Serbs in the early days of their revolt, disclaimed all
idea of enmity to the Porte, but eagerly demanded the ejection of the
Greeks and the establishment of a national Roumanian Government.
An altogether new note is struck in the fetid Phanariot atmosphere: and
we hear an unwonted appeal to "the cause of the people".

Ypsilanti of course regarded Tudor, not altogether without reason
from his own narrow point of view, as a traitor to the Hetairia. When the
two leaders met, violent words passed, and Vladimirescu dismissed all

[1] P. Eliade, *op. cit.* p. 171.

Ypsilanti's rhetoric with the burning phrase, "Greece belongs to the Greeks, but Roumania to the Roumanians".[1] When asked by what right he acted, he rejoined, "By the right which my sword gives me in my own country".[2] In his talk with Iordache, Tudor said, "I have no idea of betraying the Greeks, but their cause is not ours. Let them cross the Danube and fight on their own ground, and I promise that they shall always have an asylum in Wallachia, if things go wrong for them". There is no manner of doubt that he intended to eject Ypsilanti and preferred a direct understanding with the Porte to a revival of the old Phanariot regime. Between two such mentalities there could be no compromise.

On both sides, moreover, there was a lack of discipline among the rank and file, but while Vladimirescu showed severity towards the excesses of his followers—recruited very largely from the Pandurs[3] and frontier guards, with an admixture of broken men from among the peasantry—Ypsilanti made no attempt to restrain his rough levies, but encouraged them to acts of terror. And so it came about that a certain Sava, one of Iordache's Phanariot militia, acting on his chief's orders, managed to seize the person of Tudor, and then after some days' imprisonment, had him murdered in the open street by night. The actual murderer was never punished. The cynicism displayed by Ypsilanti in this affair is a permanent stain on the memory of the first Greek insurgent leader.

On Vladimirescu's death the popular movement at once collapsed in its original form, but events none the less took a turn highly favourable to the Roumanians. The Greek invasion was in any case foredoomed to failure in the principalities, and this was the last straw. Ypsilanti's bands were easily routed and cut to pieces at Drăgăşani, and he himself fled across the Transylvanian frontier, where he was arrested and confined for some years in the fortress of Munkács by orders of Metternich —an incident commemorated by the German Philhellene poet Wilhelm Müller. But his initiative, ill-planned and ill-executed though it was, had none the less been the signal for the real Greek revolution, which now broke out in the Morea and was only to end with the achievement of Greek independence in 1830.

[1] Aricescu, *Ist. Revoluţiei*, i, p. 291; Sturdza, *La Terre Roumaine*, p. 444.
[2] Iorga, *Gesch. d. rum. Volkes*, ii, p. 216.
[3] An ill-armed and only half organised force that had come to replace the "darabanţi".

The situation of the peasantry at this period deserves special emphasis, and may be best summed up in the words of an acute contemporary observer, William Wilkinson, the second British Consul to Wallachia. "There does not perhaps", he wrote in 1820, "exist a people labouring under a greater degree of oppression from the effect of despotic power, and more heavily burdened with impositions and taxes than the peasants of Wallachia and Moldavia, nor any who would bear half their weight with the same patience and seeming resignation. ...The habitual depression of their minds has become a sort of natural stupor and apathy, which renders them equally indifferent to the enjoyments of life and insensible to happiness...."[1] This did not prevent them from instantly responding to the call of a leader who struck the right note, but it left them as a dead and helpless mass as soon as he had been removed.

Even to this day a strange obscurity surrounds the actions and motives of this first popular leader. It is of interest to note the assurances of a group of boiars in a memorandum for the tsar, that "the people, in making Vladimirescu its chief, was not animated by a spirit of revolt, but by a patriotic zeal".[2] Another memorandum for the use of Metternich emphasised "the pitiable state" of the country and assured him that "the Wallachian people, unchained against the Government of the former Greek princes, who have deprived it of the rights and privileges accorded to it by the Porte and were unable to satisfy their insatiable appetite", had accepted "a certain Wladimiresko" as their leader, in order that he should carry its grievances to the Porte.[3] All this goes to confirm the view that Tudor looked in the first instance to Turkey rather than to foreign Powers: and that is why the fiery Maghieru, who seven years later became a volunteer in the Russian army, declined to join him, despite many ideas in common.

The Turks, in their alarm at the Greek movement, and in their desire to separate the Roumanians from the Greeks, thought it wise to grant the principal Roumanian and also Serbian demands, the more so as this left them free to concentrate their attention upon the Morean rising. In fact, the situation was a curious inversion of that which had prevailed in 1714: and the Porte put an end to the Phanariot regime for very much the same motives as had led to its establishment a century earlier.

[1] *An Account of the Principalities of Wallachia and Moldavia*, p. 155.
[2] Hurmuzaki, *Documente*, Suppl. I, i, no. 233 (undated).
[3] *Ibid.* no. 232 (also undated).

Not the least puzzling feature of that regime had been the levity with which the Turks confided in an element so essentially unreliable as the Phanariot. It is only necessary to recite the bare catalogue of those whom they actually executed for treason—Constantine Brâncoveanu in 1714, Ştefan Cantacuzene in 1716, Gregory Ghica in 1777, Gregory Callimachi in 1769, Constantine Hângerli in 1799: and to these may be added Ianache Ypsilanti in 1737, Constantine Ghica, the Chief Dragoman, in 1740; Ianache Suţu, the elder brother of Michael, the first prince of that family, in 1760 and Nicholas Suţu, the Chief Dragoman, in 1769; Stavrachi, the powerful Kapukihaya, in 1765, and Bogdan, the Grand Vestiary, in 1778.[1] But the list might be extended indefinitely, if we added the names of those whose treachery became known, but who were allowed to buy themselves off at a heavy price. Moreover, if we place ourselves at the Turkish point of view, we should expect them to have realised beyond all possibility of challenge that four of the principal international treaties of the period in question were unduly unfavourable to Turkish interests, owing to their reliance on Phanariot mediation. For it was Alexander Mavrocordato who ceded Transylvania at the Treaty of Karlowitz (1699), John Mavrocordato who ceded Oltenia to Austria at Passarowitz (1718), Gregory Ghica who arranged, however reluctantly, the cession of Bukovina in 1775, and Demetrius Moruzi who was mainly responsible for the loss of Bessarabia by the Treaty of Bucarest in 1812. But after all it was the Turks themselves who first set the example of betraying their own most vital interests for money: the Phanariots were merely apt pupils in an unequalled school of perfidy and corruption. Some writers have attempted to tone down the unqualified condemnation of the Phanariots in which most Roumanians of last century indulged. Yet the most that can be said in extenuation is that just as the Phanariots were not the authors of Roumania's degradation, but merely the tools by which it was enforced, so the swift improvement which followed was due, not so much to the eviction of the Phanariots as to the greater autonomy, order and stability achieved, mainly by foreign interference in Turkish affairs.

*    *    *    *

Faced by a decisive change in the attitude of the suzerain Power, the leading boiars showed themselves tactful and conciliatory towards the Porte, in the first instance sending one of their number, the experienced

[1] Cf. Raicevich, *Bemerkungen*, p. 24.

Theodore Balş, to present a memorial to the pasha of Silistria, who was acting as temporary administrator of both provinces. In it, while very firm in their demands, they only asked for what could be conceded without loss of prestige. They claimed compensation for the losses inflicted by the revolution, which was incidentally a way of dissociating themselves from the Greeks: and they also asked that Greeks and Albanians should no longer be allowed to purchase land in the Principalities—a restriction which was not likely to displease the Turks. They asked that the "Dedicated Monasteries" should be restored to the two Governments, who would pay over a yearly allowance to the Greek monks. (This is the first move in a quarrel which was to loom large in Roumanian history for another forty years: its significance lay in the fact that the monasteries, with their great riches, were almost entirely hellenised and thus served as direct obstacles to national culture.) The boiars further asked that the laws should henceforth be in Roumanian, that the diplomatic agents of the two Principalities at Constantinople should henceforth always be Roumanian boiars, instead of being drawn from the Phanariot clique, and above all that each prince should be chosen from the ranks of the native boiars (domnia pămînteană).

When the Russians made reproaches to the Divan for having made its appeal to the sultan, they met with the answer that it had only asked for the fulfilment of the privileges which Russia herself had guaranteed, and made further criticism difficult by appealing for deliverance from the Phanariot yoke.

Meanwhile the Turks were in military occupation of Bucarest and Jassy, and those of Ypsilanti's followers who had not fled were hunted down and massacred. There was now a prolonged struggle at Constantinople between the delegates of the boiars, many of whom had taken refuge at Kronstadt (Braşov) from the Hetairist regime, and Vogorides, the chief Phanariot candidate to the throne. But at last in June 1822 the former induced the Porte to appoint two of their own number as princes—in Wallachia Gregory Ghica and in Moldavia Ioniţa Sturdza. Ghica, it should be explained, was a nephew of the hospodar who had been executed in 1777 for treason with Russia: but quite apart from this the family had long passed as entirely Roumanised and definitely patriotic.

The newcomers found the Principalities in a lamentable state, after the long Phanariot exploitation, aggravated by the ravages of Pasvan Oglu, the requisitions of Russia and latterly the Hetairist invasion: and, as a final spasm of the old regime, the Janissaries quartered in Jassy set fire to the town on 12 August 1822 and burnt down over 2000 houses. The task of reconstruction was not rendered easier by the hostility of certain boiar emigrants whose conservatism was coloured by their desire to place their own candidates upon the throne, and who accused Ion Sturdza's liberal supporters of subversive and carbonarist leanings and hoped by this description to secure Russian support against them. A concrete proposal for constitutional reform had been put before Sturdza, and notably for the creation of a "Sfât obştesc" or Diet, chosen from a narrow circle of boiars and officials, but still elected, and enjoying full legislative and financial powers. Other suggestions related to education, reform of taxation and the exclusion of the Jews from the trades of butcher and distiller.[1]  Narrowly oligarchic as this plan was, and foredoomed from the first to rejection, it deserves to be placed on record as the first spontaneous expression of a new epoch.

The relations of the Porte and Russia were the dominant factor in the situation: and when in 1825 these relations were restored after an interruption of several years, the Russian protectorate once more became a reality.  It is significant that the emigrant boiars owed their return to the Russians and forced Sturdza to recognise the exemption of their whole class from all contributions.

The two princes were very definitely anti-Greek, and set about closing Greek schools, expelling Greek monks and appropriating their revenues: they merely assigned a fixed annual sum to the Greek convents of the East which were the legal owners of so many Roumanian monasteries. They had been selected by the Turks as immune from Russian influence and were therefore unacceptable to the Russians and during these extremely unsettled years of the Greek war and strained relations between St Petersburg and Constantinople, they lived in constant fear of a Russian inroad and felt more than ever dependent upon the Porte.  Russia on her side did not (and indeed did not wish to) make things easier for them, by putting strong pressure upon the Porte for the restitution of the monasteries to Greek hands.

\*          \*          \*          \*

For some years after Ypsilanti's failure Tsar Alexander was held back, mainly by Metternich's influence, from active intervention in the Eastern Question, although he continued to be torn between his fear of revolu-

[1] Iorga, *Gesch. d. rum. Volkes*, II, p. 248.

tion and his sympathy with his co-religionists in the Near East. But such appalling scandals as the execution of the Greek patriarch and the massacre of Chios forced him to break off diplomatic relations with the Porte in August 1822, and though the combined efforts of Vienna and London again held him back from intervention, he began in private to talk of a crusade and to listen to Frau von Krüdener's ecstatic prophecy that he was destined to deliver Jerusalem. After Castlereagh's death there was a gradual change in Britain's Near Eastern policy, and in March 1823 Canning, mainly for reasons of trade policy, recognised the Greeks as belligerents. As Canning slowly evolved on these lines, and as the Philhellene current in Western public opinion deepened, the tsar began to escape from Metternich's control and to weigh the idea of joint Russo-British action on behalf of the Greeks.

In December 1825, however, Alexander died and was succeeded by his brother Nicholas I, who, though the most autocratic of all the tsars and all the more suspicious of revolutionary movements because of the military revolt which ushered in his reign, was also on terms of personal hostility towards Metternich and so for several critical years immune from his influence. To him still more than to his brother the Greeks were mere rebels, but again the defence of Orthodoxy meant even more to him, and he hoped to reduce Turkey to subservience and thus secure an outlet to the Mediterranean. He was determined to put an end to the intolerable position, now entering its fourth year, in which he was neither at war nor at peace with the Porte: and he skilfully exploited Canning's dislike of Metternich and the Duke of Wellington's mission to St Petersburg, in order to present the Porte with an ultimatum (17 March 1826), in which, without alluding directly to the Greeks, he demanded reparation for the execution of the patriarch, but above all based his complaints on the position in the Principalities and in Serbia and the complete failure of the Turks to implement the pledges given fourteen years earlier at Bucarest.

During the summer of 1826 the Porte was reduced to virtual impotence by the grave internal crisis which culminated in Sultan Mahmud's destruction of the Janissaries. While the Turkish military power was thus disorganised, resistance to Russia would have been impossible, and on 6 October he found it necessary to conclude the Convention of Akkerman, which is a fresh landmark both in Serbian and in Roumanian history. By it the status of the Principalities was modified distinctly to Russia's advantage.

The hospodars are henceforth to be elected "among the older and most capable native boiars" by the Divan or Council, though with the Porte's approval. If this approval should be withheld, for reasons accepted as valid by both Turkey and Russia, the boiars must proceed to another election. The reigns of the two princes were henceforth fixed at seven years, and they could only be deposed for definite crimes, and only after the Russian minister had given his Government's express consent. It was laid down that the princes must take due account of the representations of the Russian Government and of its consuls in the two capitals. They were also enjoined to prepare a new "Règlement" or constitution for the better administration of the two states and the removal of obvious abuses. Russia really gained more by this convention than by previous wars: for her right to be consulted regarding changes on the two thrones was now definitely acknowledged, and assured to her a predominant influence at Bucarest and Jassy, such as no other Power could claim.

Even if from the Russian standpoint the main purpose of the Convention was to reaffirm and enforce existing treaty rights which the Turks had so persistently evaded, it remains a most curious feature that the Greek question should have been passed over in entire silence. Tsar Nicholas as yet laid far more stress upon the three vassal states which lay between him and Turkey, and in which he saw the most direct of Russian interests, than upon the Greeks, whom he still regarded as dangerous revolutionaries. But during the next twelve months he did not resist Canning's constant efforts to isolate Austria and to draw France into a Triple Alliance with Britain and Russia. Death prematurely removed Canning from the scene within a month of his successful achievement of this aim through the Treaty of London (6 July 1827): and with him disappeared the one man who could have shaped events, since the tsar was fully content to let them take their course, while the Turks were deaf to all reason and London was for the time being leaderless. Thus it came almost inevitably to the destruction of the Turkish fleet at Navarino (6 October) and the withdrawal of the three ambassadors from Constantinople.

Navarino was the turning point in the Greek revolution, for as a result the Porte lost the command of the sea and the possibility of reinforcing her army in the Morea, and long before the French sent their expeditionary force under Maison the withdrawal of Ibrahim and his Egyptians had become a mere matter of time. Meanwhile Akkerman

had altered the whole perspective of the Roumanian situation and
Russia had secured all that she could wish, without striking a blow.
Her right to be consulted as to any change upon the two thrones now
became a very definite obligation which made of her a virtual dictator,
with powers of veto or unlimited obstruction. Ribeaupierre and
Minciaky, her two consuls in Jassy and Bucarest, now occupied an altogether privileged position, and prestige such as none of their predecessors had enjoyed. The two princes were nervous and almost
powerless: everyone was apprehensively waiting for the outbreak of
hostilities between Turkey and Russia, which would more than ever
decide the fate of their country. In this lull before the storm private
committees in both capitals were engaged in hammering out the draft
of a new constitution, and though they had no authority and nothing
came of their efforts, they were symptomatic of the rapid change in the
political situation and the rebirth of national feeling.

Navarino, the logical result of Canning's progressive co-operation
with Russia and France in the cause of Greece, was followed by a
memorable reversal of British policy under the weak Wellington Cabinet
during the winter of 1827–8. But though this complicated and delayed,
it could not prevent, the final settlement, and quite inevitably the initiative passed once more into the hands of Russia, while France gave her
benevolent backing and under the Philhellenic reactionary Charles X
"held the ring" in Europe, making it impossible for Britain to act without risking a war without allies against a strong coalition. The utter
intransigeance of the Porte made war sooner or later inevitable, and, on
26 April 1828, Russia opened hostilities against it. Needless to say, her
first step was the occupation of the two Principalities.

In view of the recent transformation of the Turkish army the resistance which it offered caused general surprise: the Russians, after
capturing Varna in October, had to go into winter quarters, and it was
not until July 1829 that they effected the crossing of the Balkans, and
held Thrace, and perhaps Constantinople, at their mercy. The Peace of
Adrianople, which Diebitsch dictated on 14 September, with the help
of a Prussian intermediary, showed remarkable moderation on the part
of Tsar Nicholas. For so far from deciding upon the expulsion of
the Turks from Europe, he argued that a weak Turkey, lingering on
for an almost indefinite period, would be far more advantageous to
Russian interests. Hence Constantinople and the Straits were not
interfered with, almost all her Asiatic conquests were restored, and

the main stress was laid upon the reaffirming and stiffening of her existing treaty rights, from Kütchük Kainardji onwards. At the same time the huge indemnity of 10,000,000 ducats was imposed, and the Russian evacuation of Wallachia and Moldavia was made conditional upon its payment: and as it was obviously more than Turkey's shattered finance could hope to meet in the near future, she thereby provided herself with a plausible excuse for indefinite postponement. The Pruth remained the frontier between the two empires, but a portion of the Danubian delta was assigned to Russia, who also obtained freedom of trade on the Black Sea and throughout the sultan's dominions.

Article v reaffirmed the provisions of earlier treaties with regard to the Roumanian provinces, but in reality the special convention which was appended to the main document radically transformed the actual situation there. Henceforward the two hospodars were to be elected, no longer for seven years only, but for life, and the grounds which rendered deposition possible were still further narrowed down, in accordance with the precedent set at Akkerman. The Principalities were to have complete control of all internal affairs, "in consultation with their respective Divans", and in accordance with the treaty rights guaranteed by the Porte. They obtained the right to maintain a "militia" or armed guards for purposes of internal order, and to impose sanitary cordons and other quarantine measures on the Danube. "To ensure inviolability of their territory" the Porte undertook henceforth not to maintain any fortification on the left bank or to allow its Moslem subjects to settle there. The tribute was upheld, but the old practice of supplementary levies and payments in kind—whether grain, sheep or timber—which had opened the door to so many abuses and exactions and invasions, was finally abolished. In 1834 the tribute was fixed at 3,000,000 piastres for the two, two-thirds of this falling upon Wallachia, the larger and richer province. At the same time many of the old Turkish restrictions on trade and industry were swept away, and navigation on the Danube became free.

The Treaty of Adrianople secured to Russia what amounted to a virtual protectorate over the two Principalities, but in the five years that followed she seemed to be entrenching her position still further. While the war had lasted, occupation had brought the customary evils in its train, under the arrogant military sway of Count Pahlen—deportation of boiars and others (and even of the Wallachian metropolitan), wholesale requisitioning of livestock and means of transport, and only too often ruthless exactions and plunder without hope of redress; but, worst of all, the forced labour imposed upon the peasantry and the famine and pestilence which always accompanied an Eastern war.[1] When once peace had been concluded, however, Russian administration became mild and increasingly enlightened. Count Paul Kiselev, to whom the government of both Principalities was entrusted, was a man of high character, broad outlook and marked ability, and indeed rather a French "philosophe" of the school of Voltaire and Diderot than a Russian general entrusted by the least enlightened of all the tsars with the government of a backward conquered province.

Kiselev's rule marks an epoch in Roumanian history. It is the transition from chaos and decay to the first rudiments of ordered and decent government: and there is a decisive change in every sphere of public life. His first steps were to organise an effective sanitary cordon and a medical service, with the object of checking cholera and the other epidemics so chronic in Ottoman territory, and also to reduce the risk of famine by creating granary reserves. He then established a small but efficient native police force and frontier guards under officers trained by the Russians. The old Turkish police which it replaced had depended for its subsistence on a tithe of what it seized from robbers and evildoers, and therefore had an interest in *increasing* rather than diminishing the number of thefts. In future the gendarmerie had fixed pay and regular discipline, and though still oriental in their methods, were at least ostensibly on the side of the law.

Valuable fiscal reforms were also introduced, the old medieval tithes (ruşumători) were abolished and restrictions on the trading class removed or simplified.

Most remarkable of all, however, was the so-called "Règlement Organique", which was due very largely to Kiselev's personal theories and initiative, and which assured to the Roumanians for the first time something which could at all reasonably be described as a constitutional regime, however narrow and imperfect. From July 1829 onwards a preparatory commission discussed reform under the chairmanship of

---

[1] As early as 27 June 1828 E. L. Blutte, British Consul in Bucarest, reported on "the arbitrary, tyrannical and insolent conduct of the Russian authorities here, as well towards the natives, as towards foreigners and their protectors" (F.O. 97/402, Turkey, no. 37). On 12 September he reported that "the resources of the Principalities approach rapidly to a state of exhaustion in consequence of the unmitigated military requisitions, for which no payment whatever is made" (*ibid.* no. 56).

the Consul Minciaky. It is true that it consisted only of boiars, and only four for each Principality, and that even of these only half were chosen by the Divans (in which only the boiar class was represented at all and the reactionary greater boiars possessed a clear majority), the other half being Russian nominees. At the same time all were men of recognised standing and high character, and the two secretaries—Barbu Ştirbei and George Asachi—were to distinguish themselves in later life. Their draft, as modified and approved by Kiselev himself, was in 1830 sent to St Petersburg and there examined by a small mixed commission of Roumanian boiars and Russian officials, under Prince Dashkov. The Divans were then allowed to discuss it, but without much effect upon its final form. It was promulgated in Wallachia in July 1831 and in Moldavia in January 1832.

The main provisions of the Règlement may be briefly summarised. The election of the prince was entrusted to a special Assembly (Adunare) of 150 members, which was of course overwhelmingly boiar in complexion, for only twenty-seven belonged to the trading and middle class and no peasants were included, while the prince could only be chosen from the ranks of the higher boiars. Ordinary legislation was in the hands of a small Assembly (Adunare) in which the higher clergy sat *ex officio*, and thirty members were elected by the highest class of boiars, while nineteen more were elected by the whole boiar class, but only out of their own ranks. In other words, though the vesting of legislative and deliberative powers and of the administration of the country in a native elected body represented an enormous step forward, it must be admitted that this body was an extremely narrow caste which only considered its own class interests and filled the next thirty years with its petty brawling. Indeed the main fact about the whole regime was the deep line of cleavage which it drew between the noble and the peasant class, and its uncompromising insistence upon the boiar's absolute right of exemption from taxation.

From the first there were seeds of trouble between prince and Assembly. The prince lacked the power to dissolve: at best he could prorogue "in case of sedition or grave disorders on the part of the General Assembly" (§ 56), but in that case he had at once to report all the circumstances to the Porte and to the Protecting Power. The Assembly on its side possessed a similar right: if dissatisfied with the prince it could appeal over his head to the two courts, recounting its grievances and such remedies as it might favour. In point of fact, the Assembly was nothing but a narrow, factious little oligarchy under irresistible temptation to intrigue with the Russian consul: and this was undoubtedly part of the Russian calculations. Just as it was the aim of St Petersburg to keep the sultan and his ministers in a state of veiled dependence and to hold at arm's length the influence of all other Powers save Russia, so in the minor sphere of the Principalities it was thought better to leave a more or less nominal Turkish sovereignty but to exercise an indirect but all-pervading control of prince and boiars. This all too obvious ulterior motive in Russian policy in no way diminishes the irony of a situation in which the most rigid and intolerant autocracy of modern times planted and watered the tender nursling of constitutional government in two provinces lying immediately beyond its own borders. It illustrates the curious lack of intercourse across a frontier which was hermetically sealed then as it is again in our own day.

Meanwhile, on the economic side, the Règlement introduced changes of the very first importance affecting the status of the peasantry, and here, to the no small disgust of Kiselev himself, the details were worked out in narrow boiar interests. It is essential to bear in mind that, unfavourable as that status had become in the course of centuries (and incidentally worse in Moldavia than in Muntenia, owing to the stronger influence of the Polish nobles), serfdom had never assumed such extreme forms as under Western feudalism. There had, however, since the days of Michael the Brave, been a persistent effort on the part of the boiars to establish the equivalent of villeinage and to tie the peasant to the land. The partial reforms of Constantine Mavrocordato set certain limits to this process, but for that very reason the boiars henceforth concentrated their efforts on restricting the peasant's traditional but undefined right of cultivating all available land, and on making any concessions in this direction dependent upon an extension of labour days and servitudes. Their growing encroachments were legalised in Moldavia by decrees of 1803 and 1828, the latter under Ioniţa Sturdza, a native, not a Phanariot, prince. In a word, the boiars used the lowest ebb of Turkish and Greek rule to extend their privileges to the utmost, and now in the preliminary drafting of the Règlements they exploited their opportunity still further. The peasant's right to the use of the land was confirmed, but for the first time the boiar was established, no longer as "leader of the village, merely entitled to one-tenth of the harvest", but definitely as proprietor of the land. The peasant holdings, whose size had depended upon the number of cattle in their possession, were now reduced by more than half: and worse still, the number of days of forced service was increased to fifty-six or sixty in the year, fresh obstacles were placed in the way of the peasants moving from one village to another, and (in Moldavia, but not in Muntenia) the free use of wood for fuel was taken away. On the other hand the mass of indirect taxation was swept away, and replaced by a single fixed tax, the *bir*, on every individual peasant, but paid through the village. The net result was that the peasant henceforth knew far better how he stood, escaped from the worst uncertainty and the most arbitrary inflictions of the past, but on the other hand found some of his most fundamental rights seriously curtailed, after having survived the worst period of oppression. Kiselev himself was gravely dissatisfied, drawing certain comparisons with the neighbouring Ukraine, to the disadvantage of the Roumanian provinces, and toned down here and there the worst provisions, though without affecting the general result. He consoled himself for the imperfections of the new regime by arguing that though the masses had now more to pay, they had also more to pay it with, and that their obligations were henceforth fixed, and not fluctuating—"an inestimable advantage due to the new administration".[1] In Dr Mitrany's words: "It is saying a great deal that Europe's most reactionary government should have felt called upon to censure—with little effect—the new agrarian regime which the first autonomous Roumanian assemblies proposed to set up".[2] It is worth adding that this same Kiselev afterwards became Minister of Domains and in 1845 introduced certain Russian reforms which in some respects set a precedent for Tsar Alexander's memorable emancipation in 1861.

What gives such significance to these agrarian changes, is that the process set in motion by the development of the Black Sea grain trade had been greatly accelerated by the Russo-Turkish war, the Treaty of Adrianople, which finally ended the Turkish grain monopoly, and the famine and epidemics which followed. The result was that even between 1831 and 1833 the rent of land doubled and trebled, the price of

---

[1] Kiselev to Nesselrode, 8 March 1832—Zablocki-Desjatovski, *Graf P. D. Kiselev i ego Vremya*, IV, p. 67. In the same despatch he states that the revenues, which in 1828–9 had been 19,700,000 piastres, had already risen to 39,608,765 in 1830–31. The contribution of the Principalities to Russian expenditure was 59,511,000 piastres.

[2] D. Mitrany, *The Land and the Peasant in Roumania*, p. 33. The first hundred pages of this book give an admirable survey. See also I. L. Evans, *The Agrarian Revolution in Roumania* and General Rosetti's classic *Pământul, Ţăranii şi Stăpânii în Moldova*.

wheat rose between 1829 and 1833 from 14 to 219 piastres per "chila", the incentive to extend the area of arable land was irresistible, and the effect on the peasants' stockbreeding was unfavourable, since it meant a rapid shrinking in pasture land. It can at least be said that all this contained within itself the germ of better things: for the unshackling of Roumanian trade and the growing interest of the West in export from the Lower Danube led to a steady rise in standards and inaugurated a new era of security and prosperity as compared with the old arbitrary regime, whose utter uncertainty paralysed all initiative.

With all its limitations, then, the Règlement may be regarded as the seed from which better things were to develop. It is also providential that Russia should have favoured identical treatment for the two Principalities, thus laying the basis for that national unity which was eventually to bring emancipation from all foreign control.

It is quite possible that the new order would never have come into operation but for new developments in the Eastern Question: for there was undoubtedly a party in Russia which favoured, if not annexation, at any rate an occupation so prolonged as to accustom Europe to the final and inevitable step. Kiselev shared this view, which he had learned from Marshal Diebitsch. The arguments which he presented for the consideration of Nesselrode and the tsar were those commonly known as "the thin end of the wedge". Occupation should be maintained till the Turks had paid the uttermost farthing, or alternately "one would have in the possession of these provinces a compensation which after ten years of occupation would perhaps not be contested by an Europe which had grown accustomed to seeing Russia there....If it be objected that the aim of Russian policy is not that of territorial extension, I reply that the march of events is stronger than any foresight, and that Russia has not marched for more than a century from the banks of the Dnieper, merely to stop upon the banks of the Pruth".[1] In later despatches Kiselev moderated his tone and urged bringing home to the Porte the view that a Russian alliance was alone possible—with military help as a substitute for the promised indemnity, and a permanent protectorate over the Principalities as the outcome. The Black Sea, he argued, must sooner or later become a Russian lake.[2]

Kiselev's views undoubtedly carried great weight at St Petersburg, and indeed Nesselrode told him quite explicitly that he was to com-

[1] 19 February 1832—Zablocki-Desjatovski, *op. cit.* IV, p. 65.
[2] 21 April 1832 and 17 May 1833—*ibid.* pp. 77, 105.

mand "the expedition destined to save the Ottoman Empire".[1] But in the end Tsar Nicholas once more, as at Adrianople in 1829, decided against the partition of Turkey. Seeing that Sultan Mahmud was in the extremity of danger from his over-powerful vassal Mehemet Ali of Egypt, he had the ingenious idea of simultaneously posing as the sultan's protector before Europe, strengthening his renewed alliance with Austria, keeping the Western Powers at arm's length and converting the Black Sea into a *mare clausum* and Turkey into a virtual dependency of Russia. All this he achieved by the Treaty of Unkiar Skelessi (8 July 1833) and in September he entrenched himself still further by an agreement with Austria at Münchengrätz, amounting to a self-denying ordinance against Turkey, coupled with a pledge of close co-operation and parallel action in case of need.

The result was a *détente* in the Eastern Question for the remainder of the thirties: and there followed logically from it the liquidation of the questions still standing open from Adrianople. This was effected by the Convention of St Petersburg (29 January 1834), which provided for the evacuation of Russian troops within two months, fixed the tribute at 3,000,000 piastres, committed Turkey to a public recognition of the Règlement Organique and accepted Russia as spokesman on behalf of the Principalities.

Finally, it was agreed between the two Powers that "for this once only" the new prince should be nominated by mutual consent, the elective provision of the Règlement being postponed till the next occasion.

The princes who owed their selection to this bargain were Alexander Ghica for Wallachia and Michael Sturdza for Moldavia; and though the length of their reigns—eight and fifteen years respectively—in itself shows the growth in political stability, the manner of their appointment and their dependence on the Russian consuls placed them in a weak and humiliating position. Alexander Ghica in particular, the eighth and last of that family to occupy either throne,[2] vain, ineffective, inordin-

---

[1] *Op. cit.* p. 105. For a time there was a rumour of his being made hospodar (F.O. 97/403, no. 19—Blutte's report of 13 June 1831).

[2] He was a brother of Gregory IV, prince of Wallachia 1822–8. George Ghica had reigned in Wallachia in 1659–60, his son Gregory I in Wallachia 1660–4 and 1672–4: the latter's grandson Gregory II in 1733–5 and 1748–52, and Gregory's two sons Matthew and Scarlat thrice between 1752 and 1766, and finally Scarlat's son Alexander from 1766 to 1768. A cousin, Gregory III Alexander reigned from 1764–7 and 1774–7 in Moldavia. His two nephews were Gregory IV (1822–8) and Alexander (1834–42).

ately fond of uniforms and ceremonial, found himself the butt of constant interference from the masterful Baron Ruckman, who had most of the greater boiars on his side. Jealous, intriguing, often themselves aspiring to the throne, they transmitted their memoranda to the tsar, forced the prince to dismiss certain of his ministers or imposed upon him mere Russian nominees.

Meanwhile the first germ of a national opposition began to take shape: it as yet consisted only of boiars, more and more of whom, however, were being infected by Western ideas, thanks on the one hand to the practice of sending young men to study in Paris, and on the other to the new literary movement, to which we shall have to turn. This little group first came into prominence as critics of the Règlement itself and of its twin pillars of Russian interference and princely subservience. Already under the Russian occupation Ion Văcărescu had been confined to a monastery for his refusal to recognise the new assembly as legal: and two other big boiars, Brâncoveanu and Crețulescu, had at least gone so far as to refuse their signatures to a memorial to the tsar.[1] Egged on by the Russian consul, Ghica now rebuked the Assembly for its factious and insulting attitude, and met its unconciliatory retorts by ordering new elections in 1837. For the first time in Roumanian history, an opposition was returned to power: and though it was as yet quite impotent, it was at least the herald of a new era.

In this connection it is perhaps worth mentioning that R. G. Colquhoun, the new British consul at Bucarest—who twenty years later was to become Lord Stratford's willing agent in opposing union—reported as follows to Lord Ponsonby: "It appears beyond a doubt that the desire of the whole people is for a foreign Prince, one neither Russian nor Greek: and they are anxious for the union of the two provinces under one Prince."[2] But opinion was as yet hardly vocal.

Ruckmann now demanded that the Assembly should accept an additional article to the Règlement, rendering any change inoperative save by consent of the two courts. This he contended had been inadvertently omitted in the first instance. But the real explanation was his sense of the growth of national sentiment and his desire to keep it in check. The Assembly continued in its refractory mood and indicated its belief that the original text had been tampered with. Ruckman compelled Ghica to obtain from the Porte a firman for fresh dissolution,

[1] F.O. 97/403, no. 18—3 June 1831, report of Blutte.
[2] F.O. 98/195, no. 20—4 December 1835.

though this was a clear violation of the Règlement: and though the Assembly did not stand up to prince and consul combined, there was now a permanent, if latent, conflict. Other examples of the consul's intolerable attitude were his share in the dismissal of Vaillant, the French liberal director of the College of St Sava, and in the withdrawal of a subsidy from the new National Theatre.

By 1841 the position of the prince was growing steadily untenable, and a number of prominent boiars, led by his own cousin Ion Ghica, actually sounded Michael Sturdza as to a union of the two crowns—a suggestion that he was too bent on maintaining good relations with Russia to entertain. In the end Ghica found himself without real support from any quarter: he had from the first antagonised the nationalists, without winning either Russians or Turks, so that in the end suzerain and protector found it convenient to listen to the renewed complaints of the Assembly, and after a joint enquiry that was a foregone conclusion, to proclaim his deposition on 7 October 1842.

His successor was a younger, abler and more energetic man, George Bibescu, who came of one of the wealthiest and most influential, though not one of the oldest, Wallachian boiar families and could claim descent from Constantine Brâncoveanu through the female line. He was the first prince to be elected and was successful against a crowd of other candidates.[1] He had been educated in Paris and was already infected by romantic nationalism: on occasion he appeared in the costume of Michael the Brave and later paid a pilgrimage to his tomb. He appointed as Minister of the Interior his brother Barbu, who had taken the name of Ştirbei on inheriting from his mother: and the two embarked upon a new economic policy which would not have been possible a decade earlier.

It was not long before a fresh conflict arose between prince and Assembly, this time over the seemingly petty question of a mining concession to a Russian named Trandafilov. This was unfairly represented as an insidious form of foreign exploitation, which a patriotic Assembly must resist: it was in reality due at least as much to the alarm of the big landlords at a possible curtailment of their own profits. Instead of ordering an impartial enquiry, the Assembly insisted that the concession should be revoked. As a result, the prince perforce refused a concession to a Russian company, and the consul took his revenge

[1] The number is given by Xenopol as thirty-six, but this would seem to be an exaggeration.

by egging on Bibescu to secure a firman of the Porte suspending the Assembly for the remainder of its term.

In the vexed question of the "Dedicated Monasteries" Bibescu did his best to defend the national interests against the Russian consul. These monasteries, whose wealth and standing gave them quite undue importance in the then state of Roumanian society, had been dedicated to the Holy Places and were under the control of Greek and hellenising monks, who drew from them an income estimated at about one-fifth of the total revenue of the state and transferred them bodily abroad, on behalf of entirely alien interests. At last they were forced to consent to a certain administrative control of monastic lands and to pay an annual sum of one million piastres to the state. But Russia, who had consistently sided with the Greek monks throughout the dispute and had reinstated them in 1826, now insisted upon the supervision of her consul in the whole matter: the settlement fell through and a final solution was delayed for nearly a generation.

Perhaps the most notable achievement of Bibescu's reign was the abolition of the customs barrier between Wallachia and Moldavia by the convention of January 1846, and the establishment of that fiscal unity which in modern times has so often paved the way for political unity. Henceforth the name of "The United Principalities" came into formal use, and to the outside world they had a common frontier. At the same time the right of citizenship in Wallachia was thrown open to all Moldavian citizens who settled there, on a mere petition to the prince. The credit and initiative for this momentous change must of course be assigned equally to Bibescu and to his Moldavian colleague Sturdza.

\*     \*     \*     \*

While such was the evolution of Wallachia in this transitional period, Michael Sturdza reigned uninterruptedly in Moldavia and showed himself to be a man of great ability and ambition, perhaps unduly avaricious, but very open to modern ideas and ready to spend as well as to amass money. It is true that he was completely under Russian influence and had a personal devotion for Tsar Nicholas himself,[1] and that he had

---

[1] It is interesting to note that already in January 1830, when he was the moving spirit of a memorial to the tsar, *in favour of union under a foreign prince*, he approached the British consul Blutte, expressed "unbounded devotion" to Britain and addressed a letter to Lord Heytesbury, whom he knew personally. See F.O. 97/402, Blutte to Cowley, no. 1, 29 January 1830.

perforce to submit to much vexatious interference from Russian official-dom: but he has won his place in history as a not altogether unworthy successor to Kiselev in the sphere of reform and as the first native prince to lift Moldavia from the slough of primitive stagnation and instil modern ideas of government. It is of course obvious that the primary cause of the vast improvements wrought under Sturdza is to be found simply in the fact that Phanariot and Turkish influence was happily at an end, the tribute irrevocably fixed, a surplus attained in the annual budget, export restrictions removed, a growing stimulus provided for extending the area of cultivated land, and above all that for the first time there was a possibility of expending the revenue on public works and educational requirements. But none the less much credit falls to the share of Michael himself, who after being unduly decried as a mere Russian instrument, enjoys a higher reputation to-day than half a century ago. Unfortunately he had two grave defects, which made him deservedly unpopular: his rapacity was unbounded, and enabled him to augment an already very considerable fortune, and he seems to have been almost gratuitously arbitrary in his methods, indulging in petty personal vendettas.[1] None the less, the material improvements which he introduced constitute a very remarkable record. "At this epoch", Ion Ghica reminds us in his memoirs, "there were no chaussées in the country, or bridges over rivers: at the least inundation communications ceased, carts and carriages stopped on the bank, as at a fair, waiting sometimes for a week until the waters fell again." Sturdza—doubtless with the aid of forced labour—built roads in all directions, erected 400 bridges, established a good postal service, and equipped the first real hospitals. He constructed a whole new quarter at the rising Danubian port of Galaţ and protected it by a dyke against floods. He improved the administration of the towns—till his day mere filthy and neglected villages—and reorganised the general administration under more efficient and enterprising prefects or ispravniks. As a practical outcome of this may be mentioned the virtual extirpation of brigandage in the first five years of his reign, a convention with Austria for the extradition of deserters and vagabonds and an improvement of the very primitive prisons. Various measures were directed against usury and the undue exploitation of the peasants. Meanwhile his services in the field of education are hardly open to question. He had already been one of the

[1] See *Mémoires du Prince Nicolas Soutzo*, pp. 111–21, 146, which must however be read with some reserve.

founders of the new gymnasium which was opened in 1828 at the Church of the Three Hierarchs in Jassy: and in 1835, his second year as prince, he founded the Academia Mihăileana at Jassy, which was the germ of the later university, and besides faculties of science and law soon introduced courses of philosophy, mathematics, chemistry, architecture, aesthetics and history. It was here that in 1843 Michael Kogălniceanu, the future statesman of free Roumania, began to lecture on Roumanian history, declaring at the outset as his country all lands inhabited by Roumanians and making a frontal attack on existing social conditions. These, he declared, were "the product of oppression by an ignorant aristocracy, supported by the Porte and by the clergy, over a still more ignorant population of two million souls, whose work is exploited for the benefit of a few privileged families". This course was promptly suppressed by the Government, but historical criticism had made its first modest entry, and the liberal doctrines of Kogălniceanu and others made steady progress and bore fruit in the revolution of 1848 and the ten years' movement for unity.

The higher boiars disliked even the first faint beginnings of popular education and resented the competition of the lower classes. But the schools, at first confined to the boiar class and closed to the peasant, obviously could not exclude the sons of the clergy, and thus the peasants forced their way to education in the second generation. Moreover, the rising standard in the public services led to measures in Wallachia in 1835 and in Moldavia in 1842 restricting public office to those who possessed a diploma of studies, while at the same time the princes were in the habit of granting the title of boiar to many able youths of low birth who had finished their studies. In 1843, with the backing of the Russian consul, an attempt was made in the Moldavian Assembly to have the higher courses at the Jassy Academy suppressed, and after long opposition a majority was secured for this and Sturdza had to give way.

Sturdza, like Ghica and Bibescu in the neighbouring Principality, had much to put up with from successive Russian consuls. In 1838 Besak challenged his dismissal of the Postelnik Catargiu, on the ground of irregularities in office. There was moreover a budget deficit, and the Assembly voted extra taxation: but the consul, who was intriguing with the opposition, demanded that the prince should withhold his sanction, on the ground that this violated the Règlement: and when this was refused, he threatened a rupture. Sturdza met the deficit out of his own private fortune, but lodged formal complaints, not only with Ruckman but also with the Russian Chancellor Nesselrode, against the consul's "inexplicable proceedings".[1] Besak was hereupon recalled, but his successor Kotzebue intrigued still more actively with Sturdza's opponents, and when the prince sought to counter this by coming to terms with his chief enemy Nicholas Canta and making him minister of justice, this in its turn was condemned by the Russians, who thrived on discord, not agreement. In a memorandum addressed by Sturdza to the Imperial Government in 1842, fourteen specific grievances against Kotzebue are mentioned, and he is accused of "open opposition to the Government and animosity to the Prince".[2]

The fear of liberal ideas brought the more reactionary boiars and the Russians together in the discouragement of education—especially after the peasant rising of 1846 just beyond the Galician frontier, which of course frightened the landed class everywhere. The Russians were especially hostile to the strongly nationalist current which had captured most of the younger generation of Roumanians. Their Roman origin and affinities, the doctrine of continuity as strengthening their right to the soil held by remote Latin ancestors, the essential unity of the race despite artificial political frontiers—these three ideas struck deep root and could no longer be eradicated. They rested here and there upon questionable or extravagant theories, but in the main they could not be gainsaid.

It is time to consider more closely the intellectual movement which was at this time transforming the political and social outlook of both Principalities and preparing the way for self-government. A new generation of Roumanians was now rapidly growing up, full of Western ideas and culture, eager to proclaim their kinship with the Latin world. The bas-reliefs of Trajan's column had restored to them their spiritual ancestry and their lost national pride: but in the circumstances of the modern world it was to Paris rather than to Rome that their eyes naturally turned. Even though the glamour of the Napoleonic era began to fade, Paris asserted anew her supremacy in the romantic age of literature and in the social sphere. The practice of sending their sons to be educated in France soon took firm hold among the wealthy boiars: George Bibescu and Barbu Ştirbei, Dimitrie and Radu Golescu, were among the pioneers. But with every year more young men found their way to the

---

[1] Hurmuzaki, *Documente*, Supplement I, iv, no. 119—1 April 1838.
[2] *Ibid.* no. 179.

West, and the French language, literature and social habits became well-nigh universal in the landed and educated class, until in the second half of the century they were in positive danger of eclipsing the native Roumanian products.

Thus a number of gifted young Roumanians who had sat at the feet of Guizot and Victor Cousin, of Michelet and Edgar Quinet, came rapidly to the front in the year of crisis of 1848. But the sympathy was mutual. Quinet through his marriage acquired personal contact with Roumania, Hippolyte Desprez and St Marc Girardin visited the country and published their experiences, and the Roumanian cause aroused equal interest in Lamartine, now at the head of the Second Republic, and in Montalembert, the brilliant exponent of a mildly liberalised Catholicism. The ground had already been prepared by a number of books on the two Principalities—none, it is true, of the front rank, but none the less shedding considerable light upon a hitherto obscure corner of the Latin world.[1]

[1] For instance, Recordon, Salaberry and Laurençon in 1821, Pertusier in 1822, Anagnosti in 1837, Felix Colson (*De l'état présent des Principautés*) in 1839, Thouvenel in 1840, J. A. Vaillant (*La Romanie*, 3 vols) in 1845, Desprez in the *Revue des Deux Mondes* for 1848–9 ("La Moldo-Valachie et le Mouvement Roumain"), Bataillard in the *Revue Indépendante* for 1856, Elias Regnault, *Histoire politique et sociale des Principautés Danubiennes*, 1855, and *Mystères diplomatiques des bords du Danube*. Special mention should be made of the numerous writings and pamphlets of J. H. A. Ubicini.

# CHAPTER IX

# THE MOVEMENT FOR UNITY (1848–1859)

"Virtus Romana Rediviva"
(Motto given by Maria Theresa to Wallach Frontier Regiment)
"Aceştia aceaşĭ Români sunt"—ION BRĂTIANU (1858).

The second quarter of the nineteenth century is for the Roumanian lands a period of transition, of quiet and steady growth, which to the impatient observer may perhaps seem slow and unheroic. Despite the decisive episode of the Russo-Turkish War and the long Russian occupation, it is true to say that there are few sensational events. Yet the changes wrought in these brief decades were tremendous, and by comparison with other periods in the painful history of the Roumanian nation, really very rapid. After the utter degradation and dependence of the Turkish era a new generation required time to grow up, before anything approaching a modern political or constitutional regime could assert itself.

This slow evolution might have been prolonged indefinitely, but for the repercussions of the great year of revolution, 1848, when the sparks struck in the powder magazine of Paris speedily ran across Europe and produced explosions of varying intensity in all the main centres of Germany, Italy, Austria and Hungary. That the February revolution should have instantly affected not only Vienna, Prague, Pressburg, Pest and Zagreb, but even the remote Bucarest and Jassy, is a practical illustration of the extent to which French culture and ideas were infiltrating all classes and breaking down the old isolation of the Principalities. Many of the younger boiars and sons of the new middle class which was beginning to form, were, as we saw, in direct touch with Paris and greeted the apparent triumph of liberal ideas in the West with open and ardent sympathy. In Moldavia Michael Sturdza, despite his undoubted achievements, was isolated and without any real following: but on the other hand the new movement was completely lacking in experienced leaders, the masses were as yet entirely untouched and indifferent, and a further factor in favour of the existing order was that already nearly half the population of Jassy was Jewish, and therefore of course entirely subservient to authority. On 27 March 1848 several thousand persons met at a Jassy hotel and drew up a petition to the prince, which curiously enough laid its main stress upon the stricter enforcement of the Règlement. Michael was urged by the French consul "to take the initiative of reform", but without success. If the boiars pressed him too hard, he said, he would repel them by force, and in case of need would follow Louis Philippe into exile. In a later conversation he quoted with approval the words of the Duke of Orleans, "I prefer to be killed on the Rhine rather than in a gutter of the Rue St Denis".[1] Helped by this uncompromising mentality, he found it possible within a couple of days, by various *ruses*, and in particular by employing his two sons as a sort of decoy, to arrest the chiefs of the movement and either imprison or exile them as guilty of sedition. He then issued a proclamation of his own, vaunting that he had saved his country from the clutches of "a few malicious boiars animated by evil ideas".[2] His opponents had made no real preparations, none dared to put up a serious resistance: the brief comedy was ended without bloodshed, almost before it had begun, and Sturdza, abusing his victory without much scruple, could sleep quietly until the Russians came to his aid a few months later.

Much the most serious criticism of the old regime came from the pen of Michael Kogălniceanu, who issued two pamphlets making a frontal attack upon the prince, the Règlement and the Russian protectorate, and pleading for union with Wallachia. The second of these, "The Wishes of the National Party in Moldavia" was a clear and not really extravagant statement of the revolutionary programme: and indeed "revolutionary" is but a relative and misleading term, when applied to aims common to the whole liberal bourgeoisie of the West. But such views were as yet mere aspirations for the future, and their author found it wise to escape hurriedly across the frontier and to take refuge in Bukovina with Eudoxiu Hurmuzachi, afterwards famous as an historian and collector of sources.

Much more serious was the movement in Wallachia, where a considerable section of the younger generation was strongly infected by liberal ideas from the West, and was from the first hostile to the Règlement and to the clique of big boiars who supported it, mainly from selfish motives of advancement. To the mass of the peasantry political programmes meant but little: their whole aspirations centred in a single

---

[1] *Anul* 1848, I, nos. 36 and 42: Guéroult's reports to Paris.
[2] *Ibid.* I, pp. 180–1. A. A. C. Sturdza, *Règne de Michel Sturdza*, annexe V, no. 59.

word, Land.   None the less there was a section of them who were again ready to respond to such popular leadership as that of "Domnul Tudor": unfortunately in 1848 there was no one cast for such a rôle, though at one moment Colonel Tell and other mediocrities fondly aspired to it.   Not the least remarkable feature in Roumanian history is the fact that it was among the most down-trodden section of the peasantry, the leaderless serfs of Transylvania, that the ideas of nationality and liberty struck firmest root, found clearest expression with but little aid, and in the end triumphed over every obstacle.

On the news from Paris a revolutionary committee was formed in Bucarest, under Constantine Rosetti, Nicholas Golescu, Ion Ghica and others, and it was at first hoped that George Bibescu would be induced to place himself at their head—doubtless in the calculation that he himself belonged rather to the younger generation and had a Parisian upbringing.   His hesitation seems to have been mainly due to the assumption that Russia would intervene to crush the movement, if it proved successful.   Meanwhile a second committee had been formed by Eliade, who had performed great services as a pioneer publicist, but entirely lacked the judgment, restraint and energy necessary for leadership.[1]   The two groups coalesced in May, on the arrival from Paris of the two Brătianu brothers, Ion and Dimitrie, who with Constantine Rosetti were henceforth to dominate Roumanian liberalism and to win the confidence of the new urban and mercantile class.   Others who deserve special mention were the four Golescu, and the two Bălcescu, brothers and Ion Ghica.   Opinion among the leaders was naturally stimulated by the remarkable outburst of Roumanian national feeling in Transylvania, culminating in the meetings on the "Field of Liberty".[2] But there were from the first two contradictory currents, corresponding to the lack of clear directive in foreign policy, or perhaps more accurately, to the fact that the Roumanians had not within living memory been in a position to formulate any policy whatsoever.   Hence, while a "Great Roumania" was probably the ultimate, if vaguely defined, aim of all, the more immediate tactics were necessarily dependent upon the attitude of Turkey, Russia and Austria.   Thus some merely looked to the Porte to promote the union of the two Principalities as a barrier

[1] Regnault, who was in close relations with Eliade, draws in one of his writings a highly unconvincing comparison between Eliade and O'Connell! (*Mystères diplomatiques*, p. 33).

[2] See *infra*, p. 281.

against Russian influence; others dreamt of a Danubian confederation with Serbia and Hungary, possibly under Turkish suzerainty: while, as a conflict opened out between Hungary and Austria, others looked increasingly towards Vienna, especially as they saw their kinsmen in Transylvania espousing the Habsburg cause.

On 9–21 June one group of leaders—Eliade, Tell, Stephen Golescu and Maghieru—met at Izlaz, a village near Corabia and proclaimed a revolutionary programme. The proceedings opened with prayers from a rural altar with lighted candles, and an exceedingly wordy manifesto was read out, couched in high faluting terms. "Roumanian brothers, respect property and persons. Come together *en masse*, arm yourselves, but imitate your brothers in Transylvania. See how they assembled by tens of thousands without causing the least tumult or disorder. Have no fear save the fear of the Lord, and you can then sing without blushing, 'The Lord is with us'. Rise in His name, and the angel of heavenly justice will crush every enemy, will overthrow the rider and his horse, his chariots and arms will be scattered into dust, his projects will be dissipated like smoke. To arms, Roumanians, to the arms of salvation."[1] Coming down to solid earth, they put forward as their principal demands, independence on the basis of the ancient treaties with the Porte; a prince freely elected for five years; equal political rights, a Parliament representing all classes and a responsible ministry; a free press; a national guard; universal education for both sexes; abolition of the death penalty and emancipation of the Jews and the gypsies.[2] Those present took oath upon the Gospel to these demands, and drafted an invitation to the prince to place himself at their head. It was typical of a certain crudity of outlook that their action was postponed for some days in the hope that it would coincide with the entry of Mazzini into Rome and of Ledru-Rollin into Paris.

Meanwhile on the very day of the Izlaz meeting Bibescu decided upon the arrest of some of the leaders in Bucarest itself. But he was fired upon as he drove through the streets (the bullet lodging in one of his epaulettes), lost his nerve, tried to negotiate, and then weakly surrendered. On the 23rd he nominated a revolutionary cabinet under Nicholas Golescu, C. A. Rosetti and N. Bălcescu and signed their draft of a new constitution. The Russian consul, Kotzebue, entered a rude

[1] This was signed by Archpriest Şapca, Eliade, Stephen Golescu, Christian Tell and Pleşoianu. See Eliade, *Mémoires*, p. 79.

[2] *Anul* 1848, I, no. 287: 9 June 1848.

protest and withdrew from Bucarest, and two days later Bibescu, finding himself in a hopelessly equivocal position, retired in his turn across the Transylvanian frontier, leaving the power in the hands of a Provisional Government, presided by the Metropolitan Neofit. The leaders from Izlaz as they advanced to the capital were greeted ecstatically with the phrase, "Hosanna to those who come in the name of the Lord".[1] At the incentive of certain reactionary boiars a sudden *contre-coup* was attempted by Colonels Odobescu and Salomon, whose importance consisted in the fact that they were in control of such regular armed forces as Wallachia as yet possessed, and who were both distinctly Russophil in outlook. They began by putting the whole Government under arrest (18–20 June): but Ion Brătianu promptly roused the populace, which invaded the palace and turned the tables on the colonels: only seven persons lost their lives in the affair.

An almost bloodless revolution had thus been accomplished, and at first sight it might seem as though no excuse existed for foreign intervention. The new Government hastened to emphasise its loyalty to the existing relationship with the Porte, and appealed to the British, French and Austrian Governments for their "interest and mediation in the work of regeneration".[2] But meanwhile the very existence of such a Government was of course highly distasteful to the tsar, who was already watching with grim anxiety the course of revolution in Europe generally, and especially in the Habsburg dominions, and did not desire further complications on the Lower Danube. Kotzebue was most hostile and in his correspondence with the metropolitan, who played a weak double game, referred to "the individuals who at this moment hold the power". There were two currents inside the Government, Eliade favouring a withdrawal to the mountains, Bălcescu and Brătianu advocating armed resistance: and in the panic at the prospect of a Russian invasion, the weaker members fled from the capital, and Neofit thought fit to issue a proclamation treating this as good news and appointing a kaimakamate, or regency, of two big boiars, Theodore Văcărescu and Băleanu. Then once more the populace, led by Brătianu,

---

[1] Cf. Elias Regnault, *Histoire politique et sociale des Principautés* (1855), p. 415. This book—inspired by the more radical exiles—contains the first sympathetic and serious survey of peasant history in a western tongue (pp. 277–321). It culminates in the phrase, "In the hands of the boiars and the monks, la propriété, c'est le vol" (!) —quoting Proudhon's famous words.

[2] Colquhoun to Stratford de Redcliffe, 26 June—cit. East, *Union of Moldavia and Wallachia*, p. 20.

rose and imposed its will: the provisional Government, now composed only of the more radical and courageous elements, resumed control, appointed various commissions to study reforms, and showed its sense of the need for contacts with Europe by sending Maiorescu, Dimitrie Brătianu and Alexander Golescu as its delegates to Frankfurt, Pest and Paris (Ion Ghica had already been sent to Constantinople, to propitiate the Porte). Perhaps its most memorable act was to appoint an equal number of boiars and peasants (36 in all) for a discussion of the land question and to recognise in principle the right of the peasants to the soil. That the whole question was once more shelved, was due not so much to the shortcomings of the commission, as to the rapid and unfavourable march of events. But at least there were most interesting and fruitful discussions which created a very definite precedent.

One peasant declared, "The Règlement encloses the peasant in the property as it were in a town fortified by walls and iron gates, so that we cannot get out....To the boiars who deny serfdom to be slavery, I reply, 'Never was serfdom so oppressive as since the Règlement'.... We cannot even fly, for they illtreat and beat us". One of the most striking speeches was that of another peasant deputy, Father Negru. "If the Ciocoi could have laid his hand on the sun, he would have seized it and sold to the peasant for money the light and the heat of God. Your lands would bring you nothing if we were not there to fill your granaries with produce and your houses with gold and silver. These riches are not the fruit of the work of your arms, they are made by the sweat of our brow, under the blows of your whip and that of your Government. Would you say that you conquered this land by the sword in forgotten centuries? But we, where were we then? Were we not in your ranks...?"

Meanwhile there was a similar divergence of view on most political questions. The more advanced leaders demanded ministerial responsibility, universal suffrage and equal civil rights, full liberty of the press, association and assembly, a more equitable distribution of taxes and the abolition of all feudal dues—in short, a programme thoroughly typical of mid-century liberalism.

The Porte found itself in a somewhat awkward situation, between Russia, who pressed her treaty right to intervene for the restoration of order, and the Roumanians themselves, whose obvious distaste for Russian rule disposed the Turks to humour their vassals, all the more so when Nesselrode abused Wallachia as uncivilised. In the first instance, therefore, it appointed the moderate Suleiman Pasha as commissioner to deal with the Wallachian situation. His demand that the Provisional Government should dissolve and give place to a kaimakamate of three (Locotenenţa Domneasca) was immediately complied with, though this was an ignominious contrast to the recent meeting of protest against the sending of Turkish troops, which had been organised on the "Field of Liberty" outside Bucarest, and a severe rebuff to the deputation which had described the Règlement to him as "the scourge of the country and the humiliation of Turkey". Suleiman now came in person to Bucarest to negotiate further, and found himself greeted along his whole route from the Danube by the acclamations of the peasants. So favourable were his impressions that at an official banquet he drank to the health of Wallachia. He even remarked to a member of the Government, "There is only one thing still wanting—the union of the two Principalities. That would be a stake in the entrails of Russia".[1] But this roused the anger and suspicion of the Russian Government, who accused Suleiman of having been bought and induced the Porte to replace him by Fuad Pasha, who was frankly hostile to the Roumanian cause. On this occasion the advice offered by Stratford de Redcliffe to the Porte, merely "to wait and watch", was outweighed by Russian insistence. Russia on her side was spurred on to action by a double motive—on the one hand the desire to isolate the Hungarian revolution and secure easy means of access through the Transylvanian passes if Austria should require assistance, and on the other hand the growing hostility in Wallachia towards the Règlement and the whole regime instituted by the tsar. A picturesque, but highly characteristic incident occurred on 6–18 September, when a large crowd took possession of a copy of the Règlement from a Government office, placed it upon a funeral car, surrounded by a large train of mock-mourners and solemnly proceeded to burn it in front of the Russian consulate, forcing the time-serving metropolitan to pronounce an anathema upon it. Soon afterwards, Fuad occupied Bucarest with 20,000 Turkish troops and issued a firman describing the revolution as "inspired by the spirit of communism" and based on "principles contrary to the nature of the constitutions of the other provinces of the Ottoman Empire"—a perfectly meaningless phrase.[2] He was accompanied by the Russian General Duhamel, who was deliberately working

[1] Regnault, *Mystères diplomatiques aux bords du Danube*, p. 6.
[2] Eliade, *Mémoires*, p. 322.

to prevent any compromise between the Porte and the nationalists and found in the arrogant Turk a ready instrument. They found in the person of Constantine Cantacuzene a pliant tool, bearing the title of Kaimakam, but lacking equally authority and support. After a brief skirmish the nationalist regime collapsed, and its leaders, who were already rent by dissensions, scattered in all directions. General Maghieru withdrew into Oltenia with such troops as Wallachia possessed and for a time seemed bent upon armed resistance. He made a last appeal to Fuad, not to alienate finally "the attachment of the Roumanians to the Porte" and offered co-operation against "Muscovite intrigues".[1] Maghieru had behind him a record of active service with the Russians against the Turks: but this time the Russians had no use for him, since Duhamel held the feeble and reactionary Fuad in their hands. In the end it was the British consul Colquhoun who succeeded in convincing him that a conflict could only end in disaster. "Wallachia," he wrote, "if it remain on legal ground, preserves the guarantee of its ancient treaties, the guarantee of Europe and of Turkey: if it risks the chances of war, it may be reduced to the position of a conquered country and may lose all right to European mediation."[2] Both Colquhoun and his chief Stratford seem to have expected—and probably hoped for—a collision between Russia and Turkey over the Roumanian question: but in actual fact a working agreement was soon reached for a joint military occupation of both Principalities, and the fact that from the winter of 1848 onwards Russia's attention was absorbed by events in Transylvania left the Turks virtually undisturbed in Bucarest and in the delta of the Danube. The three kaimakams whom Suleiman had approved were now replaced by a single one, Constantine Cantacuzene, a big boiar devoted to the Règlement: and his Government was upheld provisionally by the Turks till the following spring.

On 1 May 1849 a fresh convention was concluded between Turkey and Russia at Balta Liman, by which the political status of the two Principalities was yet again revised in certain important respects. In the first place, it was decided that the princes should again be appointed for seven years only, and no longer for life: and the attitude of the two contracting parties is clearly revealed in the references to the princes as "high functionaries". Secondly, the Assemblies were suppressed as dangerously representative and open to new ideas, and replaced by the

[1] Text in Regnault, *op. cit.* pp. 471–4. Eliade, *op. cit.* p. 355.
[2] Cit. Regnault, p. 476.

so-called "Divans Ad Hoc" (a barbarous official Levantine designation), with extremely limited powers—each in fact being no better than a small aristocratic caucus, nominated by the prince. There was to be a joint occupation by Turkish and Russian troops until the country had been "pacified", and henceforth each Power was to appoint a Commissary at Bucarest and Jassy, to assist the princes with their joint advice, or in other words to control each other's activities and keep Roumania in leading strings.

It only remained to fill the thrones. George Bibescu, after his abdication, had thrown in his hand altogether and left the country: and now Michael Sturdza, who through his discreet Russophil policy had remained in nominal possession of Moldavia throughout the occupation, renounced a throne which neither pride nor a genuine, if narrow, patriotism would allow him to retain as the merest nominee, isolated from all classes. It is true that at the last moment Sturdza seriously weighed a project for the sudden arrest and exile of all the leading Moldavian boiars, and vainly hoped to win the approval of General Duhamel.[1] The two new princes, who were installed on 22 June, were Barbu Ştirbei, a brother of George Bibescu who had assumed the name of his adoptive parents, and in Moldavia Gregory Alexander Ghica, a grandson of the prince who had been executed in 1777. Both were men of some ability and of warm national feeling, and they had the wisdom to play into each other's hands, instead of intriguing against each other as so many of their predecessors. But the circumstances of the time were unfavourable, and they could do little more than wait upon events.

It is obvious that one of the prime factors in the failure of the revolution was Russian intervention. Russia, almost alone of European countries, had avoided an upheaval at home, but for that very reason the tsar was all the more determined to crush the contagion at his doors, especially in Hungary and the Principalities. The share of Polish refugees in the Hungarian movement increased his nervousness and his resentment, while the insistence upon democratic and even republican principles by the Wallachian leaders angered him further. Their doctrinaire views and lack of experience which was their weakest side, was almost at the outset sympathetically summed up by the French consul in Bucarest. "Carried away by generous instincts rather than guided by ripe conviction, still full of the emotions left by an education in our schools or gathered in our books, they ask nothing less than all

[1] Soutzo, *op. cit.* p. 165.

the political liberties so laboriously conquered by France."[1] This it was which made them play straight into the hands of Russian autocracy.

The rapid collapse of the revolution may at first sight seem disappointing, but it is only necessary to compare 1848 with 1821 in order to see how much progress had been made. The first abortive revolution had concentrated its feeble efforts upon the ejection of the Phanariots and had collapsed instantly on the death of its leader. It had successfully ended the old regime, but this had been replaced by a narrow aristocratic regime which the Règlement for a time entrenched still further in power. In 1848, on the other hand, social and political aims fill the foreground: a parliamentary regime and the emancipation of the peasantry fill the forefront of all programmes of reform, though there is still great lack of political experience and much divergence of opinion. But this time there are quite a number of young leaders capable of learning from events: and during the next decade they are very vocal in the West, and successfully prepare the ground for the next stage of development. It is but fair to add that the somewhat ineffective princes of this transitional period were no less keen upon the appeal to foreign opinion.

\*　　　\*　　　\*　　　\*

The position of the two princes was exceedingly irksome, for the Russians did not evacuate until 1851 and the tsar's Government addressed to them direct, rather than to the Porte, its demand for an indemnity to cover the expenses of an occupation which they had neither invited nor desired. Gregory Ghica was on the whole more favourably placed than his neighbour, for there had been far less disturbance in Moldavia, and he was therefore able to utilise the services of many progressives, whereas Ştirbei had no choice but to close the frontiers of Wallachia to all who had taken any part in the Revolution, and consequently found himself dependent on very mediocre advisers. On the other hand Ghica, though a man of very high character and genuinely zealous for reform, was lacking in judgment, unsystematic and incapable of sustained effort, and left his finances in confusion: whereas Ştirbei, by his economies, was able to reduce the public debt very materially during his short reign. This was all the more meritorious because he was not permitted by the Russians to enforce a levy upon the monasteries, whose wealth had grown out of all proportion to the rest

---

[1] *Anul* 1848, I, no. 34, de Nion to Lamartine, 14 March 1848.

of the national resources, but who enjoyed a status of privileged exemption from taxation, yet sent abroad much of their princely revenues.

Despite many such handicaps, both princes worked steadily at a
programme of reforms. Most important of all, in 1851 a new land
law, while increasing the number of days of forced labour for the
peasants from a nominal twelve to twenty-two, none the less really
improved matters by greatly reducing the amount of work required of
them in that period. The old *corvée* for road construction was abolished
altogether and replaced by a sort of capitation charge. It is true that
three-quarters of the burden fell on the peasant and only one-quarter
on the landlord: but still this was the thin end of the wedge, for it was
the first serious attempt to tax the privileged classes, and so had a
significance which only seems trifling to us to-day because the road
which has been travelled since then is such a long and eventful one.
Very real progress was also made in the sphere of education. The
Roumanian language asserted itself finally, and neither the reactionary
group of boiars nor the Russians found it practical to oppose it any
longer. It was characteristic of the changing atmosphere that Kogălniceanu, whose lectures on Roumanian history had been so promptly
suppressed in 1843, was now in 1852 able to publish them in a revised
form, as introduction to his edition of Moldavian Chronicles.

Among other measures for improving the material conditions of the
Principalities, special mention must be made of Ştirbei's attempt to
create the germ of a Wallachian army, and to organise a regular
gendarmerie and frontier guards.

This brief lull of four years was brought to an end by the third of the
four great Eastern crises of the nineteenth century, and its culmination
in the Crimean War. With the complicated diplomacy of the Crimean
War we are not concerned, except to trace a single thread in its very
elaborate pattern—namely its bearing upon the Roumanians. In the
settlement which followed the war, however, and in the further period
of three years during which some of the Congress's decisions were
forcibly adjusted to the hard realities of the situation, the Roumanian
problem occupied a foremost place and at times seemed likely to provoke
a fresh European conflict.

The long struggle between Tsar Nicholas and Turkey, which began
over the question of the Holy Places, was deepened and envenomed by
the bungling of the Menshikov Mission, the arrogance of the tsar, the
hesitations of the British Cabinet, the masterful attitude of Stratford de

Redcliffe as adviser of the Turks, the wavering policy of Austria and Prussia and a number of minor fatalities. The tsar's attitude towards the Roumanian question is revealed in his famous conversations with Sir Hamilton Seymour early in 1853, when he said: "The Principalities are really an independent state under my protection. That might remain as it is". Serbia and Bulgaria, in his view, might quite well be organised on similar lines, while Britain was to be bought off with Egypt and Crete, as her share in the Turkish partition. It is quite clear that these proposals were merely a very rough suggestion, in no way intended as final: for he omitted all reference to Austria's share in the booty. This does not mean that he meant to exclude her, as he unquestionably meant to exclude France (as in 1840), but rather that he took it for granted that Austria's co-operation in the Eastern Question was assured. "When I speak of Russia", he told Seymour, "I also speak of Austria; our Turkish interests are identical." In other words, he assumed that the long tradition of Austro-Russian parallel action, dating from the eighteenth century, reaffirmed at Münchengrätz in 1833, and sealed as it were by the Russian blood which he had so unstintingly poured out for Austria in 1849, was certain to be upheld now that, as he firmly believed, the supreme crisis of Turkey's fate was upon her. The solution would lie in Russia's hands, the fruits of 1774, 1792, 1812, 1826, 1829, 1833 and 1841, were now to be gathered in: fresh territory could be found for Austria in the west of the peninsula, and the main problem was to find suitable compensation for England.

In all this, however, Tsar Nicholas had profoundly miscalculated. The young Francis Joseph showed to the full that ingratitude by which Schwarzenberg had foretold that Austria would surprise the world, and included the Principalities no less than Serbia and Bosnia within the scope of his ambitions: while the statesmen and public opinion of Britain, and no one more than the masterful Palmerston, clung obstinately to the myth of Turkish regeneration and allowed Russia to become a positive obsession. This attitude was greatly strengthened by the ill-fame which Russian repression of Poland and Hungary earned for the tsar, and perhaps less consciously, though none the less effectively, by the growing importance of Levantine, as compared with Baltic, trade.

Fired by the success of the Leiningen mission to Turkey—by which Austria forced the Porte to abandon its coercion of Montenegro— Nicholas sent Prince Menshikov to Constantinople to impose his will. But this clumsy and arrogant emissary aroused resistance where it might quite easily have been avoided, and played straight into the hands of his redoubtable enemy Lord Stratford de Redcliffe, who now returned to his fifth and most famous tenure of the Constantinople embassy. Of the two main questions at issué that of the Holy Places, which had originated the crisis, was solved without much difficulty: but (as Stratford clearly foresaw) this rendered all the more difficult of solution the demand of Russia for a new treaty defining and extending the rights conferred upon her by the treaty of 1774, for the protection of the Orthodox Christians of Turkey. The alliance which Menshikov offered in his master's name, and which, if accepted, would have been equivalent to a renewal of the arrangements of 1833 (by which the Black Sea virtually became a Russian lake) was firmly rejected by the Porte, after its secret terms had first been imparted to the British ambassador: and the tsar's further demand for "moral guarantees" was also evaded by the Turkish Note of 16 June 1853.

It was then that the tsar committed a grave tactical blunder: for not content with issuing a manifesto to his subjects in defence of the Orthodox faith against the "obstinate and blinded" Ottoman Government, he gave orders for the occupation of the two Principalities as a "gage" or guarantee to be held until Turkey complied with his demands. On 2 July his armies crossed the Pruth, bringing with them a proclamation which promised to the inhabitants full respect for their treaty rights and all recent legislation: but at the same time he summoned the two hospodars to break off all relations with their suzerain and to discontinue payment of the tribute. Rather than submit to this dictation, both Ghica and Ştirbei preferred to withdraw across the Hungarian frontier; and the Russian generals Budberg and Sacken proceeded to take over the administration.

As a result of this ill-considered and precipitate action, not merely was a complete deadlock reached between Constantinople and St Petersburg, but the Western Powers were incensed by what they regarded as a clear violation of the Convention of 1841 (which had insisted upon general control by the Concert of Europe) and an attempt to reimpose an exclusive Russian predominance upon the Golden Horn, as in 1774 or 1833. Moreover, it caused acute alarm in Vienna: Francis Joseph had also rejected the tsar's proposal for parallel Austrian action in Serbia and Bosnia and in May had sent Count Gyulai, a high officer of his confidence, on a special mission to dissuade Nicholas from entering Moldavia. Annoyed at such complete disregard of her wishes, Austria none the less filled the summer of 1853 with vain endeavours to find a formula between Turkey and Russia, but the Porte paid closer attention to the parallel negotiations of the ambassadors at Constantinople and was encouraged by Lord Stratford in its unbending attitude. When, then, the Porte summoned Russia to evacuate the Principalities, Nicholas, thinking he had squared Francis Joseph and Frederick William by his recent personal interviews with them, and that he could safely defy the West, left the ultimatum scornfully unanswered and found himself at war with Turkey on the Danube. The first hostilities occurred on Roumanian territory, near Isaccea, during the winter months. The Russians suffered a series of petty reverses and it was not until 23 March 1854 that they succeeded in establishing themselves on the south bank of the Danube. Once more the Roumanians found themselves the victims of their strategic situation.

Public opinion in London and Paris became extremely restive, and the bellicose Palmerston steadily gained the whiphand over his weaker colleagues, Aberdeen, Clarendon and Graham. The correspondence of the Prime Minister, Foreign Secretary and First Lord throughout the critical months abundantly proves that they felt themselves to be slowly "drifting into war" with Russia "just when she is yielding the point in dispute", and backing Turkey "just when she acts contrary to our advice".[1] The Turks were encouraged in their arrogance by the wild language of the British press, by the notorious personal tension between Nicholas and Napoleon, and not least by their initial successes upon the Danube; and, disregarding even Stratford's advice, they sent their highly inefficient fleet to manœuvre in the Black Sea. On 30 November this fleet was surprised in the open roadstead of Sinope by a smaller Russian squadron and almost annihilated. Their reverse, which was a perfectly normal incident of war, due to the Porte's own provocative folly and to superior Russian tactics, was quite absurdly greeted in the West as a "massacre", and was the signal for an outburst of real hysterics in London and Paris. This in turn infuriated the tsar, whose nervous, half mystical moods in the closing years of his life are in marked contrast to the restraint which he had observed towards Turkey for the previous quarter of a century. The despatch of a Franco-British squadron to the Black Sea in the first week of 1854 seemed to him a deliberate insult. When, then, Napoleon suggested that Russia should evacuate Moldavia and Wallachia in return for the withdrawal of these ships, the tsar gave

[1] Clarendon to Herbert, 5 October 1853, *Life of Sidney Herbert*, I, 203.

an abrupt refusal. He remained unmoved by the rupture of diplomatic relations on 4 February and when at the end of the month the French and British presented an ultimatum, giving him two months in which to evacuate the Principalities, he not merely did not deign to reply, but promptly ordered his troops to cross the Danube at Silistria and in the Dobrogea. The result was a definite alliance of the Western Powers against Russia on 10 April, and an Austro-Prussian offensive and defensive alliance on 20 April.

The peculiar and decisive rôle of the Roumanian Principalities in the Crimean War has not received due attention from Western historians. Yet there is no more ironic situation in history than that of two sea-powers of the first rank resolved to do battle with a land colossus, and occupied for the first five months with finding a point at which they could establish contact with their enemy. The cautious neutrality of Prussia, and both her and Austria's reluctance to reopen the Polish Question, ruled out the western front of Russia as the main scene of operations: and now an event occurred which also ruled out the most obvious alternative, namely the Lower Danube, where Russians and Turks were already in conflict. Austria, fortified by her understanding with Berlin, proceeded to a gradual mobilisation of her army and on 3 June invited Russia to evacuate the two Principalities—without, it is true, indicating any fixed date or giving her action the form of an ultimatum. Yet Count Buol's remark to the Russian ambassador, Prince Gortschakov—that Austria did not intend to break the peace, but was not afraid of war—could only have one meaning.

Nicholas was frantic with rage: it was at this period that he coined the characteristic phrase, "The two most foolish Kings of Poland have been Sobieski and I, who saved Austria". But neither he nor his generals could shut their eyes to the patent military fact that Austria threatened the right flank of his armies and might only too well cut his whole communications while he was engaged upon the Danube. The failure of the Russians to reduce the fortress of Silistria had a decisive effect upon the whole war: in the first instance it made retreat at once more galling and more imperative, and at the end of July the tsar began, with extreme reluctance, to evacuate first Wallachia and then Moldavia. No sooner, however, had he taken this step than Austria, on the basis of a secret convention concluded with Turkey on 14 June 1854, proceeded in her turn to a military occupation of all Moldavia and the greater part of Wallachia, the Danubian fortresses of the latter being left in Turkish hands. The effect of this was to interpose a kind of neutral screen between Turks and Russians in the whole region of the Lower Danube and to put an end to any idea of the Western Allies advancing conjointly with the Turks from the delta, in the direction of Odessa. The French and British troops which were already being concentrated round Varna were consequently re-shipped and in September landed in the Crimea, with results too well known to require recapitulation here. It must suffice to emphasise the point that but for Austria's action the war between the Western Powers and Russia would unquestionably have taken place on Roumanian soil and not in the remote Chersonese; and that even as it was, Russia's whole military plans were vitally affected by the need for keeping a strong army of observation on the Galician frontier, to be ready for any surprise which the shifty Francis Joseph and Buol might spring upon her.

Austria's attitude was far from impressive. She did not wish for war, she preferred as her neighbour a weak Turkey rather than an aggrandised Russia: but if Turkey could no longer be saved from collapse, she hoped to supplant Russia in the Principalities, and she conceived it to be the function of the Western Powers to enable her to achieve this without actually going to war. But so difficult a diplomatic achievement was altogether beyond the powers of Buol, whose policy compares most unfavourably with that of Andrássy under analogous circumstances in 1877–8, when Bosnia was secured without a war, and on a mandate of the Great Powers.

It may be argued that Austria, in aspiring to the Principalities and taking advantage of Russia's troubles, was infringing the long-standing "gentleman's agreement" by which the two Powers divided Turkey's European possessions into an eastern and a western sphere of influence, in which their advance was to be parallel and based upon the principle of compensation. This can hardly be gainsaid, and Austria's excuse, if excuse there be, lies in her concern at the growth of Roumanian national feeling. She could not contemplate with indifference the possibility of a second Latin Piedmont springing up on her eastern frontier and becoming a centre of attraction for her own Roumanian subjects. It is not without significance that among the troops of occupation there were certain Wallach frontier regiments, and that the supreme command was entrusted to Austrian generals of Italian nationality, such as Coronini and Marziani. None the less the occupation, though it was efficiently maintained and though it brought a good many material improvements, such as roads, telegraphs, general river dredging, and plans for a railway, was never popular with the inhabitants, despite the predisposition to welcome any alternative to Russian rule. The occupation took place under the clear undertaking that Austria should guarantee the Principalities against attack and should restore them to Turkey at the end of the war.

In August, France, Britain and Austria agreed upon a series of joint demands upon Russia henceforth known as "the Four Points". Russia was asked to renounce all idea of a protectorate over Moldavia, Wallachia or Serbia, to abandon her special position as protector of the Eastern Christians, to accept the freedom of Danubian navigation and to consent to a change in the status of the Straits. The tsar abruptly refused, and for a time it seemed as though Austria, as well as France and Britain, would be involved in war. But the dissensions and vacillation of the Viennese Cabinet turned the scales towards peace. Francis Joseph himself was averse to war, and the military chiefs were afraid of complications in Italy when once they were fully involved in the East. Buol on his side, in his foolish optimism, sought to convince Francis Joseph that the two Principalities were already virtually won, and this without a war: and indeed this remained to the close of the war the main objective of Austrian policy. Alexander Bach on his side was condescendingly interested in the fate of the Roumanians as a whole, and calculated that their union under the Habsburg crown would serve as a useful makeweight against the Magyars. It would effect the further object of checking Russia's land advance southward, securing to Austria the control of the Danube mouths and promoting her trade along the river and into the Black Sea.

The allied armies first landed in September, and the battles of Alma, Balaklava and Inkerman soon followed. But all too soon the war of attrition set in and dragged its weary length through the whole of 1855, amid endless unforeseen difficulties. In all this period Austria continued to balance between the two camps, signing a treaty with the Western Powers on 2 December, but hesitating to implement it, thus leaving Sardinia to step into her place and earning the resentment and distrust of friend and foe alike. Early in March 1855 the death of Tsar Nicholas removed one of the main obstacles to peace, and Francis Joseph felt encouraged to convoke a conference of the Powers at Vienna to consider a possible compromise. It was then that Baron Bourqueney, in the name of France, launched the idea of the union of the two Principalities under a foreign prince: but Lord John Russell reserved his opinion and received instructions from Lord Clarendon to the effect that union was "inexpedient" and that it was better to leave the Porte to nominate the two princes for life. To the French ambassador Clarendon expressed the view that local conditions did not justify union. Meanwhile, it is true, Palmerston expressed to Russell the view that "Austria will want as much watching as Russia".[1]

Thanks very largely to this attitude on the part of England, the question of union lapsed when the negotiations at Vienna ended in a deadlock. The war entered on a new phase, and seemed as far as ever from conclusion, though now France blew colder in proportion as Britain blew hotter. Francis Joseph tried to improve his relations with the new Tsar Alexander II by a partial demobilisation: but without appeasing Russia he merely succeeded in alienating Napoleon III, who, quite apart from Cavour's astute policy of Sardinian intervention, was now turning his thoughts more and more towards the liberation of Italy. By the end of 1855 it was France, not Austria, that had found a possible basis of direct discussion with Russia, and early in 1856 Napoleon had secured the initiative and was able to pull back the more bellicose British Cabinet into something like moderation, to prevent Austria from again attempting the part of chief mediator, and to keep Prussia entirely in the background, as a punishment for its extreme timidity. Thus Paris inevitably became the centre of the peace negotiations. Buol, who in September had confidently exclaimed, "We have the Danubian Principalities in our pocket",[2] was to find that he had profoundly miscalculated.

Even in the preliminaries it was the question of the Principalities which provided the first basis for the coming Franco-Russian rapprochement.[3] The tsar was ready to renounce the protectorate and even listened to Napoleon's advocacy of union, which accorded with his somewhat indeterminate ideas of European reconstruction on a national basis.

Meanwhile Stratford de Redcliffe, disturbed by the growth of Roumanian national feeling, had sent Alison to Bucarest to investigate conditions, and in a memorandum of December 1855 had advised maintaining the *status quo* against both Russia and Austria, but with a

---

[1] 15 March 1855—quoted by Riker, *The Making of Roumania*, p. 32.
[2] Friedjung, *Der Krimkrieg*, p. 42.
[3] See Alfred Stern, *Gesch. Europas*, VIII, p. 137.

new and improved constitution. At the peace preliminaries which led on 11 February to the Protocol of Constantinople, he made such difficulties as to draw from his Austrian colleague, Baron Prokesch, the impatient exclamation, "He is not an Ambassador, he is a sovereign".[1] Stratford carried his recommendation that until a new constitution could be actually introduced, it was advisable that there should be no new princes, but only two kaimakamates, or regencies, nominated by the Porte. This made for delay and intrigue and was therefore welcomed by the Turks: it caused a corresponding indignation and impatience in Bucarest and Jassy, where the national movement was ablaze despite foreign occupation.

An important factor at this stage was the group of able Roumanian exiles in Paris. Their activities still await an historian, and a really authoritative account of them might be most fascinating. After the collapse of the revolution, most of the leaders, and in particular Rosetti, the Brătianus, Nicholas Golescu, Eliade, and the poets Alecsandri and Bolintineanu, gravitated back to Paris, and in the first instance devoted themselves, in the genial atmosphere of the Second Republic, to explaining and justifying their recent action. In this task they were greatly helped by a young Frenchman, Henri Ubicini, who had acted as secretary to the Provisional Government and now composed a "Mémoire Justificatif"[2] and afterwards a series of books on the Eastern Question, and also by the well-known writer Hippolyte Desprez, both in his book *Les Peuples de l'Autriche et de la Turquie*, and in his articles in the *Revue des Deux Mondes*.[3] But they also enjoyed the active literary support of Michelet, then at the height of his fame, of Quinet and Cousin and other eminent Frenchmen of the day. Encouraged by this, they attempted to publish a review: two numbers were issued under the name of "The Future Roumania" (*România Viitoare*); then followed *Republica Romăna*, which was ere long transferred from Paris to Brussels. The opening programme-article was signed by Ion Brătianu and after demanding a free and independent country "with 10 million Roumanians"—in other words, full-fledged unity—ended with an appeal to the Roumanian youth, that instead of wasting time in diplomacy and crying "Long live the Sultan" in Muntenia and "Long live the Emperor" in

---

[1] Riker, *op. cit.* p. 35.
[2] Reflecting unduly the ideas of Eliade, who on his side published in 1851 his interesting but partisan *Mémoires sur l'Histoire de la Régénération Roumaine*.
[3] Cf. also the articles of Paul Bataillard in the *Revue de Paris*.

Transylvania, they should raise the standard of a "Roumanian Republic one and indivisible".[1] Another liberal exile, Ion Ghica, probed deeper still when he pointed out that "Young Roumania" had led the revolution "up to a certain point" and thus "spared the country real misfortunes", but that the lever had always been "the discontent of the peasants against the landlords", and the knowledge, on the part of the latter, "of what had happened in Galicia and of the impunity of the insurgents".[2]

Despite many mutual disagreements all were at one on essentials. "Our Roumania exists," wrote Bălcescu, "blind is he that does not see her. Perhaps we may be forced to struggle for yet another century for its realisation. But what is a century in the life of a nation?" Nothing could be more remarkable than the manner in which the exiles were able to adapt themselves to the radically changed circumstances of France after the *coup d'état* of 1851. Their friends Michelet and Quinet could no longer lecture at the Collège de France, and there was an abrupt end to the democratic movement. There was no more hope from men like Roger-Collard or Ledru-Rollin. Yet within a very short time the Roumanians were establishing confidential relations with the Second Empire which were to have a decisive and lasting influence upon their future. Chance made Ion Brătianu acquainted with Prince Jerome Bonaparte and through him it was possible to present a memorandum to Napoleon III briefly describing the Roumanians ("occupying the country between the Tisza, Dniester, Black Sea and Danube"), insisting that the Principalities were "not a conquered country", but one which had made its contract with the Porte on terms the latter had constantly infringed, and finally emphasising that the creation of a free Roumania was necessary "if the solution of the Eastern Question was to be other than ephemeral", and that "France has become our ideal" and "has the mission to preside over the regeneration of Europe".[3] It was already the same theme which Nicholas Golescu presented to Napoleon in March 1856, in a more highly coloured form: "Roumania", he argued, "would be for France a force and a glory. You would have there more than a colony, more than a fortress. France would find there her soul. France has no need to make a conquest of us: we are open to

---

[1] *Din Scrierile și Cuvântarile lui Ion C. Brătianu*, pp. 64–5.
[2] G. Chainoi (anagram), *Dernière Occupation des Principautés par la Russie* (1853), pp. 85–7.
[3] *Din Scrierile*, pp. 70–3.

her, let her come and recognise herself in us....France in her greatness
has long forgotten us, but we have never lost her from our sight, we
have always loved and hoped in her".[1] The French consul in Bucarest
had already reported in a similar sense during the year of revolution—
"Whether she accepts or repudiates it, France has there, on the banks
of the Danube, an inevitable *clientèle*, which attaches itself to her as the
head of the Latin nations, and as its political metropolis, and which
tries every day to assimilate her language, her legislation, her literature
and even her most futile fashions".[2]

In 1855 Brătianu, continuing his unwearied campaign, issued a
pamphlet entitled *Mémoire sur l'Autriche dans la Question d'Orient*.
In it he argued that "only so long as Austria is regarded as a dyke
against Muscovite invasion will she have Europe for her", but that "if
Russia ceased to be a force, Austria herself would disappear from the
map of Europe". Meanwhile France is, above all for the whole East,
"the incarnate principle of nationality": "the reconstitution of Eastern
Europe on a basis of nationality is a *conditio sine qua non* for its civilising",
and France would gain most of all, since she would become "the idol
and arbiter of these regions, which would owe to her their return to life
and light". The Roumanians in particular had "never ceased to knock
at her doors, in order to be accepted as her advance guard in the East":
they were destined to be her natural *point d'appui*.[3] This is in essence
what Desprez had acutely observed as early as 1847—that the Roumanians aspired to form "a state strong enough to play against Russia,
in the interests of Latin Europe, the part of a vigilant and reliable
sentinel."

Such ideas found a fertile soil in the brain of Napoleon III, that
enigmatic dreamer to whom nationality, both in the abstract and in the
concrete, always made a strong appeal, and who, being more logical
than the British liberals of his day, wished to apply the principle of
nationality in Eastern Europe no less than in Italy. He was led by
parallel motives of sentiment and interest, but the sequel was to prove
him even more loyal to the Roumanian than to the Italian cause, though
to the former he did not need to sacrifice French blood and treasure. It
may be assumed that in his view the Principalities were to fulfil the
double function of a Latin sentinel on the Lower Danube and the Black

[1] Sturdza, *Acte şi Documente*, I, p. 1387; cf. also Bengescu, *Les Golescu*, p. 225.
[2] Guéroult, 31 March 1848—*Anul 1848*, I, no. 71.
[3] See pp. 23, 36–7, 43, 47 of *Mémoire*.

Sea, a medium of French culture and political influence, a convenient barrier to Russian aggression towards the coast, and at the same time a certain check on both Islam and Slavdom and a certain embarrassment for Austria, owing to her own possession of Roumanian subjects. The idea of national buffer states, as a better solution than bolstering up the incurably effete rule of the sultan, was steadily making way, and owed much to Napoleon's peculiar mentality. The worst obstacle, now and much later, was the incorrigibly Turcophil outlook of British statesmen and public opinion, at once obtusely blind to facts and arguments and resting on a blend of sentimental illusions and commercial designs.

An early step of the congress, which met in Paris on 25 February 1856, was to appoint a special commission to discuss the future status of the Roumanian Principalities. A few weeks earlier a fantastic solution had been broached by Bourqueney to Buol—that the duke of Modena, of a junior Habsburg line, should be made prince of Roumania and hand over his duchy to Sardinia: and even Cavour played for a time with the idea of using the Principalities as compensation to Austria for renunciation in Italy—an idea which was to be more seriously considered ten years later. But finding that this evoked no response either from Napoleon or from Francis Joseph, he speedily fell into line with the former's policy of Roumanian unity, and wrote to d'Azeglio, then representing Sardinia in London, "For the love of Heaven persuade Palmerston that it would be a *crime de lèse-civilisation* if he upheld the *status quo* and opposed the just wishes of the entire Roumanian population".[1]

On 6 March Clarendon discussed the question with Count Walewski —a son of the great Napoleon, in whom his cousin found a pliant political tool, and who was now French premier. Walewski explained his master's strong view that no peace would be solid or durable which did not provide for the union and independence of the Principalities:[2] and the same day the emperor gave an audience to Clarendon and pleaded personally in the same cause. Clarendon raised every possible objection, treated Austrian and Turkish opposition as "insurmountable", and even affected to regard the union as "an act of spoliation towards

[1] 6, 7 and 18 March 1856—*Lettres Inédites de Cavour.* See *Acte și Documente*, II, nos. 1391, 1392 and 1399.
[2] Clarendon to Palmerston, 7 March—Martin, *Life of Prince Consort*, III, p. 465.

Turkey". Two days later, undeterred by Clarendon's obstructive attitude, Walewski, in his capacity as President of the Congress, formally advocated union as coinciding with the wishes and interests of the Roumanian people. Clarendon did not oppose this proposal, but held that it must be subject to a definite consultation of those wishes: and this gave Ali Pasha and Count Buol an opportunity for challenging the view that the Roumanians had any such desire. In view of such strong opposition by Turkey and Austria to further discussion, the French did not press further for the moment: it was obviously impossible to risk a rupture of the whole Congress for a question of very great, but none the less secondary, importance. Fortunately Austria and Turkey were guilty of a grave tactical blunder in laying constant stress upon the alleged Roumanian distaste for union: for it led quite logically to the Congress adopting some measure for ascertaining the wishes of the population. On 12 March it was decided that in each Principality a 'Divan Ad Hoc' should be summoned, on a basis of popular election, to express its views on union, and that an international commission should be sent out to investigate conditions on the spot and report back to Paris. The result of this was to delay the settlement of the Roumanian question, to put it as it were into "cold storage" for a season: but at the same time it ensured to it the fullest possible discussion and gave it a degree of prominence before the international forum such as it had never hitherto attained. It of course marked the end of the Russian protectorate, veiled or unveiled, and ushered in a new period of transition, in which the Roumanians were to be under the tutelage of the European Concert.

There remained the question of evacuation, to which Austria stood definitely committed by her own arrangement with the Porte, but which Buol had till the last moment hoped to evade. When, then, Walewski moved for immediate evacuation by Austrian and Turkish troops alike, and Clarendon at once gave his backing, Buol "grew quite red and blew up like a rocket".[1] But he stood alone, and found it necessary to comply. To the emperor he tried to foist the main blame for failure on to the Austrian commanders, who "should never have allowed so impractical a question as union and a foreign Prince to become current":[2] but this was too futile an argument to deceive anyone. On 17 April an imperial decree announced progressive with-

---

[1] Hübner, *Neuf Ans de Souvenirs*, I, 409.
[2] Buol to Francis Joseph, 6 April—quoted by Riker, *op. cit.* p. 49.

drawal, and though Buol continued to hope against hope and was able to delay the final step till well on in 1857, Austria's prospect of remaining in possession was definitely checked.

The Treaty of Paris (30 March 1856) may be said to inaugurate a new era for the Roumanians no less than for the Serbs. On its main provisions it is unnecessary to dwell here, except to observe that it was an attempt, and a successful attempt, to substitute collective action on the part of the Concert of Europe, for separate action by Russia, and to secure for Turkey a further respite within which to re-establish herself by internal reforms. The action of the Powers, and especially of the British Cabinet, was based on the assumption that Turkey was capable of reform, and this assumption was fundamentally false. As the duke of Cambridge wrote to Queen Victoria during a visit to Constantinople, "The sick man is excessively sick, indeed dying as fast as possible: and the sooner diplomacy disposes of him the better, for no earthly power can save him....This is the opinion of every person out here of both armies, French and English".[1] But the far abler and all-powerful Palmerston was still acting upon the view so confidently expressed by him fifteen years earlier, "All we hear about the decay of Turkey is pure and unadulterated nonsense".[2] More fatal even than this assumption was the decision of the Powers to leave the execution of the promised reforms—as announced in Article IX—entirely in the hands of the sultan himself, and to disclaim all right of interference, whether collective or individual. As no other than Lord Stratford very clearly saw, the absence of "a force *from without* to keep up a steady animating pressure on the Government",[3] foredoomed the whole scheme to failure: and that was one reason why he declared that he "would rather have cut off his right hand than signed that treaty".[4]

Articles XX and XXI ordered a rectification of frontier which restored the southern portion of Bessarabia to Turkey, and gave its inhabitants the same rights as those of Moldavia proper, from which it had been amputated in 1812. The motive of this decision, however, had little or nothing to do with the just rights of the Roumanians: they were not

---

[1] *Letters of Queen Victoria*, III, p. 27: 13 May 1854.
[2] 1 September 1839—Bulwer, *Life of Palmerston*, II, p. 299.
[3] His phrase in a letter to Lord Clarendon in June 1855—S. Lane-Poole, *Life of Stratford de Redcliffe*, II, p. 439.
[4] *Ibid.* p. 436.

even consulted, and by an added irony of fate the restored territory—containing no places of any note save perhaps Chilia and Ismail—was just that portion of Bessarabia where there were fewest Roumanians, but numerous Bulgarian, Ukrainian and Tatar villages. The main aim, especially in the eyes of Austria, was to cut off Russia from direct access to the delta of the Danube and to exclude her from the number of riverine states. There was thus an intimate connection between these clauses and Articles 15–19, which laid down new international rules for the navigation of the Danube, and set up two important commissions: (a) the so-called "European" (§ 16) (consisting of Turkey, Sardinia and the five Great Powers) to supervise measures for clearing the delta channels, and (b) the "Danubian" (§§ 17–18) (composed of delegates from the riverine states Austria, Bavaria, Würtemberg and Turkey and from the three vassal states, subject to Turkey's approval) to draft rules of navigation and police control. Each of the Powers was entitled to maintain two stationnaires at the river mouth.

By Article 22 the two vassal Principalities and all their existing "privileges and immunities" were placed under the guarantee of the Powers, and it was expressly declared that no Power should henceforth enjoy any "exclusive protection" or "special right of interference in their internal affairs". The termination of the Russian tutelage unquestionably conformed to the wishes of the vast mass of the population: and though it can be argued that the new arrangement substituted a control which was every whit as interfering, and which despite all public professions was all too ready to disregard the true wishes of the Roumanians themselves, there was this essential distinction, that the Concert was at once more remote, less capable of prompt action, less harmonious and united, and therefore very soon revealed its own impotence to hold up the natural march of events.

By Articles XXIII–XXVII the Porte undertook to grant to the Principalities "an independent and national administration, as also full liberty of religion, legislature, commerce and navigation". An European commission, including a Turkish representative, was to proceed without delay to Bucarest and conduct there an enquiry into the existing situation in the Principalities and to "propose the bases of their future organisation". In each province "Divans Ad Hoc" were to be convoked with as little delay as possible. They were to be based on "the most exact representation of the interests of all classes of society", and their task was "to express the wishes of the population regarding the definitive organisation of the Principalities".

The final decisions were to be embodied in a convention signed at Paris by the signatory Powers, and were then to enjoy their collective guarantee. A national army was conceded, capable of co-operation with the Porte "against any foreign aggression". Henceforth no armed intervention from the outside was to be permitted without previous agreement between the Powers. Finally, by Article xxxi, evacuation was to follow ratification.

By these clauses and the parallel provisions regarding Serbia fundamental changes were effected in the relations of the Porte with its three vassals to the north. While putting an end to Russia's privileged position as Protecting Power, it substituted a new and utterly illogical system. Turkish sovereignty was nominally restored, but in practice hedged in on every side. For instance, in Serbia the Porte's sovereign rights were reaffirmed, yet these rights were placed under the protection of the Powers: and again, the Porte was allowed to maintain certain garrisons, and yet had to renounce the right of armed intervention. It was a makeshift which obviously could not last long: in actual fact, its overthrow came in Roumania sooner than in Serbia. These were admittedly half-solutions, but they represented a new diplomatic departure: for the right of national self-determination—of course a later phrase, then not yet in vogue—was at least tacitly recognised. The wishes of the Roumanians were proclaimed as the decisive factor. This was already a very different world from that of the Congress of Vienna, where peoples were openly bartered and partitioned according to the will of their sovereigns and without the remotest pretence of consultation. It was of course for Napoleon III a point of national honour to escape wherever possible from the tradition of 1815. None the less he was imitating the procedure of Vienna in consenting to the second treaty of 15 April 1856 by which the three Powers, France, Britain and Austria, as though distrustful of the decisions reached in the major treaty, undertook a collective guarantee of Turkish integrity. This had no meaning if not directed against Russia, but it was almost from the first day a dead letter: its contents were revealed by Napoleon himself to Count Orlov, with whom he was actively engaged in establishing a rapprochement. Indeed, the most striking development of the Treaty of Paris was the rapid improvement of Franco-Russian relations, which had remained strained ever since the fall of Charles X in 1830, and the no less marked cooling off in Napoleon's feelings towards Turkey, as revealed in his conversations with Lord Cowley[1] and later with the Prince Consort.[2]

\* \* \* \*

The Congress of Paris, while attempting a durable solution of the Eastern Question, under the auspices of the Concert, had found it advisable to postpone one thorny problem for later decision, and this at once forced itself upon the attention of all Europe as the problem of Roumanian unity. It speedily became abundantly clear that its chief advocate was Napoleon III, and that he had won over Russia to his side, that Sardinia both on principle and for ulterior motives gave her strong support, and that Prussia was benevolently, if feebly, neutral, and on occasion even ready to follow Russia. The opposition to union came from three Powers. Turkey resented her progressive dismemberment by her own allies and was quite unimpressed by the high-sounding argument that free Roumania would form a Turkish rampart against Russia. Britain still hugged the phantom of Turkish reform, and believed with Palmerston that "the United Principalities would be a field for Russian intrigue and not a barrier against Russia".[3] Austria strained every nerve to prevent union, partly from fear of its effect upon her own Roumanians, partly because she still hoped to convert military occupation into political dominion.

The Concert was thus riddled with dissensions from the very outset, and this was accentuated by the difficulty of delimiting the new frontier between Moldavia and Russia. The maps on which the clause of the Treaty had been based, proved to be inaccurate, for it had been laid down that the frontier should pass "to the south of Bolgrad", and now it was found that two quite separate Bolgrads existed, at some distance from each other, one of which suited the Russian, the other the Turkish, case. Moreover the so-called "Isle of Serpents" facing the mouth of the northern channel of the Danube, had been completely overlooked, and some Russian marines were in occupation and had hoisted the imperial flag. The dispute regarding these two points, trifling in themselves, but symbolic of larger issues, threatened for a time to divide Europe into two hostile camps and dragged on interminably. The obstinacy

---

[1] Cowley to Clarendon, 28 December 1856—cit. W. G. East, *Union of Moldavia and Wallachia*, p. 1.

[2] Martin, *Life of Prince Consort*, IV, pp. 99–102.

[3] Palmerston to Clarendon, 8 July—quoted by Riker, *op. cit.* p. 61.

with which the Russian Chancellor Gorchakov upheld his claim to the more southerly Bolgrad, was doubtless due to a hope of splitting the Franco-British alliance, based on the visit of Napoleon's half-brother and confidential agent, the Duc de Morny, to Moscow.

These delays and discords aroused the greatest alarm and excitement in the two Principalities themselves, who feared, not altogether without reason, an European conflict over their helpless bodies.[1] Meanwhile the two fugitive princes had returned to Bucarest and Jassy early in 1856, and placed themselves at the head of the movement for unity: indeed a special committee of agitation was founded in Moldavia under Gregory Ghica's auspices, with union and a foreign prince as its avowed aim. But this did not suit the game of the Porte, who now took advantage of the fact that the provisions of the Règlement Organique and subsequent Russo-Turkish conventions were still valid until the European commission could produce its new scheme. By the convention of 1849 the seven years' term of office of the two princes expired in July 1856: and therefore the Porte instead of extending it further, appointed two kaimakams, or regents, with full princely powers. Alexander Ghica in Wallachia was—to use the words of the French consul Béclard— "a worn-out and embittered old man, almost fallen into his dotage":[2] but he enjoyed the powerful backing of Colquhoun and Lord Stratford. Theodore Balş, who succeeded in Moldavia, belonged to a prominent boiar family, but was the leader of the separatist or Austrophil party, and was believed to have owed his success to a judicious bribe of 80,000 ducats (nearly one million francs) to the Porte.[3] Balş, who had at the same time purchased a half-promise of the Moldavian throne as the next stage, lost no time in replacing all prefects by pliant tools of his own, suppressing freedom of the press, closing the Academy of Jassy and other schools and appointing as his ministers open opponents of the union. In this he had the active support of the Austrian consul,

---

[1] For the history of the critical period of 1856–9 the reader is specially recommended to consult T. W. Riker, *The Making of Roumania*, and W. G. East, *The Union of Moldavia and Wallachia*, both of whom use hitherto unpublished material in the British, French and Austrian Archives.

[2] Béclard to Thouvenel, 15 July 1856—Thouvenel, *Trois Années de la Question d'Orient*, p. 19.

[3] Sturdza, *Acte şi Documente*, II, no. 501, p. 1104 (letter of Balş, confirming payment of 10,000 ducats by his cousin Theodore to Ali Pasha's secretary Adossides). According to Victor Place, it was paid through the banking house of Zarifi and Vlasto in Constantinople.

Gödel, who enjoyed a special position owing to the presence of an Austrian army of occupation. Till the very last the Austrian Government postponed evacuation, in the hope that some excuse for remaining might turn up. But France remained adamant in this question, and what was finally decisive was Russia's firm refusal to take any part in the European commission until all foreign troops had left the Principalities. When in January 1857 the Powers at last settled the boundary dispute, Austria could no longer evade her pledges, and by the end of March her last troops had evacuated Moldavia. Meanwhile the unionist party grew stronger every day, especially after the return of the political exiles from Paris as the result of Napoleon's direct intervention with the Porte.

With the discomfiture of Austria the Roumanian question resolved itself more and more into an unedifying duel between the French and British representatives in Turkey. Napoleon was by now wholeheartedly committed to the cause of union, and instructed his ambassador, Edouard Thouvenel, to use all his efforts to attain this, "with or without the consent of the Porte".[1] Thouvenel himself was not a believer in the Roumanian cause, and could only explain the emperor's attitude on the assumption that he "wished to settle on the Po questions raised on the Danube".[2] But he of course acted on orders, and he did so with growing heat and enthusiasm, owing to acute resentment at the domineering policy of his British colleague—"my special cross", as he calls him.[3] The extent to which Napoleon was engaged in the matter may be gathered from a note in his own hand on a despatch of Thouvenel—"Press strongly to obtain Reshid's support for union. Spare no effort (ne rien ménager) to obtain this result".[4] While then Stratford and his subordinates Alison, Colquhoun and others were actively encouraging the Porte against union, Thouvenel worked no less energetically in the opposite direction, and the French consuls, Béclard in Bucarest and still more Victor Place in Jassy, were the main rallying points of the whole unionist agitation, and Baron Talleyrand-Périgord, the French member on the European commission, on his way to Constantinople found himself at Bucarest the centre of public demonstrations in favour of union and of Napoleon III as Roumania's deliverer. To complete the picture of rival agents, Sir Henry Bulwer,

[1] Walewski to Thouvenel, 5 April 1856—*Trois Années*, p. 8.
[2] Thouvenel to Benedetti, 25 April 1857—*ibid.* p. 99.
[3] "Ma plaie particulière"—*ibid.* p. 99.
[4] *Acte şi Documente*, IV, no. 977: 2 April 1857.

Talleyrand's British colleague, was treated by Lord Stratford with arrogant reserve, and it came to a violent open scene between them at a session of the commission, to the scarcely veiled delight of the French party.

In April 1856 Walewski had written from the conference to Thouvenel that England "who was at first wavering, wishes Union" and that union was "in the odour of sanctity at Windsor".[1] But the irresolute Clarendon informed Cowley that the Cabinet had changed its mind and now held that "the injurious consequences of union would greatly counterbalance any advantages which it could produce".[2] By September he was already notifying Colquhoun in Bucarest that Britain disapproved of union either under a national or a foreign prince, and would oppose it "by all means that they can legitimately employ".[3] In February 1857 when the official *Moniteur* announced Napoleon's belief in union and his hope that the Powers would accept it, the British Cabinet was indignant, and Clarendon in the House of Lords pointedly alluded to the understanding between the Powers that nothing should be done to influence Roumanian opinion until the Divans had had time to meet. Cowley, after remonstrating to Walewski, wrote home that it was "difficult to argue with His Majesty, for on this question at least his philanthropy far exceeds his respect for treaties"[4]: and only a week later Napoleon in the Legislative Council reaffirmed his belief in union. Meanwhile Stratford had worked harder than ever at the Porte, and had signally proved his great influence with the sultan by securing the overthrow of the Francophil grand vizier, Ali Pasha, and the substitution of his own creature, Reshid Pasha. On the same day he had invested the degenerate Abdul Medjid with the Garter at Queen Victoria's orders.

The situation was still further complicated by the sudden death of Theodore Balş on 1 March 1857. As his successor the Porte nominated Nicholas Vogorides, son of the ex-prince of Samos, who had enjoyed the special favour of Sultan Mahmud. The new kaimakam was of Bulgarian stock, but thoroughly hellenised and like all his family entirely subservient to the Porte. His brother, as Aleko Pasha, was the first governor of Eastern Roumalia in 1878: his brother-in-law Musurus Pasha was for years Turkish ambassador in London, and his other

[1] *Trois Années*, pp. 7–8.
[2] 22 August—quoted by Riker, *op. cit.* p. 61.
[3] 9 September—quoted by Riker, p. 73.
[4] Cowley to Clarendon, 12 May—cit. East, *op. cit.* p. 201.

brother-in-law, John Photiades, was a typical Phanariot who acted as Moldavian agent at the Porte. He himself had been born in Moldavia and had married a daughter of the well-known Moldavian boiar poet Nicholas Conachi, and had been finance minister under Balş, yet he scarcely knew a word of Roumanian and was quite untouched by Roumanian sentiments. He owed his appointment very largely to the fact that France had vetoed four Austrian candidates and that he himself had cleverly induced Victor Place to recommend his name to Thouvenel, by signing a pledge[1] to do nothing which could in any way interfere with the movement for union. But no sooner was he appointed than he threw off the mask and declared that he would only support the union if he were convinced that it represented the general wishes. He then set himself to work hard in the opposite sense, prohibiting unionist newspapers, committees and meetings, publishing false programmes in the name of the opposition, and suppressing their refutations, and as he grew bolder he proceeded to numerous arrests.

In Jassy there was now an open trial of strength between the French and Austrian consuls. The lengths to which Vogorides and his prompters in Constantinople went are shown by the fact that the Greek patriarch was compelled to write a letter of reproaches and threats to the metropolitan of Moldavia, a loyal adherent of union and a friend of Place. As this failed of its effect, Safvet Effendi, the Turkish commissioner to Jassy, was fulsomely polite to the metropolitan, "kissing his hands several times, until the prelate, imagining that Safvet was a Christian dressed *à la turque*, gave him his benediction, which the other piously accepted".[2] By this time, however, it was a case of war to the knife, and the French were none too scrupulous in dealing with their rascally opponents. Through the efforts of Dimitrie Rallet, a leading member of the Unionist Central Committee in Jassy, and even of the kaimakam's own sister, a series of secret papers were abstracted and placed in the hands of Place. Their contents were highly compromising for Stratford, Alison and Prokesch, who stood revealed as encouraging Vogorides in his policy of repression: and the share of Photiades, Musurus and Gödel also became clear. For instance, Aleko told his brother that England would not allow union to be realised even if both Divans voted for it, and advised him to "follow blindly the Consul Gödel in spite of his

[1] Text in *Acte şi Documente*, IV, no. 871 (2 March 1857, in Vogorides' own hand): and in Emmerit, *Victor Place*, p. 46.
[2] Place to Thouvenel—Thouvenel, *op. cit.* p. 97.

mistakes": while Photiades imparted the Porte's instructions to work actively against union, but secretly and without betraying that he was receiving such orders.[1] Thouvenel was able to go to the grand vizier, Reshid, with the proofs of his perfidy, and reported "extreme embarrassment" and insincere pledges, but also the firm impression that "the real protector of Vogorides is Lord Stratford".[2] Reshid indeed was a mere tool in the hands of Stratford, who affected to regard him as a great man and approved the choice of his own son, Ali Ghalib Pasha, the sultan's brother-in-law, as foreign minister. The gulf between the two ambassadors is shown by Thouvenel's contemptuous reference to the new minister as better suited, both morally and physically, to the post of Court Dwarf![3] Meanwhile Stratford had told Clarendon that Reshid's fear of France was "quite puerile. It is only by acting like a bully that I can at all keep him up to the mark".[4] Thouvenel was not exaggerating when he reported to Paris that Stratford "has made of the separation of the Principalities and of the maintenance of Vogorides a personal question", and "has become, by his defects more than his merits, the 6th Great Power of Europe".[5]

In Wallachia the National party grew daily stronger: Ghica was too weak and timorous to check the movement, and his own nephew, as Prefect of Police, was not unfavourable. The big boiars had their own oligarchic interests to defend, but there was among them a sprinkling of enlightened individuals such as Filipescu, Crețulescu, Florescu, Catargiu, who together with the two ex-princes, Ştirbei and Bibescu, were working to make of the Divan a reality for the future. Béclard's influence altogether outweighed that of Colquhoun, who was in any case on the point of retiring, and the advent of the Commission to Bucarest gave the French a predominant position. But from the first Moldavia was the key of the situation: in the event of union Jassy obviously had more to lose than Bucarest, and every possible argument on this line was put forward against the unionists. But Vogorides and the Turks were not foolish enough to rely upon mere argument. A systematic attempt was made to falsify the elections, and it was cal-

---

[1] Bamberg, *Gesch. des orientalischen Angelegenheit*, p. 303.
[2] Thouvenel to Walewski, 1 July—*Acte şi Documente*, v, no. 1419. See also *ibid.* IV, nos. 1063, 1138, 1143, 1150 (the intercepted letters of Photiades).
[3] Thouvenel to Walewski—Thouvenel, *op. cit.* p. 100.
[4] 25 May—quoted by Riker, p. 105.
[5] 1 July to Benedetti—Thouvenel, *op. cit.* p. 125.

culated that if once this could be done in Moldavia, Wallachia could be made to follow suit. Hence in the first instance the registers were deliberately faked, so as to exclude the majority of the unionists, and there were wholesale disqualifications, in order to make assurance doubly sure.

Mr Riker has disinterred from the Vienna Achives a report of Gödel to Buol, containing the phrase, "I will personally see to it that every name is removed that is not fully justified according to the firman".[1] "In states like the Principalities and in face of adversaries without scruple, any means should appear good to us"[2]—so wrote Gödel's superior, the Internuncio Prokesch, only two months later. All comment is superfluous.

It was comparatively easy to employ such methods in a country where registers and statistics were a novelty and where there was no tradition of administrative routine and efficiency—in fact, very much the contrary. Appeals were made to the European commission in Bucarest regarding these illegalities, but Vogorides disregarded their findings and continued to act on the private instructions of the grand vizier, who was still encouraged by Lord Stratford and Baron Prokesch.

The Moldavian elections, held on 19 July, were so notorious and public a scandal that the metropolitan of Moldavia refused to take part in them, and that Alexander Cuza, the prefect of Galaţ, resigned his post on the ground of corrupt practices ordered behind his back in his own district by the kaimakam and his agents. An anti-unionist majority was obtained, because only 350 out of the 2000 large proprietors, only 2264 out of the 20,000 small proprietors, only 11 members of the liberal professions, were able to record their votes—in other words, only 11 per cent. of the already narrow electorate. Only 29 priests out of 3273, only 5 out of 48 archimandrites, voted.[3] Lord Stratford's first secretary, Mr Alison, was sent to Jassy to follow the situation, and therefore naturally enough was credited with an active share in preparing the elections,[4] which greatly increased the scandal. His bias, or his lack of judgment, is revealed by the fact that he duly reported to his chief that

[1] Cf. report of Place to Thouvenel, 25 March 1857 (Sturdza, *Acte şi Documente*), IV, no. 943), describing in detail the efforts of Balş in the previous December, in conjunction with Gödel, to find a Minister of the Interior ready to "make" elections, and the doubts of the two ministers selected, Nicholas Cantacuzene and Istrati, as to the possibility of success.

[2] 26 March and 13 May—quoted by Riker, *op. cit.* pp. 99, 102.

[3] *Acte şi Documente*, V, no. 1573; Thouvenel, *op. cit.* p. 133.

[4] Thouvenel, *op. cit.* p. 135.

the elections, though not altogether free from reproach, were "conducted with general regularity and propriety".[1] He appears, moreover, to have announced openly that Stratford would not permit their annulment.[2]

The result was universal indignation and protest, which vented itself against the Turkish suzerainty and even created a revulsion of feeling in favour of Russia. The French delegate to the Commission, Baron Talleyrand, said to Safvet Pasha, "You could have had a Christian Egypt: you have preferred a Roumanian Poland. In concert with Vogorides, Liehmann and Bulwer, you are working for the Emperor of all the Russias".[3] Thouvenel had meanwhile been active at the Porte and had even secured the postponement of the election for a fortnight and instructions to revise the registers in accordance with the commission's advice: but Stratford and Prokesch at once protested to Reshid, and the respite of fifteen days was cut down to eight.[4] "If Thouvenel be not curbed", wrote Stratford to Clarendon, "he will ride roughshod over the whole of us", and meanwhile he himself continued to bully Reshid and to strain every nerve against union. His idea of amicable relations with the ambassador of France, Britain's ally in a war just concluded, was to give a big dinner and reception on the anniversary of Waterloo!

The news of these events caused great indignation in Paris, and Thouvenel received instructions from Napoleon to demand the immediate annulment of the elections on grounds of illegality. On 28 July, then, the French ambassador, supported by the representatives of Russia, Prussia, and Sardinia, presented what was in effect an ultimatum to the Porte, and received the evasive and insincere answer that Turkey, as a co-signatory of the Treaty of Paris, could not annul on her own authority and must refer the question to a fresh meeting of the Powers. Thouvenel, armed with the stolen correspondence already referred to,

[1] Quoted by Riker, *op. cit.* p. 117.
[2] *Acte şi Documente*, v, no. 1578, Place to Walewski, 23 July 1857.
[3] I.e. the Austrian and British delegates, *Acte şi Documente*, IV, no. 1134 (Talleyrand to Walewski, 4 May 1857). Talleyrand in this same report wrote, "Je ne sais pas qui a inventé M. Vogorides, mais ce que je puis assurer, c'est que de tous les choix que pouvait faire la Porte, celui-là était le plus malencontreux pour elle".
[4] "The Grand Vizier told the French Ambassador that you had been the cause of his breaking his word," so wrote Clarendon to Stratford, 28 July—cit. East, *Union of Moldavia and Wallachia*, p. 123. This shows that Paris was complaining officially to London, and that London was forced to accept the complaint as reasonable.

insisted on an audience with the sultan, which was followed by the resignation of Reshid and the coming of Ali and Fuad into power. But even they only offered to summon the two kaimakams to Constantinople, and this Thouvenel rejected as inadequate. There was an open trial of strength between the two groups among the Powers. Thouvenel asked for his passports on 6 August and embarked dramatically on a French warship: and the other three ministers at the same time broke off diplomatic relations with the Porte. At this very moment the British Cabinet, at Palmerston's instance, had advised the Porte "to decline compliance with this arrogant demand", as contrary to the treaty engagement of the Powers "to respect the independence of the Sultan".[1] On 3 August Palmerston himself wrote to the French ambassador, Persigny, "We are ready for any eventualities, however painful".[2] Fortunately for the general peace, British opinion was absorbed by the Indian Mutiny, and the saner elements in the Cabinet were able to restrain the fire-eating prime minister. Indeed it was almost providential that an official visit of Napoleon III and Eugénie to Queen Victoria and Prince Albert at Osborne had been arranged for 6 August—an event which Lord Clarendon himself described to the queen as "politically a godsend".[3] Long conversations between the sovereigns and their chief ministers led to a happy compromise—happy from the standpoint of internal peace, though from that of Roumania it meant an obstinate attempt to hold back the in-rushing tide. The emperor made it clear that he "could not muster up any sympathy for such a sorry set as the Turks",[4] but that friendship with England was a paramount object of his policy. He therefore no longer insisted on "Complete union and a foreign Prince—the plan we deem the best"[5]: while Britain on her side consented to join in asking the Porte for annulment of the Moldavian elections and a revision of the registers. More important still, she agreed that the two Principalities, though not united, should obtain "similar organic institutions" and "a common system in all things civil and military".[6] Palmerston, of whose violent language Napoleon had

---

[1] 30 July 1857—quoted by East, *op. cit.* p. 123.
[2] Palmerston to Persigny—quoted by Riker, p. 130: cf. Prince Albert's memorandum of 6 August in Martin's *Life of the Prince Consort*, IV, p. 105. Napoleon complained of Palmerston's "violence".
[3] Queen to King Leopold, 12 August—Martin, *op. cit.* IV, p. 95.
[4] Prince Consort's Memorandum of 6 August—Martin, IV, p. 102.
[5] Walewski to Bourqueney, 9 August—quoted by Riker, *op. cit.* p. 135.
[6] Extract from text in East, *op. cit.* p. 131.

complained to the Prince Consort (he had, he said, forbidden Persigny to show him any more of Palmerston's letters!),[1] submitted to the compromise, while Clarendon at last asserted himself against the masterful Stratford.

The lengths to which the ambassador had permitted himself to go may be judged by the fact that though he received telegraphic instructions on 11 August to ask the Porte for annulment, he refused to act upon them for eleven days and even waited for five days after Prokesch had received parallel instructions from Vienna.[2] Not until he received a further peremptory telegram from Clarendon did he take the necessary steps at the Porte: and the fact that the Porte immediately climbed down and ordered annulment on 22 August shows that Stratford had been responsible for holding up the settlement. As the indignant Clarendon wrote to Cowley, "Stratford seems determined to defeat us, and I believe he would think his own personal triumph in this struggle would be *cheaply* purchased by dividing Europe into two hostile camps and cementing an alliance between France and Russia, founded on the extinction of the Turks".[3] This from the foreign secretary about his own ambassador throws into the shade even what Clarendon, Aberdeen, Graham and Herbert had written of the same ambassador on the eve of the Crimean War. But this time Clarendon did not merely complain to others: he bluntly told Stratford that his reasons given for delay were "insufficient" and wrote: "You seem to be creating for us as much embarrassment as the case admits, as of course the Porte does exactly what you advise".[4]

At the time there was a tendency to apportion the blame equally between Stratford and Thouvenel, London and Paris each giving the benefit of the doubt to its own man. Since the diplomatic correspondence has been published, it is no longer possible to deny that far the greater blame rests with Stratford whose bad relations with Thouvenel would not be so damning, but for the evidence that he had driven at least four of Thouvenel's predecessors—de Lacour, Sabatier, Baraguay d'Hilliers and Benedetti—one after the other to the point of frenzy

---

[1] Martin, *op. cit.* IV, p. 105.

[2] The full extracts will be found in East, *op. cit.* pp. 140–4. A colleague at the Quai d'Orsay was not far wrong in writing to Thouvenel that "Lord Stratford is evidently the true author of the crisis" (Thouvenel, p. 164). He goes on to quote Clarendon as having spoken to Persigny of "ce vieux maniaque!" (*ibid.* p. 165).

[3] Two letters of 20 August—Maxwell, *Life of Clarendon*, II, p. 147.

[4] 9 September—quoted by East, *op. cit.* p. 143.

against their closest ally. As Benedetti wrote long afterwards, "Ses collègues étaient ses ennemis". But the crowning proof of Stratford's impossible behaviour lies in the fact that even the Turks themselves were praying for his removal, and that when rumours of Aberdeen's impending fall reached Constantinople, Ali Pasha at once secretly instructed his ambassador in London to do what he could to secure a change at the embassy.[1] Thouvenel, it should be added, had no belief in, or sympathy with, the Roumanian cause, and simply acted on strict orders from Napoleon himself.[2]

Particular emphasis has been laid upon the British official attitude in this whole question, for two reasons.[3] In the first place the Roumanian dispute for a time endangered the alliance between Britain and France so recently sealed by comradeship in arms, and might very easily have plunged all Europe into war. In the second place it may be claimed as a positive moral duty on the part of the historian to place in true perspective events which have for two generations been unduly slurred over, and which illustrate the unjust and unbalanced outlook of British opinion towards the Eastern Question and especially towards Serbia and Roumania, in the middle of last century. British Liberalism, which played so notable a part in Italian liberation, became obsessed, as soon as it crossed the Adriatic, by sordid considerations of Turkish territorial integrity and British trade in the Levant, and left all the Christian nationalities of the Near East to their fate. The only British politician to raise the Roumanian question in these years was Lord Dudley Stuart, the steadfast champion of Poland, who was only moderately well-informed on Danubian problems and looked at them mainly from the angle of Russian aggression. His motion of 22 March 1849 in the House of Commons was prompted by the fear that the occupation of the Principalities would be "the first step to Turkish dismemberment": and the main stress of the debate, in which Disraeli and Urquhart took part,

---

[1] Benedetti, *Essais Diplomatiques*, II, p. 274, gives the text of the letter, dated 12 February 1855. One passage runs, "il suffit qu'un des représentants des autres Puissances dise noir pour que Lord Stratford dise blanc....Affaires extérieures, administration intérieure, patriarcat, tout est assujetti au contrôle de cet homme".

[2] See his private letters of April and July 1856 and March 1857—Thouvenel, *op. cit.* pp. 7, 11, 21, 29, 189.

[3] The extent to which Stratford's rôle in the Roumanian affair has been slurred over in Mr S. Lane-Poole's standard *Life of Lord Stratford* is a very serious blot upon the book as a whole: and it is regrettable that even Miss Malcolm-Smith in her admirable new life of *Stratford Canning* (1933), also passes it over all too hurriedly.

was laid upon the defence of Turkey against Russia, and only incidentally upon Roumanian rights.[1]

In October 1856 it proved possible to organise a public meeting at
Brighton in favour of Roumania, at which Dimitrie Brătianu spoke,
but though sympathetic messages were sent by Brougham, Gladstone
and Roebuck, no real publicity was obtained, and British opinion remained in basic ignorance of the whole Roumanian problem. It was
left to Gladstone to vindicate the honour of Britain in this question. On
4 May 1858 he introduced a motion in the House of Commons in favour
of giving "just weight" to the wishes of the Roumanians, as expressed
through their elected representatives. He insisted that "union is the
wish of almost the entire population" ("a fact deeply rooted in history"),
and its "one great and paramount object". It was "a matter which
deeply touches the principles of European policy, of public faith, and
deals with questions vitally touching the happiness of millions of our
fellow-creatures": and he besought the House "to consider well before
it determined that the fate of these two countries is to be governed by
considerations other than the welfare of the people", for that would be
"a dangerous and slippery course". Reminding the House that the
sultan was the suzerain, but not the sovereign, of the two Principalities,
he argued with great force and eloquence that "if you want to oppose
an obstacle to Russia, arm these people with freedom and with the
vigour and prosperity that freedom brings.... Do not palter with them".[2]
There is no slight piquancy in the fact that he was supported by Lord
Robert Cecil—a generation later, as Lord Salisbury, his great political
rival—who endorsed the view that the Principalities were not conquered
territory, and that they could not remain indefinitely "as mere debatable ground for the pretentions of Russia and Turkey", and who
argued that the present was "an opportunity which might never recur
of establishing those institutions to which we owe our own happiness".[3]
Gladstone was also supported by Roebuck, who argued that failure to
help Moldavia and Wallachia in their "attempts to be free and united"
would be equivalent to promoting despotism in Europe.

The incorrigible outlook of British statesmen upon Turkey is best
illustrated by Palmerston's rejoinder in the same debate. He argued
quite unabashed that if Moldavia and Wallachia "had been separate and

[1] Hansard, CIII, pp. 1134–52.
[2] Ibid. CL, pp. 45, 57, 59.
[3] Ibid. p. 79.

independent states, much as we might have regretted the invasion of their territories and the annihilation of their rights, the nations of Europe would not have taken up arms…in their defence. It was because they were outposts of the Turkish Empire, and because their invasion was a menace to its integrity and independence, which we deemed to be essential to the interests of Europe", that the Crimean War had been fought, with the author of this motion as a member of the Cabinet. He even ventured to assert that "foreign agency was the cause of the great excitement which prevailed in the Principalities". He opposed independence under a foreign prince, on the ground that such a country could not avoid becoming "the vassal of one or other of her more powerful neighbours" or being partitioned between them. Independence was contrary to the interests of Roumania and of Europe, to the engagements of the Treaty of Paris and would be "the first step towards a dismemberment of the Turkish Empire. That would be stultifying ourselves, acting in opposition to all the rules of policy which this country has of late years uniformly maintained".[1] It is interesting that Lord John Russell should have felt unable to follow Palmerston on these lines, and pleading that such an attitude would "give rise not only to disappointment but the complaint of want of faith", should have suggested that Britain should oppose a foreign prince, but should support "a united Government and legislature", in the belief that "a free and self-governing people…form the best barrier against foreign aggression—a barrier far more effective than any treaty".[2] Gladstone at the close of the debate was rightly unrepentant and declared, "I also ask why did we go to war, if after peace is established we, by violating our pledges and disappointing the expectations we have deliberately raised, exasperate the minds of a population which can never be held in permanent connection with Turkey unless it is placed in a state of contentment".[3] In a word, Gladstone, of all British statesmen, may claim to have possessed the greatest foresight and the justest appreciation of the Roumanian question.

*        *        *        *

The annulment of the elections was hailed with jubilation throughout the Principalities. A torchlight procession was organised at Bucarest in honour of Talleyrand and of Napoleon III, and the protests of Liehmann and Bulwer to Ghica were of no avail. Bulwer himself wrote

[1] Hansard, CL, pp. 85, 87.        [2] Ibid. pp. 95–7.        [3] Ibid. p. 105.

privately to Clarendon, "We must acknowledge to ourselves that almost every man in this Principality is, or says he is, for uniting the two under a foreign Prince".[1] Naturally enough, the influence of Vogorides could not survive such a shock, and Victor Place triumphantly described him as "nullifié".[2] At the new election, held in the second half of September, sixty-six declared unionists were returned out of a total of eighty-seven, only six being open opponents and the remainder doubtful. In Wallachia the result was mixed, owing to a curious faction fight between the adherents of Ghica and Ştirbei, but the main issue was never doubtful: and Talleyrand wrote home delightedly at the re-entry of "the men of '48" into political life. The two Divans met in October, and in the Moldavian the "Four Points" of the liberals were brought up for debate and eloquently expounded by Kogălniceanu. To these four—autonomy, union, a foreign prince and representative government—neutrality was now added as a fifth and they were voted by eighty-one to two, amid loud applause.[3] From the outset a high note was struck: "it is the moment to prove to the world what noble blood flows in our veins".[4] Kogălniceanu, who led the demand for union, also voiced the fifteen peasants' deputies' demand for land reform and a legislative assembly, and had in consequence to defend himself against a foolish charge of "communism". In the Wallachian Diet the "men of '48" assumed the initiative from the first day; the Assembly unanimously passed the Four Points amid cries of "Long live Roumania", "Long live the Protecting Powers", and a memorial was addressed to the Commission. Place reported that many Moldavian deputies desired to elect forthwith a French prince, and received in return a categorical warning from Walewski that Napoleon could not tolerate such a step. Clarendon would have liked the Powers to rule the question of a foreign prince altogether out of the competency of the Divans, but Walewski definitely refused this, and the Divans continued their somewhat unreal discussions of a problem in which they lacked all power of decision until, early in January 1858, they were dissolved by the Porte at the request of the Powers.

[1] 4 September—quoted by East, *op. cit.* p. 144.
[2] Thouvenel, *op. cit.* p. 169.
[3] It should be mentioned in passing that the claim of autonomy was based on references to a series of early treaties with the Turks, which were then generally accepted as authentic, but which have been exploded by modern historical criticism.
[4] *Acte şi Documente*, VI, i, no. 1980.

At this stage an ardent French advocate of the Roumanian cause, Elias Regnault, urged an understanding between Turkey and France as "the most disinterested" of the Powers, in contrast with "the feigned friendship of Russia, the haughty opposition of Austria, the hostile indifference of England". Union under Turkish suzerainty was the first essential aim; for the moment all else was secondary and would follow logically later. This sound advice was steadily taking root among the Roumanians, though the Porte remained negative to the last.

Meanwhile the fate of Roumania was influenced by a series of events both inside Turkey and in the international sphere. To the no small alarm of Vienna, Napoleon III met Alexander II at Stuttgart on 25 September, and by following the same tactics as at Osborne and not insisting upon a foreign prince, assured himself of the tsar's co-operation on all other points and thus in effect isolated England and Austria in the Roumanian question. Late in October, it is true, Thouvenel, who on his return had been graciously received by the sultan and thought that Reshid's fall had "consecrated our victory",[1] suffered one last smashing blow from the vindictive Stratford, through the reinstatement of Reshid as grand vizier: but this time the latter, who had already once hinted to Thouvenel that "he would be charmed to be delivered from his patron" (i.e. Stratford!)[2] made direct overtures to Napoleon through Sefer Pasha.[3] In December the Great Elchi went home leaving Alison to act as Chargé, and fully intending to return. But on the sudden fall of the Palmerston Government in February 1858 he was unwary enough to offer his resignation, which was accepted by the new foreign secretary, Lord Malmesbury. In the interval, early in January, Reshid had suddenly been removed by death, and the disappearance of two such figures left Thouvenel more or less in possession of the arena, and praying that "the old matador" would never re-enter it. After a certain interval—during which Talleyrand grumbled at "the barren delays" of the Commission[4]—Sir Henry Bulwer, a *bête noire* of Lord Stratford, succeeded to the embassy, and though masterful in his own way and not converted to union, he was not able to hold up

---

[1] To Gramont, in September—Thouvenel, *op. cit.* p. 166.

[2] *Ibid.* p. 182.

[3] In reality a Polish count named Koscielsky, who had acquired first French, then Turkish, citizenship, and had accepted Islam.

[4] "Nos stériles lenteurs"—8 January 1858, to Walewski—*Acte şi Documente*, VII, no. 1986.

a process that had by now become inevitable. The serpent, said the observant Thouvenel, was replacing the lion.[1] Turkish policy was again in the hands of Ali and Fuad, who blocked union whenever they could, but were in the main subservient to France.

On 22 May 1858 the deferred Conference met in Paris to consider the Commission's report and to draw up a definitive convention: Walewski, Cowley and Hübner represented their three countries, but the most interesting figure was the Russian delegate Kiselev, to whom Roumania had owed her first modern constitution and who now, almost a generation later, was to share in its transformation. At the outset Walewski, backed by Kiselev, spoke in favour of union under a foreign prince, but did not press it in face of Austrian and Turkish opposition, and was content to submit a plan for a central legislature for "the United Principalities". Hübner opposed even a common name and flag and suggested that there should merely be a revision of the existing Règlement. Cowley found himself in a very difficult position between two unbending opponents and warned London that Napoleon was ready to risk breaking up the Conference: and at a shooting party at Fontainebleau he had to defend Britain against the emperor's reproaches. The negative and confused outlook of British statesmen towards the problem is well illustrated by the fact that Clarendon and Malmesbury agreed in crediting Paris with "nothing else than a plan for establishing and perpetuating anarchy by means of an oligarchical republic".[2] Eventually the Porte itself proved less unbending than Austria and compromised upon the clumsy title of "The United Principalities of Moldavia and Wallachia". The concession of a common flag was still obstinately contested, Austria insisting on the addition of a Turkish emblem and both sides rejecting the Prussian proposal of two flags on a single pole. The stress laid by Hübner upon the flag question as "the knot of the situation" was of course due to Austria's fear that such a symbol might serve as a rallying point for her own Roumanians. Napoleon at last yielded to a personal appeal from Francis Joseph himself, but only after a semi-inspired pamphlet entitled *L'Empereur Napoléon et les Principautés Roumaines*, hinting at the possibility of an Austro-French war, had created a passing panic on the Bourse.[3]

[1] Thouvenel, *op. cit.* p. 327.
[2] Malmesbury, *Memoirs*, II, p. 124.
[3] This pamphlet contained more than one notable passage to the address of England. After quoting Disraeli's demand for a Roumanian state, as a second

At last on 19 August 1858 a new and elaborate Convention was signed in Paris, which, though it represented a further compromise between the two groups of Powers, was none the less a very great step towards constitutional government and may be said to have rendered ultimate independence inevitable. The Roumanian provinces were henceforth to be known under the clumsy title of "the United Principalities of Moldavia and Wallachia", under the suzerainty of the sultan: and the capitulations concluded with successive sultans (which we now know to be of doubtful authenticity) and the privileges established by the Treaty of Paris are reaffirmed "under the collective guarantee of the signatory Powers". There were still to be two princes, two Cabinets, two Assemblies, but a Central Commission for both provinces was to be established at Focşani, to concert measures of joint concern, and there was also to be a single supreme Court of Appeal. In each case the hospodar was to be elected for life by the Assembly and then invested by the sultan as before. Only those persons were eligible who could prove an income of 3000 ducats and had either held public office or had sat in the Assembly for at least ten years. Executive power was placed in the prince's hands, but legislative power was to be shared between him, the Assembly and the Central Commission—an entirely new experiment which in all probability would have proved unworkable, if it had ever been fully put to the test. Each Assembly was to be elected for seven years and to sit normally for a period of three months in every year, though the prince could convoke it in special session: the ministers were to be responsible to it and could be impeached either by it or by the prince. The Budget was not valid till sanctioned by the Assembly, and all taxation was subject to its approval.

Very wide powers were reserved to the Central Commission for preparing unitary legislation, proposing administrative reforms and codifying existing laws: of its sixteen members, who were to be salaried, half came from each principality, four being nominated by each prince and four elected from inside each assembly. Other clauses laid down

---

Belgium on the Danube (8 June 1855) and asking why he had changed his views, it went on: "It is a matter well qualified to overwhelm one [bouleverser l'esprit], that it should be England, constitutional and Protestant, who wants to hand over a Christian people to the mercy of the Turks. We do not know if that can serve its commerce, but certainly it will not aid its Christian and Liberal propaganda, for this act is a grave stain upon British honour in the East". It was above all because Roumanian unity had become a French cause "that certain Powers reject it with such persistence". See *Acte şi Documente*, VII, no. 2058.

the equality of all citizens before the law, equality of religion, of taxation, and of access to office: all class privileges and monopolies were
thus formally abolished. It was specially provided that a measure of
land reform should be undertaken without delay.

The annual tribute, now fixed at 1½ and 2½ million piastres for Moldavia and Wallachia respectively, was still to be paid to the Porte. It
was laid down that "in the event of foreign aggression" the suzerain
should concert with the Principalities measures for the defence of their
territory, that existing treaties between the Porte and foreign Powers
should be "applicable to the Principalities in all that shall not infringe
their immunities"—a vague phrase scarcely capable of definition—and
that in the event of the violation of these immunities the princes may
appeal through their agents at the Porte (who must be born natives of
Moldavia or Wallachia) to the ambassadors of the guaranteeing Powers
(§§ 8, 9). The two militias were to be organised on a united basis, as
if they were "two corps of the same army", and inspected in alternate
years by the nominee of one or other prince: they might not be increased by more than one-third without the consent of the suzerain
Power. It will be seen from all this that the control of the Porte over
Roumania had dwindled to negligible proportions, and that there was
scarcely any sphere of action left in which interference was still
possible.

A special annexe was added to the Convention, regulating the new
franchise for the two assemblies. The electors were divided into two
classes: (a) direct, namely those possessing a minimum income of 1000
ducats in land or an urban commercial capital of 6000 ducats, and (b)
primary, possessing an income of 100 ducats. The latter class had to
elect three electors in each district, who in their turn elected a single
deputy, whereas the former class elected two deputies for each district.
The net result was to leave the control of the assemblies in the hands of
the big landed interest, and to maintain the peasant as a negligible
quantity.

Looking upon these events from our present point of vantage, it is
difficult to conceive how serious statesmen should have believed that
such half-measures could work out in practice or hold back the tide of
national feeling that was in full flood before their very eyes. The Turks
were at least logical. When Thouvenel was first instructed, in March
1856, to press union upon the Porte, Fuad Pasha replied categorically
that a foreign prince and union were equivalent in the long run to

independence, and that the same result would follow logically in Serbia also. In 1858 the same Fuad was the Turkish representative at the Conference, and did all he could to check concessions. But the ship was now well under weigh, and Boerescu's summary of the situation was absolutely just, if politely sarcastic—"It is not complete union, but the principle is proclaimed: it is for us Roumanians to do the rest, and we owe thanks to Europe, who has shown us that union is possible". With a view to ensuring orderly elections, the Powers insisted on the appointment of provisional Governments—in each case a "Regency of Three" (Caimacamies à trois):[1] and the result was an undignified scramble among many of the big boiars to curry favour with the Porte and thus secure the princely dignity. The method of selection followed the lines of the old Règlement: and it is true that all six were declared unionists, and that while Vogorides' ministers were virtually proscribed in Moldavia, Wallachia made what Bulwer called "a clean sweep of the Ghica crowd".[2] But the situation had its dangers, since the Wallachian kaimakams were working for the ex-prince George Bibescu, while one of the three Moldavians, Stephen Catargiu, had active designs of his own upon the throne, and therefore, just because he was at issue with his colleagues, had the full backing of the Turks and Austrians.

Fortunately, the unionists in the two provinces were energetic and on the whole played their cards well, though their greatest advantage came from the dissensions of their opponents. They agreed quickly on three points—that none of the ex-princes or their sons should be selected, that the same man must be elected in both provinces and that the election in Jassy should be hastened, in order to use its outcome as a lever upon opinion in Bucarest. The third point was the most practical, for Bibescu was strong and active in Wallachia and seemed likely to carry the day. Catargiu relied on the help of the Turkish commissary in Jassy, Afif Bey, and other agents of the Porte, to overbear his two colleagues and pack the leading administrative posts and the Cabinet with creatures of his own. But the other two stood firm, and actually went so far as to order the expulsion of Afif, on the ground that his official functions had expired, and also to depose the Moldavian agent at the Porte, Photiades, the corrupt and subservient Greek who had

---

[1] Manu, Bălianu and Filipescu in Wallachia, Panu, Sturdza and Catargiu in Moldavia.

[2] To Malmesbury, 24 November—quoted by Riker, op. cit. p. 184.

been unmasked by the capture of his correspondence with his brother-in-law Vogorides.[1]

These two actions caused equal amazement and alarm at the Porte, who saw its once subservient vassals on the very verge of emancipation: and at the instance of the grand vizier the ambassadors sent a severe reprimand to Jassy for exceeding their powers under the firman. But of course this simply enabled the regents to strengthen their own position in the country by patriotic resistance, and provided the unionists with a fresh incentive to persevere. Malmesbury suggested a fresh meeting of the Paris Conference to clear up this and other disputed points, but as Buol opposed this, there was a deadlock and the Powers allowed matters to drift.

In the last week of December 1858 the elections for the new Moldavian Assembly were held on the restricted franchise already described, and they did not give the unionists the majority which they had hoped for. Out of sixty-four they obtained thirty seats, and found themselves seriously divided on the very vital question of land reform. But what saved the situation was that the majority was still more fatally divided, by twenty-one against thirteen, between the rival candidatures of the ex-prince Michael Sturdza and his son Gregory. This quarrel may almost be regarded as symbolic of the crumbling power of the old boiar oligarchy, who saw the imminent danger which threatened their privileges, and yet were incapable of uniting in their defence.

The regents in Jassy realised the urgency of action and the danger of foreign interference, and convoked the Assembly without waiting for the usual new year holidays. A further incentive was provided by the disturbing news from Serbia, where on 24 December 1858 Prince Alexander Karagjorgjević had been forced to abdicate. Austrian armed intervention seemed imminent, and the Cabinet of Vienna was only deterred by the growing tension in its relations with Paris and the prospects of war in Lombardy. For the Roumanians it seemed emphatically a case of "Now or never". During the second week of

---

[1] Some of these documents are to be found in *Acte şi Documente*, IV, nos. 1063, 1138, 1143, 1150—Photiades to Vogorides on 6 May 1857 insists on the need for hastening the elections, "because all depends on them", and for obtaining the Austrian consul's approval for ministerial changes. On 9 May he writes of his intimate relations with the grand vizier and Ghalib Pasha, and refers to himself as "secret instrument" between them and Baron Prokesch, the Austrian Inter-Nuncio. He recommends the grand vizier to use stiff language to Thouvenel as to the behaviour of the French consuls and commissioner.

January, then, the party caucus was anxiously searching for a suitable candidate for the Moldavian throne and gravely embarrassed by the refusal of either Sturdza to withdraw: the other candidates, Mavrogheni, Negri and Lascar Catargiu, were less serious. After lengthy discussions no agreement could be reached: Kogălniceanu was in despair, and another deputy, Pisoski, put his back against the door and threatened to blow out his own brains unless a speedy decision were taken. It was at this moment that a new candidate was suddenly put forward, who belonged to one of the lesser boiar families, of some antiquity but never prominent in affairs, and who had not hitherto been spoken of. This was Alexander Cuza, who in the previous summer had acquired some popularity by refusing, as prefect of Galaţ, to play the dirty game of Vogorides, and was at this moment "hetman" of the handful of troops dignified with the name of "army". At first put forward by Pisoski in the name of the National Party, he was soon joined by the supporters of Gregory Sturdza, who saw that their own man's chances were negligible: and on 17 January he was unanimously acclaimed as prince by the Assembly, after the metropolitan had spoken in his favour. Kogălniceanu, in a speech of greeting to this new heir to the throne of Stephen the Great, quoted the answer of Alexander the Good to a Byzantine envoy—"Roumania has no protector save God and her sword". Next day Place wrote to Thouvenel in high enthusiasm: "For the first time in Moldavia an election has been accomplished without expenditure of a single ducat.... The election of Colonel Cuza is the complete triumph of unionist and liberal ideas against the old system of corruption".[1]

Under the impression of the exciting news from Jassy and Belgrade, the Wallachian elections, on 22 January, gave the Conservatives a two-thirds majority, and for the moment the election of Bibescu seemed almost certain. The Democrats, whose candidate was Nicholas Golescu, had against them all the forces of Bibescu and the Ghicas alike: their sole hope lay in popular agitation, and this was in the hands of Ion Brătianu. When the Assembly met in Bucarest on 3 February, there were disorderly scenes, the mob insulted the kaimakams and shouted under the windows. An important rôle was played by Dimitrie Ghica, who as nephew of the former prince was hostile to Bibescu, and as prefect of police in the capital was able to curb or give free rein to the demonstrations. He appears to have been the first to launch the name

[1] 18 January—*Acte şi Documente*, IX, no. 2681.

PLATE XII

ALEXANDER CUZA

BARBU STIRBEI

of Cuza, but it was the young deputy, Vasile Boerescu, who turned the scale by a speech of deep fervour and simplicity. "Let us unite around this name", he cried, "and our memory will be blessed by our grandchildren.... The country will be content and our conscience will tell us that we have fulfilled the most sacred of duties." A wave of emotion swept the Assembly, and on 5 February, despite the secret reluctance of many boiars, Cuza was elected by acclamation as "Alexander Ion I". The news was received with immense enthusiasm at Jassy, where the crowd organised a torchlight procession to the French Consulate and shouted "Vive l'Empereur". Cuza himself sent a personal appeal to Napoleon III, declaring that "the fate of the Roumanians is in Your Majesty's keeping": and Napoleon played up when he addressed the French Legislature on 7 February. "If I were asked what interest France has in those distant countries which the Danube waters, I should reply that the interest of France is everywhere where there is a just and civilising cause to promote." The mere words were pointed enough, but their real significance lay in the approaching Franco-Austrian conflict and in the scarcely veiled warning to Austria to leave the Principalities alone. In one of the many "inspired" pamphlets which appeared in Paris under the Second Empire, it was broadly hinted at this moment that "Austria would like to divert to the Danube the storm which is muttering against her in Italy: but she would only precipitate events".[1] We shall realise better the fluid character of the whole situation, when we remember that on the day separating these two events Miloš and Michael Obrenović re-entered Belgrade after seventeen years of exile.

Cuza had never pleaded his own cause and now rose to a difficult occasion, showing great tact and self-restraint. He acted from the first as though the words of Victor Place's report were literally true: "It is a principle and not an individual that has been proclaimed".[2] There is little doubt that Place, who was already in intimate relations with Cuza, now advised him to summon the united Assemblies to Focşani and confront Europe with an accomplished fact. But as no guarantee of official support from Paris was forthcoming, the new prince had the wisdom not to force the pace, but to issue an eloquent appeal to the Powers for their "consecration of the great act", adding that he himself had no personal ambitions and would "always be ready to enter into

[1] *L'Autriche et le Prince Roumain* (1859), p. 31.
[2] Place to Walewski, 20 February—*Acte şi Documente*, IX, no. 2710.

private life", if that would promote the cause of union.[1] On his arrival in Bucarest, which was made the occasion of tremendous demonstrations, he assured Colquhoun that he would bow to Europe's decisions, but would resist Turkish troops by force of arms.[2]

The double election took the world by surprise and showed the futility of placing artificial obstacles in the way of union. Roumania had safely come to birth, but not thanks to the midwifery of the presiding Great Powers.

[1] *Acte*, VIII, no. 2599.
[2] Colquhoun to Malmesbury, 27 February—quoted by Riker, *op. cit.* p. 213.

# CHAPTER X

## TRANSYLVANIA FROM 1792 TO 1867

"Nimic despre noi fără noi" (No decision about us without us).
Roumanian proverb.

The year 1792 seemed about to inaugurate new political activities alike in Hungary and in Transylvania: but it was followed only too soon by the tremendous diversion of the revolutionary and Napoleonic wars, which, paradoxically enough, served at once to promote and to stifle the national movement. Promote, in that it brought new political and literary ideas surging in from the West: stifle, in that it concentrated the political efforts of the whole country upon foreign wars and almost necessarily strengthened the absolutist and centralising efforts of the Viennese court as against local interests, even when these could boast such impregnable entrenchments as the Hungarian constitution. The situation was altogether dominated by foreign issues: after the collapse of the Jacobin movement there was a complete lack of political leaders of any eminence, and the steady drain of man-power and a succession of financial crises accentuated still further the internal stagnation.

For the closing years of the eighteenth and the first quarter of the nineteenth century, then, Transylvania is but the faint reflection of Hungary—several degrees more provincial in every sense of the term, hearing only distant echoes from the great world, and living its narrow life of oligarchic and social privilege as though the institutions handed down by its ancestors were destined to last to all eternity, instead of being constantly sapped by new political, racial and economic forces.

Just as in Hungary proper Francis refused, and refused with full impunity, to summon Parliament from 1812 to 1825, when the constitutional protest at last proved too strong for him, so in Transylvania the Diet was not allowed to meet between 1811 and 1834. Recruits were levied illegally, the posts of officials were filled not by election but by arbitrary crown appointment, and the constitution became almost a farce. Even when the Diet was finally summoned, it was only after a last futile attempt to govern by a special royal commissioner: and after a year of fruitless debates and recrimination—what is known in Hungarian politics as "gravaminal policy" or the policy of putting forward grievances in rank after serried rank—Francis dissolved the Diet as disobedient, even rebellious, and deliberately obstructive. Some indication of the ideas already stirring may be gathered from the passionate oratory of the great Magyar patriot Baron Wesselényi, in which hatred of Austria and a leaning towards French liberalism were strangely blended. In one debate Kemény propounded the unfamiliar doctrine that the highest power comes from the people, while another speaker, Huszár, declaimed: "From God I expect grace, from the Sovereign I demand justice and the fulfilment of my lawful demands. We are a legislative body, the representatives of a free people. Who stands above us? I venture to answer, 'No one'". Wesselényi gave a practical turn to these ideas by producing roughly lithographed reports of the debates, in defiance of the censor, and by proposing that the orders of intruded officials should be disregarded: and a torchlight procession in his honour heralded his departure to continue his patriotic agitation as a delegate to the House of Magnates in Pressburg. Francis on his side was altogether intransigeant, and when the question of the union of Transylvania with Hungary was raised, he bluntly told a Saxon deputation that he would never give his consent, and that "in the union of a big body with a small one the latter generally loses".[1]

\*     \*     \*     \*

In all this period the Roumanians continued to be relegated entirely to the background. On the death of Bishop Gerasim Adamovici in 1796, the see of the Orthodox Roumanians remained vacant for fourteen years and was administered by a vicar, who it was hoped might be able to manœuvre his leaderless flock into the Union. But once again this failed in face of the sturdy endurance of the masses, and in 1809 an Imperial Patent was issued, granting the Orthodox the right to elect a bishop who knew their own tongue, and assigning to him a salary of 4000 gulden. Even then eighteen months elapsed before Basil Moga was approved by the emperor and could be ordained bishop by the Serbian metropolitan at Karlowitz; and even he was only second on the list, the favourite candidate not being acceptable to the authorities. A series of strict conditions was also imposed. The bishop was to regard his nomination "as a sign of Imperial grace": he was expressly excluded from the special privileges enjoyed by the Serbian nation; and he was

---

[1] F. Teutsch, *Gesch. der sieb. Sachsen*, II, p. 88.

enjoined to prevent Orthodox monks from the Principality from crossing the Carpathians and to remember that the Uniates were since 1744
on the same footing as the four Received Religions, whereas the Orthodox were merely tolerated, and that he was therefore "forbidden to
resist the spread and propagation of the Uniate religion" or to indulge
in proselytism. Finally, he was to reduce the number of his clergy and
to ensure that those remaining should be literate and should have a
knowledge of the Magyar language.[1]

This last provision vividly illustrates the neglected state of the clergy,
whose ranks may none the less be said to have formed at this time the
last refuge of Roumanian culture. Among the Uniates the situation was
less unfavourable, thanks to the unwearied efforts of John Innocent
Klein. Yet it was only under Joseph II that the first Roumanian national school was founded in Blaj (Blasendorf),[2] and not till 1811 that
a teacher's seminary was assigned to them. Meanwhile, however, three
men were laying the first scanty foundations of a Roumanian literary
revival—Samuil Klein, a nephew of the great Bishop, George Şincai
and Peter Maior. The first of these had studied at the Pázmaneum, the
famous theological college in Vienna, and after some years at Blaj returned to Vienna, to the College of St Barbara, as supervisor of studies.
It was here that he met the two young seminarists, whose five years in
Rome had not merely imbued them with classical studies, but kindled
their national sentiments in the most romantic manner possible. For
there they had been thrilled by the Column of Trajan, with its wonderful
series of bas-reliefs depicting Dacian captives gracing a Roman triumph,
and they soon had become immersed in the first uncritical study of
Roumanian origins. Full of this vision of ancestral splendour they returned to Vienna, to find the same ideas simmering in the head of Klein:
and within a year he and Şincai had produced the first modern Roumanian grammar, whose very name, despite its dry Latin husk, was a
political programme for a future age—*Elements of the Daco-Roman or
Wallach language*.[3] The preface urged the introduction of Latin in place
of Cyrilline characters, and to prove his case further Klein published
two books of prayers in the new orthography. In 1791 he became the
first censor for Roumanian books at Buda, and as he was attached to
the University library, this may be said to have been the first cultural

[1] Schaguna, *Gesch. der griech.-orientalischen Kirche in Oesterreich*, p. 134.
[2] Primaria schola nationalis Balasfelvensis.
[3] *Elementa linguae daco-romanae sive valachicae*, 1780.

centre of the Roumanians on Hungarian soil, especially after 1805, when it was provided with a Roumanian printing-press.

Klein died in 1806, but his work was carried on by Şincai, who, having quarrelled with his bishop, owed the possibility of pursuing his studies to the generosity of Count Vas, to whose sons he acted as tutor and in whose house he eventually died in 1816. The third of the little group, Peter Maior, was more fortunate and became archpriest at the little Saxon town of Sächsisch-Reen. Succeeding Klein as censor, he began in 1809 to publish collections of sermons and finally, in 1812, a *History of the Origin of the Roumanians in Dacia*. Though based largely on Şincai's manuscript, this book has a place of its own as the first *published* history by a native Roumanian writer. It cannot in any way compare with the contemporary publications of the learned Christian von Engel, a German Hungarian who had employed Şincai for the transcription of native chroniclers; but it had a deep influence on the first generation of writers beyond the Carpathians.

Şincai had already written an essay on Roumanian origins, which was to have appeared as supplement to the original "Daco-Roman grammar", but was not sanctioned by the Viennese censor. In 1813 he attempted to publish at home in Transylvania the result of his more mature studies, under the title of "Chronicon Daco-Romanorum sive Valachorum": but this time the provincial censor, at that time the Catholic Bishop, Mártonfi, forbade not merely its publication, but even the restoration of the manuscript to its author, on the ground that such a work "might have disadvantageous results for the public peace of Transylvania".[1] Later Roumanian writers contend that this veto was forfeited by the phrase "opus igne, auctor patibulo dignus", but the Magyars are able to point out that it is nowhere to be found in the original document, and its origin still remains obscure, though it certainly represents the general Magyar attitude towards Şincai and his doctrines. These were, it may freely be admitted, of a highly imaginative character and sought to prove complete continuity of the Roman tradition and purity of blood in the modern Dacians: but the underlying note was a reminder that the Roumanian nation had been robbed of its history, its monuments, its land, and sunk in unmerited neglect, but that Dacia rightfully belonged, and must one day return, to the sons of Trajan. These ideas were already in the air and admirably suited to the

[1] The book was eventually published at Jassy at the expense of Prince Gregory Ghica, vol. 1 in 1843, and the remainder in 1853.

historical and literary romanticism then prevalent alike in Germany, France and Britain and eagerly drunk in, though perhaps imperfectly digested, by the young renascent nations of the East. They became a point of departure for a number of half-baked writers of the next generation, were uncritically adopted and propagated in the decades following Roumanian independence and were clung to all the more obstinately because of the ferocious polemics which they evoked on the side of the Magyars and to a lesser degree of the Germans. It was not till the turn of the century that a more critical school arose and abandoned the more extravagant portions of the ultra-patriotic theory: and to-day these only linger among a few phantasts.

In another direction also Şincai and Maior did memorable pioneer work, in their endeavour to reform the imperfect orthography due to centuries of neglect, to shake off the Slavonic characters which served as a straight jacket to the reviving language, and to lay the main stress upon its Latin elements. This tendency, so praiseworthy in the first instance, though in its turn much exaggerated by certain writers of the later nineteenth century (who foolishly sought to rob the language of its rich and expressive Slav vocabulary and turns of phrase and to bring it into forced alignment with the other Latin tongues), was the main cause of Şincai's indifferent relations with his ecclesiastical chiefs, who took the same narrow and conservative line towards the changes which he advocated as the Serbian clergy towards the much more brilliantly conceived reforms of the great philologist Vuk Karadžić.

Nothing can well be stranger than the speedy and decisive influence which this crude pioneer work, amid the desperate handicaps of Roumanian life in Transylvania, should have exercised to the south of the Carpathians. It is all the stranger if we consider the gulf which their adherence to the Union had erected between these men and their Orthodox kinsmen in the Principalities, or again, if we remember how impervious the wealthy boiars, whose nearest route to the West lay through Hungary, were as yet to the plight of the Roumanian masses in a land which externally appeared to them more Magyar and German than Roumanian. Professor Iorga may well exclaim what salutary effects the coming of a Şincai or a Klein might have had upon the development of culture and opinion in the Principalities. In actual fact, the first link between the two movements was provided by George Lazar, who though the son of very poor parents, had achieved the as yet rare distinction of a doctorate and held a subordinate post at the

Roumanian Church in Hermannstadt, but, disappointed in his hopes and ambitions, had in 1816 gone to Bucarest as tutor to the children of a Wallachian *grande dame*. He found patrons in two of the older boiars, Bălăceanu and Iordache Golescu, and obtained permission to give free lectures on arithmetic and geometry, in a few unheated rooms of the monastery of St Sava, the object being to train surveyors for the big estates. His school was very soon full, and he was able to turn to other subjects, first geography and philosophy, and at last history, on which he lectured with an infectious fervour and conviction that withstood all the denunciations of the Greek party. The new metropolitan of Bucarest, Dionisie Lupu, granted his protection and made it possible for him to maintain himself by making very modest charges for instruction and to create a teaching staff. Lazar's homage to his Roman ancestors and to the glories of imperial Rome was every whit as uncritical as the researches of Şincai: but he was a forerunner and awakener, and his imperfect textbooks and primers were the seed of better things. He died soon after the Revolution of 1821.[1]

*     *     *     *

After the death of the Emperor Francis in 1835 the attitude of the central authorities somewhat relaxed: the attempt to supersede the constitution once more and to govern through the Archduke Ferdinand of Este as royal commissioner, was abandoned, and the Diet was allowed to meet at intervals. For instance, it sat from April 1837 till March 1838, but its activities were already overshadowed by those of the Hungarian Parliament. The language question now made its first entry, and the demand for Magyar as the official language for the whole province was put forward by two out of the three nations. The Saxons were gravely alarmed at this, but were too opportunist and narrow in their outlook to risk co-operation with the Roumanians, to whom the idea was of course still more objectionable. They could not as yet throw off the consciousness of their superiority to the despised "natio tolerata", and just at this moment they were resentful at a petition of grievances presented by the Orthodox bishop to the Diet. In it he demanded the admission of Roumanians living on Saxon territory to offices and guilds on equal terms with the Saxons themselves, the extension of tithes to the Orthodox clergy no less than to those of other

[1] The above summary closely follows Iorga, *Gesch. des rumänischen Volkes*, II, pp. 236–8.

religions, and also various reforms in taxation and in respect of mixed marriages. The petition was received with universal disapproval, and the Saxons could plausibly argue that any solution of Roumanian grievances must be for the whole country, and not merely for their territory: but their attitude was petty, and a golden opportunity was lost.

In 1839 the Hungarian Parliament again met, and the nationalist agitation among the Magyars rapidly assumed formidable dimensions. From the first it had a double character—the demand for constitutional reform on the lines of Western liberalism, notably the abolition of noble privileges and exemptions, the establishment of a direct franchise, press freedom and the emancipation of the peasantry, and at the same time a fanatical attempt to identify the two conceptions of "Hungarian" and "Magyar" and to prepare in the briefest possible period the Magyarisation of all the other races of the country. More and more, then, the struggle centred round the language question, and the Slovaks, Roumanians, Germans, Serbs, Croats and Ruthenes alike saw themselves threatened in their very existence and adopted an attitude of passive resistance. The Magyars, strong in their central strategic position (while the other races held the periphery and lacked the necessary contact with each other), overwhelmingly entrenched in the ruling class of nobles and "gentry" and in the hierarchy of the Churches, strong too in their control of the autonomous county assemblies (for centuries the bulwark of the Hungarian constitution), were able to assume the offensive all the more easily because in the forties they possessed several leaders of quite unusual ability and varying range— Count Stephen Széchenyi, known for his services to learning and to agriculture, Francis Deák, the constitutional jurist, and above all Louis Kossuth, the inspired demagogue, orator and journalist, who had already been sentenced to two years' imprisonment and was soon to receive a second sentence for organising the reports of parliamentary proceedings on more effective lines than Wesselényi's improvised effort at Kolozsvár.

In 1840, then, laws were passed at Pressburg superseding Latin by Magyar as the official language of the Government and of Parliament. Its knowledge was enjoined upon the clergy of all denominations, while all registers were to become exclusively Magyar after a lapse of three more years. Highly characteristic of the chauvinism already rampant was the reply of Pulszky—afterward's Kossuth's secretary in England —to the plea of the Free Cities for adequate representation. In his view this could not be granted, because it would mean a diminution of the power of the nobles, and above all, because the towns were mainly inhabited by Germans or Slavs.

These changes awakened an immediate echo in the Transylvanian Diet, where in November 1841 Count Kemény proposed that Magyar should at once be made the language of the Gubernium, the law courts and the provincial High Command, that the Saxon authorities should be obliged, after a respite of ten years, to conduct correspondence in Magyar, and that after a similar period Magyar should be made the language of instruction for all "Wallach" schools. Count Kálnoky actually argued that as the Saxons did not understand proper German, this would not really be a curtailment of their rights, while others openly regretted the failure to assimilate Saxons and Roumanians. When a Saxon spokesman, on the basis of the constitutional practice of four centuries, demanded that any change should respect the equality of the Germans, he was greeted by storms of protest and abuse, and warned against the dangers of isolation for a small nation like the Saxons, who had "the Bissene worm at their heart"—using the ancient Latin name of a Dacian tribe and meaning their Roumanian dependants, whose numbers were steadily growing on the "Fundus Regius". In the end, the Saxon deputies withheld their seal from the new linguistic law,[1] but even this could not avail to hold up the march of events.

It is interesting to notice the contrast between the two chief exponents of Magyar nationalism in Hungary and in Transylvania. For while Kossuth in his brilliantly edited paper *Pesti Hirlap*, urged that "we must hasten to Magyarise the Croats, Roumanians and Saxons, for otherwise we shall perish", and thereby evoked an urgent protest and warning from the wise and tolerant Széchenyi, his friend and colleague Wesselényi on the other hand was no less alive than Széchenyi to the danger of chauvinism and undue haste. In 1843 he published a pamphlet which echoed widely in its day, advocating a regrouping of the Habsburg dominions on a federal basis, as the best means of exercising a superior attraction over the Slavs inside the Monarchy and preventing them from falling into the arms of Russian Panslavism. He was far ahead of most Magyars in offering Croatia a special political and linguistic autonomy within the greater Hungarian federal unit: but in his scheme Transylvania was to become an integral part of Hungary. He

---

[1] Before 1848 each of the three "Received Nations" had to append its seal before any law of the Diet could be valid.

was of course fully alive to the capital fact that in the new era of nationalism the Magyars formed a minority in Transylvania, whereas union with the sister kingdom would at once assure to them a dominant position over the other nationalities.[1] In a word, Wesselényi hoped by the extension of sound constitutional and liberal principles throughout the Monarchy to meet the main grievances of the other races and yet assure to the Magyars their old leadership, by legitimate means. As his future was to show, he was ready, unlike most of his Transylvanian colleagues, to draw the necessary political consequences from the emancipation of the Roumanian masses. And indeed it was Wesselényi who coined the irreverent phrase, that the three Nations and the four Religions were "the seven deadly sins of Transylvania".

In this connection it is right to mention a pamphlet by another notable Transylvanian, the Saxon pastor Stephan Ludwig Roth. In *The Language Struggle*, published in 1843, he boldly defended the rights of the German language, resting on privileges which had the guarantee of six centuries behind them, and at the same time tried to prove Magyarisation to be at once undesirable and unprofitable. In the course of his argument there occurs the significant admission that if it is desired to proclaim a "Landessprache", such an one does already exist—"it is not the German, not the Magyar either, but the Wallach.... One only needs to make a journey or visit a market: before one tries to see whether the one speaks German or the other Magyar, the conversation begins in the Wallach language".[2] And again he points out that in the Estates "the Saxons have equal rights with the Magyars. But if one considers the number of those speaking, the Emperor must speak Wallach to the Transylvanians, for the children of Israel are more than we...".[3] Unhappily his only conclusion is that existing rights should be maintained and "Wallach" used side by side with Magyar, German and Latin in the dealings of the authorities with the people. But of granting real concessions to the Roumanians there is no suggestion. Nothing illustrates better the petty outlook of the Saxons than the case of a Roumanian named Secarianu who in 1845 applied for a clerk's post in Braşov and whose appeal went up to the Vienna Chancellory. In the

---

[1] *Szózat a magyar és szlav nemzetiség ügyében* (A Voice in the Matter of Magyar and Slav Nationality), 1843: cf. also M. Horváth, 25 *Jahre der Gesch. Ungarns*, II, p. 114.

[2] S. L. Roth, *Leben und Schriften*, II, p. 132.

[3] *Ibid.* p. 149.

official Saxon statement on this case occurs a sentence which speaks for itself: "During the seven centuries since the German guests were called into the country, in accordance with their privileges all public offices were exclusively administered by Saxons, without a Roumanian ever attaining a public post in all these centuries which embrace twenty-four generations".[1] And so doubtless it should have continued for twenty-four generations more.

All three men misjudged the situation in one capital aspect, in that they accepted the popular bogey of Panslavism and assumed it to be the work of an all-pervading Russian policy, whereas in reality the national movements among the Slovaks, Croats and Serbs were no less spontaneous, though weaker and more handicapped, than that among the Magyars themselves, and in reality the leaders of all four races looked far rather to Vienna than to St Petersburg or Moscow. It was only natural that Széchenyi's attention should have been mainly directed to the Slavs, while to the other two, as Transylvanians, the Roumanians also bulked largely.

*   *   *   *

Under Wesselényi the movement for union with Hungary first took clear shape. The claim of the Hungarian Parliament for the detachment of the so-called "Partes"[2] was resisted as a piecemeal solution, but the idea of transcending any such points of detail in a wider union grew in popularity as the parliamentary movement in Hungary gathered volume. Step by step the Magyar nationalists wrung fresh legislative concessions from the crown: and in 1843 Parliament introduced Magyar as the exclusive language of the legislature, the Government and official business, and also, in theory, of public instruction, though this latter decision was left to be worked out in detail and was therefore still hanging over the non-Magyar races as a sword of Damocles, when the supreme crisis of 1848 arrived. Popular enthusiasm for the "national language", as Magyar was now habitually called in this most polyglot of European states, was fanned to fever heat by Louis Kossuth—himself the son of a Magyarised Slovak "gentry" family. The mad illusion that Hungary could be Magyarised at a stroke of the pen—a proposition which at that

---

[1] A. Papiu Ilarianu, *Die constitutionelle Unabhängigkeit Siebenbürgens*, p. 37.

[2] See *supra*, p. 115. Certain easterly counties of Hungary had been left in the air by the Turkish conquest of the central plains and had escaped a like fate by incorporation with the Principality, pending a future union.

time was equivalent to every two Magyars in existence securing three renegade recruits for their nation—revealed itself in the repressive measures of the forties against Slovak nationalism, in systematic attempts to use the Churches as instruments of the Magyar propaganda, and above all in the Parliament's attitude towards Croatia, which by the laws of 1843 was only granted a respite of six years, at the end of which time it was to be subjected to the same levelling process as the minor nationalities which had never enjoyed its seven centuries of constitutional autonomy.

The movement caused growing unrest and excitement among the nationalities. The Slovaks and Croats in particular looked towards the court of Vienna, and while of course the former were weak, isolated and at a hopeless disadvantage, the latter were stiffened by the long tradition of the frontiersmen in imperial service, and when the crisis came, produced a military leader of considerable merit in Baron Jelačić. In the Parliament at Pressburg the Croats could of course effect nothing with their three delegates: Kossuth thundered his refusal to recognise Croat nationality. The other races were altogether unrepresented, though in 1847 the Slovak leader Ludevit Štúr gained entrance by the back door, as deputy for one of the royal free towns. In Transylvania the Roumanians were of course not merely unrepresented, but entirely disregarded where any political decision was in question. The only possible organised opposition came from the Saxons, whose long veiled breach with the Magyars now became open and acute.

In the autumn of 1846 the Transylvanian Diet again met, and in the following July introduced and adopted a comprehensive Language Law, by which Magyar became the language for the Gubernium, the Diet, the law-courts, and for the entire administration in the territory of the Magyar and Székely nations. The registers were to be kept in Magyar in every parish where Magyar was preached, but German was left in the Lutheran Churches. The Saxons were still left with German for the internal affairs of the "Fundus Regius", but it was already self-evident that such changes must at no distant date undermine the whole status which they had built up and maintained for over six centuries. Once more, unhappily, the Saxons could not see beyond their own narrow interests: for when the Roumanian Bishop Leményi mildly pleaded before the Diet that the grievances of his nation should at least be brought up for discussion at its next meeting, the Saxon deputy Hann protested against what he described as the bishop's communistic views regarding the status of the Roumanians on Saxon territory. A piquant situation arose when Count Dominic Bethlen took the side of Bishop Leményi.

The Diet closed on 10 November 1847, and the centre of interest was transferred to Pressburg, where the Hungarian Parliament opened two days later. Here Kossuth became more than ever before the leader of Magyar nationalism and drowned such warning voices as that of Széchenyi, who ruefully exclaimed, "He will throw our people into a situation from which God Himself will no longer be able to save it". Not content with a full programme of constitutional reform, emancipation of the peasants and equality of taxation, he must needs antagonise the Croats by his linguistic intolerance, and press for the immediate "reincorporation" of Transylvania with Hungary. But he had enthusiastic support. The movement of which he was the soul was already wellnigh irresistible when the news of the February revolution in Paris came as the bursting of the flood gates. On 15 March 1848 Parliament adopted, almost by acclamation, a far-reaching legislative programme which marks the real end of the Middle Ages in Hungary. Serfdom and all feudal exemptions and privileges were swept away, Parliament was transferred to Pest, a responsible ministry, annual Parliaments, triennial elections, a new and direct franchise, liberty of the press, religious equality, trial by jury, a national guard and a national Magyar university, were established. On 11 April the 31 Articles embodying these tremendous changes were passed into law, and a solemn oath to observe them was administered to Ferdinand in person by the Palatine, Archduke Stephen.

Not the least momentous of these laws was Article VII, proclaiming the Union of Transylvania, assigning to it sixty-nine seats in the future united Parliament and declaring Hungary's readiness to maintain "all those special laws and liberties of Transylvania which, without hindering complete union, are favourable to national liberty and unity". The details, however, were to be worked out in agreement with the Union Committee already appointed by the Transylvanian Diet.

Meanwhile in the Principality itself—then still somewhat remote even from Vienna and Pest—the three principal nationalities reacted in very different ways. The Magyars were unanimous in demanding instant union. "Let us unite, for otherwise we perish", was the watchword, and indeed their motive was as clear as daylight: for union would transform them from a nation enjoying oligarchic privilege, but numerically in a minority and conscious of its danger, into an integral part of the dominant race, entrenched in a central position and confident of success. This was crudely stated in a Magyar newspaper of the day: "He who does not see that we must undergo an immediate and thorough transformation (and indeed by as great a leap as if a powerful hand were to fling us suddenly from the Siberian sealfishery to the banks of the Mississippi)—on his thick skull all the weapons of the contemporary press will break".[1] The Saxons were divided, some, in view of their own small numbers, afraid to offend the majority and favouring an opportunist policy, others like Fabini, clearly realising that "any kind of union is surrender at discretion".[2] The Roumanians were from the outset utterly opposed, insisting that a decision must be postponed until they had been admitted to the discussion on equal terms with the other nations. The governor, Count Teleki, summoned the Diet for 29 May, and meanwhile the Saxon University[3] thought it in accordance with the new spirit to proclaim equal rights for the Roumanians on its own territory. Hermannstadt remained a stronghold of anti-unionist sentiment and displayed the black and yellow colours of the imperial house.

Among the Roumanians the first, entirely spontaneous, movement came curiously enough from a small group of officials in the Székely stronghold of Marosvásárhely: and its ringleaders, Avram Iancu and Aron Pumnul, drafted a proclamation bidding all Roumanians gather at Blaj on St Thomas's Day (Dumenica Tomei). Bishop Leményi, who approved, notified the decision to the Government, and its refusal to sanction it was simply disregarded. About 6000 persons met amid great enthusiasm on 24 April and cheered to the echo the speech of Simeon Barnuțiu, a young law student who now came rapidly to the front. Union, he argued, was a national danger until the Roumanian nation had achieved full equality. "Now is the time not to put men under the yoke, but to shake it off. Let it be borne by beasts, you have borne it long enough. Now let us be free men."[4]

This was but the merest rehearsal for the memorable assembly which met on 15 May in a meadow outside the tiny town of Blaj, there and then christened "The Field of Liberty". After an impassioned address of Barnuțiu before the two bishops, Leményi and Șaguna, and a resolu-

[1] Cit. Helfert, *Geschichte der österreichischen Revolution*, I, p. 432.
[2] Teutsch, *op. cit.* II, p. 214.
[3] The old medieval representative assembly of the Saxon nation.
[4] Teodor V. Pacatian, *Cartea de Aur*, I, p. 265.

tion of loyalty to the emperor as the Great Prince of Transylvania, the 40,000 Roumanians present proclaimed their equality as a Nation with the three privileged Nations, denounced the union and protested against the use of "Wallach" or "Oláh" in place of "Roumanian". It was resolved by acclamation to elect two deputations, one under Bishop Şaguna to the emperor, one under Bishop Leményi to the coming Diet. The petitions which they were to present included—in addition to the demand for such liberal reforms as the Magyars also advocated, e.g. personal liberty, a free press, trial by jury, equal taxation and abolition of serfdom—the claim that the Roumanian nation should henceforth be represented in proportion to its numbers in the Diet, and in all administrative, legal and military offices: that it should have its own schools, seminary and university: that the Uniate and Orthodox Churches should enjoy equal rights with the recognised religions and have general assemblies in which their bishops should be freely elected: and above all, that there should be no discussion of union till the Roumanians were fully represented in the Diet. In the popular phrase, "no decision about us, without us" (nimic despre noi fără noi).[1]

On 29 May the Diet opened at Kolozsvár, then the chief stronghold of Magyar sentiment in the Principality, in a tense and electric atmosphere. The Government put forward a programme of five points: union, abolition of feudal dues, taxation of the nobles, free speech and emancipation of the Roumanians: but the first overshadowed all else, and next day union with Hungary was voted, while the mob shouted on the streets "union or death". The Roumanian majority was not represented, and the tiny remnant of twenty-two Saxons were terrorised into compliance, though reserving their existing traditional and linguistic rights and municipal institutions. During June the Diet abolished feudal dues and was then prorogued, and not again summoned.

Meanwhile Bishop Şaguna and his colleagues were received in audience by the fugitive Emperor Ferdinand at Innsbruck on 30 May and presented the Blaj petition. They were met with the ominous argument that their future depended on the execution of the Law of Union, which had been voted unanimously. To this they replied with a protest against the action of the Diet and the assertion that "the dearest treasure of the Roumanians is their nationality and language": and after some weeks' delay they were assured that the new Hungarian Government would assure their nationality by a special law, establish Roumanian schools

[1] Teodor V. Pacatian, *Cartea de Aur*, I.

and employ Roumanians in all branches of the administration. With this Şaguna went back to Pest and met with a friendly reception from Szemere, the minister of the interior. In response to his appeals a parliamentary commission drafted a law of really liberal quality, guaranteeing the Roumanian nationality and language, the use of the latter in church and school and in the proceedings of county and communal assemblies, separating the Roumanian Orthodox Church from the Serbian Patriarchate and granting it a National Assembly of its own. On 24 August, when the question came up for discussion in Parliament, the blind Titan Baron Wesselényi pleaded the Roumanian cause in a memorable speech. "The future is darker than the night of my eyes. Only peace and understanding can save us. St Stephen told his son, happy is the country in which are many nationalities. This advice, to which our notables adhered, weighs upon us as a blasphemy, since the peoples are embittered and roused against each other.... There are several paths by which the nation can be saved from the danger that threatens us. The first is force, but we have finished with the age of force, when for instance the Slavs were extirpated by fire and sword in the German provinces. The second is assimilation, and this requires a strong culture, enormous resources and special powers of attraction, and these we lack. There remains only the third part, to unite in spirit with the nationalities, to make alliance with them, to embrace them as sisters and share all things with them." The Roumanians, he declared, deserved special sympathy, and the name should not be withheld from them, "for it is true that they are the descendants of the Romans. It is in their interest to join with us, for they, like us, are alone in this land. I implore you to accept my proposal, that we may have agreement and peace".[1] Unhappily the effect of this noble appeal was destroyed by Wesselényi's former ally Kossuth, who spoke of the Roumanians as "the spirit of the conspiracy against Hungary" and refused to recognise the special existence of Serb, Wallach or Slovak, still less to fill official posts on a basis of nationality, since that would be an attack upon "the unitary state". This from the man whose torrential eloquence had induced the House to vote by acclamation a national army and huge military credits, was decisive: and in any case events were moving rapidly to a crisis. The short-lived Prague Revolution was long since at an end, by August Radetzky had conquered Milan, and it was possible to think of the subjection of Hungary. The phantom emperor

[1] *Cartea de Aur*, I, pp. 400–2.

was made to repudiate Hungarian Independence and the March Laws, and the Croatian Ban Jelačić, at the head of 40,000 men, crossed the Drave on 11 September to impose the Imperial will upon the refractory nation. On the 28th the Royal Commissioner, Count Lamberg, was murdered by the mob of Pest, and the next day hostilities broke out.

For the relations of the Magyars with the other races this was the parting of the ways, and on all sides desperate counsels won the upper hand. On 19 September the six Saxon deputies withdrew from the Parliament as "no longer legal", and amid the ensuing tumult were denounced by Kossuth. "We may go under", he cried, "but I swear by God we shall not be the last, but shall sink into the grave under the corpses of traitors." Only a week later there was a fresh Roumanian meeting on the Field of Liberty, which reaffirmed the May resolutions, protested against the union and demanded equal representation and an extension of the new Austrian constitution to Transylvania. More ominous still, the Roumanian frontier regiments refused obedience to the Magyar national Government. There was an open trial of strength between its commissary, Baron Vay, and Baron Puchner, the imperialist general, who encouraged the Roumanians to arm and issued a proclamation promising them equal rights with the other nations.[1] While the Saxons on their side began to recruit a battalion of "Feldjäger", the Székels raided and plundered the Saxon districts, and the revolutionary journal *Kossuth Hirlapja*, commenting on one such incident, wrote, "If Sächsisch-Regen does not meet the fate of Sodom and Gomorrah, there is no justice on earth".[2] Soon there was a racial war, which though it did not assume so ferocious a character as that between Magyar and Serb in the Bačka, was none the less marked by many atrocious incidents. Avram Iancu now set himself to organise fifteen "legions" for the imperial service, each with their prefects, sub-prefects and tribunes: but the masses were entirely undisciplined, and there were serious massacres of Magyars in the little towns of Zalatna and Körösbánya (Baia de Criş), while over a hundred Roumanian and Saxon villages were sacked by the "Kossuth Hussars".[3] Under Puchner's auspices a Committee of Pacification was set up at Hermannstadt, consisting of both Roumanians and Saxons. Şaguna increasingly became the moving

[1] *Cartea de Aur*, I, p. 429.
[2] F. Teutsch, *op. cit.* III, p. 254.
[3] See Friedenfels, *Bedeus von Scharberg*, II, pp. 81–3, according to Puchner's report to Windischgrätz.

spirit of more responsible Roumanian opinion, and all the more so because the Uniate Bishop Leményi, owing to his frankly Magyarone attitude, had aroused the active protests of his own flock and was arbitrarily deposed from office by Puchner. Şaguna was never a firebrand and has even been criticised by Roumanian writers for negotiating so long with the Government in Pest and showing a readiness to discuss such inadequate offers as supplementary Roumanian classes in a Magyar academy of law, instead of a full-fledged Roumanian university. The plain truth is that he tried every path of conciliation rather than risk an open breach, but that Kossuth's intransigeance at length convinced him of its necessity.

What brought matters to a head and stiffened both sides was the abdication of Ferdinand on 2 December in favour of his young nephew Francis Joseph, who entrusted the reactionary Windischgrätz with the task of reducing Hungary to order. Kossuth, bracing himself for the struggle, gave the military command in Transylvania to Bem, the chivalrous Polish exile, a man of iron discipline, tireless resource and humane feelings. Unhappily he also sent the sinister Ladislas Csányi as civil commissioner at Bem's side, and the two men differed on fundamentals from the very outset. Bem kindled the impressionable Magyars to new effort, and soon General Urban was driven across the Bukovinian border, Kolozsvár was reoccupied, and Puchner was forced on to the defensive in Hermannstadt. In these circumstances Puchner, though with some misgivings, authorised a deputation, consisting of Şaguna, a Roumanian merchant, and two Saxons, to go to Bucarest and invite the military intervention of the Russians, who, as we have seen, were in occupation of the two Principalities since the collapse of the revolution there. In actual fact, General Lüders did not move until he received a more formal request from Puchner himself, who inflicted two slight defeats upon Bem near Hermannstadt (21 January and 4 February), but was barely able to hold his own. Even when it came, at this stage Russian help was too slight to be of much avail, and by the middle of March Bem was able to occupy both Hermannstadt and Kronstadt, and Puchner fled across the frontier. For the time being Bem was in control of all Transylvania, save the mountain districts which Avram Iancu held for the emperor. The lack of discipline of his raw Roumanian levies was sadly demonstrated by the sack of Nagy Enyed early in January, when the famous Protestant college of Gabriel Bethlen, with its valuable library, was burnt to the ground. It is too

often overlooked that it was Axente Sever's revenge for the burning of
seven Roumanian villages near Enyed by the Magyars in the previous
October. But there can be no question that many horrible deeds were
committed, and it is even alleged that a priest and fifty women were
massacred in church.[1]

The general attitude of the Roumanians to the trial of strength between Hungary and Austria, of which their question was as yet but
a fragment, was a logical sequence from their earlier attitude under
Joseph and Leopold. They looked above all to the dynasty for equality
and justice, openly repudiating the accusation of reactionary leanings
and declaring their belief in a constitutional monarchy, in which all the
nations had their share.[2] The clearest expression of their aims is contained in the petition which Bishop Şaguna laid before the young emperor at Olmütz on 25 February 1849, asking for "the union of all
Roumanians in the Austrian state as a single independent nation under
the sceptre of Austria, and as an integral part of the Monarchy", under
the sovereign as "Grand Duke of the Roumanians".[3] It is to be noted
that Francis Joseph, without committing himself to any details, accepted
"with joy and gratitude...the grave sacrifices made by the courageous
and loyal Roumanian nation for my throne and monarchy, against a
party which has violated the law and opened a civil war".[4] Nor was this
an isolated remark, for on 26 June he answered a later petition by renewed expressions of gratitude to the Roumanians and a guarantee of
equal rights and "organic institutions, in accordance with the needs of
this people and the unity of the Monarchy".[5] This, however, was only
one of many pledges made by Francis Joseph towards the subject races
of his empire: in times of stress he exploited their loyalty to the full, but
when the danger was past, he turned a deaf ear to their appeal and thus
slowly sapped the vast fund of accumulated loyalty to the throne. His
betrayal of the Roumanians is only less flagrant than his ingratitude
towards the Croats, his broken pledges to the Czechs in 1861 and 1871,
his cruel abandonment of the Slovaks to their fate after 1867.

Bem followed up his victories by an attempt at civil administration,

[1] Czetz, *Bems Feldzug in Siebenbürgen.*
[2] E.g. petition of 28 December 1848—*Cartea de Aur*, I, p. 514.
[3] *Ibid.* p. 521. Among the signatories were Ioan and Lucian Mocsónyi, and
Eudoxie Hurmuzaki, representing two of the most notable families of the Banat
and of Bukovina.
[4] *Ibid.* p. 522.
[5] *Ibid.* pp. 592–5.

and as his main principles were conciliation and amnesty, he at once came into acute conflict with Kossuth, who now dominated the Government in Pest and Debreczen, and his delegate Csányi, who declared Bem's amnesty to be invalid and set up military tribunals to execute "traitors" and confiscate their property.[1] Csányi's manifesto to the Roumanians is a classic revelation of Kossuthist mentality. It would deserve to be quoted in full, but a few sentences must suffice. It begins at top note: "You, unhappy Wallachs, deceived and led into false paths by intrigues and by Austrian officers. There is no trace in human memory or in the pages of history of a free national life on your part. You were slaves under the Romans, slaves under the migrant peoples, slaves too in the last 1000 years, and only the Magyars have extended to you also in the past year the dawn of liberty...". They have given the peasant equal rights, but "indulgence has its limits": and he therefore gives the Roumanians—"under the bloodthirsty leadership of murderers, robbers and adventurers, your tribunes, prefects and centurions"—eight days within which to submit, to abandon their "seducer" General Urban and return to their respect for the law, failing which their property would be confiscated and they would receive "corporal punishment suited to their crimes".[2]

Even at the time this was too much for many of Csányi's compatriots: for when the deputy Alois Vlad protested in the Debreczen Parliament, some applauded his quotations from the manifesto, but others tried to argue that by "corporal punishment" was meant not flogging but imprisonment.[3] In any case, it is difficult to conceive of any proclamation better calculated to defeat its own ends, and is a proof of Csányi's criminal incompetence. But there was far worse to come. The activities of Csányi's revolutionary tribunals ran entirely counter to Bem's amnesty, and Kossuth not only backed the civilian against the general, but declared invalid the chivalrous Pole's pledges to the Saxons and Roumanians. "Don't trust the Saxons", wrote Kossuth to Bem, "I am

[1] Magyar text of two manifestos of Csányi in App. 20 and 21 of G. Barițin, *Istoria Transilvaniei*, III, p. 774, and German text of stringent terms of martial law (issued by Commissary Beöthy at Kolozsvár in January 1849), *ibid.* p. 778.

[2] *Ibid.* pp. 549–50: B. Jancsó, *A román nemzetiségi törekvések története*, II, p. 719.

[3] The principal Magyar apologist, Benedek Jancsó, commenting on the affair, makes it quite clear that Vlad's interpretation was the correct one, and that in point of fact the ordinary punishment imposed by local tribunals was a flogging of twenty-five to fifty strokes (*op. cit.* p. 721).

no terrorist, but I want security against new treason of these criminal, ungrateful Saxons..., who had the impudence to summon the Russians and are thus a thousandfold guilty of godless betrayal of their country. I declare that unless they remove the Russians from the country, I shall not tolerate a single Saxon on the territory of the Hungarian Crown, but shall drive them out or deprive them of the protection and freedom of the law and sequestrate their property to meet the costs of war." Bem was therefore enjoined to arrest the principal Saxon leaders and hand them over to Csányi, who would hold them as hostages for Russian behaviour and shoot them as traitors if the Russians did not withdraw. "Kronstadt must surrender, or its obstinacy will be avenged upon Hermannstadt.... The Government reserves to itself the regulation of the future status of the Saxon territory."[1] It is interesting to find him admitting to Bem that "conditions in Transylvania are so peculiar that it is extraordinarily difficult even for me, though a Magyar, to judge as to the expedience of this or that measure". But his solution is to confine Bem to military questions and to leave all civil decisions to Csányi.[2]

So far from complying with such orders, Bem issued a general amnesty, but had to leave hurriedly for the Banat, to organise military resistance there: and Csányi took full advantage of his absence. His most famous exploit was the arrest of the Saxon pastor Stephan Ludwig Roth, one of the foremost members of the Committee of Pacification, and an ardent Austrophil, and his execution at Kolozsvár by a revolutionary tribunal, in defiance of a special safe-conduct issued to him by Bem (11 May). The charge against Roth was that he had obeyed the "rebel" Puchner and had thus aided the enemies of the fatherland, had carried the sword instead of the Bible and opposed the union which the perjured dynasty had solemnly confirmed. Roth had refused to conceal his fetters—"They do *me* no shame", he said—and now he refused to have his eyes bound and looked the shooting platoon fearlessly in the face. "Soldiers", said the captain on duty, overcome by emotion, "learn from this man how to die for one's nation".[3] Roth's brave and

---

[1] *Briefe Kossuths an Bem*, ed. Makray, pp. 3–4—letter of 17 March 1849: cf. Teutsch, *op. cit.* II, p. 274.

[2] This last phrase is quoted somewhat differently in Szemere, *Batthyány, Görgey, Kossuth*, III, p. 117. (Szemere was of course involved in acute conflict with Kossuth in the final stages of the revolution, when the one was premier and the other governor.)

[3] His last letter to his children is to be found in Teutsch, *op. cit.* II, pp. 277–8, and in Obert, *Stefan Ludwig Roth*, I, p. 216.

heroic demeanour won universal compassion: and he lives in history as the Andreas Hofer of the Saxon people. The indignant Bem, on his return to Transylvania, learning too late of this outrage, publicly re-affirmed his amnesty and wrote to Kossuth, threatening to resign his command unless Csányi were dismissed. The arbitrary methods of the revolutionary tribunals, he roundly declared, reminded him of the French Revolution.[1]

Kossuth's attitude to the Saxons and Roumanians does not stand alone. On the eve of the revolution he had in open Parliament scoffed at Croatia as "so small that it is not enough for a breakfast". He had met the demands of a Serbian deputation in the early summer of 1848 with the fatal phrase, "Then the sword will decide between us". He had roused Serbian indignation still further by his plan for settling Székels in the Banat, and a year later he was writing to Bem that "among the Serbs the only surety is to take women, children and priests as hostages".[2] But worst of all was the terrorist attitude towards his own people of origin, the Slovaks: and the gibbets erected by his orders in the northern counties are known to this day as "Kossuth gallows". Truly the great Széchenyi already in 1847 had been justified in his bitter apostrophe to Kossuth—"Incite every nationality to madness against the Magyars, throw a torch into the peasant's house, rouse the interests of the Empire to the uttermost conflict, fill to the brim the cup of vengeance with your poison, and then see what will happen".[3]

Kossuth's large measure of responsibility for the racial war cannot seriously be denied. The most that can be said for him and his sub-ordinates is that the strain of the long struggle produced in them a kind of ultra-patriotic exaltation which culminated in his solemn deposition of the Habsburgs at Debreczen on 14 April 1849 and his own assumption of the office of governor of Hungary. This crowning blunder of his career of course meant war to the knife: Francis Joseph resigned himself to asking the tsar's aid to crush the Hungarian revolution, and already in the first days of June the Russian troops began to pour across the Carpathians, from Galicia, from Bukovina and from Wallachia. Bem in particular found himself with 24,000 men, confronted by double that number of Russians and Austrians under Lüders and Clam-Gallas:

---

[1] *Wiener Reichszeitung*, 14 June 1850—cit. Friedjung, *Gesch. Oesterreichs*, I, p. 233.
[2] *Briefe an Bem*, p. 52.
[3] *Politische Programm-Fragmente*, p. 138.

and though he still put up a gallant fight, his resistance was finally broken at the battle of Schässburg (27 July), where the poet Petöfi disappeared for ever in the *mêlée*. Bem withdrew to the Banat, fought a last battle on 9 August outside Temesvár, and in the end shared Kossuth's flight to Turkey, dying there as a convert to Islam!

Meanwhile the rôle of the Roumanians was not yet ended. At the height of Bem's success Iancu still held out in the Abrud district as "King of the Mountains", and late in April, thanks to the well-meaning mediation of Bălcescu, Cesar Bolliac and other liberal refugees from Wallachia, a last attempt was made to reconcile Magyars and Roumanians. Already in March Maghieru, from his exile in Baden, had written to Kossuth, warning him of the imminence of Russian intervention and pleading for a Magyar-Roumanian alliance, but subject to the recognition of the nationality and political rights of all Roumanians under the Hungarian crown, through an official "organic Statute" and on a federalist basis. Kossuth only received this overture when the victories of Dembinski and Görgei had fired him with optimism: he rejected it and ordered measures to crush Iancu's resistance. But meanwhile Bălcescu found a hearing with Szemere and Casimir Batthyány, and a draft convention was submitted, providing for a recognition of the Roumanian name, for free use of the language in church, school and local assembly, a national guard and autonomy for both Churches. This time Kossuth accepted in principle, though a few days earlier he had said, "For the Roumanians I have only bullets and cannon". On his side Butean, Iancu's right hand, had shown complete scepticism and had answered Bălcescu's appeal for a united front against the Russians with the bitter words, "Your freedom is the gallows, your equal rights mean that the other nations who share the soil with them should be swallowed up by the Magyar element".[1] His doubts were soon to be hideously confirmed.

It was now decided to send the deputy Dragoş, a Roumanian of Magyar sentiments, on a mission to negotiate a compromise with Iancu: but his motives and prospect of success may be gathered from Kossuth's letter of instructions to him, denouncing Şaguna as a traitor on whose head rested the bloodshed of the civil war and to whom pardon could never be granted![2] While, then, Dragoş was actually treating with Iancu and Butean, another confidant of Kossuth, Major Hatvani, with

[1] Iorga, *Gesch. d. rum. Volkes*, II, p. 297.
[2] *Cartea de Aur*, I, p. 576.

a detachment of 1500 men, broke in upon them and, in clear violation of the armistice just concluded, arrested a number of the Roumanian leaders. The prefect Butean was hanged next day, and his colleague Dobra disappeared and was never heard of again. Iancu, naturally regarding this as arrant treachery, made an armed attack, sacked the town of Abrudbánya and put Hatvani to flight: and it has been alleged that as many as 4000 persons were massacred,[1] though this is almost certainly an enormous exaggeration. Dragoş, suspected of treachery, though probably quite innocent, was cut down and killed. This ended all hope of conciliation, and Iancu held out in his mountains until the Russo-Austrian troops could advance. Bem's passing hope of winning armed support from Wallachia met with no response whatsoever, mainly because of the Magyar intransigeant attitude.

As, however, the situation of the Magyars grew desperate, the madness of alienating all the other races of the country became apparent to the saner members of the Government, and notably to Szemere (the real statesmen and advocates of racial peace, Deák, Széchenyi and Eötvös had long since been eliminated). In July the Hungarian Government found it necessary to migrate from Debreczen to Szeged, and there the revolutionary Parliament devoted its expiring moments to the discussion of a law guaranteeing the free development of all nationalities on Hungarian soil. Under its provisions Magyar was to remain the official language in all administrative, legal and military affairs, the right of every citizen to use his own language in the communal and county assemblies was distinctly recognised, the language of instruction in the schools was to be that of the locality, and in it also the parish registers were to be drawn up: petitions might be presented in any language and appointments to all offices were to be made without distinction of language and religion. The Roumanians were to have a National Guard, an Orthodox faculty at the University of Pest and a general amnesty. The well-meaning premier, Szemere, in introducing these proposals, urged that they must be magnanimous enough to "offer with fraternal hand the olive branch of peace", even after "the scenes of murder" which they had witnessed. In a later speech, amid some opposition, he declared his readiness to treat all the nationalities as his brothers, and that this came not from the lips but from the heart.[2] But of course the time for such action was long since past. A law which, if voted in

---

[1] Czetz, *Bems Feldzug in Siebenbürgen*, p. 305.
[2] A. Szilágyi, *Die letzten Tage der magy. Revolution*, pp. 23, 42.

March 1848, might perhaps have rallied the whole of Hungary in support of Magyar pretensions, was worse than useless in July 1849, when the country was bleeding from the wounds inflicted by a furious racial war, and when overwhelming masses of Russian troops were closing in upon every side. The inevitable end came on 13 August, when Görgei capitulated with all his forces at Világos.

Reaction was by now rampant in Vienna, and the Austrian Government disgusted and embarrassed even its Russian ally by its brutal methods of repression. The execution of the thirteen Magyar generals at Arad, followed by that of the late premier, Count Louis Batthyány, roused the indignation of Europe and rallied opinion to the exiled Kossuth. Among the high officials who shared the same fate were the notorious Csányi and Baron Jeszenák, who had performed a similar butcher's task among the Slovaks. Over 800 individuals received long terms of imprisonment. It is, however, necessary to add that after a certain delay official lists were published, showing that 4425 men, 340 women and 69 children had been put to death without trial by the Magyar military tribunals in Transylvania, exclusive of those who fell in open fight.[1] According to a careful enquiry of the Saxon official Bedeus von Scharberg, the revolutionary tribunals were responsible for 449 death sentences and 769 were shot by their orders without trial.[2] The Roumanians on their side claim that 230 of their villages had been completely destroyed, that six of their prefects, ten tribunes, two arch-priests and eleven priests had been hanged or shot: and they give details of 1280 executions. The historian Barițiu placed these as high as 6000.[3] Meanwhile we have already seen that the Székels had sacked Sächsisch-Reen, and that the Roumanians had destroyed the Magyar towns of Zalatna and Enyed: and it is contended—for instance by Czetz, one of Bem's chief lieutenants throughout the campaign—that in the former 2000 Magyars were killed, at Jara after the fall of Enyed about 800, and at Abrud, in revenge for Hatvani's breach of the armistice, as many as 4000. That the raw Roumanian levies committed many

---

[1] *Wiener Zeitung* of 21 February 1851, cit. Friedjung, *op. cit.* I, p. 233, reproduced in full in App. 22 of Barițiu, *Ist. Transilvaniei*, II, p. 777. Of these 4425 appear to have been Roumanians, 165 Magyars, 252 Saxons and 72 Jews, gypsies, etc. A Roumanian deputation to Vienna after the pacification estimated the number of Roumanian victims from all causes at 40,000; but this can hardly be taken seriously. Barițiu, *op. cit.* p. 494.

[2] Friedenfels, *Bedeus von Scharberg*, II, p. 153.

[3] *Cartea de Aur*, I, pp 670–4. Barițiu, *op. cit.* II, pp. 492–504.

excesses, and in particular reverted to the precedent of 1783 in burning many country houses, is not open to dispute. But it is also impossible to escape the conclusion that the contrast between these later excesses and the remarkable discipline maintained during the Blaj assembly and for some months afterwards, was due to Magyar intransigeance and arming for a union which was distasteful and alarming to the Roumanian masses. As for the total casualties of the civil war, these will never be known exactly.

\* \* \* \*

The new regime is for ever associated with the name of Alexander Bach, the brilliant revolutionary turned opportunist, whose bureaucratic talents and stubborn energy recast the antiquated machinery of the Monarchy and for ten years delayed the inevitable failure. The main features of his regime were extreme centralisation, based upon a-national officials, but the use of German as the *lingua franca* of the state. The constitution promulgated for the whole empire on 4 March 1849 and at first received with high hopes in many quarters, as fore-shadowing greater equality and freer movement for the minor nationalities, was never allowed to function: after Világos it only existed in name, a series of imperial decrees were issued at direct variance with its main provisions, and finally on 31 December 1851 the perjured emperor annulled the constitution as a whole and stood forth as undisguised autocrat. But long before that date, by the proclamation of 17 October 1849, Hungary had been reduced to the status of a mere Austrian province, and it was expressly affirmed that "the former constitution of Hungary is annulled by the Revolution". The backbone of Hungarian liberties, the county administration, was destroyed, and the country was split up into five new districts: the Banat and Bačka were formed into the so-called Serbian Voivodina, while Croatia and Transylvania were detached and placed directly under Vienna. In the latter province the jurisdiction of the Three Nations was likewise replaced by six districts and a governor: the Saxons saw their ancient autonomy torn to shreds and their "University" not allowed to meet, while the Roumanians in vain reminded the Government of the solemn pledges of national union issued to them in the emperor's name, so long as their military help was of value. Iancu, deeply hurt and disillusioned at such ingratitude, withdrew to his father's house in the mountains, and sank into a state of melancholy broken by fits of excessive drinking

or of restlessness. He lived on for twenty years, adored by the mountain shepherds whose dress he wore and whose songs he accompanied
on the flute—hence the quite imaginary story that he was reduced to
beggary and earned his living as a musician at the village fairs. When
Francis Joseph visited Transylvania in 1852, Iancu failed to obtain an
audience, and when someone attempted to make this good, he is alleged
to have declined with the bitter phrase, "What could a madman like
me say to a liar like him?"

Even Bishop Şaguna was slighted by the authorities and had a very
hard fight for the rights of the Orthodox Church. His hope for a
unified Church for all Roumanian Orthodox under Habsburg rule,
whether in Transylvania, the Banat or Bukovina, still more for a Roumanian National Congress, proved quite illusory. None the less this
remarkable man, who had many of the qualities of a great medieval
churchman and perhaps owed his physical vigour and tenacity of purpose to his "Arumun" origin,[1] remained undismayed by the unfavourable
turn of events. During the ten years of absolutism he devoted his whole
efforts to the reorganisation and strengthening of the Orthodox Church,
and laid foundations capable of bearing the new superstructure of the
sixties. Meanwhile the status of the Uniates again improved after the
setback administered by the craven Leményi. In 1851 they were allowed
to elect a new bishop in the person of Alexander Sterca-Şuluţ, a member
of one of those none too numerous families of the lesser nobility which
had retained a keen sense of Roumanian nationality: and in 1855 two
new Uniate bishoprics were created at Lugos and Gherla.[2] At first
highly suspicious of possible proselytising designs on the part of
Şaguna, Şuluţ ere long changed his views, and the close co-operation
of the two metropolitans in all national questions became one of the
foundations on which the whole situation rested. Şaguna meanwhile
had to fight hard for the separation of the Roumanian Orthodox from
the jurisdiction of the Serbian patriarch in Karlowitz, and it was not till
August 1860 that the emperor even allowed a general Orthodox synod
to meet.

The Bach regime, odious as it was in many respects, undoubtedly
had redeeming features on the merely administrative side. Bach himself,

[1] His parents were merchants in Gabrova, an important Vlach centre in Macedonia, and he had been brought up in the house of a kinsman of his mother, Grabow-
ski, a merchant in Pest, and pursued his first studies there.
[2] I.e. Gherla (Szamos-Ujvár), in addition to that of Oradea Mare (Nagyvárad).

despite his abrupt apostasy, was not a mere *arriviste*, but was inspired by the soaring ambition to transform Austria into a model state, governed on paternal, but efficient lines and transcending all racial and provincial particularism in the higher unity of a centralised machine. The much abused "Bach Hussars" were, if regarded merely as bureaucrats, a distinct improvement on their predecessors. But the root error of the whole system lay in its disregard for the tide of nationality, now running more strongly than ever before, and in its reliance upon germanisation as the cement of empire. In reality, it was not long before all those nationalities which had rallied round the Habsburg throne in danger, recognised the truth of Pulszky's witty phrase, that they had received as reward what the Magyars received as punishment, and adopted an attitude of more or less sullen passivity. In Transylvania the state of siege was not abolished till December 1854, and thanks to Austria's uncertain policy during the Crimean War, her partial mobilisation and her occupation of Wallachia and Moldavia, the military authorities retained an altogether disproportionate influence alike in Transylvania and in the Military Frontiers. It is true that this bore most heavily upon the Magyars, whose privileged position was in suspense, and for that very reason was less resented by the Roumanians, and to a lesser degree by the Saxons, to whom the extension of the German language partially atoned for the infringement of their chartered rights.

An interesting light is thrown upon the mentality of this period by a correspondence between the Kossuthist Daniel Irányi and Dimitrie Brătianu, both exiles from their respective countries.[1] It was opened by the Magyar insisting that the laws of 1848 assured complete equality between all the nationalities of Hungary, that the Magyar-Roumanian quarrel was a misunderstanding due to imperialist intrigues, and urging both Slavs and Roumanians to join hands with the Magyars "in the cause of independence and liberty". Brătianu in reply expressed reluctance "to stir the still burning cinders", but then quoted most effectively from Transylvanian constitutional documents to prove the utter difference in status between Magyar and Roumanian, and ended with a phrase from the circular of Count Casimir Batthyány, dated 10 June 1849, to the effect that "the supremacy of the Magyar element, such as it has acquired for 1000 years with arms in hand", could never be renounced. Let the Magyars then cease talking of their historic kingdom and their rights of conquest, and accept the fraternal hand

[1] *Lettres Hongro-Roumaines*, published in Paris, 1851.

which so many Roumanians held out to them. Irányi in his turn drew a highly disingenuous distinction between Transylvania and Hungary, arguing that the Roumanians shared in all privileges, if they belonged to the privileged class, and that the union was voted by the same Diet which proclaimed religious liberty and abolition of feudal dues. We, he said, desire the equality of all nationalities, and a close alliance between Hungary, Poland, Roumania, and Serbia: you desire first of all the mutilation of Hungary, and only then a Danubian confederation. The choice lies with Hungary against Austria, "or against us for absolutism, treason, and perjury". Brătianu in his answer claimed to speak in the name not only of Roumanian *émigrés*, but of all Roumanians on both sides of the Carpathians. He recognised the need for union of Magyar, Slav, and Roumanian "to conquer the common enemy and make a breach in the monarchical edifice which weighs on our peoples": but he could not accept the distinction between the Hungarian nation and other nationalities. He desired to conciliate, not to incite, but he accused Irányi of wanting "at one and the same time Democracy and your right of conquest", and this was incompatible with their common aim of "Danubian fraternity".

This exchange of views was merely platonic, but the negotiations of Kossuth's emissaries with Michael of Serbia and Alexander of Roumania in 1859 were much more serious in view of the pending Franco-Austrian war: and we shall see[1] that far-reaching promises of linguistic rights were made to the Serbians and Roumanians, and a Danubian confederation was put forward unreservedly as the goal. The Peace of Villafranca shattered all these fantastic projects before they had time to take shape, but it is to be noted that what became known of them in Hungary itself alarmed public opinion, and served to strengthen the influence first of the more statesmanlike Deák and then of the more chauvinistic Coloman Tisza at the expense of the exiled governor.

The disastrous Italian campaign, and the financial crisis which it evoked, brought about the fall of Bach, and ushered in eight years of constitutional experiment in all the Austrian dominions, which very materially affected the fate of the Roumanians. Simultaneously with the October Diploma of 1860, the old Transylvanian constitution was restored, and a decree issued ordering a consultation with the representatives of all races, religions, and classes, as to necessary reforms. There was indeed very great confusion not only in the public mind, but

[1] *Infra*, p. 304.

even on the part of authorities, as to what was now to be regarded as valid—the status before or after the March laws of 1848. An active party at once formed itself among the Magyars, led by Bishop Haynald and Baron Kemény, which argued that union had received the sanction of the crown in 1848 and was therefore legally valid without further legislation: but this was strongly opposed by all the Roumanians and by the great majority of the Saxons. The October Diploma was not yet working when it was superseded, again by imperial decree, by the February Patent of 1861—the famous centralist experiment of Schmerling. This created a new Reichsrat of 343 delegates from all the legislative bodies of the empire; of these, 85 and 26 were assigned to Hungary and Transylvania. It was accepted in Hungary as a direct challenge to the nation, and the Parliament which met in Pest in April at once became involved in an acute conflict of principle with the crown, and, after memorable debates on the two addresses prepared by Deák, was dissolved in August. But before this it had expressly affirmed the validity of the union between Hungary and Transylvania, and a committee under the most enlightened liberal of modern Hungary, Baron Eötvös, had reported in favour of very wide linguistic concessions to the various nationalities of Hungary.[1]

The Transylvanian Diet was now convoked (15 July 1863) no longer to Kolozsvár, that centre of Magyarisation, but to the predominantly Saxon town of Hermannstadt. A Saxon petition and a Roumanian deputation, led by Bishop Şaguna, had already been graciously received by Francis Joseph, and the obsolete franchise of pre-March days was drastically revised, on the openly avowed ground that the Roumanian masses could no longer be ignored. In 1848 out of 300 deputies, only 90 had been elected, and of these only 3 had been Roumanians: all the rest were so-called "Regalists", nominated by the crown. In 1863 the Magyar claim that there should be 182 Regalists—134 Magyars, 29 Roumanians, and 19 Saxons—was rejected, and the total number of Regalists limited to 40. This the Magyars denounced as a breach of the constitution, and declined to take their seats, while at the same time their kinsmen in Hungary adopted the same policy of abstention towards the central Reichsrat in Vienna, thereby going far to stultify Schmerling's experiment. The Diet was thus a Rump Parliament, in which the Saxons and Roumanians had a free field. Its chief work was

[1] See translation of full text, as Appendix 1 of my *Racial Problems in Hungary*, pp. 421–4, which is to be contrasted with that of the Law of Nationalities of 1868 (Appendix III, *ibid.*).

to pass laws establishing the Roumanian nation and its two Churches on a footing of full equality with the other "Received Nations" and Churches of Transylvania, and proclaiming the absolute equality of the three languages—Magyar, German, and Roumanian—in official business of state (31 August—21 September 1863).[1] Thus when for the first time in all the centuries justice was accorded to the Roumanians, it was done in a form which Magyar public opinion was unanimous in resenting as illegal. For the brief space of two years the Roumanians breathed more freely, but all the time there was a feeling on the part of all three races that their ultimate fate depended not so much upon their own efforts as upon the result of the major negotiations between Vienna and Budapest. When, then, Schmerling's Parliament proved unworkable owing to the numerous abstentions, and when Francis Joseph resumed his interrupted discussion with Deák and Andrássy, the autonomy of Transylvania was one of the things which he found it convenient and even necessary to sacrifice.

In this brief breathing space, however, there occurred two events of great importance in the social history of the Roumanians. The foundation of the "Association for the Cultivation of Roumanian Language and Literature" by the efforts of Cipariu provided them with a cultural centre for publication, museum collections and literary effort. But above all, Şaguna at last obtained from the emperor the separation of the Roumanian Orthodox Church from the Serbian patriarchate (the death of Rajačić made this easier), and the erection of his own see of Sibiu (Hermannstadt) into an archbishopric, with two other bishoprics at Arad and Caransebeş (June 1863).[2] There were some who might regret this final recognition by the state, of the schism in the Roumanian Church: but a far sounder view was that which accepted accomplished facts which could no longer be undone and thereby made very tardy atonement for the unequal measure meted out to Uniate and Orthodox.

The abrupt fall of Schmerling in the summer of 1865 was soon followed by the dissolution of the Hermannstadt Diet and the annulment of all its legislation—and therefore of the law assuring equal rights to the Roumanians, which, it is true, had never been carried into actual force. A new Diet was at once summoned to Kolozsvár, on the old unreformed franchise, so modified as not to exclude the Roumanians

[1] For German text of these laws see Appendices 23 and 24 in Brote, *Die rumänische Frage in Siebenbürgen und Ungarn*, pp. 209–15.
[2] Those of Cluj and Timişoara were not sanctioned.

altogether, but to assure an overwhelming Magyar majority—in other words, a franchise open to the very same legal criticisms as its predecessor. The Magyars, who then formed only 29 per cent. of the population, elected 89 deputies as against 31 Saxons and only 13 Roumanians, while out of the 190 Regalists they had 132—with the result that they easily outnumbered Saxons and Roumanians combined. The latter were absolutely unanimous in declining to recognise the Union as valid, and addressing a weighty protest to the throne. The Saxons were divided, a majority disputing the legality of the Union, and all without exception insisting upon special guarantees and conditions—especially of course the maintenance of the Saxon "University" and its ancient privileges—as a preliminary to voting. But the issue was never in doubt: the Diet met with re-endorsement of the Union as its sole agenda, and the Magyar majority forthwith moved an address to the crown in this sense, requesting that Transylvanian representatives should be summoned to the Parliament of Budapest. The Diet was then prorogued and never met again. The Roumanians in their formal protest used telling and irrefutable arguments, for they had only to quote the words used by Francis Joseph himself in 1863, when he admitted that a Diet based on the laws of 1790–1 (and therefore on the old franchise) "excluding the great majority of the population from the exercise of political rights,... would lack the indispensable moral prestige to solve the internal affairs of Transylvania". He had now reverted to the very basis which he had solemnly repudiated two years before, and they were therefore entitled to affirm that an assembly thus composed "lacks the necessary moral force to ensure permanent validity to its decisions".[1] In this dignified protest there appears for the first time the bold claim that the fate of Transylvania cannot be legally decided without the participation of the Roumanian nation.

Protests were unavailing. In December 1865 Francis Joseph opened the Hungarian Parliament in person, and by that act may be said to have ended the period of pure absolutism and accepted Hungarian constitutional theory as the basis of future government. A whole year elapsed before a final agreement could be reached between Deák and the crown, and the outbreak of the Austro-Prussian War led to a pause in the negotiations. During this time all Transylvania was in a state of paralysis, waiting upon events. It was not until February 1867 that the last obstacles were surmounted, and Andrássy was appointed first premier

[1] Brote, *op. cit.* Appendices 25 and 27.

of the new constitutional Hungary. The Ausgleich or Compromise, making of the Empire of Austria and the Apostolic Kingdom of Hungary two equal sovereign states, only linked by certain common affairs at home, but forming a single unit to the outer world, obtained parliamentary sanction in March, and on 8 June Francis Joseph was crowned in Budapest, thereby receiving the mystical sanction of the Holy Apostolic Crown.

With the Dual System thus constituted we are not here concerned, except in so far as it affected the fate of Transylvania, and therefore of the Roumanians. It may none the less be well to indicate two of its most salient features, which in the end proved fatal. In the first place, in his passion for precedent and for permanence, Deák had provided no legal methods of revision, with the result that the machinery, as it became clogged, could not be repaired and eventually threatened to break down altogether. Secondly, it was not only a compact between Hungary and the crown, over the head of Austria, whose Parliament was merely invited, as late as December 1867, to ratify an already long accomplished fact: but none of the other races of the Monarchy were consulted at all. So long as we regard it exclusively from the angle of Budapest, it is perfectly possible to argue that the establishment of the Dual System was an evolution, not a revolution; that it was merely the logical outcome of the Pragmatic Sanction of 1723 and the formal recognition of Hungary's ancient constitutional rights and traditions. This is true, but it is not the whole truth. For the real motive of Dualism was a compact between the two strongest races, the Germans in Austria (on whose behalf Francis Joseph acted, though he did not properly consult them), and the Magyars in Hungary, to divide the Monarchy between them. The two next strongest races, the Poles and Croats, were bought off by special concessions of autonomy, and were thus made accomplices in holding down the remaining eight. Of these, the plight of the Czechs was comparatively easy, and improved with every decade; and none of the Austrian races save the Ruthenes had to complain of grinding oppression, as opposed to political subordination and exclusion from the control of foreign policy. But in Hungary the situation was very different, and while Croatia was allowed to preserve her ancient autonomy under new forms, the other non-Magyar nationalities—Germans, Slovaks, Ruthenes, Serbs, and not least of all Roumanians—were relegated to the position of mere political helots and predestined for assimilation by the ruling race.

# CHAPTER XI

## FROM UNITY TO INDEPENDENCE

"Quand on envisage avec désintéressement et sans passion les questions qui surgissent en Orient, on est frappé du rôle que les Principautés peuvent être appelées à jouer, et l'on convient que peu d'états secondaires sont à même de rendre d'aussi grands services au maintien de la paix européenne."

BARON TALLEYRAND-PÉRIGORD, 5 May 1858.

The new prince, Alexander John Cuza, was still under forty, his somewhat scanty education had ended in a failure to graduate at the Sorbonne, and his private morals were far from exemplary. Nor did his early career suggest any high standard of political integrity. As a member of the "Young Moldavia" group, he had been mixed up in the movement of 1848, and it is interesting to note that curiosity had brought him to the Field of Liberty at Blaj. He had shared the exile of the liberal leaders, but had soon returned under Gregory Ghica, and only came into prominence in 1857, when the notorious Vogorides selected him as his adjutant and by a specially crass act of favouritism advanced him within six weeks from ensign to major. Having thus used Vogorides as the stool from which to reach up to the first rung of the ladder of fame, he certainly was not long in kicking it from him. He threw his office of Prefect in Vogorides' face and as deputy for Galaţ in the Moldavian Divan was specially active in demanding a foreign prince and agrarian reform. Yet in 1858 Vogorides seems to have still regarded him as one of his followers, for he promoted him to the rank of colonel. Finally, the "Commission Intérimaire" selected him as war minister. In a word, he was a well-meaning man, a keen Roumanian patriot, with an all too thin veneer of liberalism, but self-indulgent, weak, an easy prey to favourites and parasites, lacking in experience, resources and method. He is reported to have greeted his election with the phrase, "Gentlemen, I fear you will not be satisfied with me".

The most vital problem which confronted him was the attitude of his suzerain and of the protecting Powers. The Porte, finding Buol ready to "protest most categorically",[1] decided to denounce the double

[1] Buol to Prokesch, 6 February—quoted by Riker, *op. cit.* p. 215.

election as illegal and to demand a fresh meeting of the Conference. But it soon transpired that France openly favoured recognition, that Russia was by no means unfavourable and in any case shared the French objection to coercion, while Malmesbury did not feel very strongly on the subject and advised the Porte to recognise Cuza as a special case, while reaffirming the *status quo* in all other particulars. Bulwer, somewhat under protest, acted as he was told, but warned his chief that "yielding bit by bit to the Principalities...must end by establishing a confederation under French and Russian protection on the banks of the Danube". In a word, Europe was far too divided to take energetic action, and the whole situation was dominated by the preparations of France and Austria for the Italian war.

One of Cuza's first acts was to send the poet Alecsandri on a special mission to Paris, London and Turin, to reaffirm his readiness to resign in favour of a foreign prince when the time for this should come, and to challenge the view that the double election in any way infringed the Convention of 1858. And indeed this was the most humorous feature in the whole situation: for amid all the elaborate provisions with which the Powers had sought to hedge round the Roumanians, there was not a phrase which actually prohibited the two provinces from selecting one and the same man as prince, and though this was manifestly contrary to the spirit and intentions of the step-motherly Concert, there was no loophole for denouncing it as illegal.

In Paris Alecsandri was cordially received, not only by Walewski and Thouvenel, but by the emperor himself, who said, "The Roumanians have given proof of great patriotism and political skill", and created in the envoy's mind the somewhat too optimistic belief that he would "warmly defend the *fait accompli*".[1] Napoleon's very genuine sympathy for the Roumanian cause, which never wavered throughout his career, was now strengthened by the consideration that under certain circumstances of the near future Roumania might easily become an effective ally of France and perform valuable strategic services on Austria's Balkan flanks. He therefore sanctioned the erection of a Roumanian diplomatic agency in Paris, made a secret present of 10,000 rifles and ammunition, and sent a military mission to Bucarest. Encouraged by this, Cuza concentrated the two militias in a newly formed military camp at Ploeşci, and obtained a vote of eight million piastres for military equipment. The result was that Austria was obliged to keep

[1] 25 February—quoted by Riker, *op. cit.* p. 241.

30,000 troops of observation in Transylvania, which she could ill spare from Italy. Cuza ingratiated himself still further with Napoleon, by a personal letter in which he declared himself in principle for dictatorship.[1]

In Turin Alecsandri was of course welcomed by Cavour and also conferred with Teleki and Klapka, the Hungarian *émigrés*. But in London his reception was definitely unfriendly, and the new foreign secretary, Lord Malmesbury, could not rise beyond an expression of horror at an act directed against the integrity of the Ottoman Empire. On this question our statesmen of both parties were almost equally hidebound. But in inconsistency the Liberals (with the shining exception of Gladstone) far surpassed the Conservatives: for while openly favouring the national movement in Italy, they did everything in their power to thwart and discourage it in Serbia and Roumania. Indeed Lord John Russell, who became foreign secretary in June 1859 on the fall of the Derby Cabinet, privately expressed himself in favour of converting the Principalities into an Austrian "Secundogenitur", not unlike Tuscany and Parma in unregenerate Italy.[2] That this was no mere passing whim could be shown by detailed references to Russell's attitude in 1863 to the Serbo-Turkish dispute, when he actually thought that an Austrian occupation of Belgrade would be the best solution!

On 7 April the Conference again met in Paris to consider the new situation. The Turkish delegate Musurus protested strongly and Hübner went so far as to propose the forcible suppression of the unionist movement. But Turkey and Austria were isolated. The meetings of the Conference coincided with an acute crisis between Vienna and Turin, in which London was vainly mediating. By 26 April Austria and Sardinia were at war, and a week later Napoleon joined the Italians. Thus the international situation helped the Roumanian cause to victory. The sittings in Paris were interrupted while the war lasted, but in September the election was confirmed. France, Russia, Britain, Prussia and Sardinia united in treating it as an infringement of the Convention of 1858, but in urging the Porte, *as a special exception*, to grant investiture to Cuza, lest fresh electoral struggles should unsettle the country. They added a threat of applying force if ever the constitution of 1858 should be infringed in any other particular. This was of course a paper menace, mainly intended to save their face and veil the surrender.

*         *         *         *

[1] See extracts in Riker, *op. cit.* p. 242.
[2] 4 September 1859, to Bulwer—*Russell Papers*, quoted by Riker, *op. cit.* p. 246.

The none too cordial attitude of the European Concert towards Roumanian aspirations naturally led Cuza to rely all the more upon Napoleon, and the outbreak of the Franco-Austrian War seemed to offer a tempting occasion for intrigue in Hungary. In London Kossuth had already come to terms with Prince Michael of Serbia and his Magyar wife, a Countess Hunyady, and after a talk with Napoleon he sent General Klapka to negotiate with Alexander Cuza, bearing with him an introduction to Victor Place in the terms, "He is no revolutionary in the obnoxious sense of the word, but a Magyar patriot and an adversary of Austria".[1] With Place's aid Klapka concluded a secret convention with Cuza, permitting the Magyars to form depots of arms in Moldavia and along the Transylvanian frontier, and some of the French rifles supplied to Cuza were to be dealt out to Magyar insurgents. Rifles were actually sent to Roumania, but the plans for a campaign in Transylvania[2] were not yet ripe when the Peace of Villafranca rendered them nugatory. What would have happened if the war had continued it is quite impossible to forecast, but it is to be noted that the Magyar *émigrés*, in striking contrast to their allies in 1848–9, pledged themselves to proclaim "complete reconciliation between Serbs, Wallachs and Magyars", equality for all races, language rights in commune and county and in the army, and autonomy for Transylvania, if a special Assembly should vote for it at the end of the war. Above all, they declared that the fraternal principle must guide them and that their goal must be "the confederation of the three Danubian states—Hungary, Serbia and Moldo-Wallachia".

How far Cuza was sincere in his dealings with the Magyars is open to question. A year later he had the assurance to say to the Austrian consul, Eder, who had wind of Klapka's activities, "Fundamentally a rift separates us from these Asiatics: we are of quite another race and blood. We sympathise with all nationalist tendencies, but not so far as to sacrifice our interests to the Hungarians".[3] None the less he allowed Garibaldi and the Magyar Redshirt General Türr to import rifles secretly to Galaț, and when the secret was betrayed, only very reluctantly yielded to the representations of the consuls, and after trying to confiscate them for his own use, had to allow them to be shipped back.

[1]  20 March 1859—cit. Emmerit, *Victor Place*, p. 87.
[2]  See memoranda of Place in Emmerit, *op. cit.* pp. 93–7: text of Klapka's Convention in Kossuth, *Meine Schriften aus der Emigration*, I, pp. 417–21.
[3]  Eder to Rechberg, 13 June 1860—quoted by Riker, *op. cit.* p. 268.

After this, Magyar-Roumanian relations faded into the background, and we shall see that the next great crisis, in 1866, developed, and passed, too rapidly for Klapka, who led a Hungarian legion in the Prussian ranks, to establish any fresh contacts with Bucarest.

At home Cuza's position was one of great difficulty. He had to meet the jealousy of all the leading boiars, not merely as an upstart, but above all as the insistent advocate of land reform. He had at first to govern with two Cabinets and two Assemblies, and the Central Commission as well, which interfered at every turn, reminding him without much circumlocution that he was merely a stopgap for a foreign prince, and pressing upon him the draft for a new unitary constitution. This Cuza refused, as going too fast. He could not risk a conflict with the Powers, and wisely felt that in such a position the first essential was to reach an understanding with the Porte. These differences of opinion involved him in constant changes of Cabinet and eventually in a dissolution: he was already developing a strong contempt for constitutional government, and confided to the British consul that he "had to choose between traitors and fools", but relied upon their own folly to defeat them.[1]

In October 1860 the prince paid his official visit to Constantinople, announcing to his subjects that he was going there to "enforce Roumanian interests": and indeed he pleaded very effectively for a wider franchise and for a real instead of a personal union. His arguments and general behaviour seem to have favourably impressed the grand vizier, Ali Pasha, and after long negotiations he at last obtained in December 1861 a firman of the sultan sanctioning the unification of Governments and Parliaments. But the Porte never did anything save by halves and with reservations, and this time it limited its sanction to the reign of Cuza himself. This was so obviously unnatural and unsatisfactory, that the Powers strongly demurred, and so we see by an irony of fate the Porte's own bad tactics once more driving Europe in a direction which it would fain have avoided. On 5 February 1862 the two Assemblies were fused into one at Bucarest, and the Central Commission ceased to exist. Henceforth Roumanian unity was a reality and irrevocable. Separate customs had already been abolished, and the financial and judicial systems were now unified.

These three first years were a period of instability, intrigue, and continual ministerial changes, sometimes involving fresh elections and always the dispossessing of officials. But still there was a slow crystalli-

[1] Green to Bulwer, 7 June 1860—quoted by Riker, *op. cit.* p. 256.

sation of something which might be described as party government. Two main groups emerged, known in those days as "Whites" and "Reds"—Conservatives and Liberals. The Conservatives found an able leader and a notable orator in Barbu Catargiu, the first premier of an united Cabinet, who rallied the reactionary boiars in favour of their privileges and especially against land reform, round which the struggle raged most bitterly. Among the Liberals the two most notable were Ion Brătianu, a keen adherent of French political and administrative methods, and Michael Kogălniceanu, the Moldavian orator and historian.

Catargiu was a strong-willed and passionate defender of the old order: he suppressed rioting with a high hand, and on the anniversary of the revolution of 1848 he prohibited a meeting on the Bucarest "Field of Liberty". A week later his conflict with the progressive forces culminated in tragedy: for he was assassinated in the street on his way home from the Assembly (20 June 1862). Though various attempts were made at the time to apply the maxim "Cui bono?" and to incite party passions by unproved insinuations, the murderers were never discovered, and to this day the crime remains shrouded in mystery. Undoubtedly it freed Cuza from his most formidable adversary and the Conservatives from a leader of the first calibre; but he hesitated to expel them from office, and for another eighteen months a trial of strength took place between him and the new Conservative chief Crețulescu, who blocked the prince's projects of a loan, new railways, and above all land reform. But at last in October 1863 he broke with the Conservatives and summoned to power Michael Kogălniceanu, the spiritual leader of the Moldavian Liberals, a man pre-eminent for his ardent patriotism, wide learning, and serious way of life. Not many months were to pass, however, before it became clear that land reform, the main aim of prince and premier, could not be carried in the teeth of so reactionary an Assembly and that they were not in agreement as to alternative methods of enforcing it.

That a breach between the prince and his party opponents was so long in coming was mainly due to the recrudescence of a question whose solution had long been overdue and upon which national sentiment might be encouraged to concentrate. The so-called "Dedicated Convents" owed their very existence to one of the best traditions of the Principalities, namely the constant generosity of princes and boiars to the Church, and especially to the monasteries, who, as in pre-Reformation England, had long fulfilled valuable social functions. But under a regime as unsettled as that of the Turkish period special charters had been found necessary to protect these endowments, and gradually the practice had grown up, of placing monasteries under the protection of the Holy Places in Jerusalem, Sinai, Athos, or one of the great patriarchates of the Levant. The result was that, as Greek and Phanariot influence asserted itself both in church and state, the "Dedicated Convents" passed more and more into the control of alien monks, who diverted the revenues abroad, for purposes in which Roumanians had no interest and from which they derived no profit. By the end of the Phanariot era these monasteries owned in Wallachia about a quarter, in Moldavia almost one-third, of the total area: and the fate of their revenues had become a burning question which vitally affected the welfare of the population and the income of the state. We already saw that after 1821 an attempt was made to remedy the abuse, but that the monks found a protector in Russia, and induced her to uphold the *status quo*. Under the Règlement Organique a certain control was established, and the Ministry of Cults was authorised to farm out the monastic lands by an auction every five years. Kiselev appointed a mixed commission of monks and officials to work out a new arrangement, but the monks successfully obstructed: and again in 1843, when George Bibescu tried to solve the question, they managed to induce Russia to intervene and insist upon a respite of ten years. The fact is that a postponement suited Russian policy very well on the eve of the Crimean War, since it helped to secure the support of the higher clergy throughout the Levant, whose financial interests were at stake. During the war their annual income was estimated at about nine million francs, of which nearly five million found their way abroad.

After the war the international Commission suggested as a fair settlement, that the main revenue should be applied to social work, in pursuance of the original purpose of such foundations, and that the state should take over the administration, paying a fixed annual sum to the Holy Places. But again Russia succeeded in obtaining a postponement. At last in 1859 the Wallachian Government proposed levying a quarter of the monastic revenues, and the egumens who protested were threatened with expulsion. But the question remained a subject for interminable negotiations between the Powers, until in May 1860, in view of the economic depression, the farmers of monastic revenues demanded either the termination of their contracts or a reduction of their dues. This was carried out in Wallachia, while in Moldavia an inventory was taken, and a quarter of the monastic revenue since the year 1853 was claimed by the state, the monks being informed that if they did not comply they must leave the country. The Porte lodged a protest, and France and Russia now urged arbitration: but meanwhile the monks declined Barbu Catargiu's offer to negotiate, doubtless reckoning with foreign help. In November 1862 Cuza issued a decree sequestrating the disputed revenues, and placing them in the hands of the state: and when both the Porte and the ambassadors of the protecting Powers protested, he adopted the attitude that the question was a purely internal one, and issued a further decree forbidding the use of Greek in all churches and monasteries, and ordering the arrest of recalcitrants. The strength of the Roumanian Government lay in the knowledge that while its own people were solidly behind it, the Powers could not agree, and that their discussions were tapering out in an insincere battle of words between Bulwer and Moustier at Constantinople. Russell, who about the same time took an openly anti-Serbian line in the affair of the Turkish bombardment of Belgrade, was no less hostile to the Roumanians and told Bulwer to inform Cuza that his proceedings were "illegal, tyrannical, and subversive".[1]

But Roumania by now had the bit between her teeth, and in December 1863 a law of expropriation was passed by the Assembly, fixing the compensation at 84 million piastres; but in view of representations from the Porte and the Powers, this was soon raised to 150,000,000. But apparently on the advice of General Ignatyev (now beginning his long and stormy career as Russian ambassador in Constantinople), the monks and the patriarch refused to compound—thus acting in very much the same way as the Vatican towards the Italian state after 1870: and eventually in 1867 the Roumanian Chamber declared the offer of compensation to have lapsed. The whole treatment of the question may seem somewhat high-handed according to Western standards, but there is no doubt that it put an end to a most crying abuse, which had been unjustly and artificially prolonged in favour of a parasitic class, at once alien and incompetent. The Greek monk had long been the very reverse of an asset to the state.

The passage of this reform ended the truce between the prince and the Conservatives, and Kogălniceanu's democratic measure of land reform was keenly resented and on 25 April 1864 rejected by the Assembly. Cuza saw that he must surrender or fight: and as personal reasons made

[1] Quoted by Riker, *op. cit.* p. 365.

him the enemy of the big boiars, and as his mental processes followed the same autocratic lines as those of Napoleon III, he now decided on an appeal past the oligarchy to the masses, to support him as dictator. The peasants, he confided to the French consul, "are the state's active force. The rest do not matter, and the day an effort is made to overthrow me, I shall have three million peasants with me".[1] On 14 May, then, he not merely dissolved the Assembly, but carried out what is known in Roumanian history as the "Coup d'État". He issued a proclamation to the nation, appealing against "the irreconcilable resistance of a factious oligarchy" and demanding a plebiscite of all Roumanians above the age of 25 on the subject of a new Constitution and a wider franchise. The Statute which he submitted to them, as an extension of the Covenant of 1858, embodied certain highly important changes. Henceforth the prince was to possess the sole initiative of legislation. Side by side with the existing Chamber there was to be a Senate nominated by the prince himself. At the same time the franchise for the lower house was extended for the first time to the peasant masses—though admittedly in such a way that, in the then state of political education, it could be manipulated only too easily by the prefects in the interest of the Government of the day.

The plebiscite—a rough and ready imitation of Cuza's model, Napoleon III—endorsed his proposals by 682,621 to 1307: and it is unnecessary to add that the prevailing illiteracy and the speed with which it was pushed through made it somewhat of a farce. But the prince retained the initiative which he had so boldly seized. The once formidable consuls were left gasping, and the anger of the suzerain was swiftly turned away by the announcement that Cuza was hastening to Constantinople "to place at the Sultan's feet his own homage and that of the entire Roumanian nation".[2] Bulwer and other ambassadors refused to attend the official Turkish dinner in the prince's honour, but he remained imperturbable, good-humoured, and unyielding, and in the end convinced the Porte that a graceful acceptance of his homage on his own terms was preferable to an attempt to impose its will by force of arms, with all the international risks which that would involve. Meanwhile he listened patiently to Bulwer's none too palatable lecture, and left upon Prokesch the impression that "if he is lying, he is doing so with the appearance of truth.... He has the power in his hands and

[1] Tissot to Drouyn, 13 May 1864—quoted by Riker, *op. cit.* p. 437.
[2] Moustier to Drouyn, 15 June—quoted by Riker *op. cit.* p. 453.

is now exclusively responsible for its use".[1] And so on 28 June, within five weeks of the plebiscite, the Powers ratified the innovations as an "Acte Additionel"—"as homage to the dear defunct", to quote Mr Riker's not unduly sarcastic phrase. Moreover they added the provision that henceforth the United Principalities might effect internal legislative changes without any interference from outside, in all matters save those affecting relations with the suzerain power.

This striking success encouraged Cuza to make a further bid for popularity by promulgating the famous Agrarian Law of 24 August. But though this will always remain one of the great landmarks in Rou-manian history, and has earned for Cuza himself the undying gratitude of the peasantry, it must be confessed that it was too much the work of theorists, and so far from solving the land question, gave rise to many unseen complications which were to survive till after the Great War. None the less no criticism can obscure its fundamental merits. The per-sonal liberty of the peasant at last became a fact, all restrictions upon his movements, all feudal dues and tithes, were swept away, the landlord receiving as compensation "state bonds representing the tenfold value of the yearly servitudes owed by each category of peasants, with five per cent. interest",[2] and annual cash payments, spread over a period of fifteen years, being also exacted from the peasants themselves. The former serfs were then settled on holdings varying in size according to the district. Two-thirds of the arable land were to be taken over from the landlords, "but on small estates only, where there was not enough to go round".[3] The forests remained the unrestricted property of the boiars. There was soon a serious shortage of grazing land, and "the patrimonial land reserve was lost to the peasants without any compensation whatever". Kogăl-niceanu had desired from the bottom of his heart "to level up society, to lower the highly-placed, and to raise the humble".[4] But unhappily the new holdings were as a rule not large enough to be self-supporting, and so, as in Russia, emancipation had the unexpected effect of depressing the peasantry to a lower level. In the words of a recent critic, the law was "hastily conceived, imperfectly prepared, and frequently badly applied....The preliminary statistical survey which was really indis-pensable was not made, with the result that the boiars were often able

---

[1] Prokesch to Rechberg, 23 June, 1864—cit. Schlitter, p. 109.
[2] D. Mitrany, *The Land and the Peasant in Roumania*, p. 50.
[3] *Ibid.* p. 51.
[4] *Ibid.* p. 55.

successfully to assert a claim to land to which they were not entitled. Moreover the actual distribution was carried out in such a manner that all the worst land fell to the share of the peasantry".[1]

Despite many imperfections this reform was the first charter of a new era, leading to the two tragic dates of 1907 and 1917: in its own smaller sphere it was hardly less epoch-making than the almost parallel emancipation in Russia, which cannot have failed to serve as an incentive, though there is no sign of imitation. But in the meantime, though it changed the legal status of the peasants, "it did not give them sufficient economic strength to stand up against political inequality, nor did it give them sufficient power to withstand economic oppression".[2]

Scarcely less momentous was a second law promulgated by the dictator in 1864, that on Public Instruction, which laid down—in theory —free and obligatory education, established new primary schools, gymnasia and lycées and the two universities of Jassy and Bucarest, and set up a system of bursaries which enabled poor children of merit to pass from the village to the high school. Many provisions of this law were to remain on paper for over a generation to come, and even towards the close of the century were hotly contested by reactionary politicians. But it too was a charter and a programme, upon which all future progress was solidly grounded.

These two reforms will always stand to the credit of Cuza, but they were his last solid achievements. Power demoralised him, though it was certainly no mere pose when he publicly reaffirmed his readiness to make way for a foreign prince, and he was too genuine a patriot to plunge his country into civil war. But he was surrounded by a camarilla of the worst kind, the finances again fell into disorder, salaries were in arrears, corruption was rampant, and there was much peculation with army contracts. Foreign commercial firms obtained concessions which enabled them to exploit the country. Meanwhile Cuza's private life became a public scandal, even in the lax society of Bucarest, his treatment of his wife "Domnea Elena"—a Rosetti by birth and noted for her high character and devotion to charity—caused much offence. His mistress, Marie Obrenović—a daughter of Costin Catargiu and widow of a younger brother of Prince Miloš of Serbia—lived with him in the palace, but had many rivals to his favour. Their liaison left a fatal legacy to Serbia, for Marie's son by her own husband grew up neglected and

[1] Ifor Evans, *The Agrarian Revolution*, pp. 41-3.
[2] Mitrany, *op. cit.* p. 62.

unprincipled in the care of a gipsy woman, and as King Milan Obrenović transplanted the evil lessons of his childhood to the palace of Belgrade. Meanwhile, as Elena had no children, Cuza made his children by Marie his heirs, and it was even rumoured that he thought of the succession for one of them.

During 1865 discontent grew very rapidly throughout the country. Kogălniceanu, disillusioned and out of sympathy, could no longer work with a man with whom he had so little in common, and the feeble Crețulescu took his place. In August, while the prince was taking a cure at Ems, and at the very moment when he was planning state visits to the West, an *émeute* broke out in Bucarest, which was at once repressed with some brutality, but whose effect was to drive the rival Conservative and Liberal factions into each other's arms. A secret committee was formed, of which Lascar Catargiu, Ion Ghica, and his cousin General I. C. Ghica, Văcărescu, the Golescus, the two Brătianus, Dimitrie Sturdza, Rosetti, and Peter Carp were all members: its deliberate aim was to overthrow Cuza and to secure a prince belonging to one of the reigning families of the West. While the main threads of the conspiracy at home were placed in the hands of C. A. Rosetti, Ion Brătianu went to Paris and set himself to prepare French opinion for a change in Roumania, by publishing a violent pamphlet against "the usurping Prince", who instead of devoting himself to the welfare of his country, displayed nothing save "a mediocre personality and an immense vanity", and who was making of Roumania "a governorship of St Petersburg", and surrounding himself with Russian agents.[1] In reality this was an absurd exaggeration, for the Russian court was by this time definitely hostile to Cuza, and only deterred from action against him by the desire to remain on good terms with Paris. Much more justified was Brătianu's outspoken conclusion that "the Roumanians only ask one thing—that the Emperor should let them know whom he would regard with benevolence as Prince of Roumania".

Meanwhile he was pulling many wires behind the scenes, and used his personal relations with Drouyn de Lhuys and his wife, and with the minister of instruction, Duruy, who enjoyed Napoleon's confidence. But above all he relied upon the benevolent influence of Mme Hortense

---

[1] General Florescu, the Minister of Interior, had been aide-de-camp to the Russian General Lüders during the occupation of 1848; Mme Crețulescu was a Russian. Alexander Cantacuzene and Moruzi were also denounced as slavish Russophils.

Cornu, a foster-daughter of Queen Hortense, and as a child at Arenenberg the playmate of Louis Napoleon, who still listened to her advice and valued her high intelligence. By February 1866 Brătianu was sufficiently sure of the success of his efforts to telegraph to Rosetti the secret signal which meant that the conspirators could safely proceed to action. In diplomatic circles Cuza's position was widely regarded as precarious, and Clarendon, fearing possible complications from a change, instructed Green, the British agent in Bucarest, to urge the prince "to correct the errors of his administration". But the interview was a complete failure, since Cuza treated the adoption of ministerial responsibility, which alone could have reconciled his enemies, as quite impossible, and on the other hand emphasised his readiness to retire, if the Powers would choose a foreign successor, which was the very opposite of Clarendon's desire.[1] Sunk in indolence and self-indulgence, Cuza made no attempt to escape from the impasse, and even disregarded an urgent secret warning of his danger: and so events took their course.

On the night of 23 February 1866 a number of prominent officers, won over by the Central Committee, carried out a successful palace revolution. Cuza was roused from his bed after midnight, and forced to dress hurriedly while his mistress hid behind an improvised screen: an officer knelt and offered his back as a rest for the act of abdication, and no sooner had Cuza appended his signature, than he was hurried to a carriage and driven off to Cotroceni, whence, after an interval of some days, he was escorted to the frontier. Not a moment was wasted by the successful conspirators, and when the inhabitants of Bucarest left their houses in the morning, they found at every corner a proclamation in the name of a Regency—composed of General Nicholas Golescu, Dimitrie Sturdza (acting for the Conservative leader, Lascar Catargiu, who was absent), and Colonel Haralambi—announcing its devotion to constitutional government, and the intention to elect a foreign prince, and thereby at length fulfil the long deferred aspirations of the "Divans ad hoc" of 1857. A new Cabinet was formed under Ion Ghica, who had played a worthy part in the events of 1848, had been made prince of Samos in 1854, and was supposed to enjoy the favour of the Turks and of England, though Bulwer regarded him as "an artful and determined intriguer".[2] In the afternoon the two Chambers met and elected by

---

[1] 20 December, Clarendon to Green, and 5 Jan. 1866, Green to Clarendon—quoted by Riker, *op. cit.* pp. 486–7.
[2] Bulwer to Russell, 6 March 1861—quoted by Riker, *op. cit.* p. 494.

acclamation Philip Count of Flanders, the younger brother of Leopold II of Belgium. This was really in the nature of a demonstration, to prove how united Roumanian opinion was, and to forestall any action by the Porte or the consuls, who this time found themselves quite helpless. There had never been any chance of acceptance, and Philip at once declined the proffered throne: as a grandson of Louis Philippe, he would scarcely have been acceptable to Napoleon.

Meanwhile, however, Ion Brătianu had been more active than ever in the West, and with the discreet connivance of Napoleon III, was sounding another candidate. This was Prince Charles of Hohenzollern Siegmaringen, of the elder South German and Catholic branch of that family. His father, Karl Anton, had voluntarily renounced his position as a reigning sovereign, and had acted for three years as Prussian premier until Bismarck took his place in 1861: at this moment he was military governor of the Rhine, residing at Düsseldorf. The young Charles, though brought up as a Prussian officer, was as much French as German by blood, for his paternal grandmother was a niece of Joachim Murat, while his maternal grandmother, Stephanie of Baden, was by birth a Beauharnais, and adoptive daughter of the great Napoleon. He was thus actually a cousin of Napoleon III, through the latter's mother Hortense as the daughter of Josephine Beauharnais.[1] His own sister, Stephanie, had recently married King Pedro V of Portugal.

The exact manner in which the candidature of Prince Charles first emerged is even to-day obscure, and it is not certain whether it will be altogether clear even when the jealously guarded Brătianu family archives are at last given to the world. The initiative seems almost certainly to have lain with Ion Brătianu himself: and though he consulted Mme Cornu as to Napoleon's sentiments, it is doubtful whether she ever handed on the enquiries. After the event, at any rate, Napoleon affected great surprise and told her that "they have saddled me with it".[2] He must have known the main lines of the project, but remained passive, did not consult his ministers, and was doubtless pardonably absorbed in the approaching struggle in Germany.

[1] "J'ai en moi de Son sang", he wrote to Napoleon III on 13 May 1866—*Aus dem Leben König Karls*, I, p. 36.

[2] Ollivier, *L'Empire Libéral*, VIII, p. 84. See also Henry, *L'Abdication du Prince Cuza*, pp. 60–3. It is however known that Mme Cornu wrote to Ali Pasha (who had formerly been Turkish ambassador in Paris), describing Charles as a "favourite" of Napoleon, and as "French in feeling". See Henry, *ibid.* no. 274 (Prokesch to Mensdorff, 15 May).

The Austrian representative in Bucarest, Baron Eder, looking on with hostile eyes, reported in the first instance that the older boiars favoured the return of Bibescu, while the more radical groups were thinking of General Nicholas Golescu as prince, or of Ion Brătianu as president of a republic. He even recorded the foolish rumour that Brătianu might proclaim himself prince.[1] Eder's informants ascribed Charles's candidature above all to Italian intermediaries, but as time passed he more and more suspected the hand of Bismarck.[2] Meanwhile Prince Metternich in Paris received the French ministers' profession of ignorance with thinly veiled scepticism: when Drouyn told him of an intrigue between Prussia and Russia on Charles's behalf, he "could hardly help laughing", so he wrote home to his chief.[3] The Austrian Government was doubtless encouraged by learning from its London ambassador, Count Apponyi, that Lord Clarendon was talking of an open conflict with Paris in the Roumanian question and actually threatening to separate himself from France if she adhered to the idea of a foreign prince.[4] In view of London's attitude it became more than ever Napoleon's cue, and therefore of course Drouyn's, to play the ignorant and decline all responsibility.

On 31 March Brătianu visited Charles and Karl Anton at Düsseldorf, and made an offer of the Roumanian crown: and though he failed to obtain a binding answer, he was sufficiently encouraged to take the necessary steps for creating an accomplished fact. The uncertainty at home could not be allowed to continue, especially in face of protests from the Porte and the doubtful attitude of the Conference, reassembled in Paris to discuss the situation. On 14 April, therefore, the Provisional Government proclaimed Charles as their candidate, and instituted a plebiscite in the country, with the result that 685,969 votes were polled in his favour, and only 224 against. It was high time, for there was an outburst of separatist feeling in Moldavia, which might easily have opened the door to foreign intrigue, and which for a few days led to rioting and bloodshed in Jassy.

For the second time an international crisis came to the aid of Roumania. The struggle of Prussia and Austria for hegemony was rapidly

[1] Eder to Mensdorff, nos. 179 and 202—Henry, *L'Abdication du Prince Cuza*.
[2] *Ibid.* p. 303—14 and 15 April—nos. 199 and 202.
[3] *Ibid.* no. 291—21 May, Metternich to Mensdorff.
[4] "Lutte ouverte et corps à corps" were Clarendon's own words. Apponyi to Mensdorff, 7 April—Henry, *op. cit.* no. 185.

coming to a head, and warlike preparations were being made on both sides. Austria, still further preoccupied by the discontent of Hungary, and by the fear of a Prusso-Italian alliance, could not pay due attention to the affairs of the Lower Danube, let alone concentrate troops or threaten occupation, as she might have done under other circumstances. Charles and his father still hesitated until they could be sure of the attitude of King William, as the recognised head of their whole family, and William very rightly preferred not to commit himself too far, and while showing a certain distaste for the idea of a Hohenzollern prince as vassal of the sultan, hinted that the essential point was to be sure that neither France nor Russia would oppose.[1] As he had by now—rightly or wrongly—been led to reckon upon Napoleon's definite support, and at the same time upon the tsar's passivity, Charles decided to take the necessary risks. Bismarck, whom he consulted, deliberately strengthened his resolve: "You have been unanimously elected by a whole nation: follow this call, go straight to the country....The Powers most interested, Russia and the Porte, will protest most decidedly against your election, France, England and Italy will be on your side, and Austria will do all it can to upset your candidature. But there is not much fear from this side, as I think of keeping Austria busy for some time". Prussia, he added, if approached officially, would have to oppose, in order not to offend Russia, but "by acting on your own account you will rescue the King from an awkward situation, and I am sure he would not be ill-disposed, though he could not give his consent as head of the family. If Your Highness is once in Roumania, the question will soon be solved, for if Europe sees itself faced with a *fait accompli*, the Powers most concerned will protest, but a protest remains on paper and the facts won't be altered". He should write a flattering letter to the tsar, and perhaps a Russian marriage might be arranged later.

In effect Bismarck's advice meant that Europe could safely be disregarded, and that in the event of failure, his personal position in Prussia would be the same as before: "you would return home and could always remember with pleasure a 'compliment' which can never be made a reproach to you". The prince was then received in audience by King William, who gave him leave of absence from his regiment, and his own private blessing: and he significantly assured the king that he was "ready to recognise Turkish suzerainty for the moment, but with the tacit reserve that he would free himself from it by force of arms

[1] *Aus dem Leben König Karls*, I, pp. 12–13.

and conquer full independence on the battlefield". It was in such a mood that the young Prussian knight-errant set out to win his kingdom: and it is interesting to note that Brătianu and Davila, when received for the second time at Düsseldorf, laid before him a map depicting all the countries inhabited by Roumanians and left upon him, according to his diary—published, it is true, in 1894—a somewhat "adventurous" impression.[1]

When his mind was at last made up, there was still a very practical difficulty to overcome: how was the prince to reach his new Principality? The sea route took three weeks, and led through Constantinople: the Russian route was equally impracticable. The sole alternative was through Austria: but hostilities between Austria and Prussia might break out at any moment, and Charles would be in danger of arrest as a Prussian officer, and in any case, if identified, would certainly not be allowed to proceed to Roumania. He therefore made his way to Zürich, procured a Swiss passport in the name of "Karl Hettingen" bound for Odessa, and travelled for some days across Austria and Hungary, in trains overcrowded and disorganised by the order of mobilisation: he wore goggles and went second class (evidently for the first and last time, to judge by his naïve diary comments on the dirty carriages), and he narrowly escaped recognition by Austrian officers whom he had known in the Schleswig campaign. After an anxious wait of forty-eight hours for a Danube steamer at Baziaş, he was joined by Ion Brătianu, who had travelled direct from Paris, and now sat in the first class, studiously ignoring the bogus Swiss "drummer". When the steamer at last touched Roumanian soil at Turnu Severin, Charles was in too great a hurry to land, and the captain, who knew he had a ticket for Odessa, called out to him to stop. But Brătianu and his suite hustled him unceremoniously down the gangway, and he landed in his future kingdom with an angry voice ringing in his ear, "By God, that must be the Prince of Hohenzollern".[2] But Brătianu had already turned hat in hand to greet his new sovereign, who after a two days' drive in an open carriage with postilions and eight horses, across the still primitive Wallachian roads, was joyously greeted in Bucarest on 22 May 1866. The torrential rain that welcomed his arrival after a drought of three months, was accepted in oriental fashion as a happy omen.

How well advised the Roumanian leaders were in pressing for a speedy decision is proved by certain tentative negotiations which re-

---

[1] *Aus dem Leben König Karls*, I, pp. 17–18, 26.  [2] *Ibid.* pp. 38–43.

mained entirely secret at the time and have only emerged from the darkness of the archives in our own day. In the search for a formula which would solve the Italian question without a fresh war, it occurred to the Italian Government that Austria might be induced to renounce Venetia if she could obtain the Danubian provinces as compensation: and this idea was actually taken up by Lord Russell, discussed in the British Cabinet in November 1864, and despite Palmerston's scepticism, cautiously put forward both to Drouyn de Lhuys in Paris, and to the grand vizier.[1] Of course nothing came of a project which illustrates the very unequal measure adopted by Russell towards national problems in Eastern and Western Europe. But Cuza's fall occurred at a moment when the Venetian problem was in a certain sense the finger on the balance between Austria and Prussia: and Nigra, with the approval of the Italian premier, General La Marmora, at once sounded Napoleon III as to such an exchange.[2] The emperor was evasive, and it was on this occasion that he advised Florence to make terms with Berlin, thereby unwittingly initiating that Prusso-Italian alliance which was to prove of such vast advantage to Bismarck by tying the hands of Western Europe during the victorious campaign of Königgrätz. The idea of compensation still lingered in the European chancelleries, and a proposal that Austria should take Serbia, Bosnia and Hercegovina in exchange for Venetia came from Baron Talleyrand, now French ambassador in St Petersburg, and was quoted approvingly by the Empress Eugénie to Prince Richard Metternich as "une politique large et grandiose" for Austria.[3] The Roumanian project seems to have lingered till May, when Ali Pasha said that if the Principalities were to be lost, Turkey would sooner see them Austrian than independent.[4] Russia on her side made it clear that their annexation by Austria would involve a breach with Russia.[5] But as nothing succeeds like success, what finally blew the plan sky-high was the victory of Prussia in the Seven Weeks' War, which left the Powers incapable of prompt action upon the Lower Danube and led the Porte to reflect that its new vassal must be treated with the respect due to his victorious cousin.

[1] See Riker, *op. cit.* p. 511; Alfred Stern, *Gesch. Europas*, IX, p. 453.

[2] De La Gorce, *Histoire du Second Empire*, IV, p. 581.

[3] Oncken, *Rheinpolitik*, I, no. 50, 22 March.

[4] H. Schlitter, *Aus der Regierungszeit Franz Josephs*, p. 114. In 1869 Ali, as grand vizier, actually proposed to Francis Joseph and Beust the cession of Roumania to Austria-Hungary.

[5] A. Stern, *op. cit.* IX, p. 457.

All these moves took place behind the back of the Paris Conference, which met early in March 1866 at Napoleon's suggestion and eventually dispersed on June 4 without reaching any conclusion. The Turkish delegate, Safvet Pasha, argued that the expulsion of Cuza had automatically dissolved the union, but no other Power endorsed this thesis, and when Russia proposed a fresh consultation of the population, Drouyn de Lhuys took the line that their wishes had already been expressed beyond the possibility of a doubt. The Porte formally protested against Charles's election as altogether illegal, massed troops along the Danube and was with difficulty held back from a military occupation: it was the French Government that assured Constantinople that the choice of the new prince was directed not against Turkey but Austria.[1] Fortunately the Turks were debarred by the Treaty of Paris from sending troops without the sanction of the guaranteeing Powers.

Meanwhile a strong Government was formed under Lascar Catargiu, mainly Conservative in colour, but with the two notable exceptions of Ion Brătianu and C. A. Rosetti, who held the portfolios of Finance and Education. Their main task was to push through a new Constitution as rapidly as possible and thus provide a firmer foundation for the new regime: and in point of fact it received parliamentary sanction as early as 11 July, when the prince at once took oath to it.

The new Constitution was based mainly on the Belgian Charter of 1831, and at the time of its adoption might fairly claim to fulfil the boast of its framers that it was one of the most liberal then in operation. But it was not enough to pass enlightened laws: it remained to enforce them and to imbue public opinion and the governing class with respect for the principles which they embodied. If, however, many most important provisions remained more or less on paper or were conveniently evaded, this was almost inevitable in a country only slowly emerging from the appalling conditions of arbitrary and corrupt government depicted in earlier chapters. Its more salient features deserve to be briefly summarised, since it was to remain in force, save for certain specific changes in 1879 and 1884, for two generations to come. Its earlier provisions lay down a number of abstract principles—liberty of conscience, of instruction, of the press and of assembly, and again, equality before the law, eligibility for office and the abolition of all privileges, monopolies and titles. Certain of these principles remain somewhat ill-defined, but others are interpreted in such detail as to give

[1] Schlitter, *op. cit.* p. 113.

pretty effective guarantees. Though education was henceforth to be free and obligatory, it is true that the number of schools erected and the endowment of those already in existence remained entirely inadequate throughout the reign, though undoubtedly standards were rising slowly yet steadily all the time. The provisions regarding the press were framed on extremely liberal lines (§ 24). Trial by jury was instituted for press offences, and no preliminary authorisation or deposit was required for the publication of a newspaper, as in contemporary Hungary: nor could a newspaper be lawfully censored, suspended or suppressed. Again, § 26 laid down the freedom of public meeting, without preliminary authorisation, to discuss any question—open-air meetings, it is true, being expressly excluded: and this at a time when no right whatsoever of assembly or association existed in Hungary.

The legislative power was to be shared by the prince and the two Chambers, and the initiative for a bill could come from any one of the three. The duration of Parliament was for four years. The powers of the sovereign were defined with some precision. The throne was settled on Prince Charles and, failing children of his own, on his brothers and their heirs (§ 82). He had the right to nominate and dismiss ministers, to dissolve Parliament and also to adjourn it, but in the latter case only for one month at a time. He enjoyed the right of absolute veto on legislation and the right of political amnesty. He was to be head of the army, and might conclude treaties with foreign states: but this latter prerogative was hedged in by the very important proviso that "in order that they may have obligatory force, they must first be submitted to the legislature and approved by it" (§ 93)—a clause of which much will be heard when we come to consider Prince Charles's foreign policy at moments of supreme crisis. The princely authority was further limited by a clause enjoining that the two Chambers should meet automatically on 15 November in every year, whether summoned by the prince or not (§ 95)—the intention obviously being to make it impossible for him to govern legally without Parliament. Again, while ordinary laws could be initiated by the prince or by either Chamber, in the case of financial and military measures the initiative was reserved to the Chamber of Deputies (§ 33)—a point striking at the very root of absolutist tendencies. The Budget must be voted annually by the Lower House (§ 113).

Parliament was to consist of two Houses—a Senate and a Chamber of Deputies, and the franchise rested upon a somewhat complicated and artificial system of electoral colleges, devised to favour the propertied classes—a practice which could still be justified by the backward state of the masses, and for which there were numerous contemporary precedents. For the Lower House there were then still four colleges, the first and second respectively consisting of voters whose income from land exceeded 300 ducats, or amounted to between 100 and 300 ducats. The third was purely urban, being open to business men and tradesmen paying over 80 piastres in direct taxes, and duly recognised members of the liberal professions, without any money qualification. In the fourth were grouped all remaining taxpayers, but here every fifty electors chose a delegate and these primaries together elected a restricted number of deputies. Thus of course the great majority of voters only elected indirectly, and the wealthier classes had an altogether disproportionate share in political power: and this survived, though in a modified form, even after the very mild electoral reform of 1884.

It should be added that at the time discussion centred round three main points: (1) The adoption of the bi-cameral system, which has survived all political changes and which probably assured to Roumania greater stability than to some of her Balkan neighbours, which have at times experimented with an Upper House, only to discard it once more. (2) The princely veto upon legislation, which was made absolute, and not merely suspensory, as at first proposed. (3) The restrictions upon citizenship under Article 7, which laid down that "only foreigners belonging to Christian persuasions can obtain naturalisation". With the European and Jewish aspects of this provision it will be necessary to deal later.

That a Government of such discordant elements should have brought into being a constitution destined to survive, almost unaltered, till the United Principalities became "Great Roumania", is no small testimony to the realism, initiative and skill by which the Roumanian statesmen of that age made good their lack of parliamentary tradition and experience. But before the month was out, the two groups fell apart, and Catargiu gave place to the more moderate, if more rusé, Ion Ghica, who tried to govern without the Liberal leaders Brătianu and Rosetti. It was Ghica's special function to employ his former good relations with the Porte in order to secure Turkish recognition, and after long haggling an agreement was at last reached on 20 October, which owed at least as much to the battle of Königgrätz as to any other cause. By it Charles was recognised as hereditary prince and might maintain an army of

30,000 men,[1] but was not allowed to increase its numbers without the Porte's consent. He obtained his own coinage, but not the right to confer decorations and the tribute was to be "augmented", but the time and method of this was left entirely vague.[2] The Turkish ministers persistently continued to refer to the "United Principalities" and to the "Moldo-Wallachians" instead of "Roumania" and the "Roumanians". The prince paid his state visit of investiture at Constantinople, and was received with very special honours by the sultan. In January 1867 the recognition of the Powers followed, more or less as a matter of course, and instead of the half-baked status inaugurated by the events of 1859 Roumania now enjoyed a new and regularised position.

After suffering for centuries from an exposed geographical situation, Roumania had at last been able to profit decisively and on successive occasions, from a favourable political constellation in Europe: and there were therefore not unnaturally some of the new prince's subjects who entertained the rash illusion that Austria's defeat offered a tempting prospect of realising what now began to be spoken of as "Daco-Roman Unity"—or the union of all sections of the Roman province of Dacia. But the prince sternly discouraged what were still the merest day-dreams, though it is to be noted that throughout life he invariably showed a keen interest in the Roumanians of Transylvania and, undeterred by hostile comment, made a point of receiving those of their leaders who visited Bucharest. For the time being phantasy of this kind was effectually checked by the conclusion of the Dualist settlement of 1867 between Austria and Hungary, which at first immensely stimulated the development of the Habsburg Monarchy, and which, by assuring to the Magyars a political monopoly inside Hungary and a growing influence upon diplomacy and foreign policy, correspondingly depressed the status of their 3,000,000 Roumanian subjects.

As a Prussian officer, Prince Charles had, in June 1866, been firmly convinced of Prussia's superiority over Austria, just as in August 1870, in the teeth of all opinion in his new home, he maintained that Prussia would smash France within two months. But he had also brought with him from the West sound judgment and a sense of proportion, and he soon realised the length of the road which Roumania still had to travel. He therefore set his face resolutely against any policy of adventure, in whatever direction, and to quote but a single instance,

---

[1] Its actual strength in 1866 was only 17,648, with 1696 officers.
[2] § 10 of Convention—cf. *Aus dem Leben*, I, p. 88.

showed the greatest possible reserve when the ardent Rosetti engineered a secret meeting between him and the Magyar Garibaldian *émigré* General Türr, whose object was to make Wallachia the base for a madcap rising in Hungary. "My sole task", Charles told him, "is to revive by good administration a country which has been utterly ruined, morally and financially."[1] This represents the prince's policy during the first ten years of his reign, and indeed also his settled policy after the inevitable interruption of 1877–8: and to his sane and tireless insistence upon it Roumania owes a debt that is simply incalculable.

He soon realised that conditions were very bad and unhealthy in every branch of public life. The finances were in disorder: and serious peculation and corruption had just been discovered high up in various Government departments. As he wrote to his father in July 1866, "We literally haven't a groschen".[2] Communications were very primitive: there were as yet no railways open. Cholera and bad harvests had aggravated the agricultural situation. Education was a mere mockery outside the principal towns. The National Guard was insubordinate, the army ill-disciplined and badly equipped, partly owing to the usual dishonest contractors. One of his first acts showed both the extent of the evil and the courage with which he faced it. A large number of officers demanded of him the dismissal of those concerned in the *coup d'état*: whereupon he delivered to them a public harangue explaining why he could not consent to such a thing and why he must, as army chief, insist upon unqualified obedience from all his officers. It struck a note that was at once Prussian and didactic, but it had the desired effect. Even without this incident he required but little incentive to devote his main effort to army organisation, and he would scarcely have been human, especially in the years following Königgrätz, if he had not sought his models at Berlin rather than Paris, alike in discipline, in instruction and in armament. This was, however, keenly resented by Napoleon III, whose hostility to Prussia grew in proportion as he realised the extent to which he had misjudged her strength and been outwitted by Bismarckian policy. His tortuous designs for compensation on the Rhine and the Scheldt continued to go awry, he viewed with resentment the speed with which the new Italy had emancipated herself from his guidance and allied herself with his potential enemy, and he suspected his other Latin *protégé*, Roumania, of following on the same

[1] *Aus dem Leben*, I, p. 89.
[2] *Ibid.* I, p. 93.

path. His attitude to Roumania was inevitably complicated by the growing rapprochement between France and Austria, who of all the Great Powers had hitherto shown the strongest opposition to Roumanian unity and to a foreign prince.

Napoleon's changed attitude was embarrassingly revealed in his suspicion of Brătianu as "an instrument of Mazzinian policy",[1] and in the utterly unproved allegation that he had been mixed up in the Orsini plot a decade earlier. Brătianu's energetic measures against the Moldavian Jews, which the Alliance Israélite in Paris exploited to the full, and which led to official protests from London and Vienna, gave Napoleon the desired pretext for demanding the obnoxious minister's dismissal; and Duruy tried to gild the pill for Charles by arguing that "men who are good at making revolutions and overthrowing governments are never good at governing ".[2] But for the prince it was a very serious issue, for not merely was Brătianu unquestionably the ablest and most forceful personality in Roumanian public life at the moment, but also one who held the key position of the Ministry of the Interior and on whom he relied more than any other to introduce some order into a slovenly administration and debased finances. Ambitious, eloquent, aggressive, nationalistic, denounced by superficial observers for his revolutionary past, he was really, in terms of the mid-century in Western Europe, essentially *bourgeois* in outlook, though in private life he preserved the traditions of a lesser boiar family. In contrast to his intimate friend Rosetti, who remained a supreme sentimentalist to the very end of his life, Brătianu's character had a hard note of realism which struck some kindred chords in Charles and rendered him politically almost indispensable. Feeling him to be standing the test more and more as a proved statesman, the prince neither could nor would drop him overboard[3] and found a gallant compromise. In August 1867 the Crețulescu Cabinet, of which Brătianu, though a Liberal, was the life nerve, resigned in favour of Stephen Golescu, and Brătianu visited Paris in order to clear himself of the charges levelled against him and to assure the French Government of Roumania's devotion. On his return he was once more entrusted with the portfolio of Finance, and placed in control of the Interior during the new elections. But the prejudice was not overcome, and Moustier, now for a brief space the

[1] Letter of Mme Cornu in *Aus dem Leben*, I, p. 202.
[2] *Ibid.* p. 212.
[3] To his father, 7 March 1868—*ibid.* I, p. 253.

French premier, spoke of Brătianu as "representing revolution, agitation and a future cataclysm", while Rouher denounced "the revolutionary despotism of the Brătianus" and the ever reckless Gramont thought of "showing Charles to the door".[1] The murder of Michael Obrenović and an abortive Bulgarian rising, whose organisers came from Roumanian territory, caused further alarm in France, and Charles wrote to his father that Moustier "wants at all costs to pick a quarrel with Roumania" and to force the Government to resign.[2] The attitude of London was also far from friendly: the Chamber had early in 1867 voted Roumanian citizenship to Gladstone and Roebuck,[3] but no other British politician showed any comprehension of the Roumanian cause and shortly before his death Lord Clarendon expressed himself to Count Kálnoky in the most unfriendly terms towards Roumania.[4] Austria remained unfriendly, Prokesch had told the prince to his face that Roumania had let itself "be misused by the European Revolution and turned into a nest of enemies of the Monarchy",[5] and Beust spoke of "the Daco-Roman swindle" and even suspected Brătianu of intrigue with Russia.[6] Even Prussia's attitude was doubtful, the crown prince facing the possibility of having to "sacrifice my cousin Charles" to Austria;[7] and the Prussian representative was instructed to inform the prince that Roumania's good relations with Prussia depended on the avoidance of any activities which might offend Hungary,[8]—now the bulwark of Francis Joseph's throne.[9]

In a situation of such difficulty internal consolidation had to take precedence over external adventure. Prince Michael of Serbia, during his state visit to Bucarest in April 1867, urged upon him that Roumania

[1] Oncken, *Rheinpolitik*, III, nos. 657, 658 and 645 (17 November). On 5 March 1869 Napoleon wrote quite openly to Charles of his suspicions of Brătianu, adding "I see with pleasure that experience has taught your Highness the danger in politics of relying on men accustomed to opposing the principles of order and justice". *Aus dem Leben*, I, p. 340.

[2] *Ibid.* I, p. 284.

[3] At the same time as Michelet, Quinet, St Marc Girardin, Ubicini and Bataillard.

[4] Schlitter, *op. cit.* p. 146.

[5] *Ibid.*

[6] Oncken *op. cit.* II, p. 515, note to no. 551—5 February 1868.

[7] *Ibid.* II, no. 543—Metternich to Beust.

[8] Wertheimer, *Graf Andrássy*, I, p. 455.

[9] Prince Charles recorded in his diary that "Roumania has links with three of the Great Powers—that of race with France, of religion with Russia, of family with Prussia, but the latter concerns the Prince alone".—*Aus dem Leben*, I, 253.

and Serbia must combine to shake off the yoke of the Porte; and Charles admitted that he regarded Turkish suzerainty as "oppressive and humiliating".[1] But he also insisted that the first essential was to re-organise their armies, and that till they were ready it was necessary to remain on good terms with Constantinople and not provoke the Powers. A year later he did conclude a secret convention with Serbia, which formed part of Michael's ambitious network of Balkan alliances: but if Michael had within the near future attempted to organise an offensive —and such seems to have been his intention—it is almost certain that Charles would have exercised a restraining influence and refused to stake the existence of his own country. The assassination of Michael, her ablest modern ruler, was a grave setback for Serbia: but it probably averted a premature outbreak of war for which neither she nor Rou-mania nor Greece possessed the necessary strength or resources.

In 1869, then, pursuing his policy of caution, Charles paid visits of ceremony to the courts of Europe, and in particular to the tsar at Livadia and to Napoleon III in Paris. Most important of all, through the mediation of the Prussian crown prince, he returned home with a wife, in the person of Princess Elizabeth of Wied, the future "Carmen Sylva", who brought him great domestic happiness and was to devote a long life and very genuine artistic and literary talents to raising na-tional and moral standards in her adopted country and making it better known to the outside world. The princess was a Lutheran, and Charles, who, though himself a Catholic, had already taken oath to educate his children in the Orthodox faith, refused to submit to the terms imposed by the Pope, and was married at Neuwied in the presence of Queen Augusta of Prussia, a German chaplain being found to risk excom-munication by granting the nuptial benediction. The royal idyll, resting upon Charles's manly and loyal character and on Elizabeth's vivid and charming personality, had a steadying influence in days of uncertainty and gave to the dynasty a prestige and stability which were con-spicuously lacking to the Serbian court under Milan and Alexander.

Despite his marriage and state visits Charles's position on his return was somewhat precarious. An open breach had at last come between him and the Liberals, not so much owing to persistent foreign advice as to purely personal incidents at home. In a talk of five hours early in 1869 Brătianu had warned the prince of "internal catastrophe" and had earned the proud rejoinder that "a Hohenzollern cannot be overthrown

[1] *Aus dem Leben*, I, p. 188.

so easily as a *parvenu* Prince".[1] That same spring we find the prince's father advising him against the retention of Brătianu in power, despite all his merits, owing to Napoleon's deep distrust of that statesman. "Without the support of France", he adds, and the advice carries all the more weight because it comes from a Prussian source, "the existence of Roumania is continually menaced, because in any project of a Franco-Austrian alliance Roumania becomes an object of compensation from the political and territorial point of view." A dissolution followed, and the methods of electoral pressure, for which Roumania was henceforth to become proverbial, reduced the Opposition to ten deputies in a Chamber of 157, with the result that Liberal agitation was transferred to the street and to the press, which was irresponsible and often scurrilous. Charles tried to govern by a succession of centre Governments, eliminating the strong personalities of both Left and Right: but this ended by alienating even such men as Kogălniceanu, who early in 1870 declared, "This dynasty can't be upheld any longer!"[2] Nor did it help matters when foreign affairs were entrusted to Peter Carp, who had till then edited the anti-dynastic paper *Le Pays Roumain*, and whose assistant editor Blaramberg now continued his campaign in the Chamber.

Charles already seemed in grave danger of falling between two stools, when the complications of 1870 brought matters to a head. There was a spontaneous outburst of Roumanian sympathies towards France, and Carp, in answer to an interpellation, declared that "where the flag of France flies, there are our interests and sympathies". Instead of tactfully recognising that the prince's feelings must inevitably be with his kinsmen and his former comrades-in-arms—and all the more so since it was his own brother Leopold whose candidature for the Spanish throne had been used as a pretext for the fatal Franco-Prussian quarrel—a large section of Roumanian opinion deliberately set itself to insult him and render his position untenable. "We cannot fight the Prussians in France", so ran the demagogic phrase, "but we will do it here!"[3] In August 1870, while the scale was already wavering in favour of the Prussians, an abortive attempt at revolution was made at Ploeşci: the prince was to be expelled, a republic proclaimed, Nicholas Golescu made Regent and Brătianu Minister of War. The movement was quickly suppressed, but the jury's acquittal of those implicated threw a signifi-

[1] *Aus dem Leben*, I, p. 335.
[2] *Ibid.* II, p. 61.                    [3] *Ibid.* II, p. 159.

cant light upon popular feeling at this moment. The prince took it calmly, but told his angry premier, Iepureanu, that it was "a blow to liberal institutions in Roumania".[1] The Address voted in the following December by the Chamber contained passages which he felt to be a reflection upon himself: and for a time he thought very seriously of abdication. A confidential letter addressed to the German novelist Auerbach and published by a calculated indiscretion, referred to the Address as "a *chef d'œuvre* of Phanariot perfidy", bitterly criticised the "inexperienced and utopian" agitators and made it quite clear that he was making "a last effort" in the teeth of calumny and misconceptions.[2]

This heated state of public sentiment coincided with very serious scandals connected with the new Roumanian railways. As the young state enjoyed no credit abroad, only somewhat speculative contractors could be found to finance such enterprises, on terms both exorbitant and elastic. The first line, from Suceava to Jassy and Roman, was built by the firm of Ofenheim, and proved fairly satisfactory. But the contract for the still more important lines connecting Roman on the one hand with Galaţ, and on the other with Bucarest and Verciorova (and so with Hungary and the West), was unfortunately carelessly worded and entrusted to a Prussian Jew named Strousberg, who used bad material, became involved in scandalous mismanagement and delay and only completed the work with the utmost difficulty. In the winter of 1870 it transpired that he could not pay the coupons to his shareholders, but had the impudence to claim that the full liability lay with the Roumanian state. Prince Charles, who had been swift to grasp the immense importance of these railways to Roumania's economic development, had exposed himself by hurrying through the contracts, and now, by a perversity of fate, von Ambronn, another German who had for years been in his own and his father's service, and had been appointed official supervisor of contracts, was found to have speculated away the company's reserves by selling the guaranteed deposit in Berlin for worthless papers. Matters were made still worse when the Prussian state, in the interest of numerous Prussian shareholders, insisted that the obligation must be taken over, even though the treasury was almost empty. All this supplied the malcontents with fresh capital for a really scurrilous anti-dynastic campaign, which fortunately overshot the mark by suggesting that to resign now would be to play the deserter and the traitor.[3]

[1] *Aus dem Leben,* II, p. 128.    [2] *Ibid.* II, p. 138.
[3] Damé, *Hist. de la Roumanie contemporaine,* p. 224.

By now the prince's pride and his sense of realities were thoroughly roused. He felt that he could not abandon foreign shareholders who had relied mainly upon the solvency of a Hohenzollern ruler: but his heart also was far too deeply engaged in Roumania for him to be able to contemplate the dangers of foreign intrigue and intervention which a fresh vacancy on the throne would certainly involve. The action of Russia in repudiating the Black Sea settlement of 1856 at a moment when France was prostrate and the German Powers in secret collusion, made him fear for southern Bessarabia and even for Roumania's new-won status in Europe. The Liberals, now thumping the French drum for tactical quite as much as sentimental reasons, summoned the country through their organ *Romậnul* to celebrate "23 February" as the day commemorating "the overthrow of a Prince who had violated the constitution and wasted the public money".[1] Meanwhile Charles had been warned by Bismarck to expect "no help, but rather ill-will, from abroad", and this seemed proved when the confidential feelers which he had made in other European capitals were allowed to leak out. No less illuminating is the comment of the veteran Prokesch Osten: "If Prince Charles succeeds in making Roumania governable, it will be the greatest *tour de force* of the last half-century—simply prestidigitation".[2]

The crisis was brought to a head on 23 March 1871, when the Bucarest mob broke the windows of a hall in which the German colony and the Prussian consul-general von Radowitz were celebrating their victories: the police and Government remained completely passive, despite the republican tinge given to the demonstration. Next day the prince sent for Lascar Catargiu and Nicholas Golescu (by whom as Regents,[3] in 1866, he had been solemnly installed) and placed his abdication in their hands: and he only yielded to their supplications, in return for the assurance that he could henceforth rely upon a rally of all the Conservative forces in the country. It was on this basis that Lascar Catargiu formed a new Cabinet, which for five years to come was to remain the exponent of "resolute government" and address itself to the ungrateful task of calming overwrought political nerves. As his colleagues the new premier took Crețulescu and Florescu, who had been prominent under Cuza, the veteran General Tell, who had played his part in 1848, and as Foreign Minister, Costa-Foru, a jurist and

[1] Schlitter, *op. cit.* p. 164.
[2] Damé, *op. cit.* p. 225.
[3] The third, General Haralambi, was absent from Bucarest.

professor of some repute. It must, however, be confessed that in one respect Catargiu created a fatal precedent: for it was under him that the inordinate control of the prefects over the elections became a permanent feature of public life. This meant that under so narrow and artificial a franchise the Government of the day would tend more and more to hold the electorate in its hands, unless some exceptional questions provoked a crisis of the first water. Out of this fact there gradually evolved a system by which the political leaders—in this the successors of the old boiar factions—fell into two, or at most three, competing groups and the length of their tenure of office came to depend upon the judgment or calculations of the crown. A crude illustration was afforded by the elections of May 1871, at which only six members of the Opposition were elected, with the result that C. A. Rosetti withdrew in helpless disgust to Paris.

The weak point of the Conservatives was their lack of contact with the masses, but this was of course true of all parties throughout Charles's long reign and until the coming of unity and universal suffrage, when new devices were contrived to perpetuate so far as possible the old system. The Conservatives, however, were in the main, though not exclusively, recruited from the boiar class and stood for the large landed interest, and this of course made them vulnerable to their opponents. But the Liberals, on their side, though their programme corresponded with the main tenets of Western liberalism, were in no sense a party of the masses, but essentially the exponents of the middle class, which was still something of a novelty in Roumania and was absorbed in the pursuit of narrow materialist aims. Politically the peasantry were as yet amorphous and indifferent, and both parties still treated them as virtually negligible.

The Strousberg affair still caused acute trouble: for the law by which Parliament proceeded to regulate it—and notably the annulment of the original concession, the purchase of the bonds issued by Strousberg and their re-issue at 4 instead of $7\frac{1}{2}$ per cent.—was not acceptable to the German Government and therefore not sanctioned by the prince. Bismarck took a very high line and showed a marked animus against Roumania, and his intervention with the Porte as the suzerain Power was intensely resented in Bucarest and led to mutual recriminations. His dictatorial attitude was cleverly exploited by the "Reds" against the "German Prince", and gave General Ignatyev an excuse for denouncing the new empire at the Porte. Bismarck's uncompromising support of the *louche* Strousberg has always remained somewhat of a mystery, and attempts have been made to explain it by the fact that the latter was a dependent of the great Berlin banking house of Bleichröder, upon whom Bismarck relied almost unreservedly in all financial questions. This does not, however, account for the quite needlessly hectoring and provocative tone which he adopted.

One immediate effect was to ease the tension which had prevailed between Bucarest and Vienna during the opening years of the reign. The hostility of the Ballplatz under Beust (Francis Joseph's Saxon chancellor) to a Hohenzollern prince had been paid back with interest by the Liberal leaders, who were strongly tinged with irredentist feeling: and it was only natural that Roumania should resent the marked deterioration in the status of their Transylvanian kinsmen, as a result of the Compromise of 1867 and the intensive Magyarisation that so soon followed. It is true that Andrássy, as the first premier of the restored Hungary, showed a more conciliatory spirit towards Roumania, and both Bismarck himself and the Marquis Pepoli—Charles's uncle by marriage, and at that time Italian minister in Vienna—urged the prince to accept the overture. It is highly significant that even as early as 1868 Charles, while discouraging extravagant day-dreams among his own subjects, replied that friendship would be made easier, if only the Magyars would restore to the Roumanians those rights which they had enjoyed under the Austrian provisional regime of the sixties![1] Soon after, Bismarck warned him very flatly that what was attainable for Roumania was the title of "la Belgique des bouches du Danube", but that Prussia would never support her in aspiring to Transylvania.[2] Andrássy appears to have warned Bismarck in 1870 that he must choose between Hungary and Roumania, and this led the chancellor to advise Charles to keep the irredentist Brătianu at arm's length.[3] None the less Andrássy, when he succeeded Beust as foreign minister, thought it worth while to woo Roumania, and when he at last met Charles in Vienna in June 1873, used such sympathetic language that the prince referred very frankly to the difficulties caused to him by the growth of irredentism, and asked whether it would not be possible to assign to the Roumanians of Hungary a status similar to that of the Croats![4] To this Andrássy naturally did not respond, but he assured Costa-Foru that

---

[1] *Aus dem Leben*, I, pp. 309, 331; II, pp. 89, 315.        [2] *Ibid.* I, p. 332.
[3] Wertheimer, *Graf Andrássy*, I, p. 573.
[4] *Aus dem Leben*, II, p. 319.

Austria-Hungary had every interest in seeing a strong and consolidated Roumania. The prince's relations with Francis Joseph now grew increasingly cordial and were eventually to become one of the strongest personal ties of his later life. But this was hardly more acceptable to public opinion than his not unnatural sympathies with his own native country: and the comic press denounced him alternately as licking the boots of Bismarck or kneeling in supplication to Andrássy.

The five years of the Catargiu Cabinet were a period of relative calm, in which the main problems were the further extension of the railway system, the creation of an agricultural mortgage bank, the conclusion of commercial treaties with Austria-Hungary and other states, the introduction of a tobacco monopoly and, above all, financial reforms to meet the ever-present budget deficit. But Catargiu shed one by one his leading colleagues, and though men of real talent such as Titu Maiorescu and Alexander Lahovary took their place, by the spring of 1875 the Conservative party was visibly crumbling. A group of younger Conservatives, who had grown up in Paris under the Second Empire with its hybrid ideas on political and party government, forced themselves to the front and ere long allied themselves with the Liberals, among whom Ion Brătianu and Rosetti still held a dominant position.

This natural process was hastened by external events. In the summer of 1875, when Europe had scarcely recovered from the fit of nerves induced by the famous Franco-German "War Scare" of April and May, the rising in Hercegovina and Bosnia reopened the whole Eastern Question, imposed a fresh strain upon Austro-Russian relations (which the League of the Three Emperors had done so much to improve), and in particular provoked a dangerous nationalist ferment in the two Serbian principalities, Serbia and Montenegro, with whom the insurgents desired to unite. Prince Milan, then a young man of twenty-three, of loose morals and unbalanced temper, was already revealing his arbitrary tendencies and had utterly failed to win the affections of his people. Fully aware that his army was undisciplined and ill-equipped, and subject to constant remonstrances from the Powers, he also knew that to hold back his people indefinitely was beyond his powers and would be almost equivalent to abdicating his throne in favour of his rival Nicholas of Montenegro or of Peter Karagjorgjević, who soon joined the ranks of the Bosnian rebels. The sole hope of peace lay in the Powers producing a compromise between the Porte and the insurgents; but unhappily first the consular intervention of the autumn, then the Andrássy note of 30 December 1875, and finally the Berlin memorandum of May 1876, proved completely abortive—very largely owing to the negative attitude of the Turcophil British Cabinet. This last failure convinced the Serbs that nothing was to be gained from Europe, and the Turkish Revolution of 29 May, following upon Turkish bankruptcy and such incidents as the Salonica murders, encouraged them to believe that Turkish dissolution was at last imminent: and at the end of June, encouraged by a crowd of Russian volunteers, they rashly declared war upon the Porte. Austria and Russia looked on, with the secret agreement of Reichstadt in their pockets.

It had long since become clear to such keenly interested observers as Prince Charles and his advisers that unless Europe could impose a settlement—and this seemed increasingly doubtful—war between Russia and Turkey was wellnigh inevitable and that in that event Roumania could hardly fail to be involved. When Prince Milan's uncle, Alexander Catargiu, came to announce Serbia's decision and to urge Roumanian co-operation in the common cause of independence,[1] Charles showed extreme reserve. But he was not inactive, for all through the previous winter urgent steps had been taken to prepare the Roumanian army for any emergency. Above all, he realised the danger of a factious and malcontent Opposition in face of a Government which had lost all drive and prestige and was increasingly negative. The threats of Brătianu, that only a change of regime could avert a revolution,[2] angered him, but were wisely taken to heart. In May 1876 the Conservatives were definitely dropped, and at the June elections almost wiped out of existence by the application of their own well-tried methods. Under the premiership of the somewhat neutral Iepureanu, the real driving force was supplied by Brătianu and Kogălniceanu, as ministers of finance and foreign affairs. Rosetti returned from self-imposed exile to be president of the chamber and to dream of social reforms. So long as Russia remained neutral, Roumania was resolved to follow her example, but Kogălniceanu lost no time in addressing a memorandum of "seven points" to the Porte, which aimed at extracting concessions in return for benevolent inaction.[3]

---

[1] *Aus dem Leben*, III, p. 15.     [2] *Ibid.* p. 16.
[3] Recognition of the historic Roumanian name, of Roumanian consular jurisdiction in Turkey, of passports, of the agent in Constantinople as member of the diplomatic corps, of the middle channel in the Danube delta as the Turco-Roumanian boundary.

The Liberals, once back in the saddle, could not resist an offensive against their rivals, and proceeded, much to Charles's annoyance, to impeach Catargiu and eleven of his ministers for infringement of the constitution and squandering of public revenue, and to order the charges to be placarded in every commune. This had the effect of forcing the premier to resign, since he had, not many years previously, been a colleague of Catargiu: and so in August 1876 Brătianu himself at last became premier, and laid the foundations of an almost uninterrupted dictatorship for the next twelve years. The old understanding between the prince and Brătianu now seemed to be restored: and both were agreed that the moment for decisive action was rapidly approaching. At the beginning of October, while Serbia was being rapidly overrun by the Turks, and Russian intervention seemed certain, the new premier, with Charles's full approval, visited the tsar at Livadia and negotiated with him, Gorchakov and Ignatyev the conditions under which the Russian armies might cross Roumanian territory in the event of a rupture with Turkey. As in so many previous Russo-Turkish wars, Roumania's geographical and strategic position made it impossible for her to stand aside: but for the first time in modern history she had ceased to be a mere pawn on the board, unable to move except at the direction of others. The long years devoted by the prince to military organisation were now to bear fruit: for Roumania once again had an army which would weigh something in the scales of war. None the less, Gorchakov would not hear of the Roumanian claim to be admitted to the status of an ally, like Victor Emanuel of Sardinia in the Crimean War, and talked of forcible occupation. In that case, Brătianu rejoined, the Roumanians would resist, and their destruction by the Russian arms would be a singular prelude to a campaign in favour of the Balkan Christians. After this sally the two statesmen parted on the best of terms.

The final decision was postponed for some months by Turkey's unexpected acceptance of the Russian ultimatum in favour of beaten Serbia, and by Derby's proposal for a Conference at Constantinople. But the Conference ended in a complete fiasco, for two main reasons: firstly, because the new grand vizier, Midhat Pasha, was determined to resist foreign dictation in the matter of reforms, and secondly, because he had convinced himself (thanks very largely to the Turcophil attitude of Sir Henry Elliot and despite the warnings of Lord Salisbury) that Britain would fight on the Turkish side against Russia, as in 1854. The tsar, genuinely pacific, but faced by many internal difficulties and unable to keep his armies indefinitely on a war footing, knew that if the Conference failed war was inevitable, and therefore concentrated his main effort upon secret negotiations with Austria-Hungary. The Budapest Convention (of 13 January and 18 March 1877) re-established the principles laid down at Reichstadt and committed Austria-Hungary, in return for the right to occupy Bosnia-Hercegovina, not only to benevolent neutrality, but also to "paralysing by diplomatic action" any intervention by other Powers. Russia thus averted the dangers which had forced her to evacuate the Principalities in 1853, and could now, if war came, advance across Roumanian territory without fear of any flanking attack from Galicia or through the Transylvanian passes.

Meanwhile Charles pushed on his preparations, telling his father that the army was "burning to show its worth", but that "we shall do all in our power to prevent Roumania from becoming the theatre of war". He was not, of course, initiated into the Austro-Russian plans, but he was far too near to realities, on the Lower Danube, to be able to share the illusions of London. The new Turkish "paper" Constitution proclaimed by Midhat, with the deliberate purpose of checkmating the reforming efforts of the Powers, served to rally the Roumanians round their prince, for its marked reference to "the privileged provinces" and their "chiefs" was resented as a direct attack upon the autonomy of all the vassal states. The Chamber invited the Government to vindicate Roumanian rights and found the Porte in an unconciliatory mood, even after Abdul Hamid had ejected the pseudo-reformer Midhat and assumed power through his own nominees. The conflict suited the prince's book,[1] for he had long since reached the conviction that since Roumania lay in the direct line of collision, all attempts at neutrality were bound to fail. He could not, however, at first persuade his ministers of this, and found it expedient to convoke a Crown Council, consisting of the Cabinet and prominent ex-ministers—a practice which was eventually to become a special feature of Roumanian constitutional life. The premier took the line that resistance to Russia was quite impossible and that alliance with her would not be unduly dangerous, since in no circumstances would Europe tolerate the substitution of Russian for Turkish suzerainty, but there was still a majority for neutrality. All that he could do was to appoint the interventionist Kogăl-

[1] "Kam mir sehr erwünscht", he writes to his father—*Aus dem Leben*, III, p. 192.

niceanu as foreign minister instead of the Russophobe Nicholas Ionescu, and meanwhile to concentrate the Roumanian army west of the Olt, in such a position that it would in effect constitute the right wing of the advancing Russians. On 16 April Kogălniceanu signed a convention with Russia which assured to her armies free passage across Roumania, provisioning and the use of roads and railways, and pledged her to respect Roumanian laws and institutions. When the Porte in its turn summoned Roumania to co-operate in resisting invasion, Kogăl- niceanu gave the evasive answer that so grave a matter must be referred to Parliament; an extraordinary session was convoked, and the con- vention with Russia adopted by sixty-nine to twenty-five, Dimitrie Sturdza and Peter Carp, as inveterate Russophobes, voting in the minority. That very day the Russians declared war on Turkey and began to cross the Pruth, excusing their action by urgent strategic necessity. The prince, though indignant with the Grand Duke Nicholas for issuing a proclamation to his own people without consulting him, showed quite remarkable tact and self-restraint: and by withdrawing his troops from the Danube he at one and the same time forced the Russians to treat him with greater consideration and gained time with the Turks by leading them to hope for his neutrality.

The Roumanian attitude was very frankly stated in the Circular Note addressed to the Powers in the middle of May: they had "no other aim", it declared, "save to ensure respect for our neutrality. The Great Powers, while invoking the inadequacy of the provisions on this question, and not taking account either of the gravity of the situation or of our well grounded perplexity, refused to comply with a demand subsequent events have proved to be only too justified". It could of course be argued that a declaration of neutrality would have been a breach of the Treaty of Paris and that the Powers in endorsing such a step would have been committing themselves to war with Russia. Their refusal was therefore almost a foregone conclusion, but it completely absolved Roumania, and inevitably drove her straight into the arms of Russia.

Meanwhile the Russian attitude was very disquieting. There was a tendency to override or ignore Roumanian susceptibilities and treat the country as a mere Russian dependency—an attitude which doubtless finds its explanation in the repeated occupations and treaty provisions of the previous hundred years. Roumania's co-operation on equal terms was airily rejected by the vain and pompous Gorchakov: the most that he would concede was that she might join the war uninvited, but in that event there must be complete fusion and unity of command. "Russia", it was stated quite explicitly, "does not need the assistance of the Roumanian army."[1]

Such an attitude inevitably forced the Roumanians to a further step. Already on 11 May the two Chambers adopted a resolution declaring Roumanian Independence and rupture with Turkey to be accomplished facts (21 May). The grand duke and tsar himself were most cordially welcomed by the prince and Government, but the prince limited himself to the defence of the strategic points of Giurgiu and Calafat and steadfastly maintained these Fabian tactics while the Russians effected the crossing of the Danube under considerable difficulties. In June Gurko seized the Balkan passes, but was forced on to the defensive by superior Russian forces, and thus the main issues of the war came to centre round Plevna, a series of strong positions on rolling downland ten or twenty miles south of the Danube. Here a formidable Turkish defence was organised by Osman Pasha, and in the second half of July the Russians suffered more than one reverse, and finding themselves in urgent need of reinforcement, pressed the Roumanians to come to their aid by occupying Nicopolis. Prince Charles, with a fresh army of 50,000 men and 180 guns at his disposal, was this time able to lay down specific conditions for co-operation, and the Russians, dismounting from their high horse, gracefully offered him the command of the united armies before Plevna. This had its obvious drawbacks and dangers, for it involved in some sense the very fusion which he had so consistently opposed, and it would have thrown much of the discredit of defeat upon the newcomers. But it was a very high compliment which perhaps only a Romanov could have offered to a Hohenzollern, and not a tsar of Russia to a vassal of the sultan: and while Charles might hope that eventual success would accrue to the profit of his adopted country, he also knew that refusal would be highly dangerous.

On 8 September the Roumanian army had its real baptism of fire in the redoubts of Grivița, before Plevna: and the foreign attachés and correspondents were unanimous in their praise of its extreme gallantry and steadiness, which contributed very materially to the final defeat of the Turks. The costly assaults upon the fortress had, however, been decided against the prince's better judgment, and in the end it was his

---

[1] Text in *Aus dem Leben*, III, p. 167 and in Bamberg, *Gesch. der orientalischen Angelegenheit*, which rests on Roumanian sources.

policy of close investment that carried the day.[1] After Osman Pasha's surrender on 9 December, Charles resigned his command, and took no part in the Russian march across the Balkans, his attitude being in marked contrast to that of Prince Milan, who, having in the previous summer been forbidden by the tsar to enter the war, now fell upon the disorganised Turks and hurriedly occupied Niš without any serious resistance. It is but fair to add that but for this Serbia might have been wholly abandoned by the Powers and left without any territorial gains at the peace. Roumania's position was essentially different: she had held the Danube line, and kept the war for the most part off her own territory. Any immediate menace on the part of the Turks was now over, and it seemed positively contrary to Roumanian interests to carry the war further into what was nominally Turkish, but really Bulgarian, territory. In order, however, to have something in hand for future bargaining and to prevent any possible Turkish flanking movement, the siege of Vidin was continued, and both it and Belogradčik surrendered towards the end of February.

At this point Roumanian and Russian interests very definitely parted. Nothing could induce the tsar to pledge himself to the admission of Roumanian representatives at the peace negotiations: every time the question was raised he was politely evasive, while full of vague assurances that Roumania would not be left out of account and that he would never forget the sacrifices her sons had made.[2] In January 1878, after Sofia had fallen, and Skobelev had crossed the Shipka pass, the Grand Duke Nicholas proceeded to armistice negotiations, first at Kazanlik, then at Adrianople, and though he treated the prince's delegate, Colonel Arion, with great courtesy, he did not admit him or even discuss Roumanian claims with him. These claims were recognition of independence, the razing of all Danubian fortresses, the surrender by Turkey of all the channels of the Danube delta, and an indemnity of 100,000,000 francs. Meanwhile in St Petersburg, General Ion Ghica appealed in vain to the tsar and the chancellor: the invariable answer came that Roumania could not be a full contracting party until her independence had been recognised by Europe.

What lay behind this attitude was the firm resolve of the tsar—at last

[1] An excellent and scholarly account of "Roumania's share in the War of 1877" by General R. Rosetti, will be found in the *Slavonic Review*, no. 24 (March 1930).
[2] *Aus dem Leben*, III, 379.

officially communicated to General Ghica on 29 January—to demand
the "retrocession" of those three districts of Southern Bessarabia
which had been taken from her by the Treaty of Paris. Alexander II
appears to have set his heart upon this as an essential satisfaction of
the national honour, and used many strange arguments—as that the
cession in 1856 had been made to Moldavia, not to Roumania(!) and
that Russia could not be expected to hold to this clause alone of a treaty
which the war had rendered entirely inoperative. The plea that the
territory in question had been for centuries an integral part of Moldavia
and had fallen to Russia for the first time only forty-four years before
the Treaty of Paris, seems to have made not the slightest impression
upon either tsar or chancellor, who for all their devotion to the cause of
Balkan nationality saw through distinctly imperialistic spectacles and
felt that a war could not be regarded as victorious unless it brought
access of territory. "Whatever arguments you may invoke", Gorchakov told Ghica, "you cannot modify our resolutions, for they are
unchangeable. You are faced by a political necessity." Moreover, the
Russians resented almost impatiently the tenacious devotion of the
Roumanians to their own flesh and blood and their indifference to the
generous compensation offered. This was the province of Dobrogea,
in other words the territory situated between the mouths of the Danube
and a line drawn eastwards from Silistra or from the point at which the
Danube turns away to the north-east, to some point on the Black Sea
south of Kustendje or Constanţa. It was a barren and neglected land,
best known to history as the unhappy Ovid's place of exile, and thinly
populated by a very mixed population of Turks, Tatars, gypsies,
Gagaoutzes, Bulgars, Ukrainians and Roumanians. There was, it must
be admitted, a strong element of insincerity in Alexander's attitude, for
already in the secret conventions of Reichstadt and Budapest he had
expressly reserved his right to Bessarabia; and from the moment that
the armistice terms became known, it was abundantly obvious that
Bessarabia would be used by the Powers as the only safe and convenient compensation which could be allowed to Russia in Europe—
as it were, a consolation for her failure to secure a foothold in
Bulgaria.

The question had already been aired in the press, and indeed the
Government had from the very first known that such a claim was to
be expected. But it wavered between two opposite extremes, on the
one hand a reluctance to look hard facts in the face and a naïve hope that

at the last moment some new complication, such as a conflict between Russia and Britain, would avert the danger; and on the other a reluctant recognition of the extent to which Roumania's situation in 1878 resembled that of Italy in 1860. While Brătianu and even the prince hugged their illusions to the very last, Kogălniceanu was far-sighted enough to realise that in the given situation of Europe, the sacrifice of Southern Bessarabia was the necessary price of independence and of Russian help, no less surely than the cession of Nice and Savoy had been the price of Italian unity. But, perhaps not unnaturally, the Government lacked the courage to avow the necessity, though this had unquestionably been its attitude when the question was first considered. Brătianu and his colleagues thus found themselves in a thoroughly false position. They were perfectly aware that behind the diplomatic *coulisses* the Great Powers had accepted Russian views on this point, throwing Roumanian interests to the wolves in order to press points which affected more closely their own selfish interests. Yet a futile attempt was made to negotiate with the Grand Duke Nicholas, and Ion Ghica was sent on a mission to London, to see how far Disraeli's anti-Russian policy could be exploited in Roumania's interest. In actual fact he found but scanty sympathy there, since the true-blood Turcophils were apt to look askance upon the ally of Russia, now hoist with its own petard: his own hope lay in the false calculation that Britain might intervene in the war.

Ignatyev, on his way to negotiate the final peace at San Stefano, was instructed to visit Bucarest in the hope of inducing Roumania to yield without protest; and in return for such complaisance the boundaries of the Dobrogea were to be enlarged to include the key fortress of Silistra, and an indemnity of 100,000,000 francs was to be extorted from the bankrupt Turks. He even threw out vague hints of a personal union between Roumania and the new Bulgaria, perhaps even of the cession of the whole right bank of the Danube as far as the Balkan range —though it is difficult to believe that this last offer could have been seriously meant. Once more Kogâlniceanu was in favour of acceptance, but Brătianu, with the prince's approval, overruled him and applied himself to the easy task of rousing public opinion. On 6 February, then, the Chamber acclaimed a motion affirming the intangibility of Roumanian territory and worded in such a way as indirectly to challenge the good faith of the tsar, who had solemnly guaranteed it less than a year earlier.

There was every reason for indignation, but no ground whatsoever for expecting outside help. The attitude of the Powers was one of complete cynicism. The London Cabinet was completely indifferent to Roumania, and Lord Salisbury, in his complicated parallel negotiations with Russia, Turkey and Austria, found in Bessarabia an invaluable object of barter. France was still extremely timorous and actively interested in Greece alone of the Balkan nations. Italy was well-disposed to her young Latin sister, but counted as yet but little in Europe. Austria-Hungary was already committed up to the hilt by the secret convention with Russia, while Germany was above all concerned in preventing a quarrel between her two imperial allies, and playing the honest broker at the impending Congress. Indeed the attitude of Bismarck and the old Emperor William was specially disappointing to Charles as a Hohenzollern, for he had fondly hoped to manœuvre Russia into a position before Europe in which, by insisting upon Bessarabia, she would incur the charge of rankest ingratitude. But it soon transpired that Bismarck had not the slightest intention of offending Russia for the sake of Roumania, and in fact he not merely backed Russia consistently throughout on this point, but continued to cause grave embarrassment by his attitude on the railway dispute and the Jewish question. Vienna was outwardly more benevolent, and Francis Joseph received Brătianu in audience in March: but acquiescence in the cession of Bessarabia was Austria-Hungary's tit for Russia's tat in Bosnia, and the Roumanian statesman came away empty-handed.

Hence the Roumanian memorandum circulated to the Powers in March, and the formal protest lodged in St Petersburg, were entirely ineffective, and Roumania's indignation at the Treaty of San Stefano, from which her representatives were again entirely excluded and in which Russia dealt direct with Turkey as to the evacuation of Russian troops across her territory, failed to arouse an echo even in London and Vienna, where that treaty was most strongly challenged. But the Russians were indignant at their victim's anger. The tsar expressed to Ghica his regret that Roumania was already forgetful of the immense services conferred on her by Russia, and Gorchakov warned him that if Roumania dared to protest against Article VII of San Stefano, the tsar would occupy her territory and disarm her army! This provoked a truly gallant rejoinder from Prince Charles. Refusing to believe that such a threat could ever have been uttered by Tsar Alexander, he declared that an army which fought before Plevna under the tsar's eyes, "will let itself be annihilated, but not disarmed".[1] This retort, made public by an indiscretion, echoed through Europe, and Prince Gorchakov found it expedient to give an official *démenti* of the original phrase. But Brătianu feared either war or a Russian *coup de main*, and the idea of transferring the Government from Bucarest to Craiova was seriously considered.

By the beginning of June the prince had realised that as not a single Great Power would take up the Roumanian cause, Bessarabia must be regarded as lost: and he therefore strongly urged Brătianu and Kogălniceanu, who were now sent as Roumanian representatives to Berlin, to come to a direct understanding with Gorchakov and Shuvalov before the Congress opened. He hoped thereby to secure Roumania's admission to the Congress (on the same terms as Greece, which for a short time had serious grounds for hope), and in any case to obtain, as compensation for voluntary submission, a larger cession of territory. Kogălniceanu approved these tactics, but both Brătianu and Rosetti held to the more doctrinaire view that as Europe had assigned Southern Bessarabia to Roumania in 1856, only Europe could now decide its ultimate fate, and that voluntary acceptance of surrender or exchange might create a precedent for further amputations in the future.

The cause of the small Powers at Berlin was already prejudged. For tactical reasons both Waddington and Salisbury advocated the admission of Greece, but when other Powers opposed it, they dropped the idea. With this the already faint hope that Roumania too might be admitted, faded into thin air, and meanwhile the famous indiscretion of the *Globe* (in publishing the text of the secret Anglo-Russian Agreement, which alone had made the Congress possible) revealed the fact that Bessarabia had already been sacrificed to Russia by her chief opponent. It soon became obvious that Bismarck would do nothing for Roumania, and Andrássy made it clear that he could not risk a war with Russia for Bessarabia, thus skating over the still more essential fact that Russia already held his written promise in this question. Italy and France alone were sympathetic, and even Waddington soon advised submission to the inevitable.

On 1 July, then, Brătianu and Kogălniceanu, "nervous and unhappy",[2] were allowed to read their memorandum before the Congress

---

[1] *Aus dem Leben*, IV, p. 19.
[2] Radowitz, *Denkwürdigkeiten*, II, p. 52.

PLATE XIII

MICHAEL KOGĂLNICEANU

ION C. BRĂTIANU

and then politely dismissed. Their five demands were: (1) that no territory should be detached from Roumania; (2) that the Russian right of transit should come to an end; (3) that she should recover the Danube mouths and islands; (4) that she should receive an indemnity; and (5) that she should be recognised as both independent and neutral. Gorchakov refused to allow any discussion of Bessarabia, and Beaconsfield entered a formal protest—"and that was that", as Radowitz, one of the acting secretaries of the Congress, records in his diary.[1] Beaconsfield had received the two delegates that morning, listened courteously without expressing any opinion and warned them that "in politics ingratitude is often the price of the best services". He gave out that in his opinion the exchange would be "a very good bargain for Roumania"; but his real views are contained in a letter to the queen, announcing that "the compensation allotted to the rebellious tributary states for their alliances with Russia would be as meagre as practicable".[2] In his speech of justification before the House of Lords he significantly left out all reference to the Bessarabian question, and the omission was at once pointed out by Lord Granville. Lord Derby on the same occasion remarked that "Russia has turned a devoted and submissive ally into an enemy", but marred this effective phrase by adding that Roumania "made war as a matter of speculation and has only her own Government to thank"—thus showing that as foreign secretary he had never grasped the inexorable nature of Roumania's dilemma.

Once more Gladstone's attitude was in marked contrast to that of his great rival and may be claimed by posterity as saving the honour of Britain for the second time in the Roumanian question. Already in February he had expressed the hope that "the peace to come" would not be marred by "the alienation of Bessarabia", and in March that Russia would not "stoop to this petty spoliation of a humble but brave ally": and on 8 April he spoke in the House of Commons against an "impolitic and culpable spoliation". After the Congress he again protested, accused the Government of "selling Bessarabian liberty to Russia", who would now reimpose "her despotic institutions": and in the final debate he denounced the premier's speech at the Congress against the cession of Bessarabia, "when all the time he had made known his consent". Joseph Chamberlain endorsed this protest against

---

[1] "Und damit war es fertig"—*ibid.* p. 52.
[2] Buckle, *Life of Disraeli*, VI, pp. 332–4.

"a comedy rehearsed in private".[1] It is impossible to read the premier's Congress speech—in which he treated the cession of Bessarabia as an interference with the treaty of 1856 and as affecting an engagement taken towards Europe respecting the freedom of Danubian navigation[2] —without marvelling at his assurance in hoodwinking the British public as to the perfectly concrete pledges which he himself had already given to Russia. In intimating privately to St Petersburg that Britain had no intention of resisting the accomplished fact, Beaconsfield was guided by the obvious impossibility of making Bessarabia a *casus belli* if once the other questions were settled. But to pose meanwhile as still defending a position which long ago he had criticised Palmerston for not upholding sufficiently, was not unnaturally regarded by its victims as a sinister and discreditable farce.

No less than fifteen articles of the Treaty of Berlin directly affected Roumania. The Powers were unanimous in refusing her the neutral status of a Belgium of the East, and she had to be content with independence. But even this was made dependent on two conditions—the cession of Bessarabia to Russia, and the removal of all religious disabilities not merely in respect of office in the state, but even of admission to citizenship. That this was also imposed upon Serbia, where the question was far less acute, did not diminish Roumanian resentment: indeed the minor circumstance that Europe gave this clause precedence over that relating to Bessarabia, served to increase the resentment beyond all bounds. Subject to these conditions, the delta of the Danube with its islands and the whole Dobrogea as far as a line from Silistra to Mingalia, were to be assigned to Roumania, and an European Commission of delimitation appointed. Five other clauses dealt with Roumania's new commercial status, while Articles LII–LVII regulated anew the navigation of the Danube. This time Roumania obtained a seat, on equal terms, in the international Danubian Commission, which, with revised powers, was to have its seat at Galaṭ. All river fortresses were to be dismantled, and the regulation of the Iron Gates was entrusted to Austria-Hungary.

For Roumania the Treaty of Berlin is the last great international landmark before the still more memorable events of our own time. The fruit of independence proved to have a bitter core, and it was long before public opinion could accommodate itself to the sacrifices de-

[1] 1 August 1878.
[2] Protocol of 9th Sitting, 29 June.

manded. But it was unhappily inherent in the situation, that Bessarabia should be the "small change" which the Great Powers could employ for purposes of major bargaining, and which was not in itself worth a quarrel. The prince was able to restrain the Chamber from any formal protest, and the loss of Bessarabia was duly ratified on 12 October by eighty-three to twenty-seven. He himself tried to salve his pride by the specious argument that the Dobrogea was not compensation, but a war indemnity freely offered from Europe. But its occupation by Roumanian troops was not tolerated until the last Roumanian authorities had withdrawn from the lands beyond the Pruth.

# CHAPTER XII

# THE REIGN OF KING CHARLES

A considerable time was to elapse before the conditions imposed by the Powers were accepted: indeed it was neither the first nor the last occasion on which the Roumanians displayed surprising powers of resistance to the will of Europe. It had been left to Andrássy to make clear beyond all possibility of mistake that not one of the Powers would recognise Roumania or accredit ministers to its Government until formal submission had been made to the terms of the Treaty. The Chambers sought a compromise by voting the surrender of Bessarabia on 12 October—and as in 1877, Russia actually took possession the very next day—and by undertaking that outstanding questions (which meant the status of the Jews) would be solved in a constitutional manner. But this was not enough for either Germany or France: and though the British Government shared their views on the Jewish question, Lord Salisbury became increasingly nervous at the delay, because it gave an opening to Russia to postpone the evacuation of her armies and to make her withdrawal from the Dobrogea conditional upon free military passage over Roumanian territory. He and Andrássy were agreed in opposing this, and on 12 November 1878 even urged upon Berlin immediate recognition, in order to strengthen Roumania against Russia and avert any possible danger of her throwing herself into the arms of the tsar: but neither Bismarck nor even Waddington would believe this to be a real danger, or would yield an inch on the Jewish issue.

All this affected the minor, but by no means unimportant, question of frontier delimitation. The international Commission to which the details were left favoured the inclusion of Silistra in the ceded territory, on the ground that this key fortress dominated the whole province and was a necessary adjunct to the Dobrogea itself. Unfortunately the Roumanian Government, impatient at the attitude of the Powers and hoping to counterbalance its concessions in other directions, occupied the lines of Arab Tabia near Silistra on 3 January 1879, on its own initiative. This led both the tsar and Giers, his acting foreign minister, to use very sharp language to General Ghica: and on 19 February, on the explicit advice of all the Powers, Roumania had the further humiliation of evacuating rather than risk an open conflict with Russia. On the Commission Arab Tabia was eventually assigned to Roumania, but the Russian delegate obstinately opposed the cession of Silistra, and finally carried the day with his complaisant colleagues (June 1880). The motives were obvious enough. Russia at this time assumed that Bulgaria would remain virtually her vassal, and therefore welcomed an arrangement by which the latter would secure great strategic advantages on the Danube against her northern neighbour. Once more Roumania had perforce to submit, but the decision rankled: it completed the process of disillusionment towards Russia, and it was never regarded in Bucarest as definitive, with the result that from 1908 onwards it formed the point of departure in Roumania's attitude towards Bulgaria and Turkey.

Infinitely more delicate was the question of Jewish disabilities. Article VII of the Constitution of 1866 laid down that "only foreigners belonging to a Christian confession can obtain naturalisation": and therefore the complete abstract equality of all religions demanded by the Powers under Article XLIV of Berlin could not become valid without constitutional revision. The Roumanians, already in a state of acute irritation and tension owing to the loss of Bessarabia, were not in the mood to make further concessions which would cut deep into the social structure of the country and might, in the view of the more conservative classes, work a veritable "social revolution", even though on peaceful lines.

Though Western propagandists claimed that Jews had been settled in the Principalities from time immemorial, the truth is that Jewish immigration was a comparatively recent event. This is proved by the fact that almost all the newcomers bore German names. The lack of any statistical data under Turkish rule naturally makes exact calculations difficult: but it appears certain that at the opening of the nineteenth century there were not more than 2000 Jewish families in Moldavia, and hardly any in Wallachia. Partly as the result of conditions in Russia and Russian Poland (the "Pale" was hideously overcrowded and both the authorities and the Christian inhabitants intensely hostile) but above all owing to the rapid growth in prosperity, the removal of trade restrictions and the increased importance of the Black Sea grain trade, there was a rapid influx of Jews into Moldavia, especially after the Treaty of Adrianople: and under the Règlement Organique of 1833 they were classified as a nation apart, under certain specific restrictions and privileges (§§ 50–4). During the next generation they came to form an actual majority of the population in such towns as Dorohoiu, Falticenĭ, Botoşani and even in the capital Jassy itself: but they none the less tended to remain apart in distinct communities, as aliens, not possessing the rights of citizenship. As in many other parts of Europe, they developed superior trading instincts, indulged in usury and especially in the villages exploited native agriculture and at a later stage acquired a hold over many landlords and occupied the position of middlemen. M. Theodore Reinach has ably summed up the factors which go to make up the character of the modern Jew—"the Bible (Thora and prophets), Talmudic education for long generations, prolonged persecution, enforced abstention for centuries from certain occupations, and the exclusive practice, also enforced, of other forms of activity, the brusque change from oppression to full liberty, from misery to ease and riches, from ignorance and docile faith to complete emancipation of the intellect. There is not one of the qualities or defects of the Jews of to-day which cannot be explained by one or other of these six causes".[1] This passage goes to the very root of the problem with which we are briefly concerned.

From time to time restrictions were placed upon the influx of the Jews, but the authority of the state was too low to ensure their proper enforcement: and in the same way attempts to prevent them from settling in the villages or following the trade of innkeepers (for instance the law of 1844 and decrees of 1839 and 1850) were never made really effective.[2] Undoubtedly many obtained entry or evasion by corrupting the very inefficient subordinate officials. None the less in theory these various restrictions were upheld, and the Jewish element was in the main concentrated in the towns of Northern Moldavia, in a manner and to an extent which made it more and more difficult for the state to digest them. By 1859, then, there were already 118,000 Jews in Moldavia, but only 9200 in Wallachia: forty years later, in 1899, there were 201,000 in Moldavia and 68,000 in Wallachia. In the northern districts especially the disproportion between Jews and Christians was as great as in the worst places in the Russian Pale or Galicia: and during the fifties and sixties the former speedily acquired a virtual economic hegemony in Moldavia. For to say that there were 250,000 Jews in a total population

[1] *Grande Encyclopédie*, XXI, p. 273.
[2] In 1858 there were 12,814 Jewish heads of families in Moldavia. Verax, *La Roumanie et les Juifs*, p. 20.

of 5,000,000 gives no real idea of the situation: as late as 1900 the total urban population of Roumania was 700,000, and of this 300–400,000, or more than half, were Jews. By 1878 it was already obvious that they could no longer be expelled, it was quite impossible to assimilate them, and their unrestricted naturalisation *en masse* would have made of the Moldavians, at any rate, a minority in large tracts of their own country, and removed all restraint upon the economic exploitation of peasant and boiar alike. The nation, then, was unanimous in regarding unreserved compliance with the demands of the Powers as a grave menace to the state. Religion cannot be said to have played a part in the question which now arose (except in so far as it perpetuated the gulf between the two races): but the periodic outrages upon synagogues, as the real centre of Jewish life, helped to perpetuate this illusion abroad, and the Jewish organisations may perhaps be excused for doing nothing to disabuse public opinion. In reality, however, it was an essentially economic problem, in which the Jews showed their economic superiority, their greater agility and alertness and, it must be added, their greater readiness to work. The Conservative statesman Peter Carp, who had a gift of blunt speech, was perfectly right when he told his countrymen in 1879, "Work, civilise yourselves, and you will rid yourselves of the Jews".

The agitation in favour of the Jews centred in the influential "Alliance Israélite" in Paris. Already in 1866, when the new Roumanian constitution was in preparation, Crémieux, the founder of the Alliance, visited Bucarest and offered to raise a low-term loan of 25,000,000 francs in return for clauses declaring that "religion constitutes no obstacle to naturalisation" and promising the gradual extension of political rights to the Jews. But this evoked violent protests, culminating in the sack of the new synagogue at Bucarest and other discreditable incidents: and it was then that Article VII was adopted. The strong line taken by Ion Brătianu in the Jewish question in the late sixties led the Alliance to organise a press campaign against Roumania in more than one country in Europe, and Napoleon III was induced to intervene on behalf of the Jews. The agitation was increased by an astonishing incident near Galaţ, where an attempt on the part of the Roumanian authorities to deport ten Jewish vagabonds into Turkey and the refusal of the Turks to admit them ended in the wretched victims being thrown into the Danube and two left to drown. The clamour of the press and the skill with which the Alliance mobilised Western finance against Roumania, contributed very materially to the fall of Brătianu in 1869 and to the alienation of French public opinion towards the close of the Second Empire. Kogăl-niceanu, whom no one could accuse of illiberal ideas, issued a vigorous defence of the Roumanian attitude and disclaimed "all claim to be in 1869 more civilised than were the French between 1806 and 1812".[1] After 1870 the agitation died down, but all through the seventies there were periodical riots and assaults upon the Jews, notably at Vasluĭ, Ploeşci and Darabani, which the Alliance Israélite exploited to the full. The Treaty of Berlin gave it its opportunity: Article VII of 1866 was clearly indefensible on any ethical basis, and it was easy to mobilise opinion through the Parisian press and through the bankers of Paris and Berlin. Waddington and Bismarck were at one with Disraeli and Salisbury, and Andrássy, though milder in form, took the same side. Article XLIV of the Treaty was accordingly drafted as follows: "In Roumania the distinction of religious creed or confession cannot be brought up against anyone as a motive for exclusion and incapacity, as regards thè enjoyment of civil and political rights, admission to public employment and honours, or exercise of different professions or in-dustries. The freedom and open practice of all religions shall be assured to all citizens of the Roumanian state, as also to foreigners, and no obstacle shall be placed in the way of the hierarchic organisation of the various communions, or of their relations with their spiritual chiefs. Citizens of all Powers, merchants or others, shall be treated in Rou-mania, without distinction of religion, on a footing of perfect equality".

It was generally agreed that Article VII must be abandoned, but there was acute divergence as to what should take its place, and intense ex-citement prevailed both in the Chamber and throughout the country. In December 1878 Brătianu reconstructed his Government, including his recent critic and future successor, Dimitrie Sturdza, and early in April 1879 elections were held for a Constituent Assembly. The prince's father anxiously warned him that it was impossible "to fight against the will of Europe", and the Speech from the Throne contained the signifi-cant and two-edged phrase, "The Great Powers demand that we should adapt ourselves to the ideas prevalent in civilised states, before they admit us into the European family of states". But the Chamber was in almost open revolt: men like Lascar Catargiu and General Florescu made violent attacks on the Government and the Congress, and Brătianu threatened resignation, to show that constitutional enforcement of

[1] An allusion to the decrees of Napoleon I.

Article XLIV could not be attained. The prince was exceedingly anxious, and not without reason, for already in March, Bismarck was fulminating against the Roumanians, threatening intervention through a collective note of the Powers and applying the screw through the perennial railway question. To Lord Odo Russell he accused them of "dishonesty and arrogance", and "deplored that they were not within his reach, so as to administer the whipping they so richly deserved".[1] Meanwhile, he insisted on treating Roumania as a subordinate state, whose affairs still fell to be discussed with the Porte! Salisbury, once more afraid of driving Roumania into the arms of Russia, launched a compromise scheme by which she should be asked to embody Article XLIV in a new edition of Article VII of the Constitution: but though this was adopted by the Western Powers and by Austria-Hungary, the German attitude remained unchanged.

On 5 July the Commission of the Chamber presented proposals which were little short of a challenge to Europe. It declared that "there are no Roumanian Jews and never were, but only such as were born in the country, but are assimilated neither in language nor customs and do not aspire to be": it then insisted on a special law of naturalisation for each individual, and declared the right of ownership in land to be "a political, not a civil, right". On this Brătianu again resigned, and Prince Charles had some trouble in inducing him to reconstruct the Government, with Kogălniceanu at the Interior and Boerescu at the Foreign Office. The country seethed with excitement, the Chambers were flooded with petitions, and being unmanageable, were prorogued, in spite of German warnings that this would irritate the Powers.

Brătianu now sent Boerescu to the West, but entirely without success. But the new finance minister, Sturdza, himself a German in outlook, went to Berlin, submitted to Bismarck's lectures,[2] and discovered (what Salisbury already suspected) that the railway question was an obstacle to good relations and that behind the chancellor stood Bleichröder, both as a Jew and as the mouthpiece of the Prussian shareholders. He therefore set himself to evolve a Railway Convention which was eventually to buy out the shareholders on favourable terms and in the meantime secured them by a mortgage on the tobacco monopoly. The old emperor did nothing for the scion of his house, though he confessed to

---

[1] Russell to Salisbury, 2 March—cit. Medlicott, *Recognition of Roumanian Independence*, II, p. 574 (*Slavonic Review*, No. 33).
[2] *Aus dem Leben*, IV, p. 235.

sharing the Roumanian view of the Jewish question, and tried to divert Charles's annoyance from Germany to England, who "sees in every Jew a cultured Rothschild".[1]

It undoubtedly seemed to contemporaries both puzzling and highly unreasonable that the Roumanians should oppose such obstinate resistance to a measure which was simultaneously imposed upon the Serbs, and to which the latter scarcely demurred. But this was due to the utterly different nature of the problem in Serbia, where the Jews were a mere handful, mainly confined to Belgrade itself, belonging to cultured Sephardim families with a long Balkan tradition and therefore easily assimilable, and where Jewish immigration was negligible and usury played no part, since the ruling class was to a man drawn from the peasantry.

It was not till 18 October 1879 that a solution of the question could be reached. On that day the Chamber, by 133 votes to 9, amended Article VII in the sense that "difference of religious creed does not constitute an obstacle to the acquisition or exercise of civil and political rights". On the other hand, though naturalisation could now be obtained "without distinction of religion", a special act of Parliament was required for each individual case, a formal petition and a ten years' domicile were demanded in all save exceptional cases, and, above all, it was expressly provided that only Roumanian citizens could acquire land. There can be little doubt that this last limitation was wise and necessary, for without it, during the thirty years that followed, the Jews would almost certainly have been able to establish a strangle-hold over the Roumanian landowning class. But it cannot be denied that the theoretical equality accorded with one hand was rendered illusory by a host of restrictions, and that the majority of the Jews in Roumania, though entirely free to exercise their religion, remained in certain respects citizens of the second rank. Specially unjust was the fact that the lack of citizenship on the part of a family which might have been domiciled for two or even three generations did not carry with it the corresponding exemption from military service. The new law, then, removed the most glaring disability, but it left ample room for evasion, obstruction and abuses: and the Jewish question in Roumania continued to exercise and alienate important sections of Western opinion, with noticeable effects upon Roumania's position in the bourses of Europe and the New World. It was not until the great land reform which

[1] *Aus dem Leben*, IV, p. 237.

followed the War that the question entered upon a new, and on the whole less acute, phase.

The settlement just summarised fell considerably short of that demanded by the Powers, and the one conciliatory gesture to which the Chamber would consent was to vote the naturalisation of 1000 Jews *en bloc*. But this sufficed, for by this time the Powers were only too eager to get it out of the way, and even Bismarck, seemingly influenced by the impending railway agreement, was less categorical. In November he admitted to the French ambassador that the time for recognition had nearly come, but "said that a few weeks more of 'strangulation' would do the Roumanians good, before they were allowed to enjoy an independence which they had done nothing to deserve".[1] Lord Odo Russell's reports show that by the end of the year Bismarck's attitude was simply dependent on the railway question, which lay between Sturdza and Bleichröder: he actually forbade the ambassador ever to mention the question, either verbally or in writing, until he had recovered from the acute biliousness to which he was so often a prey. On 20 February 1880, then, the Powers, though careful to point out that the new clauses did not entirely meet the case, none the less notified their readiness to recognise: the last obstacle to Roumania's admittance to the European commonwealth had been removed.

It remained for Prince Charles to set the crown upon his work in more senses than one. During the summer of 1880 he paid a series of ceremonial visits to Vienna, Berlin, Dresden and to his parents, after eight years of separation: and one result was the regulation of the succession in favour of his brother Leopold's eldest son, Prince Ferdinand of Hohenzollern. The goal of a royal crown was already in sight, when party dissensions flared up once more, and were still further embittered by an attempt on the life of Ion Brătianu in December 1880. The Conservative party, reconstituted under Lascar Catargiu, assumed an aggressive note and revived against the Liberals the old charge of following republican ideals and not being, like themselves, a party of order in the state. One of the most violent of the Conservatives was Titu Maiorescu, a savant of high distinction and a Transylvanian by origin, who did more than any man to win over his party to the German connection, and became Charles's trusted premier during the Balkan wars.

Such a charge was peculiarly explosive at such a moment: for on

[1] Russell to Salisbury, 26 November—cit. Medlicott, *op. cit.* p. 587.

13 March Tsar Alexander II, who had long since carried his life in his hand, was blown to pieces by Nihilists, and the possibility of revolution in Russia became a disturbing factor to her small neighbour. It was felt to be impossible to wait, as originally intended, till the national festival of 22 May, and so on 25 March 1881 General Lecca—significantly enough one of the leading conspirators who had dethroned Alexander Cuza—proposed to the Chamber the immediate proclamation of the Kingdom of Roumania: and this was carried by acclamation in an overwhelmingly Liberal House, including C. A. Rosetti who had never made any concealment of his original republican views. The Conservatives thus got more than they had bargained for: but they at least assumed *belle mine à mauvais jeu*, and Prince Charles became king without a single dissentient voice. On 22 May he and Princess Elizabeth were crowned at the Cathedral of Bucarest, and it was characteristic of the man that the new crown was made from the metal of a Turkish cannon captured at Plevna. "It will show to future generations", he said, "the heroism of the Roumanians of to-day, and the intimate union of the country and its sovereign." There was a natural dignity, a calm and steadfast serenity, about the new king which outweighed his occasional tendency to pessimism and his inveterate love of balancing both in home and in foreign politics, and which inspired confidence and seemed a guarantee of continuity.

The final ceremony found Ion Brătianu out of office. For reasons which still remain obscure after the lapse of fifty years, he retired on 23 April in favour of his brother Dimitrie, then still Roumanian agent to the Porte. The new premier, though he had long since rallied to the monarchy, remained sincerely devoted to those principles of democratic nationalism which he had learned in years of exile from the greatest exile of the century, Mazzini. Still believing that a Liberal party existed to translate into practice the liberal theories of the forties, he imagined that his summons to power would enable him to purge the party of its many bosses and professional "Panamists". In his programme speech before the Chamber he had the temerity to speak of "hungry wolves", and was listened to in resentful silence by the alarmed majority. His parliamentary career was thus finished before it had really begun: as soon as the coronation was over, there was a general clamour for the return of Ion Brătianu, to whom the interlude had given added strength. From June 1881 till April 1888 the Liberal leader exercised virtually dictatorial powers, framing the administration upon French centralist

PLATE XIV

KING CHARLES

lines, exploiting to the full the narrowly oligarchic and unequal franchise and making of his prefects a series of petty satraps without whom political agitation was difficult even for the boiar class. He himself was a man of high character and wide sympathies, but he considered that the somewhat doctrinaire ideals of his brother Dimitrie and their old associate C. A. Rosetti were ill adapted to the iron age upon which Roumania was entering; he attached great value to the rapid creation of a new middle class, strongly nationalist in feeling and able both to hold the Jews at arm's length and to outstrip in economic development the more primitive and less wealthy communities of the Balkan peninsula: and he therefore, like more than one statesman in contemporary Europe, while maintaining his own private standards, found it convenient to encourage the "spoils system" and to build up his party organisation on the basis of "Enrichissez-vous". This led to a break with most of the comrades and colleagues of early days, Kogălniceanu consoling himself with the Paris Legation: and indeed Dimitrie, founding a new journal *Naţiunea*, conducted henceforward a veritable blood-feud against Ion, in the name of the "pure" as opposed to the "impure" Liberals! But the Opposition was hopelessly divided. The defection of the purists was counterbalanced by the adherence of others, notably Dimitrie Sturdza, who became more and more Ion Brătianu's understudy, alike in home and foreign affairs. The Conservatives, though Lascar Catargiu retained their nominal leadership, also fell into two groups—the "Tory Die-Hards" of the old unregenerate boiar class, and the Junimists—so called after the Moldavian literary society "Junimea" (Youth)—among whom the most eminent were Peter Carp, Titu Maiorescu, Theodore Rosetti and Alexander Marghiloman. Most of these latter had studied in Germany rather than in France, and looked towards the Central Powers, while the Old Conservatives continued to be Russophil, not so much from innate sympathy as for tactical and social reasons. Unlike them, the Junimists realised that in the modern world which Roumania had now definitely entered, a social programme was no less necessary for a Conservative than for a Liberal party. For this there were ample openings, and they laid the main stress upon administrative and financial reforms, on the irremovability of judges, and on improving the status of the peasantry, which, it could no longer be denied, had been steadily deteriorating since the notable, yet altogether inadequate, reforms of Alexander Cuza. The main canker in the land question was the fact that while little or nothing was done to satisfy the land hunger of the peasant or to facilitate the purchase of small, as opposed to large, holdings, there was nothing to check, and indeed much to render automatic, the increase of the already far too extensive *latifundia*.

By the law of 1881 Brătianu made a mild attempt to redeem some of the pledges given to the landless peasants whom the war of 1877 had mobilised: it now became possible for the first time to put up land for sale in small lots, at a fixed price. Under the stress of Junimist agitation Brătianu introduced a further law in 1884 (amended in 1886), encouraging the subdivision of state domains at twenty years' purchase, and giving certain preferences to the peasants, teachers and priests, but still restricting the amount available for small holdings. But the only immediate effect of these laws was that 641 state domains (covering an acreage of 153,000 hectares) passed into the hands of 760 large owners, while 39 were bought by peasants.[1]

Another concession which the Opposition agitation wrung from the veteran Liberal statesman was his decision in 1883 to reform the Constitution; but the elections for the Constituent which was to decide it were managed with such skill and so little scruple that a Liberal majority of 134 was faced by only twelve opponents. Even Dimitrie Brătianu's election was prevented, and when the Government then offered him a seat in the Senate, he furiously declined: while as a further protest against governmental pressure, half the scanty band of survivors—including such men as Catargiu, Kogălniceanu, Tell, Vernescu, Lahovary—committed the tactical blunder of resigning their seats. Despite this, acute dissensions continued within the Chamber itself, and it was not until after the premier had openly threatened to resign and Rosetti had protested against "the strangling of free speech by a Liberal Government" and withdrawn from public life, that the new reform passed into law (10 June 1884). The principal change related to the parliamentary franchise. Henceforth the electorate in each district was to be divided into three instead of four "colleges"—the first consisting of persons with an income of over 1200 francs; the second, of urban dwellers, paying at least 20 francs in direct taxes (members of the liberal professions, retired officers and functionaries being exempt from this); and the third of all others who paid a tax, however small. In the third college, however, every fifty electors were to elect one delegate for the final election of a deputy. The total number of deputies was 183,

[1] Mitrany, *Land and Peasant*, p. 69.

of whom fifty-four chosen by the first, and forty by the third, college.[1]
In other words, the main weight of an extremely narrow franchise in
an overwhelmingly agricultural country was deliberately thrown upon
the urban, professional and official class, and greatly strengthened and
simplified the hold of the Government of the day upon the electorate.
Politically the peasantry was an almost negligible quantity, except when
social unrest made emergency measures, whether of concession or
suppression, advisable.

There was, however, one other important innovation in the revised
Constitution, which affected a section of the peasantry. Article 94
detached from the land owned by the state—mostly due to the monastic
expropriation of 1863—no less than twelve large estates, extending to
118,000 hectares, and formed them into a Royal Domain, the revenues
of which accrued to the crown, but were administered by a special
minister. Brătianu announced his desire that the king should be the
"First Peasant" of Roumania, but of course this measure really tended
to make him "First Boiar", and as time passed and the domain grew
larger and larger, much spiteful and even dangerous criticism was heard.
The truth is that King Charles had all the instincts of a big landlord,
thrifty, cautious, efficient, and his estates would in any case have
flourished: but under the guiding hand of Ion Calinderu, a brilliant
jurist of Greek origin, whose life-work it became, they developed into
a model of scientifically applied agriculture, due regard being taken for
schools, housing, hygiene and rural industries of every kind.

The king's attitude towards party government requires brief comment. In the opening years of his reign he had almost identified himself
with Brătianu and the Liberal regime, and it required more than one
severe wrench in home and foreign affairs to detach him from them. The
way in which he reconciled himself to ministers whom events forced
upon him, first in 1871 in the case of the Conservatives, and then in
1875 in the case of the reviving Liberals, is faintly reminiscent of Queen
Victoria's early attitude to Melbourne and Peel. Certain it is that by
the eighties he had again grown so accustomed to the Liberals as to
tolerate, or even encourage, the redrafting of the Constitution on lines
which seemed to make the Government all-powerful, so long as it
enjoyed the royal favour. But as the process of party disintegration

[1] In the year 1905 the number of inscribed voters in the three colleges was as
follows: (1st) 15,973 direct; (2nd) 34,742 direct; (3rd) 42,907 direct and about one
million indirect, through delegates.

grew more marked, the king did all in his power to encourage political evolution in the direction of a "two-party system". After the fall of Brătianu in 1888 he found himself much freer, and his ideal for the remainder of the reign was the maintenance of "Ins" and "Outs", so that when one set of politicians had had as much of power and its many perquisites as he thought was good for them, there should always be an obvious alternative Government, waiting and eager for office on terms to be arranged with the crown. The rise of a third party, whether Junimists or Conservative Democrats, embarrassed him, as likely to lead to undue bargaining and demagogy, and he therefore looked askance at the leaders of any such movement. In the main, he succeeded in making of the crown the finger on the political balance and retaining for it the fullest initiative of summons and dismissal. Hence, though a man of upright standards, steadfastly opposed to any return of Phanariot methods, and incapable of the crude tactics adopted in Belgrade or Sofia, he closed his eyes to the fact that the very system which he was evolving in the interest of the royal prerogative, inevitably strengthened oligarchic tendencies and promoted the rise of a greedy and cynical *petite bourgeoisie*, eager to share with the old boiar class, subservient, and bent on material gain. He had a genuine admiration for the Roumanian peasantry, but it does not seem to have occurred to him that they were entitled to, or fit for, a share in political power.

After the reforms of 1884 Brătianu still remained in power for four years, but in growing isolation, and surrounded by men of lesser calibre, who none the less were strong enough to checkmate his passing inclination for an alliance with the Junimists on a basis of further reform. His autocratic leanings had grown with age, and as his young and aggressive opponents pressed hard upon him, his attitude was vague and negative. There was one famous occasion on which, when asked for his programme, he would only say, "My programme is 1821, 1848, 1857, 1859: it is 1866, 1877, 1883: it is the Revolution, the demands of the "Divans ad hoc", the Union, the foreign Prince, independence and royalty": and one of his lieutenants, pointing to a portrait of Michael the Brave, called out, "That is our programme".[1] This theatrical allusion to Roumanian unity could not conceal the sterility which had come upon the Liberal party.

The Bulgarian *coup d'état* of 1886 not unnaturally caused great excitement to the north of the Danube, and a fresh attempt on Brătianu's

[1] Damé, *op. cit.* pp. 367, 399.

life in September appears to have convinced him that there existed a plot to apply to Roumania, in the interests of Russian hegemony, the hectoring methods adopted against Prince Alexander of Bulgaria. He even suspected complicity on the part of his brother Dimitrie, who on his side continued to fulminate against a "regime of arbitrary corruption, lies and violence" and allied himself with Catargiu, Vernescu and Nicholas Fleva, the chief orator of those days. During 1887 popular agitation against Brătianu grew, and though the elections to which he resorted brought in the usual governmental majority, the regime was shaken to its foundations by charges of malversation brought forward and proved against two of the highest officers in the army—a scandal which touched King Charles upon the raw. By the end of March 1888, despite his huge re-cast majority in the Chamber, Ion Brătianu had obviously lost prestige in the country and withdrew from office, never to return. Thus ended a memorable career to which posterity has rendered the justice which party passion withheld at the moment of his fall. Ion Brătianu's keen sense of reality had led him decade by decade to pour water into the rich revolutionary wine of his youth: but in this he merely followed an evolution common to all, but especially to Latin, countries. He had shown great statesmanship and constancy in exile, great wisdom in his choice of a foreign prince and in the delicate task of his instalment, and a just balance in drafting the Constitution: and if in his two long and eventful periods of office he had shown certain autocratic *allures* and given a somewhat oligarchic interpretation to the pure doctrine of liberalism, he stands only second to King Charles himself among the makers of modern Roumania and may be said to have inaugurated the most prosperous era in all her history. Indeed this very prosperity which he had done so much to promote and which spread with almost American suddenness, was responsible for the all too materialistic outlook which the great statesman adopted in his final phase and bequeathed as a legacy to his sons.

What gave the finishing touches to Brătianu's ascendancy over the king during the eighties was their complete agreement in the sphere of foreign policy. The bitter experience of 1878 had fatally alienated Brătianu from Russia and filled him with profound distrust and fear of further Panslav aggression. In his consequent search for a powerful ally, France—despite his own Francophil past—had to be ruled out owing to her temporary eclipse in Europe, while Britain, with all her Russophobia, was too remote and uncertain. There remained Austria, relations with whom were complicated by the Roumanian question in Transylvania, and Germany, whose leading statesman had shown a curiously brutal indifference, if not antipathy, to the Roumanian cause. To the king even Bismarck's whims were as nothing compared to his veneration for the Emperor William, his close friendship with the crown prince and his desire to be closely linked with the Hohenzollern empire: and he therefore did all in his power to turn the Liberal leader's thoughts towards Berlin and Vienna. Moreover, Bismarck was already coming to feel that his new alliance with Austria-Hungary would be greatly enhanced in value if the young Balkan states could be attracted into its orbit: whereas if they remained hostile, "an effective promotion of Austria-Hungary's interests in the Peninsula, which we consider it our duty to support, will thereby be materially hampered".[1] Already in 1880, then, he was urging Baron Haymerle, in a friendly way, to show more consideration for Roumania, and about the same time he promised Brătianu support, in order to bring him towards Austria-Hungary.[2] He was afraid of Russia out-trumping Austria-Hungary in Bucarest, arguing to himself that the latter could at best only offer Roumania a guarantee of her existing possessions, whereas Russia could promise her—as was actually done in the Great War—new territory in Transylvania. It is interesting to note that the possibility of her recovering Bessarabia does not enter Bismarck's head, whereas from the very first the spectre of the loss of Transylvania hovers in the background. The fact that Roumania is a mere detail in his major aim of reconstructing the somewhat damaged Three Emperors' League, makes it all the more significant that he does not place Bessarabia and Transylvania on all fours.

By 1882 Bismarck, forgetful of his own bullying attitude in the Jewish and railway questions, finds it difficult to understand why Austria is "so discourteous to the Roumanians".[3] He is still somewhat contemptuous of Roumania's quality, but thinks her well worth winning, as the final strategic link in the elaborate series of agreements which he is building up—the Dual Alliance in 1879, the Dreikaiserbündniss in 1881, the successive adhesions to the former of Serbia in 1881, of Italy in 1882, of Roumania in 1883, and finally, most ingenious of all, the super-secret Reinsurance Treaty of 1887. For a whole year

[1] Quoted by Caprivi to Reuss, 26 March 1891—*Grosse Politik*, VII, no. 1469.
[2] Bismarck to Reuss, 3 October 1880—*ibid.* XII, i, no. 2949.
[3] Hatzfeldt to Reuss, 4 May 1882—Anlage II to ditto.

after this querulous complaint nothing happens, but in the end it is Bismarck who takes the decisive initiative, Haymerle having died in the interval and been succeeded by Count Kálnoky, whom Bismarck prefers despite his cynical and uncompromising nature. In the meantime relations between Vienna and Bucarest had not improved: and an awkward incident in June 1883 provided a stimulus to all parties concerned to clear the air. The statue of Stephen the Great was unveiled in Jassy, and at a banquet which followed a toast was drunk, in the presence of the king (he was even alleged to have clinked glasses with the speaker) to "The Absent"—meaning the "unredeemed Roumanians".[1] As Charles was on the point of paying visits to the German courts, the indiscreet Frenchman who had published the facts in *L'Indépendance Roumaine* was expelled from Roumania, and the king gave personal apologies and assurances when he reached Vienna. Bismarck struck while the iron was hot, and suggested to Kálnoky that during his Gastein cure they should discuss "an extension of our league of peace with Italy eastwards, to include Roumania".[2] Kálnoky replied that as he was "practically certain of Serbia", the addition of Roumania "would fill a very noticeable gap", but added that Roumania had actively opposed Austria-Hungary in the Danubian question and shown no sign of conciliation, and that he must therefore leave it to Bismarck to find the right formula.[3]

It was the right psychological moment for Bismarck's talks with Brătianu. For some years Roumanian antipathy had been directed almost equally against Russia and Austria—Bessarabia, Silistra and the bullying of Bulgaria on the one side balanced the Danubian question and Magyar repression on the other. What forced on a decision was not only the impossibility of standing alone, the knowledge that neutrality was not attainable, the alarming object-lesson of Russian arrogance across the Danube, but above all the fact that while Russia had no ally against Austria, the latter now definitely had Germany behind her. Charles's dynastic and national sentiments pushed him towards the Central Powers, and his soldier's instinct in favour of a connection with the strongest military power in Europe impressed his all too realistic ministers. The fact that Serbia was simultaneously being drawn into

[1] Peter Gradişteanu spoke of "precious jewels" which had fallen from the crown of Stephen the Great.

[2] 19 August 1883—*G.P.* III, no. 583.

[3] Reuss to Bismarck, 21 August—*ibid.* no. 584.

the orbit of Austria-Hungary was not without its influence, though of course the sober and sagacious King Charles had nothing in common with King Milan, the flashy and unprincipled neurasthenic who sat so uneasily on the throne of Belgrade. Above all, the fear lest Russia might, if an alliance gave her the opening, attempt to apply in Roumania the same crude dictatorial methods as in the new Bulgaria, and so establish her hegemony over the whole peninsula, still further weighed the scales in favour of the Central Powers.

On 8 September 1883, then, Bismarck discussed the situation in great detail with Brătianu at Gastein and laid the foundations of a new Roumanian policy.[1] It is interesting to find the chancellor confessing afterwards that the Roumanian's aversion to Russia was altogether too strong for his taste, and that he had to stress the desire of the Central Powers to avoid any quarrel with Russia. This had the immediate effect of making Brătianu express the fear lest Roumania should be the scapegoat in an agreement between the three empires, and Bismarck only calmed him by insisting on the need of maintaining the non-Slav elements in that part of Europe. Brătianu said he was convinced that Roumania could only assure her independence by leaning against Austria and Germany, and that the only menace to this independence came from Russia: Germany could therefore rely on Roumania's support in the event of Russian aggression. Bismarck gathered the impression that Brătianu aimed not so much at a defensive alliance, as at "an offensive and defensive alliance, with share in the profits", and therefore felt it necessary to warn him that for Austria and Germany, "a war with Russia, even if victorious", was something which there was every ground for avoiding. The two men cannot have been drawn to each other. Bismarck, writing of Brătianu, expresses annoyance that he should send his son to Paris to be educated. "The mere fact that he does so, is characteristic", he says, and he wonders how far it is due to the influence of Rosetti, "whose intimacy with the Reddest parties in France is beyond doubt". He seems to have accepted Brătianu's professed belief that only in reliance upon the Central Powers could Roumania preserve her independence: but his private calculation was that Roumania could be relied upon so long as King Charles reigned, but that it would then be uncertain whether "the French party of upheaval" would gain the upper hand.[2] He noted as suspicious signs the

[1] G.P. III, no. 585—Bismarck to Reuss, 8 September.
[2] Ibid. no. 586—Bismarck to Reuss, 15 September.

fact that the king had appointed as his aide-de-camp Captain Condianu, who had been mixed up in the republican "Putsch" of 1871 and that Brătianu left at the legation in Constantinople a man like Mavrogheni, who was a kinsman of Cuza and Karagjorgjević. (Here he misjudged: the two facts were a sign of strength in the king and of deliberate magnanimity in the premier.) The general conclusion, however, was, let us take Roumania, but let us continue to negotiate with Russia on the lines of Saburov's proposals.

The conversation clearly left a tinge of suspicion in the chancellor's mind, for a week later he complains of Brătianu's "cupidity" (*Begehrlichkeiten*). He resented the assumption that Germany would not be able to retain Italy's alliance save by promising her territory as the result of war: and when, to draw out his innermost thoughts, he quoted Corsica and Nice, he seemed to detect the further assumption that the Italians would want even more. The obvious inference which Bismarck drew was that Brătianu's own demands after victory would not be modest: the instinct was sure, but in actual fact it was left to his son to stretch Roumanian claims to their uttermost limit.

The ground having been thus cleared, Brătianu on his way home saw Kálnoky and soon reached an agreement: and on 30 October 1883 a secret treaty was signed at Vienna between Austria-Hungary and Roumania, to which Germany adhered by a special protocol of the same date.[1] Brătianu would have preferred an arrangement *à trois*, but this was not approved by Germany, one reason being that Bismarck had a certain amount of difficulty with the Emperor William, whose strongly Russophil feelings always had to be taken into account. In the original draft one clause referred to the event of Roumania or Austria-Hungary being attacked "*par la Russie*", and this had to be altered to please the emperor, though of course the kernel and sense of the agreement were not altered. Bismarck, remembering his Gastein talks, was ready enough to avoid any phrase that might seem to encourage Roumania, with two million German and Austrian bayonets behind her, to dream again of the Dniester frontier.

The essential provisions of the Treaty can be speedily summarised. (1) "Peace and alliance" is the aim, and a mutual undertaking is given "not to enter any alliance directed against one of their states, and to lend mutual aid within the limits of their interests". (2) In the event of

---

[1] Pribram, *Geheimverträge Oesterreich-Ungarns*, pp. 32sqq.; *G.P.* III, nos. 587, 598.

an unprovoked attack upon Roumania Austria-Hungary is bound to bring timely help against the aggressor. If Austria-Hungary were attacked in the same circumstances in a portion of her states bordering upon Roumania, the *casus foederis* would at once present itself for the latter. (3) If either is threatened by aggression, the two Governments are to concert military measures together. (4) In the event of war there shall be no separate peace. Extreme secrecy is prescribed. The treaty is valid for five years in the first instance, and for three years longer unless one year's notice is given on either side. Translated into every-day terms, Article II meant that while Austria-Hungary undertook to help Roumania against aggression "from any quarter" (which meant in practice Russia, Bulgaria, Turkey or Serbia), Roumania could only be held liable to help Austria-Hungary if attacked by Russia or Serbia.

The adhesion of Germany gave Roumania the guarantee of the two Great Powers against aggression, and in 1888 Italy's adhesion also was added: so that her position was almost unassailable. Kálnoky made it quite clear to the German ambassador[1] that he had no illusions as to the possible friendly feelings of Roumania for Austria-Hungary. Roumania, he saw, felt the necessity of going with Austria-Hungary, but to her the real guarantee of existence consisted solely in the covering signature of Germany. That this was the bare truth was to be made abundantly clear at a later date both by the king himself and his ministers. None the less, it also had its advantages from the standpoint of Vienna: for it brought Roumania as well as Serbia into the Austrian sphere, shut off Russia from the Danube except at its very mouth, and for the time restricted her sphere of Balkan interest to Montenegro and Bulgaria. The one hardly weighed in the international scale, though Tsar Alexander, in a moment of pique, toasted her prince as his only friend in Europe. In the other Russia was rapidly turning public opinion against the Liberator, owing to the tactless and aggressive interference of her civil and military agents. Meanwhile a thoroughly practical result of the new agreement was that Roumanian military plans and fortifications could now be directed solely in the direction of Russia, and that the Transylvanian frontier could be left unfortified.

Brătianu and Sturdza, in their conversations with the German minister[2] on the eve of signature, expressed the conviction that the treaty would strengthen Roumanian independence and check Russian in-

---

[1] *G.P.* III, no. 590—Reuss to Bismarck, 1 October 1883.
[2] *Ibid.* no. 595—Saurma to Bismarck, 13 October.

fluence. They spoke of Russian efforts to foment internal strife, and asserted categorically that more money than ever before was being sent from St Petersburg to the Roumanian Opposition and to the press: and that the king shared this belief is to be seen from a later letter of his to Prince Alexander of Bulgaria.[1] In a word, fear of Russian intrigue was a main motive for signing, though doubtless any argument likely to impress the to them unduly Russophil Bismarck would obviously receive full emphasis.

The most significant thing about the treaty was its extreme secrecy.[2] Brătianu, with the king's approval, promised that it should not be submitted to Parliament, and this of course applied to Austria-Hungary, where foreign policy was definitely a preserve of the monarch, and the control of the two Delegations upon the joint foreign minister was far too loose to prevent secret agreements. In Roumania, however, an almost unique situation resulted. In the Constitution of 1866 a curious loophole had been left, which gave king and premier their opportunity. Article 93 expressly laid down that the king concludes "conventions of commerce, navigation and others of the same nature", but that they must be approved by Parliament before they can become valid. Nothing is said of foreign treaties in the wider sense, yet it is expressly stated that the king "has no powers save those attributed to him under the constitution", and the conclusion of treaties is not on the long list of his powers. On the other hand no act of his is valid unless countersigned by a minister, who thereby takes the responsibility. The secret treaty is in the name of Francis Joseph and Charles, but it is countersigned by Dimitrie Sturdza as foreign minister, and thus the letter of the law would seem to have been fulfilled, though hardly the spirit. Seldom at any rate has a secret been better kept, and though the existence of a certain *rapprochement* with the Central Powers was patent to all the world, and indeed openly admitted, it was not until 1914 that the existence of a specific and binding alliance became known. Throughout these thirty-one years only a tiny handful of men were in the secret, and in the first instance only the king and the two Liberal chiefs.

During the remainder of the eighties, then, though the world did

---

[1] Corti, *Alexander von Bulgarien*, p. 288.
[2] An early example of this will be found in *F.D.D.* 1st series, v, no. 99. On 22 September 1883 the Roumanian minister informs his French colleague that in Brătianu's talks with Bismarck there was no question whatsoever of Roumania entering the Triple Alliance.

not know it, Roumania was a vassal of the Central Powers, occupying the same relative position as that of Serbia since 1881. But there were two very important differences. In the first place, there could be no greater contrast than that between the dignified, balanced, sagacious Charles, fortified by many dynastic connections, and the highly intelligent but dissolute and unstable Milan, born of an upstart family and a no less dissolute mother and in constant and scandalous dissension with his wife: and this difference of character was reflected in Milan's scarcely veiled contempt for his subjects and his abject abasement before Vienna. While it lasted, the Serbian treaty with Austria-Hungary (signed in 1881, renewed in 1889, but allowed to lapse in 1895) was a no less jealously guarded secret than the Roumanian, but the vassalage of Belgrade was open and humiliating. Moreover, Serbia's treaty was with Austria-Hungary alone, Germany standing aloof, and its terms were such as expressly to preclude Belgrade from conducting an independent foreign policy of its own. Hence Roumania, while retaining the respect of the world and never reaching the same degree of subordination, yet extracted from the alliance far greater advantages than did Serbia, whose treaty rested mainly on the dynastic fears and fantasies of Milan.

For a whole generation after Berlin distrust of Russia was an obsession with most Roumanian statesmen: and Russia's treatment of Bulgaria and her first prince, Alexander of Battenberg, with whom King Charles was on intimate, even affectionate, terms, only served to strengthen this feeling. Charles had sometimes had his dreams of adding Bulgaria to an expanding Dacian kingdom, and late in 1878, while encouraging his friend "Sandro" to accept the new throne, told him in all seriousness that "if this new profession does not work, I am ready to take over your cares of government".[1] When, however, it came to the bloodless union of the "two Bulgarias" in 1885, and the defeat of Serbia at Slivnitsa, Charles was careful to avoid Milan's precipitate and dog-in-the-manger attitude, and like Austria-Hungary, frankly accepted the new situation. Milan, he told Alexander, "should get out of the mess into which his headstrongness and megalomania has thrown him".[2] The result was that Bucarest was quite naturally chosen as the scene of the Serbo-Bulgarian negotiations, ending in that shortest of all treaties, a single clause restoring the *status quo* (3 March 1886).

[1] Corti, *Alexander von Battenberg*, p. 56.
[2] *Ibid.* p. 288.

But the Bulgarian *coup d'état* of the following August, under Russian auspices, and the final abdication of Prince Alexander, caused great alarm in Bucarest, and the prolonged interregnum, with all its dangerous reactions upon international policy, still further strengthened Roumania's tendency to lean upon Vienna and Berlin. The proposal put forward in some quarters while the Bulgarian throne was going begging, that it should be offered to King Charles in "personal union", was politely declined, not without some inward reluctance, but in the knowledge that compliance would have offended Russia and Austria-Hungary equally.

The fall of Ion Brătianu in March 1888 and the temporary eclipse of the Liberal party confronted King Charles with a situation of equal uncertainty at home and abroad. For the first time there was no straight issue between the "Ins" and "Outs", such as it was the king's constant aim to create: for a series of dissident Liberal fractions had drifted into alliance with the Old Conservatives, whom he regarded as unsound in foreign policy, while the Conservative dissidents, though sound in foreign policy, were in his view increasing the confusion at home by breaking away from the main party, yet not co-operating with the Liberal reformers. He thought for a moment of calling the veteran Kogălniceanu, but as that proved impossible, he compromised by forming a Cabinet of Junimists, led by Theodore Rosetti, till then president of the Supreme Court. The Germanophile Peter Carp took foreign affairs, and was supported by two men for whom history reserved a special part, the Transylvanian Titu Maiorescu and Alexander Marghiloman. The reckless agitation which had precipitated the crisis had been misunderstood by the masses, and scarcely was the new Government in the saddle, when a serious peasant rising broke out—not, it is to be noted, in the remote and backward mountain districts, but in the rich plains that surrounded Bucarest itself. In many cases the mayors' offices were sacked, grain reserves pillaged, and an attempt made to cut up the large fields. "Something had changed after all in Roumanian agriculture after 1864", writes Dr Mitrany, "but less in the manner of cultivation than in the mode of management." The root evil was the rapid growth of absenteeism among the landlords and the rise of a new class of middlemen, "not professional farmers...but farming speculators, renting for short periods at exorbitant rents", and bent on realising swift and high profits for themselves and their employers. The sudden challenge of King Demos was a severe shock for the propertied class: and the Junimists, whom M. Damé has aptly called "a brilliant general staff without an army", were not equal to such an occasion: the elections held in the autumn of 1888 strengthened the Old Conservatives, and after reconstructing his Cabinet—a compromise which satisfied nobody—Rosetti finally resigned in January 1889, and the king had no choice but to summon the veteran Conservative leader, Lascar Catargiu, to power. The Conservatives were to remain in power till October 1895, though with constant re-shufflings— General Manu and General Florescu filling the office of premier for exactly a year each, but then giving place to Catargiu once more.[1]

As so often happens, it was thus left for a Conservative administration to introduce legislation such as usually figures on Liberal programmes. Certain vitally necessary financial reforms were passed— the adoption of the gold standard and the improvement of the currency. The rapid commercial development of the country necessitated the introduction of a new Mining Law and the conclusion of various commercial treaties. In 1891 the irremovability of judges was carried, thus removing one very dark blot on Roumanian public life: but the no less odious practice of changing prefects and a mass of other administrative officials at every change of government, had by now entrenched itself as one of the foundations of the existing order, and it was destined still to survive many an upheaval. Special mention must be made of the law of 1893 on primary education, due to the initiative of Take Ionescu, a brilliant young lawyer who had passed from the Liberal dissidents to the Junimists and was more than once again to plough a lonely political furrow. His was the first serious attempt to make a breach in the illiteracy of the peasant masses by founding village schools: and the rôle of the primary schoolmaster, not only as a teacher of youth, but as an enemy of usury and alcohol and a promoter of rural banks, was henceforth to become the bright feature in an agrarian system marked by neglect and social contrasts.

The new Land Law of 1889 was an attempt to take the edge off the land hunger of the peasantry, and it authorised the sale, in small lots, of all the domains still in the hands of the state, amounting to 1,200,000 hectares. None the less the result was not satisfactory, and much of the available land appears to have passed into wrong hands. Demand far exceeded supply, and when in 1896 the Liberals amended the law so as

[1] Manu 17 November 1889 to 18 November 1890, then Florescu to 9 December 1891, then Catargiu to 16 October 1895.

to limit the new holdings to 5 hectares, there was again such a rush that prices rose too high, and when bad harvests followed, many of the new owners were insolvent. Moreover the state of the law on agricultural contracts, even as modified in 1893, remained extremely unsatisfactory: and through it, in the words of Dr Mitrany, "the constitutional guarantees for personal liberty and for the sanctity of domicile could be set aside for 95 per cent. of the population at the will and whim of a village mayor, and this not in exceptional circumstances, but in every-day life, in matters arising out of the daily work—the only means of subsistence—of the people".[1] The decades that followed were the Golden Age of irresponsible landlordism, and in some respects the peasant found himself as much exploited, as fatally tied to the soil, as in the vanished days of serfdom.

Speaking broadly, however, the Conservative achievement in these years was a creditable one. It could not resist paying the Liberals back in their own coin, by demanding the impeachment of Brătianu and his colleagues: but after violent dissensions between the rival groups, the proposal was substantially rejected by the Chamber, Take Ionescu, in one of his most brilliant speeches, urging it not to pursue a policy of vengeance such as would only discredit it in the eyes of Europe. Meanwhile the Liberal party was undergoing a process of transformation: Ion Brătianu and Kogălniceanu died within a few months of each other in 1891, and Dimitrie Brătianu followed a year later, after helping to reconcile the two hostile sections of the party, and Dimitrie Sturdza stepped naturally into the leadership.

The twenty-fifth anniversary of Charles's accession directed attention anew to the question of his heir: and on 10 January 1893 Prince Ferdinand was married to Princess Marie of Edinburgh, the grand-daughter at once of Queen Victoria and of Tsar Alexander II and niece of the king's close friend and kinsman the late Emperor Frederick. From the dynastic point of view this not only brought added prestige to Roumania, but seemed a fresh move towards the Triple Alliance, both in view of the close kinship between the British and German royal families and of the apparent strengthening of political ties between their respective countries during the second Salisbury ministry: while the mother of the future queen linked her with the court of Russia. Her own beauty, versatility and *joie de vivre* soon won many hearts.

During these seven years of Conservative rule the king had skilfully

[1] Corti, *op. cit.* p. 79.

adjusted himself to new internal developments, but in foreign policy his position was at the first, and indeed for several years, highly equivocal and insecure. This was the verdict of some of the keenest contemporary observers in Europe, though events show them to have taken too gloomy a view. In September 1888 Bismarck and Kálnoky agreed in the view that Charles "is making a false calculation in counting on the boiars, whereas they would see nothing more gladly than the overthrow of the new kingship and the restoration of elected hospodars under the Russian or Turkish protectorate. King Charles over-estimates the strength of his position, as his great purchases of landed property show, and seeks the friendship of the aristocracy instead of winning the devotion of the peasantry against it and against Russia".[1] This is only quoted as a political curiosity: for if the second half hits the nail on the head, the first half was a patent distortion, though not utterly without foundation.

Only a fortnight later Francis Joseph, in conversation with Count Herbert Bismarck, passed a strangely severe verdict upon Charles—so different from the view which he afterwards came to hold of one of his rare friends among crowned heads. The emperor actually called him "a vain and short-sighted gasbag" and expressed real concern as to the future of the new dynasty. "If he goes on managing things as clumsily as at present, and does not even ensure the visible continuity of the dynasty" (a reference to the fact that Prince Ferdinand's position as Heir Apparent was still a little fluid) "he might easily meet with the fate of Cuza. This would bring grave embarrassment to Austria, for she could not look on while Roumania became a Russian dependency."[2] He added that the activities of the German and Austro-Hungarian ministers in Bucarest were hampered by the king's "self-willed conceit".[3] It is important to note that the two ministers in question were Bernhard von Bülow and Count Goluchowski, who were, ere many years had passed, to direct the policy of the Triple Alliance. Indeed in the thirty years preceding the Great War, the witty saying of a French diplomatist was amply justified: Bucarest served as the "springboard for Ambassadors", and among those who won their spurs there were not only Bülow and Goluchowski, but Kiderlen, Aehrenthal, Czernin, White, Lascelles and the second Giers. "A hot soil for your début",

[1] G.P. vi, no. 1351—Bismarck to William II, 20 September 1888.
[2] Ibid. no. 1352—Memorandum of Herbert Bismarck, 5 October.
[3] "Besserwissenden Eigensinn."

said the veteran ambassador Schweinitz to Bülow when he left for Bucarest in May 1888 to take up his first post as minister.

What with party brawling, a veritable peasant revolt, occasional riots in Bucarest and even shots against the palace windows, it was indeed a hot soil. Above all, the alliance was in danger. Hitherto only the Liberals had shared the dire secret with the sovereign: but not having been denounced under Clause 5, it would now automatically become valid for another three years. Someone else had to be initiated, and this was a decisive factor in the king's selection of the Junimists, despite their lack of following; for Carp and Maiorescu in particular were open Austrophils. But when a year later it proved necessary to admit the Old Conservatives to office, the king resolved to keep foreign policy strictly in his own hands, and thus an incredible situation arose, in which successive premiers and foreign ministers pledged themselves publicly before the Chamber to absolute neutrality as the only possible policy, in complete ignorance of the fact that their predecessors had committed the country to an alliance which under certain circumstances might involve it in war with Russia. It is true that at the same time they got Parliament to vote extensive grants for fortifications, but this barely served to alleviate the disquiet of the allied ministers at a situation so irregular and so fraught with danger for the crown and for their own interests. It was Bülow's task to press the king discreetly in favour of converting the secret alliance into an open one, but Charles steadily opposed this both for reasons of party politics and for fear of closing all roads towards St Petersburg. Matters were therefore allowed to drift till the spring of 1891, when the question of renewal became imminent, since the treaty was due to expire in October. At this moment its existence was known only to the king, the two Brătianus (who both died within the next year), Dimitrie Sturdza, its actual signatory, and Beldiman, who had been at the Roumanian Legation in Berlin when it was signed and remained throughout life an ardent Germanophil.[1] Goluchowski, starting from the assumption that it was "desirable" that there should always be at least one informed member of the Roumanian Cabinet with whom the Central Powers could negotiate, suggested to his colleague Bülow that the king should either admit Carp to office, or else initiate Manu and Lahovary, the premier and foreign minister! But Charles objected, arguing that renewal would scarcely

---

[1] Bülow reported home that Carp also was in the secret, but at this time not even he knew (*G.P.* VII, no. 1464).

be possible until the Liberals returned to power, and for this they were not yet ripe. Neither Manu nor Florescu, he said, would have the courage to sign (presumably because it would mean signing away their principles); Lahovary lacked the necessary authority, Lascar Catargiu would demand too many counter-concessions; to Carp he refused to reveal it (whether owing to his personal dislike for that outspoken statesman, or because Carp was at once brother-in-law, and deadly enemy, of the Liberal leader Sturdza, is not quite clear). It would not matter, he added, if the treaty went out of force till more stable conditions returned, since the danger of a European war in the next few years was very slight.[1] The two ministers had to hide their concern and contented themselves with arguing that Roumania had a far stronger interest than her greater allies in not breaking the thread of the alliance. But this was the very moment at which the king saw himself obliged to accept a purely Conservative Cabinet, pledged more than ever to neutrality and to leave the making of elections in their hands! It was also a period when the fall of Bismarck led to considerable stocktaking at Berlin in the whole field of foreign policy. Caprivi, new to his job, consulted his soldier-ambassador at St Petersburg, General von Schweinitz, and the two agreed that Germany's "obligations towards King Charles could not be brought into line with the provisions of the Russian agreement", and that the various secret agreements conflicted with each other. They made a joint representation to William II in this sense, and thus the Roumanian treaty seems to have been a contributing factor to the fateful decision not to renew the Russo-German Reinsurance Treaty.[2]

Bülow's report to the new German chancellor, Caprivi, contains the caustic comment: "The King acts on the principle, 'To the most savage dog the fattest morsel'. In always trying to pacify first of all those who seem most dangerous to him, he sets a premium on disloyalty, with the result that no party trusts him, and hardly any politician is personally devoted to him".[3] This is undoubtedly too severe, but it reflects the outlook of many towards what may fairly be described as the least impressive incident in King Charles's whole career.

It is at this awkward moment that a new factor begins to assume increasing importance, alike in home and foreign policy. The policy of

[1] G.P. VII, no. 1464—Bülow to Caprivi, 27 February 1891.
[2] Schweinitz, Denkwürdigkeiten, II, p. 404.
[3] G.P. VII, no. 1466—Bülow to Caprivi, 17 March 1891.

Magyarisation pursued in Hungary during the fifteen years of Koloman Tisza's rule, so far from dying down after his fall, assumed even sharper forms during the nineties, and especially against the Roumanians of Transylvania, who on their side at last began to show signs of resistance, after the long period of barren abstention. In 1891 the University youth of Bucarest drew up a memorandum recounting the grievances of their kinsmen beyond the mountains, and this was answered by the Magyar students of Budapest University—polemics which led to the eventful Memorandum Trial (see p. 413). In the following winter the so-called "League for the Cultural Unity of all Roumanians" was founded at Bucarest and began a lively press agitation to which public opinion was not slow to respond. This increased the delicacy of maintaining a secret alliance with the oppressors of unredeemed Roumania. It is highly instructive to find that one of the very first to express concern at Magyar policy in Transylvania as directly affecting the Triple Alliance as a whole was no other than the German Chancellor Caprivi. He very sensibly recognised that Transylvania was the real cause of Roumanian estrangement and that unrest was bound to continue so long as Hungary's attitude remained unchanged, and indeed that if the treaty lapsed, the estrangement was likely to grow. From the specifically German standpoint this would mean a serious handicap upon Austro-Hungarian military action, and "therefore", he added, "for us too an increase of the dangers of war".[1] Acting on Caprivi's instructions, Prince Reuss sounded Kálnoky on this delicate subject, but got little out of him beyond a general admission of tactlessness, qualified by the view that the Magyars could not be blamed for desiring to spread their language, especially among the officials. He then tried to sail away upon another tack, putting forward as reasons for King Charles's reluctance to renew the treaty "the lack of energy noticeable in him latterly", and "the influence of the Queen, whose outlook is growing steadily more peculiar and in politics more and more confused....Though so highly gifted" added Kálnoky (though on what grounds it is difficult to conceive), "the Queen is by no means friendly towards her German fatherland".[2] In the following August Bülow, on his way through Vienna, broached the same subject with Kálnoky and quoted complaints of the king and leading Roumanian statesmen. This elicited from Kálnoky the admission that "the Magyars are often influenced more by short-

[1] G.P. VII, no. 1469—Caprivi to Reuss, 26 March 1891.
[2] Ibid. no. 1470—Reuss to Caprivi, 30 March 1891.

sighted passion than by considerations of cool reason. Fortunately, being in this somewhat Asiatic, they fall into lethargic inactivity just as quickly as they foam up". He then assured Bülow that he had succeeded, by personal intervention, in holding up the execution of the Kindergarten Law—a notorious instrument of Magyarising policy— and that the Budapest students had received an official hint to moderate their polemics with the Roumanians.[1]

Meanwhile Prince Reuss was not exaggerating when, after one of his talks with Kálnoky, he reported to Berlin[2] that the king was simply afraid to let his present Cabinet into the secret, though he may have gone too far in asserting that men like Florescu, Catargiu or Vernescu simply could not conceal it from Russia. The various schemes suggested for getting round the difficulty show the utter artificiality of the whole situation. One was that the treaty should be allowed to run on auto-matically for another three years: but even this would not work unless at least one minister was let into the secret, so as to cover it by min-isterial responsibility. Another was that autograph letters should be exchanged between Francis Joseph and Charles, containing a pledge for another three years: and meanwhile they would live in the hope of regularising the position by a change of ministers. This idea was dropped because Goluchowski was certain that King Charles would never consent to such a step. By August 1891 a solution seemed as far off as ever. The king was very touchy on the question and much depressed at the *impasse*.

Naturally enough, as Bülow pointed out to Caprivi,[3] the king was reluctant to admit that he had not merely kept the Conservative chiefs for years in the dark as to the vital obligations of the country, but positively denied their existence. How sensitive he was in the matter was shown by his outburst against Austria-Hungary for trying to place him before "a kind of aut-aut". This, he said, was "unwise" (*nicht klug*): they should give him a certain latitude and not affront him. It was a dangerous game, and they were driving him into the opposite camp! Bülow soothed him down by denying all idea of pressure and

---

[1] *G.P.* VII, no. 1471—Bülow to Caprivi 4 August 1891.

[2] *Ibid.* no. 1468—Reuss to Caprivi 26 March 1891. The reader is urged to com-pare the attitude of official Germany in 1891 towards the Transylvanian question, with its attitude twenty-two years later, on the eve of the Great War—see *infra*, pp. 463–4.

[3] *Ibid.* no. 1471—4 August.

by assuring him that the Central Powers were content "to leave the time and method of renewal to his own loyalty and tact".[1]

Meanwhile the king's mind was working steadily towards a solution. It was in this very month of August 1891 that a French squadron visited Russian waters, and that the first foundations of the "Franco-Russe" were laid. This made a considerable impression on the Roumanians, and there were some who argued that they should attach themselves to the new combination. But in the end the attraction of the Triple Alliance proved stronger, and even the Francophil statesmen Esarcu and Lahovary confessed to Bülow their fear lest the French, "*hypnotised by the gap in the Vosges*, might be ready to sacrifice all the Balkans, and especially Roumania, for the left bank of the Rhine".[2] They were fully alive to the possibility that if they drew away from the Central Powers, Germany might have to look for other allies in the Near East, and that after a decade of successful penetration in Turkey she might not look in vain. For Roumania the dangers of isolation were by no means negligible.

In October King Charles saw Caprivi in Berlin and gave him a verbal guarantee of Roumania's loyalty even without a treaty, pointing out, as one soldier to another, that all her military preparations were directed towards a single front—in other words, against possible Russian aggression. While assuring the chancellor that the delay was due to party politics at home, he none the less pointedly referred to the embarrassment which Magyar chauvinism caused him.[3] In January 1892 Charles met Francis Joseph, who showed his usual tact, and refrained from pressing him: but Kálnoky, eager to strike while the iron was hot, put forward the idea of an entirely new treaty. This, the bitter-tongued Kálnoky told the German ambassador, "would save King Charles from the painful confession that with the exception of Mr Carp, he had led his government by the nose for ten years past"—of course an overstatement of an undoubted fact. A piquant detail further illustrates the king's methods: it was found that only a single copy of the treaty existed in Roumania, and this was in the king's private safe at Sinaia, which was shut up for the winter! There was no copy in the Foreign Office at Bucarest.[4]

[1] *G.P.* VII, no. 1472—Bülow to Caprivi, 7 August.
[2] *Ibid.* no. 1473—Bülow to Caprivi, 11 August.
[3] *Ibid.* no. 1475—Memorandum of Caprivi, 29 October.
[4] *Ibid.* no. 1480—Reuss to Caprivi, 3 March.

At last on 18 March the king took the necessary plunge, by revealing the whole position to Alexander Lahovary, now once more foreign minister, and winning him for the idea of renewal. But it took him two further months of preparation, before he could broach the subject to the Conservative premier, Catargiu, and history only records the latter's consent, but not his feelings.[1] In June a formal overture to Vienna was made by Lahovary: but once more there is a marked difference of attitude towards Austria-Hungary and towards Germany. The king spoke very frankly to Bülow of the grievances of the Roumanians of Transylvania, while admitting that it was perhaps tactless of them "to ogle the Young Czechs, Slovenes and anti-Semites". He went so far as to say that in the event of a successful joint war against Russia he would like to put in a claim for Bukovina, though realising that he could not possibly raise such a question. And then he added, "If it were a question solely of a Roumanian-Austrian Treaty, no Roumanian would sign it: it is only the future accession of Germany that makes the Treaty possible, and gives it its real value in my eyes and in the eyes of my Ministers".[2] In his memoirs Bülow long afterwards records a similar opinion expressed by the king about the same period: the alliance, he held, could only survive so long as Germany kept the leadership in her hand, for if neither Germany nor Russia existed, a conflict between Roumania and Hungary would be quite inevitable.[3]

On 25 July 1892, then, the treaty between Roumania and Austria-Hungary was formally renewed, Germany acceding as before, and Italy adding her signature in November.[4] On this occasion only Catargiu, Lahovary, Carp and Calinderu were admitted to the secret, and it is characteristic that the Roumanian ministers in Vienna and Berlin were not informed! Of any reference to Parliament there was now less question than ever. The only change was that four years were fixed instead of five, with three more years automatically if the treaty were not denounced in 1895. King Charles had at last extricated himself from an awkward, not to say impossible, position. The policy inaugurated by the Liberals and sanctioned by the Junimists was now formally adopted by the Conservatives. Thus one by one each of the three parties committed themselves to the foreign policy so consistently advocated

---

[1] *G.P.* VII, nos. 1481 and 1482—Bülow to Caprivi. 20 March and 16 May.
[2] *Ibid.* no. 1484—Bülow to Caprivi, 8 June 1892.
[3] Bülow, *Denkwürdigkeiten*, I, p. 621.
[4] Text in Pribram, *op. cit.* pp. 70–2.

by the king, and the last fear of a challenge to his dynastic position seemed to have been removed. Henceforward the alliance had the endorsement of all parties in the state, and its subsequent renewals were little more than formalities—in September 1896 and April 1902 under Sturdza, and finally in February 1913 under Maiorescu. The fluctuations of opinion will be alluded to in their own place. It should be added that meanwhile the Serbian alliance with Vienna, after being renewed in 1889, was allowed to lapse in 1895.

It is highly characteristic of the growth of Roumanian national sentiment that in the years immediately following the Conservative endorsement of the alliance, it should have been the first signatory of that alliance, Dimitrie Sturdza, who took the strongest public line against Magyar policy. The nineties were a period of social transition and political rearrangement, corresponding to the unexampled material prosperity, the growth of a new commercial class and the passing of old leaders. The outrageous treatment meted out to the Roumanians of Transylvania by successive Hungarian Governments evoked widespread indignation south of the Carpathians, and while Sturdza shared such feelings to the full, it was an admirable platform on which to rally public support for the reconstituted Liberal party and to discredit a Government which lacked the power to enforce any real protest at Budapest. And indeed, if it could be argued that the Conservative party was a mere preserve of the old boiar class, or at least of its more intelligent members, there was also an uncomfortable grain of truth in the contention that the Liberal party in its turn merely sought to create a rival caucus, resting on a less aristocratic basis and better versed in trade and finance, but no less oligarchic in aims and outlook.

Already in 1890 Sturdza, who had studied in Bonn and Munich and was a frank admirer of German culture, had published a pamphlet called "Europe, Russia and Roumania", in which he warned against a Russian Constantinople, treated the Roumanians as "a dam against the advance and designs of union of the Slav races" and claimed that "a policy of neutrality not only has no sense, but simply means treason to the nation and the betrayal of its highest interests". In October 1893, having in the interval been elected leader of his party, he wrote two short memoranda on the difficulties created for the alliance by Magyar chauvinism. He freely recognised that the Magyars and Roumanians had certain common interests against the Slav danger, but insisted that the latter were too tough to yield to Magyarisation and that the quarrel between them was equivalent to joint suicide. "The Magyars", he pointed out, and here he touched the very kernel of the problem during the fifty years of Dualism, "will not see that Hungary only assumes an important position in the European commonwealth because it forms part of the Habsburg Monarchy." Much of his argument was devoted to proving that "irredentism" had as yet but little hold upon the Transylvanian Roumanians, who looked above all to Vienna and to the house of Habsburg for deliverance, but, he continued, the Magyars by their brutal persecutions (and he might have added the Habsburg monarch, by condoning them) were doing their very best to turn their imaginary terrors to reality and to make Bucarest the centre of the movement. It was above all his closing argument—that the Magyars were undermining Roumania's adhesion to the Dreibund and so opening the door to Russian aggression—which appealed so strongly to King Charles and led him to show the memoranda to Bülow and warmly endorse their contents.[1]

Perhaps encouraged by this approval, Sturdza on 9 December 1893 addressed the Roumanian Senate at great length on Magyar-Roumanian relations. His central note was that Roumania was surrounded by Roumanians—almost as many outside as inside the kingdom —and that it was for her a capital interest that not one of them should go under. After a full statistical survey of the racial problem in Hungary, 1867, he asserted that since Hungary had been detached from Austria in the old principle inscribed on the Vienna Burg—"Justitia regnorum fundamentum"—had been discarded. He was however careful not to endorse the claim of autonomy for Transylvania, but simply to insist that the Roumanians should be immune from the danger of Magyarisation, assured full equality with other citizens, and free to petition the throne without punishment. For the Roumanian Parliament to remain silent as to the fate of its kinsmen would mean, he forcibly argued, that "we had only exchanged our vassalage to the Turk for vassalage to Hungary". In conclusion, he repudiated all idea of conquering Transylvania, firstly because it was beyond the strength of Roumania, but above all because the maintenance of the monarchy was "an European necessity of the first order".[2]

Though Sturdza's speech secured for the first time European publicity for the question at issue, it did not for a moment check the

[1] *G.P.* VII, no. 1488—Bülow to Caprivi, 16 October 1893.
[2] Text as Appendix 42 of Brote, *Die rumänische Frage.*

Magyar onslaught. The Memorandum Trial of May 1894 caused intense excitement and anger, and this was accentuated by the public pronouncements of Wekerle, and other leading Magyar statesmen. The result was renewed activity on the part of the Cultural League, public meetings and violent press agitation; and this was in turn the subject of strong protests by Count Albert Apponyi and Albert Berzeviczy in the Hungarian Delegation. Count Kálnoky made a long answer, emphasising the unofficial character of the League, the powerlessness of the Roumanian Government in face of its own very liberal press laws, the relative insignificance of Daco-Roman aspirations, the desirability of friendly relations between the Monarchy and Roumania and the entire goodwill of official Bucarest[1]—in other words, he buried the question in amiable platitudes and evaded the central issue. Meanwhile Sturdza, it must be admitted, continued to make party capital out of the whole affair. He had some excuse for hinting that the ruling boiars had more in common with the Magyar magnates than with their former Roumanian serfs: but he knew full well that intervention on the part of the Government was quite impossible, and he was gratuitously stirring the embers when he made known the details of public moneys assigned for the support of Vlach schools in Macedonia, which exceeded tenfold the grant to the needy denominational schools in Transylvania.

When Sturdza stated that no responsible person in Roumania dreamt of the conquest of Transylvania, he only spoke the bare truth: the European constellation of the nineties made such a programme fantastic and the Russian danger still darkened the whole Roumanian horizon. Even as late as 1910 or 1912 it is safe to assert that the overwhelming majority of Roumanians, though convinced in their inner consciousness that unity would some day come, did not expect it in their own lifetime and were content to think that it would be realised by their grandchildren. There were even many earnest and deserving patriots who, realising that universal war would be too high a price to pay for unity, were ready to contemplate its achievement through some kind of federal union with the Habsburg Monarchy, assuring the survival of their monarch, Parliament and institutions on the same honourable terms as Bavaria then enjoyed within a federal Germany. A compromise which to-day, with "Great Roumania" before our eyes, may seem treason to the national ideals, was not really so at the close of last century: and we shall see later that men as diverse as Aurel Popo-

[1] Text as Appendix 48 of Brote, *op. cit.*

vici, the Archduke Francis Ferdinand, Lueger and Conrad were not building merely upon air. What really rendered such a dream impossible and, as the years passed, won an increasing number of converts to the more drastic solution, was the stubborn hardening of the Magyar Pharaoh's heart, and the long series of provocations that followed the Memorandum Trial—the muzzling of the non-Magyar press, the notorious elections of 1896, the demonstrations at the Millenary Exhibition, the law on place-names and many other incidents. Moreover it followed logically that an increasing number of Roumanian intellectuals from Hungary crossed the Carpathians—among them Maiorescu, the poet Coşbuc, Ioan Slavici, and Aurel Popovici, of whom we shall hear later: and they would not have been human if they had not attached themselves to the super-patriots of the League. The mentality of the average Roumanian of the kingdom from the nineties onwards cannot possibly be summed up more clearly than in the words of Mr Take Ionescu when I first met him in Bucarest in 1909: "If I thought that Magyarisation could succeed, I should simply withdraw from public life altogether, for in that case it would not be worth while going on even here in the Kingdom. We should have no future".

Parallel with the growth of national feeling went a considerable agitation against foreign capitalists, and the Liberals denounced the new Mining Law for its undue liberality in the matter of leases, and in particular oil-field concessions, to foreigners. The party quarrel on this subject and the parallel issue of railway contracts grew so acute that the Liberals withdrew from the Chamber and attempted to boycott its proceedings. The king, realising the declining forces of the Conservatives, called Sturdza to power on 15 October 1895 and entrusted him with new elections, the result being that the Liberals obtained the usual superfluity of mandates, and the Conservatives shrank in their turn to a tiny fraction. In calling Sturdza, however, Charles had his eye upon foreign affairs: he was straining every nerve for improved relations with Austria-Hungary, and office imposed a muzzle upon the champion of Transylvanian rights. In September 1896 the newly regulated channel at the Iron Gates was inaugurated with great ceremony, and Francis Joseph went on from it to pay a state visit to Bucarest. The king found it tactful to pay his return visit at Budapest rather than at Vienna, though his own subjects resented this compliment to the Government of that rabid Magyariser, Baron Bánffy: and he used the added prestige which these visits brought in order to visit Tsar Nicholas II at Moscow in the summer of 1898, and thus restore relations which had remained all too formal since 1878. During the nineties Roumania made gigantic strides from the purely material point of view. The railway system was greatly extended and improved, so that in the decade preceding the War, thanks to the use of oil fuel, it was at once cleanly, cheap and efficient. In 1894 the new Sulina Canal was opened, and in the same year the great Danubian bridge of Cernavoda (stretching for twelve miles across the river and surrounding marshes, and costing 34,000,000 francs) was opened for traffic. The Black Sea terminus of Constanţa was then converted into a modern harbour, and a subsidised line of steamers began to ply to Constantinople and Egypt. A whole series of imposing public buildings began to rise in the capital, whose population increased from some 100,000 early in the century to close upon 300,000 in 1900. But in 1898 there was a disastrous failure of the harvest, and in the following year the value of Roumanian exports suddenly dropped from 283 to 149 million francs; import duties also fell by half, and a serious deficit resulted. The Alliance Israélite took advantage of the crisis to revive agitation in the Jewish question, and indeed economic stress in the north Moldavian towns and villages did lead to occasional anti-semite riots. International Jewish capital was increasingly disposed to impose a financial boycott upon Roumania.

Meanwhile the Liberal party encountered other unexpected difficulties. There were internal quarrels between Sturdza, Fleva and Aurelian, and Sturdza unwarily became involved in a dispute with the Orthodox hierarchy. The Metropolitan Gennadius attempted to secure personal control of the wealthy philanthropic foundations of Princess Brân-coveanu, but this was frustrated by her kinsmen and trustees, Prince Ştirbei and Prince George Bibescu: the tables were turned upon Gennadius, who was tried and convicted before the Holy Synod of simony and heresy and sentenced to deposition. But Sturdza turned public sympathy towards the delinquent prelate by his needlessly draconic action in sending the police to evict him from his palace and deport him to a monastery. Sturdza found it necessary to resign office, while a belated attempt was made to smooth over the worst of the scandal: but Aurelian, the stop-gap premier who succeeded him, developed a sudden appetite for power and could only be dislodged by a scandal impinging upon foreign policy—the affair of the Jeszenszky[1] decoration—and internal party unity proved to be badly shaken. Sturdza remained premier

[1] The public prosecutor in the Memorandum Trial. See *infra*, p. 415.

for exactly two years (April 1897–April 1899): what brought him down was the factious accusation of having betrayed the cause of his kinsmen in Hungary. The Bánffy Government had taken exception to Roumania's practice of subsidising certain national schools in Transylvania, in particular the Roumanian gymnasium at Braşov, and Sturdza had had no choice but to yield. But this and the fresh dues imposed by Budapest upon Danubian traffic roused public opinion to the length of street riots, and he was forced to resign.

The Conservatives were in no enviable position. Their veteran leader Catargiu died on the very day of Sturdza's fall: G. G. Cantacuzene, the new premier, and his foreign minister Lahovary, lacked prestige and experience, and despite the presence of Fleva, Manu (Finance), and Take Ionescu (Education) in the Cabinet, the key to the position lay more and more in the hands of Peter Carp, leader of the Junimist group. The new Government was unable to cope with the heavy deficit, Carp confessing openly to the Chamber that he lacked both the moral and material power to effect the necessary reductions in expenditure. Meanwhile the scandals connected with the harbour works of Constanţa reverberated through the country—the French contractor Hallier stopped work and then copied Strousberg's example by demanding compensation from the Roumanian Government. Pressure from Paris led to the appointment of an international court of arbitration, which awarded Hallier three million francs in excess of the contract, and the court had to be defended by a cordon of gendarmerie against the anger of the mob. The scandal assumed fresh forms when a brother of the ex-premier, General Manu, claimed a commission of 12 per cent. on the sum awarded to the French capitalists.[1] A loan was secured in Berlin, but only under most unfavourable terms, which were further stiffened by the necessity of appealing to a Paris bank to take up what remained unsubscribed. Carp tried to save himself by a visit to Berlin and openly Germanophil demonstrations: "all the world knows", he told the *Neue Freie Presse*, "that we lean towards the Triple Alliance. This is not a new policy, there is no party controversy upon it. Sturdza is as Germanophil as I am". This is to be explained not only by the perennial fear of Russia, but by an acute passing quarrel with Bulgaria, due to the murder of the Vlach schoolmaster Mihaileanu in Bucarest itself by a Bulgarian komitadji, and by anxiety for the fortifica-

---

[1] See Freiherr von Brackel, *Rumäniens Staatskredit in deutscher Beleuchtung*, p. 118.

tions of the new Cernavoda bridge. But the king was already longing for the return of the Liberals, and though Carp rallied the two Conservative factions for a month or two, he fell definitely on 25 March 1901.[1]

Sturdza may be said to have saved Roumania from financial distress and by orthodox budget methods to have brought her back to credit and prosperity. It was widely held that his rigid insistence upon economies and the abolition of sinecures would earn him the enmity of crown, army and bureaucracy: but he provided yet another proof that nothing succeeds like success. In the first year he balanced the budget at 218,500,000 francs, proclaimed "By ourselves" to be the Liberal motto, and announced that Roumania did not intend to go knocking at the doors of others, as though she lacked confidence in the moral force and energy of her own people. There was in Sturdza's pronouncements a certain note of xenophobia, which was to be even more marked in the premierships of Ionel and Vintila Brătianu. During the same period the Liberal minister of education, Spiru Haret, carried a stage further the reforms initiated by Take Ionescu and did much to reduce the heavy handicap of illiteracy among the peasant masses.

In foreign policy there had been a certain lull as the new century opened, due in very large measure to the steadying effect of the Austro-Russian agreement of 1897 for co-operation in the Near East. But ere long there was a recrudescence of komitadji activity in Macedonia (of which the Mihaileanu murder was simply an offshoot), and in 1903 it came to an open insurrection, which the Turks only quelled with some effort and no little bloodshed. The Bulgarians were the main aggressors and the chief sufferers, but the Roumanians became very anxious for their Vlach kinsmen—the so-called "Aromânii" or Macedo-Roumans. Sympathy and calculation played an equal part. The first Vlach school had been founded as early as 1864 at Tirnova, near Monastir, and ever since 1879 special subsidies for the benefit of Vlach schools in Turkey had been included in the Roumanian budget. At first it was only 14,000 francs, but by the turn of the century it had reached 500,000 and by 1912 a million francs! As the forging of statistics—racial, religious and educational—was an important function of all the rival propagandas, and as Turkish statistics were merely farcical, it is not surprising that the figures relating to the weakest of the five Macedonian nationalities, and also the latest in the field, should show most surprising contra-

[1] See the well-informed reports of the French minister in Bucarest. *F.D.D.* Series II, i, nos. 14, 57, 101, 151, 179.

dictions. That the Roumanian element absorbed into the Greek and Slav mass may have been as numerous as a million and a half is possible, though quite incapable of proof. The elaborate statistics claiming the number of Kutzo-Vlachs in the five western Vilayets as 516,000 about the year 1910, are almost certainly an exaggeration, while their opponents generally considered it generous to admit a fifth or a quarter of that number! Perhaps 250,000 would be near the mark, but it is a mere estimate. As the war of rival racial propagandas grew fiercer and concentrated upon the schools, the Vlachs, who were infinitely weaker than the Bulgarians or Greeks, or even the Serbs, found an able leader in Apostol Mărgărit, an Orthodox priest who founded a Roumanian gymnasium at Monastir. He was encouraged by the Porte as a counterweight to Bulgar and Greek, by the French Catholic missions in the hope that a Latin race might in the end be more amenable to proselytism, even by the Austrians, who were glad to divert Roumanian attention from their kinsmen north of the Carpathians. Needless to say, no one in Bucarest was naïve enough to suppose that the Vlachs of Perister or Pindus could ever be united with Roumania, in however loose a form: and the money expended upon this propaganda was in the nature of bread cast upon the waters, or as a cynic would have it, a speculative investment which events might justify. When Count Goluchowski bluntly asked Take Ionescu what possible use a group of Roumanians in the Pindus could be to Bucarest, that statesman replied that they might become "an element of compensation at the right moment".[1]

Meanwhile the Porte continued to play off the rival races against each other: typical of its tactics were the concessions made to Bulgaria in 1894 and again in 1897 in order to secure the neutrality of Bulgaria during the Turko-Greek War, and again the creation of a Serbian bishopric at Üsküb (Skoplje) in 1902, in order to divide the Balkan Slavs. Encouraged by this, the Roumanian Government kept pressing the Porte for a Roumanian bishopric at Monastir, and the Vlachs themselves curried favour at Constantinople by protests against the cession of Thessaly to Greece. A compromise was achieved in May 1905, when the Porte withheld the bishopric, but recognised a separate Vlach *millet*, no longer subject to the Greek patriarchate and possessed of a national liturgy. Here too the motive of promoting friction between Greece and Roumania was only too obvious, and indeed only too successful: for the chauvinists of Athens, who affected to regard the

[1] Quoted by the French minister, 25 June 1901. *F.D.D.* 2nd series, I, no. 301.

Vlachs (like the southern Albanians) as Greeks, were vocal in their protests; anti-Greek riots in Roumania soon came as an answer; and diplomatic relations between the two Governments were broken off for several years.

By this time Sturdza had already fallen from power. His last energies had been most successfully concentrated on financial reforms, but he was rapidly ageing, and inside his own party there was once more a powerful "Fronde" of younger men, led by Ion Brătianu's two able sons, Ionel and Vintila. At the end of 1904 the king recalled the Conservatives, still led by the somewhat colourless G. G. Cantacuzene: and Take Ionescu as finance minister carried through the conversion of the loan from 5 to 4 per cent. and effected the much-needed reform of exempting treasury officials from the vicious "general post" that followed changes of ministry. His attempt to found an Agrarian Bank was less successful, being opposed by the Liberals, whose great achievements in industrial and urban development led them for a time to overlook the crying needs of the agricultural population and the extent to which the new middle class was ready to exploit it in the mad hunt for swift fortunes. Roumania was one of the most fertile agricultural countries in Europe, and yet, as the more far-sighted of her sons recognised, the peasant was sunk in misery and neglect and had no say in the government of a country of which he was the real backbone. Even the king, his fears for the alliance long since allayed, allowed himself to be lulled into a false security by the rapidity with which Roumania recovered from the economic crisis of the late nineties, and reverted to the old panacea of Government by "Ins" and "Outs", retaining in his own hand the power to drive each successive drove from the trough of office when its appetite seemed to him sufficiently appeased.

The Great Peasant Rising of March 1907 came as a rude awakening. To the outside world, which took its scanty news about Roumania at second or third hand, the event seemed like a thunderbolt from a clear sky. But to the discerning few it caused no surprise. Already in 1904 Professor Basilescu had spoken of "the volcano trembling under our feet", and had prophesied that "a day will come when fire will devour the palaces, the granaries and all the property of those who exploit the peasantry". A year later the more moderate Spiru Haret, a truly liberal Minister of Education, and a prophet of peasant democracy, had referred to "the menacing character" of the situation and the "extreme urgency" of reform. Professor Saulescu, the Bucarest economist, in October 1906 expressed his view that if no reforms were introduced, "the Agrarian question will be solved by a dreadful *jacquerie*". Above all, Constantine Stere published a series of warning articles in *Viaţa Româneasca*, which were unhappily addressed to deaf ears. Yet no one in Roumania could speak with greater authority on peasant problems, for he added to his theoretic knowledge as an economic expert the practical insight which his own past life afforded: he came of a boiar family in Bessarabia, and his sympathies for liberal institutions and peasant wrongs had earned him banishment to Siberia, whence he had made his way to the free Kingdom and had not unnaturally become a confirmed enemy of Russia. "Thanks to the peasant's work", Stere had argued in 1906, "the country can export six times as much grain to-day, and yet the peasant has in no way profited by his work and productivity: on the contrary, his condition is increasingly miserable". It was the bare truth to affirm that "the peasant sells his labour at famine prices and pays an exorbitant rate for his land".[1]

The revolt broke out with remarkable suddenness on 15 March 1907 near Botoşani, and soon spread all over Moldavia. In the first instance there was plundering of Jewish houses, but it soon assumed a definitely agrarian, rather than anti-semite, character and was directed against the large tenant farmers and absentee landlords. The troops were called out and engaged with the rioters near Jassy itself, but as the movement spread southwards they were outnumbered near Văslui, and had to beat a retreat. The political situation was obscure, owing to the sudden death of the foreign minister, General Lahovary, on the first day of the outbreak, and owing to dissensions between the premier and Take Ionescu. Finding himself unequal to the task of restoring order, Cantacuzene resigned on 25 March, and the king summoned the Liberals under Sturdza, with Ionel Brătianu in charge of the Interior, and with Haret and Stelian as ministers of Education and Justice. Peter Carp spoke in the Chamber in favour of strong measures of repression, and two days later the new minister of War, General Averescu—a staff officer of high promise, trained in the Italian school—proclaimed a state of siege in Bucarest itself. Still the disorders continued. Bands of peasants in-

---

[1] The arable land of Roumania had risen from 19·9 per cent. of the total area in 1860 to 46·8 per cent. in 1906, the exports of cereals from 547,000 to 3,281,000 tons. Cf. C. Georgescu, *La Réforme Agraire*, p. 73.

vaded Galaţ, demanding the division of the great estates, and 4000 others from Teleorman began to march upon the capital. There was a fresh crop of pogroms, and wholesale systematic destruction of property. The Brâncoveanu estates in Oltenia, those of Ştirbei, Pherekyde, Florescu and Arion suffered especially severely. The revolt spread westwards into Wallachia and then up into the mountains. There were signs of anarchist organisation, subversive manifestos passed from hand to hand, and rumours of King Charles's death were put abroad. By the beginning of April 120,000 troops were under arms, the banks were everywhere guarded, a cordon was drawn round Bucarest itself, and the parliamentary session was closed, after Sturdza had made an appeal for urgent legislation and had shaken hands dramatically with Take Ionescu as leader of the Opposition, on the floor of the House. A royal proclamation promised the abolition of middlemen on the state lands, an uniform system of valuation, the restriction of agricultural leases to a maximum of 8000 acres and the extension of small holdings.

In this situation Averescu, Brătianu and the king between them agreed upon still more drastic measures. The whole country was divided into rayons, the pursuit of the marauders was undertaken by flying columns with mounted artillery, and reprisals were taken wherever the peasants refused to lay down their arms. In the Vlaşca district, not very far from Bucarest, three villages were bombarded and destroyed: and at Băileşci near Craiova there was something like a pitched battle between the troops and 10,000 insurgents armed with guns, axes, knives and scythes, who were in the end ruthlessly mown down. In many cases peasant soldiers showed a natural reluctance to fire upon their own kith and kin, but discipline was sternly enforced. It was estimated that within three days over 10,000 peasants were killed, and whole villages razed to the ground.[1] A bad impression was created by the arrest of Vasile Kogălniceanu, son of the great Moldavian statesman and a tireless worker in the cause of peasant education and the co-operative movement, and by the charges brought against the historian Professor Iorga and the anti-semite specialist Professor Cuza, both of whom had shown an all too rare comprehension for the peasants.[2] *The Times*

[1] Cf. G. D. Cioriceanu, *La Roumanie Économique*, p. 328; T. Dragu, *La Politique Roumaine après les troubles agraires*, p. 8.

[2] It was at this time that Christian Rakovsky, a Bulgarian of Roumanian citizenship, and founder of the infant Socialist party in Bucarest, was illegally expelled from the country, and began that career of agitation which was to end as Russian Bolshevik commissary and ambassador.

correspondent, J. D. Bourchier, when received in audience by the king, was amazed to find that he looked at the whole affair through narrowly military spectacles and was almost solely concerned with its disciplinary side.[1] Charles received characteristic congratulations from Francis Joseph, who had begun to concentrate troops along the Transylvanian border, in case foreign help should prove necessary: and it has been freely hinted that repression was the price paid for averting intervention both from Austria and from Russia, and again that the king threatened abdication, if a single Austrian soldier crossed the frontier.[2]

The full facts about the rising will probably never be known: for some years after the War it transpired that the official *dossiers* containing its innermost secrets had disappeared from the ministries of War and Interior, having presumably been removed by those politicians upon whose political past they threw a lurid or embarrassing light. But when once the revolt was over, a genuine, if still quite inadequate, attempt was made to redress the worst of the peasant grievances. In post-war retrospect Vintila Brătianu admitted very frankly that "none of the earlier reforms had sufficiently eased the needs of the peasant class" and affirmed that the outburst had "roused the conscience of the political parties". A very competent economic authority in reference to these events has cynically noted that "as a result of the repression the Liberal party took the title of the National Liberal Party".[3] It would be fairer to say that when the danger was over, both parties breathed again and contented themselves with homœopathic remedies which did not probe to the root of the evil, but also that henceforth agrarian reform remained as a foremost plank in the Liberal programme and was carried through—at the eleventh hour, it is true, but not too late to avert utter disaster.

The new law on agricultural contracts, passed in December 1907, was intended to redress the balance which had hitherto been weighed down against the labourers, to check the old system, or lack of system, under which land leases and labour contracts had been inextricably mixed, and the peasant thus exposed to many abuses. It was made

[1] Mr Mitrany alludes to the "baffling fact" that in the "four crowded volumes" of the king's memoirs (*Aus dem Leben*), "the peasant question is remembered in not one single line".

[2] Marghiloman, *Note Politice*, I, p. 62. To that statesman the king said on 22 March 1907, "Toute la Roumanie est à refaire, car tout a sombré" (*ibid.* p. 60).

[3] Cioriceanu, *op. cit.* p. 328.

possible to forbid the peasant to gather in the maize, pending some unsettled debt, and district commissions in which peasant as well as landlord were represented, were set up to fix a minimum wage. The restriction placed upon the use of school children in the fields was well
meant, but sometimes worked out in a contrary sense. An attempt was
also made to solve the vital problem of grazing, by assigning lands to
the communes: here conservative opposition whittled down the concessions, though the main difficulties were really due to the fairly recent
inroads of the boiar class upon the secular right of enclosure. Finally
a new Casa Rurala, or Land Office, was created, provided with the
necessary capital by the state and enjoying a monopoly of thirty years:
its main object was to promote the transfer of land from the big landlords to the peasants, and scientific commassation of existing holdings,
on lines adopted with such beneficial effects in Germany at the close of
the century. The real flaw in all this legislation was that its execution
still remained in the hands of the dominant class. It is not too much to
say that "the big landlord was himself the law", since he and his tenant
were entrenched in control of the commune, thanks above all to a
regular tariff for the bribery of all officials, even up to the sub-prefect.[1]
In 1913 Vintila Brătianu—then it is true, in opposition—admitted that
the new law on contracts had been "deliberately ignored"[2] and while
commons for grazing had really been created on all the numerous state
domains, this process had by the eve of the Great War only been
carried out on one quarter of the private estates, thanks above all to the
passive resistance of the landed class. "If the riches of one social class
increase out of all proportion, without productive activity worth mentioning on its part, this can only happen at the expense of other classes"[3]:
and this is exactly what was taking place in Roumania. The decade
following the great harvest failure and the consequent financial crisis
was on the contrary a period of unexampled prosperity and commercial
development for Roumania, as for many parts of Europe: but thanks
to the narrow political structure of the state, the agricultural masses did
not share to any appreciable extent in the expanding profits of the boiar
and the big tenant farmer: and they were by now well able to contrast
their lot with that of the Bulgarian and Serbian peasant, who owned his
land, and was in each case the decisive factor in the state.

[1] M. Şerban, *Rumäniens Agrarverhältnisse*, pp. 87–92. The most authoritative
account is in R. Rosetti's *Pământul, Ţăranii şi Stăpanii în Moldova*.

[2] Mitrany, *op. cit.* pp. 85–90.          [3] Şerban, *op. cit.* p. 87.

CHAPTER XIII

# TRANSYLVANIA UNDER THE DUAL SYSTEM

"Flere possim, sed juvare non"—ŞAGUNA, 1865.

"Ihr habt bei Nacht und Nebel gekriegt,
Und euer Feind, er liegt besiegt:
Doch als man die Leiche beim Licht erkannt,
Da war's euer eigenes Vaterland."

"Ungarn"—GRILLPARZER.

The political transformation of the Habsburg Monarchy, consummated by the victory of Prussia and the urgent necessity of appeasing Magyar discontent, had most disastrous results for the Roumanian subjects of the emperor. The cup was dashed to the ground when it had almost touched their lips. The national and linguistic rights which the despised helots of Transylvania had for so many generations demanded in vain, had at last been accorded by the Diet of 1863: but their validity had been strongly challenged, and Schmerling's constitutional experiment collapsed before they had ever come into force. Moreover, so long as Transylvania remained an unit, the Roumanians inside it, however curtailed of their rights, formed an absolute majority of the population and had a reasonable certainty of asserting themselves in the future. But its incorporation with Hungary reduced them, even in conjunction with their brethren of the border counties, to a powerless minority, comprising only 15 per cent. of the total population of the lands of the Holy Crown. The life of the smaller unit was to be merged in the wider history of Hungary, and there was no redress, as that other privileged nation, the Saxons, was soon to learn to its cost.

Their abandonment by the emperor came as a cruel shock to the whole Roumanian community, and there were at once two currents of opinion. The one, led by the historian Bariţiu and Ioan Raţiu, the advocate of the Uniate metropolitan, favoured an active campaign of agitation and resistance, the other, under Archbishop Şaguna, held that such tactics would only endanger such national concessions as they might still hope to secure. In February 1865 Şaguna had been received in audience by Francis Joseph, who had publicly expressed "complete confidence" in him and in the Roumanian people: in August he was again received, but to the end of his life preserved rigid silence as to what then passed between them.[1] All that is certain is that Şaguna, in still hoping to conduct to a successful issue the negotiations for Church autonomy (now in an advanced stage), declined to sign any memorial to the crown unless it was couched in such terms as need not offend the new regime. Bariţiu and Raţiu then acted alone, and the latter was able to present their joint memorial to the emperor on 31 December: but though it contained an able summary of constitutional development and a moving appeal to save the identity of Transylvania, it of course remained entirely without effect.[2]

It was in this connection that Şaguna coined the memorable and moving phrase which was to remain the motto of the ensuing period— "Flere possim, sed juvare non". In a private letter about the same time he argued that the main task was to "consider those fledglings which remain true to their nature. Duck's eggs, put under a hen, hatch out ducks, but hen's eggs, put under a turkey, hatch out chickens. And so we must always remain Roumanians, whatever may be the regime and its motto. It goes without saying that, as hitherto, so in future, we shall hold with immovable faith to the Emperor and the legal order established by him.... My whole doctrine reduces itself to the proverb, 'Act and be silent (fă şi taci)'".[3] Or, as he said in another connection, "Vana sine viribus ira": the essential thing was "that with Roumanian vigour we may give effect to the principle of equal national rights".[4] There were of course at the time some who condemned Şaguna as sterile and negative, but before he died even they recognised that he was a great constructive statesman who, realising the political constellation to be unfavourable, for that very reason concentrated all the more upon the task of church organisation. Success had nearly crowned his efforts before the change came, and he was resolved to do nothing that might compromise the result. Already in 1864 the Serbian metropolitan and synod had at long last consented to the separation of the Serbian and Roumanian Orthodox: the first draft of an Organic Statute had been completed (significantly enough by a commission of four priests and

[1] Bariţiu (*op. cit.* III, p. 315), quotes the alleged saying of Şaguna: "Your Majesty's will is a command for the Roumanian nation", but admits that it is not vouched for or proved.
[2] Full text in Appendix 27 of Brote, *op. cit.* pp. 225–31.
[3] Lupaş, *Istoria bisericească a Românilor Ardeleni*, p. 206.
[4] Lupaş, *Mitropolitul Şaguna*, p. 240.

eight *laymen*), and on 24 December 1864 an imperial decree had established a Roumanian metropolitan see at Sibiu (Hermannstadt), with two suffragan sees at Arad and Caransebeş. It is true that he had pressed for three more sees at Timişoara, Cluj and Oradea Mare and for the inclusion of the Bukovina within his jurisdiction: but the Magyars objected to any strengthening of the Roumanian element in the two towns which were to be centres of Magyarisation in Transylvania and the Banat, the Uniates quite reasonably opposed the erection of a rival bishopric in Oradea Mare, while the claim to Bukovina was rejected as suspect and all too likely to encourage unionist sentiment.

None the less there remained much that was of the utmost importance, and it was above all Şaguna's tactical reserve, and the prestige which his person enjoyed in Vienna and even in Budapest, that led to the embodiment of the draft statute in Law IX of the new Hungarian Parliament (24 June 1868). This new constitution deserves closer attention than it has hitherto received, not merely because it proved to be the real bulwark of Roumanian nationality in the next half century, but because it was an almost unique experiment in ecclesiastical government, blending as it does to a remarkable degree the episcopal and presbyterian systems and assuring unusual importance to the lay element and to the principle of democratic election. While retaining all matters of dogma, ritual and discipline in their own hands for decision in the Episcopal Synod, the hierarchy rests upon popular election—the metropolitan by the Church Congress, each Bishop by his own Episcopal Synod, and the clergy in each case by the vote of the Parochial Synod—in other words of all male parishioners, being self-supporting and of good character. Throughout each ascending grade of church representation the lay element is very strong. In the Eparchial Synod there are twenty clerical and forty lay members; the diocese being divided into twenty districts, each sending three deputies—that is, one priest elected by the clergy and two laymen elected by the Parochial Synod. In the National Church Congress again, there are thirty clerical and sixty lay members: but when a vacancy in the metropolitan see occurs, Congress is specially convoked with an augmented membership of 120 and is bound to elect (by ballot, in the Cathedral Church), within three months of the last prelate's death. The Consistory, in which again elected laymen play their part, is divided into a Church Senate for ecclesiastical appeals, a School Senate for disciplinary matters in the Church schools, the examination of candidates and the provision of catechists, and an Epitrophal Senate for the administration of Church funds and property, library, vestments, etc. There is also a Protopresbyteral Court, consisting of seven clergy, for disputes between the clergy, complaints against them, electoral enquiries and matrimonial suits; and the archpriest who presides has undergone a special election in a lower court.[1] There can be no doubt that the proximity of the Magyar Calvinists and the influence which they had already exercised (though doubtless by intrusion) upon the Orthodox since the sixteenth century, had familiarised the Roumanian Orthodox leaders with democratic methods of Church government, and using a foundation which the Magyar authorities would be disposed to welcome as their own, they built a superstructure admirably adapted for national defence. As Alexander Mocsónyi once said, after the system had undergone three decades of testing, "clergy and people, priests and laymen, stand at every point in most intimate contact one with another, and from the constant co-operation of these two constituent elements of the Church a vital process takes its source".[2]

Şaguna steered this statute through the rocks of the Budapest Parliament and through the first meeting of the Church Congress, where some foolish hotheads were inclined to fancy him as "sold to the Magyars".[3] But he did not stop there. Starting from the standpoint that "schools and literary institutions are an essential part of the Church",[4] and deeply conscious of the backward conditions of his people, he established a printing press at Sibiu, issued liturgies and religious books, put the theological seminary on a new footing, extended the library and above all, spared no effort in increasing the number of primary schools maintained by the Orthodox Church and equipping the all too few Roumanian gymnasia, notably at Braşov, Lugoş and Brad. In all this he put forward as his motto, "Loyalty to the throne, freedom in order, order in freedom". When he died in 1873, it was already possible to survey the immense progress made since he first became bishop, and it is not too much to say that he was already venerated, even by many Roumanians outside his fold, as "a man sent from God". George Bariţiu, who held very different political

---

[1] Full and precise details are to be found in Silbernagl, *Verfassung und gegenwärtiger Bestand sämmtlicher Kirchen des Orients*.
[2] Lupaş, *Mitropolitul Şaguna*, p. 295.
[3] Cf. *Cartea de Aur*, v, p. 5.
[4] Lupaş, *op. cit.* p. 297.

views and certainly cannot be suspected of blind adulation, gave public expression to this feeling and declared that Şaguna "had a plan so wide and grandiose as to leave his successors at least 100 years of work before it could be realised in its entirety".[1] An orator in the Roumanian Senate justly celebrated him as "the Star of Orthodoxy, who has won for the Roumanians north of the Carpathians rights for which they have shed tears through many centuries". His imposing personality, flowing beard and piercing eyes, strengthened the impression which he made upon friend and foe alike. He was indeed of the same type as those medieval churchmen who towered above the mediocrity and ignorance of their age: and his services to the Roumanian national cause were no less signal than those of his great contemporary, Bishop Strossmayer, to the cause of Jugoslav culture and national unity.

Meanwhile the Ausgleich settlement was an accomplished fact, and the main current among the Roumanians was as yet in favour of attending the reconstituted Hungarian Parliament. But when Macelariu attempted to speak there in Roumanian, he was abruptly brought to order and forbidden by the president, who declared that "without use of the mother tongue, fatherland and nationality are a mere illusion". This may stand as a classic illustration of the Magyar mentality, which identified the fatherland with one particular race, and then denounced the other races as unpatriotic in protesting. The Roumanian deputies abandoned the attempt to use their own language, but they boldly put forward a programme of Transylvanian autonomy and thus roused great indignation among the Magyars. It is interesting to cite the attitude of one deputy in particular. Paul Hunfalvy, a Magyarised German whose original name was Hundsdorfer, and who now became prominent as an historical controversialist and wrote several standard works on Hungarian ethnography and Roumanian origins, allowed himself during a debate to fling at the Roumanians this revealing phrase: "Don't provoke us to employ towards the other nations the methods of total extermination employed by the Anglo-Saxons towards the Red Indians of North America".[2] This outburst was a mere foretaste of what was coming. It was doubtless encouraged by the attitude of Koloman Tisza—then still in partial opposition as leader of the Left and critic of the Dual System—who challenged the arguments of the Roumanian deputies as to "equal rights" and declared that the nationalities

[1] Lupaş, op. cit. p. 327.
[2] Iorga, *Histoire des Roumains de Transylvanie*, II, pp. 361-4.

PLATE XV

ANDREIU ŞAGUNA

must follow the Magyar proverb, "Be silent and pay". Their interest, he said, was not to learn their own language in school, but to become assimilated as quickly as possible.[1]

In December 1868 Parliament passed a law professing to regulate the details of the Union (XLIII). By it the special privileges of the various nationalities were abolished, and the equality of all citizens was proclaimed, irrespective of race or religion. But how this was already being interpreted is shown by the fact that as early as March 1867 the ministry was empowered by Parliament, pending final legislation, "to carry out the necessary measures with regard to the government, administration and justice in Transylvania, *on its own responsibility and according to its own views*". On the strength of this, the Saxon count, Conrad Schmidt, was promptly forbidden to summon the Saxon University (the autonomous body by which the nation had been governed for centuries), and in February 1868 was relieved of office, though he had been appointed for life, and not by the Government, but by the University. By Law XLIII (§ 9) the Saxons were deprived of the historic right of electing their count, and the appointment was vested in the crown, under the advice of the Hungarian Cabinet. The privileges of the University were solemnly guaranteed by § 11, and the ministry was to prepare a more detailed law regulating self-government on Saxon territory (the Fundus Regius or Königsboden), after previous consultation with those concerned.

A short digression is necessary to show how these pledges were kept: for if the new regime rode thus roughshod over one of the three privileged Nations, it may be imagined how much consideration was shown to the despised Roumanians. When county government was reorganised in 1870 (Law XLII), formal reference was again made (§ 88) to the special law which was to be devoted to Saxon affairs, but year after year passed, and no such law was ever introduced. Meanwhile the minister of the interior, exercising his provisional powers, aimed repeated blows at the autonomy which he was solemnly pledged to respect. In January 1869 he issued a decree annexing sixteen Roumanian communes to the See (or Stuhl) of Hermannstadt, and ten Magyar and Roumanian communes to that of Kronstadt, the object being to undermine their purely German character, and in March of the same year a further decree imposed fresh rules for the election of representative bodies and local officials, and dispensed with proofs of legal training.

[1] "Csit, hallgas és fizés"—debate of 23 November 1868 on primary education.

In 1871 the new law regulating the communes was applied to the Saxons also, in direct contravention of the Act of Union. The Magyar language was introduced into the Saxon administration (in virtue of XLIV, 1868), which had hitherto been conducted in German only, and became the official language in the courts of first instance (in defiance of the same law, §§ 7, 8 and 9). At last, in April 1876 a law was introduced, not carrying out, but directly violating, the pledge of the Act of Union (XII, 1876). The office of Saxon count was annulled, the University's sphere of influence was restricted to control of its property, and its general assembly placed at the discretion of the high sheriff of Sibiu county. Further inroads on Saxon rights were made by Law XXXIII of 1876, which redistributed the counties in such a way as to play off Saxon and Roumanian against each other and to leave the Magyars whenever possible as the finger on the balance. All these measures were justified publicly as a necessary curtailment of medieval anachronisms: Baron Kemény declared that the Saxons had forfeited their rights by sending deputies to the Reichsrat under Schmerling: while Koloman Tisza argued that parliamentary power stands higher than any rights.[1] The small numbers of the Saxons made them an easy prey, and though their wealth, culture and independent habits delayed the process of decay, the citadel of their autonomy had been stormed, and for the next generation they played a losing game, without much help from their kinsmen in Central Europe.

It is necessary to turn back to the Ausgleich settlement, of which three essential corollaries were the Union of Transylvania, the Compromise with Croatia and the Law of Nationalities. This latter law (XLIV, 1868) was peculiarly the work of Deák himself and still more of Baron Joseph Eötvös, a profound student of political ideas and the theory of nationality, and the regenerator of Hungary's educational system: and there can be no doubt that it was framed in perfectly good faith and inspired by liberal ideas. It is true that even they, and far more Tisza and his chauvinist young guard, regarded assimilation as the ideal solution of the racial problem: but they differed from him radically in their choice of methods. They held that a policy of mildness and concession would prove more efficacious than restrictive measures, and that Magyar culture, if it was to prove equal to the task of assimilation, could only conquer in virtue of its innate superiority and moral force.

[1] *Preussische Jahrbücher*, XLVIII, p. 168. See also Löher, *Das Erwürgen der deutschen Nationalität in Ungarn.*

For two generations to come this law, guaranteeing the Equal Rights of the Nationalities, was to be quoted before the world as the proof of Hungary's unexampled racial tolerance: but while no one who studies its text can deny that it was generously planned and adequate in its pledges, it suffered from one fatal defect—that from the very outset it remained a dead letter. It rested in the first instance upon a fundamental confusion between "Hungarian" and "Magyar", or rather the deliberate refusal to distinguish between the two. "A magyar nemzet" was applied to the whole Hungarian nation—"the indivisible unitary Magyar nation", to quote the text of the law—but was continually identified with "the ruling nation" (*az uralkodó nemzet*): while another phrase in common use was "foreign inhabitants" (*idegen ajkuak*), applied to all the non-Magyar races, whether indigenous or domiciled in Hungary for many centuries.

The most important provisions of this law may be summarised under five heads[1]: (1) The right of every member of a County Assembly to speak in his mother tongue; the use of a second language for the minutes, if one-fifth of the members should desire it, and still wider linguistic rights in the local communal assemblies. This was evaded by a peculiar franchise, which left half the seats in the hands of the "Virilists" (or principal taxpayers) and assigned seats to a number of permanent officials, with the result that the Magyars almost invariably had a crushing majority and prevented such rules from ever coming into force. On the rare occasions when a serious attempt was made to assert the right, it was repudiated with energy by the chauvinists and dismissed by the more moderate as superfluous, since the non-Magyar representatives almost without exception understood the Magyar language. (2) The obligation upon administrative officials to know and use the language of the districts where they were employed. Not merely was this deliberately disregarded from the outset, but it soon became the practice to insist upon (at any rate external) Magyarisation as a qualification for office, to draft the few non-Magyars who ran the gauntlet of the public service to purely Magyar districts and to serve the non-Magyar districts with ardent Magyars who often could not speak the local language and sought to spread a knowledge of the "language of state" by their own stubborn insistence on its use. How little attempt was made to apply

[1] For a detailed analysis, see my *Racial Problems in Hungary*, pp. 147–60, and Appendix III for a full translation of the text. The German text is to be found in Appendix 29 of Brote, *op. cit.* pp. 236–40.

this section of the law, may be gathered from a significant circular issued by Count Andrássy the younger, as minister of the interior a whole generation later, in December 1907: for in it he urged the need for making it effective if the officials were not to remain like foreigners among the non-Magyar population. (3) The promise to employ non-Magyars in administrative and judicial posts; and not to allow nationality to be a disqualification for any post, especially that of high sheriff of a county (föispán). Yet in actual practice, though in eleven counties the Roumanians, in seven counties the Slovaks, formed a majority of from 66 to 96 per cent. of the population, no Roumanian or Slovak was ever appointed high sheriff or vice-sheriff after 1870. At that date nearly one-third of the officials in Transylvania were Roumanian by birth, but even by 1891 they had sunk to under 6 per cent. instead of about 60 per cent. on a basis of population, and only held subordinate positions: and this tendency was still further accentuated during the next two decades. The Memorandum of 1892 was able to point out that in the sixty-five District Courts of Hungary (twenty-three of which were in Roumanian territory) only one single Roumanian had ever been appointed president, that in the ministries the Roumanians were virtually unrepresented, that there was only one Roumanian inspector of education, and only one Roumanian holding a chair at the two Universities. (4) The rights of the mother tongue were strictly guaranteed in the district courts of justice, and special rules were laid down for interpreting at the court's expense and issuing the verdict in the language of the parties concerned. But the Law of Nationalities had barely been two years in existence, when the whole judicial system of Hungary was reorganised by Law IV of 1869. This involved the abolition of the old county courts, and as the rights assured to the nationalities in them were not extended to the newly created courts, the most essential judicial concessions fell at once into abeyance and were never renewed in any subsequent legislation.[1] In other words, Hungarian justice, from the first instance to the last, was completely Magyarised: and the Slovak patriot, Father Andrew Hlinka, spoke the bare truth when he declared that "the non-Magyar peasant stood like an ox, dumb before the courts of his native land"—a phrase which brought down upon its author a severe sentence for "incitement of one nationality against another". (5) Most vital of all, perhaps, was the solemn educational pledge given by the state under

---

[1] Yet Magyar writers of the pre-war decade continued to quote the judicial sections of XLIV, 1868, as though they were still in force.

§ 17. "Since the success of public instruction, from the standpoint of general culture and wellbeing, is one of the highest aims of the state, the latter is bound to ensure that all citizens, of whatever nationality, living together in considerable numbers, shall be able in the neighbourhood of their homes to obtain instruction in their mother tongues, up to the point where the higher academic culture begins." In other words, the state pledged itself to provide primary and secondary education for all its citizens in the mother tongue. In practice, however, the state schools were made the medium of unrestrained Magyarisation. The non-Magyar languages were completely banned at the universities, and we shall see that the new University of Kolozsvár was soon to become a focus of propagandist effort against the Roumanians. In all the gymnasia and modern schools maintained by the state, neither German, Slovak, Ruthene nor Roumanian were in use, and the same applied to all grammar schools, industrial, commercial and agricultural schools under state management. A terrific premium was set upon Magyarisation.

This was not all. The Slovaks had three *denominational* secondary schools of their own, but these were closed in 1874, and for the next forty-four years the whole Slovak nation was deliberately kept without any secondary school—being given none by the state and being repeatedly refused permission to found any by private enterprise. The Ruthenes never had a secondary school of their own under Hungary, the Serbian Orthodox Church possessed one Gymnasium at Novi Sad. The Swabian Germans had none, but the Saxons, thanks to their ancient autonomy as a "Nation" and the cultural funds which they had accumulated, and also to the close identity between their nationality and the Lutheran faith, were able to maintain no less than five Gymnasia, one "Realgymnasium" and two other incomplete middle schools.[1] The position of the Roumanians in education was a somewhat special one and will become clearer when we come to deal with the Apponyi Education Acts of 1907. During the eighties and nineties they possessed two Uniate Gymnasia at Blaj and Beiuş (Belényes), one Orthodox Gymnasium and one incomplete Real School at Braşov and a private Gymnasium at Năsăud (Naszód). In 1870 the Orthodox and Uniate Churches respectively possessed 1604 and 2058 primary schools, three-quarters of the former and

[1] At Bistritz, Kronstadt, Mediasch, Hermannstadt and Schässburg; at Hermannstadt; and at Sächsisch-Reen and Kronstadt. All these institutions still exist, though they have fallen upon hard times.

four-fifths of the latter being Roumanian (the balance being Serb and Ruthene).[1]

It is essential to realise that the first census taken after the Ausgleich, in 1869, revealed the facts that 63 per cent. of the whole population of Hungary was altogether illiterate, while another 9.7 per cent. could read but not write: that 1598 communes were without any school whatever: that 24 per cent. of the teachers were without diplomas, that there was only one qualified teacher for every 170 children liable to attend school, and that of these barely 48 per cent. attended. The Primary Education Act (XXXVIII) of 1868 was a gallant and enlightened attempt to remedy these evils, and was quite definitely based on the assumption that among so backward a population normal conditions could only be attained through the medium of the mother tongue.[2] But unhappily its creator, Baron Eötvös, with whom this idea was fundamental and unchallengeable,[3] died in 1871, and henceforward the whole trend of Hungarian education was in the very opposite direction. "The secondary school", wrote a well-known Magyar political writer, Béla Grünwald, the accomplice of Koloman Tisza in destroying the Slovak Gymnasia, "is like a huge machine, at one end of which the Slovak youths are thrown in by hundreds, and at the other end of which they come out as Magyars":[4] and exactly the same applies to the Roumanians, though they were better organised for resistance than their fellow-victims. "The primary school", wrote a Hungarian official report, "is one of the most powerful means of consolidation for the Hungarian national state." And again, "For the Magyars it (i.e. the state school in mixed districts) guarantees the augmentation of their expansive force and extends the race towards the frontier".[5]

---

[1] The numbers rose to 1809 and 2220 in 1880, to 1823 and 2166 in 1890, and to 1792 and 2067 in 1903. By the latter year, out of a total number of 16,405 primary schools, 9294 were purely Magyar, 3740 others mixed, only 305 German, 477 Slovak, 64 Ruthene, 154 Serbo-Croat. The Roumanians had 2339 *all denominational*, and clung to them as their last stronghold. See *Ungarisches Statistisches Jahrbuch*, XII (1904), p. 357.

[2] This is expressly stated by the official publication of the ministry of education in 1900—*L'Enseignement en Hongrie*, pp. 94–5.

[3] See his books *Über die Gleichberechtigung der Nationalitäten in Oesterreich.* (1850), *Der Einfluss der herrschenden Ideen des XIXten Jahrhunderts auf den Staat* (1854) and *Die Nationalitätenfrage* (1865). "Nationality", he wrote on one occasion, "is, like religion, a matter of the spirit, and so belongs to those affairs which cannot be finally decided by the commands of a majority, but only through mutual understanding" (p. 65).

[4] *A Felvidék*, p. 140.          [5] *L'Enseignement en Hongrie*, pp. 94–5, 169.

In the period of feverish legislative activity which followed the Ausgleich, the Roumanians took their part in the parliamentary debates. In 1869 they had twenty-five deputies, the foremost of whom were Alexander Mocsónyi, Vincent Babeş, Macelariu and Alois Vlad: and it is worth noting that they followed Şaguna's line of argument—that unsatisfactory laws, once sanctioned, could only be undone by legal means[1]—whereas Bariţiu advocated passivity and abstention. As the wave of Magyar chauvinism rose in the seventies, it became increasingly difficult for the non-Magyars to make headway against constant insult and intimidation. The classical plea of Mocsónyi (30 June 1870) in favour of racial equality and compromise—listened to with marked attention and respect by Deák himself[2]—was the last speech of its kind from the non-Magyar benches. Already one deputy had roughly warned them that "those whom the Act of Union does not please can emigrate, but he who remains must make the best of it". The appeals of Saxon and Roumanian alike were more and more greeted by cries of "Go to Dresden" or "Go to Bucarest": their request for a subvention for a Roumanian national theatre was rejected almost as an insult.[3] One last effort to obtain a hearing was made in a memorandum addressed to Parliament in 1872[4]—which recited the many points in which the Law of Nationalities was not applied or directly contravened, and appealed for a constitutional discussion of Roumanian grievances and an address to the sovereign.

With Deák in retirement, Eötvös dead, and Andrássy transferred as foreign minister to the Ballplatz, Koloman Tisza came rapidly to the front as leader of the reconstituted Liberal party, and for the fifteen years of his premiership (1875–1890) was far more truly dictator than Kossuth or Deák had ever been, establishing his predominance on a far-reaching system of electoral corruption and administrative trickery. The Magyars of the central plain had always formed the backbone of Kossuth's following, and still elected many deputies of the Party of Independence. Tisza therefore hit upon the ingenious method of turning the parliamentary scale by his control of the non-Magyar districts of the periphery: and for this purpose the non-Magyars either had to be reduced to complete subservience or kept from the polls by special devices. This explains the revised Electoral Law of 1874, which, in the

[1] Cf. *Cartea de Aur*, v, p. 5.
[2] *Ibid.* p. 407.        [3] *Ibid.* p. 287.
[4] Text in Appendix 31 of Brote, *op. cit.* pp. 251–75.

words of the official government organ, was so involved that "the confusion of Babel has really been erected into law".[1] Gerrymandering, unequal distribution, a highly complicated franchise, public voting, inadequate legal checks upon corruption and a deliberate mobilisation of officialdom in favour of the Government candidates—all this combined to produce Koloman Tisza's famous "Mameluke" system. This law still further increased the difficulties of election for non-Magyar candidates and did more than anything else to turn the scale in favour of abstention. A few Serb stalwarts still penetrated to Budapest, but from 1875 to 1906, with only the rarest exceptions, the Roumanians and Slovaks adopted and maintained the fatal policy of passivity. They thus not only lost all representation in the central Parliament and exercised a demoralising effect both upon the peasant masses and upon the rising generation of intellectuals, but also greatly increased the overconfidence of the Magyar chauvinists and created in them illusions which even the Great War has failed to dispel. As a result, Koloman Tisza acquired an almost despotic control of 250 constituencies and his party a safe majority for exactly thirty years. These seats he bestowed upon his followers as largesse for their loyal support: and in this way many a decayed aristocrat repaired the broken fortunes of his family, many a pliant official rose to riches and honour. This pseudo-Liberal regime rested above all upon a programme of Magyarisation.

Other incidents besides the new electoral law led to this sudden collapse of non-Magyar resistance. During 1874 the three Slovak Gymnasia—two Protestant and one Catholic—were closed by the Government on vague allegations of "Panslavism" (since the thirties an habitual nickname for Slovak national feeling): and in April 1875 the "Matica Slovenska" was also dissolved, and its entire funds, building, library and museum arbitrarily confiscated. In the following winter the Serb deputy Dr Polit ventured to interpellate the premier on this drastic action and to suggest that the funds should at least be restored to the original donors, in other words, to the Slovak nation. It was on this occasion, that Tisza made his famous retort, "There is no Slovak nation". Less known is his earlier sally against the Roumanian deputy Vincent Babeş, who had urged that the non-Magyars also should be taught their national history in school. There was no such thing as a "national" history of the non-Magyars, Tisza hotly contended. The reason why Babeş hated the Magyars so (here he begged the question)

[1] Pester Lloyd, 24 July 1894.

was clear enough: he had always gone to a non-Magyar, to a German, school, if indeed he had ever visited a school at all! The turn of the Serbs came in 1876, when amid the excitement of the Eastern crisis their leader Svetozar Miletić appealed for volunteers from the Banat, to fight for Serbia against the Turks. The Hungarian Government, which was ardently Turcophil and much alarmed at Russian policy, promptly arrested Miletić and Kazapinović without troubling about the former's parliamentary immunity. After awaiting trial for over a year he eventually received a sentence of five years for separatist tendencies, lost his reason, and did not long survive his release. The parting words of his political career were "hodie tibi, cras mihi" and "We meet again at Philippi": and his chief disciple Dr Polit quoted them in his maiden speech almost a generation later, when at last a small band of non-Magyar deputies re-entered the Hungarian Parliament.

A conference of Roumanian voters convoked at Sibiu in May 1875, declared that "the activists are not Roumanians, but traitors and Magyarone renegades".[1] This petulant outburst of despair was far removed from statesmanship: its excuse, if excuse there be, is to be found in the provisions of the new franchise, which were deliberately framed to promote Magyar supremacy. Based upon a combination of property, taxation, profession or official position and ancestral privileges, it left the proletariat almost unrepresented, and indeed barely 6 per cent. of the population had the vote. As there was no ballot, the "small man" was subjected to gross intimidation, and it was the commonest thing for voters to be brought between the fixed bayonets of gendarmes, to vote for the official candidate. Even by the turn of the century nearly one-third of the deputies were elected by less than 100, and close upon two-thirds by less than 1000, votes.[2] But perhaps the most interesting feature of the new law was its maintenance of a special franchise for Transylvania—only 3·2 per cent. of the population being enfranchised, as against 6·5 to 7·5 per cent. in the central districts of Hungary proper. The more Roumanian a county was, the fewer voters did it possess. Thus out of the seventy-four deputies whom Transylvania sent to Budapest, thirty-five represented the four Magyar counties and the chief towns, which together formed only 20 per cent. of the population, whereas only thirty deputies represented the remaining 72 per cent. of the population, which was predominantly Roumanian.

[1] *Cartea de Aur*, VI, p. 511.
[2] For full details, see Chapter I of my *Corruption and Reform in Hungary* (1911).

In other words, there was among the Roumanians an average of one deputy to every 50–60,000 inhabitants, but among the Székels one to 4–5000! Moreover in Transylvania the qualification was from three to six times lower in the towns than in the rural districts, for the simple reason that the Roumanians were in a hopeless minority in most urban communes. Finally, in the rural districts of Transylvania the qualification was infinitely higher than in Hungary proper.[1] It has been calculated that owing to the greater poverty of the soil and the primitive conditions still prevailing, the Roumanian peasant, before he could obtain the franchise, must own at least six times as much land as his Magyar equivalent.

The different measure still meted out to Transylvania, despite the centralising tendencies of the Government, was strikingly illustrated in two other directions. While in Hungary proper the Liberal press law passed in 1848 was revived after 1867, Transylvania was left saddled with the reactionary old press law which had been imposed by arbitrary decree under the Bach regime.[2] This gave the public prosecutor special discretionary powers, which he was able to use against the Roumanian press. This is one reason why the leading Roumanian newspapers of the Dualist period came to be published in Arad and Budapest. Another peculiarity of the regime was the establishment in 1871, by ministerial order, of special Jury Courts for press offences. The high income qualification for jurymen deliberately handicapped the Roumanians, who were man for man so much poorer, and thus left the courts mainly in the hands of the Magyars and Saxons. But as in Hermannstadt the jurymen were mainly Saxons, and often acquitted the Roumanian editors brought before them, the minister of the interior abolished that court in 1885,[3] and Roumanian cases came before the ultra-chauvinistic court of Kolozsvár.[4] Acquittals were almost unknown, and the most

---

[1] In the latter the vote fell to all owners of "a quarter urbarial session" (roughly fourteen acres), in the former it was limited to taxpayers who could show a net income of 159 crowns.          [2] Imperial Patent of 27 May 1852.

[3] The incident which decided the Government deserves to be recorded, and the reader may easily form one of two opposite opinions upon it. In February 1885 there occurred the centenary of the execution of Horia and Cloşca (see p. 187), and the veteran historian Bariţiu wrote an article in *Observatoriul*, to the effect that the event could only be celebrated "after a Hungarian Plevna, when the Roumanian nation recovered those inalienable rights and liberty of which the Dualist Pact had robbed it". The Court in Sibiu acquitted him on 13 December 1884. See *Cartea de Aur*, VII, p. 144.

[4] Ministerial decrees of 10 July 1871 and 27 June 1885.

monstrous convictions were made on the standard charge of "incitement of one nationality to hatred against another"—a charge entirely one-sided in practice, since prosecution of a Magyar for inciting to hatred of the Roumanians was simply unknown, though the offence was of daily occurrence. *Laudatio criminis* was a scarcely less frequent charge. There was indeed a systematic attempt to make a really national Roumanian press impossible, by heavy sureties, fines, confiscations, imprisonments and petty annoyances.[1]

In 1879 the new law on primary education marked a further stage in aggressive Magyarisation, by making a knowledge of the language of the state compulsory for every teacher, imposing a state control upon all training colleges in this sense, and giving the ministry of education power to decide the number of hours to be devoted to the teaching of Magyar and to close any institution which failed to conform.[2] Most illuminating are the parliamentary debates on this law. The well-known deputy Helfy (formerly Heller) boldly argued that "there should be no nationalities, but only a Magyar nation", while Madarász quoted the Law of Nationalities in order to prove "*that the Magyar nationality is the political nation and hence Hungary is not a polyglot, but a Magyar state*". Orban, after contrasting the modest claims of the Magyars with the action of the English, "who have violently Anglicised ten million Irishmen and Scotsmen" (*sic*), declared that the new law would only be effective if beside the Magyar-speaking teacher were placed the Magyar-feeling and Magyar-speaking priest. When Partheniu Cosma, one of the few Roumanian activists still in the House, described the new policy as an attempt "to Magyarise the non-Magyar races at all costs with iron and fire", he was greeted with general cries of assent and approval, and in the same way the gallant plea for justice for the nationalities put forward by the Kossuthist stalwart, Louis Mocsáry, evoked general protest and eventually led to his expulsion from the Party of Independence.

In 1883 the same tendencies were applied to secondary education,

[1] Between the years 1886 and 1908, 362 Roumanians were sentenced to 134 years' imprisonment and fined about 100,000 crowns for political offences, mainly incurred through the press. This statement will of course make no impression upon the reader unless he is able to project himself backwards into the pre-war atmosphere: for what was then a most formidable indictment (for which there was no contemporary European parallel save perhaps in Russia), has become an everyday occurrence in half of the states of Europe, and leaves public opinion altogether indifferent.                     [2] Law XVIII, 1879, especially §§ 2, 4 and 6.

and here their success was really phenomenal. On the eve of this law there were 151 "middle schools" in Hungary, of all categories, and of these all save fourteen[1] were Magyar. By 1903 the number had risen to 190, but the thirty-nine new institutions were all exclusively Magyar. The earnest desire of both Slovaks and Roumanians to found and support additional middle schools out of their own resources, met with strong official obstruction. A sufficient instance of this is the fact that a petition signed by the representatives of eighty-four communes, led by General Trajan Doda, for leave to found gymnasia at Arad and Caransebeş, failed for ten years even to obtain an answer.

In other words, the growth of the towns—whose decisive rôle as centres of Magyarisation was early recognised—kept pace with the process of imparting a fanatically Magyar instruction and outlook to the vast majority of the rising generation, and of putting every obstacle in the way of any corresponding educational expansion among the non-Magyars. The most for which the latter could hope was to cling desperately to the scanty resources which still remained to them.

As the pace of Magyarisation in the elementary schools did not correspond to the ardent hopes of its promoters—especially in many districts where the non-Magyar population was compact and heard scarcely a word of Magyar in their daily lives—further projects were devised during the eighties and nineties. In 1902 Dr Wlassics, as minister of education, issued a decree enjoining that from eighteen to twenty-four hours in the week should be devoted to Magyar instruction in the denominational schools, which were the last stronghold of the nationalities. As the number of hours of instruction in Hungarian primary schools never exceeded twenty-six in the week, this meant that all ordinary subjects of instruction were to be subordinated to the mania for Magyarisation—in defiance of every known rule of pedagogy. But even this was eclipsed by the demand put forward by Eugene Rákosi before the School Commission in 1904, that the nationalities should be compelled to teach nothing in their schools for three whole years save speaking, reciting and singing Magyar! And this was not the demand of some isolated fanatic, but of the editor of *Budapesti Hirlap* (then

[1] Of these the Roumanians had four complete and two incomplete, the Serbs one. The rest were Saxon (the Swabians having none). Of the pupils in the secondary schools in 1903, 3549 were Roumanians, as against 47,907 Magyars. Of a total number of 3953 secondary school teachers only 98 were Roumanian. *Ungarisches Statistisches Jahrbuch*, XII (1904), pp. 390–2, 396.

the leading newspaper of Hungary), himself a leading dramatist and publicist of the new era.

Still more symptomatic of Magyar aims was the Kindergarten Law (xv) of 1891, which avowedly aimed in the first instance at the assimilation of the rising generation of non-Magyars, and only in a lesser degree at reducing infant mortality and the evils which lay at its root. It was officially laid down that the kindergarten movement had been losing its humanitarian character since 1867 and that in Hungary it was its *"national mission"* which distinguished it from similar movements abroad.[1] Elaborate clauses provided for "practical exercises in the language of State" from the age of three upwards: and "for at least half the day" Magyar was to be used with the children. But the attempt to provide prayers of a general "inter-denominational" character for use among children of different faiths, overshot the mark and aroused the doubts of the various church authorities. Their passive resistance and the lack of adequate state funds prevented the system from becoming universal, and by 1903 only 190 kindergarten had been opened: but these contained 233,000 children of whom 90,000 were non-Magyar.[2] This onslaught upon babes and sucklings was highly dangerous among the Slovaks, and the poets Hurban Vajansky and Adolf Hejduk have crowned with lasting infamy the system of virtually selling children for the purpose of Magyarisation. The Roumanians were better able to resist, thanks to their church organisation, but they too were gravely alarmed.

Meanwhile the Roumanian language was not tolerated officially. Public notices, and even danger warnings, whether on a railway, in a post-office or on the streets, were exclusively Magyar. Expulsions were frequent, from schools or seminaries, of young men who dared to use their mother tongue, or to speak it "ostentatiously" in the streets. Official sanction was persistently withheld from the formation of Roumanian societies.[3] There were continual incidents due to the pro-

---

[1] *L'Enseignement en Hongrie*, pp. 53–4 (published by the Ministry of Education).

[2] 11,925 Roumanian. In 1909, 241,211 (of whom 11,139 Roumanians). *Ungarisches Statistisches Jahrbuch*, XII, p. 345; XVIII, p. 321.

[3] E.g. in 1870 a proposed students' union, "Minerva", was forbidden on the ground that there were enough academic societies already and that seventy students were not enough to form a society. In 1890 an Association of Roumanian ladies in aid of the Uniate schools was forbidden on the ground that the Roumanian schools needed no help! At Arad attempts to found a Roumanian Literary Society were repeatedly thwarted. Such instances could be multiplied indefinitely for the thirty-five years preceding the War.

hibition of Roumanian songs or national colours. A classic example was that of the funeral of Mureşianu, the poet of "Deşteaptă-te Române" (Roumanian, Awake!). A wreath decorated with the Roumanian tricolour had been sent by the Society of Journalists in Bucarest, but as the coffin was being carried to the hearse, gendarmes appeared and forcibly removed the colours. Some years later seventeen schoolboys were brought before the police of Braşov for placing a wreath upon the poet's grave. Some years before the War, at Brad, a small girl of six was arrested by gendarmes for wearing Roumanian colours in her hair: father, mother and nurse were fined and sent to gaol for three or four days, and the father was suspended from his post as secretary of the commune.

At the same time constant pressure was put upon all non-Magyars, especially those in subordinate positions, to Magyarise their family names, and the ease with which this could be done gave rise to the nickname of "Crown Magyars" (the price of registration being one krone, or 10d.).[1] But while Hungary thus was rapidly filled with Magyarised Slavs and Germans in high positions, and while the Jews availed themselves of the opportunity by thousands, it is remarkable that the Roumanians once more opposed the most stubborn resistance. The number of Roumanian renegades was relatively small, and this is one reason why the number of Roumanian officials so steadily decreased. In all the long lists of public men in Hungary who have taken fresh names since 1867 hardly a Roumanian is to be found:[2] and it became more and more the practice among Roumanian intellectuals in Hungary not only to give their children specially *Roumanian* or *Roman* Christian names, but wherever possible to select such names as do not lend themselves to Magyarisation. Julius becomes Gyula, Alexander Sandor, but nothing could be made of Octavian, Virgil, Ovid, Tiberius, Hortensia, Lucretia, Caius, and so on.

During the whole period under review Kolozsvár (Cluj) was the centre of the Magyarising current in its most exaggerated and aggressive

[1] Decree of the minister of the interior, April 1881, reducing the charge from 5 gulden to 50 kreutzer. There are statistics showing that while in 1848–9 there were 670 adoptions of Magyar surnames, and 933 between 1853 and 1867, the number rose to 4284 between 1867 and 1880, and to 42,437 between 1881 and 1905. But in the ten years preceding the War the habit almost certainly increased still further, and since 1930, a special agitation has been on foot in "Rump Hungary" for the further Magyarisation of surnames.

[2] Cf. Lutz Korodi, *Siebenbürgen*, p. 93, and my *Racial Problems in Hungary*, p. 187.

form. It was in this spirit that a new university was founded there in 1876: and at it the Roumanians were only on sufferance, though the disabilities imposed upon students going from Hungary to foreign universities made it almost impossible for young Roumanians to escape from the hateful atmosphere and study at Bucarest or Vienna—just as the Slovaks found it hard to make their way to Prague and on their return found all avenues closed to them as "Panslavs". Kolozsvár partially retained its old character as provincial capital. The Magyar nobility had town houses there and gave the social tone. They also made it the centre of the "Emke" (Transylvanian Magyar Cultural League), the richest and most active of a group of similar bodies, whose whole *raison d'être* was Magyarisation in every sphere of public life.[1] In 1892 Emke already had 20,000 members, an income of 140,000 crowns and a capital of over 1,000,000, and maintained numerous schools, infant homes, book stores and singing societies. Some county assemblies, thanks of course to the narrow franchise, even went so far as to levy a rate in favour of the Emke. Meanwhile it is the bare truth to say that in every town of Transylvania or the Banat the Roumanians were relegated to the suburbs and the countryside. The only place where they were in undisturbed possession was Blaj, the seat of the Uniate metropolitan: and this, like the equivalent Slovak stronghold of Turčiansky Sväti Martin, was no more than a big village.

\*        \*        \*        \*

The party of "activism" lost ground steadily after Şaguna's death, and the barren policy of abstention carried the day. It was not till 1881 that any serious attempt was made to define more clearly the Roumanian political attitude. In May of that year a conference of 153 delegates from all the Roumanian constituencies was summoned to Sibiu —the initiative coming from the veteran Bariţiu and from Nicholas Popea, formerly Şaguna's vicar-general and now bishop of Caransebeş. The result was the foundation of the "Roumanian National Party", which at once issued a statement of policy and a new programme of action. It protested openly against the Union, the Law of Nationalities, and the educational and electoral laws, as in its view serving "the falsely conceived interests of a single nationality, the Magyar". It took note of "the systematic degradation of the Roumanian nation in the common

[1] In 1894 the Magyar National Union (Magyar nemzeti egyesület) was founded, for all Hungary, and in the same year another cultural league for the north-west.

fatherland" and of "the deep political, moral and economic decay" of recent years: and while treating passivity as still necessary, it proclaimed the need for union in common defence, and to this end appointed a permanent electoral committee. The main demands now put forward were: (1) the restoration of Transylvanian autonomy; (2) the use of the Roumanian language in administration and justice throughout Roumanian territory; (3) the employment of officials acquainted with the language and customs of the people; (4) revision of the Law of Nationalities and loyal enforcement of all laws; (5) church autonomy and state contributions to church schools; (6) universal suffrage, or at the very least a vote for every direct taxpayer. It denounced Magyarising tendencies as definitely "unpatriotic", announced its readiness to co-operate with all who desired the extension of public liberties, and expressly refrained from any opinion on the Dual System, on the ground that it was not at present in question.[1] The Roumanians thus ranged themselves definitely on the side of liberal progress, while demanding the restoration of those national rights which they had secured for one brief moment in the sixties, and which in no way ran counter to the free development of neighbouring races, though of course fatal to Magyar hegemonist designs. There was nothing in the programme which could seriously be regarded as "irredentist", but it was of course denounced in Budapest as "dangerous to the state" and of course, truly enough, as incompatible with the unity of the Hungarian crown. From the very outset no compromise was possible between the two ideals. The Roumanians could not accept "the idea of the Magyar state", without dooming themselves to ultimate extinction: the only question was whether Roumanian sentiment could still be reconciled with the higher interests of the Habsburg Monarchy as a whole, or whether the Magyar claim was to be allowed to override all else and to make a question of international policy of what was as yet mainly internal.

The new programme did not at first alter the general political tactics: and the third conference of delegates, in 1887, decided, in view of the gross corruption and excesses at the last general elections, to contest even fewer seats than before, but to prepare a memorandum of Roumanian grievances and lay it before the emperor-king himself. In this year only a single Roumanian ran the gauntlet of official methods, and

---

[1] *Cartea de Aur*, VII, pp. 37–8; *Racial Problems in Hungary*, Appendix 14. For the German translation of the text see Appendices 34 and 35 of Brote, *op. cit.* pp. 299–302.

he, Trajan Doda, a retired general of the imperial army, notified the president of the Chamber that he would not take his seat, in order to reveal to the sovereign and to the outside world that the Roumanian people had been "by violence and intrigue ejected from all its positions" and that there was "at present no place for it within the framework of the Hungarian constitution". It was not, he added, merely a vote in Parliament, but the national honour that was at stake. For this address, the general was sentenced by the Arad press jury court to two years' imprisonment and a fine of 2000 crowns: as a fit of apoplexy prevented the old man from appearing, verdict was pronounced *in contumaciam*.[1]

The general party meeting of 1890 was convoked under the impression of these brutal sentences, and it is significant that now for the first time the Roumanian leaders ventured upon the slippery ice of foreign policy. Speaking as members of "a great Roumanian family of over 11 million souls", they demanded free cultural development for them all, but while repudiating Daco-Roman tendencies and desiring "a strong Austria-Hungary", in close friendship with Roumania, they drew a contrast between the currents of racial conciliation in Austria and the situation of the non-Magyars in Hungary and pointedly suggested that the Roumanian element had "an importance for the Triple Alliance". Little did they know that Caprivi and another future German chancellor were already only too conscious of this aspect of affairs, and that it was to bulk very largely in the calculations of Berlin on the eve of the greatest of all conflicts.

The controversy was beginning to widen. We have already seen that in the year 1891 the Roumanian Cultural League was founded in Bucarest as the direct result of the ill-treatment of the Roumanians north of the Carpathians, and as an answer to the activities of the various Magyar cultural leagues. The main initiative came from a group of teachers and students at the two Roumanian universities, and the latter circulated a manifesto which aimed at enlisting foreign opinion on the side of the non-Magyars. A no less outspoken "Reply", published by the Magyar students of Budapest, led the younger generation of Roumanians in their turn to abandon the mistaken passivity of their fathers and to issue, under the title of "The Roumanian Question

---

[1] He was specially pardoned by the crown. The well-known author Ioan Slavici, who had reproduced Doda's address in the *Tribuna*, and treated it as a sign of national awakening, was sentenced in April 1888 to a year's imprisonment. See Brote, *op. cit.* p. 399.

in Transylvania and Hungary" a lengthy "Réplique", describing with a great array of detailed information and legal argument, but often in tactless and provocative language, the many wrongs and grievances of their race. The only result was to draw down upon their heads a savage sentence from the jury court of Kolozsvár—Aurel Popovici, the student mainly responsible for the Réplique, being sentenced to four years, and N. Roman, as director of the printing press, to one year's imprisonment, for incitement against the Magyar nationality. Popovici escaped to Roumania and, significantly enough, became a protagonist of Austro-Roumanian friendship and of the Triple Alliance, and a decade later, a trusted adviser of Francis Ferdinand.

It was in this sort of atmosphere, and in view of an impending general election that a fresh party conference took place at Sibiu on 20 January 1892 and resolved that the long postponed memorial to the crown should be drawn up without further delay, in view of the fact that the Government's openly proclaimed aim was "a direct negation of the fundamental ideas of the modern state and a disastrous utopia". On 1 June a deputation of 300 Roumanians conveyed this "Memorandum" to the Hofburg in Vienna; but not merely were they not admitted to an audience with Francis Joseph, but some weeks later the document was returned to them unopened by the Hungarian premier, Count Szapáry, with the remark that its signatories had no legal right to speak in the name of "Hungarian citizens of Roumanian tongue"! In July, it is true, in answer to an interpellation, the minister of justice, Szilágyi, admitted the clear constitutional right of all citizens to petition the crown, even for illegal things,[1] and for a time the Government wavered in its attitude. But eventually the chauvinist current definitely gained the upper hand, and as meanwhile the rejected document had been printed and made public, the entire committee of the Roumanian National Party was brought to trial for "incitement against the Magyar nationality" incurred in this very petition (7 May 1894). The memorandum itself erred on the side of length, as such documents are apt to do, and it is therefore impossible to do more than indicate its main thesis: but it is no exaggeration to say that it contains a full arsenal of unassailable facts and arguments, so masterly in its cumulative effect as to leave no course open to the Government save either to enforce laws which it regarded as the merest camouflage against foreign opinion, or to strike home ruthlessly with all the forces at its command. The main

[1] *Cartea de Aur*, VII, p. 585.

contention—that the regime which was now celebrating its first quarter of a century had been dominated by a desire for national hegemony, contrary to the historical development of Hungary for 1000 years past—could not seriously be denied. To challenge the further contention that the Union was "an open defiance of all the rights of the Roumanian people and of the fundamental laws of the Principality" involved in effect a denial of the constitutional character of the Roumanian claim for Transylvanian autonomy: and this was in fact the attitude of Budapest. The main part of the document was devoted to a minute examination of the electoral, municipal, educational, press and agrarian laws, as instruments for the repression of the Roumanian element, and above all of the Law of Nationalities itself, which, it was asserted "beyond its title, contains no trace of the noble idea of Equal Rights", but rested upon a confusion of political and ethnical conceptions which could be shown, paragraph by paragraph, to have remained a dead letter from the outset. A surprisingly good case was made out for the questionable policy of political passivity. Finally, it was roundly affirmed that the main aim of successive Hungarian Governments had been, "not good administration", but the Magyarisation of the whole public life"—in other words, "to convert the polyglot Hungarian state into a Magyar national state", and this the past twenty-five years had shown to be a dangerous utopia. Shut out from all political influence, and destined to be absorbed as "alien elements", the Roumanians had no course left but to appeal to the crown, to whom they had shown signal loyalty in the past, and especially in 1849, though this was one of their main crimes in the eyes of official Hungary.

The trial took place before a Magyar chauvinist jury at Kolozsvár, and at an early stage in the proceedings counsel for the defence—among whom, it is significant to note, three leading Slovak advocates of the day were serving as volunteers[1]—found it necessary to withdraw from the court owing to the attitude of its president. Elaborate precautions were taken to supply the foreign press with a garbled version of the trial and to prevent the true facts from leaking out: and on the second day the minister of the interior sent urgent instructions to all county authorities to arrest any "agitators" whom they might find stirring up the people. But the firm attitude of the accused overbore all their pre-

[1] Miloš Stefanovič, Matthew Dúla (who lived to be president of the Slovak National Council which in October 1918 declared for union with the Czechs), and Stephen Fajnor.

cautions. In the name of all his colleagues the party chairman, Dr Ioan Rațiu, read aloud a fiery declaration, declining to recognise the jurisdiction of a court "where the Magyars figure both as accuser and judge". "What is under discussion here is the very existence of the Roumanian people, and *the national existence of a people is not discussed, but affirmed....* There can be no question of judgment: you can condemn us as individuals, but not as the representatives of our people....But though you are not competent to judge us, there is none the less another tribunal, larger, more enlightened, and assuredly more impartial—the tribunal of the civilised world, which will condemn you yet more severely than it has hitherto done. By your spirit of medieval intolerance, by a racial fanaticism which has not its equal in Europe, you will, if you condemn us, simply succeed in proving to the world that the Magyars are a discordant note in the concert of European nations."[1]

Under such circumstances the result was a foregone conclusion. Rațiu himself, Pop de Bașesti, Father Vasile Lucaciu, Teodor Miháli, Comșa, Bărcianu and nine others were sentenced to a total of thirty-two years' imprisonment.[2] An incident which followed the trial is worth mentioning, because it illustrates the mentality of both sides. Dr Rațiu on his return to Turda was greeted by a Magyar mob, who attacked his house and broke up his furniture. Rațiu came out on the balcony and called out "Thank you, gentlemen, that's how I always pictured you". One Budapest newspaper even went so far in its comments on the trial, as to regret that the good old practice of affixing the heads of traitors to the city gates had fallen into disuse.

A month later these sentences were followed up by the dissolution of the Roumanian National Party, by order of the new minister of the interior, Hieronymi, who had already publicly expounded the view that to demand the undoing of the Transylvanian Union or any federalist settlement was treason to the fatherland and not open to discussion.[3] Now again he declared that no Government would ever deal with a party whose programme was directed against the Union, and that it would "apply the law against such agitators with pitiless severity and with an energy that allows no bargaining".[4] The premier, Dr Wekerle,

---

[1] Text in *Racial Problems in Hungary*, pp. 472–4; *Cartea de Aur*, VII, pp. 666–9.
[2] Five other members of the central committee who had not attended the meeting which decided for publication, were not charged: Eugene Brote and Aurel Popovici had fled to Roumania.    [3] 3 November 1892—*Cartea de Aur*, VII, p. 555.
[4] 19 July 1894—*ibid.* p. 679.

in his turn indignantly denied all idea of forcible Magyarisation, treated the whole question of the nationalities as quite a novelty, but justified the dissolution of the Roumanian National Party, and hinted vaguely at "steps against assistance from abroad". But meanwhile, with the Memorandum Trial, the Roumanian question in Hungary had made its entry into the field of European politics, just as surely as the Zagreb Treason Trial, twenty-five years later, served to advertise the Croatian question before the wider forum. In France and Belgium it aroused considerable attention, just as the woes of the Saxons occupied sections of German opinion, and especially such societies as the "Verein für das Deutschtum im Ausland" and the "Gustav Adolf Verein": while in Roumania it kindled intense indignation and excitement and reacted upon foreign policy in the manner already described.[1] With sudden candour the public prosecutor, Jeszenszky, as he left the court, had greeted one of the accused with the words, "*You* are the condemned, but *we* are the vanquished".[2]

The intervention of Sturdza and of Kálnoky in no way allayed the Magyarising tendencies, and indeed chauvinism grew still more extreme under the premiership of Baron Bánffy (January 1895–February 1899). His avowed aim was to create the "Unitary Magyar State", and to create it at top speed: and the remarkable Millenary Exhibition of 1896 was from one aspect an attempt to convince Europe that the experiment was succeeding, and of course relegated all the non-Magyars entirely to the background. The ardent demonstrations to which the exhibition gave rise and the crop of controversial literature on Magyar claims, not unnaturally provoked counter-demonstrations in neighbouring countries. The use of heraldic symbols of Hungarian medieval suzerainty aroused the resentment of Balkan chauvinists, and the Hungarian tricolour was burnt first on the streets of Belgrade and then, in imitation, by the students of Bucarest before the statue of Michael the Brave. In the Austrian Reichsrat Dr Lueger, the famous clerical and anti-semite mayor of Vienna—who had coined the nickname of "Judapest" for the Magyar capital, and had demonstratively welcomed the Roumanian delegates when their memorandum was rejected by the Hofburg—now declared that every German who made common cause with Hungary was a traitor to the German idea.

One solitary concession had been made by Bánffy to the nationalities

[1] See *supra*, pp. 373, 379.
[2] Sirianu, *La Question de Transylvanie*, p. 328.

—a sign of condescension which he afterwards recognised as mistaken: they obtained permission to hold a joint political congress in Budapest in August 1898. This was the beginning of close co-operation between the Roumanians, Serbs and Slovaks, led respectively by George Pop de Başesti, Michael Polit and Paul Mudron: and the programme which they drafted, and to which they invited the adherence of the Germans and Ruthenes also, was a further step away from the barren policy of abstention. With the example of the Memorandum Trial before their eyes, they were careful to recognise the political integrity of the Crown of St Stephen, but at the same time condemned the idea of a Magyar national state as running counter to the ethnical and historical traditions of Hungary. They then demanded the due fulfilment of the Law of Nationalities, a redistribution of the counties so far as possible on a linguistic basis, and a cessation of the infringement of Church autonomy. Their other demands—in particular universal suffrage, the ballot, free elections, freedom of association and assembly, the extension of press freedom and reform of the jury courts for press matters—belonged to the general category of liberal reform in Europe, though their absence weighed with special rigour upon the non-Magyars. There was never any prospect of even the more moderate of their wishes being granted, and the meeting was intended by its organisers as a reminder of existence and a point of departure for common action. Even united, they were as yet too feeble to run the gauntlet of the electoral system. The "Bánffy elections" of October 1896 outdid all previous records of violence and corruption. Tisza's "Mameluke" system was upheld and secured for the Government a mass of safe seats in the non-Magyar districts: but real war was waged against the Magyar Opposition of the central plains, and whole regiments of the joint army were employed to "prevent excesses" and "maintain order"—which really meant preventing "undesirable" voters from reaching the polls. In the indignant words of Count Albert Apponyi, "the laws were merely an instrument for concealing the arbitrary action of the Government".[1]

Bánffy pursued his racial policy quite unabashed. The campaign for the wholesale Magyarisation of family-names was conducted from the ministry of the interior itself, and great pressure exercised upon county and municipal officials: while a new law enjoined the exclusive use of Magyar place-names throughout the country. Thus not merely Cluj,

[1] 25 October 1896, at Budapest.

Sibiu and Braşov, but even Klausenburg, Hermannstadt and Kronstadt gave place to Kolozsvár, Nagy Szeben and Brassó: and henceforth the post offices and railways of Hungary were carefully purged of anything that might reveal its polyglot character to the traveller. The non-Magyar central committee issued a public protest against the new law, but it was of course entirely disregarded.

Baron Bánffy's misuse of power roused the Magyar Opposition to fresh efforts. In the words of Count Apponyi, the Parliament of 1896 had been "bred in sin and born in sin", and was condemned by a moral law to suffer like a fever patient from continual crises. Meanwhile acute social unrest found expression in wholesale emigration, harvest strikes and rioting in the agricultural districts: and the Government threw itself into the arms of the big landlords by forming a large reserve of foreign labourers, as strike breakers, at low wages. Social Democracy was still in its infancy in Hungary, but made its first entry into Budapest and the larger towns. Early in 1899 Bánffy found it necessary to resign, and under his successor Koloman Széll there was a certain lull in the situation. In particular, the new premier adopted milder tactics towards the nationalities, adopting as his motto "Law, Right and Justice", greatly reducing the number of prosecutions against the Roumanian and Slovak press, dissolving the notorious "Nationalities Section"of the premier's office and introducing a law against bribery and corruption. His attention was more and more concentrated on the military and commercial disputes with Austria, and the fierce obstruction of the Opposition groups drove him on to the defensive. The milder Széll gave place in November 1903 to Count Stephen Tisza, the most forceful and in many ways most characteristic of Hungary's pre-War statesmen, combining the arrogance of the "gentry" and the fatalism of the strict Calvinist with an ardent belief in Magyar predominance. This man, of whom his no less masterful father Koloman once said that he was a fine rider, but a bad driver, came into power with the definite object of rallying the Liberal party—now undermined by faction after thirty years of uninterrupted office—and of saving the Dual System and reconciling the crown. Francis Joseph had for a whole generation past been the firm upholder of Dualism and of its corollary, Magyar hegemony, and as the Matica and Memorandum incidents clearly showed, had definitely thrown the non-Magyars to the wolves. But the history of his long reign shows that there were two things which could rouse him from his opportunist love of half-measures, namely any attack upon his double prerogative in military and in foreign affairs: and the Army Order of Chlopy (13 September 1903)—denouncing all idea of dividing up the Joint Army or interfering with the language of command—was a clear warning of his rising wrath. On his side military and strategic considerations outweighed all others: but what imported such venom into the question was the ulterior aim of the Magyar parties to use the Joint Army as an instrument of Magyarisation against the Roumanians, Slovaks and Germans. Tisza's sole remedy was to meet force by force. But his illegal strategem for securing revision of the standing orders led the Opposition to wreck the House by using broken lids and benches as bludgeons and missiles (December 1904). They then united in an anti-Liberal Coalition, which at the general elections of 1905 inflicted a crushing defeat upon the Liberals, the first since the fusion of 1875! Tisza fell, and Francis Joseph, unwilling to admit that his sacrosanct Joint Army could ever become an object of barter with the victors, took the risk of governing without a majority and appealed to a veteran cavalry general, Baron Fejérváry, to form a Cabinet as an act of obedience to his military chief. The new Government, consisting of untried men, was from the outset denounced as unconstitutional and, knowing that it would be simply howled down in Parliament, looked elsewhere for support. The new minister of the interior, Joseph Kristóffy, was allowed to place universal suffrage in the forefront of his political programme and so to appeal to the masses against the ruling caste.

Throughout this period of crisis, the Roumanians and their non-Magyar allies had watched the progressive degeneration of parliamentary life, without of course being able to throw any real weight into the scales. But they felt encouraged to abandon abstention and issued a revised programme at the elections of 1905, reaffirming that of 1881 (and therefore with it the claim to autonomy) but adding a number of further democratic demands, such as universal suffrage, the ballot, redistribution, press freedom, right of association and assembly, free education (with the Roumanian language wherever the Roumanians were in a majority), abolition of virilist mandates, of entails, of taxation upon necessaries, the inalienability of a minimum of property, and of course the enforcement of the Law of Nationalities and of a knowledge of the local language by all public officials. Significantly enough, it included a clause approving the single language of command in the Joint Army, with due recognition of the individual regiments (in other words, leaving German on its pedestal, and placing Magyar, Roumanian and all other languages on a lower, but equal, footing) and demanding the abandonment of Magyarising tendencies in the army. It is true that "activism" at first bore but scanty fruit: only eight Roumanians, led by Theodore Miháli, entered the new House. But the events of 1905 brought them fresh courage, and above all the more conciliatory attitude of Kristóffy on the vital question of franchise reform, which involved a relaxation of official pressure both upon the nationalities and the Magyar urban working class. Moreover it became known to them that in this Kristóffy had the approval—none the less vehement because it was not publicly expressed—of the Heir Apparent, Archduke Francis Ferdinand, who viewed with increasing alarm the disintegrating effects of Magyar Chauvinism alike upon home and foreign policy and saw in the non-Magyars a conservative element and a bulwark of the dynasty against Hungarian separatism.

During the years which still separate us from the great catastrophe an intimate secret alliance was established between the Roumanian and Slovak leaders and "Belvedere", the archduke's palace in Vienna: and this is the crowning proof that in neither case was there any truth in the reckless charges of irredentism levelled against them by the Pan-Magyars. In 1906, as in 1848 and 1892, the "Panslavs" and "Daco-Romans" still looked to Vienna: and we have already seen that the responsible statesmen of the Roumanian kingdom, Liberal and Conservative alike, shared the Germanophil sentiments of their Hohenzollern king and in their desire to lean upon the Central Powers and their readiness to contemplate some kind of federal link, found the main obstacle in Magyar treatment of their kinsmen north of the Carpathians.

Meanwhile "the idea of the unitary Magyar state" (a magyar állam eszme) became a dogma of Hungarian public life. "Either Hungary will become a great national state", declared Gustav Beksics, the most noted publicist of the Liberal era, "or it will cease to be a state at all"[1]: while Eugene Rákosi, a brilliant dramatist and editor of the coalition journal *Budapesti Hirlap*, preached all his life the doctrine of "the thirty million Magyar State" as a goal at which the eight million Magyars of his day should aim! Baron Bánffy on 11 July 1906 openly declared: "The legal state is the aim, but with this question we can only concern ourselves when we have already assured the national state.... Hungary's interests demand its erection on the most extreme Chauvinist lines".

[1] *A Dualismus*, p. 240.

27-2

A year later he went still further: "In a peaceful manner this question cannot be solved...for we wish the unitary Magyar national state, while they wish the polyglot state, with equal rights of the nationalities".[1] Bánffy, it is true, had lost his following in general political questions, but when he spoke on the racial question he met with applause from all sides of the House. And indeed his views only differed in emphasis from those of Count Stephen Tisza, who on 16 January 1905 officially declared: "A cardinal condition for the enjoyment of rights by other nationalities is that the citizens of other nationalities should recognise unreservedly that this state is the Magyar state—that state which the politically unitary Magyar has created": and he added the naked threat that the Magyar nation had never given any binding promise to maintain the Law of Nationalities "for all time..., when we perceive that through it we grant to our opponents rights against ourselves". Even the mild Széll insisted vigorously on "the idea of the Magyar State", arguing that "this country must first be preserved *as a Magyar country*, and then it must be cultured, rich, enlightened and progressive".[2]

The tacit alliance of Kristóffy with Labour and with the non-Magyars—of which an outward sign was the withdrawal of restrictions on the young trades unions and on the right of public meetings—caused acute alarm among all the older parties. It seemed to justify the view of the old Liberal Guard that the main prop of the Magyar hegemony was the support of the crown and that the withdrawal of this might injure the whole structure. It took some time for the Coalition leaders to convince themselves that Francis Joseph was really in earnest: but drastic proof was provided by his dissolution of Parliament in February 1906 and by the manner in which it was done. The Parliament building was surrounded by strong military forces, among whom Roumanian regiments were prominent: a royal decree was read aloud, not by the premier or one of his ministers, but by Colonel Fabricius, a Honvéd officer in full uniform, and no writs were issued for a new election.

[1]    31 October 1907. On 1 January 1908 he again repudiated any possibility of a compromise. "Without Chauvinism nothing can be achieved."

[2]    21 June 1908, at the Congress of Magyar Cultural Leagues, "Every citizen", he also said, "is equal before the law, *with the single limitation regarding language*, which is demanded by political unity and unity of administration and justice". Count Apponyi, who by reason of his wide European culture was to be accepted outside Hungary in after years as a champion of moderation, fully endorsed Széll's point of view and pleaded for "an energetic national policy" as the only means of solving the racial question.

Despite action so obviously in conflict with the constitution, the country remained passive, and the masses were eagerly awaiting electoral reform. The panic-stricken Coalition set on foot secret negotiations with the crown and on 9 April 1906 accepted office on terms which enabled it to save its face by a few showy outward concessions, but left the crown's essential position unimpaired and gave him a secret written pledge whose betrayal two years later undermined the fast declining credit of the Government.

The details of this transaction lie beyond the recent narrative, but it was a turning point in the racial question from two aspects. It proved once for all that Francis Joseph was completely indifferent to the fate of the non-Magyars and had used them and their rights as a mere instrument to render the ruling class more amenable to his wishes. This meant that their last hope from the dynasty depended upon whether Francis Ferdinand succeeded to his uncle's throne before the situation was irretrievably compromised. Secondly, it made of electoral reform the central issue of Hungarian public life, from a social and racial no less than from a political point of view. Without this reform there could be no legal assertion of non-Magyar rights, and it was sufficiently obvious that the existing franchise represented the maximum of political monopoly, and that the ruling class had nothing to gain, and the workers and non-Magyars nothing to lose, by its extension in any form, however inadequate. Indeed it is not too much to affirm that for the next ten years the real issue was a struggle not *for*, but *against*, universal suffrage. Stated more crudely, the Coalition strained every nerve to evade its secret pledge to introduce reform on "at least as broad a basis" as the Kristóffy plan, under which the minimum was to have been universal and equal suffrage for all literates.

At the elections of April 1906 the Liberals abstained, and the "Mamelukes" went over bag and baggage into the camp of the Coalition, which obtained 380 out of 413 seats. The non-Magyars at last entered the House as a tiny but compact group of twenty-five, with a common programme of racial equality and democratic reform. The Roumanians were strongest, with sixteen seats, and the able, but somewhat colourless Miháli was now reinforced by two future leaders of great ability, Alexander Vaida-Voevod and Julius Maniu, and the fighting priest Vasile Lucaciu, the hero of the Memorandum Trial. From the very first they were received with open hostility by the new majority. It was seriously argued that the mandates of the whole Roumanian party should be annulled, on the ground that their programme was hostile to the state: and Aurel Vlad had to defend the name "Roumanian National Party" by such analogies as the Irish Nationalist party in Britain or the republican parties in the monarchical states. A deliberate device for frightening the non-Magyars into silence was the suspension of their parliamentary immunity and the condemnation of the Slovak deputies Juriga, Hodža and Ivánka to various terms of imprisonment. But it was obvious that the main centre of resistance was among the Roumanians, who, amid the many difficulties of their situation, had been able to entrench themselves in their church autonomy and in their denominational schools[1]: and it was therefore quite logical that the new regime should direct a concentric attack upon the non-Magyar primary school.

The debates which preceded the famous Apponyi School Laws of 1907 throw a flood of light upon the whole situation. The elaborate statistical investigations of Paul Balogh—published in 1902[2]—had revealed the fact that during the heyday of Liberalism Magyardom had gained 261 communes from the non-Magyars, but had lost no fewer than 456, and this despite the fact that the scale had been weighted in its favour by the whole resources of the state! In particular the Roumanians had gained 362, and had only lost 64, communes! Balogh himself treated "the territorial losses of the Magyar element as the most striking refutation" of the charges of oppression put forward by the other races. But public opinion took up the question from another angle and clamoured for more stringent measures against the non-Magyars, arguing that unless the pace were hastened still further, Magyarisation would still be incomplete before European complications supervened.

The temper of Parliament was revealed by its attitude to a speech of the Roumanian deputy Goldiş in April 1907. He had quoted the phrase of a Magyar colleague "that it was both mistaken and impossible to bring up Magyar children in a German spirit", and was greeted with loud applause: but when he added, "equally mistaken and impossible

---

[1] In 1900 the Roumanians, though they only had four secondary schools, had by a concentration of effort been able to maintain 3279 primary schools—1984 Orthodox and 1295 Uniate.

[2] *A Népfajok Magyarországon* (The Races in Hungary), over 1100 pages with hundreds of tables and a large portfolio of maps—a book unique in Europe! See especially pp. 949–50.

is it to educate Roumanian children in a Magyar spirit", the applause changed to loud and angry protests. But the classical example is provided by the Vaida incident of a few days later. Towards the end of a long speech against the Education Bill, Dr Vaida recited two Magyar poems, one written by a Magyar chauvinist in violent abuse of the Roumanians, the other by a Roumanian patriot repaying these insults with interest in the language of his opponents. This latter poem, he argued, went far to prove the futility of the policy of Magyarisation in the schools; for instead of converting the Roumanians into Magyars, it merely made some of them bilingual, and therefore doubly dangerous to the Magyars. He had spoken to a thin and inattentive house, but next day, when the stenographic report came into the hands of the deputies, there were violent protests, and Count Apponyi himself argued that after such a speech there was nothing left for Vaida but to resign his seat: the apology which he offered was not accepted, he was howled down, forced to absent himself for a couple of months, and when he again appeared was greeted on all sides by abuse as "a traitorous villain", whom "a sense of honour and patriotism and the sovereignty of the Magyar nation...must surely forbid from appearing" in Parliament.

The Education Acts which were the occasion for such scenes were a deliberate and deep-laid plan for the capture of the last non-Magyar stronghold, the denominational school. Law xxvi regulated the salaries of teachers in the state elementary schools, and while genuinely planned to improve their material condition and efficiency, did this at the expense of their freedom and subjected them to close control in national matters. Law xxvii applied similar control to teachers in the church schools, who were declared to be state officials and hence at the mercy of state inspectors. By imposing a minimum salary and new standards of equipment known to be beyond the financial powers of the Orthodox and Uniate Churches, it faced them with the alternative of closing down (to be superseded by purely Magyar state schools) or of accepting state grants such as involved far-reaching control, both of the textbooks in use (especially geography and history) and of the linguistic attainments of the teachers. The teacher must henceforth be able to read, write, and teach Magyar correctly, and must give instruction in the manner and to the extent laid down by the ministry, which in certain cases acquired a veto on appointments and even power to nominate without consulting the school authorities (§§ 20, 21). Stringent provisos for the inculcation of Magyar patriotism were introduced, a special oath of loyalty in the Magyar language was exacted from all teachers, steps were taken to punish "tendencies hostile to the State" on the part of the teacher or committee of management, and teachers were liable to dismissal unless they could ensure that "the child of non-Magyar tongue, on the completion of its fourth school year, can express its thoughts intelligibly in the Magyar language, in word and writing" (§§ 18, 28). These and other clauses were of course a fresh violation of the Law of Nationalities both in letter and in spirit, and when fully applied, were bound to render church autonomy illusory. From the pedagogic standpoint they would have been a monstrosity even in mixed districts, and for a language as easy as Roumanian: in wide districts where the peasants scarcely ever heard a word of Magyar in daily life, it was obviously impossible in the case of a language as difficult as Magyar. It became as it were a sword of Damocles. Those who tried to carry it out had to devote about eighteen out of twenty-three hours a week to Magyar linguistic instruction—but of course the result was failure to learn either Magyar or anything else.[1] Well might a Roumanian deputy bitterly denounce the Apponyi Laws as little better than "an addition to the criminal code, such as will encourage espionage and demoralise the teaching staff". In 1909 Count Apponyi went a step further and issued a decree ordering that the religious instruction of all Roumanians at state middle schools must be given in the language of the state, and when the hierarchy forbade the clergy to comply, he threatened to withdraw their state stipends (the so-called Congrua).

If it be asked why the Roumanian schools were not taken over altogether, a number of reasons can be found. In the first place the budget could not have met so great an expense, and the state wisely preferred to leave as much of the burden as possible on the shoulders of the churches, thus securing a maximum of control through a minimum of expenditure. Secondly, the pretence of church autonomy had to be kept up, for the Roman Catholic Church, and even the Protestants, though thoroughly Chauvinist in sentiment, began to take alarm at possible precendents. And the tactics adopted enabled Apponyi, a true pupil of the Jesuits, to undermine the whole basis of the non-Magyar

---

[1] For detailed analysis see my *Racial Problems in Hungary*, pp. 227–33. As a result of the new laws there were in 1912 only 2635 Roumanian schools and 2767 teachers, as compared with 2975 and 3086 in 1907. See Ghibu, *Viaţa şi Organisaţia Bisericească şi Scolara*, p. 165.

church school, while preserving appearances abroad and boasting the liberality of the church grants!

The bitterness and alarm engendered by this law was increased in 1908, when Count Andrássy introduced a project of electoral reform which sought to counteract possible gains to the non-Magyars by a combination of open voting, plural voting and a literacy test: but the bill was stillborn and soon consigned to oblivion. The Army Bills of 1909 again evoked strong Roumanian protest, and Julius Maniu was howled down for his bold criticism of racial policy under the Dual System. He and Stephen Cicio-Pop contended that "the army is not there in order to Magyarise, but to defend, the country": but they were insulted from all sides as "traitors" and "dirty thieves" and told to "go to Bucarest" or to Austria. The president found it necessary to suspend the sitting, and on resuming warned Maniu that he had forgotten he was in Hungary, adding, "We want to introduce into the army the language of state, the nation's true form of expression" (16 February 1909).

It was at this period that the Roumanian leaders in their despair turned more and more towards the Archduke Francis Ferdinand and established close confidential relations with him, thereby again disproving their alleged irredentist leanings. This was in no small measure due to Aurel Popovici, the exiled author of the "Réplique",[1] who in 1906 published a provocative but highly remarkable book entitled *The United States of Great Austria*, treating Dualism and Magyarisation equally as failures and aberrations, discussing the constitutional issue with a wealth of illustrations from the political theory of all Europe, strongly affirming the mission of the Habsburgs and Austria's rôle in deciding the Eastern Question, but arguing that the only sound solution was to annul the Dual System, that "mater discordiae", and to establish in its place a federal state of fifteen units, framed as nearly as possible on a racial basis, with German as the *lingua franca* of joint affairs. Such a reform, he contended, could never be achieved by parliamentary means: the emperor alone had the power, and the duty, to carry out "the *coup d'état* of all the peoples". Magyar tyranny had made of Hungary "a Bastille of the nationalities", but if the crown once showed the necessary courage, "ils morderont sur du granit", and the Monarchy would be stronger and greater than ever, the union of all Roumanians would be accomplished within the new federal framework and

[1] See pp. 380, 412.

a Balkan federation, also under Habsburg overlordship, would logically
follow. There was an undercurrent of Grillparzer's famous phrase,
"When will the Emperor mount his horse?"[1]—which was at this time
much quoted by the Christian Socialists, with many a side-glance
towards the Belvedere Palace.

That such ideas were in the air in Austria is shown by the
almost simultaneous publication of an even more remarkable political
essay entitled *Foundations and Tendencies of the Austro-Hungarian
Monarchy*,[2] by Karl Renner, then junior librarian of the Reichsrat. In
it the future Socialist chancellor of post-War Austria—after a most
searching criticism and contrast of constitutional development in Austria
and in Hungary, and of the conflict of three ideas, nationalism, parlia-
mentarism and absolutism—tore to shreds the legal fictions upon which
the Hungarian constitution and the policy of Magyarisation rested,
emphasised the impossibility of Hungary standing alone, "girt by a
solid ring of states akin to her other races" and argued that a break-up
of the Monarchy must inevitably be followed by the partition of
Hungary. Austria might even stand as "*tertius gaudens*" in the struggle
of Magyar against Roumanian and Serb. For Renner the true solution
was to be reached in three stages—extension of local self-government,
democratic in character and divided wherever possible on ethnographic
lines: secondly, the erection of a political structure on this basis, at once
territorial and national—each race being organised in a kind of national
"University" (as the Saxons had once been in Transylvania), cutting
across the geographical and economic divisions: and thirdly, the formation of a central representative body for the whole Monarchy. Writing
as he did when the agitation for universal suffrage in Austria was in full
swing, he argued very plausibly that Austria simply had to go about
her own business of reform and set her own house in order, and Hungary
would soon be forced to follow suit.

Of these two books the second was far the most profound and closely
reasoned, but coming from a Socialist it met with but little response in
the mind of the heir apparent: whereas the first, with its frank recognition of imperial unity and its dynastic appeal, flattered all his prejudices

---

[1] "Wann steigt der Kaiser zu Pferde?" Cf. novels of Adam Müller-Gutten-
brunn, which were a glorification of Habsburg enlightenment as against Magyar
tyranny.
[2] *Grundlagen und Entwicklungsziele der oesterreichisch-ungarischen Monarchie*,
under the pseudonym of Rudolf Springer.

and came to him almost as a revelation. "Great Austria" became the watchword of the Christian Socialist party and of Dr Lueger, and it was generally known who stood behind it. Henceforth Francis Ferdinand and his intimates from time to time explored the question of constitutional reform and viewed with growing misgiving and anger the racial policy of Budapest. In one of his letters to his military secretary, Colonel Brosch, there occurs the significant phrase, "I *must* keep the nationalities for me, for this is the only hope for the future":[1] and he was in the habit of receiving certain Slovak and Roumanian leaders and allowing them to speak with surprising frankness. On one such occasion he coined the two phrases, "I am surprised, after what has happened, that your people should have any loyalty left", and "It was bad taste on the part of the Magyars ever to come to Europe":[2] and here he spoke from the deep conviction that Magyar racial policy was digging the Monarchy's grave, and that his uncle was blind to the facts.

Francis Ferdinand showed special favour to the Roumanians on both sides of the Carpathians: and his visit to King Charles at Sinaia in the summer of 1909 had a high political significance. On his journey his own Roumanian subjects made a silent demonstration by lining the railway tracks in their thousands and greeting his train as it passed. Even the most obtuse intelligence could understand this, and the annoyance of Budapest was intense, and openly expressed. The king, on his side, won his guest by special attentions to his morganatic wife, the duchess of Hohenberg, and doubtless laid the same stress as in former years to Andrássy, Kálnoky and Caprivi, upon the complications which Magyarisation had introduced into his relations with Vienna and Berlin. How little either he or his people had as yet adopted an irredentist programme was further shown by the positively royal reception accorded to Dr Lueger on his visit to Bucarest and by the genuine enthusiasm shown for Austria as opposed to Hungary.

By the end of 1909 the Coalition Government had crumbled, and early in 1910 the Liberals were re-constituted as the Party of National Work. The new premier was Count Khuen-Hedérváry, who during his twenty years as Ban of Croatia had corrupted a whole generation and played off Serb and Croat against each other. The Khuen elections of 1910 eclipsed even Bánffy's record for bribery and violence: and the

---

[1] Chlumetzky, *Erzherzog Franz Ferdinand*, p. 323.
[2] These phrases were repeated to me in 1913 under seal of secrecy, by those to whom he used them: the need for secrecy has long since vanished.

premier's understudy, Jeszenszky, devoted special attention to his old enemies the non-Magyars. Troops were employed in 380 constituencies, and when this was criticised in Austria, an official *communiqué* explained that "only" 194 battalions of infantry and 114 squadrons of cavalry had been used. Even the Party of Independence was decimated, while the little band of non-Magyars sank from 26 to 8—five Roumanians and three Slovaks. Ten Roumanian electors were killed, and the vanquished spoke bitterly of "a real civil war". Under the impression of this victory Count Stephen Tisza addressed the House on the racial question and defined pre-War Magyar policy more authoritatively than ever before. The whole House without distinction of party must, he agreed, welcome "with patriotic joy" the fact that the elections had "virtually wiped the nationalist agitators out of public life". It was now time to solve the burning racial problem and to establish harmony with the small Balkan nations, "who can find the surest guarantee of their existence in the political power of the Magyar nation". But "our non-Magyar fellow-citizens must first of all reconcile themselves to the fact that they here belong to a national state, which is not a conglomerate of different races, but which one nation has conquered and founded, upon which one nation has stamped the ineradicable impress of its individuality". He then demanded "pitiless severity" against the agitators, but "the fullest brotherly fairness" towards the non-Magyar masses. But "with nationalist parties" he would never make compromises. He appealed in particular to the Roumanians, "because of all races in the country national consciousness beats most strongly in their breast", because he saw in them "the greatest material, spiritual and moral strength" and because "beside the frontier the proud Kingdom of Roumania rises in undreamt-of splendour". But the Roumanians must not form parties on the basis of nationality, for "in that moment they are already denying the political unity of the Magyar nation. With this shade of opinion there can be no negotiations: it must be fought, and if we conquer, we must destroy it" (12 July 1910). Khuen-Hedérváry, on his side, announced his intention of introducing universal suffrage, "but in such a form as will safeguard in future also the character of the Hungarian state, in accordance with its 1000 years' history". The Roumanians were defeated, but undaunted: Vaida, Maniu and Miháli upheld the original programme, and though there was a *fronde* within their ranks—led by the poet Octavian Goga—it was more, not less, intransigeant, and no one could be found to negotiate on Tisza's terms.

Simultaneously there went on an unequal struggle between the ruling oligarchy and the working classes as a whole, Magyar and non-Magyar alike. And as the non-Magyars were mainly engaged in agricultural pursuits and the successes of Magyarisation were confined to the towns (in great part owing to the complaisance of the Jewish element), the Socialist movement came late in Hungary, and, when it came, struck root mainly among the Magyars and the Jews. The working class was entirely unrepresented in Parliament. Everything was done to hinder the growth of trade unions (as late as 1908 the Government dissolved the federations of ironworkers and timbermen). The imprisonment of strikers was an ordinary occurrence. Meanwhile housing conditions for the labourer actually grew worse. The working day for farms was from "sunrise to sunset". Government had devised special measures to prevent harvest strikes, and to supply the big estates with underpaid workers imported from other districts. The Agricultural Law of 1907 even legalised flogging for labourers up to eighteen by the landowner. In 52 per cent. of the Hungarian factories there were children under fourteen working twelve or more hours per day. In the richest county, Bács-Bodrog (Bačka), tuberculosis was rampant and the main certified cause of death. Emigration rose by leaps and bounds owing to bad labour conditions, coupled with political repression. Between 1900 and 1906, 657,000 left Hungary out of a population of 19,000,000: and from 1906 to 1914 the rate exceeded 200,000 a year.

One other vital factor in the Hungarian situation must be mentioned —the economic transformation, which expressed itself on the one hand in the decay of the gentry, the class which had long been Hungary's political backbone, and on the other hand in the virtual capture of industry, banking, commerce and the press by the Jews. Two results of this were a struggle for offices on the part of the gentry class, and the consequent multiplication of state officials. From 1892 to 1902 their numbers were increased by 37,500. In 1904 they numbered 207,000. By 1908 they had already risen to 235,000. Meanwhile, however, the big entailed estates and the land held in mortmain by the Roman Catholic Church had doubled since 1867, but the number of independent owners of land had diminished by 118,000 between 1870 and 1900. In Transylvania there were relatively fewer large estates—the great *latifundia* being in the southern plains, in Slovakia and in Ruthenia: but a few big feudal families, like the Bánffys, Bethlens, Telekis, Josikas, were very notable exceptions and had an altogether disproportionate control of the political situation. There was a deep gulf fixed between the Magyar ruling class and the Roumanian peasantry, whose land-hunger was still unassuaged and which still occupied (*mutatis mutandis*) the same position of political and social helotry in which its ancestors had lived for generations. Virtually banished from the towns, or at least relegated on sufferance to the suburbs, excluded from public office and deliberately cramped in education and culture, they found a focus of democratic resistance in church and school alone, and this the Apponyi Laws were steadily setting themselves to undermine.

A fresh conflict with the crown over the army question led to Khuen's fall in April 1912, and his successor Dr Ladislas Lukács, in taking over the pledge of universal suffrage, defined it "in such a way as to preserve the due influence of the more developed and riper strata of society and also the unitary national character of the Hungarian state". Lukács himself came of a Transylvanian family of Armenian origin, and had been left as an infant among the wreckage of a sacked country house in 1849. Only a year later he was driven from office by the outcome of a libel action: the Opposition deputy Désy had described him as "the greatest Panamist in Europe" and was acquitted by the jury when it transpired that Lukács had in 1910 accepted three million crowns from a leading bank for electoral purposes. At last on 5 June 1913 Count Tisza again became premier and set himself at one and the same time to crush parliamentary obstruction, even by an armed guard; to check the democratic onslaught by a carefully doctored Franchise Reform (XIV, 1913) resting on differentiation by age, literacy and taxation; and finally, to reach a settlement with the nationalities, or at any rate the Roumanians, whom alone he regarded as a real danger. His genuine desire to reach agreement was never in doubt, but its prospect was vitiated by his feudal and arrogant outlook: to him the Magyar must be "master in his own house", and the Roumanian was a citizen of the second rank, whose mere survival was a proof of the unexampled generosity of the "Herrenvolk" (az uralkodó nemzet).

The atmosphere was rendered still less favourable by the scandalous incident of Hajdudorog. In June 1912 the Hungarian Government obtained from the Vatican the Bull "Christi Fideles", detaching seventy-five parishes from the Roumanian Uniate Church, placing them under a Magyar Vicar-General and introducing Magyar as the language of the liturgy. Meetings of protest followed, and a memorandum was sent to the Pope, reminding him that Leo XIII by the

Encyclical "Praeclara Gratulationis" had solemnly guaranteed the inviolability of the Uniate Church in Transylvania. A sinister turn was given to the affair when in March 1914 an infernal machine sent through the post blew to pieces two of the chief dignitaries of the new diocese. The feud was continued by a monster trial at Satu Mare, where Father Mureşianu and fourteen of his parishioners were sentenced to varying terms of imprisonment for their resistance to Hajdudorog.

Tisza was of course well aware of the precarious situation arising from the Balkan wars, and it was this above all which led him in October 1913 to propose a discussion with the Roumanian National Council.[1] No meeting ever took place, for when Tisza's proposals were submitted to them, the Roumanians—and here Goga and the younger men were in full agreement with Maniu, Miháli and Pop—unanimously rejected them as inadequate and reaffirmed the programme of 1881, which of course included Tisza's red rag, Transylvanian autonomy. The breach again widened, and on the eve of the Great War a fresh series of press trials was pending against Roumanian journalists. Goga's brilliant play, *The Village Notary*, had caused keen annoyance in Magyar circles, especially when it was staged by the National Theatre of Bucarest.

The murder of the archduke was a death-blow to Roumanian hopes, and henceforth Bucarest inevitably took the place of Vienna in all plans for the future. But we shall see that the cautious and equivocal attitude of the Roumanian kingdom during the first two years of war forced the Roumanian leaders in Hungary to be even more negative and temporising.

[1] It is interesting to recall an article of Dr Vaida-Voevod entitled "Slawen, Deutsche, Magyaren und Rumänen" in the *Oesterreichische Rundschau* for January, 1913—an article then thoroughly representative of Roumanian opinion in Hungary. He denounces as "beer-table fantasy" the idea of a Daco-Roman Empire to the Theiss, achieved by Russian aid. He demands a strong Habsburg Monarchy and treats the double hegemony of German and Magyar as the root of all evil. Count Tisza—"the uncrowned King of Hungary"—is working not for the consolidation of the Monarchy, but for the rule of the Gentry oligarchy over "inferior races." A final phrase is obviously addressed to the Archduke Francis Ferdinand—"We need a strong hand and a powerful will: Providence must send them to us."

# CHAPTER XIV

# ROUMANIA AND THE BALKAN PROBLEM
## (1908–1914)

Roumania was still recovering from the severe shock administered to her prestige at home and abroad by the Peasant Rising of 1907, when the crisis in Balkan affairs assumed a more acute form. For over a decade from 1908 onwards foreign policy was to remain the predominant issue, upon which internal reform was also to depend.

Thanks very largely to the Austro-Russian agreement achieved in 1897 by Counts Lamsdorff and Goluchowski and to the success of the Powers in localising the Cretan question, there had been a period of relative calm in the peninsula for the following six years. But it was already quite obvious that Macedonia was a dangerous storm centre, torn by rival propagandas in church and school, which the Turks played off against each other with no little skill. As yet the main struggle was between Greeks and Bulgars, but the Serbs and Albanians were already asserting themselves in the northern and western districts, and even the Vlachs, as liberally subsidised from Bucarest as their neighbours from Athens, Sofia and Belgrade, became a by no means negligible factor. The events of 1903, however, created a new situation: for the Bulgarian insurrection, though drowned in blood, revealed the full intensity of racial feeling, posed the whole question before Europe, and forced the Powers to intervene. By a pure coincidence there was in the same year a change of regime in Serbia (the overthrow of the Obrenović dynasty), in Croatia (the fall of Khuen Hedérváry), and in Bosnia (the death of Kállay) which, though it as yet passed unnoticed abroad, altered the focus of the Southern Slav question and set new forces in motion.

From 1903 to 1908 the question of Macedonian reform was one of the main preoccupations of European policy, and went through successive phases relating to finance, administration and gendarmerie. Austria-Hungary and Russia, it was generally recognised, were of all the Powers the two most directly interested in the Near East: the agreement reached between their foreign ministers at Mürzsteg in October 1903—literally a few hours before the more far-reaching proposals of Lord Lansdowne reached Vienna—remained for some years the foundation upon which all attempts at settlement had to rest. Friction was averted as long as Lamsdorff and Goluchowski remained in office, and indeed in proportion as Russia became involved in a gigantic struggle with Japan for the mastery of the Far East, she found co-operation with Vienna in the Balkans convenient and even necessary. For some time after the Peace of Portsmouth, though again free to look westwards, she was still sufficiently exhausted to dislike the prospect of fresh foreign complications; and Austro-Russian relations might have continued good but for the personal element which was introduced in 1906. Baron Aehrenthal owed his appointment as foreign minister very largely to the Russophil reputation which he had acquired during many years at the Embassy in St Petersburg: but ere long his relations with Izvolsky, Lamsdorff's successor as Russian foreign minister, grew increasingly strained, and the friction which first became apparent in connection with the abortive Sandjak Railway project of February 1908 resolved itself, during the long Bosnian annexation crisis, into an embittered trial of strength between the two men, resting upon mutual recriminations and charges of bad faith. In the background were Aehrenthal's acute distrust of Britain and his annoyance at the Anglo-Russian *rapprochement*: and indeed his political outlook may be measured by the fact that to him Izvolsky and Stolypin passed as "Liberals", in no small measure owing to their Anglophil tendencies. Yet another dangerous ingredient in the situation was Aehrenthal's complete indifference to the cause of Turkish reform and his desire to exploit Turkish difficulties for his own ends. Thus while Sir Edward Grey, as early as December 1907, was gravely alarmed at the anarchy and unrest in European Turkey and earnestly working for common action of the Powers, as the sole means of averting disaster,[1] Aehrenthal made his own private bargain with the Porte for a railway concession at the expense of Macedonian reform, and meanwhile expounded to Berlin his desire for the isolation of Britain.[2] The Young Turkish Revolution widened the gap between the rival statesmen and precipitated events: for while Grey, without any foolish illusions, regarded the Young Turks as the least of evils inside Turkey and honestly strove to smooth their path by holding back Russia and discouraging the formation of "two opposing camps" in Europe,[3] Aehrenthal quite erroneously assumed that the meeting of

[1] *British Documents*, v, nos. 173, 179, 182.
[2] *Ibid.* no. 184; *Grosse Politik*, no. 7676—30 April 1907.
[3] *B.D.* v, nos. 219, 388, 408.

King Edward and the tsar at Reval had been the signal for the revolution, and now decided upon the annexation of Bosnia, without any regard for possible consequences to the new Turkish regime. His attitude to Serbia, following upon the so-called "Pig War", was rigid and hostile: he simply insisted that the Bosnian question was no affair of hers, and that she must be refused any direct access to the Adriatic or territorial contact with Montenegro, and he allied himself at home with the Magyar Chauvinists in their campaign against the dominant party in Croatia, the Serbo-Croat Coalition. The Zagreb Treason Trial was staged in order to convince the world of Serbian guilt, and clinching proof was added by an inspired article of the historian Friedjung, published on the day when a declaration of war against Serbia seemed certain. But the whole plan failed, the Zagreb and Friedjung trials developed into an European scandal, while Serbo-Croat unity became a prime issue of Austro-Hungarian internal and external policy, and Serbia began to assume the rôle of a Southern Slav Piedmont in proportion as Vienna, and above all Budapest, alienated those sympathies from the Habsburgs which a tradition of three centuries had engrained in a large section of the race. It followed almost automatically that Austria-Hungary, not content with the attempt to set Serb and Croat against each other, sought to exalt Bulgaria at the expense of Serbia and to place the latter between two fires. Her general staff, under the masterful Conrad von Hötzendorf, propounded the view that Austria-Hungary's strategic line of advance to the Aegean inevitably lay up the valley of the Morava, through the heart of the Serbian kingdom.

This highly complex and changing situation could not be indifferent to Roumania, though she played at first a somewhat passive rôle. Her distrust of Russia, inculcated by the bitter experience of 1877–8, had become little short of an obsession: and the Pan-Slav bogey not merely drove her into the Triple Alliance, but was responsible for her submitting to many things from Hungary which would normally have thrown her into the rival camp. But with the defeat of Russia in the Far East a load seemed to have been lifted from Roumania's shoulders: her statesmen breathed again and attached themselves more confidently than ever to Berlin and Vienna, whose undiminished prestige and military power seemed to them the surest guarantee of the existing European order. From 1900 to 1910 the post of German minister in Bucarest was held by Kiderlen-Waechter, a man of outstanding ability whom William II for reasons of personal pique kept in relative diplomatic exile, but who won the confidence of both the king and his ministers and of course did nothing to discourage their view that "Roumania's road to Vienna leads through Berlin".[1] For them Germany, not Austria, still less Hungary, was the key to their alliance policy.

The Bosnian crisis shook Roumanian complacency: for while it was satisfactory to realise that Russia, much as she might sympathise with Serbia, was not ready to face another war for her sake, it was by now apparent that Austria-Hungary was bent upon the destruction of Serbia and that one method of attaining that end was to encourage the aggrandisement of Bulgaria. Indeed, during the decade preceding the Great War it was generally believed that Bulgaria was superior to all her neighbours, alike on moral and on military grounds and was predestined for the hegemony of the Balkan peninsula at no distant date. This idea was highly distasteful to Bucarest, where Bulgaria now tended to replace Russia as political bogey, and all the more so because neither Serbia nor Greece was valued very highly as a counterweight. King Charles's nervousness was increased by his suspicion of King Ferdinand —a suspicion which he shared with almost all the crowned heads of Europe, whether related or unrelated to the Coburgs: but his aversion to the Karagjorgjević dynasty, and to the events which had brought it to the throne, as yet held him back from any *rapprochement* with Serbia. None the less he admitted to General von Conrad that he regarded Serbia as "a flank position against Bulgaria".[2] Moreover, he was not blind to the parallel nature of Serbian and Roumanian interests in so far as their kinsmen in Hungary were concerned. He saw with a certain disquietude the gradual decay of the Dual System and the rapid increase of Magyar Chauvinism, and already in 1903 he had privately advised the Roumanian leaders in Hungary to abandon the policy of abstention and make a stand against Budapest. To Take Ionescu he actually let fall the remark, "Do you suppose that Austria is eternal, and that we shall never see its dismemberment?"[3]

Early in 1909 failing health forced Dimitrie Sturdza to resign the premiership. His place was taken by Ionel Brătianu, the eldest son of the great Liberal statesman, and already leader of a younger Liberal

---

[1] E. Jäckh, *Kiderlen-Waechter*, II, p. 180.

[2] 22 June 1908—Conrad, *Aus meiner Dienstzeit*, I, appendix 24, p. 589.

[3] *French Diplomatic Documents*, 2nd series, nos. 252 (19 May) and 378 (29 July 1903).

*fronde.* At home Brătianu rested his policy, like his father before him, upon the expansion of the new urban middle class—though some of his younger colleagues, and notably Ion Duca, devoted a sympathetic attention to the agrarian problem. Abroad, his attitude was one of suspicious, but realistic, nationalism, determined to maintain the existing balance of forces in the peninsula or to exact ample compensation for any change. He was impressed by the success of the Central Powers against Russia and accepted it as a proof that the rumours of internal disintegration in Austria-Hungary were quite unfounded. It was already abundantly obvious that his main preoccupation was to be on the winning side, and to leave sentiment to others.

In the summer following the crisis the Archduke Francis Ferdinand visited Sinaia and expended all his great personal charm, with very real success, upon the Roumanian statesmen. He was all the more effective because he made it quite clear both to the king and to the premier that he sympathised with Roumanian aspirations, disapproved of Magyar policy in Transylvania and was actually very pleased at the annoyance which his visit to Roumania had caused in Budapest. A few days afterwards Brătianu came to Prince Schönburg, the Austro-Hungarian minister, and declared "I am no *phraseur,* but I shall never forget the way in which the Archduke spoke to me and his genuine sympathy for the Roumanian people".[1] But it is highly characteristic of Brătianu that he then paid visits in Vienna and Berlin and sounded Aehrenthal as to possible compensation for Bulgarian expansion and talked vaguely of impending war. Kiderlen, who by now knew Roumanian politics through and through, reported very unfavourably upon Brătianu, who, he said, "cannot sleep for fear of Greater Bulgaria", and consoled himself for the prospect of a Turkish collapse by the hope of obtaining not merely Silistra—the town denied to Roumania in 1878—but even the Rushchuk-Varna line.[2] Brătianu did not attempt to conceal from Schönburg that "Roumania will do all in her power to prevent one-sided aggrandisement of Bulgaria": but he utterly failed to extract any pledge from Aehrenthal and resigned himself to a watching game. It was at this time a very common pose on the part of Roumanian statesmen to declare, as did the king to Schönburg in March 1910, that "we belong to the Balkans neither ethnographically nor geographically nor in any other way".[3] But this deceived no one; for Roumania was as

[1] *Austro-Hungarian Documents,* II, no. 1676—15 July 1909.
[2] *Ibid.* no. 1726—24 August.      [3] *Ibid.* no. 2089.

vitally concerned in the transformation of European Turkey as in the fate of her own kinsmen north of the Carpathians.

At more than one moment during the Bosnian crisis an European war had seemed inevitable, and when a peaceful settlement was at last reached, the relief was correspondingly great. But this only served to obscure the fact that, though certain jagged rocks had been avoided and the water now seemed deeper, the current was stronger and the river positively racing towards the edge of a stupendous cataract. The internal situation in Turkey was long past recovery: the chief criminal, Abdul Hamid, was overthrown by a second revolution in April 1909, but the dominant Committee of Union and Progress now threw off the mask of racial conciliation and plunged into a policy of rabid Turkification, which inevitably drove the Christian races into rebellion or alliance with their kinsmen across the borders. Thus from 1909 to 1911 there was a rapid recrudescence of komitadji activities in Macedonia, while Shevket Torgut Pasha waged regular war upon the Albanians and thus incidentally alienated from Turkey the one race which had shown real loyalty and devotion in the past. Meanwhile Izvolsky, still smarting from his defeat at the hands of Aehrenthal, set himself to promote a Balkan League, ostensibly for the greater independence of the smaller states, but of course in reality under the aegis of Russia. What completely vitiated his first effort was that it was conceived merely as an alliance of the three Slav states—Bulgaria, Serbia and Montenegro—with a reconstituted Turkey: it left out Greece, presumably owing to her Pan-Hellenic aims, and Roumania as too completely in the orbit of Austria-Hungary. It thus betrayed the ulterior object of undermining the influence of the Dual Monarchy, and indirectly of the Triple Alliance, in the affairs of the Near East. During 1910 both King Peter and King Ferdinand visited Constantinople, and the Turkish heir apparent paid return visits to Sofia and Belgrade: while the proclamation of Montenegro as a kingdom provided an excuse for further discussions among Balkan sovereigns. But any wider alliance in the sense advocated by Charikov, Izvolsky's enterprising representative at the Porte, was rendered impossible by Turkish racial intolerance and by what a British diplomat called the "almost unrealisable ambitions" of the Christian states.[1] Meanwhile to all this Roumania adopted an attitude of extreme reserve. Brătianu was resolved to prevent "any

[1] *B.D.* IX (i), no. 135—10 March 1910, Cartwright to Grey.

one-sided aggrandisement of Bulgaria":[1] to Kiderlen he expressed a preference for the *status quo*, both towards Turkey and Austria-Hungary,[2] but he shared, though reluctantly, the view of his Serbian colleague Milovanović, that internal causes rendered Turkey's collapse inevitable, and in that event his solution was parallel aggrandisement and compensation for all the Christian states, which for Roumania meant extension in southern Dobrogea.[3] He was in entire accord with King Charles's resolve to maintain peace as long as possible, but "as soon as the balance of Balkan power was disturbed, to throw his sword into the scales".[4]

During the winter of 1910 the king decided upon one of his periodical reshufflings of the party cards: but on this occasion he had a choice of alternatives. Peter Carp had succeeded to the leadership of the Old Conservatives on the death of G. G. Cantacuzene, but Take Ionescu—who after the Peasant Rising had been offered the leadership by one wing of the party, but had refused to "add a harem revolution to a civil war"—none the less seceded a year later and formed a group of Conservative Dissidents, sometimes nicknamed "the party of malcontents". The king had many reserves about Carp despite his strongly Germanophil outlook: "I can influence them all," he once told Schönburg, "Sturdza, Brătianu, even Take, but never Carp, though I like him".[5] But he definitely distrusted Take Ionescu, alike for his western connections, his demagogic gifts, and his mercurial temperament, and felt that the active support which Take gave to the Standard Oil Company in its exploitation of the Roumanian oilfields went too far in the opposite direction from the Brătianu brothers' xenophobia.[6] It was therefore Carp, not Ionescu, who became premier in January 1911, with Marghiloman as minister of the interior and Titu Maiorescu and Filipescu as his other two most prominent colleagues. Their programme contained numerous administrative and other reforms, but only a small portion of these could be realised, and the electoral methods employed in 1911 envenomed still further the party feud. The Liberals, reduced

---

[1] *A.H.D.* II, no. 1740—17 September 1909, Schönburg to Aehrenthal.
[2] Jäckh, *op. cit.* II, p. 183.
[3] *B.D.* IX (i), no. 172—12 August 1910, Cartwright to Grey.
[4] *A.H.D.* III, no. 2563—13 July 1911, Fürstenberg to Aehrenthal.
[5] *A.H.D.* II, no. 1907—18 December 1909.
[6] On 27 November 1910 the king expressed to Marghiloman the fear that Take Ionescu "as chief of the Government, might become the man of the Americans and the instrument of Rockefeller". *Note Politice*, I, p. 82.

to a mere handful, withdrew in dudgeon from the Chamber and organised a violent campaign in the country, in conjunction with the "Takists". A panamist affair connected with the Bucarest tramways gave only too welcome an opportunity for mutual mud-flinging. It was during this period of opposition that Ionel Brătianu fell under the influence of Constantine Stere, a Bessarabian boiar who had been banished to Siberia for his liberal views, and who now sought to convince the statesmen of his adopted country of the need for fundamental reforms in land tenure and the franchise. Stere never occupied the front of the stage and his rôle as the "éminence grise" of the Liberal party may well have been exaggerated: but it seems certain that he first matured a definite design for outbidding the Conservatives and attaching the masses to the Liberal party by structural changes in the state.

During 1911 Roumania was increasingly reserved and vigilant towards Balkan developments: dominated by the narrow conception of compensation, she weighed the possibility of a Turkish alliance only to reject it, not for reasons of principle, but from a well-grounded feeling that Turkey's dissolution was at last in sight. This process was greatly hastened by the outbreak of the Tripolitan War in September 1911: for it encouraged, and indeed almost compelled the various Balkan Governments to debate every possible combination, with a view to being "in at the death" and securing a due share of the booty. Italy acted for her own interests and while occupying the Dodecanese wisely restricted her military action to African soil: any attempt at operations in the coveted Albania would have at once involved Austria-Hungary, since it would have run counter to the self-denying ordinance into which Rome and Vienna had entered in 1907 when renewing the Triple Alliance. But the renewed unrest in Albania, a massacre at Istip in December 1911 and the excesses of the Turkish elections, which reduced the opposition to a handful of ten, served as so many warning signals of urgency. The majority of Crown Prince Boris in February 1912 was attended by the crown princes of Roumania, Serbia, Greece and Montenegro and was the occasion of an unique demonstration of inter-Balkan solidarity, which was unhappily not to endure. The absence of Turkey from the gathering was a no less marked and ominous fact, which corresponded only too well with what was happening behind the scenes. During the winter secret negotiations had been proceeding between Serbia and Bulgaria and quite separately between Bulgaria and Greece: in the former case the initiative had come from Milovanović in

Belgrade, in the latter from Venizelos in Athens. Russia was admitted to the secret at an early stage, but Sazonov as foreign minister was at once less energetic and less assertive than his predecessor Izvolsky, and played a consultative rather than a directive rôle. Indeed it is quite evident that the idea of a Balkan Alliance had taken quite a different turn from that put forward by Charikov with the full sanction of St Petersburg; and his recall from Constantinople really marked the final failure of the attempt to include Turkey, though this was of course not realised at the time. Sazonov looked at the Balkans through narrowly Slav and Orthodox spectacles and laid the main weight of his calculations upon Bulgaria and Serbia, thinking that Greece could be relegated to the background and Roumania paralysed by her geographical position: by the close of the year he saw that he could not ride the whirlwind and in vain strove to hold back the forces which he had let loose.

The main foundation of the whole alliance was the Serbo-Bulgarian Treaty of 13 March 1912, supplemented by the military convention of 12 May: the corresponding Bulgaro-Greek engagements were signed on 29 May and 23 September, while the Serbs and Greeks eventually entered the war without any precise political understanding. The essence of the Serbo-Bulgarian treaty consisted of a mutual guarantee of territory, mutual assistance with all their forces in the event of either becoming involved in a war with Turkey, and an indication of the lands which each would annex if their joint arms were crowned with victory. Macedonian autonomy was envisaged, though not defined: but it was agreed that if this should prove impossible of attainment, certain districts lying to the south-east of the Šar mountains should be regarded as a neutral zone, and the decision regarding its fate should be left to the arbitration of the tsar of Russia, to whom the whole arrangement was to be communicated. The main purpose of the military conventions was to lay down the respective forces to be employed against Turkey, but a special clause committed Bulgaria to sending 200,000 men to the aid of Serbia, in the event of an attack from the side of Austria-Hungary. If on the other hand Roumania should attack Bulgaria, Serbia was bound to declare war immediately and send at least 100,000 men to Bulgaria's aid: and Bulgaria was also bound to defend Serbia against a Roumanian attack, though this time the number of troops was not specified. The Bulgarian premier, Geshov, who conducted the whole negotiations, states in his memoirs that King Ferdinand's consent to the clauses against Austria and Roumania was only obtained because he knew the text of an Austro-Roumanian military convention of September 1900, giving Roumania under certain circumstances the right to annex not only Silistra, but perhaps even Rushchuk, Shumla and Varna![1] No such convention has ever seen the light, but it may possibly be one of the documents upon which the post-war Roumanian veto upon Austrian official publications has descended.

In this extremely fluid and uncertain situation King Charles seemed to be aging rapidly, and his nervous irritation was reflected in talk of abdication.[2] Feeling that the Conservatives were not strong enough to stand alone in a foreign crisis of the first magnitude, he pressed for a reconstruction of the cabinet through the inclusion of the Dissident Takists. But he was not prepared to take Brătianu's advice and make Take Ionescu premier: this would, he considered, be "un malheur national", and his old prejudice revived in the phrase that "he hoped not to end his reign by the shame of a Take Government".[3] The utmost he would concede was the Ministry of the Interior to Ionescu, if the latter would take office under Brătianu as premier: but the latter in his turn was not prepared to share power with a faction in which the brilliancy of its chief could not conceal the mediocrity of the rank and file. Finally, after long bickering and intrigue, Carp gave place in April 1912 to Maiorescu; and negotiations were set on foot with Take Ionescu for a fusion of the two Conservative groups. Two other notable changes about the same time had a very important bearing upon the Balkan situation. On 29 February Count Aehrenthal died and was succeeded by the nonchalant and superficial Count Berchtold, and on 1 July the premature death of Milovanović, the ablest Serbian statesman of this century, brought into power the less scrupulous Nicholas Pašić, a blind devotee of Russian conservatism and orthodoxy.

The Balkan agreements, though hedged round with the utmost precautions, afford the classical proof that the old diplomacy was breaking down and that real secrecy could no longer be assured. Russia was already in the plot, and we now know that the British minister in Sofia, Sir Henry Bax-Ironside, was able to report every stage to London.[4]

---

[1] I. E. Gueschoff, *The Balkan League*, p. 36.
[2] Marghiloman, *Note Politice*, I, p. 78.            [3] *Ibid.* pp. 78, 105.
[4] *B.D.* IX (i), nos. 543 (18 June), 555 (26 February), 558 and 559 (14 March), 560 (16 May). It is important to note that so far from expressing approval or satisfaction, the British Government held that it was "most unfortunate that such a Convention has been concluded, especially under Russian auspices" (Nicolson to Cartwright, 18 March—*ibid.* no. 560).

Geshov, while giving him this information with the knowledge and approval of Russia, did not impart it to the French minister: but this may merely have been because Sazonov himself, after a certain interval, kept Paris much more fully informed of every detail.

Meanwhile, within a few weeks of the original agreement, Kiderlen Waechter, now German foreign secretary, informed King Charles that Berlin knew—from an unimpeachable source which he could not reveal[1]—of the existence of a Serbo-Bulgarian alliance under direct Russian auspices: and had assumed Russia's aim to be "to hold the Balkan states in her hand and prevent them from independent action".[2] In actual fact Sazonov had been quite genuinely concerned to end the internecine quarrel between Serbia and Bulgaria by fixing their mutual spheres of influence: but behind this there of course lay the old desire for a common Slav policy in the Balkans. The would-be allies did not, however, initiate Russia into the details beforehand: Sazonov was confronted with the clause on Russian arbitration as an accomplished fact, and was afraid that if he refused they might turn elsewhere.[3]

It is highly characteristic of the relations between Berlin and Vienna that Kiderlen did not let Vienna into the secret. The Austro-Hungarian minister in Sofia, Count Tarnowski, well informed though he was, remained quite sceptical during the summer as to the various rumours of a Serbo-Bulgarian alliance, and in his reports to Berchtold did not hesitate to treat it as impossible.[4] Even as late as October, he maintained the same attitude and argued from parallel action, rather than concrete agreements, between the belligerent governments.[5] Meanwhile Kiderlen continued to criticise Berchtold to King Charles; and the two men agreed that every effort must be made to prevent the conduct of policy passing from Berlin to Vienna, as Aehrenthal had achieved against Bulow, "for one day that might cost us dearly".[6] He was only paying back, with some interest in the way of resentment, Berchtold's

[1] It is difficult to avoid the conclusion that this source was King Ferdinand of Bulgaria.

[2] Jäckh, op. cit. II, p. 186.

[3] B. v. Siebert, Diplomatische Aktenstücke, pp. 560–1—Sazonov to Benckendorff, 31 October 1912.

[4] A.H.D. IV, no. 3703 (16 August). He was still sceptical on 4 September (ibid. no. 3764).

[5] Ibid. nos. 4064, 4065 (12 October), 4161 (23 October).

[6] Jäckh, op. cit. II, p. 188. The king told Prince Fürstenberg a month later that Kiderlen had informed him of a close relation between Bulgaria and Serbia, to counterbalance Roumania's alliance with the Dreibund. A.H.D. IV, no. 3530—21 May.

own tendency to keep secrets and confront his ally with accomplished facts. "We are not bound", he told his chief, the Chancellor Bethmann Hollweg, "to support Austria-Hungary in her Eastern adventures.... We don't want to play the Austrian satellite in the East."[1] There was no doubt in this the tacit implication that the chancellor was no match for Vienna in the sphere of foreign policy, but that Kiderlen himself might save the situation. It may not have been modest, but it was probably true, and the latter's sudden death in the last days of the year was a real disaster from the standpoint both of a firm and constant German policy and of an unravelling of the Balkan tangle.

During the summer of 1912 the pace of events was hastened by fresh troubles in Albania: the Turkish Government was obviously losing control, and both the scheme of reforms proposed by Count Berchtold in August and the very inadequate concessions offered by the Porte in September entirely failed to ease the situation. The Powers' belated effort at collective action, with its endeavour to soothe Turkish susceptibilities and its insistence upon a *status quo* which had become untenable, caused genuine alarm in all the Balkan capitals: and the sudden promise to enforce the Treaty of Berlin (after it had been allowed to remain on paper for thirty-four years) seemed little short of a mockery. On 13 October 1912 Bulgaria, Serbia and Greece presented a series of drastic demands for national autonomy, such as would virtually have created a series of states within the Turkish state and subjected the central authorities to the control of the ambassadors. It cannot be doubted that they neither expected nor desired a favourable answer, and as the Turks preferred to ignore the Note altogether, war followed two days later. The allies were not deterred by the warning of the Powers that they would insist upon the maintenance of the *status quo*: for they calculated—and, as events showed, rightly—that Europe was too profoundly divided to be able to enforce its will.

The Great Powers on their side, though for very different reasons, were all opposed to war. Russia was extremely annoyed at her inability to control the movement to which she had been privy, and feared the possible consequences: indeed Sazonov, who was on a visit to the West, made it clear to Poincaré that in the event of war he hoped for a check to the allies, and especially to Bulgaria, since the Powers could then

---

[1] *G.P.* XXXIII, no. 12135—2 September 1912.

extract concessions from Turkey, whereas complete victory "would upset everything".[1] Austria-Hungary, on her side, having by now obtained an inkling of the secret clause against herself, was mainly concerned with destroying the harmony between the new allies and, above all, preventing any aggrandisement of Serbia. Britain, though sufficiently disillusioned by the Young Turk regime, would still have liked to postpone the catastrophe and was most anxious to avoid dividing Europe into two hostile camps.[2] France was frankly alarmed at the European aspect of the affair, while Italy was absorbed in her African spoil, but anxious to check Austrian influence in Albania. Germany by no means saw eye to eye with her ally, being highly suspicious of Bulgaria and her king, not indisposed to sympathise with Serbia and especially anxious that Roumania should be humoured and not alienated from the Triple Alliance. On one point only did the Powers seem to have been united on the eve of war—namely in the belief that the Turks would be victorious and that the refractory Christian states would soon have to submit to a settlement dictated from without. It was this which gave the League a brief respite and enabled it to confront Europe with accomplished facts of the most drastic kind. King Charles did not share this view, though he did not foresee a complete Turkish *débâcle*: but he felt that the greatest possible reserve was enjoined upon him in so fluid a situation, when events might swiftly dislocate his relations with the two main groups in Europe.

The overwhelming successes of the allied armies radically transformed the situation. By the end of November 1912 Turkish rule in Europe was restricted to the lines of Chataldja and Gallipoli and the three fortresses of Adrianople, Janina and Skutari. It was abundantly obvious that the fallen structure could never be re-erected and little more was heard of the Powers' insistence upon the *status quo*. William II had hit the nail on the head when he described the attempt to restrain the allies as hopeless—a mere "*testimonium paupertatis* for Europe": and he was now quick to accept the Turkish defeat and to insist upon "free fight and no favour" for the allies in their "justifiable storm of victory".[3] But it followed logically that the various agreements between the allies were already quite out of date and would have to be drastically

---

[1] Poincaré, *Les Balkans en Feu*, p. 234.
[2] *B.D.* IX (i), no. 722.
[3] *G.P.* XXXIII, marginalia on nos. 12235, 12246, 12297, 12320, 12321.

revised. Large areas were not provided for at all, and the problem assumed quite a new form if the three main victors were to acquire a common frontier somewhere in the centre of the peninsula: while the position of Albania in the west and Roumania in the north, the general aspects of Balkan balance of power and the attitude of the neighbouring Great Powers, introduced further complications. Most serious of all was the acute friction which now flared up afresh between Austria-Hungary and Serbia: for not merely was the former Power enraged at such a disturbance of all her political calculations, but was watching with pardonable anxiety the wave of enthusiasm for the Balkan allies and the Serbian "Piedmont" which swept through the Southern Slav provinces of the Dual Monarchy. The movement took all the more acute forms because by an irony of fate the Balkan deliverance coincided with a renewed Magyar-Croat conflict and the Cuvaj dictatorship in Croatia. It is not surprising that such swift success went to the allies' heads. The Serbs, in Sazonov's phrase, were "taken by a kind of *vertige*",[1] and talked of Dušan's Empire: the Greeks assumed that Crown Prince Constantine was destined to wear the crown of the last Paleologus: while King Ferdinand forgot his Coburg caution and prepared for a state entry into Constantinople and a coronation in purple buskins in the Church of the Holy Wisdom.

Meanwhile the official press in Vienna and Budapest adopted a menacing tone towards Serbia, which the Serb gutter press repaid with interest, and the story of gross insults to the person of Prochaska, the Austrian consul in Prizren, threw Vienna into a ferment and was kept alive by the Ballplatz long after its falsity had been established. As the Serb army approached the Adriatic, Austria-Hungary mobilised, and for a time a conflict seemed inevitable. Count Berchtold's main aim was to prevent the aggrandisement of Serbia in any form, and to hold her in check by a predominant Bulgaria: but in the end, finding no support from any of the Powers and restrained by Berlin's highly critical attitude, he fell back upon an irreducible minimum, by which (1) Serbia was to be excluded from all access to the Adriatic and to sign commercial treaties with the Monarchy, (2) an independent Albanian state was to be created, (3) Salonica was to be a free port, and (4) Roumania was to receive territorial compensation.[2] It followed inevitably

[1] Poincaré, *op. cit.* p. 323—Sazonov to Georges Louis, 10 November.
[2] Cf. *G.P.* xxxiii, no. 12320—Kiderlen to William II, 3 November; *F.D.D.* no. 392—8 November; *A.H.D.* iv, no. 4673—28 November.

from this that Serbia, if a western port were denied to her, would be forced by geography, quite apart from politics, to seek compensation to the south, in other words to claim the valley of the Vardar, which was her sole alternative route to the sea: and this again, as Vienna was well aware when she defined her veto, inevitably involved Serbia in conflict with Bulgaria for the populations living to the west of the Vardar.[1] Signs of friction between the allies were thus only too apparent during the Peace Conference which met in December in London: but so long as there was a possibility of renewed hostilities and the Serb siege guns were still needed to reduce Adrianople, a rupture was avoided. If peace had then been concluded under the pressure of the Great Powers—who on the whole worked together with remarkable cordiality —all might still have been well: but at the very last moment Kiamil Pasha was overthrown by a palace revolution in Constantinople, the commander-in-chief Nazim Pasha was assassinated and the Young Turks under Talaat and Enver adopted an uncompromising attitude. Hostilities were resumed on 28 January, and during the two months that elapsed before Adrianople and Skutari could be forced to surrender, the Balkan rivals were entrenching themselves in their new possessions, peaceful readjustment became increasingly difficult, and foreign fishing in troubled waters correspondingly easy.

This brief outline was essential to any understanding of Roumanian policy during the Balkan Wars, which was determined by a cautious balancing of forces and a resolve to avoid all commitments so far as possible till the very last moment. Roumania thus became to some extent the finger upon the scale, and doubts as to her possible attitude played a decisive part in restraining Austria-Hungary from armed intervention.

On the eve of Balkan hostilities King Charles summoned a cabinet council, in which he treated war as ultimately inevitable, but in the meantime advocated a waiting attitude and a concentration of the Conservative forces, as safer than the transfer of power to the Liberals. This last aim was achieved by the admission of Take Ionescu to the Maiorescu Cabinet as minister of the interior, with portfolios for three

---

[1] As early as 16 December the Serb Delegation to the London Peace Conference informed Izvolsky that this would be Serbia's attitude. The situation is very neatly summed up in a telegram of Georges Louis to Poincaré on 10 November (Poincaré, *op. cit.* p. 322); "Pousser la Serbie vers la mer Égée, c'est vouloir la brouiller avec les Bulgares et avec les Grecs".

of his adherents. From the first the king warned Vienna that he could not allow any notable change of the Balkan *status quo* without compensation for Roumania: but at the same time he promised to take no important step without first consulting Austria-Hungary and Germany.[1] He brushed aside Turkey's overture for a military convention[2] and as the allies pushed forward, he pinned his hopes for a moment upon the intervention of the Great Powers, an European Conference and the grant of independence to Albania and Macedonia: this would avert undue expansion on the part of Bulgaria and any armed conflict between the rival races.[3] Bulgaria's military success and soaring ambitions roused all his old suspicions and forced him to change his tactics: for Turkey was ceasing to be a counterweight, and he must therefore look more towards Serbia and Greece. Meanwhile public opinion took alarm, and gave open expression to the fear that Austria-Hungary aimed at a Big Bulgaria and was trying to hold back Roumania from action until it was too late. Prince Fürstenberg, who was both well informed and sober in judgment, warned Berchtold that the Dual Monarchy was steadily losing popularity and that the alliance would be compromised if Roumania obtained nothing.[4]

It was at this stage that the Archduke Francis Ferdinand, in his capacity as inspector-general of the army, sent General Conrad von Hötzendorf on a special mission to Bucarest—the pretext being condolence with the king on the death of his sister the countess of Flanders, but the real aim being to explore Roumania's military and political intentions and to make sure of her in the event of complications. Acting on instructions, he assured King Charles that Austria-Hungary would watch over Roumanian interests and obtained from him the verbal pledge that in the event of an European war, "Roumania would play her part as a loyal ally".[5] He conferred with the Roumanian chief of staff, General Averescu, who, being a native of Bessarabia and closely acquainted with conditions in the Russian army, was, Conrad reported, far more reliable from the standpoint of the Triple Alliance than either the Liberal leader Brătianu or the two brilliant Conservatives, Take Ionescu and Filipescu. Conrad dropped a few hints in favour of the

---

[1] *A.H.D.* iv, nos. 4111 (16 October), 4212 (31 October).
[2] *F.D.D.* 3rd series, iv, no. 257.
[3] *A.H.D.* iv, no. 4226—1 November.
[4] *Ibid.* nos. 4418, 4442.
[5] *A.H.D.* iv, no. 4719; Conrad, *op. cit.* ii, p. 351.

project of Dr Riedl[1] for a customs union between Roumania and Austria-Hungary, and returned home eager that Roumanian claims should receive fuller consideration in Vienna. Only a month later he was reappointed chief of general staff, but was unable to win either Francis Joseph or Francis Ferdinand for his firebrand schemes of a preventive war against Serbia or Italy. His insistence upon the strategic importance of Roumania and its bearing upon the whole policy of the Triple Alliance appears to have played no small part in holding back the Monarchy from more radical alternatives.

Austria-Hungary indeed found herself between Scylla and Charybdis: for in proportion as she pressed the claims of Bulgaria against Serbia she drove Roumania to support Serbia and Greece as a counterweight to Bulgaria's dream of hegemony. On the other hand, her efforts to win Bulgaria for concessions were far from successful. The Russophil statesman Dr Danev, then no less powerful than the premier Ivan Geshov, passed through Bucarest after a visit to Vienna and Budapest, but his intransigeance made a very unfavourable impression upon the king and his ministers: the most that he would consider was the renunciation of any Bulgarian claim to Dobrogea, a few minor rectifications of frontier, and a guarantee for the Vlachs of Macedonia. But the old grievance of 1877 had been reopened by events: the Roumanians, so far from regarding this as a concession, had always held the view that Silistra had been filched from them by a Russian intrigue, and that its restoration was but their due. Maiorescu laid the main stress upon Silistra, which he called "a wedge in Roumania's flesh", arguing that the frontier of 1878 had been imposed upon both countries and that it was now time to make their own arrangement.[2] But Chauvinist opinion, as voiced by many Liberals, talked of the "quadrilateral" of Shumla-Silistra-Rushchuk-Varna. The intermediate line demanded by the Bulgarophil Take Ionescu and favoured by the king was to run from Turtucaia to Balchik: and it was this demand which became the basis of negotiations between Mişu and Danev in the wings of the London Conference. Take Ionescu, who had an English wife and old associations with London, was sent there on a less formal mission, but was accused by jealous rivals of talking too much, and certainly failed to soften the unflinching Danev.[3]

---

[1] A high Austrian official who enjoyed the confidence of Francis Ferdinand.
[2] *A.H.D.* v, no. 4878—12 December.
[3] Cf. *A.H.D.* v, nos. 5208, 5281, 5289, 5369, 5370.

At the turn of the year it was plain that the negotiations were going badly, and Fürstenberg sent fresh warnings as to Roumanian susceptibility. Francis Ferdinand, it is true, sent a warm New Year's message to the king, and hoped Roumania's services to world peace would earn "suitable recognition": while Conrad urged that the Monarchy should range itself "openly and unreservedly" on Roumania's side.[1] On 6 January, then, Fürstenberg was instructed to inform the king that as a result of Austria-Hungary's sustained pressure in Sofia, Bulgaria was at last willing to cede something more than a mere strip of uninhabited land.[2] But by now Maiorescu no longer laid the whole weight upon Silistra, but spoke of it as an absolute minimum, while the party leaders on both sides spoke of putting Bulgaria "against the wall", and coined the catchword of "plucking out the thorn from Roumania's flesh".[3]

The London Peace Conference was protracted into January 1913 owing to dissensions among the delegates: none of them, and the Bulgarians least of all, showed any perception of the principle of "do ut des", while the Turks played for time and foresaw the coming quarrel between their enemies. The complicated diplomatic negotiations of this period would lead us far beyond the scope of this narrative; and it must suffice to point out two essential features illustrating the mainly pacific outlook of the Powers. Germany, who had genuinely welcomed the choice of London, exercised a restraining influence upon Austria-Hungary, while Britain spared no effort to hold back Russia. The German foreign secretary, Kiderlen, as early as 3 November had expressed the fear that "behind Austria's silence large territorial plans are concealed",[4] and Tschirschky, his ambassador in Vienna, sent a report to Berlin, treating Austria-Hungary as "an uncomfortable ally", accusing the Ballplatz Press-bureau under Kánya of stirring up unauthorised mischief in the Balkans, and explaining Berchtold's failure to notify his plans against Serbia by the fact that "he has no clear plans!"[5] William II for his part had long since reconciled himself to the redistribution of forces in South-East Europe, and pictured to himself the Balkan League "as the 7th Great Power, leaning on Austria-Hungary and the Triple Alliance".[6]

[1] *A.H.D.* v, no. 5152; Conrad, *op. cit.* III, p. 48.
[2] *A.H.D.* v, no. 5217.        [3] *Ibid.* no. 5240.
[4] *G.P.* XXXIII, no. 12315—to Tschirschky.
[5] *Ibid.* XXXIV, no. 12593—29 December, to Zimmermann.
[6] *Ibid.* XXXIII, no. 12320.

Danev's obstinate resistance to all serious concessions was of course duly reported to Bucarest by Mişu and Ionescu: and Roumanian public opinion flared up dangerously. It is not too much to ascribe to the Roumano-Bulgarian dispute a decisive influence upon the attitude of Vienna, where the atmosphere was still electric and talk of war was by no means confined to hotheads. For it was clear that if Roumania attacked Bulgaria, the latter would find herself between two fires and would in any case have great difficulty in dislodging her allies from the disputed Macedonian lands, and that a difference of outlook towards Serbia would rapidly emerge between Bucarest and Vienna, thereby endangering Roumania's relations with the Triple Alliance. This last aspect of the problem appealed especially to Berlin, where Zimmermann insisted strongly that the Dreibund must support Roumania's demands; and Lichnowsky in London was instructed to put pressure upon Danev. This seemed all the more essential because the Alliance itself had just been renewed in November, and as the question of the renewal of the secret Roumanian alliance was automatically up for discussion, a luke-warm attitude to Roumanian interests might have proved fatal. King Charles held two cards in his hand—firstly, the probability that the Liberals would ere long supersede the Conservatives, and the fact that Brătianu was by no means as complaisant as Maiorescu; secondly, his insistence upon secrecy "in order to be able to ensure the backing of Russia".[1] In both cases there was an undercurrent of doubt and detachment which alarmed Berlin: and even in Vienna the desire for active measures against Serbia was driven into the background by Conrad's demand for going "openly and unreservedly" with Roumania—a view which, he convinced himself, was shared by Francis Joseph and by Berchtold himself.[2] In actual fact the Austro-Roumanian treaty was signed on 5 February, and Germany's adhesion on the 21st.[3]

On the other hand, it proved possible to hold back the Roumanian Government from its threat to occupy the Turtucaia-Balchik line with 50,000 troops, in order to force Bulgaria to negotiate seriously.[4] But

---

[1] *G.P.* xxx (ii), no. 11298—Waldthausen to Bethmann Hollweg, 21 January 1913. On 9 February Jagow wrote to Lichnowsky that the coming of the Roumanian Liberals to power would be a grave danger to European peace, *ibid.* xxxiii, no. 12810. On 13 March Berchtold wrote to Jagow that if Brătianu came in, he would certainly resort to force, "and *this would conjure up an European conflagration*", *A.H.D.* v, no. 6162.    [2] Conrad, *op. cit.* iii, p. 48.

[3] Pribram, *Geheimverträge*, p. 110; *G.P.* xxx (88), nos. 11302 to 11306.

[4] *A.H.D.* v, no. 5262.

Fürstenberg, who understood the Roumanian mentality to a remarkable degree, warned his own Government that if the crisis should end without Roumania securing the concessions on which she had set her heart, the alliance would be undermined with public opinion, and even the crown's prestige would be gravely affected.[1] Party feeling ran high, and the frontier question was used as an instrument of Liberal agitation for office. Mişu, hitherto a loyal adherent of the Triple Alliance, was reported as saying that if the Balkan League consolidated, Roumania would be between it and Russia and might have no choice save to adhere to it.[2] When the Balkan War broke out again, there was a moment when even a section of the cabinet clamoured for action, but Berchtold begged the king not to force the situation and thus appear as the ally of the Turks against the whole League,[3] and Sazonov warned Bucarest that Russian opinion might force him to act if Bulgarian territory were occupied.[4] By the middle of February there was talk of mobilisation, ministers were working themselves up into a fury, the opposition press attacked the Dual Monarchy, using Magyar policy as an easy object of attack, and openly criticised the crown for its monopoly of foreign policy. The king was in a state of nervous excitement, not far from collapse, and told Fürstenberg that unless Austria-Hungary guaranteed Silistra to him, he should have to call in the Liberals. The minister told Maiorescu quite frankly that Vienna might easily interpret this as blackmail, and that it would be impossible to make anyone in Europe understand why Silistra had suddenly become a matter of life and death.[5] Both points were only too true, but what really mattered was that Silistra had come to figure as a catchword of party politics and that King Charles—*débordé*, as Sazonov called him—was no longer strong enough to stand up to public opinion. The premier himself was ready to offer Bulgaria an indemnity or Silistra, but his colleagues were more concerned to outbid Brătianu, who talked of prestige and a possible change of policy. Even Carp was openly for war, while Averescu, as chief of staff, favoured an immediate attack on Bulgaria, in alliance with the Porte—arguing that, by smashing her once for all, Roumania would be safe for a whole generation in the event of a general war against

---

[1] *A.H.D.* v, no. 5438.    [2] *Ibid.* no. 5575.
[3] *Ibid.* no. 5727—Erlass to Bucarest, 9 February.
[4] *Ibid.* no. 5739.
[5] *G.P.* XXXIV, no. 12835—Waldthausen to Jagow, 12 February; *A.H.D.* v, no. 5827—Fürstenberg to Berchtold, 16 February.

Russia.[1] At length, when a rupture seemed imminent, a British proposal for the mediation of the Powers was accepted: a collective *démarche* on 2 March gave the king the backing which he needed, and the dispute with Bulgaria was then referred to a conference of ambassadors at St Petersburg.

Berchtold—aided by his two ministers at Bucarest and Sofia, Prince Fürstenberg and Count Tarnowski, both much abler than he—continued against growing odds his efforts to retain the friendship of both Roumania and Bulgaria and to bring them to a direct agreement. Germany threw her whole weight into the Roumanian scale and, while making it clear that Austria-Hungary could count on her armed support if vital interests were at stake, hinted at the need for defining those interests and at the unwise and incalculable effects of a resort to force against Serbia. Austria-Hungary had obtained her two chief aims, an independent Albania and Serbia's exclusion from the Adriatic, and it would be madness to risk a conflict from which Russia could not abstain without fatal loss of prestige.[2] The chancellor at the same time emphasised the satisfaction which his growing collaboration with England caused him. The German Government was perhaps strengthened in this attitude by the marked difference of Sazonov's attitude to Berlin and Vienna. There was even an occasion when he told the German representatives that he only had hope for the future, "if German influence remained decisive inside the Triple Alliance"![3] Under the influence of such views the new foreign secretary, Herr von Jagow, spoke very frankly to Szögyény as to the designs of "the war party" in Vienna and refused to hear of any suggestions to the contrary.[4]

Meanwhile Conrad as usual pressed for the conquest of Serbia and wished to keep Roumania quiet by the offer of the Timok district, which is mainly Roumanian by race. But Francis Ferdinand turned the scale by his strong disapproval of a war with Russia: to him the true solution lay in a renewal of the Three Emperors' League and such a recon-

---

[1] *G.P.* xxxiv (i), no. 12864—Bronsart von Schellenberg, 15 February; *A.H.D.* v, no. 5794—Fürstenberg to Berchtold, 14 February.

[2] *G.P.* xxxiv (i), no. 12818—Bethmann Hollweg to Berchtold, 10 February; no. 12797—Tschirschky to Bethmann Hollweg, reporting conversation with Chlumecky. On 4 December Grey said very much the same to Lichnowsky: "Russia would not retreat a second time [as in 1909], and would rather resort to arms" (*G.P.* xxxiii, no. 12481).

[3] *G.P.* xxxiv (i), no. 12649—8 January 1913, Lucius to Bethmann Hollweg.

[4] *A.H.D.* v, no. 5680—5 February, Szögyény to Berchtold.

stitution of the Habsburg Monarchy as would win the Southern Slavs and Roumanians to its side, and meanwhile the Balkan states might be left to kill each other off.[1] Berchtold, then, fell back upon the triple aim of keeping Serbia away from the sea, creating a "viable" Albania and satisfying Roumanian claims, and to this extent both Berlin and Rome endorsed his views. But when—in his eagerness "not merely to keep Roumania on our side, but also to rely in some measure on Bulgaria or at least prevent it from joining Russia and the Entente"—he urged that the Triple Alliance should openly support the cession of Silistra to Roumania and of Salonica to Bulgaria as a makeweight, he met with a definite refusal from Berlin, for dynastic reasons.[2] William II was already disinclined to make concessions to his bugbear Ferdinand of Bulgaria, but under no circumstances at the expense of his own brother-in-law Constantine of Greece.

It is easy after the event to criticise the Bulgarian statesmen for their inelastic attitude: but it was asking a great deal of them, that at the height of a victorious war they should yield up territory to an unfriendly neighbour. The argument used by King Charles to Danev, that it was a slight price for the lasting friendship of Roumania,[3] was specious and unconvincing: and it must be added that Bulgarian public opinion, arrogant and intoxicated by success, took almost for granted an open conflict between Serbia and Austria-Hungary, which would force Greece to keep quiet and would leave Bulgaria quite able to deal with Roumania alone. This attitude was comprehensible enough in March and April 1913, when Serbia's share in the siege of Scutari rendered the Austro-Serbian quarrel more acute than ever before, and Berchtold was held back from armed intervention only by the device of an international naval demonstration and a joint *démarche* of the Powers in favour of an Albanian solution. Yet another miscalculation of the weak, if well-meaning, Geshov and the intractable Danev, was that Russia would force Serbia to respect the terms of the original convention and evacuate Macedonia: both statesmen shut their eyes to the complete change in the strategic situation due to Serbia's eviction from the Adriatic, her common interests with Greece and the Roumanian menace

---

[1] *G.P.* XXXIV (i), no. 12788—Duke Albrecht of Württemberg (Francis Ferdinand's brother-in-law) to Prince Max Fürstenberg. Conrad, *op. cit.* III, p. 127: "Of Serbia not one plumtree", said the archduke.

[2] *A.H.D.* v, nos. 6227 and 6246—Berchtold to Berlin, Rome and St Petersburg, 20 and 21 March.

[3] *Ibid.* VI, no. 6399 (1 April).

on the Danube. In reality, only Austro-Hungarian intervention could have saved Bulgaria, and this only at the risk of a general conflagration: and when early in May Montenegro yielded to the inevitable and consented to evacuate Skutari, public opinion was set and resentful both in Sofia and in Bucarest. The award of Silistra by the Protocol of St Petersburg (10 May), which would have satisfied Roumania three months earlier, was now treated by Bucarest as an altogether inadequate equivalent for neutrality, but by Sofia as groundless and excessive. The moment for an agreement had been missed, Serbia and Greece were concocting an alliance for the defence of their Macedonian conquests, and their overtures to Bucarest became increasingly tempting. To complete the deadlock, the energetic war minister Filipescu left the cabinet and joined with Carp in an agitation against the Protocol, and public opinion was more hostile to Bulgaria than ever before. It became known in Bucarest that the Austrian ambassador in St Petersburg had thrown his weight into the Bulgarian scale, and this served to fan suspicions against Austria-Hungary.

Yet again Austria-Hungary had carried her way in the matter of Serbian access to the Adriatic, but had stopped short of an armed conflict, thanks, it may be argued, to the combined efforts of Berlin, London and St Petersburg. Henceforth the catastrophe in the east of the peninsula was well-nigh inevitable: for Berchtold's assurances that he could not get more for Roumania because of the Entente Powers did not convince either Charles or Maiorescu. The further argument that a *rapprochement* with Serbia would run counter to the Triple Alliance[1] left them cold: for almost at the same time Germany was trying to bring Roumania and Greece together. More than this, Germany was as distrustful as ever of Bulgaria and definitely opposed to her acquiring a dominant position in the peninsula.[2] Bulgaria lulled herself in the fatal illusion that Roumania would not dare to move against the will of Vienna, and that her neutrality being thus assured, it would be easy to finish with Serbia and Greece.[3]

On 22 May Berchtold sent an almost peremptory message to Bucarest, but without any effect. He could not understand the sudden change of opinion regarding Silistra, which some months earlier had been treated as the key and was now dismissed as a mere bagatelle: and he strongly

[1] *A.H.D.* vi, no. 6630—Berchtold to Fürstenberg, 15 May.
[2] *G.P.* xxxiv (ii), no. 13292—Memorandum of Jagow, 11 May.
[3] *A.H.D.* vi, no. 7031—16 May, Geshov's statement to Tarnowski.

dissuaded King Charles from asking more, since the allies might then agree on the Macedonian question under the aegis of Russia, and Roumania might well be left out. He added the warning that "in case of a Serbo-Bulgarian conflict we [i.e. Austria-Hungary] shall be compelled to take sides against Serbia and *in a given case oppose her by force of arms*".[1] But this led to plain speech on the part of the king. There was a difference of policy between them, he told Fürstenberg: for Austria-Hungary wanted a Big Bulgaria at Serbia's expense, while Roumania counted upon Serbia to hold Bulgaria in check. The Bulgars were, in his view, far less reliable than the Serbs; they were Roumania's "historical rival and enemy"; despite the cession of Silistra Bulgarian opinion was agitating against Roumania, and an "éclatant" proof of friendship was still required. If Vienna should try to hold Roumania's arm, "while seeking her right against Bulgaria", this would completely undermine the position of the Dual Monarchy in Bucarest.[2] Fürstenberg, now thoroughly alarmed, reported that a "deep resentment" was growing up against the Monarchy, and that the king was probably "the only really firm support" of the alliance policy. But Berchtold replied that the king's remarks must not be left unchallenged and that he must be "urgently warned" that "*in view of the open and deep-seated conflict between the Monarchy and Serbia, the military co-operation of Roumania with Serbia and Greece was incompatible with the alliance*".[3] Count Hoyos, one of Berchtold's assistants at the Ballplatz, confided to Fürstenberg that Vienna's policy "had been throughout the crisis directed towards breaking up the Balkan League", and that in the Serbian question Roumanian and Austro-Hungarian interests "ran directly counter to each other".[4]

Under strong pressure from the British Government the Balkan delegates signed the Treaty of London on 30 May 1913: but in one sense

[1] *A.H.D.* VI, no. 7103—22 May, Berchtold to Fürstenberg. Fürstenberg did not communicate this telegram, but read it to Take Ionescu, who reported its contents to the king. On 15 December 1914 Ionescu revealed this in an article in *La Roumanie*, to which after an interval of three weeks Fürstenberg opposed a formal *démenti*. The Austrian Diplomatic Documents prove Take Ionescu to have told the truth (see his *Souvenirs*, p. 96). On 10 June Berchtold formally denied to Tschirschky having sent instructions in this sense (see *G.P.* XXXIX, note to no. 15828).

[2] *A.H.D.* VI, nos. 7153 and 7189—25 and 28 May.

[3] *Ibid.* no. 7194—29 May.

[4] *Ibid.* no. 7399—18 June.

this only added to the tension, for Bulgaria, assuming that all danger from the Turkish side was thus at an end, was less than ever disposed to make concessions in Macedonia, while Serbia, having signed a secret convention with Greece, now publicly demanded a revision of the original treaty of partition. This forced the moderate Geshov to resign, and decided King Ferdinand and General Savov to concentrate their troops in Macedonia. The tsar's personal appeal to the two Slav brethren, to resort to the arbitration which they themselves had proposed, was disregarded; and the Russophil reputation of the new premier, Dr Danev, was more than counterbalanced by the rigid chauvinism which he had already revealed in his negotiations with Mişu and Ionescu.

While the two sides were glaring at each other across a sealed frontier, Count Stephen Tisza became Hungarian premier and delivered a re-sounding speech on foreign policy. He affirmed the Monarchy's desire for the independence of the Balkan peoples and disclaimed all idea of "protectorate, privileged position or expansion". But then, alluding to Russia's separate action, he insisted that here too the Balkan states were "free to choose their own method of settling their differences. They may—and we should deplore it if they did so, but they are entitled to do so—choose the method of war, or they may choose mediation or a tribunal of arbitration". But they must be quite untrammelled in their decision, and Austria-Hungary could not allow any other state to acquire special prerogatives in the Balkans. This had an immediate stiffening effect in Sofia, where it was interpreted as tying Roumania's hands. But this was yet another miscalculation. King Charles refused Berchtold's suggestion that Roumania should guarantee her neutrality beforehand and on the contrary made it clear that if it came to war he would occupy the Turtucaia-Balchik line and perhaps even take steps to prevent any excessive Bulgarian victory. To Fürstenberg's plea that this "meant entering the enemy's camp" he replied that he was very sorry, but Vienna had always known that he could not tolerate a Big Bulgaria.[1] On this Berchtold made a last desperate effort in Sofia: as the strengthening of Serbia would be altogether contrary to Austria's in-terests, "Bulgaria can count in certain circumstances on our active support", but only if she met Roumania's desire for compensation.[2] But Danev was absolutely rigid: on 29 June he told Tarnowski that Serbia's refusal of arbitration must mean war and that Roumania would

[1] *A.H.D.* VI, no. 7466—23 June.
[2] *Ibid.* no. 7486—24 June, Berchtold to Tarnowski.

not be given her *pourboire*.[1] Well might Maiorescu say that Bulgaria was waiting till the knife was at her throat.

The final tragedy came that very night. General Savov, believing that he could cut through Serbs and Greeks "like a knife through rotten cheese", evict them from the disputed territory and end the whole matter in a few days without a real war, gave orders for a treacherous midnight attack. That upon the Serbs was sanctioned by King Ferdinand behind the back of his premier: that on the Greeks was ordered by Danev against the king's wishes![2] But the despised allies were fully prepared, repelled the attack, and soon in their turn assumed the offensive. The series of battles known under the collective name of the Bregalnica raged until 9 July, and ended in a general Bulgarian retreat. Meanwhile the political calculations of Sofia again went wrong. Count Berchtold talked of intervention in the event of a Serbian victory, but found almost equal disapproval in Berlin and in Rome. Tschirschky argued that neglect of Roumania had put the whole Alliance into a false position, since they had definite obligations towards her, but none towards Bulgaria,[3] while Zimmermann treated Bulgaria's friendship as a "chimaera" and Great Serbia as a "cauchemar".[4] In Rome San Giuliano could see no excuse for an Austrian *coup de tête*, and conveyed to Jagow his view that the overpowering of Serbia could not be allowed.[5] Berchtold's isolation was completed by Berlin's growing interest in the cause of Greece. Roumania, on the other hand, took immediate action: her minister had already given notice to Danev that she would at once move if it came to a conflict,[6] and now, on 3 July, a general mobilisation was ordered. Anti-Austrian demonstrations were organised in the streets of Bucarest by the Chauvinists of the Cultural League: and Berlin took fright at the risks of driving Roumania into the arms of Russia. All that Berchtold could do was to urge upon Sofia immediate concessions to Bucarest, but to the very last moment Danev counted

---

[1] *A.H.D.* VI, no. 7553.

[2] King Ferdinand to Tarnowski—*A.H.D.* VI, no. 7838—18 July. "C'est à n'y pas croire" is the comment of the French military writer whose articles in *Revue Bleue*, December 1913, remain the best account of the Second Balkan War.

[3] *G.P.* XXXV, no. 13477—2 July; *A.H.D.* VI, no. 7584: Bericht of Berchtold on his conversation with Tschirschky—in which he complains of Berlin's erroneous estimate of Austria's policy towards Bulgaria and Roumania.

[4] *G.P.* XXXV, no. 13490—6 July.

[5] *Ibid.* no. 13493—7 July, Jagow to Tschirschky.

[6] *A.H.D.* VI, no. 7543—29 June.

upon Russian help and King Ferdinand hesitated between the rival policies. When Roumanian troops were already engaged in crossing the Danube, he reminded Maiorescu of a promise—made in a situation which had altered out of all recognition—not to take any step beyond occupying the territory claimed.[1] The Roumanian declaration of war had already given an indirect answer: for it pointed out that Roumania had given Bulgaria fair warning of its intentions,[2] but had never even received an answer: on the contrary, Bulgaria had attacked her allies "without any observance of even the elementary rules of preliminary notification, which would at least have testified to a respect for the conventions of international usage".

To complete the tragedy, the Porte, having first demanded and obtained the withdrawal of all Bulgarian troops to within the new frontier, announced its intention of reoccupying Ottoman territory. Bulgaria found herself ringed in by advancing foes, resistance was hopeless, and on the 20th Enver Pasha and the Turkish cavalry entered Adrianople unopposed. Berchtold now saw that in the event of armed intervention he must lose Roumania, and to add to his perplexity he found Berlin opposed to his idea of an European Conference,[3] while San Giuliano politely threatened to hold him back "by the tails of his coat".[4] Even at this stage the unhappy Bulgaria hugged her illusions, and General Racho Petrov notified Count Tarnowski that a decisive victory against Serbia was still possible, if Austro-Hungarian support were assured.[5] King Ferdinand sent his secretary to ask whether Vienna would look on at the downfall of Bulgaria and her dynasty and Serbia's preponderance in the peninsula. But the most that could be extracted from Berchtold was the assurance that Austria-Hungary had identical interests and favoured Bulgarian expansion, subject to the two conditions that she must not form a new Serbian alliance "in the service of the Pan-Slav idea" and must come to terms with Roumania. After an interval of two days he advised King Ferdinand to address a direct appeal to Bucarest, ceding the territory demanded and explaining the danger in which the Coburg dynasty found itself.[6]

[1] A.H.D. VI, no. 7738—12 July.
[2] Cf. also Conrad, op. cit. III, p. 379.
[3] G.P. XXXV, no. 13505—Jagow to Tschirschky, 12 July.
[4] A.H.D. VI, no. 7748—Mérey to Berchtold, 12 July.
[5] Ibid. nos. 7769 and 7781—Tarnowski to Berchtold, 14 and 15 July.
[6] Ibid. nos. 7797 and 7814—Berchtold to Tarnowski, 17 July.

On 17 July, then, King Ferdinand resigned himself to the inevitable and made the necessary appeal to King Charles, receiving in reply the suggestion of a Conference of the five Balkan states on Roumanian soil. At the same time he dismissed the Russophil Danev and called the old Austrophil party into power, with Radoslavov as premier and Genadiev as foreign minister. To Count Tarnowski he denounced Russia's hostility to Bulgaria, but in the same breath declared that he had merely used Russia against Turkey in order to obtain the indispensable co-operation of Serbia and Greece. How could he expect that Austria-Hungary would leave him in the lurch and not use an unique opportunity for crushing Serbia? He had only ordered the night attack on the "odious Serbs" in the hope of Vienna's help! One kick would still suffice,[1] and William II was rendering Austria-Hungary a very bad service by deterring her from attacking Serbia. Tarnowski wisely restricted himself to enquiring why in that case the king had not initiated Vienna after war broke out against Turkey, and on the contrary had kept a Panslav Government in power. This was another way of saying that King Ferdinand had brought disaster on himself by playing fast and loose with both sides.[2]

Even at this stage Bulgaria tried to make her cession of territory conditional upon the Roumanian troops withdrawing across the Danube: but the mild Maiorescu made it clear that they would not be withdrawn until it was certain that Bulgaria would not resume war against Serbia.[3] On this, Bulgaria made complete submission and consented to Bucarest as the seat of the negotiations, and in return Maiorescu promised that the Roumanian army would not occupy Sofia unless the Serbs and Greeks insisted on doing so, and even then not out of hostility, but in order to prevent unrest and save the dynasty. Meanwhile preliminary discussions were being held at Niš, but though

[1] "Un coup de pied suffirait pour assommer la Serbie", *A.H.D.* VI, no. 7838—18 July.

[2] It is worth noting that King Ferdinand's audience to Tarnowski on 18 July 1913 was the first since August 1912, and that he tried to excuse this by his belief that Tarnowski's correspondence was betrayed to Russia (he implied, rather than said, by Geshov and Danev!). Tarnowski reports this without comment, but clearly does not believe him (see *A.H.D.* VI, no. 7883).

[3] How wise a precaution this was is seen from Count Tarnowski's report of 5 August (*ibid.* no. 8234), which shows that even when the Bulgarian delegates went to Bucarest they still hugged the plan of making a separate peace with Roumania, thus getting a free hand against Serbia and Greece, and going on with the war *à outrance*.

the Greeks in particular put forward rather exorbitant claims, there was soon general agreement that they should be transferred to Bucarest. While all the Powers were protesting against the Turkish seizure of Adrianople, King Charles made two friendly gestures towards Sofia by urging upon the sultan due respect for the Treaty of London, and by indicating that Serbia could not be allowed to take Vidin.[1] King Ferdinand had meanwhile telegraphed to William II, but was very bitter at a reply which he described as full of "irony and insults": his real complaint was that the emperor, in order to avoid a war with Russia, had prevented Austria-Hungary from attacking Serbia. An excellent opportunity, he said, had been lost for making Serbia disappear from the map![2]

Genadiev, who was less personal and more concrete, now offered on behalf of Bulgaria an alliance with Austria-Hungary and Roumania,[3] and this overture Berchtold greeted with alacrity. But he found no corresponding enthusiasm in Berlin, which continued to distrust Bulgaria, and favoured a Greco-Roumanian agreement. Germany remained equally unconvinced when Berchtold talked of Franco-Russian designs for a reconstituted Balkan League, and when he argued that the breach between Vienna and Belgrade was "permanent and unbridgeable".[4] The sudden plunge from a Russophil to an Austrophil policy can only be described as Bulgaria's crowning folly: for it decided Russia, the only power from whom armed intervention against Turkey could be expected, to adopt a passive attitude just when she was considering either action on her own part or a mandate to Roumania in Adrianople.[5]

The Conference opened at Bucarest on 30 July, under the presidency of Maiorescu, and lasted less than a week. The Balkan states had every motive for haste, since there was a constant danger of intervention by the Powers: they therefore only granted an armistice for a few days at a time, and in the end warned Bulgaria that Sofia would be occupied unless she at once accepted their terms. An agreement was reached on 6 August, Austria and Russia, through their ministers at Bucarest, reserving the right of subsequent revision, but the others making this subject to unanimity on the part of the six Great Powers. King Charles

[1] *A.H.D.* VI, nos. 7985 and 8018—24 and 25 July.
[2] *Ibid.* no. 8074—27 July.
[3] *Ibid.* no. 7937—22 July.
[4] *G.P.* XXXV, no. 13564, 22 July and *A.H.D.* VII, no. 8157—Erlass to Berlin, 1 August 1913 (*G.P.* XXXV, no. 13724).
[5] *G.P.* XXXV, no. 13615—30 July.

lost not a moment in telegraphing to the Emperor William that "after grave difficulties have been overcome, the conclusion of peace is assured, and *thanks to you it remains definitive*". William II in his turn thanked Charles for his "wise and truly statesmanlike policy" and rejoiced at their "co-operation in the cause of peace"—a telegram which the king acknowledged "with pride and sincere gratitude". The three telegrams were at once published, with the full permission of the emperor, and the sensation which they produced throughout Europe was not diminished by the fact that they had never even been submitted to the Berlin Foreign Office, still less to the Austrian Government. Bethmann Hollweg objected, but admitted that he could not restrain his master, while Zimmermann consoled himself by the thought that Vienna, though annoyed, would be less zealous in the cause of revision.[1] Berchtold caused the greatest possible offence to everyone from the king downwards, by sending pointed congratulations on "the provisional peace".[2] Meanwhile King Ferdinand bade his soldiers, "indignant at the felony" of their allies, "exhausted but not conquered, ...furl their glorious standards till better days".

The point most in dispute at Bucarest was the possession of the Aegean port of Kavala by Greece: and here the Emperor William, taking full control of foreign policy, threw his whole weight in favour of his brother-in-law King Constantine, whom he demonstratively made a German field-marshal. Jagow, acting on orders, was able to remind Berchtold that as late as 14 July he had favoured "strengthening Greece as much as possible", and Tschirschky, who had a truly Prussian plainness of speech, warned him that he would find himself isolated and would come up against "la force des choses". "Without Kavala", said Jagow, "Greece can hardly conclude peace": and it would be sheer folly to back Bulgaria against her or to compete with Russia for her favour: "after provoking war, Bulgaria cannot complain if she has to pay costs".[3] On 12 August Tschirschky was instructed to announce that Germany regarded the treaty as definitive and now desired above all to restore the old relations with Roumania: but when he saw Berchtold, the conversation centred no longer round Kavala, but the "Great Serbia" which the treaty had recognised on the Monarchy's southern borders and whose danger Germany overlooked.

[1] *G.P.* xxxv, nos. 13736 and 13737; *A.H.D.* vii, no. 8414.
[2] *A.H.D.* vii, no. 9066.
[3] *G.P.* xxxv, nos. 13700, 13701, 13703, 13725—1–5 August.

Tschirschky answered tartly that revision was impossible without war, and were Štip and Kočana worth an European conflict?[1] William II for his part treated Vienna as "completely cracked".[2]

By the middle of August the question of revision was virtually dead: France and Germany united in favour of Greece, Russia yielded to French influence in the question of Kavala, and, finding the Bulgarian Government so ardently Austrophil, left it to their new friend to save Adrianople for them: while Britain, after protesting against Turkey's violation of the Treaty of London, took fright at the Indian Moslem agitation and left the invader in possession. Berchtold was indeed isolated and had to content himself with his one solid achievement, Albanian independence, in which incidentally he had the full sympathy of Roumania, both because the Vlachs hoped more from the Albanians than from either Greeks or Serbs, and because the new Prince, William of Wied, was a nephew of Queen Elizabeth. "We are sitting on the ground between all the stools", wrote Conrad to one of his generals: "we shall have peace all right, if we abdicate in all directions."[3]

It was natural enough that King Charles and Maiorescu should insist upon the permanence of the new settlement: for it had greatly enhanced Roumanian prestige both at home and abroad, and had turned fickle opinion once more in favour of the crown. They had acquired the long-coveted strategic frontier in Dobrogea, and indeed almost their only losses had been from cholera, since the Bulgarian troops were engaged on other fronts. King Charles had preserved the Balkan balance of power, and played the rôle of mediator between the rival forces, while showing that, in the words of Maiorescu himself, Austria-Hungary could no longer dictate the policy of Bucarest.[4] The Conservative leader, by this time over seventy, could now rest on his laurels and give place to the Liberals, whose appetite for office recent events had greatly stimulated.

In one very important respect the Liberals, on the eve of office, showed themselves more far-sighted than the king. One effect of the war had been to reveal to the peasant soldiers the contrast between agrarian conditions in their own country and in Bulgaria. South of the Danube they found everywhere prosperous small holdings, better

---

[1] *G.P.* xxxv, nos. 13741 and 13749; *A.H.D.* vii, no. 8345.
[2] *G.P.* marginalia to no. 13740.
[3] Conrad, *op. cit.* iii, p. 404.
[4] *A.H.D.* vii, no. 8407.

methods of cultivation and a complete absence of big landlords and grasping middlemen. Ionel Brătianu, and still more Constantine Stere, the theorist of the party, were swift to grasp the dangerous reactions of this discovery upon the mind of the masses: and the result was a new political programme with which the Conservatives could not hope to compete. Its two main points were land reform and reform of the franchise, and though they were considerably watered down in order to ally the nervousness of the crown, they none the less gave Brătianu a popular support in wide circles, which, it is hardly too much to affirm, was to prove, in the hour of supreme peril, the salvation of Roumania. In the autumn of 1913, then, Brătianu proclaimed in the Liberal organ *Indépendance Roumaine* the need for satisfying the land-hunger of the peasantry: while the veteran Dimitrie Sturdza closed his public career by pronouncing the ominous word of "expropriation" as a necessity of the not far distant future. The Conservative Democratic group of Take Ionescu hastened to accept the reform in principle, and thus it was obvious that the Old Conservatives—again divided into two groups, the reactionaries under Marghiloman, and the opportunists under M. Cantacuzene—were already fighting a losing game, in which their best cards were the conservatism of the fast failing king and the avoidance of all foreign complications.

\*         \*         \*         \*

The Balkan Wars had put a very severe strain upon the two great European alliances and produced some quite unexpected combinations: and the Treaty of Bucarest left a considerable aftermath of friction between Vienna and Berlin. William II, who hoped that the incompetent Berchtold would now be superseded, felt it incumbent on him to convince Vienna of his entire loyalty to the Triple Alliance. He justified his insistence upon retaining Roumanian friendship and winning over Greece, as essential interests of the alliance, which had to be upheld "even at the risk of temporarily offending Austria".[1] He was much relieved to receive a letter from Francis Ferdinand early in September, expressing "admiration" for the success of William's policy and declaring that "in all modesty" he "fully identified himself with it".[2] Soon after, the archduke attended the centenary celebrations of the Leipzig "Battle of the Nations", and exchanged visits at Konopiště and Springe; and for the brief remainder of his life the two men were

[1] *G.P.* xxxvi (i), no. 13781.
[2] *Ibid.* xxxix, no. 15709—Treutler to Foreign Office, 7 September.

on terms of real intimacy. The emperor also saw Francis Joseph in Vienna and took occasion to discuss Balkan policy with Berchtold, who admitted that to win over Bulgaria without alienating Roumania was almost like "squaring the circle". Carried away by his own eloquence, William assured him that Austria-Hungary must enjoy a hegemony over all the Balkan states; that if Serbia refused to place her army at Vienna's disposal, "Belgrade will be bombarded and occupied, until the will of the Emperor Francis Joseph is carried out": and here with hand on sword he added that he was ready "to draw the sabre and stand behind the Monarchy if ever your action makes it necessary". If it should come to a "death struggle" in Europe for the monarchical principle, Vienna "could always count upon him to the full, and whatever came to him from the Vienna foreign office was for him a command". That this was no passing whim, but a definite attempt to recapture Vienna's good graces, is shown by the emperor's conversation with the Austro-Hungarian chargé at Munich five weeks later, in which, after denouncing Bulgaria and King Ferdinand, he argued that the Serbs, as a serious factor in Europe, simply "must be harnessed before the car of the Monarchy—in one way or another". If it came to "a serious armed conflict,...we Germans stand with you and behind you: but we can in no case be indifferent as to whether the twenty divisions of your army are tied up for operations against the Southern Slavs, or not".[1]

Emperor and archduke were completely at one in their desire to win back Roumania for the Triple Alliance, and well aware that just as Roumania had originally tied herself to Vienna not for its own sake, but as the ally of Berlin, so to-day it was only Germany's prestige that could retrieve the situation.[2] The emperor even considered the idea of himself visiting Bucarest,[3] and it was only abandoned as likely to offend and excite Russia. It was, however, the same motive which inspired Francis Ferdinand in securing the appointment of one of his own special intimates, Count Ottokar Czernin, as Austro-Hungarian minister in Bucarest. He had instructions from Berchtold to clear away misunder-

---

[1] These two documents were given to me confidentially in 1928 and published for the first time in an appendix to my article "William II's Balkan Policy" (*Slavonic Review*, no. 19, June 1928)—in extenso English translation. The originals were afterwards published in *A.H.D.* vii, nos. 8934 and 9096.

[2] This argument was lucidly put forward by the Roumanian minister in Berlin, A. Beldiman, to Jagow on 7 September 1913—*G.P.* xxxix, no. 15794.

[3] *Ibid.* xxxix, no. 15713—Tschirschky to Jagow, 18 February 1914.

standings, to convince Bucarest of Vienna's benevolence and to insist that close relations between Roumania and Serbia were incompatible with the Alliance, since there was "*no possibility of mitigating or composing*" the Austro-Serbian conflict. He was to do all in his power to elicit from the king a clear statement as to Roumania's attitude "in the case of great decisions", and to urge an abandonment of the extreme secrecy which hedged round the treaty. It was not necessary to publish its terms, but it was high time that the world should know that Roumania had been the ally of the Central Powers for over a quarter of a century.[1] The choice of Czernin was in itself significant, for he had long paid close attention to the delicate "question of nationalities" in the Dual Monarchy, had some years earlier published a pamphlet openly criticising Magyar racial policy, and was known to share the heir apparent's strong views as to the need for drastic reforms in Hungary and his specially marked sympathy for the Roumanians of Transylvania. The appointment was violently attacked in the Hungarian Parliament, but the premier, Count Tisza, who in his own very different way was fully conscious of the need for a *détente* with the Roumanians, gave Czernin his backing and remained in close and direct contact with him. It was widely known that Francis Ferdinand was violently hostile to Tisza, and had with difficulty prevented Francis Joseph from putting the Magyar Calvinist leader in Berchtold's place.[2] His own candidate was no other than Czernin, who eventually owed his selection as foreign minister to the Emperor Charles's reliance upon his uncle's former confidants.

Czernin was not long in reaching the conclusion that publication of the treaty was quite impossible unless a change in Roumanian popular feeling towards the Dual Monarchy could be effected, and that this in its turn depended upon a Magyar-Roumanian understanding inside Hungary. Like his predecessor Fürstenberg, the military attaché Hranilović[3] and their subordinates, he insisted that the internal and external aspects of the Roumanian question could not be separated, and that the sins of former Hungarian Governments were bearing bitter fruit.[4] In this view he was confirmed by conversations with the king and his statesmen. The old man, taking care to speak as a private

[1] *A.H.D.* VII, no. 9032—Erlass of Berchtold, 26 November 1913.
[2] Cf. *G.P.* XXXIX, no. 15789.
[3] Cf. Conrad, *op. cit.* III, pp. 482, 553, 562.
[4] *A.H.D.* VII, nos. 9051 and 9052—5 December.

individual, and not as sovereign to a foreign envoy, quoted some of the chronic incidents which disturbed relations—such as the arrest of Madame Take Ionescu by Magyar officials—and said quite bluntly that "the seat of the evil lies in Transylvania". He sincerely hoped that Tisza's negotiations would lead to a settlement on the lines long ago advocated by Deák, and added that if he had ulterior aims, he would rejoice at the quarrel, which played straight into the hands of the irredentists.[1] Their conversations culminated in the king's confession —uttered "with a visible effort" and great embarrassment—that as matters then stood, and in view of unanimous public opinion, the Alliance could not be put into force:[2] Roumania would not turn her arms against the Monarchy, but to fight shoulder to shoulder was impossible, unless Vienna could do something to mitigate the Magyar-Roumanian conflict. Meanwhile Czernin judged rightly that Charles wished to play the part of an arbiter in the Balkans, having lost little of his suspicion towards Bulgaria and taking every opportunity of offering mediation between Belgrade and Vienna.

Tisza on his side saw the desirability of appeasing the Roumanians of Hungary, but his arrogant nationalism would not allow him to pay anything even remotely resembling the necessary price. Thus the pourparlers which took place during the winter between his representative and the Roumanian National Party were foredoomed to failure. On 14 February 1914 the party executive rejected Tisza's offer as inadequate and reaffirmed the autonomist programme of 1881, and it was widely believed that in doing so its leaders had the approval of the heir apparent. They were certainly in touch with him through his military secretaries Colonels Brosch and Bolfras, through Dr Funder, editor of the official Christian Socialist organ *Reichspost*, and, not least, through Aurel Popovici, the ardent promoter of "Great Austrian" ideas. The failure of the negotiations, and a tactless speech of Tisza—stating that friendship with Roumania was the best Balkan combination, but that others were possible—caused a recrudescence of feeling against the Monarchy, not merely in social and academic circles but even in the army, and fully confirmed the accuracy of Czernin's diagnosis. If public opinion in the kingdom made the proper treatment of its kinsmen in Hungary the touchstone of diplomatic relations, Hungarian opinion was no less bent upon Magyarisation and quite indisposed to concede

[1] *A.H.D.* VII, no. 9039—30 November.
[2] "Nicht effectuirbar", *ibid.* no. 9066—8 December.

equality to the despised "Wallachs". None the less an understanding was as yet genuinely desired not merely by Brătianu who, though unquestionably the most chauvinistic of all Roumanian statesmen, had exchanged confidential letters with Tisza on the subject,[1] but even by such a man as Filipescu, the very able and energetic Conservative minister of war, who sought an exit from the blind alley in a highly original manner. His idea was that Transylvania should be ceded to Roumania, but that in return the whole of Roumania should be incorporated constitutionally within the Monarchy, and that her Hohenzollern king should accept the same position under the Habsburg dynasty as that of Bavaria or Saxony inside Germany.[2] This was not an entirely new idea: for Ion Maiorescu, father of the premier, had evolved such a project in the middle of the nineteenth century, and already in 1911 Aurel Popovici had discussed it with Filipescu and offered to transmit it to Francis Ferdinand through the influential Jesuit, Count Galen.[3] When the story came to light after the Great War, the dead statesman was charged with lack of patriotism: but in reality, given the totally different circumstances of 1913, he was merely acting with foresight and sanity, and such a scheme, if realised, might have helped to avert a world-catastrophe, while ensuring Roumania's future. In any case, Czernin, though cordially approving, at once realised that Magyar policy was a fatal obstacle.

Tisza on his side was far too clear-sighted not to realise this. The fact was that he was not prepared to make the necessary concessions, and, in a memorandum addressed to Francis Joseph on 15 March, set out an alternative policy. "The conquest of Transylvania", he wrote, "always remains the greatest bait" for Roumania, hence it was essential to win over Bulgaria to the Triple Alliance by a firm promise of future compensations in Macedonia. It should then be possible to detach Roumania and Greece from Serbia, reconcile them with Bulgaria, and bring

---

[1] *G.P.* xxxix, no. 15795—Waldburg to Bethmann Hollweg, 16 September 1913; *A.H.D.* vii, no. 9255.

[2] *A.H.D.* vii, no. 8463—11 March 1914. Already published by Conrad, *op. cit.* iii, appendix x.

[3] Marghiloman, *Note Politice*, i, p. 87. Field-Marshal Conrad (Conrad, *op. cit.* iii, p. 551) records a conversation in January 1914 with the Roumanian military attaché Major Eremie, who admitted that a party existed in Roumania that favoured the inclusion of "all lands of Roumanian tongue under their own King", within the framework of the Monarchy. Conrad replied, "Ohneweiters", but pointed to the "Hungarian State Idea" as the main obstacle.

them to heel. "Austria-Hungary's task", he argued, was "difficult in itself: of success there could be no question, unless we have the full assurance that we are understood, appreciated and supported by Germany."[1]

On 16 January 1914 the long expected change of Government took place, and Ionel Brătianu succeeded Maiorescu as premier. To the last King Charles maintained the most unnatural precautions as to the secret alliance. Only now was Brătianu initiated into the fact that the alliance had been renewed a year previously: and the new foreign minister, Porumbaru, a mere cipher, was not even allowed to know that it existed! Yet Czernin was right in suspecting that the king was no longer, as in the eighties, undoubted master of the situation: and indeed the real reason why he shrank from revealing the treaty was his consciousness that it was rejected by the bulk of the nation. Meanwhile Brătianu had his way in home affairs: and in order to fulfil his double programme of agrarian and electoral reform, a Constituent Assembly was convoked, with power to revise certain articles of the existing constitution. In actual fact the parliamentary commissions were only convoked for June 1914, and had not yet begun their work when the outbreak of the world crisis rendered postponement advisable.

The breakdown of negotiations in Hungary, and the disastrous bomb outrage at Debreczen—which was traced to the sinister figure of Cătărau, a Bessarabian Roumanian, who served as Russian spy in the Bucarest police and seemed to enjoy some mysterious immunity from arrest—led to fresh recriminations between Bucarest and Budapest. During the winter and spring demonstrations became chronic, notably when the Cultural League induced the National Theatre to perform *The Village Notary*, a play of strongly anti-Magyar tendency by the brilliant young Transylvanian poet Octavian Goga. Brătianu assured Czernin that official intervention would only make matters worse, but the minister told the king that he was "less interested in the street or in the League than in the passive attitude of the Government", and even this failed of its effect.[2]

The widening gulf between Bucarest and Vienna was obvious to all Europe, and encouraged Russia in renewed efforts to establish her predominance in the Balkans at the expense of Austria-Hungary. Roumania formed as it were the pivot upon which the two great rivals

[1] *A.H.D.* vii, no. 9482, previously published by *American Historical Review* for January 1924.    [2] *A.H.D.* vii, no. 9547—3 April.

could make the minor Balkan Powers revolve, and her adhesion meant a very great strategic advantage to one side or the other. To the Austrians she meant an addition of five army corps on the right flank, within striking distance of Odessa: to the Russians she gave direct access to Bulgaria and Serbia, the possibility of invading Hungary through the unfortified Transylvanian passes and the complete dislocation of all Austrian plans of offensive.

The air, then, was full of rumours and "combinations". The Serbian crown prince and premier visited St Petersburg to thank the tsar personally for his support of the Serbian cause, and received the characteristically Romanov answer that he had simply done his "Slav duty". They were followed by the Greek premier, Mr Venizelos, and both statesmen broke their journey in Bucarest and conferred with Brătianu as to the possibility of a reconstituted Balkan League—if not with Bulgaria, then without her. Both Roumania and Greece were willing to link such a combination with the Triple Alliance, with the double object of isolating Bulgaria and guaranteeing their own conquests: Berlin fully shared both their distrust of Sofia and their desire to bridge the gulf between Serbia and Austria-Hungary. King Charles in particular clung to the idea of mediating in the quarrel, and Pašić assumed a readiness which was probably more tactical than sincere. The Emperor William, in his impromptu style, had actually suggested to Czernin that the Roumanian difficulty could best be solved by an offensive and defensive alliance of the Monarchy *with Roumania and Serbia against Bulgaria*! This seems to have fermented in Czernin's mind till in June he broached it as a means of confronting Bucarest with a direct "Either-Or"—preferably through the medium of Berlin—and so clearing up an equivocal situation.[1]

In February Crown Prince Ferdinand paid a much delayed visit to St Petersburg, and there was some talk of a marriage between his eldest son, Prince Carol, and a daughter of the tsar. Sazonov remarked with mild sarcasm that it was not every day that an Orthodox Hohenzollern could be secured: but nothing came of the project, since Nicholas II wished his children to make their own decisions. On this occasion the perspicacious Czernin warned his Government that in the near future Roumanian policy might well come to depend not so much upon Ferdinand as upon his versatile wife Princess Marie, who had strong Russian sympathies. "Her character and mentality", he wrote, "is one

[1] *A.H.D.* VIII, no. 9902—22 June.

of the most important reasons for putting relations with Roumania on quite another basis."[1]  She was certainly delighted when in the early summer the tsar himself paid a visit to King Charles at Constanţa: and though the sovereigns refrained from politics, Brătianu and Sazonov had long discussions and went off together on a brief excursion into Transylvania by motor car, which provoked a most violent protest from Tisza.[2]  Sazonov was highly pacific in his professions: he of course had to be cautious with Brătianu, for he knew that Roumania looked askance at "Panslavism" and was very sensitive about the Straits, and that the king had strong Dreibund proclivities (of the treaty he was of course unaware).  His tone was therefore reassuring—"provided that Austria does not touch Serbia": and here he was probably sincere, for he said the same thing in more than one quarter during the spring, thus conveying the warning that Russia could not be indifferent to the fate of Serbia and would not revert to her attitude of 1909.  It is of course true that in speaking thus he was approaching Brătianu at the point where accord was most likely.

It may reasonably be affirmed—though the full proofs would lead us far beyond the limits of this volume—that at this period of lull before the storm both St Petersburg and Berlin believed themselves to be working for peace, but that the mining and countermining in which they both indulged, and of which the Liman von Sanders Mission to Turkey and the St Petersburg military and naval discussions were the most striking examples, inevitably created an atmosphere of unrest and flux, in which any incident might easily produce an explosion.

Meanwhile there was a renewal of conversations between Francis Ferdinand and William II, and one of the subjects to which they devoted special attention was the Roumanian question.  The whole Wilhelmstrasse, taking the cue from its master, argued that "everything depends on the way the Roumanians in Hungary are treated".[3]  Late in March the emperor was in Vienna and broached the question very frankly with Count Tisza, whom he met for the first time.  Tisza talked confidently of still winning over his own Roumanians by concessions in school and church, and so of reconciling Roumania with the Dreibund.  The im-

[1]  *A.H.D.* VII, no. 9619—28 April.
[2]  "A direct incitement of our Roumanians and a provocative demonstration of Russian interest in Transylvania", Tisza to Berchtold, 14 June—*A.H.D.* VIII, no. 9861.  Czernin had given his permission (*ibid.* no. 9873, Czernin to Berchtold), though he afterwards denied this.
[3]  Baernreither, *Fragments of a Political Diary*, p. 276.

pressionable William saw in him a really strong man, got talking of Slav and Teuton, and charmed the Magyar statesman by saying that the best defence lay in "a Germanic Austria and a Hungarian [meaning a 'Magyar'] Hungary".[1] Characteristically enough, when he talked a few days later with the archduke, he spoke only of a German Austria and of "washing the Czechs' heads", but not a word of a Magyar Hungary: by now he knew his archduke.[2] In May they met again at Miramar, and this time the emperor spoke of Tisza in warm terms of commendation, but Francis Ferdinand's opinions were reflected in the remark that he would not keep Tisza twenty-four hours at the head of a cabinet, for fear of his organising a revolution against him in forty-eight hours![3]

There was one last meeting between the two friends amid the rose-gardens of Konopiště, on 13 June 1914: and once again the Roumanian question bulked large in their discussions. They agreed that the best way of saving the alliance was to reassure the Roumanian Government as to the maintenance of the Treaty of Bucarest: but the conversation then naturally turned to Hungary, and the archduke denounced the Magyar oligarchy for their ill-treatment of the non-Magyars and Tisza for his dictatorial methods, and finally the emperor, to appease him, promised to instruct Tschirschky, whenever he met Tisza, to greet him with the phrase, "Lord, remember the Roumanians".[4] It was in this direction that the archduke's mind was moving, when he started on the fatal journey to Bosnia. Unlike his uncle, who had by this time become a bureaucratic automaton, Francis Ferdinand was fully conscious of the manner in which internal and external policy had become interlocked in the fateful Southern Slav question, above all owing to the racial fanaticism of the Magyars: and he now saw exactly the same process at work in the relations of the Monarchy with Roumania, this time with momentous effects upon the whole strategy of the Triple Alliance.

*　　　*　　　*　　　*

The murder of the archduke at Sarajevo on 28 June 1914 was at once realised as a deadly blow to hopes of peaceful evolution. Nowhere did it cause greater consternation than among the Roumanians, on both sides of the Carpathians, who had consoled themselves for the vexations

[1] *G.P.* xxxix, nos. 15715, 15716—23 and 24 March.
[2] *Ibid.* no. 15720—27 March.
[3] *Ibid.* no. 15732—Tschirschky to Jagow, 10 May.
[4] *Ibid.* no. 15736—Treutler to Zimmermann, 15 June; no. 15737—Tschirschky to Bethmann, 17 June. Cf. Baernreither (*op. cit.* p. 275), to whom the emperor had already used this phrase, on the analogy of "Lord, remember the Athenians".

of Magyar policy and its reactions upon external relations by the certain knowledge that the future emperor was their genuine and devoted friend, and by the hope that on his accession, which could not long be delayed, drastic political changes would be effected. It now became obvious—and this was driven home by the scarcely veiled satisfaction in wide circles of Magyar public opinion—that no such hopes could be set upon the new heir apparent, who, however amiable in disposition and devoted to his uncle's memory, altogether lacked the force of character, the experience and the prestige which alone could have achieved the difficult task of constitutional reform.[1] Whether Francis Ferdinand would have succeeded, or merely precipitated disaster, will always remain an open question: but no one can deny that he was one of the strongest personalities whom the House of Habsburg has produced—one of the great "might have beens" of modern history. Overcome, then, with dismay and disappointment at the loss of their most influential friend in the Dual Monarchy, the Roumanians at the same time saw the quarrel between the Monarchy and their Serbian neighbour break out in an acuter and more dangerous form than ever before, and were only too conscious that the Serbian and Roumanian questions were more and more following parallel lines.

Vienna too was not blind to this aspect of affairs, and in the elaborate statement of policy addressed by Count Berchtold to Berlin on 3 July 1914 (but already drafted before the murder and therefore not influenced by it) very special attention is paid to the rôle of Roumania. It is assumed that irredentist feeling is driving her away from Vienna, and leading her, despite the secret alliance, to aim at "a policy of free hand", and that King Charles might not be able to fulfil the *casus foederis*, perhaps not even to enforce neutrality. The Roumanian alliance could therefore no longer be regarded as the pivot of Austria-Hungary's Balkan policy, and as its military value was thus in question, support must be sought elsewhere—in other words, from Bulgaria—in the struggle against Russia's designs of "encirclement".[2] William II read this with obvious reluctance, but none the less, while reiterating his suspicions of Bulgaria and her king, promised to use his influence on King Charles, in the sense that the Bosnian tragedy had destroyed the latter's favourite project of an Austro-Serbian *rapprochement*.[3]

---

[1] As Filipescu said to the Russian minister, the hope of improvement had vanished!—*Russian Documents*, IV, no. 81.

[2] *Deutsche Dokumente*, I, no. 14.          [3] *D.A.* I, no. 6.

When, however, the subject was broached to the king by the German and Austro-Hungarian ministers, he clung desperately, if nervously, to his former view, insisted on the complete loyalty of Pašić and official Serbia, denied all idea of a new Balkan League aimed by Russia at the heart of Austria, showed himself firmly opposed to a Bulgarian alliance, accused Berchtold and Vienna of having lost their heads, offered to bring personal pressure upon Belgrade for a regulation of the conflict, and characteristically declared that he would never lend himself to any project for the conquest of Transylvania. "We shall not live to see that", he said, turning to Crown Prince Ferdinand, who was present at his conversation with Count Waldburg: "your son perhaps!"[1] He was perfectly ready to meet the emperor's wishes by "drawing back from Serbia" and trying to rein back the anti-Austrian agitation which was once again noticeable in the press: but, if his action was to be effective, Hungary must make things easier for her Roumanian subjects.[2] Meanwhile in conversation with Count Czernin he expressed "great pessimism" as to the future of Austria-Hungary and insisted strongly on the distinction between the assassins (*Mordbuben*) and official Serbia.[3]

The only effect of Charles's insistence upon the practicability of mediation, and his belief that Russia would join him in pressure upon Belgrade, was that Berchtold left Bucarest severely alone on the eve of the ultimatum to Serbia. Mediation was the very opposite of what he wanted: and if at any time he had been disposed to relent, he was "surrounded by a clique which wanted war because they regarded an arrangement as impossible"[4] and the Treaty of Bucarest as untenable. But King Charles not unnaturally shared the annoyance of the Roman statesmen at Berchtold's secretive tactics, and at his failure to keep his allies informed as to action which might so easily involve them also in war. Czernin records that when at last he read out the ultimatum already despatched to Belgrade, the king at once assumed that a world war

[1] *D.D.* I, no. 41—Count Waldburg, German Chargé, to Berlin, 11 July. He said very much the same thing to Marghiloman a fortnight later, in answer to the question "whether he considered the question of Transylvania to be ripe enough for risking everything for it". No, he said, but in twenty years Austria would break up, *owing to Hungary's attitude* (see *Note Politice*, I, p. 277).

[2] *D.D.* I, no. 66—14 July.

[3] *Ibid.* no. 39—quoting Czernin's report, as sent on to Berlin.

[4] These are the considered words of Rudolf Sieghart, who knew as few others the secrets of the Dual Monarchy (*Die letzten Jahre einer Grossmacht*, p. 168). He specially names Forgách, Musulin and Hoyos. Kánya had by this time gone to Mexico, but Macchio was still there.

would be inevitable. A week later the king told the German minister that he was trying to prepare Roumanian public opinion for the possibility of war with Russia, but that there were great difficulties in the way of his fulfilling his pledge.[1] Two days later, he quoted the Italian minister, Baron Fasciotti, as affirming that his Government was not bound by the Alliance in a quarrel which Austria-Hungary had provoked: and he added that a similar clause was contained in his own treaty. He had exacted a promise from Brătianu to uphold the alliance if at all possible, but in that case something must be done to remedy the Transylvanian situation. A promise of Bessarabia, he argued, had no value for Roumania, except in a situation when Russia had lost a great deal of other territory also and Roumania could therefore be sure of keeping her gains.[2]

Roumania's attitude on the eve of the catastrophe was one of distrust and irresolution. Public opinion was bitterly hostile to Austria-Hungary, but not yet ripe for an alliance with Russia, and inclined to discount the Western Powers as too far off to be effective allies. Roumania's main concern was to retain her hold upon her recent conquests and to prevent any change in the Balkan balance of power established by the Treaty of Bucarest. She was entirely sceptical towards Austria-Hungary's disclaimer of all territorial conquests, and assumed that war must inevitably lead to Serbia's destruction and Bulgaria's aggrandisement, to which she could not reconcile herself. She was therefore above all disposed to wait upon events and avoid all diplomatic entanglements until the guns had spoken and it was possible to weigh the chances of military success.

[1] *D.D.* II, no. 463.
[2] *Ibid.* III, no. 582—1 August.

# CHAPTER XV

# ROUMANIA AND THE GREAT WAR

The lists were now set, and when the trumpet sounded across Europe, Roumania found herself torn in two directions. Loyalty to the Power within whose sphere she had lived for a whole generation meant strengthening the Magyar hold upon her kinsmen, and also probably the aggrandisement of Bulgaria: adhesion to the Entente meant exposing Roumania to all the dangers of an advanced strategic position: even neutrality might mean the loss of friendships and a precarious isolation after the struggle was over. In face of these dire alternatives and the challenge to his personal honour, the king's health visibly weakened: he felt himself almost alone, after close upon half a century of devoted service to his adopted country, and he can hardly have been blind to the nemesis which his secretive methods had at last brought upon him.

At the height of the crisis the Germans were even more insistent than the Austrians. On 2 August Bethmann Hollweg appealed to Bucarest for an immediate mobilisation against Russia, and Bessarabia was already promised as Roumania's share in the spoils of victory. Germany further offered to extract from Bulgaria a pledge of renunciation of the Dobrogea, in the event of Roumania moving against Russia:[1] and by revealing the secret Turkish alliance, concluded that very day, it was hoped finally to turn the scales at Bucarest.[2] All that the king could do was to summon a Crown Council and to promise that he himself would advocate mobilisation.

The momentous council was held at Sinaia on 3 August 1914 and, according to precedent, included not only the members of the cabinet, but the leaders of both Opposition groups[3] and the heir apparent. King Charles, speaking in French contrary to his usual habit, read a declaration condemning any "policy of sentiment". Neutrality would only destroy the position which Roumania had won for herself in Europe; public opinion would not tolerate an alliance with Russia: interest and honour alike pointed to action on the side of the Central Powers. His words were greeted with ominous silence. After an

---

[1] *D.D.* III, nos. 646, 699, 729.     [2] *Ibid.* IV, no. 743.
[3] Except Filipescu, who was doing a cure at Baden-Baden.

interval the fiery Carp urged immediate war on behalf of Germanism against Slavdom: it was useless to show undue consideration for the Roumanians across the Carpathians, who had never desired incorporation and would be the first to fire against their brethren. Roumania had a treaty and must help the king to keep his engagements. Bessarabia was the prize, and if the key-point of Hotin were assigned to Austria-Hungary, she and not Roumania alone, would be engaged in its defence. Carp found himself entirely alone. The finance minister, Costinescu, who afterwards earned the nickname of "Minister for the Entente", spoke against Russia, but declared that to join Austria-Hungary in the field would provoke a civil war. Marghiloman, now acting as accredited chief of the Conservatives, argued the objections to active intervention on either side, and insisted that the *casus foederis* did not exist: and in this view he had the support of Take Ionescu, who clung to the Treaty of Bucarest, while recognising that events were likely to overthrow it. Brătianu showed an unusual reserve and encouraged the others to declare themselves, but his advocacy of armed preparation without commitments and at the same time of preparing uninformed public opinion as to all eventualities, ended by carrying the day.

All save Carp were agreed, openly or tacitly, as to the impossibility of holding the nation to a treaty whose very existence had been concealed from it and which in any case ran counter to all constitutional practice. The king was in almost as weak a position as in the early nineties: for the renewal of the treaty in 1913 had not been communicated to the Opposition leaders, according to what had become a tacit understanding, and the foreign minister, Porumbaru, had remained in ignorance of its text even after taking office. The mere reminder that it had never been, and could not conceivably now be, submitted to Parliament, was enough to force its author on to the defensive. Still more decisive was the clearly defensive character of the alliance, which could not be claimed as valid in the event of Austrian aggression against Serbia. The king's last arguments for intervention were destroyed by the news which reached Bucarest that very morning, that Italy had denied the *casus foederis* and declared her neutrality. In yielding to the inevitable, he could not repress the remark, "Gentlemen, you cannot imagine how bitter it is to find oneself isolated in a country of which one is not a native": to which there came the crushing rejoinder, "In peace time it was possible for Your Majesty to follow a policy contrary to the sentiment of the country, but to make war in defiance of that sentiment is impossible".[1] In falling back upon the position of "a constitutional monarch, who would not declare war alone", he was of course making a virtue of necessity. His written declaration, he said, was his political testament, which he would not renounce, and this led Carp to expect his abdication.[2] But it is probable that Charles felt that such a decision must be reserved for the supreme moment when his ministers came to urge intervention on what he regarded as the wrong side: till then, it was his duty to save what could be saved. There can be no doubt that the events of the summer filled him with real agony and shortened his life. It was not merely that he felt his own honour to be at stake, and that the German and the Hohenzollern in him responded to the call to arms: he was also sincerely convinced of German invincibility and of the vital necessity for cordial relations with Berlin and Vienna, as the sole alternative to open conflict with Budapest and so with Vienna also, and finally he never could shake off the distaste for Russia which his experiences in 1878 had bred.

The one concession made by the Cabinet to the views of the king and his allies, was the intimation that it would no longer insist upon the exact maintenance of the Treaty of Bucarest and would not react to Bulgarian intervention against Serbia.[3] Austria-Hungary hoped that this would suffice to bring in Bulgaria, but King Ferdinand, finding that his appeal to King Charles for a joint understanding met with no response, knowing that his lack of munitions would expose him to grave danger, and being at the same time subjected to the strongest possible pressure from Russia, decided for the present to watch events and if possible extract concessions from Turkey.

There now began an undignified and none too scrupulous competition between the two belligerent groups for the favour of the lesser Powers. While the Central Powers offered Bessarabia, Sazonov as early as 1 August pledged Russian support in acquiring Transylvania, if only Roumania would ally herself with the Entente, and soon added other pledges regarding the supply of munitions and the purchase of grain stocks. A convention was actually drafted, by which Russia

---

[1] When in Bucarest in January 1915, I was informed on very high authority that the king, as a last resort, instituted a private and informal kind of plebiscite among the Roumanian officers' corps, as a result of which only 110 out of about 6000 openly declared in favour of marching against Russia.

[2] Marghiloman, *Note Politice*, I, pp. 230–7.

[3] *D.D.* IV, no. 811, Waldthausen to Berlin, 4 August.

undertook not to make peace until all the Roumanian lands of Austria-Hungary were united with the kingdom: but Brătianu presumably knew that he could never obtain the sanction of the king to such a document, and he grew suspicious when he found that Sir Edward Grey refused the same guarantee of integrity for Roumania as for Belgium.[1]

Meanwhile both sides were making similar offers in Athens and Sofia. The Entente suggested that Greece should make concessions to Bulgaria and receive ample compensation in Epirus at the expense of Albania, while Bulgaria was to have Štip and Radovište for her neutrality: the Central Powers had the much easier task of offering Bulgaria *carte blanche* against Serbia and merely leaving Greece undisturbed. Most important of all was the case of Italy, to whom the Entente were already offering Trento, Trieste and Valona, but who preferred as yet to study the fortunes of war.

As August waned, Roumanian public opinion demonstrated strongly in favour of France and Belgium, but the German victories gave the Government pause. Brătianu, whom Czernin in a moment of irritation had described as "anointed with every oil", needed every conceivable wile in order to thread the path of neutrality, and set himself to play off Czernin and Poklevski, the two protagonists in the diplomatic corps of Bucarest. To him, knowing how inadequately supplied was the Roumanian army, the decisive problem was the Eastern front, and while the danger to Paris grew, he watched two great events seemingly cancel each other—the Russians capturing Lemberg and flooding westwards across Galicia and southwards to the Carpathian passes, and Hindenburg triumphantly checking the advance of their armies in East Prussia.

Early in September, King Charles was thrown into fresh embarrassment by a telegraphic appeal of the German Emperor: the Austrian failure at Lemberg had undone Germany's great achievement in the East, the Russian wave was threatening to submerge Europe and dominate the Balkans, and it was for Roumania to play the same part as at Plevna and decide the issue. Crude as this was, it set Charles again thinking of intervention in aid of a distressed ally. It was at this moment that Marghiloman revealed to the German minister his grounds for fearing that the Russians, once in occupation of Bukovina, might offer it to Roumania, and that the king might thus be placed in a most

---

[1] *Iswolski im Weltkriege*, nos. 10, 27, 49, 59.

embarrassing position.[1] While Conrad, from the purely military stand-point, urged upon Berchtold the need for an arrangement with Rou-mania, Tisza took alarm at the extent to which Transylvania was denuded of troops, but was even now reluctant to make concessions. Germany, prompted by Marghiloman, who had allies inside the Liberal Cabinet, proposed the cession of Suceava and other Roumanian districts of Bukovina, and the grant of a charter to the Roumanians of Transyl-vania.[2] Tisza at once made it clear that this was impracticable, since "the Roumanian question is not a Transylvanian question, almost 40 per cent. of its population being Magyar and German, whereas almost half the Hungarian Roumanians live outside Transylvania".[3] He was, however, ready to receive the Roumanian leaders and promised that their patriotic behaviour would bear its fruit.

In these early months the Roumanian regiments of the Austro-Hungarian army suffered very severely on the Eastern front: it has been calculated that at least 400,000 Roumanians were under arms, of whom 50,000 were made prisoners by the Russians and another 20,000 deserted, forming the nucleus of the later legions on the Entente side. At first they were roused to enthusiasm by assurances that their brethren of the kingdom were about to join them against the Russians: and for a time they were misled by the permission to wear Roumanian national colours and to sing "Roumanians, awake!"—two actions which had always been sternly proscribed in pre-war Hungary. But gradually their mood turned to one of sullen despair, and they came to believe that they were being used by the authorities as "cannon-fodder".[4] Tisza, on the contrary, seems to have genuinely persuaded himself (or at least constantly assured the Austrians) of the loyal enthusiasm with which the non-Magyar races were fighting for the common cause: but Mihali, the president of the Roumanian National Party, told his friends in Bucarest of the restlessness of the Transylvanian population, and how it was awaiting the Russians almost as deliverers, while the Magyars openly rejoiced at the losses of the Roumanian regiments, as tending to free them from the irredentist spectre.[5]

[1] In point of fact, Sazonov on 16 September announced to the Roumanian Government the occupation of part of Bukovina by Russian troops, as "the first step towards liberation from the Austro-Hungarian yoke"—*Iswolski im Weltkriege*, no. 211.　　　　　　　　　　　　　　　　[2] Conrad, *op. cit.* IV, p. 790.

[3] Tisza, *Összes Munkai*, II, no. 260, 13 September.

[4] The 23rd Brigade in particular earned the nickname of the "Forwards Brigade", because of its phenomenal losses.　　　　　　　[5] *Note Politice*, I, p. 261.

The Roumanian political leaders were reduced to utter helplessness. The murder of the archduke had knocked the bottom out of their whole plan for the future, and in view of Roumania's neutrality they had no choice but to wait upon events, and in the meantime to make loyal declarations of support to the Habsburg throne and the Hungarian fatherland. Earlier in the year Dr Alexander Vaida-Voevod, with the full approval of both Bucarest and Vienna, had made a pronouncement in Parliament in favour of the Triple Alliance, intended to pave the way for concessions from Tisza. It was inevitable that he and his colleagues, and still more the hierarchy of both Churches, should adopt the same attitude after the outbreak of war; for so long as there was a possibility of Roumania joining the Central Powers, any other course would have been sheer madness, and they had virtually no control over the decision. This also explains the close contacts which they maintained throughout the war with the Austro-Hungarian High Command and even with Berlin. Their foremost motive was to screen their compatriots from the reprisals and persecutions which would have followed the slightest signs of wavering. After the war, their opportunism was thrown in the teeth of men like Vaida, Ciceo-Pop and Mihali, both by their enemies in Budapest and by their party opponents in the New Roumania, in the hope of discrediting them politically. But it then transpired that what had finally determined their tactics were the messages sent to them by Brătianu, Take Ionescu and other leading statesmen of Bucarest, strongly urging upon them the necessity for public pronouncements of this kind, in the interests of the population, and assuring them that this would not be misunderstood in Roumania, which was for the time condemned to inaction.

Vienna and Berlin continued to urge concessions upon Tisza, and he on his side to "deal out small doses with a teaspoon" and to insist on a binding declaration of the Roumanian Government as a preliminary. At the end of September there were only 7000 troops in all Transylvania, and the strange idea was broached that the Roumanians should be invited to occupy that province as neutrals, in order to avert a Russian invasion. This not unnaturally roused Tisza's scorn: rather a Russian than a Roumanian occupation, he said, and when the possibility of ceding territory came up, he roundly told Czernin that anyone who ceded one square yard of Transylvanian soil would be shot. Bucarest should be warned beforehand that any attack would be resisted to the death, and that there was no hope of a mere military promenade.[1] The Germans wanted the immediate entry of Roumania, because the Austrians would then be able to divert a corresponding number of the troops from Galicia to East Prussia and so help them to complete the Tannenberg victory. But Tisza banked upon a Russian defeat in Galicia as an essential preliminary to concessions, and so the whole negotiation dragged.

At this stage the internal situation was modified by the death of King Charles on 10 October. The world war shortened the life of Pope Pius X, and the trial of strength with his ministers and the obscurity of the future undoubtedly had the same effect upon Charles, who foresaw intervention on the side of the Entente and was positively glad that he would not live to see it. The utterly abnormal situation of the moment dwarfed an event which would otherwise have been recognised as ending the most prosperous and pacific era in all the troubled history of the Roumanian race. The nation was not in a mood for calm estimates and retrospects: it was holding its breath before a plunge, which instinct told it was sooner or later inevitable, into murky waters whose depth it could not fathom, and for the moment it felt out of sympathy with its dead monarch. But to-day there is no sane Roumanian who would deny the essential greatness of its first king, his untiring efforts to raise and to fix the standards of public and private life in a country demoralised by corrupt alien rule, his rigid insistence on the example that the court must set, his rare qualities as an administrator and as a soldier, his devotion to duty, the realist methods which he applied to problems of foreign policy, his constant encouragement of intellectual effort in every sphere. His weak points have become apparent in the course of this narrative—the artificial balancing by which he sought to retain his control of politics, the exaggerated secrecy in which he shrouded his relations with other Powers, above all his narrow outlook towards the peasant masses, which he scarcely admitted as a factor in his political calculations. But these were limitations due to the environment from which he came and to a period which had created the illusion of permanence upon contemporaries, but was in reality essentially fluid.

The new king, Ferdinand I, lacked his uncle's prestige and political associations. Though well-read, versatile and a good judge of character, he was deficient in will power, slow to reach a decision: a natural diffidence made him uncertain in the expression of opinion, and he was

[1] Tisza, *op. cit.* II, nos. 264, 290.

thus more amenable to the influence of a powerful minister. His first and natural impulse—in which Queen Marie, despite her natural sympathies with Britain and Russia, wisely encouraged him—was to husband the resources of the country and avoid all complications until it became possible to form a clearer estimate of the main struggle in Europe. There were as yet too many factors of complete uncertainty: Russian promises required much closer definition, England was suspected of Hungarian sympathies, Bulgaria could not be trusted to remain neutral if Roumania joined the Entente. Above all, there was still much doubt as to the rôle of Italy, with whom the Roumanian Government had on 23 September signed an undertaking to act in common. The death of the Italian foreign minister, San Giuliano, a week after King Charles, inevitably tended to postpone action: and during the winter Roumania watched with mingled trepidation and imitative zeal, the tortuous parallel negotiations of Sonnino with both Triple Alliance and Triple Entente. Meanwhile the entry of Turkey increased the resemblance between Roumania and Bulgaria, each wooed by the rival groups, each playing for rival bids of territorial and other advantage, but each mainly interested in the Galician battlefields and after January 1915 in the struggle for the Dardanelles.

Early in November, the Hungarian Government announced a series of mediocre concessions to the Roumanians—the official use of national colours, the extension of the Roumanian language in church, school and lawcourt, and a political amnesty: but neither the lay leaders nor even the cautious metropolitan could be induced to accept them as a definite settlement: they fell completely flat in Bucarest, and were even unfavourably criticised in the German press. A fortnight later Hindenburg transmitted from the German East Command an appeal to Tisza for further concessions, as the only means of winning Roumania.[1] Tisza reacted somewhat acrimoniously to Berchtold, Burián and Archduke Frederick: he had "already made all imaginable concessions", and in any case Roumania's aim was not to improve the lot of her kinsmen, but to annex Transylvania and Bukovina, so that to beat Russia was the real way to win her over.[1] A picquant detail is supplied by the fact that *Ziua*, the subsidised organ of the German Legation in Bucarest, was at this time filled with denunciations of Hungarian tyranny.

[1] Tisza, *op. cit.* II, nos. 525, 533, 558. To the German Ambassador Tisza flatly refused to admit that the unfavourable atmosphere in Roumania was in any way due to Hungarian racial policy (*ibid.* no. 494, 5 November).

Brătianu decided to wait at any rate till the spring, to build up his scanty stock of munitions, and to watch Bulgaria. Meanwhile he put a strict embargo upon the transit of war material from the Central Powers to Turkey, while Sofia took the same line towards Russian supplies for Serbia. Public opinion in Bucarest was keenly divided, not so much between Dreibund and Triplice, as regarding the date at which intervention against Austria-Hungary might safely be undertaken. Immediate action was vociferously demanded by a group of nationalists at Bucarest university, led by the rector, Thomas Ionescu, but above all by his brother Take and by Nicholas Filipescu, who quarrelled violently with Marghiloman, formed the so-called "Acţiuna Nationala" and to all intents and purposes seceded from the Conservative party. They were joined by a small group of Transylvanian exiles, led by the poet Goga and the militant Uniate priest and deputy Vasile Lucaciu. The impetuous Filipescu, who had threatened "one fine day to break King Charles's windows", now transferred his animosity to Marghiloman, as leader of the Germanophils. The shrill discord of voices was heightened by the fact that the rival belligerents set themselves to buy up certain newspapers and to found thinly camouflaged organs of their own: calumny and rumour celebrated veritable orgies. Bucarest was also a paradise for speculators in grain and maize, on which the rival Powers squandered vast sums in order to forestall each other and which provided showers of corrupting baksheesh.

The triple failure of Austria in Serbia, culminating in the evacuation of Belgrade in December 1914, increased Bulgaria's disinclination to commit herself: and for the first nine months of 1915 Serbia, weakened by typhus epidemics, was left undisturbed, while the Entente bargained with her property, actual and prospective, as baits to Sofia and Rome. To all the Balkan states it seemed obviously better to await the result of the British onslaught on the Dardanelles: for Roumania in particular—as indeed for Russia herself—success would solve the problem of her supply of munitions, and at the same time probably cure Bulgaria of any inclination to throw in her lot with the Central Powers.

The military situation on the Eastern front during the first four months of 1915 justified the Allies in straining every effort to win over Italy, whose entry they believed would be absolutely decisive: and the obstinacy with which Francis Joseph, Burián (who succeeded Berchtold as foreign minister in January) and Tisza resisted the Italian claim to Trentino and Gorizia, with Trieste as a free port, made it easy for the

Entente to out-trump the rival group. The secret Treaty of London (26 April 1915) secured Italian support mainly at the expense of the Jugoslavs: and the negotiations which Sonnino still continued with Vienna were henceforth merely intended as a blind. How serious the situation was for Austria-Hungary may be gathered from the fact that the High Command seriously contemplated a withdrawal to the line of the Save (thereby abandoning Trieste and the whole Karst and endangering its connections with Dalmatia and the fleet).[1] Even more significant is the fact that the fiery Conrad warned Tisza on 23 April that a war on four sides was impossible,[2] and that a week later Tisza himself was facing the prospect of a joint drive by Italy, Serbia and Roumania into the very heart of Hungary, and wondering whether a peace feeler could be put out through Spain or Denmark.[3] Meanwhile it was known in Vienna that on 6 February Roumania had renewed and extended her agreement with Italy for four months, and Czernin fully shared the view of Conrad that Italy's entry would involve that of Roumania also.[4]

In these weeks Austria-Hungary was on the very verge of disaster. What saved her, and incidentally held back Roumania once more, was the success of Conrad's great counter-offensive in Galicia—the long and carefully prepared *coup* upon which everything was staked. In the early summer, therefore, Bucarest and Sofia were wooed more insistently than ever by the rival suitors; and with such an object-lesson in greed and cynicism on the part of Europe it is scarcely possible to launch charges of perfidy against Brătianu or Radoslavov. It soon became obvious, however, that the Treaty of London, in proportion as it promised Jugoslav territory along the Adriatic to Italy, made it more difficult for the Serbs to yield the Vardar valley to Bulgaria: while every time the Entente increased its offer to Serbia, the suspicions of Roumania and Greece, to say nothing of Serbia, were correspondingly augmented. To the very last the Entente preserved its illusions, though

---

[1] This transpires from confidential documents of Marshall Boroević and Archduke Eugene, published after the war. It is not clear whether the French and British Intelligence Departments were aware of these facts; if so, it would explain the advice which they gave to their Governments, that Italy's entry might decide the war. Unfortunately the first Italian attacks were not pushed home, and Austria-Hungary did not evacuate as originally intended.

[2] Tisza, *op. cit.* II, no. 1024, Conrad to Tisza.

[3] *Ibid.* no. 1047, Tisza to Conrad, 1 May.

[4] Pribram, *Austrian Foreign Policy*, p. 85.

it should have been obvious that the Central Powers had far more to offer to Bulgaria than the rival group. In the end their promise of "the undisputed zone" in Macedonia, *without* immediate occupation, was completely out-trumped by the Porte's actual cession of land in Thrace (3 September), followed by the German and Austrian promise of both the "disputed" and "undisputed" zones,[1] together with all Serbia east of the Morava, ample compensation if either Roumania or Greece attacked, loans and munitions and the help of German storm troops under Mackensen (6 September).[2]

The main line of these rival negotiations was not unknown to Brătianu, and confirmed him and the new king in the need for extreme caution and binding guarantees—admittedly difficult to define, even with a complete honesty of purpose which they failed to detect among any of the belligerents. They rightly assumed that the war would still be long and strenuous, and felt that their own best hope was to husband their resources and only to enter the fray at a moment when this new weight might be expected to turn the scales decisively in one direction or another. Hence Brătianu allowed the interventionists to shout at intervals, but veiled himself in extreme reserve, maintaining a strict veto on the transit of munitions, but permitting many highly profitable transactions in the sale of grain and oil.

Czernin was of course much relieved at the turn of events in Galicia and the failure of the Italian offensive, but he positively "besought" Tisza to abandon his "rigid attitude of rejection" and discuss an offer of territory to Roumania.[3] He got the reply that the loss of Transylvania would mean the end of the Monarchy as a Great Power in Eastern Europe, and that the idea of ceding any portion of Hungarian soil was to be rejected *a limine*.[4] On the other hand he was ready to discuss the cession of the three southern districts of Bukovina, if the Germans on their side would cede to Austria the Sosnowice coal mines. Bethmann Hollweg and Jagow were so frightened at the possibility of the Dardanelles being forced, owing to Turkey's lack of munitions, that they urged Burián to ask Brătianu what he would take (as compensation or "Entgelt") for letting munitions through.[5] But it was the old story

---

[1] Under the secret Serbo-Bulgarian treaty of 1912—see *supra*, p. 440.

[2] These events may best be followed in Radoslavov, *Bulgarien und die Weltkrise*, and in Marcel Dunan, *L'été Bulgare*.

[3] Tisza, *op. cit.* III, no. 1094—23 May.  [4] *Ibid.* nos. 1100, 1101, 1135.

[5] *Ibid.* v, no. 1686*k*—25 June, 1915.

of being more liberal with his neighbour's territory than with his own. Bukovina belonged to Austria, not Hungary.

It was at this time that Erzberger, the German Centre deputy who enjoyed considerable influence in Austrian Catholic circles and even in the entourage of the young heir apparent and his wife, made an appeal to Tisza for concessions to the Roumanians. But he received in reply the sledgehammer warning to drop this "poisonous mixture of little truth with much fiction": every German who wished to pre-serve his country from fresh danger, wrote Tisza, "would do well to leave alone the theme of concession to our Roumanians".[1] The German learnt with silent scepticism that conditions in Transylvania were far better than in Roumania and that no country was so just to its nationali-ties as Hungary.[2] After this snub, however, Tisza did consent to a certain revision of the terms offered to the metropolitan Meţianu in November 1914: he was now ready to modify the franchise in such a way that the Roumanians might hope for thirty-five or forty seats, to assign a certain number of administrative posts to Roumanians, to increase the endowments of the Orthodox and Uniate Churches, to recognise the Roumanian language in lawcourt and office, and to extend its sphere in the schools. But he refused even to discuss Transylvanian autonomy and poured derision upon Czernin's suggestion of a Rou-manian university as "a cultural monstrosity" which "would injure the practical interests of the Roumanian youth" and (here lay the real reason) "create an impossible situation towards the other nationalities" of Hungary.[3]

After this Czernin seems to have given up Tisza as hopeless: and as the summer passed and the Central Powers won their smashing victories in Poland, the danger of Roumanian intervention could once more be safely shelved. Czernin reported home that the king was altogether in Brătianu's hands, the queen much more passive, Brătianu himself "cowardly and false": and he now concentrated upon a scheme for a "National" government under Marghiloman and the now decrepit Maiorescu—Carp having made himself impossible by offensive criticism of the queen. Nothing, however, is more characteristic of the Rou-manian situation than the attitude of these very men. Carp, the in-corrigible Germanophil, had in a moment of candour assured Dr Münz,

[1] Tisza, *op. cit.* III, no. 1130—5–12 June, 1915.
[2] Erzberger, *Erlebnisse im Weltkrieg*, p. 80.
[3] Tisza, *op. cit.* no. 1180—30 June.

"We are the allies, but not the friends, of Austria",[1] while Marghiloman, always the mainstay of the Central Powers, never ceased, in all his discussions with Czernin, to harp upon what he called his "leitmotiv" of a charter for the Transylvanians and freely admitted to Mihali that of every hundred Roumanians ninety-five were decidedly anti-Austrian—by which of course he really meant anti-Magyar.[2] Marghiloman got so far as to assure Czernin that in return for a written pledge of Bukovina and concessions to the Transylvanians he could win the king for a reconstruction of the Cabinet (dropping the Ententephil ministers, Costinescu and Anghelescu), the withdrawal of the veto on Turkish munitions and the promise of intervention against Russia by a specific date. But once again, despite pressure from both general staffs, the scheme broke down against Tisza's opposition: and this time it is not surprising, for the demand (as submitted to and sanctioned by Maniu, Vaida and Aurel Popovici) culminated in autonomy for the Roumanians of Hungary on the analogy of Croatia, a local Diet, proportional representation at Budapest and a Roumanian minister without portfolio![3]

Even before Warsaw fell on 4 August, all real hope of forcing the Dardanelles had vanished, though we now know that the Turks were twice on the point of surrender, that the dire shortage of Turkish munitions was the main motive of the German staff in harping upon the Roumanian question, and that there was a moment when Roumania could have had Suceava in return for free transit. Even after her treaties of 3 and 6 September, Bulgaria continued to fool the Entente for another five weeks: then on 14 October she suddenly declared war upon the Serbs, while the shock troops of Mackensen and Köves fell upon them from across the Danube. Roumania, more isolated than ever now that King Constantine was leaning so openly towards the German side, had to look on in dismay while Serbia was overrun and the remnant of her armies was condemned to a long and disheartening defensive in conjunction with the Entente forces so grudgingly dispatched to the Salonica front. Bulgaria now obtained all and more than she had hoped, and prepared to annex all Serbia east of the Morava, including the Roumanian district of the Timok. King and premier urged upon Vienna not merely the expulsion of the Karagjorgjević, but the com-

[1] Baernreither, *Fragments from a Political Diary*, p. 256.
[2] *Note politice*, I, pp. 325, 362: cf. also pp. 251, 283, 296.
[3] *Ibid.* pp. 480–4: Tisza, *op. cit.* v, no. 1686*l.*

plete partition of Serbia between her neighbours. To this, however, Count Tisza objected, not on any moral grounds, but simply because he feared that the annexation of several million Serbs would stimulate some form of Jugoslav union within the Habsburg Monarchy. He therefore suggested that she should lose her eastern and southern provinces to Bulgaria and Albania, that she should be cut off from the Save and Danube (losing Belgrade in the process) and that Montenegro should at the same time be cut off from the sea. There would thus remain "a poor mountainous country, cut off from waterways and for the most part unfertile, shut in between powerful neighbours and in complete economic dependence on the Monarchy".[1] Not the least of his motives in promoting the destruction of Serbia was that Bulgaria, aggrandised at her expense, would reduce Roumania to complete impotence and set free Transylvania from all danger.

Elated by their Balkan victories, the Central Powers adopted a more arrogant tone at Bucarest. Goga and Lucaciu, the exiled Transylvanian agitators, stood as candidates for the Roumanian Chamber, and when Waldburg made it known that their election would be regarded as a hostile act not merely by Austria-Hungary, but by Germany, the Government found it convenient to manipulate their defeat. More serious was the conclusion of a big corn deal with Great Britain, involving an advance of £10,000,000 through the Bank of England. Czernin, who had already secured fifty thousand trucks of grain for Austria, was annoyed that the Entente should lay its hands upon the surplus, and his German colleague, Von dem Bussche, informed the king that Berlin could no longer trust Brătianu and refused all dealings with him: the German Staff, he said, favoured an ultimatum to Bucarest in the matter of corn supplies, and one more drop of water would make the cup overflow.[2] There was fresh talk of a Conservative Cabinet under Marghiloman and Maiorescu: but Brătianu was firm in the saddle and was not to be dislodged. Cautiously, fortifications were begun in the Carpathian passes, but none upon the Pruth, as Marghiloman demanded. The death of Queen Elizabeth early in March snapped another tie between the court and its German kinsmen.

The first half of 1916 was on the eastern and southern fronts the quietest period of the war, and Roumania again resigned herself to

[1] Tisza, *op. cit.* IV, no. 1444*b*, Tisza to Francis Joseph, 4 December 1914; no. 1468, Tisza to Burián, 29 December.

[2] *Note politice*, II, p. 17.

await events. Conrad, freed from Balkan anxieties, planned the *coup de grâce* for Italy and after dangerously denuding Galicia, won a brilliant success at Asiago. This gave Brusilov his opportunity; the Russian counter-offensive at Lutsk effectually destroyed Conrad's hope of "finishing the War" in Italy, cost Austria 200,000 men and brought the Russians once more within reach of the Carpathian passes into Hungary. The result was that the Germans, tired of continually rescuing their ally from the consequences of enterprises begun without their knowledge, insisted on the need for unity of command, and obtained the somewhat reluctant consent of Francis Joseph. Events in Roumania speedily proved the wisdom of this decision.

In March and April Brătianu, still balanced on the sagging tight-rope of neutrality, appeased Berlin and Vienna by two commercial export agreements, as a counterpart to the January contracts with London. To his critics he had the unanswerable reply that Roumania was swimming in her own grease and simply had to find an outlet for her surplus products. To have allowed the Entente to pay for and pile up stocks which it could not use, while all the time famine was already assailing large sections of the German and Austrian population, would assuredly have brought an ultimatum upon Roumania's head: and this, as the Entente had to recognise, would have involved an attack upon Roumania at the psychological moment best suited to their enemies, and not, as they still hoped, at the moment of really decisive advantage for themselves.

The resounding victories of Brusilov convinced Brătianu and even the king that this moment was at last at hand. Already at the beginning of July the secret reports of the General Staff in Teschen estimated the relative strength of Austria and Russia on the Eastern front at 450,000 and 780,000,[1] and the disproportion seemed to grow as Brusilov advanced: while the main Bulgarian army was tied to the Macedonian front. Tisza sent an anxious memorial to the emperor, pointing out that Transylvania was so denuded of troops as positively to invite a Roumanian "military promenade". In his belief the further aggrandisement of Bulgaria at Serbia's expense was now the sole means of holding back Roumania: in return for this Bulgarian troops could be used for the defence of the Transylvanian passes.[2] Even in this emergency, however, Tisza and his entourage were quite intran-

[1] Tisza, *op. cit.* v, no. 1674*i*—9 July.
[2] *Ibid.* nos. 1673*c* and *i*—7 and 22 July.

sigeant. He told Czernin that in his belief the only hope of holding back Roumania lay with the king; yet when the king had spoken—most tactfully, according to Czernin—of the unfortunate effect produced upon Roumanian opinion by fourteen death sentences passed on Transylvanian intellectuals (including six Orthodox priests), Tisza declined to hold out any prospect of pardon, insisting that this could only be the spontaneous àct of the emperor-king.[1] By this time Czernin's reports were full of warnings that Roumania would move as soon as the essential harvest had been gathered in.

In July and August 1916 Bucarest witnessed the same unedifying spectacle as Rome and Sofia in the spring and summer of the previous year. Roumania had twice held back at moments when her intervention might well have been decisive—while the Russians were capturing Przemysl early in 1915, and again while Bulgaria was attacking Serbia in the following autumn. By holding back a third time, she risked being reduced to complete impotence and alienating both groups of belligerents. The German minister pressed Brătianu for a definite declaration of neutrality, but failed to tie down this master of obscurity and prevarication. Meanwhile, with the utmost secrecy, negotiations were conducted with the Entente, who, though still hopelessly handicapped by the lack of any unity of command, were groping towards the idea of a general attack on all fronts—Verdun, the Somme and Galicia, to be supplemented by the Isonzo, Macedonia, Mesopotamia and Transylvania. On 17 August 1916, then, a treaty of alliance was concluded between Roumania and the four Entente Powers, by which in return for a territorial guarantee and a free hand to annex certain specified territory, she undertook to declare war on Austria-Hungary not later than 28 August with all her available forces. There was the usual mutual undertaking against a separate peace and a clause (to which Brătianu assigned quite exaggerated importance), assuring Roumania equal status with her greater allies in all peace negotiations. But all else paled before the scandalously immoderate promise of territory: for Roumania was to receive not merely Bukovina to the Pruth, all Transylvania, the Banat, Maramureş and Crişana, but a line reaching to within a few kilometres of both Debreczen and Szeged and thereby including large tracts of fertile plain inhabited exclusively by Magyars, where there was no shadow of ethnographic or strategic excuse. It is impossible to suppose that the Allies were unaware of this; they were

---

[1] Tisza, *op. cit.* v, nos. 1676 *a* and *c*—25 June and 10 July.

recklessly ready to pay almost any price for a new recruit, so long as it was at the enemy's expense. The military convention which was signed at the same time contains several points of interest. Under § 1 Roumania's entry was to be preceded by one week by an allied offensive from Salonica. Under §§ 2 and 3 Russia undertook to continue her offensive along "the whole Austrian front" and with special energy in Bukovina, but also to send one cavalry and two infantry divisions to the Dobrogea for joint action against Bulgaria. Roumania was to be supplied "uninterruptedly with at least three hundred tons a day of war material".[1]

Nothing whatever was said of Germany, with whom Brătianu hoped to the very last to avoid a conflict, although Bussche had warned him, in the bluntest possible fashion only a week before signature, that any attack on Austria-Hungary would lead to an immediate counterattack by both Germany and Bulgaria. On the very eve of his departure Bussche received, through the Conservative chiefs, a highly characteristic message from the premier: the Government had refused to declare war on Germany or to commit itself to economic war, and hoped for a speedy renewal of normal relations. This would be possible if aerial bombardments and any other needless cruelties against the civilian population could be avoided. Bussche was not reassuring, and talked of Belgian *francs-tireurs* and reprisals for the "Barralong" and the bombing of Karlsruhe.[2] And sure enough the first Zeppelin raided Bucarest as early as 5 September, causing panic and no little damage.

The decisive Crown Council was held on 27 August; beside the Liberal ministers there were present the ex-premiers, Rosetti, Carp and Maiorescu, Marghiloman as Conservative leader and the interventionists Filipescu and Ionescu. The king declared that the victory of the Central Powers was now impossible, and that after ripe reflection and internal struggles which they would understand, he agreed with the necessity of war and appealed for their support and for "silence as of the confessional". Brătianu argued that the whole Latin world was opposed to Germany and that Italy's action had quite altered Roumania's relations towards Russia: nor was it possible to go with Germany now that she was encouraging Bulgaria "to take our place in the East". Take Ionescu applauded with enthusiasm, Marghiloman

---

[1] German text of both in *Iswolski im Weltkriege*, nos. 301, 302.
[2] *Note politice*, II, pp. 164–6.

warned against Russian designs upon Constantinople and showed scepticism as to the chances of war, but was ready to remain silent and not to strike a discordant note in face of national unity. Only the implacable Carp blurted out, "I wish that you may be beaten, for your victory would be the ruin of the country!"[1] Brătianu advised him to recall his sons and send them to the German army! Marghiloman told the king very frankly that he could not endorse the declaration of war, but that it might be just as well to have someone to fall back upon: "If things go badly, I shall be there to help". It cannot be denied that he had a prophetic instinct.

War was declared on Austria-Hungary that same day—the day of Italy's formal rupture with Germany: but Italy's earlier example was followed and no similar act committed against Germany. But it was from Berlin that the most violent and immediate reaction came. There was an outburst of press abuse against the "par nobile fratrum", the Latin traitors who were proving their descent from the deported criminals of ancient Rome. The degenerate Hohenzollern was contrasted with the frank and soldierly Constantine of Greece, who had wisely espoused the cause of his brother-in-law. But these mouthings were followed by deeds of extreme prowess. The German Government was fully aware that the whole alliance was at stake, unless Austria-Hungary could once more be saved from ruin and an ocular demonstration provided for Bulgars and Turks.

# CHAPTER XVI

# WAR AND DEFEAT

From the very outset Roumania was dogged by failure and ill fortune. Her plan of campaign, which had been submitted for approval to both Joffre and Alexeyev, rested on the assumption that Germany would be fully occupied at Verdun and on the Somme, that the Italians would attack again on the Isonzo, and above all, that the Brusilov offensive would absorb all the energies of Austria-Hungary and that a determined allied offensive from Salonica would keep the Bulgarians fully occupied and thus leave the Roumanians free to overrun Transylvania, join hands with the Russians in Bukovina and threaten the Austrian right flank in the Carpathians. After the event it was easy to argue that Roumania should have first reduced Bulgaria to impotence by a swift thrust at Sofia, and perhaps Varna also. But on the other hand it was an absolute dogma of the Russian high command, that Bulgaria would not dare to attack the "Liberator", and that the Dobrogea was in no serious danger; while on the other, Roumanian popular sentiment clamoured for the immediate deliverance of Transylvania, all the more so as its garrisons had once again been dangerously depleted. In the facile phrase of the day, the Roumanians gave a rendezvous to Brusilov at Dorna Vatra (in Bukovina) and to Sarrail on the Mureş, but neither of them kept tryst.

This is not the place for an account of the operations and strategy of the war: the barest outline must suffice, all the more so because the most essential documents are not yet accessible and may perhaps never be forthcoming. But nothing can obscure two salient facts. In the first place the successful Russian offensive ceased at the very moment when its continuance seemed likely to be decisive, and the Central Powers were thus able to detach the necessary forces to deal with the Roumanian invasion. In the second place, the promised operations in Macedonia were half-hearted and bungling and never deserved the name of a real offensive, and the Bulgarians not merely had surplus troops available, but found it safe to employ them in an attack of astonishing vigour upon the combined forces of Roumania and Russia. These two main facts are not open to question, but complete mystery still envelopes the underlying forces. It is known that an important section of official Russia was by no means as enthusiastic for the entry

of Roumania as were its Western allies, holding that her territorial
claims were altogether excessive and at any rate in Northern Bukovina
conflicted with Russian interests. It is also known that General
Alexeyev and his staff were highly critical of the Roumanian army and
inclined to think that it might prove a strategic liability rather than an
asset. Finally, it is a simple fact of chronology that Sazonov, who as
Russian foreign minister was mainly responsible for the negotiations,
fell from power on 23 July, and that with the advent of Boris Stürmer
in his place "the dark forces" which were soon to prove Russia's ruin,
asserted themselves in a sense that was increasingly hostile to the Allies
and to a vigorous conduct of the war. But it is a very long way from
this to the suggestion that there was deliberate treachery on the part
of the Russian staff and Government, and that Petrograd was by
no means reluctant to see Roumania overthrown and permanently
weakened. Indeed Sazonov himself, a declared enemy of Stürmer and
all his ideas, has left it on record that Alexeyev pressed very strongly
in August for Roumania's immediate entry—in Sazonov's own view,
quite mistakenly—and that Stürmer saw in the accomplished fact "a
great diplomatic success" of his own.[1] Yet no less an authority than
General Iliescu, Roumania's chief of staff throughout the campaign,
published a statement in the French press soon after the first Russian
revolution,[2] accusing Stürmer of forcing Roumania to move at an
inopportune moment and then deliberately abandoning her in order
to negotiate a separate peace with Germany. It must be added that
hitherto no concrete proof of such allegations has been forthcoming,
and they may be relegated to the realm of fairy tales. The most that
can be said is that the advent of Stürmer increased the tension between
Petrograd and its armies in the field, paralysed Russia's powers of
offensive and diminished the chances of cordial co-operation with all
her allies, old or new.

[1] Sazonov, *Les Années Fatales*, p. 286. Neratov (at that time Sazonov's chief
helper) gave evidence before the Provisional Government's Commission of
Enquiry, to the effect that Stürmer had pressed strongly for Roumania hastening
the date of entry, and that G.H.Q. also attached great importance to this. The
Foreign Office, he maintained, acted equally under pressure from the military and
from the Western Allies. *Padenie Tsarskogo Rezhima*, VI, p. 215.

[2] *Le Matin*, 3 April 1917; *New Europe*, 12 April 1917. This was strongly denied
in the *Novoye Vremya* of 26 April (that is, under the revolutionary regime). There
are indeed many who explain Iliescu's eagerness for intervention as a gambler's
throw to divert attention from the deficiencies of the army.

On the Balkan front it is more possible to reach the truth, though the details still remain extremely obscure. All through the summer of 1916 differences of opinion had continued between London and Paris as to the value of maintaining the Salonica expedition. This and the anomalous position in Greece (where there was an open trial of strength between King Constantine and Mr Venizelos, as protagonists of the rival groups in Europe) sapped the initiative of General Sarrail and complicated his relations with the generals of the allied forces, behind whose back there were periodical intrigues—fatuous but dangerous—for a separate peace with Bulgaria at Serbia's expense. During June and July Sarrail received instructions to prepare an offensive, with a view to "holding" Bulgaria's entire forces, "depriving the enemy of his liberty of movement" and thus promoting Roumania's entry. But he found that General Milne had still more precise orders "not to take the offensive until Roumania definitely opens her campaign".[1] Sarrail, therefore, had to operate with French and Serbian troops only; himself almost as much a politician as a soldier, he was fully aware of the conflicts between Paris and Chantilly, complicating still further the Anglo-French disagreement, and he was justifiably uneasy at the refusal to place adequate resources at his disposal.

To complete his disarray, the Bulgarians launched an attack of their own on 17 August, three days before the obstacles to a general allied offensive had been overcome. The Allies countered, it is true, but it was not till 10 September that the counter-offensive became at all serious: and after endless delays and a violent quarrel between Sarrail and Cordonnier in front of allied officers, it tapered out in October, without ever having fulfilled its purpose of destroying Bulgaria's freedom of movement. Of the reoccupation of Serbia and of a rendezvous with the Roumanians on the Mureş there was never even the remotest question, though the heroic Serbs persevered on their section of the front, until Monastir was reoccupied in the middle of November. Well might the Roumanian troops chant the half ironical, half plaintive lines:

> O Sarrail, Sarrail, Sarrail.
> Noi ne batem, şi tu stai!
> (We are fighting, and you stand still!)

Yet another of the many obscurities of this situation is the fact that Colonel Rudeanu, the Roumanian military representative in France,

---

[1] 23 July, Robertson to Milne—Sarrail, *Mon Commandement*, p. 137.

signed at Chantilly on 23 July a convention binding Roumania to dispatch 150,000 troops without delay against Bulgaria, in conjunction with Sarrail's attack from the south, but that Brătianu categorically refused to attack Bulgaria.[1]

After the declaration of war the Roumanians at once threw their main armies upon Transylvania, intending to occupy the Mureş valley as rapidly as possible, as this would enable them to reduce the length of their fighting line by almost one half, and thus counteract the imperfections of road and railway communications south of the Carpathians. General Averescu entered by the Tömös Pass and took Braşov, while Prezan forced the Tölgyes Pass and occupied the northern Székely districts: other armies advanced by the Red Tower upon Hermannstadt and by the Vulkan and Iron Gates in the extreme west, but did not make the same progress.

When the invasion began, the Austrian commander General von Arz (himself a Transylvanian Saxon and the future Chief of Staff), only had about 25,000 men at his disposal and had to withdraw northwards. The result was a panic and flight among the Magyar population, and violent attacks were launched in the Parliament of Budapest against both the Government and the High Command for being taken unawares. But Tisza held his ground, gallantly (and accurately) defended Czernin against all charges, and meanwhile concentrated his main efforts upon mobilising German support for the crumbling edifice. Nor did Germany waste a moment's time in demonstrating that she was indeed a friend in need. While Falkenhayn was sent to the aid of Arz, Mackensen with a limited number of storm troops won the confidence of the Bulgarians and stirred them up to a swift counter-offensive from the south. Brătianu, for all his subtlety, had profoundly miscalculated the attitude of Bulgaria, who had acquired an altogether inordinate appetite since the downfall of Serbia and was now eager for revenge against her enemy of 1913.

From the very first day Mackensen was singularly successful. As early as 6 September he had captured Turtucaia on the Danube, with many guns and 25,000 prisoners: Silistra was hurriedly evacuated, and Roumania's hold upon the Dobrogea was endangered. The whole Roumanian plan of campaign was thus dislocated: instead of pursuing the offensive into the heart of Transylvania, it was now necessary to assume defensive positions and transfer considerable forces to the

[1] Paléologue, *La Russie des Tsars*, II, 323–7.

south-west front. The Russians, who had lightly promised 50,000 men for the Dobrogea without expecting that they would ever be required, now only sent 20,000. As a minor tragedy, these included the Czech and Jugoslav Legions formed out of Austro-Hungarian prisoners on the Russian front: they fought with the heroism of despair, but were left without support and decimated, their wounded shooting each other to avoid falling into the enemy's hands.[1] By the third week of September Mackensen had occupied the old Bulgarian frontier and was threatening the great bridge of Cernavoda. In the Kokel valley a fresh Roumanian advance was attempted, really for political quite as much as for military reasons. But Arz and Falkenhayn were now massing their forces, and on 26 September Manolescu was defeated near Hermannstadt and thrown back across the Red Tower Pass into the old kingdom. Retreat was now inevitable, and by the middle of October the last fragments of Transylvania had been evacuated by the Roumanian armies, who brought away with them thousands of refugees, flying from the fear of Magyar reprisals.

Falkenhayn's next task was to cut off the Wallachian salient and join hands with Mackensen and the Bulgarians outside Bucarest. The battle of Târgu Jiul (26 October) brought a passing gleam of success to the Roumanian arms: the Germans fell into a skilfully laid trap in the Vulkan Pass and suffered a serious reverse. But this passing advantage was speedily wiped out by the death of General Dragalina and by the treachery of a staff officer who joined the Germans.[2] The

---

[1] They were regarded with suspicion, and barely tolerated by the Russian High Command, and dependent for medical service upon an unit of the Scottish Women's Hospitals, under Dr Elsie Inglis and Mrs Haverfield, who went through the whole Dobrogea campaign. Dr James Berry and his wife Dr Dickinson Berry also organised a private hospital of their own, first in Serbia, then on the Roumanian front.

[2] Early in the war a singular accident proved to me that there were traitors inside the Roumanian army. Through an unimpeachable source which I am even now not able to mention, I learned that on 26 September 1914 a meeting had taken place at Braşov between two Austrian agents named Freitag and Ionescu Cananan, and the wife of a certain Roumanian officer, then adjutant to General Lambrino, of the Jassy Corps Commando. This lady, acting for her husband, handed over the Roumanian plan of mobilisation (32 pages): and it was arranged that at the commencement of the actual mobilisation of which the document provided the key, a telegram should be sent, containing the words, "Je vous félicite". A sum of 4000 kronen was paid over.

These facts were duly communicated to the proper quarter and transmitted officially to Bucarest, but I never learned whether they were acted upon.

German advance into Wallachia was resumed, a fresh army effected the passage of the Danube, between Zimnicea and Giurgiu, and by the middle of November Bucarest was in grave danger. The group of forts erected round the capital by Brialmont in the eighties proved to be even more ineffective against modern weapons than those which he had planned round Liége.

In this dangerous situation Russia once more showed a curious indifference: the despatch of reinforcements to the Dobrogea under General Sakharov did not prevent the fall of Constanţa. A last gallant effort was made by Generals Prezan and Berthelot to check the Germans on the river Argeş, and for a time Mackensen's forces were in real danger. Unhappily the whole plan was ruined by the incompetence and panic flight of General Socec, who was afterwards tried by court martial and degraded. As a result the Roumanian forces were cut into two portions, and the Government had to resign itself to the evacuation of the capital and a hurried withdrawal into Moldavia. On 6 December the Germans entered Bucarest in triumph, but only after great accumulations of grain and other stores had been destroyed by the retiring army. A special technical mission under Colonel Norton Griffiths wrought such elaborate destruction in the abandoned oilfields as to make it impossible for the enemy to use them for many months to come.

The year closed with a prolonged battle along the fortified line of the Seret. This time the Russians sent the necessary reinforcements, realising that the loss of Moldavia would probably involve the evacuation of Galicia and Bukovina and an enemy threat to Odessa. By January 1917 the Seret front was stabilised, and providentially for Roumania the mad project of withdrawing army and Government into Southern Russia, on the analogy of the Serbs at Corfu, was abandoned. The gold reserve and archives were sent for greater safety to Moscow, and were eventually sequestrated by the Bolshevist Government.

Parliament met at Jassy late in December, and a kind of concentration Cabinet was formed. Brătianu remained premier and took over Foreign Affairs from its titular holder, Porumbaru; Take Ionescu became a minister without portfolio, while three other members of the Ententophil Opposition[1] were also included. Nicholas Filipescu had died shortly before Bucarest fell: the three Germanophils, Carp, Maiorescu and Marghiloman, remained behind, and were destined to perform the ungrateful but useful function of buffer between Roumania

[1] Michael Cantacuzene, Greceanu and Mîrzescu.

and the arrogant victor. Marghiloman had warned the queen that by suing for peace there was still time to save the country and the dynasty, to which she had replied, with grave dignity, that this alternative had never been examined.[1] And indeed, amid all the confusion and panic, heightened by the discovery of much corruption and poltroonery, there was never any serious question of surrender. Those in whose hands Roumanian destinies lay set their teeth and refused to lose faith in the ultimate success of the Allied cause. So far as the Germans were concerned, they had straightened out the salients of the Eastern front and reduced it to a minimum: they had not annihilated Roumania, but had at any rate for many months to come destroyed her powers of offensive, and their surplus forces could now be better employed elsewhere. For the first half of 1917 there was the same sort of pause as after the conquest of Serbia almost exactly a year before.

\* \* \* \*

Roumania's tragic failure coincided with, or heralded, a series of tremendous events which speedily transformed the whole aspect of the war. The death of Francis Joseph on 21 November marked the end of a great era and was followed by a change of regime in both halves of the Dual Monarchy. The young Emperor Charles, a man of high character and ideals, but lacking in balance and experience and utterly unequal to the problems by which he was faced, turned to new men and methods that were often highly amateur and inadequate. The hide-bound officials of the court were all replaced, the Archduke Frederick lost the supreme command, and headquarters were transferred from Teschen to Baden. In Hungary Tisza only maintained himself with difficulty, came into conflict with the crown over the thorny question of electoral reform, and disapproved, though he could not prevent, the summons of the Austrian Reichsrat, the grant of a political amnesty and the opening of a period of concession to the non-Germans. Above all, Tisza's nominee at the Ballplatz, Baron Burián, was replaced by Count Czernin, known to Charles as the candidate of his uncle Francis Ferdinand for that post and the legatee of his political ideas. Both Charles and Czernin realised that only by reconstituting the Monarchy on federal lines could its disintegration be averted: both were aware that its resources were subject to a dangerous strain and

[1] *Note Politice*, II, p. 298.

that peace was an imperative necessity. They were, however, fatally handicapped in both directions, in the one case by Charles's coronation oath as Apostolic King, which involved a solemn pledge to respect the territorial integrity of Hungary, in the other by the unyielding attitude of Berlin and the interlocking of the military forces of the two allies, which rendered a separate peace almost impossible. They were on the horns of a dilemma: and the need for action was increased tenfold by the outbreak of the Russian Revolution and the entry of America. Henceforth there was to be a war of ideas and principles, far more disintegrating than the highest explosive: the question of nationalities, which had so long gnawed at the vitals of the Habsburg Monarchy, was now being restated in terms of national unity and "self-determination". Czernin's secret memorandum of early April assured the young emperor that "another winter campaign would be absolutely out of the question: in other words that in the summer or late autumn the war must be ended at all costs".[1] That information of so ultra-confidential a character should have become known to the Entente has generally been ascribed to the treachery or indiscretion of the clerical deputy Erzberger;[2] in reality it was the work of the anti-Austrian "Maffia" organisation in Prague, which had its ramifications in the very highest circles. That the betrayal played its part in predisposing the Entente against the famous peace negotiations of Prince Sixtus of Bourbon is also certain: but these were foredoomed to failure for other reasons which lie outside our present field of investigation. It was not until a year later that the negotiations became known, through Clemenceau's ferocious exposure of Czernin's mendacities; but behind the scenes the essential facts were known to many. It is probably true to say that the dismay caused among the lesser nationalities by the discovery that the Entente statesmen no longer refused all discussion of a separate peace, was counterbalanced by the knowledge that Austria-Hungary was showing signs of extreme exhaustion and that her statesmen recognised their danger.

All these factors weighed with the Roumanian Government in exile and encouraged it to hold its ground instead of retiring beyond the Pruth into Russian territory. We know now how fortunate this decision was, quite apart from the internal state of Russia following upon the Revolution: for if once Moldavia had been evacuated, the Germans

[1] Czernin, *In the World War*, p. 14.
[2] For his defence see his *Erlebnisse im Weltkrieg*, pp. 117-21.

would have established a Government of their own in Bucarest and raised the question of King Ferdinand's dethronement.[1] This was the course favoured by Peter Carp, whom a high German functionary in Bucarest criticised as "more reactionary than the most reactionary Prussian"; it was also favoured by Constantine Stere, who began to issue a newspaper in the interest of the Central Powers and who desired a "personal union" with Austria—either under the Emperor Charles or his young son—as the only means of bringing the kingdom and Transylvania closer together. What really proved fatal to this discreditable intrigue was the attitude of Marghiloman and Maiorescu who, more true to Conservative principles than their former chief, had scruples even as to the abdication of King Ferdinand and felt that to eject the dynasty altogether would create a very dangerous precedent in an Eastern Europe honeycombed with revolution.[2] Marghiloman, as President of the Red Cross, enjoyed a prestige among the Germans which none of his colleagues possessed, and was able to obtain many alleviations from the occupying authorities and even the repatriation of many Roumanian prisoners from Germany.

Meanwhile what was achieved in Moldavia, amid the utter disorganisation and discouragement produced by defeat and the appalling overcrowding and disease which tens of thousands of refugees brought with them, was little short of miraculous. In the six months of relative calm before fresh storms General Berthelot, as head of the French mission, succeeded in completely reconstituting the Roumanian army, ruthlessly weeding out incompetent and corrupt elements, showing court favourites and "political" staff officers to the door, and re-equipping with French guns and supplies, specially shipped to Murmansk and escorted through Russia by armed guards, whose task grew increasingly onerous as the control of the Provisional Government weakened. Much was due to the personality of Berthelot himself, massive, unflinching, self-reliant—dominated, in M. Paléologue's admirable phrase, by "une volonté calme, souriante, inflexible".[3] At the same time Transylvanian legions, corresponding to those already formed out of the Czecho-Slovak and Jugoslav prisoners on the Russian front, were organised at Jassy, very largely at the instance of MM. Goga and Sever Bocu; and their numbers were rapidly growing,

[1] *Note Politice*, II, p. 382.
[2] *Ibid.* pp. 539, 544.
[3] *La Russie des Tsars*, III, p. 45.

when the Russian *débâcle* made further recruiting wellnigh impossible.[1]

When, then, the Russians made their final offensive early in July 1917, the Roumanians, under the competent leadership of Averescu, Prezan and others, were ready to play their part and successfully held their own against the combined German and Austro-Magyar forces of Archduke Joseph at the battle of Maraşti (22 July). Unhappily this remained an isolated action, for in the meanwhile the process of disintegration in the Russian army had been rapidly gathering strength and proved fatal to any sustained offensive. The gallant stand of the Czechs at Zborow was a last flash in the pan, followed by collapse upon a wide front, and during August the Austrians reoccupied the whole Bukovina. But the devoted work of Berthelot bore its fruit, for the attack launched by Mackensen and the Archduke Joseph was vigorously repelled at Maraşeşti in fighting lasting over a week (12–19 August). The valour of the Roumanian peasant soldier, when worthily led, was now signally vindicated, and ungrudgingly admitted by the discomfited but ever gallant Mackensen and his staff.[2] With the Russian army in full disintegration on their flank, it was impossible for them to assume the offensive in their turn; and indeed the frequency of fraternisation between the Russian and German trenches often left the Roumanians in an extremely precarious position. But it is not too much to say that their maintenance in being, in a strong defensive attitude, saved Odessa from occupation by Mackensen, and perhaps even Moscow from Leopold of Bavaria.

With the fall of the Russian Provisional Government early in November and the advent of Lenin and the Bolshevists to power,

---

[1] The total number of volunteers on Roumanian soil has been estimated at 29,000 and 1816 officers (Clopoţel, *Revoluţia din 1918*, p. 138). In November 1917 three regiments were formed under the names of Alba Iulia, Avram Iancu and Turda. One battalion was left behind in Moscow and had to go out through Siberia, like the Czechoslovak army. The legionaries published at Chişinău a paper called *Ardealul* (Transylvania), afterwards rechristened *România Noua*, which exercised a notable influence upon the Bessarabians at a most critical period. The chief organisers were Colonel Stârcea, MM. Ghibu and Ghiţa Pop, and Octavian Goga, "the sweet singer of our sufferings" (Cântăreţul pătimirii noastre), whose poetic note was still high and clear, and not yet contaminated by political ambitions.

[2] Marghiloman's diary records several instances of German military admiration for the Roumanian troops: what might they not have done if they had been on the right side!

Roumania found herself completely isolated from all Allied help, and surrender became a mere matter of time. The disintegration of the Russian army had the most alarming effects, for at many points along the common front Russian and Roumanian regiments were interlocked. There were constant attempts to undermine the loyalty of the troops, to establish the system of soldier's soviets and to preach the overthrow of the existing order. Trenches were surrendered, without warning, to the Germans, in such a way as to leave the Roumanians in the air. On one occasion a plot to waylay the king and queen and either murder or deport them to Russia, was only just discovered in time. In such a situation, with masses of undisciplined troops on the move, with refugees often ill-supplied with papers of identity, with famine and disease rampant, it is really surprising that the authorities maintained the necessary control. The full history of this harassing and chaotic period will perhaps never be written, for no records exist as to many important transactions; and it must suffice for our present purposes to affirm that not even the sufferings of Serbia or of Belgium will compare with those of Roumania, one half of whose population were exiles in their own land, while the other half were bled white by a conqueror whose ruthlessness had the excuse that his own people were starving.

Nothing is more surprising than that in this supreme crisis the peasant masses should have refrained from drastic revolutionary action and should have been so little affected by the propaganda of their Ukrainian and Russian neighbours. But this does not mean that they remained indifferent, and if revolution was avoided, it was above all due to the fact that the leaders of both parties at Jassy were fully alive to the dangers of the situation, possessed the initiative and strength to impose their views upon the rank and file of their followers, and not least of all, were able to convince the king of the necessity for instant action. It would be absurd to suggest that King Ferdinand was a man of genius or of profound intellect; and indeed he often suffered from fits of irresolution and doubt. But on this occasion he showed a noble courage and saved his country from certain disaster. Early in April 1917 he visited the front and addressed the troops in words which have become historic: "Sons of peasants who, with your own hands, have defended the soil on which you were born, on which your lives have been passed, I, your King, tell you that besides the great recompense of victory which will assure for every one of you the nation's gratitude, you have earned the right of being masters, in a larger measure, of that soil upon which you fought. Land will be given you. I your King, am the first to set the example; and you will also take a larger part in public affairs".[1]

He even went so far as to assure the veteran journalist Costa-Foru that the idea of granting land was his own, thereby perhaps unduly minimising the undoubted share of Brătianu and Take Ionescu. But he had achieved something which could no longer be undone, he had electrified the masses to whom General Berthelot was striving to impart a new ardour and discipline, and he had immunised the nation against Bolshevik propaganda. On 22 May the official *Indépendance Roumaine* announced that it had been decided no longer to postpone reform, in spite of the many difficulties of war and invasion, and that an understanding had been spontaneously reached between the crown and Government. In June, then, a Constituent Assembly—sitting at Jassy, not many miles behind the battle line—inevitably formed on highly irregular lines and not counting one single peasant among its members, adopted at Brătianu's invitation the two principles of electoral reform and land expropriation, which, he claimed, would already have been accomplished but for the delays caused by the war. This involved a modification of Article XIX of the Constitution: private property might henceforth be expropriated not merely for the usual reasons of public utility, subject to the ordinary compensation, but also for reasons of national interest. It was decided that all lands belonging to foreigners, absentee landlords, corporations and institutions should be completely expropriated; that this should also apply to the domains of the crown; and that the big landlords should surrender two million hectares (nearly five million acres) for subdivision among the peasantry, each individual estate being henceforth limited to a maximum of 500 acres. Payment was to be made in Government stock, redeemable at 5 per cent., and the prices were to be fixed by special appeal tribunals. At the same time the franchise was to rest on universal suffrage, proportional representation and compulsory voting. It is quite true that even now voices were heard complaining that the reform was altogether inadequate; and certainly the method by which settlement was reached was peculiarly unfortunate, for not a single expert in constitutional law was consulted, and the draft was secretly hammered out and bargained over by Ionel Brătianu and Take Ionescu, for their respective parties.

[1] Mitrany, *Land and Peasant*, p. 101.

But the result was probably as much as could have been carried without open discord: even as it was, Mr Argetoianu, a leading Conservative boiar, denounced the new measure as "a law of persecution, directed against a whole class", and the Senator Gradişteanu made an altogether unmeasured personal attack upon Brătianu, even charging him with the appointment of traitor and Germanophil officers. The bill was carried by 130 to 14 (in the Senate by 179 to 5), and the main opposition came from the new Labour Party of Dr Lupu, which regarded it as altogether inadequate. In the end the amount of land to be expropriated was reduced from $2\frac{1}{2}$ to 2 million hectares, and the subsoil was exempted. The method of fixing compensation, the period at which the reform was to begin to operate, were left somewhat vague: but this after all was almost inevitable, in view of the uncertainties of the general situation. Much was left upon the knees of the gods: yet it may reasonably be claimed that the landed class rose to its responsibility to an extent for which there are not many parallels in history, and was eventually rewarded by escaping from a revolutionary upheaval.

At this point it would be unpardonable to omit a brief eulogy of the sustained heroism of Queen Marie. For months she courted danger daily amid the epidemics of the hospitals and the overcrowded city, and set an example of calm and confident endurance which many Roumanian women were proud to follow, and which did much to uphold British prestige in South-east Europe.

Throughout the same period inside the occupied territory strange intrigues were on foot. The veteran Carp, more autocratic than ever after the sudden death of Maiorescu in July, was prepared to form a Provisional Government, for the specific purpose of proclaiming a new king and making immediate peace: but fortunately he was almost impossible to work with, and his views were unacceptable even to the somewhat questionable group of men upon whom he relied. He refused all collaboration with Stere, as "a man who had offered Roumania to Austria": his own idea was implicit reliance upon Berlin. He would not even consider land reform or universal suffrage, whereas Stere, for all his hostility to the refugee Government in Jassy, treated its two great measures of reform as something which could never be undone and must be recognised as fundamental for the future. Most incredible of all, Carp wished to make his own son-in-law, Colonel Sturdza, minister of war in the projected Cabinet and had already induced the Germans to give a sinecure to Sturdza's intimate colleague, Major

Wachmann. This was indignantly rejected by Marghiloman, who greatly understated the facts when he said that Sturdza was "for the army a deserter". The relations of the two statesmen grew exceedingly strained, the occupying authorities came to realise that Carp had no real backing, and that the plebiscite which he desired was unworkable: and when the Emperor William passed through Roumania on his way to Sofia and Constantinople, Carp was not even offered an audience.

What saved the situation in the occupied territory, however, was not the dearth of pliant instruments, but the lack of a clear-cut Roumanian policy on the part of the victors, and above all the divergent views of Berlin, Vienna and Budapest on the subject. In the dynastic question one candidature after another was considered—the "Hungarian" Archduke Joseph, the emperor's younger brother Archduke Max, King Ferdinand's younger son Nicholas (then still a boy), the king's brother Prince William of Hohenzollern, even a Bavarian or a Prussian prince: but none ever received permanent or serious backing. In the still more important territorial question there was the same uncertainty. Early in 1917 there was loose talk of appeasing Russia by the cession of Northern Moldavia beyond the Seret (inhabited by Ukrainians) and leaving Austria with her ancient province of Oltenia. This was soon abandoned owing to the Russian Revolution, for the statesmen of the Central Powers lost all desire to conciliate a Russia which had rejected the Romanovs, and began to coquet with the idea of an independent Ukraine. Czernin's whole policy was directed towards winning Germany for renunciation in the West (Belgium and Alsace) in return for compensation in the East: and a new plan was evolved which would assign "Congress Poland", and perhaps Galicia also, to Germany, while leaving Austria-Hungary a free hand in Serbia and Roumania. In Czernin's own words, "it was a return to the original idea of the Archduke Francis Ferdinand, the union of Roumania with Transylvania, closely linked to the Monarchy".[1] The rich wheat lands and oilfields of Roumania would make good the loss of Galicia. It was also calculated that the Entente, though committed to Serbia, would show less interest in Roumania, and would probably leave her to her fate if agreement could be reached on all other points. Czernin kept as a trump card the double concession that Serbia should be allowed to unite with Montenegro and thus obtain an outlet to the sea. But Prince Sixtus, when he came to negotiate with Mr Ribot and

[1] *In the World War*, p. 297. Pribram, *Austrian Foreign Policy*, p. 107.

Mr Lloyd George, soon found that it would not be safe even to mention the Roumanian project: and letters passed between Paris and London insisting on the impossibility of abandoning an ally who had timed his entry in response to their urgent appeals.

As time passed, Vienna and Berlin found it increasingly difficult to clear their ideas as to the eventual fate of Roumania. In proportion as Germany's hope of establishing permanent control over Poland, and even Lithuania and Courland, grew stronger, it seemed only reasonable that Roumania should fall within the Dual Monarchy's sphere of influence. But her great economic importance fascinated Berlin, whose conceptions of "Middle Europe" included direct control upon the Lower Danube, and in particular of the ports of Constanţa and Galaţ. From this angle, indeed, Roumania was infinitely more important than Bulgaria, and the heads of the German occupation in Bucarest were constantly dropping hints that Germany needed a strong Roumania and would respect her territorial integrity. Marshal Mackensen himself was "fire and flame against the annexation of the Dobrogea".[1] The disagreement gradually became a four-sided one: for quite apart from rival German and Austrian dreams of economic mastery, the Bulgars were above all concerned with this very annexation of the whole Dobrogea, while Hungary, though much to the disgust of both Berlin and Vienna and with a minimum of encouragement from either, pressed incontinently for rectifications along the whole Carpathian frontier, and aimed at vengeance and indemnity for the events of September 1916. Even the Turks played their part in complicating the discussion: for if Bulgaria was to be aggrandised in the north, they were determined that she should restore the territory which they had so reluctantly ceded as the price of her entry in 1915.

One of the first acts of the Bolshevik Government was to make peace overtures to the Central Powers, and Roumania simply had no choice but to take her part in the armistice which this involved, since she would otherwise have exposed herself to a crushing offensive. When, however, the Peace Conference opened at Brest-Litovsk, on 20 December 1917, the Brătianu Government declined the invitation to take part, and maintained an attitude of anxious reserve. Its Conservative members, in their fervour against the idea of a separate peace, were even now prepared to face the retreat of army, Government and king into Russia or to some allied country: but Brătianu wisely refused

[1] Marghiloman, *op. cit.* III, p. 387.

to take such an engagement, in view of the marked hostility of the new regime in Russia and the geographical impossibility of seeking any other place of refuge. What rendered an armistice indispensable was the fermentation inside the Russian army: General Shcherbachev, a loyal supporter of the Provisional Government, could no longer control the forces under his command, which threatened to desert wholesale and march upon Jassy. Under such circumstances the Entente ministers, forced to act without reference to their Governments, drew up a protocol which recognised that Roumania had only yielded to *force majeure*. King Ferdinand resigned his nominal command in favour of General Prezan, hitherto Chief of Staff.

The peace negotiations at Brest-Litovsk continued throughout January 1918. They were conducted publicly, on the ostensible basis of "peace without annexations or indemnities", and the great importance attached to them was shown by the presence of the German and Austro-Hungarian foreign ministers, Herr von Kühlmann and Count Czernin, in addition to that marked personality, General von Hoffmann, commander on the Eastern front. From the first it was obvious that there was no common ground on which the generals and statesmen of the Central Powers could meet such men as Trotsky and Yoffe. Behind the scenes there were also acute dissensions between the military and civil authorities, German headquarters aiming at wholesale annexations in the East and caring nothing for the impression which this might produce upon America. In this situation Czernin— rendered desperate by the breakdown of the food supplies of the monarchy and by rioting and public unrest in Vienna, and bent on securing at all costs a "Bread Peace" such as would diminish the economic crisis by giving access to the grain stores of Odessa—successfully concentrated his efforts upon sowing dissension between the Great Russian and Ukrainian delegations at Brest. This was not so difficult, because the latter, though revolutionary in character, was not under the spell of Bolshevik doctrine, but laid its main stress upon nationalist and agrarian aims, looking to Kiev rather than to Moscow. Finding Trotsky resolutely opposed to a federal solution, the Ukrainians, on 24 January, declared their complete independence as a People's Republic, and on 9 February concluded a separate peace with the Central Powers. Czernin's concession of the district of Cholm to this new state ruined the prospects of an Austro-Polish settlement, but everything was subordinate to economic needs: in his own words, he signed "under pressure of imminent famine".[1] The Austro-German forces now set themselves to a more or less friendly occupation of Ukrainian territory, in the hope of collecting food supplies for their own half-starving populations at home.

These developments in the Ukraine reacted very directly upon Roumania, who naturally found the National Rada of Kiev less dangerous than the Bolshevik Government of Moscow, and therefore cultivated friendly relations with it. A certain proportion of the Russian troops in Roumania was Ukrainian in sentiment and ready to co-operate in measures for the disarming and expulsion of the undisciplined and refractory military units which were spreading through the country and deliberately striving to undermine all authority. Specially dangerous were the Bolshevik headquarters at Socola, outside Jassy, which was a centre of armed intrigue and militant propaganda, and whose chiefs were secretly incited by Trotsky himself to seize the persons of the king and his Government and extend to Moldavia the benefits of the proletarian revolution. The rapid spread of outrage and pillage throughout the villages forced the Government to grasp the nettle firmly; and on 21 December Socola was occupied by Roumanian troops, and its 5000 Bolsheviks were disarmed and deported to Russia, while similar disarming was effected at Neamţ, Galaţ, and other places.

With the restoration of comparative order in Moldavia, the centre of interest was transferred to Bessarabia, where the Russian Revolution had wrought a surprisingly rapid transformation. Immediately after the fall of the tsar in March 1917 a National Democratic Party had been formed by the "Moldavians" of Bessarabia, led by Stroescu, Gore and Halipa: and far-reaching autonomy on a national basis was proclaimed as its primary aim. But in the first instance the local soviet was formed on a purely Russian basis, without a single Roumanian member, whereas the chief opposition to it came from the extreme reactionaries and anti-Semites.[2] It was not till late in July that Bessarabia became really vocal, and this was above all due to the military committee formed at Odessa, which represented close upon 200,000 soldiers belonging to the province. During the summer of 1917 there was growing

[1] *In the World War*, p. 251.
[2] It is interesting to note that men like Krupenski, Purishkievich (of the Black Hundred), Krushevan and others were all of "Moldavian" boiar origin, though their families had long been completely Russified.

anarchy in the Ukraine; the returning troops pillaged in the villages, and the murder of Murafa and Hodorogea, two of the most active "Moldavian" intellectuals, caused special excitement. In order to stem these currents, and in protest against the tendency of the Kiev authorities to catch up Bessarabia in the current of Ukrainian nationalism, the military committee, now claiming to represent over 300,000 soldiers, convoked a congress of 989 delegates, officers and privates. At its meetings on 21–23 October unanimous resolutions were adopted in favour of "the historical and political autonomy of Bessarabia", and side by side with the principle of self-determination there appeared a significant phrase expressing "the desire to unite the whole Roumanian nation". It was therefore decided to convoke a National Assembly (Sfatul Ţarei) of 120 members (of whom 84 were to be Roumanians).

The Russian Provisional Government had already fallen before the Sfat could meet, but its delegate to Bessarabia, Mr Ion Inculeţ, who had been a lecturer at the University of Petrograd, was at once elected president. From the very outset the Sfat was pronouncedly nationalist in character, and almost equally out of sympathy with the old and the new currents in Russia, with Conservatism and Bolshevism. Its opening ceremony on 21 November 1917 was marked by scenes of ecstatic enthusiasm, from the Roumanian *Te Deum* at the cathedral and the parade of the Bessarabian troops to the unfurling of the Moldavian flag and the singing of the hymn of Roumanian unity, Deşteaptă-te, Române (Roumanian, Awake!). For the first time in history Bessarabia had a really representative governing body of its own and it was not slow to act. Already on 1 November four hundred Roumanian schools were opened, and on 2 December the "Democratic Federative Moldavian Republic" was proclaimed; and one of its first steps was to appeal to the Roumanian Government and the Entente ministers at Jassy for practical help in the struggle against the Bolshevisation of the country. During December and early January a critical stage was reached, and in proportion as Moldavia rid itself of anarchic elements and expelled the wandering units of demoralised Russian soldiers, the Bolshevik onslaught was concentrated against the weak and inexperienced Bessarabian Government. At the very eleventh hour, thanks not least of all to the urgent representations of General Berthelot and M. de Saint Aulaire, the Brătianu Government, already on its last legs, took the decisive step of sending a division of Roumanian troops under General Broşteanu to restore order. It was only just in time: for it found that the Bolsheviks had already established their "Staff" at Chisinău, under Perper, Levinson and Kabak, suspended the sittings of the Sfat, driven out the members of the Government and arrested the Inter-Allied "Commission de Ravitaillement". The tables were now turned; Perper and his hordes withdrew first to Bender and then across the Dniester into Russian territory, and something like order was gradually restored. There could now be no turning back, and on 6 February 1918 the Sfat unanimously proclaimed the full independence of the Moldavian Republic.

It was self-evident that this was but a temporary expedient, that Bessarabia could hardly hope to maintain its independence against an aggressive Bolshevik Russia, that union with Roumania would bring an access of strength to both parent and daughter, and that it was simply a question of arranging terms and reconciling two exceedingly different mentalities. To the exiled Roumanian Government, more-over, this issue offered an honourable compensation for shattered hopes in other directions, and rendered easier the now quite inevitable negotia-tions with the enemy. Indeed, even the Central Powers looked upon such a solution with favour; for not merely was any diminution of Russian strength acceptable to them, but both Ukraine and Roumania figured increasingly in their plans as useful counters to the Bolsheviks. Needless to say, the events at Chisinău involved a complete breach between Jassy and Moscow. Trotsky declared a war of ideas upon the Roumanian oligarchy. The Roumanian treasure at Moscow was con-veniently confiscated, though with the assurance that it would be restored to Roumania when she regained her "freedom". Diamandi, the Roumanian minister at Petrograd, was actually arrested as a kind of hostage, and only extricated himself with the greatest difficulty. Christian Rakovsky, the Dobrogean Socialist agitator who had been illegally expelled from Roumanian soil after the rising of 1907, was now sent by his Moscow friends to promote revolution among the Roumanians, and began by organising a reign of terror in the Rou-manian colony at Odessa.[1] His failure, which was materially promoted by that remarkable Canadian soldier of fortune, Colonel Boyle, was none the less most surprising: it serves very well to illustrate the fundamental difference of character between Roumanian and Russian and the deep-seated mutual antipathy not of one, but of all classes.

The treaty concluded at Brest with the Ukraine almost coincided

[1] For his own version see his *Roumania and Bessarabia* (London, 1925).

with an ultimatum addressed by Marshal Mackensen to the Roumanian Government. Take Ionescu and his Conservative colleagues maintained their intransigent attitude against the bare idea of a separate peace, and reaffirmed their readiness to face the prospect of a withdrawal into Southern Russia or even the Caucasus, the nearest point from which contact with the Entente could have been established! This was magnificent, but it was not war; and it is impossible even to-day to contemplate the probable results of taking them at their word. The more realistic Brătianu was not prepared to take such fantastic risks, especially after General Averescu and other army chiefs had laid before him the strategic aspects of the problem. King Ferdinand, however, had a further reason for reconciling himself to the bitter prospect of negotiation. The former Austrian military attaché in Bucarest, Colonel Randa, had been despatched by the Emperor Charles and Count Czernin on a secret mission, without the knowledge of Berlin, and had given the assurance that Vienna disapproved all talk of "punishment for treachery" and that there was still time for an honourable peace with the Hohenzollern dynasty. This manœuvre, which was unquestionably inspired by generous feeling on the part of Charles, none the less illustrates the divergent outlook of the two central allies in the Roumanian question; and King Ferdinand would have been most unwise, in such a situation, to ignore the hint, and might indeed reasonably hope to extract concessions from the evident conflict of interests. Czernin in his post-war memoirs described his motives with convincing bluntness: "At this time there was already a certain decline in the value of kings on the European market, and I was afraid that it might develop into a panic, if we put more Kings off their thrones".[1]

On 8 February Brătianu resigned, and at his advice the king appointed General Averescu, then still the idol of the whole Roumanian army, as premier, for the express purpose of making peace. As all the most eminent politicians were deeply committed to the Entente cause, it was decided to send delegates of secondary importance, but meanwhile an appeal was addressed to Mişu, the very able minister in London, to take over the crucial portfolio of Foreign Affairs and to this he patriotically responded, with the tacit approval of the Entente. Meanwhile in Bucarest the Germans began to waver on the subject of terms. Carp and Beldiman, the minister in Berlin—both more Prussian than the Prussians—wished them to refuse all dealings with

[1] *In the World War*, p. 261.

the king and his Government; Stere was willing that Roumania should be placed under a German viceroy on the analogy of Canada or South Africa.[1] The German emperor was still resentful against the "traitor" Hohenzollern, but Mackensen, on the spot, opposed deposition and would have appointed a regency (his own candidate being Duke Albrecht of Mecklenburg) and left the nation to decide in calmer time as to the future of the dynasty. The final decisions represented a compromise between the standpoints of Mackensen, Czernin, who came to Bucarest in person, and Marghiloman, the one man in occupied territory who showed gleams of statesmanship and never lost his head. To him the two capital questions were always how to save the dynasty and the Dobrogea; he remained quite unmoved by Carp's senile violence and Stere's personalities, kept his counsel as to the Randa overtures, and when the Jassy delegates came to see him at the king's request, gave, according to his lights, a faithful exposition of the tactics most likely to rescue something from the wreckage. In order to save the Dobrogea, he would have been ready to offer an alliance to the Central Powers by substituting the Roumanian for the Bulgarian army on the crumbling Russian front. His subtle, essentially "Phanariot" mind quickly grasped the implications of the kaleidoscopic events in Bessarabia and Ukraine: at last the moment seemed to have come when Bessarabia could not only be won but kept, and as he said, "Russian anarchy was establishing a sort of confraternity of arms", and the king's position might be regarded as saved.[2]

On 24 February Czernin arrived in Bucarest: some days later he had a meeting with King Ferdinand behind the front and warned him that the terms now to be offered were not a subject for haggling, but to be "taken or left", and that they represented the dynasty's last chance.[3] Two Crown Councils were held before the inevitable sur-

---

[1] In the calculation, it is true, that this would reduce Bulgaria's chances of securing Dobrogea and that as Austria was destined to be Slavised, Germany would in the end be instrumental to an union of Transylvania and Roumania. "Les misérables de Jassy", he said venomously, "will sign anything to save themselves". In the first number of his newspaper *Lumina*, Stere declared that "standing on the ruins of our country, we must ask ourselves" whether "a crown without prestige, ... a public life without honesty and solidity" could be allowed to continue to "poison the whole moral atmosphere". His solution therefore was unreserved political and economic attachment to the Central Powers—see *Note Politice*, iii, pp. 286, 338. [2] *Ibid.* p. 362.

[3] "J'oublie ma haine", was his theatrical phrase to Marghiloman. *Note Politice*, III, pp. 367, 379.

render. Take Ionescu continued to plead with all his eloquence against a separate peace, while Brătianu, though more resigned to hard facts, doubted whether it were possible to give up Dobrogea without further armed resistance. But discussion made it clear that the sole alternatives to acceptance were the formation of a frankly Germanophil Cabinet to which better terms might be offered by the enemy (and for this opinion in Jassy was still not quite ripe) or of a War Cabinet under Averescu (and this was dismissed by the General himself as an act of sheer madness from the military point of view). Meanwhile there was an object-lesson beyond the frontier. Trotsky's rejection of terms at Brest had only resulted in a fresh German advance and a strengthening of German-Ukrainian relations: Rovno had fallen on 20 February, and on 1 March the Germans entered Kiev as allies of the new order. The news that Bolshevik Russia had after all resigned herself to the signature of peace at Brest-Litovsk on 3 March proved decisive, and four days later the Averescu Government signed peace preliminaries at Prince Ştirbei's castle of Buftea near Bucarest.

The full details were left to be worked out later, but four salient features were at once apparent. (1) The whole Dobrogea had to be ceded, not to Bulgaria but to the Central Alliance, whose individual members were then free to discuss its fate among themselves. (2) Substantial rectifications were made in favour of Hungary along the whole length of the Carpathian frontier, with the object of placing Roumania strategically at the mercy of her northern neighbour. (3) Roumania had to consent to ruthless economic exploitation on the part of the victorious Powers for a period of years. (4) She was obliged to dismiss the Entente military missions, to demobilise eight divisions without delay and to allow the passage of the Austro-German troops across her territory to Odessa. In return for all this she received a free hand in the Bessarabian question.

A logical consequence of the surrender was the appointment of Alexander Marghiloman as premier, in the hope that by his personal relations with the victors and his known hostility to the Entente cause—based on a firm belief in Germany's ultimate triumph—he might earn some alleviation of the final terms. The king not unnaturally received him without enthusiasm, but had the strongest grounds for believing in his good faith and devotion to the dynasty. On his side he made the condition that the new Government should not attempt to upset the reforms "which were his work": while Marghiloman secured his consent to a dissolution of Parliament and insisted that Roumania must now "go whole-heartedly" with the Central Powers. The king somewhat lamely pleaded that he could not make an immediate volte-face. In actual fact, Marghiloman put up a very gallant uphill fight. He began by making it clear to Czernin and Kühlmann that he would not accept office at all unless concessions were made both as to the Carpathian frontier and as to the regime of occupation: and this extracted a letter from Czernin to the king, assuring him that concessions were granted solely to the person of the new premier. Hungary had originally demanded Sinaia (the king's summer residence) and the oilfield of Câmpina; and now Czernin renounced not only these, but Turnu Severin and Ocna also. At this the Budapest Government, under the pressure of a chauvinist Parliament, imposed an absolute veto on further renunciation, and Count Tisza, out of office, but still the most influential man in his country, claimed that Hungary's peace terms were "of so mild a nature as to amount to a generous gift to a conquered Roumania". Czernin now had to comply with explicit instructions, and soon afterwards fell from power, as the result of Clemenceau's revelation of the young emperor's secret peace offer. His successor, Count Burián, was mild in tone, but being a Magyar himself, shared the views of Budapest, and Marghiloman got no further help either from Kühlmann or from Mackensen.

Meanwhile, within the ranks of the Central Powers there were acute dissensions. Germany was above all concerned to secure stocks of grain, food and oil, but she also regarded Roumania as an essential link in the framework of a future "Mid-European" combination and wished to retain her own direct control, instead of leaving either Austria or Bulgaria in possession of the Danube delta. Austria shared Germany's dislike to the Cernavoda-Constanţa line falling into Bulgarian hands, but was above all bent upon bringing Roumania wholly and finally within the Habsburg orbit. Hungary regarded this project with mixed feelings, as likely to strengthen Roumanian influence inside the Dual Monarchy, and therefore to weaken the Hungarian hegemony over her own Roumanians: and she was anxious not to let slide an opportunity for strengthening the chains which bound them and promoting the cause of Magyarisation. Bulgaria was bent on securing not merely the districts which she had lost to Roumania in 1913, but the whole Dobrogea, and if possible even the northernmost channel of the Danube at its exit to the sea. Berlin and Vienna were united in opposing this and placing the "Old Dobrogea" under a Condominium of the four Powers: they would have quite genuinely preferred to leave it in Roumanian hands, but feared, and not without reason, the rise of an Entente party at Sofia and the scarcely veiled propaganda for a separate peace. Turkey played her part in intrigue and counter-intrigue, because it was obvious that the Condominium diminished her chances of recovering Thracian territory from the Bulgarians. Czernin has left it on record that he and his fellow negotiator Kühlmann had to steer their way through many shoals—"to avoid mortally offending the Roumanians, to observe so far as possible the character of a peace of understanding, and yet to keep both Turks and Bulgarians on our side".[1] In the end everyone was dissatisfied.

The final Treaty of Bucarest, which was signed on 7 May 1918, was described at the time by the leading Munich newspaper as "a model of the peace to be imposed on all our enemies". To Bulgaria was ceded outright the territory which she had lost in 1913, with certain minor rectifications; but the Dobrogea proper was left as a Condominium of the victorious Powers, who undertook to assure Roumanian's commercial outlet to Constanţa. By Articles 24–26 the international regime of the Danube was calmly ignored, and a new Commission was established for the control of the mouths and their main ports Galaţ and Brăila, membership being restricted to riverine states. The territory assigned to Hungary (under § 11) was very much smaller than that originally demanded by the Wekerle Government and by Hungarian public opinion. There had been a determined attempt to secure the oil-fields of Câmpina and Bacău (which would incidentally have involved the "Roumanian Balmoral" Sinaia, which lies between them and the old frontier) and the salt-mines of Slanic and Prahova, and again to establish direct territorial contact between Hungary and Bulgaria, by annexing Turnu Severin and the Jiu valley. This was resisted by Czernin as incompatible with the principle of "no indemnities and no annexations", which formed the basis of his discussions with the Bolsheviks at Brest: and in the end Hungary had to content herself with a series of "rectifications" along the whole length of the Carpathian frontier, which were to serve a double purpose—to place all the strategic points of the watershed in the hands of the Monarchy and thus render invasion from the south extremely difficult, and to facilitate the project of an artificial "cultural zone", intended as a solid

[1] *In the World War*, p. 209.

ethnical wedge between the Roumanians of the kingdom and their kinsmen of Transylvania. Even these modified cessions of territory involved a purely Roumanian population of 150,000 in 170 villages: but the Magyars were of course entitled to point out that the districts in question were but thinly populated, though rich in forest wealth. But at the time they regarded them as quite inadequate.

The remainder of the treaty was economic in character. War indemnities were expressly renounced, but the result was effectually achieved under another name. The victors had originally intended to assert their control of the Roumanian state railways, the crown domains, the harbours and the oil-fields, and to place the finances of the country under a German supervisor. But if these draconic intentions were abandoned, what remained was severe enough. (1) Roumania had to take over within six months all the notes issued by the Germans in occupation through the Banca Generala—amounting in round figures to one milliard lei (then £40,000,000); to indemnify the Central Powers for all the coupons (*bons de réquisition*) with which their purchases of grain and other commodities for the army had been paid—amounting to another milliard; and to meet all individual claims in respect of injury to health and property (estimated at about £75,000,000 more). (2) The Central Powers established a monopoly of the whole agricultural produce of Roumania for nine years. A joint commission was to establish the amount of surplus available in a given year, and no export to other countries was allowable, until a fixed amount had been delivered. An Austro-German company, with a capital of 70 millions, was set up for the farming of Roumanian land and for the direct purchase of the harvest. (3) All the oil-fields controlled by the state were leased for a period of thirty years—renewable for two further periods of thirty years!—to a special Austro-German monopoly company: and this company, from which all other foreign capital was expressly excluded, was to enjoy the exclusive right of export of raw petrol, and had the power to fix the annual amount which might be reserved for Roumania's internal consumption. (4) The wharves of Turnu Severin were to be leased for thirty years to Austria-Hungary, for the nominal sum of 1000 lei a year, and all products shipped there were to be exempt from duty. A similar arrangement was made with Germany for forty years in respect of the wharves of Giurgiu. (5) An army of occupation of six divisions was to be maintained in Wallachia until the conclusion of a general peace, at Roumania's expense, with the right of requisitioning: and its expenditure upon public works, over which of course Roumania had no control, was to be made good afterwards. (6) Hungary ensured the inclusion of special clauses relating to nationalist propaganda and restricting the naturalisation by one state of subjects belonging to the other. This was of course directed against the many thousands of Transylvanian refugees, who would presumably have found themselves in the same equivocal situation as the Jews, if this provision had been enforced.

No attempt has been made to analyse in detail this memorable treaty: this must be left to the economic experts of the Carnegie Foundation. The best commentary upon it is to be found in the answer of a high German officer at Bucarest to the lamentations of Marghiloman's secretary: "A harsh peace? Just wait till you see what we are preparing for France and England!"[1] Nothing illustrates more clearly the gulf in mentality between the two groups of belligerents than the fact that each believed itself to be infinitely less draconic than the other. In the particular case of Roumania the Germans unquestionably believed themselves to be magnanimous,[2] and would have been more so but for Bulgaria.

Soon after his return from Bucarest Herr von Kühlmann addressed the Berlin Chamber of Commerce on the underlying aims of the treaty. He laid great stress upon the importance of the Danube and Black Sea for Germany and explained the reasons for demanding special wharves for German and Austrian shipping at Turnu Severin and Giurgiu, and for excluding all other Powers from any say in the Danubian Commission. "Having secured the possibilities of increased use of the Danube route, unrestricted traffic on the railways and 'through' cable and telegraph communication, it was important to obtain the necessary guarantees, both for the fundamental conditions of our commercial intercourse for long years to come, and for securing the surrender of such cereals and other natural products and oil production as Roumania is in a position to deliver. . . . Roumania will have to suffer heavily from the consequences of the war into which she rushed so lightly. The pecuniary burden alone, which according to the estimate of her present statesmen, will certainly not amount to less than nine milliard lei,[3] is not easy for a relatively small country to bear. Roumania had before the war 7½ million inhabitants. The loss, as a result of the war

---

[1] *Note Politice*, III, p. 340.

[2] Burián in his Memoirs, written in 1922, still regarded the treaty as "moderate and just"—*Drei Jahre*, p. 240.          [3] Then at par = £360,000,000.

and the directly ensuing epidemics, is estimated at 800,000 to 1,000,000, so that with the accession of Bessarabia Roumania's population after the war may be put at 9–10,000,000. . . . Even though a war indemnity in cash has not been exacted, yet the damages which Roumania will have to pay under the treaty itself and various supplementary agreements, will amount to very considerable sums in the long run—not differing very substantially from what might presumably have been obtained through an indemnity".[1]

Throughout these months Roumania had figured very prominently in the discussions in the German press, constant emphasis being laid upon its importance as a factor in the problem of "Mitteleuropa", especially now that Ukraine seemed likely to become a separate state under some kind of German suzerainty. It was even suggested that Germany required a port and even "an independent colony of her own" at the mouth of the Danube, and that her claim to the Dobrogea or a section of Southern Bessarabia was "on ethnical grounds at least as good as Bulgaria's, in view of the numerous German colonists already settled there.[2]     *       *       *       *

Amid the bitterness and humiliation of this treaty the one consolation lay in the course of events in Bessarabia. It was by now abundantly obvious that the Moldavian Republic had no chance of surviving, and that the choice lay between partition and union with Roumania. Menaced on all sides, by Russian Bolshevism, by the Austro-German occupation of the Ukraine, and by the claims of Kiev upon the whole north of the province, the Bessarabian leaders Inculeţ and Ciugureanu appealed to the Bucarest Government and to the Entente diplomatists at Jassy. At their invitation, Marghiloman visited Chişinău, and at this critical juncture was manfully supported by Constantine Stere, who enjoyed great influence with all classes in Bessarabia and now atoned for his deplorable subservience to the Central Powers by an impassioned if inflammable speech in favour of union. After a reference to the tyranny which had sent him to a Siberian dungeon, "We are called here", he said, "in that elemental process which pulverises Bastilles and creates new life. You have here lighted a torch which has burned all feudal parchments and annihilated all privileges of caste, and you remain a people based upon nothing but the farm and intellectual effort. You must carry the torch yonder, to consume dry-rot

[1] Cit. *Norddeutsche Allgem. Zeitung*, 23 May 1918.
[2] See e.g. a long and closely reasoned article in *Hamburger Nachrichten* of 27 Feb. 1918.

and injustice, to defend the whole Roumanian nation at the most critical hour of its history".[1]

On 8 April, then, the Sfat, voting publicly by name, declared for the union of Bessarabia with Roumania. But the decision, which was carried by 86 to 3, 36 abstaining,[2] was made subject to a number of stringent conditions. The Diet was to remain in being until it could draft and carry into effect an agrarian reform suited to its own special problems: and even later Bessarabia was to retain administrative autonomy and a Diet elected by universal suffrage. The Zemstvo organisations were to be upheld. The rights of all minorities were to be guaranteed. Two Bessarabian ministers, elected in the Diet, were to sit in the Roumanian Cabinet. The future constitution was to include full guarantees of freedom of the person, of the press, of speech, assembly and religion. A few days later, a large delegation from the Sfat visited Bucarest, joined the Government at an official *Te Deum* in the Cathedral, and acclaimed King Ferdinand as "King of the Peasants".[3] Inculeţ and Ciugureanu took oath as ministers without portfolio. During the summer the ties between Bessarabia and Bucarest and Jassy—whose political relations with each other throughout 1918 can only be compared to that of the Siamese twins—were gradually strengthened; and it was but natural that the Roumanian authorities should set themselves wherever possible to discourage the revolutionary tendencies which their Bessarabian kinsmen brought with them as a legacy from Tsarist and Bolshevist Russia. It must be added that the centralising measures which they conceived as a panacea only increased the confusion: and for years to come Bessarabia was a hotbed of intrigue, official incompetence and corruption, and popular disillusionment, constantly fomented from Moscow. This was all the more unfortunate because both Russia and Ukraine protested vigorously against the Union (each claiming the province for itself), while the Bulgarian press showed a lively resentment at such mild treatment of Roumania, and especially against the introduction of compulsory Roumanian into all the Bessarabian higher schools.

For the moment, however, Bessarabia provided an absolutely unique example of a country crushingly defeated in war, yet aggrandised at the expense of one of her own allies.

[1] Cit. by C. U. Clark, *Bessarabia*, p. 197.
[2] The 138 deputies were divided racially as follows: 103 Roumanian, 13 Ukrainian, 7 Russian, 6 Jewish, 5 Bulgarian, 2 German, 1 Pole, 1 Armenian.
[3] Marghiloman, *op. cit.* III, p. 464.

# CHAPTER XVII

# THE COMPLETION OF NATIONAL UNITY

"The existence of the Hungarian national state has been entirely bound up with the position of the Monarchy as a Great Power."

Tisza to Burián, 29 Dec. 1915.

With the Treaty of Bucarest Roumania was condemned to an entirely negative rôle during the decisive months of the Great War; and the centre of gravity in our narrative shifts to Hungary.

The ill-starred invasion of Transylvania had deplorable results in both directions. Large sections of the Magyar population fled before the Roumanian army, suffered many privations, and quite naturally returned full of anger and suspicion towards their Roumanian fellow-citizens. On the other hand, a large section of the latter received the invading army with open arms, and, having compromised itself, was forced to withdraw with it into Moldavia, where it shared all the terrible experiences of defeat, exile and disease. Some idea of the true senti-ments of the Roumanians in Transylvania may be gleaned from facts published by the Magyar deputy Paul Szász,[1] showing that about 80,000 Roumanians fled during the winter of 1916–17, of whom 34,000 had evaded military service and 2000 were Austro-Hungarian reservist officers who joined the Roumanian army. The result of this was whole-sale confiscation of the property of those who fled, and many thousands of the Roumanian intelligentsia were interned or imprisoned—in par-ticular the wives and daughters of fugitive clergy and teachers. Some months later, when the Roumanian deputy Şerban complained in the Budapest Parliament of the sufferings of these people, Count Tisza—who for the first two years of the war had constantly laid public stress on the loyalty and gallantry of the vast majority of the Roumanians and other non-Magyars—retorted that "the majority of the intelli-gentsia fraternised with the invaders", and that "to say that we are throwing into chains the mothers and sisters of the Isonzo heroes is an impudent calumny unparalleled in history. . . . We all know where the thousands of deserters went, and everyone who has studied the question knows that none displayed such incredible ingenuity in

---

[1] In the Hungarian Parliament during the franchise debate, 27 February 1918.

evading military service, or at least in haunting the hospitals, as a portion of the Roumanian intelligentsia".[1]

Magyar opinion, as voiced by Tisza, was of course perfectly right in regarding the priests and schoolmasters as the ringleaders of the Roumanian national movement. Those clergy who had fled were treated as traitors:[2] of those who remained, a very large proportion was deported; and for the rest of the war, and in the final period of Bolshevik effervescence, many Roumanian parishes in Transylvania were left entirely without religious observances or pastoral care. Even baptisms and marriages were impossible. The whole Orthodox consistory, with the teachers of the theological seminary and other notables, were removed to Oradea Mare, in cattle-trucks marked in chalk "oláh pap" (Wallach priests) and there interned. Worse still, in many districts thus deprived of their clergy a policy of forced conversion was carried out. Drummers announced that the "Wallach law" was no longer recognised, and it was indicated that failure to join the Uniate Church would result in their being sent to the front or to forced labour in Serbia. Of this policy, however, the Uniate hierarchy was completely innocent: the pressure came from the civil authorities, and the villages in question were instructed to ask for new priests, not from the Roumanian bishops, but from the Magyar Uniate bishop of Hajdu-dorog,[3] whose whole *raison d'être* was Magyarisation.

Tisza fell in June 1917, but the appointment of Count Albert Apponyi as minister of education in the new Esterházy Cabinet marked a fresh offensive against the Roumanians. Declaring that it was "among the Roumanian teachers that we have had the most deplorable experiences", he announced his intention of creating "a strong military, ethnographic and cultural Zone" along the whole southern frontier, with the deliberate object of driving a racial wedge between the Roumanians of the two sides of the Carpathians. Throughout this zone all denominational schools were to be closed and replaced by state schools, conducted on strictly Magyar lines: the process was to begin with the eighty schools from which teachers had "disappeared". The Orthodox consistory answered the minister somewhat lamely, urging that it was unfair to generalise from these 80 cases as to the guilt of the whole

[1] 25 June 1917.

[2] As a single example, no less than 28 out of 42 priests in the Făgăraş district fled.

[3] See *supra*, p. 430. *Magyarország* of 26 August 1917 reports "the conversion of many thousands of Orthodox Roumanians, on such a scale that the suffragan and priests cannot supply all the need".

teaching profession, giving facts as to the 400 teachers mobilised at the front and pleading that the best way to defend a frontier was not to suppress state aid, but to assist the Church in its administrative work. This naturally did not impress Apponyi, who in October nominated Baron Emil Horváth, as Royal Commissioner, to regulate the whole question of Roumanian church schools, and on 17 December notified the metropolitan that in the coming Budget he intended to ask for powers to erect 1600 primary state schools in the new zone and 800 "Fröbel Schools" in the neighbouring districts—in other words, a project of Magyarisation throwing utterly into the shade the most questionable provisions of the Apponyi Education Laws of 1907. In March 1918 he took a further step: in his Bill for the state endowment of religious bodies, he expressly omitted the two Roumanian Churches, and at the same time announced the withdrawal of state aid from all Orthodox schools in the 18 border areas—238 in all. He had already ordered the closing of the Orthodox and Uniate training colleges.[1] In a further Bill guaranteeing Catholic autonomy, he included insidious clauses, intended to bring the Roumanian and Ruthene Uniate hierarchy under the control of the Roman Catholic primate of Hungary: and at the time of his resignation from office in May there was already an acute conflict, the metropolitan of Blaj and his suffragans declining to attend a conference convoked by Cardinal Csernoch, and the Papal Nuncio in Vienna finding it necessary to intervene.

One of Apponyi's last acts was to notify the Roumanian Church authorities that he intended to exercise to the full the state's right of inspection in the Church assemblies: and this was upheld by his successor Count John Zichy, despite all remonstrances. The utter subservience of the Metropolitan Mangra—whom Budapest had imposed upon the Church in October 1916, on the death of that worthy veteran Meţianu—proved unable to extract a single concession from the fanatical Apponyi: and Mangra was universally regarded as a renegade and traitor to the national cause. Hungary pursued this cultural policy to the very last, and even in August 1918 the minister of commerce, Baron Szterényi, was threatening the Church authorities with the actual confiscation of school buildings in the Zone.[2]

Parallel with this went a new colonising policy, avowedly framed

---

[1] Sibiu, Arad and Caransebeş: Blaj, Oradea Mare and Gherla.
[2] The documents relating to these conflicts will be found in L. Triteanu, *Scoala Noastra: Zona Culturală* (Sibiu, 1919).

upon the Posen model. In the autumn of 1917 the minister of agriculture, Mr Mezőssy, issued a decree forbidding land to be sold or let on long lease without special Government permission, in 31 non-Magyar counties and in certain Transylvanian towns—the aim being to prevent the Roumanians in particular from extending their holding in land. The minister of the interior, Mr Ugron, in connection with the proposed redistribution of the border counties, let it be known that the Government were considering schemes for the exclusion from public life of all whom they might choose to regard as "hostile elements", for a more severe criminal code for political offences, and for systematic Magyar colonisation in Roumanian districts. Count Klebelsberg[1] put forward the idea of "breaking the Roumanian ring" by the settlement of Magyars to connect the Székel districts with the main Magyar territory to the west of Transylvania. Meanwhile, in marked contrast to Austria, where the Emperor Charles issued a complete political amnesty in June 1917, the prisons and internment camps of Hungary remained almost as full as ever.

Most enlightening of all was the Hungarian attitude towards the non-Magyars in connection with the renewed agitation for electoral reform. It was the utter inadequacy of the Government proposals—"turning to derision the beautiful promise of the Sovereign", to quote the official *Fremdenblatt*—that led to Count Tisza's fall in June 1917; and it was Count Bethlen's disapproval of franchise reform that prompted him to refuse the ministry of the interior in Count Esterházy's short-lived Cabinet. Esterházy soon proved unequal to the task of squaring the circle, and was in his turn succeeded by the veteran "Swabian" statesman and financial expert, Dr Wekerle, who left to the Jewish lawyer-demagogue Vázsonyi, as minister of justice, the almost impossible task of drafting a bill acceptable alike to the masses, the crown and the oligarchy. For the rest of 1917 there was a trial of strength between the rival forces, Tisza openly denouncing the "fatal idea" of giving the vote to all holders of the "Charles Cross":[2] "a current of radicalism would set in and the knell of the Hungarian national state would soon sound". In Transylvania Magyar political circles

[1] 12 March 1918, in Parliament. He was minister of education under Count Bethlen from 1922 to 1928.

[2] The only qualification for this was to have spent at least 12 weeks in the firing line, and it was estimated that about 1,500,000 men would thus obtain the franchise.

were also unanimous against reform. Count Bethlen declared, "We must advance with democracy, but only so long as the Magyarisation of Transylvania is not attacked. *The franchise struggle must stop at the gates of Transylvania*".[1] At his instance the demand was put forward that the franchise should be restricted, "as in other civilised states", not only to literates, but to persons who were literate in "the language of state"; that the qualification of four school classes should be restricted to those schools which gave adequate instruction in the Hungarian language, history and constitution; and that the "Charles Cross" qualification should only apply to those who could read and write Magyar.[2]

It is unnecessary to indicate the many complicated provisions of the Franchise Bill as finally drafted by Vázsonyi in December 1917; but though the ballot was restricted to the 88 urban constituencies and though Vázsonyi produced elaborate statistics to show that the proportion of Magyar voters would be increased from 61 to 62.7 per cent., the opposition of Tisza, Bethlen, Jósika and the Transylvanian Magyars continued. "A radical franchise", Tisza claimed, "constitutes a great danger for our nation and party: all who desire our ruin seek to present us with it. The intellectual standard is a great danger for the Magyars, since a large proportion of the non-Magyars can learn to read and write, and then there will be an end of Magyar supremacy." The deputy Vargha underlined this by denunciations of the Roumanians and by the argument that "in this country only one culture has any rights, and that is Magyar culture". This opposition led to the fall and reconstruction of the Wekerle Cabinet in April 1918, and a new qualification was introduced, of the ownership of eight yokes (12 acres) of land, but with the special exclusion of Transylvania. The Roumanian peasantry had to be kept from the polls so far as possible. In the words of Count Bethlen, "the question of democratisation is one of life and death for Transylvania, and threatens the existence of every class of society".[3] During the same debate Count Andrássy denounced self-determination as "a dangerous catchword, the realisation of which would mean the end of the Hungarian State", while Count Klebelsberg treated it as "a formula whose object was to force upon us by words

[1] 31 July 1917 at Maros Torda.   [2] 9 February 1918 at Kolozsvár.
[3] 1 March 1918. In July he even proposed an amendment exacting from all electors a test of reading and writing in the Magyar language, which would have meant virtual disfranchisement of the nationalities, but this was not adopted.

what could not be imposed by force of arms ". The latter speaker also argued that since 1880 the proportion of Magyars to the rest of the population had increased by 3 per cent. in each decade, and had reached 54 per cent. in 1910: some decades of a victorious peace might reasonably be expected to raise the proportion to 75 per cent.! Vázsonyi himself was rash enough to describe the war as a crushing blow to irredentism, to prophesy the complete absorption of the Ruthenes, to advocate a more severe penal code and the permanent exclusion from the franchise of all who fled with the Roumanian army.[1] Finally, the premier, Dr Wekerle, explained to the House that under the new scheme the proportion of Magyar voters in Transylvania had risen from 49·8 to 53·6 per cent., while that of the Roumanians had fallen from 36·3 to 29·6 per cent.[2] At the same time he announced that with the passage of the reform into law the idea of a war election had been abandoned, thus saving the country, according to Tisza's belief, from "the most terrible anarchy".

*     *     *     *

It will be abundantly clear from the above narrative that by the summer of 1918 the Roumanians had been reduced to an attitude of complete passivity—those of the kingdom by the draconic Treaty of Bucarest, and their kinsmen north of the mountains by the aggressive policy of Budapest. But the great tragedy in Europe was now rapidly reaching its climax, and nowhere was the political transformation which it wrought more sudden and overwhelming than among the Roumanians.

The internal situation in Austria had by this time become desperate, and the central authorities were at the mercy of the Hungarian Government, which used its relative surplus of food stocks to extract political concessions, or better still, to hold back the Emperor Charles from that last-hour federalisation which might still perhaps have saved the Habsburg Monarchy as a whole, but was only possible at the expense of Hungarian integrity. Ever since the convocation of the Austrian Reichsrat on 30 May 1917 the malcontent nationalities had possessed a public forum before which to air their political grievances, and the very fact that their kinsmen were so effectually muzzled in the Budapest Parliament served as an added incentive to spokesmen from Bohemia, Slovenia or Bukovina to champion the cause of Slovakia, Croatia or

[1] 16 March.          [2] 7 May.

Transylvania and to proclaim the doctrines of self-determination and national unity. The periodical speeches in the Reichsrat led to sharp recriminations in Budapest; but the Austrian Government was by now quite unable to restrain its recalcitrant subjects. A fresh stimulus to nationalist ferment was given by the Congress held in Rome on 8 April 1918, at which all the non-German and non-Magyar races of Austria-Hungary were represented:[1] and in May a similar Congress was held at Prague, in honour of the jubilee of the Czech National Theatre, and was skilfully exploited as a demonstration of solidarity between the Czechs, Slovaks, Serbs, Croats, Slovenes, Poles, Italians and Roumanians.

In the interval the revelation of the emperor's secret overtures to the Entente, and the consequent downfall of Czernin, had dealt a further blow to the Monarchy's prestige and encouraged nationalist hopes. The failure of the Austrian offensive on the Piave, the spread of mutiny, desertion and the so-called "Green Cadres", the recognition accorded by the Allies and America to the Polish and Czechoslovak armies and National Councils abroad, the hesitations and fall of Seidler, the Austro-German disagreements regarding Poland—all these were so many stages in the progressive disintegration of the Habsburg state, and hope sank to zero as the tide at length turned even against Germany on the Western front. At last on 10 August Charles informed his ally in Berlin[2] that if no general peace could be secured by the end of the year, Austria-Hungary would be compelled to act separately. Before the month was out Foch had provided the most cogent of reasons for swift action, by the great allied offensive from Soissons and Arras: Hindenburg drew back to the Siegfried line, and the abandonment of the St Mihiel salient was like the forcible opening of a trap whose jaws were wearing out. By the middle of September Burián, urged on by the emperor and shamefacedly defiant of Berlin, launched his peace offer to President Wilson, only to find that the moment had passed and that the victorious Allies stood irrevocably committed to the cause of nationality in Central and South-eastern

---

[1] While, however, the Czechs and Slovaks were represented by Beneš and Štefaník, and the Jugoslavs by Trumbić, Meštrović and many others, the Roumanians present were mainly from the kingdom (notably the future premier, Mr Mironescu): the leading Transylvanian exiles, such as Goga and Lucaciu, had not as yet reached the west of Europe.

[2] Cramon, *Unser Oesterreichisch-ungarischer Bundesgenosse*, p. 514.

Europe. In more than one crisis of the war they had wavered and prepared to sacrifice their publicly proclaimed principles, but now there was no longer any motive for hesitation or concession. The ball was at their feet.

The process of disintegration was hastened still further by the swift collapse of Bulgaria in the second half of September and by the knowledge that Turkey's defection was now only a matter of weeks.[1] The Central Powers saw in this a grave menace to their weak army of occupation in Wallachia and even to their control of the Ukraine, while their forces in Albania were compelled to withdraw hastily northwards into territory where a Jugoslav revolution was now imminent. Even the Marghiloman Government, which in June had conducted farcical elections to secure a subservient Germanophil majority, now played for time and successfully evaded the urgent German demands for the ratification of the Treaty of Bucarest. The alarm of the Central Powers was reflected in the increasingly broad hints of Mackensen's delegate, Colonel Horstmann, that the Dobrogea might be restored to Roumania in the event of Bulgarian desertion, and even that the new Carpathian frontier might be revised in return for ratification (which of course would have ended the possibility of renewed military activity on Roumania's part). Throughout the late autumn Bucarest and Jassy watched each other doubtfully and waited upon events: prevarication was inherent in such a situation, and the real decisions inevitably lay beyond Roumania's control.

The Austrian Parliament met on 1 October, under the impression of Bulgaria's surrender, and the premier, Baron Hussarek, announced a programme of national autonomy for Austria. But this, while deeply offending the Austrian Germans, fell far short of the wishes and hopes of the Czechs, Poles and Jugoslavs and was at once publicly repudiated by their leaders, while Dr Wekerle, speaking for Hungary, ominously declared, "We are no longer faced by the same Austria with whom we came to terms in the past", and turned to "Personal Union" as the best solution. Meanwhile Charles and some of his Austrian advisers, only too conscious that the time for half-measures had passed, were eager to proclaim a full-fledged federalist programme for the whole Monarchy. But when this came to be discussed by the Crown Council on 15 October, Wekerle threatened to cut off Hungarian food supplies from

[1] The Emir Feisal entered Damascus on 1 October. The Turkish armistice was signed on 30 October, and the Straits were opened to the British fleet.

starving Vienna unless Hungary's territorial integrity were expressly safeguarded, and at the last moment the unhappy emperor felt bound by his coronation oath to respect this view. Thus it came about that the manifesto of 18 October, announcing the federalisation of Austria, was not merely stillborn and rejected with scorn by the non-German races, but actually precipitated the disintegration of the state, since every race outbid its neighbour in the enunciation of radical nationalist programmes. Moreover the abstract recognition accorded by the manifesto to "National Councils" as the mouthpieces of their respective nations made the centrifugal process almost irresistible.

Meanwhile, intransigent to the last, Count Tisza had visited Croatia and Bosnia in September, in order to effect an understanding with the Southern Slavs: but when he found that all responsible leaders in the south insisted upon the co-operation of Serbia in any solution, he lost his temper, said that after the war Serbia would be so small as to serve Bulgaria for breakfast one morning, and ended with the thunderous phrase, "It may be that we shall be ruined, but we shall have strength left to crush you first".[1] The mad arrogance of this feudal *homo regius* did more than anything else to complete the alienation of the Jugoslavs from Hungary and even from the crown, and to precipitate their revolt: when known in Budapest, it also had its share in convincing the Roumanians and Slovaks that there was nothing to be hoped from official Hungary. As a supreme instance of his combined tactlessness and realism, Tisza launched on 17 October, in the lobby of Parliament, the memorable phrase, "Károlyi is right: we have lost the War". Coming from the most redoubtable champion of the Magyar cause, this contributed more towards the ensuing dry-rot than all the utterances of his more radical opponents or the defeatism of the now crumbling Isonzo front.[2]

Among the National Councils which now sprang up in every part of the Dual Monarchy, the most powerful were the Czech Narodni Výbor, which now set itself to prepare the bloodless revolution of 28 October in Prague, and the Narodno Vijeće, whose headquarters were in the Croatian capital, but which was equally representative of Slovenia, Bosnia and Dalmatia. The Roumanians, despite their weak position, did not remain behind. On 12 October the executive of the

---

[1] Nowak, *Der Sturz der Mittelmächte*, p. 227. Glaise-Horstenau, *Collapse*, p. 195.
[2] Cf. *ibid.* p. 213—"a terrible act of *harakiri*"; and again Schmidt-Pauli, *Graf Bethlen*, p. 82—"That was the real signal for the revolution".

Roumanian National Party met at Oradea Mare: Maniu was still absent at the front, but MM. Goldiş, Vaida, Ciceo-Pop, Vlad and Mihali were all present, and drafted a resolution which invoked the right of self-determination for the Roumanians of Hungary, denied to the Hungarian Parliament and Government all right to represent them at the Peace Conference, and declared Budapest's decisions as in no way binding upon them.[1] Dr Vaida, whose courage, eloquence and mordant wit well fitted him for the delicate task, read aloud this message in the Hungarian Chamber on 18 October, greeting the ideas of Wilson as the most memorable since the first days of Christianity, boldly reproaching Wekerle and Tisza for their grossly repressive policy and contrasting it with Wilsonian principles. Utter consternation fell upon the House when Father Juriga adopted a similar line on behalf of the despised Slovaks. For the moment both Roumanians and Slovaks only needed to hold aloof and watch events moving in their favour. The steps now taken by Parliament to promote Hungary's separation from Austria did but further the very evils which they sought to avert: to the last moment Hungarian public opinion, reactionary and progressive alike, seemed oblivious to the fact that "the existence of the Hungarian national state had been entirely bound up with the position of the Monarchy as a Great Power".[2]

When summoned to an audience with the Archduke Joseph, recently returned from the broken Italian front, Dr Vaida was able to present himself as the first Roumanian politician who had been publicly admitted to the presence of a Habsburg since the early eighties, and adhered resolutely to the claim of self-determination. Meanwhile Maniu had been allowed to leave the front, and was invited by the National Council to represent their interests at Vienna, where amid the general confusion he soon formed a "Sfat" of Roumanian soldiers and had 100 officers at his beck and call. In Prague a large section of the garrison consisted of Roumanian troops, who at once rallied to the Czech cause, and by their attitude contributed towards the bloodless character of the revolution: they were at once organised as a "Roumanian Legion" and established contact with their political leaders in

---

[1] "The Roumanian Nation which lives in the Monarchy awaits and demands, after the sufferings of centuries, the achievement of its inalienable rights, in full national life."

[2] These words occur in a letter of Tisza to Burián, 29 December 1915—Tisza, *op. cit.* IV, no. 1468.

Transylvania. Various local councils sprang up in that province during the second half of October, but it was at Arad that the central organisation was established, and that Stephen Pop publicly took the oath to the "Roumanian National Council for Hungary and Transylvania". After a brief trial of strength with the local patriots of Cluj, the Arad Committee fully asserted its authority in all directions, received the full support of the bishops of both Churches and revived the suppressed newspaper *Românul*, under the editorship of Goldiş. By the end of October contact with Budapest was virtually at an end; the exchange of notes between Count Burián and President Wilson, culminating in the latter's full recognition of the Czechoslovaks and Jugoslavs, dealt the last deathblow to central authority, alike in Vienna and in Budapest; the Italian front crumbled and the troops of all nations poured homewards in disorder, and before the Armistice could be concluded on 3 November, the Habsburg Monarchy had of its own accord dissolved into its component parts. The Polish and Ruthene provinces seceded, the Czechoslovak Republic was proclaimed in Prague, the Slovak National Council in St Martin resolved upon union with the Czechs, the Jugoslav National Council in Zagreb declared its independence, the fleet and arsenals mutinied and fell into Jugoslav hands. The ruling party in Budapest shared in the general eclipse, the Radical forces led by Count Michael Károlyi rapidly asserted themselves and formed a revolutionary Government on 31 October, and Count Tisza, the representative of the old order, brave and unbending to the last, was assassinated in his house by undisciplined soldiers.

The Roumanians, then, in the first fortnight of November saw themselves isolated from the main theatre of political and military decision, but able to disregard with impunity a beaten Hungary, which was obviously in complete disintegration. In such a situation the perfectly genuine appeals of the Károlyi Government, in its desperate effort to save Hungarian integrity by a twelfth-hour adoption of full democracy, fell upon deaf ears among all the non-Magyar races. The new "Minister of Nationalities", Oskar Jászi, was known and recognised as a true friend, who had for years faced abuse and calumny in his campaign for equal justice.[1] Jászi in particular was in the same unhappy position as

---

[1] He belonged to the small group of democrats who published the monthly review *Huszadik Század*, one of the most remarkable sociological journals in prewar Europe, and had also written in 1912 *The Development of National States and the Question of Nationalities* (A nemzeti államok kialakulás és a nemzetiségi kérdés).

men like Lammasch and Redlich in Austria: prescient and untiring in their warnings, the power with which they were entrusted at the twelfth hour turned to water and trickled through their helpless hands. In the same way in Hungary a programme which would have won the grateful co-operation of the Slovaks and Roumanians ten years earlier, offered no attractions at a moment when the intoxicating cup of full independence was already within their grasp. Hence on 10 November the Roumanian National Council notified Budapest that it had taken over power for the twenty-three counties inhabited by Roumanians and parts of three others.[1] Three days later Dr Jászi opened negotiations at Arad with Pop, Goldiş and other Roumanian leaders, and offered them Transylvanian independence and complete racial equality, as the basis of a new Danubian Confederation of free peoples. The commune, and no longer the county, was to be the unit of political organisation, and this unquestionably offered true democratic guarantees. But Károlyi and Jászi themselves were only too well aware that they had come too late: the offer was refused, and Maniu had an unanimous party behind him in demanding "complete separation".

The Magyar-Roumanian dispute was unhappily still further enravelled by the impossible provisions imposed upon Hungary by the Belgrade armistice. Not merely did the short-sighted General Franchet d'Esperey treat Károlyi and his colleagues with great indignity and utterly ignore their Ententophil record—thereby undermining their already wavering prestige at home and preparing the way for extremists of the Right and Left: but the line of evacuation which he prescribed for Transylvania[2] ran counter to every known principle of race, geography or strategy, and to this day it remains a mystery how it came to be adopted. Even the evacuated territory was to remain under Hungarian administration and gendarmes. At the same time the general, who had had no dealings with any race save the Serbs, authorised the occupation not only of Bačka, Syrmia and Bosnia, but of the entire Banat, by Serbian troops, simultaneously restricting their advance towards Croatia and the Adriatic. He thereby seemed to be diverting Serbia's attention from the goal of Jugoslav unity towards

[1] Békés, Csanád, Ugocsa. It is important to note that the native Roumanians made no attempt to claim the monstrous frontier of August 1916.

[2] The rivers Sumeş, Bistriţa and Mureş to its juncture with the Tisza. In other words the capital Cluj and a >-shaped territory penetrating the very heart of the Principality.

the purely Orthodox territory north of the Danube, and in so doing needlessly provoked a conflict, with very dangerous possibilities, between Serbs and Roumanians, since the eastern portion of the Banat was overwhelmingly Roumanian in character.

This hastened Roumanian action. A manifesto in favour of union was issued to the world, and a national assembly, on the analogy of 1848, was summoned to Alba Iulia. On 1 December 1918 this memorable meeting, attended by 1228 delegates and many thousands of peasants, from all the various Roumanian districts of the crown of St Stephen, passed amid unending acclamations a resolution in favour of the union of all Roumanians in a single state. Local autonomy was to be retained until a Constituent Assembly, elected under universal suffrage, could be convoked. Greetings were sent to the Roumanians of Bucarest, to all the "liberated peoples of the former Monarchy" (including the Germans of Austria), gratitude was expressed to those who had fallen in the cause of liberty and national unity and to the Allied Powers, and the Peace Congress was invited to assure "the union of all free nations", justice and right for small and great nations alike, and the avoidance of war in future conflicts. The third resolution attempted to define the fundamental principles on which the new Roumanian state should rest, and it is interesting to compare them with the interpretation soon given to them by the politicians of the Old Kingdom. There was to be (1) full national liberty for all races, with use of the mother tongue in education, administration and justice; (2) full autonomy for all religious creeds; (3) "a purely democratic regime in all branches of public life"—general, direct, equal and secret suffrage, by communes, on proportional representation, for both sexes from the age of twenty-one; (4) complete liberty of press, assembly and association, and "free propagation of all human thoughts"; (5) radical agrarian reform, on the basis of "social levelling and increased production"; (6) "the same advantages to the industrial workers as are secured to them by law in the most advanced industrial states". It is highly significant of the spirit of the moment, that they freely recognised the right of the Peace Conference to settle "the definitive boundaries of the state thus constituted", and also that they pledged themselves to treat their minorities "in accordance with the principles enumerated by President Wilson".

The assembly then proceeded to call into being a "Directing Council" (Consiliul Dirigent), under the presidency of Julius Maniu, with a

Cabinet of fifteen members: Dr Vaida-Voevod was entrusted with the portfolio of Foreign Affairs, Ciceo-Pop with War, Vlad with Finance, Goldiş with Education. The new Government dispatched telegrams to King Ferdinand and Queen Marie, announcing union with the "Regat" as an accomplished fact, exchanged cordial greetings with the Roumanian Academy, and sent a deputation to Bucarest, headed by Bishop Miron Cristea of Caransebeş, the most marked personality among the Orthodox clergy of Transylvania. It was at this time, amid the ruin of all his projects, that the unhappy Metropolitan Mangra died at Budapest, unwept, unhonoured and unsung. The formal protest of the Károlyi Government against the Alba Iulia decisions passed entirely disregarded, and the union was effected without opposition and almost without bloodshed, so completely in abeyance were Hungary's powers of resistance. The secular dream of the Roumanian race, when at last it came, came "as a thief in the night", when preparation had ceased and hope had almost vanished.

\*        \*        \*        \*

While these momentous events were radically transforming the whole situation in Transylvania, that of Roumania itself remained extremely obscure. The collapse of Bulgaria relieved Bucarest of one great anxiety, but there were disturbing rumours that the Entente, influenced especially by America, had recognised the retention of Southern Dobrogea by the Government of Sofia, which since the abdication of Tsar Ferdinand was in the hands of their friends. During October King Ferdinand played for time, shifting uneasily between Marghiloman's crumbling Government, the reviving Liberals under Brătianu—now in close alliance with Mişu—and General Averescu, who hoped to supersede them both and argued that if the Chambers had any legal value whatsoever, it was impossible for Brătianu to pass "from the bench of the accused to the bench of ministers".[1] But here he altogether miscalculated, for no one in the country cared two straws for the validity of a Chamber elected in such circumstances as those of June 1918, and Brătianu only had to bide his time till the army of occupation melted away and the irresolute king capitulated before him. Marghilo-

[1] The foolish story that he had accepted 2,000,000 francs from the German propagandist agent Günther was put about on the basis of an obviously forged document, yet appears to have been believed even by so shrewd an observer as Take Ionescu!

man was in the position of the Moor who had done his duty: the Moor could now go. On 6 November the king received him in audience as usual, and informed him in somewhat embarrassed language, that the Entente ministers had expressed their lack of confidence in the existing Government and their desire to see a change. Marghiloman resigned on the spot, but had the spirit to assert that "thanks to my Government, the dynasty is strong, and the country has an army, munitions and Bessarabia". A Brătianu Government, he added with a spice of personal and party malice, would be "a moral impossibility". The fallen statesman was loaded with obloquy by many whose own conduct was not above reproach: but in the calmer atmosphere of to-day it is possible to admit that he was inspired by the same patriotism as his opponents and rendered signal service to the country. His failure to foresee the Entente victory in 1918 certainly cost Roumania less dearly than the failure of Brătianu to foresee the outcome of intervention two years earlier.

Not Mişu, as Marghiloman had expected, but General Coanda now became premier, but as an obvious stop-gap until the retreat of Marshal Mackensen should render all danger of a military relapse impossible. He at once proceeded to repeal the laws enacted by his predecessor, and ordered a partial mobilisation, to which the response was most inadequate. War was declared anew upon Germany, under the exceedingly flimsy pretext that she had violated the Treaty of Bucharest by increasing her army of occupation beyond the agreed strength. This was a fatal line to take, for it knocked the whole bottom out of the Roumanian contention that the treaty had no legal validity and that the alliance of 1916 had never ceased to exist. But for the time all thought of logic, precedents or legal consequences was swallowed up in the one desire to reoccupy Transylvania. At the same time the effervescence into which the revolutionary outcome of the war had plunged the greater part of Europe was especially apparent in Roumania, with the extreme object lesson of Russia just beyond her borders. The German army of occupation had, it is true, everywhere maintained order, and in Bucharest itself had even introduced many improvements: but their requisitioning had drained the country almost dry and exasperated every class of the population. The king was therefore undoubtedly wise in issuing, with as little delay as possible, a fresh proclamation in which he solemnly reaffirmed the pledges which he had given in 1917. There was to be universal suffrage and expropriation of two million hectares of private property, in addition to the crown domains and the estates of charitable institutions. "By means of these reforms", he said, "we will ensure to all those who labour a social and material existence more just and more plentiful."[1] No reference was made to Transylvania and Bukovina, whose status was as yet unregulated, and even the allusion to Bessarabia was somewhat open to criticism, since the Sfat, though it had decreed union, had specially reserved the right to carry through land reform on its own lines.

Meanwhile steady pressure was put upon the king to end this obviously provisional situation by recalling to power those responsible for the alliance with the Entente, which had after all proved to be the winning side. On 14 December Brătianu became premier once more, and after a somewhat halfhearted attempt to secure the co-operation of Take Ionescu, proceeded to form a mainly Liberal Cabinet, though assigning Foreign Affairs to the late minister in London, Nicholas Mişu, and admitting Vaida-Voevod and two others as representatives of the Directing Council of Transylvania. There was the same rapid hardening of public opinion in Bucarest as in some other capitals—the same aggressive and partisan spirit, the same inclination towards reprisals and boycott. The idea of a national representation at the Conference was speedily abandoned: and Brătianu completely dominated the whole Delegation.

Even before his arrival in Paris the premier had missed a great opportunity for securing to Roumania a strong moral position in the counsels of Europe, and this was undoubtedly partly due to his lack of direct contact with the West throughout these critical years. After his temporary fall from power it had been suggested that he should go to Paris and prepare the ground for the Conference: but in the end he quite rightly decided that it was necessary for him to be within reach in so utterly fluid a situation. His chief colleague, and at the same time his only serious rival, Take Ionescu, decided otherwise and eventually received a German safe-conduct for the journey. His house in Bucarest had already been systematically sacked by the Germans, and now demonstrations against him were arranged by the occupying authorities at the main stations through which his train passed: at one place a squad of gypsies, acting on orders, pelted his carriage with rotten eggs.

The months which followed were in many ways the culminating period of Take Ionescu's career. All his cosmopolitan sympathies, his

[1] Mitrany, *Land and Peasant*, p. 111.

long training in international thinking, now stood him in good stead. "He saw clearly that peace was near and that Roumania was not prepared for it: he appreciated in full that such unreadiness would involve a danger of isolation and disregard."[1] He therefore lost no time in pleading the cause of Roumania before the statesmen of Paris and London, and was relieved to find that they were already more sympathetically disposed than ever before towards the lesser nationalities of Eastern Europe, and capable of appreciating Roumania's sufferings and the categorical imperative which had dictated peace. Above all, however, it was his aim to promote a close understanding between Roumania, Serbia and Greece, such as might give them the status of a Great Power at the crucial discussions in Paris: and he was glad to have arrived at the psychological moment when the allies were according recognition to the reconstituted Polish and Czechoslovak nations. He already had good personal relations with the Greek and Serbian premiers, Venizelos and Pašić. With the former, a far-sighted and practical statesman, he was at once in accord, and even with the tortuous Pašić he found it easy to agree, because the problems that concerned them jointly of course lay at the Balkan, not at the western, end of the future Jugoslavia. He was, however, alarmed to discover the profound dissensions inside the Jugoslav ranks, which alone prevented France and Britain from according full recognition to the unified Jugoslav state in September, or at latest October.[2]

The most delicate point at issue was the future of the Banat, which by the iniquitous treaty of August 1916 had been assigned in its entirety to Roumania, though the south-west corner of it was purely Serb in character. If this clause had been put into effect, the Jugoslavs would

[1] *History of the Peace Conference*, IV, p. 221. (The Roumanian section, though unsigned, is known to be by a tried British friend of Roumania, who was intimately associated with the whole course of the negotiations which he describes.)

[2] Early in October 1918 MM. Pašić and Venizelos were in London, and Mr Take Ionescu asked me to arrange a private meeting between him and Dr Trumbić, the President of the Jugoslav Committee, whom he did not as yet know personally. At the time Mr Ionescu was inclined to blame Trumbić for failure to agree with Pašić, and was unwilling to accept the very detailed facts and arguments which I laid before him, regarding the Committee's troubled relations with the Serbian Government. But when we next met, in Paris after the Armistice, he regretfully admitted, on the basis of official information from many quarters, that the facts were as we had presented them, and that Pašić, by his narrow Panserb policy, was jeopardising the cause of Jugoslav unity, and indirectly of wholehearted Balkan co-operation.

have looked across the river from the windows of their capital to Serbian territory which had been wrested from Hungary merely in order to be assigned to an ally who had never possessed it and had not conquered it. It is difficult to conceive a better method of turning two friendly neighbours into enemies, than to provide such an obvious bone of contention: and those responsible for the secret treaty deserve the strongest condemnation. In October 1918, however, Take Ionescu, in adopting a conciliatory attitude on the question of the Banat, had other unanswerable arguments on his side. In the first place, the treaty had been consistently concealed from Serbia, the country most directly concerned, and could not therefore be regarded as in any way binding upon her. But above all, it had of course been concluded without the knowledge or co-operation of the United States, and in the eyes of President Wilson was simply non-existent and in flagrant contradiction to the Fourteen Points. The Western Powers took a view halfway between Serbia and America: "Though they had no wish to embarrass Roumania by public declarations on the subject, they did not regard the Treaty of 1916 as any longer valid, since Roumania had technically violated it by the conclusion of a separate peace".[1] Take Ionescu was statesman enough to realise the blunder originally committed and the desirability of reaching a direct Serbo-Roumanian agreement before ever the question swam seriously into the ken of the Great Powers. He therefore negotiated with Pašić and reached an amicable understanding by which far the greater portion of the Banat was assigned to Roumania, including the whole southern bank of the Mureş to its junction with the Tisza,[2] and the whole of the important railway connecting Timişoara and the little Danubian port of Baziaş. This was of course contingent upon the approval of Bucarest, and unhappily it leaked out gradually in the press and was denounced by chauvinist opinion as a betrayal of the national cause. The result was that Brătianu drew back from his original intention of making Take Ionescu the second peace delegate: he offered him, it is true, a seat in the Cabinet, but in such a way that he would have exercised no control over policy, and therefore had no choice but to decline. While, then, most European nations took care that their delegations should be representative of all parties in the state, Roumanian policy was in the hands of a single

[1] *History of the Peace Conference*, IV, p. 222.
[2] This was in its turn an encroachment upon purely Magyar territory near Szeged, and was not eventually upheld.

party and to all intents and purposes of a single man. Another result was that the Banat question was left open for nine months, and in the end was settled on lines distinctly less favourable to Roumania than those for which Ionescu was so unjustly denounced.

Take's conception of policy may be summed up very succinctly: he desired a Balkan bloc capable of resisting the pressure of the Great Powers, a durable peace resting upon Wilsonian principles and the definite failure of "Mitteleuropa". No greater contrast can be imagined than that between this brilliant cosmopolitan demagogue full of intuition and improvisation, and the massive, slow-moving Brătianu whose mind revolved within the limits of a rigid and unbending patriotism and to whom the whole ideology of Wilson was at once meaningless and highly suspect. In the words of that mysterious but singularly acute observer, Dr E. J. Dillon, Brătianu and Wilson "moved on different planes, and spoke different languages":[1] and the Roumanian statesman, from his first arrival in Paris, was in more or less open revolt against the whole aims, tactics and decisions of the Conference. It was an added misfortune that Brătianu should have chosen Mişu as the second delegate: for the latter, while fully deserving his reputation as a pliant and versatile diplomatist, had latterly lost his initiative and developed fatalist traits for which his friends had not been prepared,[2] and which soon made of him a mere adjunct to his masterful chief.

The estrangement of Roumania was in some ways a comedy of errors, but it had its tragic side and contributed very materially to that lowering of tone which so soon followed the first days of Wilsonian enthusiasm. The ideals so glibly proclaimed on all sides meant little or nothing to Brătianu: he saw only the sinister figures that lurked in the coulisses. His own basis was "the treaty [of 1916], the whole treaty and nothing but the treaty": and from this nothing could move him. Deeply resenting the Allies' initial refusal to regard it as still binding, he was cut to the quick by finding that its rejection also destroyed his favourite design of ranking Roumania as one of the Great Powers

[1] *History of the Peace Conference*, IV, p. 167.

[2] The present writer well remembers one occasion on the eve of the Conference when Mr Mişu persisted in discussing Dean Inge's studies on Plotinus, as far more profitable than the inanities of European policy. The philosopher in him may have been right, but then he should have shunned such a post as that of foreign minister. The key to Mişu undoubtedly lies in his Macedo-Vlach origin and in his remarkable linguistic attainments.

(which he fancied himself to have secured by Article VI of the Alliance). To this were added other grievances, such as the refusal of a third delegate to Roumania, though one was assigned to the yet unrecognised Jugoslav state. He could not be brought to see that the Council had commitments to Serbia also, and that by framing his demands upon a new basis, more in accordance with the spirit of the times, he could obtain nine-tenths of his whole programme without any effort. He staked his personal dignity upon obtaining every jot and tittle of the original claim, and offended the whole Council by his rigid overstatement. Thus no agreement was possible between him and Belgrade, and the dispute came before the Supreme Council of Ten on 8 February 1919. His argument that only wide river frontiers such as the Danube, Tisza and Dniester could maintain the peace between Roumania and her neighbours was more than coldly received by the Council, who were far more favourably impressed by Dr Trumbić's persuasive presentation of ethnical conditions and the share of the Banat Serbs in the national movement for a whole century past. When a plebiscite was proposed, the Jugoslavs at once accepted, but Brătianu was cautious and evasive. Finally, a Committee was appointed (including two representatives each of America, Britain, France and Italy), to consider the territorial claims of Roumania and not least her dispute with Serbia.

With the labours of this Committee we are not concerned: but since it has often been affirmed that the post-war treaties were hurried through by ignorant statesmen, it is essential to insist that on the contrary the frontier problem was subjected to prolonged and strenuous inquiry by a number of highly trained experts,[1] who, after working through the material, submitted proposals for adoption by their chiefs, who were in the nature of things concerned with broad policy rather than details. Indeed it is not too much to affirm that never at any European Congress had such careful study been devoted to the ques-

[1] On 1 February 1919 President Wilson informed the Council that "ever since the United States entered the war, he had had a body of scholars continuously studying such questions of fact as racial aspects, historical antecedents and economic and commercial elements". See "Minutes of Supreme Council" in David Hunter Miller, *My Diary*, XIV, p. 180.

On the British side Messrs Headlam-Morley, Harold Nicolson, Allen Leeper, and General Mance, on the American side Professors Archibald Coolidge, Seymour, Douglas Johnson and others, on the French side Prof. E. de Martonne. Cf. H. Nicolson, *Peace Making*.

tions involved, by so many competent persons. To-day it is possible to admit that the exclusion of the enemy's representatives from these discussions was a serious blunder: but it must not be forgotten that their voluminous memoranda, statistics and maps received the fullest consideration, and—a very important point—that German and Hungarian (and not Polish, Czech or Roumanian) official statistics were taken as the basis on which the new frontiers were drafted. One of the British experts has admirably summed up the methods adopted. "Failing recourse to plebiscites on a large scale for which the necessary machinery of control, in the shape of occupation of territory by Allied troops was lacking, it was clearly necessary for the Committee to assume as a general principle that a community of race implied a common racial consciousness. Ethnic considerations took the first place in determining the committee's decisions. But it could not be exclusively ethnic considerations, for there were certain broad principles of geography and economics, certain imperative considerations of transport and communications, which had to be allowed to play their part."[1]

The discussion of the new Roumanian frontiers fell into four main sections. (1) That of Bessarabia presented no difficulty, for it possessed clearly marked river boundaries; historically it had always formed part of Moldavia till the rape of 1812; while ethnically the Roumanians formed a majority, and the next strongest element was Ukrainian, the Great Russian element being negligible, except from the social point of view. Hence the only questions still open were whether Russian susceptibilities must be spared, and whether the undoubted discontent which had taken possession of wide sections of the Bessarabian population since the union was due to passing causes of economic stress and corrupt administration, or reflected a permanent opposition to union. We shall see that a considerable period was to elapse before Europe recognised Roumanian sovereignty over Bessarabia.

(2) The problem of Bukovina was also solved without much effort, though not in accordance with ethnical principles. It was at first suggested that the frontier could with advantage be rectified to include in Eastern Galicia close upon 80,000 Ukrainians, living in a compact mass in the north of the province. But by the time the question was ripe for discussion, Galician autonomy was already collapsing, there was no longer an Ukrainian state to claim its co-nationals on the Pruth and Dniester, and it was thought useless to augment still further the

[1] *History of the Peace Conference*, IV, p. 227.

already excessive number of Ukrainians under Polish rule. Bukovina in its entirety was assigned to Roumania.

(3) The frontier with Hungary presented great difficulties.

(*a*) Transylvania was from the first outside the discussion: for the Roumanians there formed a strong majority in eleven out of its fifteen counties, and, as the Saxons had rallied to the new regime (at a National Assembly held at Mediasch early in January), the irreconcilable Magyar minority probably did not exceed a quarter of the total. The uncomfortable fact remained, that a compact mass of over 500,000 Székelys[1] occupied the south-eastern bend of the Carpathians, at the farthest possible point from the Hungarian frontier: they are indeed the exact geographical centre of "Great Roumania"—the kernel in the fruit.

(*b*) Roughly 300,000 more Magyars live in scattered islets and enclaves all over Transylvania, and of these about one-third in and around Cluj, so long the centre of rabid Magyarisation under the old regime.

(*c*) There remained the western counties of Maramureş, Satu Mare (Szatmár), Salagiu (Szilágy), Bihar, Arad and the Banat (comprising in its turn Timiş, Torontal and Caraş-Severin). The commission was unanimous in rejecting the line of the Tisza, as laid down by the Treaty of 1916, for that would have assigned to Roumania, without rhyme or reason, a wide plain solely inhabited by Magyars. But it was equally unanimous in ruling that to follow the main ethnic lines between Roumanians and Magyars would create an unworkable frontier, since it would run across the "tangled cross-hills" to the west of Transylvania and make proper communications from north to south quite impossible. They therefore assigned to Roumania the three key towns of Arad, Oradea Mare (Nagyvárad) and Satu Mare (Szatmár Németi), but at a point between Szalonta and Kisjenö, where it seemed possible to construct a substitute railway, they decided in favour of the Hungarian claim. It is but right to add that though all three towns had an overwhelming Magyar majority, this was the result of two generations of intensive Magyarisation, in which the large Jewish element acted as the ready instrument of the ruling race, and that both Arad and Oradea Mare had remained, even at the height of the Magyarising period, centres of Roumanian culture, the one of the Orthodox, the other of the Uniate, Church.

(4) There remained the thorny problem of disentangling Serbian

[1] In the counties of Csík (86 per cent.), Háromszék (83 per cent.), Udvarhely (95 per cent.), Maros-Torda (57 per cent.).

and Roumanian claims in the Banat. The county of Caraş-Severin was overwhelmingly Roumanian and not really in dispute. In Timiş out of a total population of 500,000 there were only 70,000 Serbs and 169,000 Roumanians, as against 150,000 Germans and 78,000 Magyars: geography in any case ruled out the possibility of uniting the Germans with Austria or Germany. The real trouble lay in the county of Torontal, where the races were more hopelessly intermingled than ever, and no human skill could avail to draw an ethnic boundary. Here there were 199,000 Serbs, as against 86,000 Roumanians, 125,000 Magyars and 158,000 Germans. In the end an attempt was made "to balance, so far as possible, the numbers of Serbs under Roumania and of Roumanians under Jugoslav rule". Unhappily at the last moment it was decided to assign the towns of Vršac and Bela Crkva (Versecz and Weisskirchen) to Serbia, thus cutting the railway connections of Timişoara and Arad with the Danube, and foredooming (as subsequent events have shown) both towns to stagnation and decay. Incidentally this decision ran directly counter to the principles followed along the Hungaro-Roumanian frontier.

The recommendations of the Committee were adopted unaltered by the Supreme Council. But Brătianu refused to endorse them and protested vigorously against the manner in which Roumania had been excluded from decisions which so vitally concerned her. Undoubtedly he was entitled to protest against the "conferential Tsarism" of the "Big Five", especially as voiced by the brutally outspoken Clemenceau: and many of the other smaller states shared his resentment at the lack of consultation. He was unquestionably right in resisting the Council's demand, or rather command—as arbitrary as it was ill-founded—that Roumania should disarm by a specific date, in complete disregard of the fact that Bolshevik Russia was steadily arming for an attack upon her and Poland, as a preliminary to penetrating Central Europe and raising the standard of world revolution. The mysterious favour displayed towards the Bolsheviks is one of the still unexplained features of the Conference and is nowhere more apparent than in its dealings with Roumania. The reverse to this medal was the alleged attempt to extract from Roumania far-reaching industrial concessions for a group of Jewish-American financiers, under peril of losing America's support at the Conference. It is easy to understand how such experiences deepened the xenophobia of one who was suspicious by nature and all the more restive under dictation because of his own dictatorial leanings.

Much more questionable was his opposition to the inclusion in the treaty with Austria of a clause binding the Succession States, and therefore among others Roumania, to accord minority rights within the newly acquired territory, according to the discretion of the Allied and Associate Powers. He did not attend when the first draft of the treaty was presented to the Austrian delegates on 2 June, and, when the frontiers were made public ten days later, he withdrew in high dudgeon to Bucarest, leaving the already all too negative Mişu with instructions, "not to negotiate but to resist".[1]

The publication of the frontiers had been rendered necessary by events in Hungary. As early as 4 March 1919 the weak Liberal-Socialist Government of Count Károlyi had collapsed, the final blow being the demand put forward by the Allied military representative in Budapest, Colonel Vyx, for the evacuation of Southern Slovakia. Károlyi was succeeded by a Soviet Republic under Béla Kun and other unknown adventurers, and most of the old political leaders were arrested or fled the country: but the Red Army, which Kun and Boehm organised, received a certain support from officers of the old regime, as the one hope of averting further encroachments by the neighbouring states. In this case, as in that of the Russian Soviets, the Supreme Council at first showed a moderation which strikingly contrasted with its treatment of its own smaller allies: and General Smuts was sent to negotiate with Kun. When this led to no result, the Roumanian Government, highly alarmed at the establishment of such a regime at its very doors, in one of the strategic centres of Europe, resorted to military measures and in the middle of April drove back the Red Army to the line of the Tisza. This greatly increased the friction in Paris: the Council peremptorily forbade any Roumanian occupation of Budapest, but were not prepared to adopt the alternative proposed by Brătianu, namely the dispatch of an inter-Allied force to restore order. Kun, encouraged by the Council's strange tenderness towards him, proceeded to reorganise his army on lines of the older discipline, and at the very end of May launched an offensive against Slovakia, where the new Czechoslovak army was as yet scarcely in being. In this he followed the double aim of saving Slovakia for Hungary and establishing

---

[1] V. V. Tilea, *Acţiunea Diplomatica a României* 1919–20, p. 18. This book, written as an intelligent and convincing defence of Dr Vaida's policy, is hitherto the only serious contribution from the Roumanian side, on this most controversial subject.

direct contact with Russia across Galicia. The lively protests of Dr Beneš roused the Big Ten to strong action: an ultimatum was dispatched on 8 June, and Kun evacuated the disputed territory, in order to save the Soviet regime. But this had fatal results upon the morale of the army, and internal anarchy seemed imminent. The Supreme Council upheld its veto against Roumania's offer to "make order" in Budapest; and it must be admitted that Brătianu's intransigent temper in Paris and his exaggerated territorial demands justified them in fearing reprisals against Hungary if he were given a free hand. But at last they authorised Foch to draw up a joint plan of action with the Roumanian military authorities, and this was to have been launched on 20 July. Béla Kun, however, forestalled this by 24 hours. In a last hope of regaining popularity at home by a gambler's throw, and incidentally of securing the rich harvests of the Tisza districts for hungry Budapest, he launched an offensive against Roumania with 85,000 troops, impudently informing Paris that his aim was to force the refractory Roumanians to respect the frontiers prescribed by the Supreme Council.

The Roumanians had been closely watching the Hungarian situation and were not taken by surprise. After five days of stiff fighting, the Red Army collapsed, and with it the Bolshevist regime: Kun and some of his colleagues escaped to Vienna, while the bloodthirsty Szamuély shot himself to escape capture. In the first days of August, while the Archduke Joseph, in close co-operation with the Entente representatives, was engaged in creating order out of temporary chaos and establishing contact with the counter-revolutionary Government of Szeged, the Roumanians occupied Budapest and the surrounding country, and calmly ignored the ineffective thunderbolts of Paris. Brătianu now revenged himself for a long series of affronts. Starting from the assumption that "the Great Three are unconscious Bolsheviks" and that their whole attitude was "malicious and dangerous",[1] he made not the slightest effort to conciliate the Allies, and speedily and most effectively destroyed the gratitude he might have won from the Magyars by his share in their deliverance. Tact and moderation did not figure in his vocabulary, and the Roumanian military authorities were left a free hand to requisition on an altogether ruthless scale. It is characteristic of his curious mentality that at the very moment when he was kindling intense resentment among all classes of Magyars,

---

[1] These phrases were used in conversation with the all too sympathetic Dr Dillon (*History of the Peace Conference*, IV, p. 18).

"he toyed with schemes for a Hungaro-Roumanian alliance, perhaps to be cemented by a union of the two crowns", and to be rendered invincible by an understanding with Poland and Ukraine.[1] Undoubtedly Brătianu, with his inside knowledge of the disgraceful story of concession-hunting by Allied and associate interests in the Banat, the Ukraine and other places, felt that the Supreme Council lacked an adequate moral basis for its fulminations against him. His Commissary in Budapest, Diamandi, the former minister in Petrograd, refused to take orders except from Bucarest, and calmly quoted to an Entente general the Roumanian proverb, "Even a donkey will not twice fall into the same quicksand".

The discreditable story of Roumanian requisitioning must not be glossed over. Not merely were enormous stocks of corn, fodder, cattle and machinery commandeered, not merely were the Roumanian railways replenished with locomotives and rolling stock, but in numberless cases private houses were plundered and stripped bare. It was freely alleged that factories were wantonly dismantled, not in order to make use of their plant, but merely to cripple their powers of competition or export.[2] There were certainly many cases of blackmail, corruption and revenge. But as these incidents have been trumpeted to the world by a persistent propaganda, it is also necessary to point to the other side of the medal. Two blacks can never make a white, but there is a difference between gratuitous and unprovoked rapacity and plunder, and reprisals for two years of requisitioning on a gigantic scale. The army of occupation of the Central Powers was known to have removed from Roumania 2,500,000 tons of wheat, and untold quantities of livestock. Before the war the Roumanian railways were served by 1200 locomotives; but only fifty were left behind. More than one factory was stripped bare, and thousands of houses were emptied of their contents.[3] The victims were of course entirely helpless, but they

[1] *History of the Peace Conference*, IV, p. 232.

[2] Certainly much of this material was simply wasted. The present writer, as late as November 1920, saw hundreds of open trucks, laden with the spoils, standing in railway sidings near Cluj, long since ruined and unusable; and this was but a single casual instance.

[3] When in Belgrade, in December 1914, ten days after the Austrian evacuation, the present writer learned that furniture removal vans had been brought across the river from Hungary and had been sent to certain selected houses (which could be named), and had systematically removed their contents. Similar things happened in Bucarest, the crassest example doubtless being the house of Take Ionescu, which was emptied by a squad of eighty men, working to order.

were often able to compare notes and identify the plunderers: and when the chance of revenge came, human nature did not stop short at mere replacement or even equivalent values, but often resorted to usurious interest or downright plunder.

The breach between Bucarest and Paris was complete. The Roumanians remained in occupation of Budapest, and Brătianu, whom the Council had so often ignored and who had only been allowed to see the draft of the Austrian treaty a few hours before it was handed to the Austrians, now revenged himself by leaving unanswered their urgent telegrams. An impossible situation had thus arisen: Roumania by prompt action had saved the Danubian countries from communism or anarchy, but she could not be allowed to flout indefinitely the authority of the Peace Conference. It was decided to send Sir George Clerk to Bucarest, to extract from Brătianu a clear statement of his intentions and if possible to insist upon binding declarations for a settlement of the reparation question. Meanwhile the treaty between Austria and the Allies was signed at St Germain on 10 September, without the concurrence of Roumania. Brătianu met this by a highly characteristic move of his own: he resigned office, as a protest against Article LX of the treaty, and assumed that he would thus rally the country against foreign dictation, that the king would follow his lead and that his artificial parliamentary majority rendered his position unassailable. But he had made a triple miscalculation. King Ferdinand showed unexpected firmness, for it did not suit the dynasty to embroil itself with the whole Western alliance. He therefore formed a non-party Cabinet under General Vaitoianu, with Mişu as foreign minister, and decided to put the country to the test of general elections, on the grounds that the Chamber elected during the German occupation was a fake, but that a reconstruction of the Chamber of 1914 was no less impracticable.

For the first time in Roumanian history official pressure was relaxed, and virtually free elections were held, with the surprising result that the Liberals were reduced to 93 out of 244 seats in the Old Kingdom, and were scarcely represented in the other provinces. In Transylvania the National Party, under Maniu and Vaida-Voevod swept all before them, and speedily allied themselves with the newly constituted Peasant Party of the Kingdom. Both Take Ionescu and General Averescu had abstained, and thus the "National-Peasant Bloc" became for the time the sole alternative Government. The king, still hypnotised by Brătianu and fearing radical currents among the peasantry, clung for a time to the colourless Vaitoianu Government and left it to negotiate with Paris. The conversations between the premier *in statu demissionis* and the delegate of the Powers were conducted with the utmost urbanity, but Brătianu remained absolutely rigid on the minority question and on the partition of the Banat, and though he promised to issue instructions against further requisitioning in Hungary, nothing was done to implement the pledge. After Sir George Clerk's return to Paris there was a pause of some weeks, but by the end of November it became only too obvious that the Vaitoianu Government was insincere in its professions towards the Conference, and an ultimatum was therefore transmitted to Bucarest, demanding immediate acceptance of the allied decisions, under pain of a complete diplomatic rupture.

There could be no real question of continued resistance, despite the combative mood of Brătianu: and the crisis was solved by the resignation of General Vaitoianu and the formation of a Cabinet based upon the Transylvanians and the new Peasant Party. Mr Maniu remained in charge of the "Directive Council", but his closest colleague Dr Vaida-Voevode became premier. The inclusion of Ion Mihalache, a young peasant-schoolmaster of high ideals and great eloquence, and of Dr Lupu, the only serious critic of agrarian reform in the abnormal Jassy Parliament of 1917, was a sympathetic democratic gesture, but alarmed the Court and was from the very first made the basis of calumny and intrigue. General Averescu, with the halo of the "Peasant-General" still about his head, also joined the Cabinet, but left it within a fortnight, with the intention of organising a "People's Party" of his own.

Dr Vaida was confronted with the thankless task of repairing the windows which his predecessors had broken, and in the brief space of four months wrought a complete transformation in Roumania's relations with the outer world. On 9 December General Coanda, on behalf of the new Cabinet, signed the Minorities Treaty which Brătianu had so long and obstinately resisted. On a careful study of the document itself, it is quite impossible to detect any valid grounds for this resistance, except injured *amour propre* at its having been administered as a pill to a naughty child instead of being jointly concocted. The other ground, on which Poland has so often insisted—namely, that such treaties ought to be binding upon all Powers, great and small alike—is one which must appeal to all who regard the solution of minority problems as one of the fundamental issues in post-war Europe. But to refuse all commitments towards the minorities until this demand for equality has been granted, comes dangerously near evasion of obvious duties, and it is perhaps not unnatural, in view of their strained relations with Brătianu on all questions, that the Supreme Council should have interpreted his attitude in this sense.

Its most essential provisions guaranteed full equality of civil and political rights to all citizens of the new state "without distinction of race, language or religion" and recognised that "all persons born in Roumanian territory who are not born nationals of another state, shall *ipso facto* become Roumanian nationals" (§ 6). Roumania was bound to admit to full citizenship all former Austro-Hungarian subjects born in the territory transferred to her, but, during a period of two years after the treaty came into force, such persons retained the right to opt for "any other citizenship which may be open to them". In such an event they would have to transfer themselves within one year to the country of their choice, but would be entitled to retain immovable property in Hungary.

It was further specifically laid down that Roumania should provide "adequate facilities" in the language of the minorities, both in the law-courts and in the primary schools (§§ 8 and 9), and, in districts inhabited by "a considerable proportion" of non-Roumanians, should accord "an equitable share" of the public monies granted for educational or religious purposes. In particular the Saxons and Székels were to enjoy "local autonomy in scholastic and religious matters" (§ 11) and all minorities were to be free to maintain school and other institutions at their own expense (§ 9). Article 7 prescribed the automatic naturalisation of all "Jews inhabiting any Roumanian territory, who do not possess another nationality". It would be idle to pretend that all these provisions have been fulfilled to the letter: but only those who are wilfully blind or have assimilationist aims can deny that the treaty contains nothing which runs counter to the paramount interests of state unity and all that is essential for a just settlement of this vexed question.

It is a great misfortune that the course of internal politics in Roumania from 1920 to 1928 followed rigidly centralised lines and, by driving the more liberal-minded Transylvanian leaders into the political wilderness, left the solution of the racial question in the hands of men from the Old Kingdom, to whom the whole conception of a polyglot

state was unfamiliar, and whose bureaucratic ideals were those of the
First Empire. When at length the Transylvanians came into power after
the fall of Vintilă Brătianu in 1928, one of the first steps of Dr Maniu
was to institute a thorough inquiry into the problem of the minorities,
and it was his intention to introduce a kind of Charter or Statute of
Nationalities, granting the maximum of local autonomy compatible
with a strong central executive. But before this could assume concrete
shape, the great economic crisis engulfed Roumania, like its neighbours, and all surplus energies were devoted to emergency legislation
and to the brutal problem of "making ends meet": a semi-dictatorial
regime followed, and though this baneful experiment was abandoned
before retreat from a blind alley had become impossible, the favourable
moment had been allowed to pass and the Charter, to which many
attached high hopes, is still awaiting the Greek Kalends.

*       *       *       *

The signature of this treaty rendered possible a resumption of friendly
relations between Roumania and the Powers. Dr Vaida paid personal
visits to Paris and London, where his dignified and conciliatory attitude
won him golden opinions. Particularly cordial were his relations with
Mr Lloyd George and his reception by the king. Nor was the confidence placed in him unjustified. In the thorny question of the Banat
he accepted the arbitration of the Supreme Council, which was of course
an honourable way of consenting to partition, on the lines of the
frontier already determined in Paris. The dispute with Czechoslovakia
regarding the northern frontier of Maramureş was no longer left to
drag out its weary length, and was ended by a fair compromise. The
technical difficulties relating to the Danubian Statute were speedily
cleared out of the way by an attitude of mutual conciliation. But
Dr Vaida's crowning success was won before the Conference at its
meeting in London on 3 March, when the Allied Powers unreservedly
recognised Bessarabia as an integral part of Roumania, despite the
claims advanced upon it by the Soviet Union.

Unhappily even the most effective statesman is not able to be in
two places at the same time, and while Dr Vaida was successfully
re-establishing Roumania's shattered international prestige, active intrigues were on foot in Bucarest, which ended in his abrupt dismissal
from office on 13 March, without previous consultation and without
his even being invited to discuss the situation. This, the most ques-

tionable act of King Ferdinand's reign, cannot be reconciled with the spirit of the Roumanian constitution; and the contemporary alarm at the radical outlook of Dr Lupu as minister of the interior, must be dismissed as a transparent pretext. Undoubtedly it was due to pressure from reactionary agrarian circles, who feared more drastic action in the land question from the Transylvanians and their peasant allies than from the politicians of the Regat. The appointment of General Averescu as premier was an attempt to canalise the agrarian movement through the personality of an idolised general, himself a peasant. By entrusting him with power all fear of a Boulanger seemed to be averted, and if step by step he should exhaust his reserve of popularity and cease to be a political force of the first rank, the way would have been opened for a return to pre-war methods of party government. Averescu at once ordered elections, and by artificial means stamped out of the ground a hitherto non-existent "People's Party", holding 209 out of a total of 369 seats. He then greatly strengthened his position by a pact with Take Ionescu, who himself became foreign minister and secured the thorny portfolio of Finance for Mr Nicholas Titulescu, his most brilliant supporter and afterwards his political heir.

The decisive factor, in what was really a thinly-veiled *coup d'état* from above, was the agrarian question. Mr Mihalache, as minister of agriculture, had been pressing strongly for an extension of the reform beyond the arbitrary figure of two million hectares and for the extension to the Old Kingdom of the more radical principles already adopted in Bessarabia; and he all too rashly challenged his opponents by affirming that they dare not let his bill through, since such a "certificate of ability for the new parties" would also be "a sentence against those who had ruled the country hitherto".[1] The big boiars not merely secured access to the palace and insistently denounced the Cabinet for its "Bolshevist" tendencies, they even prevented Mihalache from obtaining an audience to expound his views. His place was taken by Mr Garoflid, the ablest spokesman of the great landed interests, and it was he who now gave its final shape to the Agrarian Reform. His law, not promulgated till 21 July 1921, respected the differences of method and application in the Old Kingdom and the new provinces, but very rightly aimed at their eventual co-ordination. It is essential to add that the Garoflid reform, though it did not go so far as the more ardent spirits had hoped, remained true to the pledges of 1917 and 1918 and

[1] Mitrany, *op. cit.* pp. 115–19.

may fairly be described as a reasonable compromise between the two extremes. Politically, however, the sudden change of regime seriously strained the machine and retarded consolidation, for the Transylvanians were aggrieved and affronted, and it became the considered policy of the Bucarest party cliques to maintain their exclusion from office until appetite forced them to accept on terms of gross inequality. It was sought to stereotype this unnatural situation by artificial correctives to universal suffrage, and by methods of electoral corruption which soon threw pre-war Hungary into the shade. When the artificial majority of Averescu disintegrated and death prematurely removed the more generous and imaginative Take Ionescu, the Liberals inevitably regained power, on the old basis of centralisation, xenophobia and a network of party banks favouring the towns against the peasants. King Ferdinand, especially as his health failed, became more and more the prisoner of the Liberal party, and the situation was complicated still further by Prince Carol's renunciation of the throne.

The death of the king in 1927 left the nominal control of affairs in the hands of a clumsy and almost unworkable Regency of three and the country was faced by the disturbing prospect of at least twelve years of minority of a boy-king. But death again exercised a decisive influence upon the course of events, and the successive elimination of Ionel Brătianu, his brother and successor Vintila, and finally the Regent Buzdugan, weakened the Liberal oligarchy, rendered a National Peasant Government possible and removed the obstacles to Prince Carol's return from exile. After 1928 it seemed as though healthier political conditions were slowly returning: above all, the long and arbitrarily delayed reconciliation between the Regat and Transylvania became an accomplished fact. Unhappily the World Crisis all too soon played havoc with the new Government's whole programme of social and economic recuperation, and created an unstable situation in which dictatorial and fascist solutions found an increasing number of advocates. There can be little doubt that if revolution has been averted, this was above all due to the much-criticised land reform of 1917–20, which immunised the peasant masses against the infiltration of communist doctrine from Russia. To-day there is much suffering and discontent in the villages; but since Stalin's ruthless destruction of peasant economy in the Soviet Union, even the most foolish knows what is happening to his luckless neighbour Eucalegon's house, and keeps his fire hose ready.

*    *    *    *

It only remains to describe the final stages leading to the conclusion of peace. Our brief summary of events has already shown the extent to which the new Hungary's relations with her three neighbours were ruined by the incredible bungling of successive armistices. It was absolutely necessary that their terms should be revised, for they contained oversights or blunders which vitally affected the Succession States: but it was only natural that each change should be felt in Budapest as a breach of faith, or at best as a further blow of fate. The advent of a Bolshevik regime in Hungary and the impossibility of normal dealings with it, inevitably delayed the settlement still further, quite apart from the natural absorption of the Council in the major problems of world policy. Finally, the invasion of Slovakia introduced a fresh complication, for it almost compelled the Allies to fix the future frontiers of Hungary and make their decision public, at a moment when serious discussion with representative Hungarians was altogether precluded by the political situation, even if the evil precedent of dictation rather than discussion had not already been adopted at Versailles. "And this decision was in fact irrevocable, for the Great Powers could not reverse it without breaking faith with their smaller Allies."[1]

The Red Terror was followed by the Roumanian occupation, the fall of Kun, the White Terror and for a time chaotic conditions; and it was not until 26 November that a concentration Cabinet could be formed in Budapest, under the regency of Admiral Horthy, and Allied recognition accorded. The peace terms were communicated to the Hungarian Delegation on 16 January 1920, and this was the occasion of a remarkable speech by the veteran Count Albert Apponyi, who protested against their exclusion from discussions, as contrary to the basic principles of President Wilson. Nearly a month elapsed before their first formal reply, and then their request, that Hungary should not be described in the preamble as a Republic, was granted, but their appeal for plebiscites before dismemberment—which they themselves described as "the chief and fundamental demand"—was definitely rejected. They now promised to the non-Magyars "a wide cultural and even territorial autonomy" and "a special solution for Transylvania". The Allied reply of 6 May 1920 claimed that plebiscites were superfluous and "would not give results substantially different from those at which they had arrived after a minute study of the ethnographical conditions and national aspirations. The wish of the peoples

[1] *History of the Peace Conference*, IV, p. 416.

was expressed in October and November 1918 when the Dual Monarchy disappeared under the blows inflicted by the Powers, and when long oppressed populations welcomed their Roumanian, Jugoslav and Czechoslovak brethren".[1] All that the Allies were prepared to concede was a boundary commission, whose duty it was to report on any matters "not corresponding to ethnic or economic necessities". The Council of the League could then offer its services to secure "rectification of the original tracing" by friendly agreement between the parties concerned. This phrase, which occurs in the covering letter signed by President Millerand on 6 May, aroused altogether exaggerated hopes in the minds of the Hungarian delegates at Paris and has been constantly quoted since that date as involving an Allied pledge of revision. It is difficult to understand, on a careful perusal of the text, how this regrettable misunderstanding could ever have arisen, for it quite obviously refers to minor points of local rectification, and not to anything which deserves the more ambitious title of revision. Indeed, it stands to reason that in May 1920 the Allies, even in order to secure Hungarian military aid against Bolshevist Russia, could not possibly have pledged themselves to what would have involved them in instant and acute conflict with three of their own allies. Count Apponyi resigned from the Hungarian Delegation in protest against the Allies' attitude, but resistance was hopeless, and on 4 June 1920 the Treaty of Trianon was signed, on the lines already laid down a year earlier. Roumanian Unity was an accomplished fact.

*        *        *        *

The Treaty of Trianon ends the most momentous epoch in the whole history of the Roumanian race: what follows belongs very definitely to contemporary history and lies outside the scope of this present narrative. Gigantic problems of reconstruction confronted the new country, and after fifteen years are still to a great extent unsolved. Two generations of peace and clean government might make of Roumania an earthly paradise, for she has great natural resources and all that is necessary to a well ordered economy. But her chief asset is the Roumanian peasant, who amid adverse political surroundings has shown a virility and endurance that border on the miraculous.

[1] *History of the Peace Conference*, IV, p. 423. See also *Justice for Hungary*, p. 102.

PLATE XVI

KING FERDINAND AND QUEEN MARIE

At their coronation in Alba Iulia

# BUKOVINA AND BESSARABIA UNDER FOREIGN RULE

While Transylvania always of necessity formed the central problem of Roumanian racial policy, alike numerically and for reasons of geography and tradition, there were two other important provinces which in the century and a half before liberation evolved on lines of their own and to which we must devote a brief survey, in order that the reader may estimate the relative position of all the Roumanian lands on the eve of the Great War.

It will be remembered that the first partition of Poland saved Turkey from a similar fate and that Russia at the memorable Treaty of Kütchük Kainardji in 1774 preferred a loose protectorate over the Christians of Turkey to actual annexations of the two Principalities, and the acute friction with Austria and Prussia which that would have involved, but that no sooner had the Russian armies evacuated Moldavia than Joseph II ordered the occupation of its northern districts by his own troops. These were gradually augmented throughout 1774, while lengthy negotiations were set on foot at the Porte, still further protracted by wrecking intrigues from the courts of St Petersburg and Berlin. The Turks had already consented in principle to the cession of Oltenia, as held by Austria from 1718 to 1739, but Joseph attached still greater importance to Northern Moldavia, as forming the strategic link between Transylvania and Galicia, and succeeded in winning over Kaunitz to his views. The claim to Pocutia, as the ancient possession of that portion of Poland so recently acquired by Austria, was too flimsy a pretext to impress even the exponents of grab in which that century was so rich. The cession of Turkish territory was finally legalised by the Convention of 7 May 1775, but Baron Splényi had already established his headquarters at Cernăuţi or Czernowitz in the previous August.

The new province was officially named Bukovina—"the Beech Wood"—a suitable title, since it still consisted in the main of enormous forests, very thinly inhabited. The great majority of the inhabitants were Roumanians, but along the Dniester and towards Cîmpolung the

Ukrainian population was already spreading westwards at their expense, while in the market towns trade was largely in the hands of Armenians and Jews. The Austrians when they took over found not a single doctor or apothecary in the whole country, no bridges, and scarcely any roads, and only two recognised schools, apart from two or three private institutions. The greater part of the land belonged to the monasteries, of which there were twenty-six,[1] the more venerable of them still living upon the rich endowments of Stephen the Great and other Moldavian princes, but, like everything else, fallen into decay under Turkish rule and shockingly mismanaged by alien monks.[2] Their reform was one of the first tasks of the new military administration and had permanently beneficial results. Bukovina was formed into a separate diocese, transferred from Rădăuți to Cernăuți, and detached from the jurisdiction of the metropolitan of Jassy. After a short interval it was placed by Joseph II under the Serbian Orthodox metropolitan of Karlovci, but for obvious reasons distance and civil control, in the one case by the Austrian, in the other by the Hungarian, authorities, prevented all serious danger of interference. Above all, the so-called "Religionsfond" was created in 1786 out of the revenues of the monasteries, all but seven of these being closed; and henceforth these lands were administered by the state and the surplus income applied to the endowment of the episcopal see, a school for priests, a seminary, and other ecclesiastical purposes. The grave financial crises of the Napoleonic period in Austria reacted upon the "Religious Fund" also and delayed the effects of reform. But from the second half of the nineteenth century onwards there was steady improvement, and constant surpluses were applied to augmenting the stipends of the clergy, securing pensions for their widows, endowing Orthodox schools, and eventually to erecting a cathedral and metropolitan palace at Cernăuți— the latter indeed on lines of altogether regal extravagance. It is right to place emphasis from the very outset upon the ecclesiastical aspect of affairs, for the enlightened attitude of Joseph II in respecting, while reforming and controlling, the pious foundations of earlier princes, did

---

[1] There were also three nunneries.

[2] The most important were Stephen's foundation at Putna (1466), Suceava (1514, founded by his son Bogdan III), Moldavița (1531 by Peter Rareș), Suceavița (by the Movilă family) and Dragomirna (in 1602 by the Metropolitan Anastasius Crimca)—for the most part strongly fortified and still preserving many interesting frescoes, relics and other treasures.

more than anything else to ensure the survival and progress of the Roumanian element during the 150 years of Austrian rule.

The basis of the new order was laid by efficient military commissioners, such as Splenyi and Enzenberg, the latter of whom was specially well qualified because he had commanded one of the Wallach frontier regiments and knew the character of the people whom he had to govern. The chancellor, Count Blumegen, also gave the sound advice that the Bukovina should be governed according to its own traditions and that every effort should be made "to win the confidence of the Moldavian nation so far as possible".[1] But in 1786 Joseph yielded to his passion for centralisation and decided to unite Bukovina, as a single "Kreis" or district, to Galicia, then as ever much the largest of the seventeen Austrian provinces. At the same time he abolished the titles of boiar and mazil and merged their holders in the Galician nobility, disregarding the almost unanimous protest of those affected. Bukovina undoubtedly suffered from these decisions, which in actual fact were never carried to their legal conclusion or fully applied. Indeed after Joseph's death the Aulic Chancellory proposed their immediate reversal, and though Leopold II did not endorse this suggestion, the province occupied a somewhat hybrid status for two generations to come, this being doubtless mainly due to its remoteness and to the stagnation which followed the great wars. Though it failed to obtain a Diet of its own, it took no part in the proceedings of the Galician Diet until the year 1817, and it preserved its own separate lawcourts and fiscal arrangements. It should be added that the Austrians immediately set themselves to raise—or it might be more accurate to say, to set up—educational standards; and in the first decade 9 schools (6 Roumanian, 1 Latin, 1 Greek and 1 German), 3 normal schools (of mixed Roumanian and German character) and a seminary were established. These were undoubtedly meagre results according to our modern outlook, but by no means so meagre if compared with contemporary effort in neighbouring countries.

Bukovina, then, may be said to have vegetated for the first half of the nineteenth century: and the only event of more than local importance was the meeting of the emperors Francis and Alexander at Cernăuți in 1823. It shared in the effervescence of 1848, but this took the form of renewed protests against the connection with Galicia and a demand for a separate diet and an autonomous position under the

[1] Nistor, *Der nationale Kampf in der Bukovina*, p. 174.

Habsburg crown. It found a worthy leader in Eudoxiu Hurmuzaki,[1] a man of wide culture and political restraint, whose name will be for ever associated with the great collection of documents illustrative of Roumanian history, issued by the Roumanian Academy under his auspices and completed long after his death. He and other notables signed a petition to the emperor, and this was repeated in a modified form to Francis Joseph soon after his accession. Under the centralist Austrian Constitution of 4 March 1849, Bukovina was duly constituted as an autonomous Duchy, and though representative institutions fell into abeyance when the as yet untested Constitution was arbitrarily suspended in 1851, bureaucratic autonomy remained, and in 1853 the last vestiges of the unwelcome connection with Galicia were swept away, and a Landespräsident was appointed. In 1861, when the experiment in constitutional Government was renewed, Bukovina became one of the seventeen "Länder", or provinces of the Austrian empire— actually the smallest after Trieste, Gorizia and Vorarlberg—and in April of that year its first Diet met in Cernăuţi. It is again characteristic of the prestige enjoyed by the Orthodox Church that the masterful Metropolitan Eugene Hakman should have become the first Landes- hauptmann. Of this prelate it is possible to take two very conflicting views. There can be no question of the great services which he rendered to the cause of Orthodoxy and no less of Roumanian nationality in Bukovina: but the reverse of the medal is revealed by his long conflict with the Metropolitan Şaguna of Sibiu. When the latter, thanks largely to his favour at court during the absolutist period of Alexander Bach, at length succeeded in detaching the Roumanian Orthodox Church of Hungary from the irksome jurisdiction of the Serbian patriarch, it was widely suggested, and seemed only natural, that all the Roumanians of the Habsburg dominions should be placed under a single ecclesiastical authority. To this design, however, Hakman opposed an obstinate and successful resistance, and the metropolitan see of Cernăuţi remained to the end in the enjoyment of its peculiar autonomy and its splendid endowments. But the result was to accentuate the dangerous isolation in which this diminutive fragment of the race found itself amid the rising Slavonic flood.

In many ways the chief event in the quiet annals of Bukovina under the Dual System was the foundation of the University of Cernăuţi in

[1] The family originally came from Chios in the sixteenth century and inter- married with the princely family of Movilă.

1875, in honour of the centenary of Austrian rule. In it the Orthodox seminary established in the twenties was now expanded into a full theological faculty. At the same time it is true that the new seat of learning was too often regarded by Vienna as an instrument of spreading German culture farther eastwards, and a great proportion of the chairs were held by Germans—some, it must be added, of real eminence in their day. The underlying tendency was clearly marked, and Victor von Scheffel, the hero of German student lore in its greatest days, having a few years earlier addressed a poem of greeting to the new University of Strasburg, reconstituted as a bulwark of Germanism in the West, now addressed an ode to this more distant outpost of German culture on the Pruth. A bronze statue of "Austria" was erected, in miniature imitation of those ponderous "Germanias" and "Bavarias" so dear to the heart of Imperial Germany in its early days. It must at once be added that while German method and discipline permeated the whole organisation, and the majority of the students were German,[1] every effort was made to promote Roumanian and Ruthene culture at the same time. Yet though the official attitude of the Government towards the Roumanians was benevolent—in the most striking contrast to that of Budapest to their kinsmen in Hungary—there emerged more clearly in every decade the disturbing fact of a decline in the Roumanian population in comparison with the other races of the province. This was all the more disturbing because it was a natural, not an artificial, process—due in the first instance to Bukovina's lack of contact with Transylvania, and even with Moldavia, and to the cessation of Roumanian immigration from both these directions, but above all to the fact that, parallel with this, Ruthene immigration from Galicia was growing steadily in volume and was proving the stronger element. Indeed it is not at all easy to explain why the Roumanians should be so immune from Russifying influences, and so susceptible to Slavisation in its Ukrainian form. The process may indeed, if more closely examined, provide a key to the folly of forcible assimilation from above, in contrast to the immense possibilities of natural assimilation from below.

Whatever may be the true explanation, the facts are hardly open to question. The Ruthenes, who were a negligible factor when the province first fell to Austria, numbered 108,000 in 1848 as against 209,000

---

[1] In 1900, out of 392 students, 218 were German, 89 Roumanian, 35 Ruthene, 40 Polish—see *Festschrift* of 1900.

Roumanians. From that date onwards the proportion altered steadily, as will be seen most clearly from the following table:

|  | Roumanians | Ruthenes | Total |
|---|---|---|---|
| 1880 | 190,005 | 239,690 | 568,453 |
| 1890 | 208,301 | 268,367 | 642,495 |
| 1900 | 229,018 | 297,798 | 730,195 |
| 1910 | 273,254 | 305,101 | 794,424 |

This means that between 1880 and 1890 the Roumanians declined by 4 per cent., and that during the next two decades there were again declines of 10 and 9 per cent., as against increases by 12 and 11 per cent. Meanwhile the Jews, of whom there were only 175 families in 1786, had increased to 102,000 in 1910. The real German population amounted to 66,000, living for the most part in compact villages: they were descendants of miners from the Zips who were brought to such places as Kirlibaba, Eisenau and Freudenthal at the very end of the eighteenth century, of peasants from the Palatinate and Southern Germany who were settled about the same time and finally of others brought from Bohemia towards the middle of last century. Being more remote in custom and tradition, and speaking what quite inevitably became the *lingua franca* of the administration, these Germans had no difficulty in retaining their individuality. But it is only necessary to visit the country to find many traces of villages essentially Roumanian in type and in name, which are now entirely Ruthene. The whole country between the Pruth and Dniester is to be regarded as overwhelmingly Ruthene, whereas the southern portions of the province are as decidedly Roumanian and, as our narrative has shown, contained the earliest nucleus of the Moldavian state.

\* \* \* \*

Very different were the fortunes of Bessarabia, which the Porte ceded to Russia in 1812, by the first of the four treaties of Bucarest, as the price for evacuation of the remainder of Moldavia and Wallachia.

Tsar Alexander's attitude was a combination of liberal sentiment and tactics: he hoped that Bessarabia was but a foretaste of future annexation and desired to win over the inhabitants. He therefore nominated Scarlat Sturdza, one of the foremost Bessarabian boiars, as head of a provisional Government which was to respect "the ancestral laws and customs of the country". The instructions sent to Sturdza through General Chichagov are well worth quoting: "You must endeavour to lay the foundation for a larger building. Protect property and its owners: make it as easy as possible for those who settle there to acquire property. The public burdens must be equally distributed: the honesty of the administrative officials must make the inhabitants forget the lack of a regular system of laws. Let the inhabitants feel the advantage of a fatherly and liberal administration. Draw the attention of neighbouring peoples to this province by making it happy. The last war had aroused great hopes among the Christian peoples: now that our army has been called away to another field, one must take care to preserve that devotion towards us and to withdraw them from the influence of our enemies. The Bulgars, the Moldavians, the Wallachians, the Serbs, seek a fatherland: you can contribute towards finding one for them".[1] These hopes do not seem to have been realised. The first Russian officials, both military and civil, were both incompetent and corrupt, and Count Kiselev, who afterwards played so memorable a part in Roumanian history, told Alexander, "Everything is for sale, and the prefects are obliged to steal more than the rest, as they have paid 20 or 30 thousand roubles apiece for their nomination".

There was a very large exodus of the peasantry, who had had recent experience of Russian requisitioning in war and had grounds for fearing a deterioration of status under the Russian system of serfdom. Even without this the province was only thinly populated: according to the not very reliable estimates which we possess, there were only about 250,000 inhabitants in 1812, though they grew very rapidly to 412,000 in 1829, to 990,000 at the end of the Crimean War, to 1,935,000 at the census of 1897 and to 2,393,000 in 1909. This was mainly due to a high birthrate, but immigration was steadily encouraged. The Russian officials and generals to whom extravagant grants of land were made during the first twenty years of the occupation, brought in serfs from the interior of Russia, while the stream of Bulgar colonists which had already begun about 1770 still continued, and German and even French Swiss settlers were imported and formed prosperous villages, living a life of their own.

Meanwhile Gabriel Banulescu-Bodoni, a native of Bistriţa in Transylvania, was nominated metropolitan of Chişinău and Hotin and played a beneficent rôle for the first ten years. He established a theological seminary in which three languages—Russian, Roumanian,

[1] Zinkeisen, *Geschichte des osmanischen Reiches*, VII, p. 7.

and Latin were on an equal footing: he built 200 new churches in the much neglected province, and above all he was allowed to set up a Roumanian printing press which issued catechisms and liturgies. Not merely was this not opposed by the Russians, but in 1819 a Roumanian Bible was specially printed at St Petersburg—being a reprint, not of "Serban's Bible", then still in use in the Principalities, but of the version printed at Blaj in 1795.

In April 1818 Alexander I issued an ukase regularising the local autonomy of Bessarabia. The main feature of the new system was a Supreme Council consisting of six members elected by the boiar class and five nominated by Russia—in other words, on the narrowest possible oligarchic lines. The two languages were on an equal footing in the administration, and the tribunals were instructed to govern in accordance with the local laws and privileges "accorded for ever" to the province.

The reign of Nicholas I brought changes for the worse; and even the liberal-minded governor, Prince Vorontsev, an ardent admirer of English constitutional ideas, found it necessary to swim with the current, while Banulescu's successor as metropolitan was the first of a series of Russifiers in the Church. In February 1828 another ukase abolished the Supreme Council and created in its place a body which was purely consultative and whose members were nominated by the authorities. The courts were reorganised on Russian lines, Russian became the exclusive language of the administration, and power was concentrated in the hands of a military governor, directly dependent upon the governor-general of Odessa.

If the reign of Nicholas was marked by a slow infiltration of Russian influence, clothed in absolutist-bureaucratic forms, there are no outstanding events which require emphasis in this brief sketch. Nor did the territorial changes following the Crimean War bring any relief for the "Moldavian" population. For the problem was treated by Europe rather from the strategic than from the national point of view, the paramount considerations being Danubian navigation and Turkish defence against Russia; and by an irony of fate the three southern districts—Ismail, Cahul and Bolgrad—which were now reunited with Moldavia, were the very districts where the Roumanian population was least numerous!

When even these three districts were reannexed by Russia after the war of 1877, and with the sanction of Europe, a strong wind of

Russification began to blow in Bessarabia, as in other non-Russian provinces of the tsar's dominions. Even the introduction of the Zemstvo system of local government in 1869—which elsewhere may be said to mark the first faint dawn of liberalism—had only served to exacerbate the situation, since it fell from the outset into the hands of the most reactionary elements in the province. Henceforth Bessarabia remained a stronghold of reaction, and the natural breeding ground of such movements as the "Black Hundreds".

At the same time the metropolitan Paul Lebedev (1871–82) became an ardent exponent of Russification through the Church. Henceforth all ecclesiastical records were kept in Russian only; Russian schools were installed in the monasteries, and in 1878 the priests of the three reannexed districts were given two years in which to learn Russian or to lose their cures. Lebedev found it difficult to attract the requisite number of Russian-speaking clergy, but, undeterred by this, he even went so far as to close a number of churches altogether rather than leave them in the hands of Roumanian priests. The Roumanians were helpless, and indeed the name of "Roumanian" was altogether proscribed: the national feeling was driven underground and seemed doomed to extinction. But the vitality of the peasant survived all trials, and a local proverb summed up the whole situation in a phrase: "Father is Russian, mother is Russian, but Ivan is Moldavian" (Tata rus, mama rus, dar Ivan moldovan).

The last two decades of the sixteenth century were a period of absolute reaction, on lines hostile to the non-Russian nationalities, and Bessarabia, where the old nobility was swamped by Russian elements, where there was virtually no intelligentsia and where the small tradesmen were mainly Jewish, led what was really a vegetable existence. But here, as in other provinces, a change occurred after the Russian Revolution of 1905 and the coming of the Duma. Roumanian newspapers were for a time allowed to appear. The teaching of Roumanian was revived at the theological faculty in Chişinău, and the diocesan press, originally founded by the metropolitan Banulescu, again began to issue Roumanian publications. The Marshal of the provincial nobility, Paul Dicescu, founded a "Moldavian Cultural Society" and appealed to St Petersburg, though without success, for the establishment of Roumanian schools. Meanwhile a more democratic current made its appearance under an advocate of Chişinău, Emanuel Gavriliţa, and a group of young writers and poets soon centred around the newspaper *Bessarabia*. But these activities alarmed the Russian authorities, and within less than two years the Roumanian press had again been suppressed.

In 1908 militant Russification found an aggressive leader in the new metropolitan Serafin Chichagov, a former colonel who had been obliged to resign his commission, had embraced the monastic career and owed his appointment as bishop to certain reactionary ladies of the capital. He allied himself closely with the Krupenski family whose influence was so all-pervading that liberal publicists gave Bessarabia the nickname of "the Krupenskian Province" (Krupenskaya Gubernia). They were agreed in treating all Roumanian national tendencies as "separatism" and in prohibiting the teaching of the language and the circulation of books from across the Pruth. Serafin's excess of zeal in Church affairs had the unexpected result of evoking a widespread sectarian movement known as the "Innocentist". It took its name from a certain Ion Inocenţie Ţurcan, a monk from the neighbourhood of Balta, who was credited with miraculous powers of healing and preached the approaching end of the world. So great were the crowds of pilgrims who flocked to him, that the authorities transferred him to a monastery in the far north of Russia; but hundreds of his peasant admirers sold all that they possessed and followed him to the White Sea. His great influence, resting on emotional eloquence, was symptomatic of the unsound conditions in which all culture and progress in their mother tongue was denied to the "Moldavian" peasant masses. It is not surprising that Bessarabia became the happy hunting ground of the reactionary "League of True Russians", better known as the "Black Hundred", and of the grossest form of anti-Semitic calumny. The centenary of the Russian occupation was celebrated in 1912, amid utter repression, and this had in no way been relaxed when the Great War broke out.

\*     \*     \*     \*

## BIBLIOGRAPHICAL NOTE

There is no really satisfying book upon Bessarabia, though that of Z. C. Arbore, *Basarabia* (Bucarest, 1898), is a most painstaking and thorough publication for the period of last century. Mr C. Upson Clark's *Bessarabia* (New York, 1927) is a useful summary, but is full of gaps.

A certain amount of controversial literature was issued during or after the Peace Conference, and falls into three groups: (1) six pamphlets by Ion G. Pelivan (a Bessarabian deputy)—"La Bessarabie sous le régime russe"; "L'Union de la Bessarabie à la Mère-Patrie"; "Le Mouvement et l'Acroissement de la Population"; "L'État Économique de la Bessarabie"; "Chronologie de la Bessarabia"; "Les Droits des Roumain sur la Bessarabie". (2) Four pamphlets purporting to be answers to the above, by A. N. Krupenski (the Russian reactionary leader) and Alexander Schmidt (former mayor of Chişinău under Russia). These are entitled: "The Bessarabian 'Parliament' 1917–18"; "Bessarabia and Roumania; What is the 'Bessarabian Question'?"; "Summary of events in Bessarabia". (3) Two more serious Russian pamphlets entitled "Mémoire sur la situation de la Bessarabie" (by the Comité pour la Libération de la Bessarabie) and "The Case for Bessarabia" (Russian Liberation Committee, London) with preface by Professor Paul Milyukov. The Bolshevik view will be found in the pamphlet of Christian G. Rakovsky, entitled *Roumania and Bessarabia* (London, W. P. Coates, 1925, 1s.).

## APPENDIX II

# THE POPULATION OF ROUMANIA

1899. Total 5,956,690, of whom 5,489,296 (92 per cent.) were Roumanian; 467,394 non-Roumanian.

Of these 5,451,787 were Orthodox, 266,652 Jew, 149,667 Catholic.

1912. Total 7,234,920, of whom 6,693,853 were Roumanian; 541,067 Jew, Turk, Tatar, Bulgar, German.

1930. Total 18,025,237, divided as follows:

| | |
|---|---|
| Old Kingdom (Regat) | 8,766,932 |
| Transylvania and Banat | 5,546,896 |
| Bessarabia | 2,865,600 |
| Bukovina | 845,903 |

Of these 14,505,740 were Roumanian;

3,519,497 non-Roumanian—1,305,753 Magyar, 681,502 German, 536,006 Jew, 550,000 Ukrainian, 300,000 Bulgar, 230,000 Turk and Tatar, 120,000 Russian, 48,000 Serb, 35,000 Pole.

The racial distribution in Transylvania and the neighbouring counties of Hungary at the last pre-war Hungarian census (1910) was as follows:

| I. *Transylvania* | Roumanian | p.c. | Magyar | p.c. | German | p.c. | Total |
|---|---|---|---|---|---|---|---|
| Alba de Jos (Alsó-Fehér) | 171,483 | 77·4 | 39,107 | 17·6 | 7,269 | — | 221,618 |
| Bistriţa-Năsăud (Bestercze-Naszód) | 87,564 | 68·5 | 10,737 | 8·4 | 25,609 | — | 127,843 |
| Braşov (Brassó) | 35,091 | 34·7 | 35,372 | 35·0 | 29,542 | — | 101,199 |
| Făgăraş (Fogoras) | 84,436 | 88·7 | 6,466 | 6·8 | 3,236 | — | 95,174 |
| Huniedoara (Hunyad) | 271,675 | 79·9 | 52,720 | 15·5 | 8,101 | — | 340,135 |
| Târnavele-Mici (Kis-Küküllö) | 55,585 | 47·9 | 34,902 | 30·1 | 20,272 | — | 116,091 |
| Cojocna (Kolozs) | 153,717 | 68·0 | 60,735 | 26·9 | 6,710 | — | 225,879 |
| Town of Cluj (Kolozsvár) | 7,562 | 12·4 | 50,704 | 83·4 | 1,676 | — | 60,808 |
| Târnavele-Mari (Nagy-Küküllö) | 60,381 | 40·6 | 18,474 | 12·4 | 62,224 | — | 148,826 |
| Sibiu (Szeben) | 113,672 | 64·3 | 10,159 | 5·7 | 49,757 | — | 176,921 |
| Solnoc-Dobaca (Szolnok-Doboka) | 189,443 | 75·2 | 52,181 | 20·7 | 6,902 | — | 251,936 |
| Turda Arieş (Torda-Aranyos) | 125,668 | 72·1 | 44,630 | 25·6 | 576 | — | 174,375 |
| Muraş Turda (Maros-Torda) | 70,192 | 36·2 | 111,376 | 57·4 | 7,706 | — | 194,072 |
| Town of Marosvásárhely | 1,717 | 6·7 | 22,790 | 89·3 | 606 | — | 25,517 |
| *The Székely Counties* | | | | | | | |
| Csík | 18,032 | 12·4 | 125,888 | 86·4 | 1,080 | — | 145,720 |
| Háromszék | 22,963 | 15·5 | 123,518 | 83·4 | 617 | — | 148,080 |
| Udvarhely | 2,840 | 2·3 | 118,458 | 95·4 | 2,202 | — | 124,173 |
| | 1,472,021 | 55·0 | 918,217 | 34·3 | 234,085 | 8·7 | 2,678,367 |

| II. *Hungary Proper* | Roumanian | p.c. | Magyar | p.c. | German | Ruthene | Total |
|---|---|---|---|---|---|---|---|
| Maramureş (Mármaros) | 84,510 | 23·6 | 52,964 | 14·8 | 59,552 | 159,489 | 357,705 |
| Satu Mare (Szatmár) | 118,774 | 32·8 | 235,291 | 65·1 | 6,041 | — | 361,740 |
| Town of Satu Mare (Szatmár Néméti) | 986 | 2·8 | 33,094 | 94·9 | 629 | — | 34,892 |
| Salagiu (Szilágy) | 136,087 | 59·1 | 87,312 | 38·0 | 816 | — | 230,140 |
| Bihar | 261,494 | 44·9 | 307,221 | 52·8 | 2,183 | — | 582,132 |
| Town of Oradea Mare (Nagy-várad) | 3,604 | 5·6 | 58,421 | 91·1 | 1,416 | —<br>Serb | 64,169 |
| Arad | 229,476 | 65·3 | 78,130 | 22·2 | 34,330 | 322 | 351,222 |
| Town of Arad | 10,279 | 16·3 | 46,085 | 73·0 | 4,365 | 1,816 | 63,166 |
| Timiş (Temes) | 160,585 | 40·1 | 47,518 | 11·9 | 120,683 | 57,821 | 400,910 |
| Town of Timişoara (Temesvár) | 7,566 | 10·4 | 28,552 | 39·4 | 31,644 | 3,482 | 72,555 |
| Town of Vršac (Versecz) | 879 | 3·2 | 3,890 | 14·2 | 13,556 | 8,602 | 27,370 |
| Torontal | 86,168 | 14·5 | 125,041 | 21·0 | 158,312 | 191,036 | 594,343 |
| Town of Pančevo (Pancsova) | 769 | 3·7 | 3,364 | 16·2 | 7,467 | 8,714 | 20,808 |
| Caraş-Severin (Krassó-Szö-rény) | 336,082 | 72·1 | 33,787 | 7·3 | 55,883 | 14,674 | 466,147 |
| | 1,437,259 | 39·6 | 1,140,670 | 31·4 | 496,877 | 285,467 | 3,627,299 |
| Total in all Roumanian counties of the former Hungary | 2,909,300 | 46·1 | 2,058,887 | 32·6 | 731,962 | 285,476 | 6,305,666 |

# BIBLIOGRAPHY

## 1. GENERAL HISTORIES

### (*a*) ROUMANIA

ENGEL, J. C. VON. Geschichte der Moldau und Walachey. 2 vols. 1809.
HURMUZAKI, EUDOXIU. Fragmente zur Geschichte der Rumänen. 5 vols. Bucarest, 1878.
*IORGA, N. Geschichte des rumänischen Volkes. 2 vols. Gotha, 1905.
—— Histoire des Roumains de Transylvanie et de Hongrie. 2 vols. Bucarest, 1915.
—— A History of Roumania. London, 1925.
—— A History of Anglo-Roumanian Relations. Bucarest, 1931.
JIREČEK, CONST. Geschichte der Bulgaren. Prague, 1876.
—— Geschichte der Serben. 2 vols. Gotha, 1911–18
KOGĂLNICEANU, M. Histoire de la Valachie. Berlin, 1837.
—— Histoire de la Dacie des Valaques transdanubiens et de la Valachie. Berlin, 1854.
SINCAI, G. Hronica Romînilor. 3 vols. Bucarest, 1886.
STURDZA, A. A. C. La Terre et la Race Roumaine. Paris, 1904.
UBICINI, J. H. A. Les Origines de l'Histoire Roumaine. Paris, 1886.
URECHIA, G. Chronique de Moldavie. Ed. J. Picot. Paris, 1878.
URECHIA, V. A. Istoria Românilor. 2 vols. Bucarest, 1891.
*XENOPOL, A. D. Istoria Romînilor din Dacia Traiană. 6 vols. Jassy, 1888–94.
—— Histoire des Roumains. 2 vols. Paris, 1896.

### (*b*) HUNGARY

ACSÁDY, IGNÁCZ. A Magyar Birodalom története. 2 vols. Budapest, 1903.
ANDRÁSSY, COUNT JULIUS. The Constitutional Development of the Hungarian Nation. London, 1908.
ENGEL, J. C. VON. Geschichte des ungrischen Reiches und seiner Nebenländer, 1806.
FESSLER, IGNAZ A. Geschichte von Ungarn. 2nd ed. 5 vols. Leipzig, 1869.
FRIEDJUNG, HEINRICH. Oesterreich von 1848 bis 1860. 2 vols. Stuttgart, 1908–12.
HORVÁTH, MICHAEL. 25 Jahre aus der Gesch. Ungarns. 2 vols. Leipzig, 1867.

HUBER, ALFONS and REDLICH, OSWALD. Geschichte Oesterreichs. 6 vols. Gotha, 1888–1921.

KNATCHBULL-HUGESSEN, HON. C. M. The Political Evolution of the Hungarian Nation. London, 1908.

KRONES, FRANZ VON. Handbuch der Geschichte Oesterreichs. 4 vols. Berlin, 1881.

MAILÁTH, GRAF JOSEPH. Geschichte der Magyaren. 5 vols. Regensburg, 1852–3.

MARCZALI, H. A legújabb Xor története. Budapest, 1892.
—— Hungary in the Eighteenth Century. Cambridge, 1912.
—— Ungarische Verfassungsgeschichte. Tübingen, 1910.
—— Magyarország története. Budapest, 1913.

MÁRKI, A. and BEKSICS, GUSTAV. A modern Magyarország (vol. x of A Magy. nemzet története). Budapest, 1898.

REDLICH, JOSEF. Das österreichische Reichs- und Staatsproblem. 2 vols. Leipzig, 1922–9.

TIMON, AKOS VON. Ungarische Verfassungs- und Rechtsgeschichte. Berlin, 1904.

SAYOUS, ÉDOUARD. Histoire générale des Hongrois. Paris, n.d.

SZALAY, L. Geschichte Ungarns. 3 vols. Pest, 1866–74.

SZEKFÜ, J. Der Staat Ungarn. Budapest, 1918.

## (c) THE EASTERN QUESTION

BAMBERG, F. Geschichte der orientalischen Angelegenheit. Leipzig, 1888.

DRIAULT, E. La question d'Orient depuis ses origines. Paris, 1912.

GORIAINOV, SERGE. Le Bosphore et les Dardanelles. Paris, 1910.

*HAMMER, JOSEPH VON. Geschichte des Osmanischen Reiches. 2nd ed. 4 vols. Pest, 1836.

IORGA, N. Geschichte des Osmanischen Reiches. 5 vols. Gotha, 1908.

MARRIOTT, SIR JOHN. The Eastern Question. Oxford, 1915.

MILLER, WILLIAM. The Ottoman Empire. 2nd ed. Cambridge, 1923.

ROEPELL, R. Die orientalische Frage in ihrer geschichtlichen Entwicklung. Breslau, 1854.

SAX, CARL VON. Geschichte des Machtverfalls der Türkei. Vienna, 1913.

SOREL, ALBERT. La question d'Orient au XVIIIᵉ siècle. Paris, 1883.

ZINKEISEN, J. W. Geschichte des Osmanischen Reiches. 7 vols. Gotha, 1840–63.

## 2. PRINTED DOCUMENTS AND SOURCES

Anul 1848 în Principatele Române: Acte şi Documente. 6 vols. Bucarest, 1902–10.

*Aus dem Leben König Karls von Rumänien. 4 vols. Stuttgart, 1894.

*BALOGH, PÁL. Népfajok Magyarországon. Budapest, 1902.

BRĂTIANU, ION C. Din Scrierile şi Cuvântarile lũi Ion C. Brătianu: Pagini de Istorie Contemporana. Bucarest, 1921.

Dépêches inédites du Chevalier de Gentz aux hospodars de Valachie 1813–28. 3 vols. Paris, 1876–7.

HENRY, P. L'Abdication du Prince Cuza. Paris, 1930.

*HURMUZAKI, EUDOXIU. Documente privitore la Istoria Românilor. 30 vols. Bucarest, 1887–1908.

IORGA, N. Acte și Fragmente cu privire la Istoria Românilor. 6 vols. Bucarest, 1895, etc.
—— Correspondance diplomatique roumaine sous le Roi Charles I (1866–80). Paris, 1923.
—— Studii și Documente. 4 vols. Bucarest, 1901.
KOGĂLNICEANU, M. L. Acte și Documente. 2 vols. Bucarest, 1893.
ONCKEN, HERMANN. Die Rheinpolitik Napoleons III. 3 vols. Berlin, 1926.
*STURDZA, D. A. Acte și Documente relative la Istoria Renascerei Românieĭ. 9 vols. Bucarest, 1900–1.
—— Charles I Roi de Roumanie. 2 vols. Bucarest, 1899, 1904.
Ungarisches Statistisches Jahrbuch. 18 vols. Budapest (to 1912).

### 3. THE EIGHTEENTH CENTURY

BALTIMORE, LORD. A Tour to the East in the years 1763–4. London, 1767.
BAUER, GEN. VON. Mémoires historiques et géographiques sur la Valachie. Bucarest, 1884.
BLANCARD, T. Les Mavroyéni. 2 vols. Paris, 1893.
BOHRER, JOS. Bemerkungen auf einer Reise von der türk. Gränze über die Bukowina. Vienna, 1802.
BOSCOVICH, GIUSEPPE. Giornale d' un viaggio da Constantinopoli in Polonia. Bassano, 1784.
*CANTEMIR, D. Beschreibung der Moldau. Frankfurt, 1771.
CARRA, J. L. Histoire de la Moldavie et de la Valachie. Neufchâtel, 1781.
DAPONTES, CONSTANTINE. Éphémerides Daces. Ed. E. Legrand. Paris, 1880.
DEL CHIARO. Istoria delle moderne rivoluzioni della Valachia. Venice, 1718.
FILITTI, J. C. Rôle Diplomatique des Phanariotes de 1700 à 1821. Paris, 1901.
HAUTERIVE, COMTE. Mémoire sur l'État ancien et actuel de la Moldavie. Bucarest, 1902.
IORGA, N. Documente privitoare la familia Callimachi. Bucarest, 1902.
—— Documente privitoare la Constantin Vodă Brîncoveanu. Bucarest, 1901.
PERTUSIER, CHARLES. La Valachie, la Moldavie et l'influence politique des Grecs du Fanar. Paris, 1822.
POUQUEVILLE. Voyage dans la Grèce. Paris, 1824.
*RAICEVICH, F. Osservazioni storiche intorno la Valachia. 1788.
REGNAULT, ELIAS. Histoire politique et sociale des Danubiennes. Paris, 1855.
SOUTZO, NICHOLAS. Notions Statistiques sur la Moldavie. Jassy, 1849.
STURDZA, A. A. C. L'Europe Orientale et le Rôle Historique des Maurocordato (1660–1913). Paris, 1913.
THORNTON, T. Present State of Turkey. London, 1809.
VAILLANT, J. A. La Romanie. 3 vols. Paris, 1844.
*WILKINSON, WM. An account of the Principalities of Wallachia and Moldavia. London, 1820.
*ZALLONY, M. P. Essai sur les Fanariotes. Marseilles, 1824.

### 4. THE NINETEENTH CENTURY

ANAGNOSTI, M. La Valachie et la Moldavie. Paris, 1837.
ARICESCU, C. D. Istoria Revolutiei de la 1821. 2 vols. Bucarest, 1874.
BATTHYÁNY, GRAF VINCENZ. Reise nach Constantinopel. Pest, 1810.

BENGER, G. Roumania in 1900. London, 1901.
BERGNER, RUDOLF. Rumänien. Breslau, 1887.
BIBESCU. Le Règne de Georges Bibescu. 2 vols. Paris, 1893.
BLARAMBERG, N. Essai comparé sur la Roumanie. Paris, 1885.
BOITOS, O. Bataillard et la Révolution roumaine. Paris, 1930.
BOLLIAC, CÉSAR. Mémoires pour servir à l'histoire de la Roumanie. Paris, 1855.
BRATISCH, L. Dr Strousberg und seine Ingenieure. Berlin, 1872.
COLSON, FÉLIX. De l'État présent et de l'avenir des Principautés. Paris, 1839.
*CORTI, E. C. Alexander von Battenberg. Vienna, 1920.
*DAMÉ, F. Histoire de la Roumanie Contemporaine. Paris, 1900.
*EAST, W. G. The Union of Moldavia and Wallachia. Cambridge, 1927.
*ELIADE, I. Mémoires sur l'histoire de la Régénération roumaine. Paris, 1851.
ELIADE, POMPILIU. Histoire de l'esprit public en Roumanie. 2 vols. Paris, 1905.
* —— De l'influence française sur l'esprit public en Roumanie. Paris, 1898.
GOLESCU, A. G. De l'abolition du servage dans les Principautés. Paris, 1856.
GROTHE, HUGO. Zur Landeskunde von Rumänien. Halle, 1907.
KOSSUTH, L. Meine Schriften aus der Emigration. 3 vols. Pressburg, 1880.
LAURENÇON. Nouvelles Observations sur la Valachie. Paris, 1821.
LINDENBERG, PAUL. König Karl von Rumänien. Berlin, 1908.
MEDLICOTT, W. N. The Recognition of Roumanian Independence (Slavonic Review, nos. 30, 31).
NISTOR, I. I. Der nationale Kampf in der Bukowina. Bucarest, 1918.
RECORDON. Lettres sur la Valachie. Paris, 1821.
REGNAULT, ELIAS. Histoire politique et sociale des Principautés Danubiennes. Paris, 1855.
*RIKER, T. W. The Making of Roumania. Oxford, 1931.
ROSETTI, R. Pământul, Ţaranii şi Stâpaniĭ în Moldova. Bucarest, 1907.
La Roumanie 1866–1906. (Publication of Ministry of Agriculture.) Bucarest, 1907.
SALABERRY, COMTE DE. Essai sur la Valachie et la Moldavie. Paris, 1821.
SAMUELSON, J. Roumania Past and Present. London, 1882.
SCHLITTER, HANS. Aus der Regierungszeit Franz Josefs. Vienna, 1899.
SLAVICÍ, J. Die Rumänen. Vienna, 1883.
SOUTZO, PRINCE NICHOLAS. Mémoires. Vienna, 1899.
STURDZA, A. A. C. De l'histoire diplomatique des Roumains (1821–59). Paris, 1907.
THOUVENEL, ED. La Hongrie et la Valachie. Paris, 1840.
WHITMAN, SIDNEY. Reminiscences of the King of Roumania. London, 1899.
*XENOPOL, A. D. Domnia luĭ Cuza-Vodă. 2 vols. Bucarest, 1902.
—— Les Roumains. Paris, 1905.
*ZABLOCKI-DESJATOVSKI, A. P. Graf P. D. Kiselev i ego Vremya. 4 vols. St Petersburg, 1882.

## 5. THE TWENTIETH CENTURY

ANTONESCU, C. G. Die rumänische Handelspolitik 1875–1910. Leipzig, 1915.
AUERBACH, B. Les Races et les Nationalités en Autriche-Hongrie. Paris, 1917.
BAERNREITHER, J. M. Fragments of a Political Diary. Ed. J. Redlich. London, 1930.

Bănescu, N. and Mihăilescu, Ioan Maiorescu. Scriere Comemorativă. Bucarest, 1912.

Barbulescu, Ilie. Relations des Roumains avec les Serbes, les Bulgares, les Grecs. Jassy, 1912.

Bratter, C. A. Die kutzowalachische Frage. Hamburg, 1907.

Bülow, Bernhard von. Denkwürdigkeiten, iii, iv. Berlin, 1931.

Clopoţel, Ion. Revoluţia din 1918. Cluj, 1926.

Cramon, A. von. Unser öst-ung. Bundesgenosse. Berlin, 1922.

Creanga, G. D. Grundbesitzverteilung und Bauernfrage in Rumänien, 1907.

Dillon, E. J. The Peace Conference. London, 1920.

Djuvara, T. G. Mes Missions diplomatiques 1887–1925. Paris, 1908.

Dragu, T. La politique roumaine après les troubles agraires de 1907. Paris, 1908.

Eisenmann, Louis. Le compromis austro-hongrois. Paris, 1904.

Emmerit, M. Victor Place. Bucarest, 1931.

Encyclopaedia Britannica (12th, 13th, 14th Editions). Articles on Roumania, Serbia, Hungary, Austria, Bulgaria.

Evans, Ifor L. The Agrarian Revolution in Roumania. Cambridge, 1924.

Erzberger, M. Erlebnisse im Weltkrieg. Berlin, 1920.

Georgescu, C. C. La Réforme agraire en Roumanie. Paris, 1908.

*Glaise-Horstenau, E. von. The Collapse of the Austro-Hungarian Empire. London, 1930.

Hilfferich, K. Der Weltkrieg, iii. Berlin, 1919.

Horváth, Eugene. Responsibility of Hungary for the War. Budapest, 1933.

Iancovici, D. Take Jonesco. Paris, 1919.

—— La Paix de Bucarest. Paris, 1918.

Immanuel, Col. Der Balkankrieg 1912–13. 6 Hefte. Berlin, 1913.

Ionescu, Take. Souvenirs. Paris, 1919.

—— La politique étrangère de la Roumanie. Bucarest, 1891.

Jászi, Oscar. The Dissolution of the Habsburg Monarchy. Chicago, 1929.

Logio, G. Clenton. Roumania, its History, Politics and Economics. Manchester, 1932.

Maiorescu, Titu. Zur politischen Lage Rumäniens (Deutsche Revue, Jan. 1881).

*Marghiloman, A. Note Politice 1897–1934. 5 vols. Bucarest, 1927.

*Mitrany, D. The Land and the Peasant in Roumania. Oxford, 1930.

Nagy, V. A Románia elléni hadjárat. Budapest, 1925.

Naumann, Friedrich. Bulgarien und Mitteleuropa. Berlin, 1916.

Noua Constituţia României. Ed. D. Gusti (23 essays). Bucarest, 1922.

Nowak, K. F. Chaos. Munich, 1923.

Ollivier, Émile. L'Empire Libéral, viii. Paris, 1906.

Opočensky, Jan. Umsturz in Mitteleuropa. Dresden, 1931.

Pittard, E. La Roumanie. Paris, 1919.

*Popovici, Aurel C. Die Vereinigten Staaten von Gross-Oesterreich. Leipzig, 1906.

—— La Question roumaine en Transylvanie et en Hongrie. Paris, 1918.

Roucek, Joseph S. Contemporary Roumania and her Problems. Stanford (U.S.), 1932.

Rubin, A. Les Roumains de Macédoine. Bucarest, 1913.

Russu Sirianu, M. La Question de Transylvanie et l'unité politique roumaine. Paris, 1916.

SARRAIL, GENERAL. Mon Commandement en Orient. Paris, 1920.
SCHMIDT-PAULI, EDGAR VON. Graf Stefan Bethlen. Berlin, 1930.
ŞERBAN, M. Rumäniens Agrarverhältnisse. Berlin, 1914.
SETON-WATSON, R. W. Racial Problems in Hungary. London, 1908.
—— Corruption and Reform in Hungary. London, 1911.
—— Sarajevo. London, 1926.
—— Roumania and the Great War. London, 1915.
SOSNOSKY, THEODOR VON. Franz Ferdinand. Munich, 1929.
—— Die Politik im Habsburgerreich. 2 vols. Berlin, 1912.
STIENON, C. Le Mystère Roumain. Paris, 1918.
Studi sulla Romania (Istituto per l' Europa Orientale). Naples, 1923.
TILEA, V. V. Acţiunea Diplomatica a României. Sibiu, 1925.
URSU, J. Pourquoi la Roumanie a fait la Guerre. Paris, 1918.
WACE, A. J. B. and THOMPSON, M. S. The Nomads of the Balkans. London, 1914.
WEDEL, O. H. Austro-German Diplomatic Relations. Stanford (U.S.), 1932.
WERTHEIMER, E. VON. Graf Julius Andrássy. 3 vols. Vienna, 1910–13.

## 6. TRANSYLVANIA

ASZTALOS, M. Wesselényi Miklos az elsö nemzetiségi politikus. Budapest, 1927.
BARIŢIU, G. Parti alese din Istoria Transilvaniei. 3 vols. Bucarest, 1889–91.
BENKÖ, JOSEPH. Transsilvania. 2 vols. Vienna, 1778.
BERGNER, RUDOLF. Siebenbürgen. Leipzig, 1884.
BETHLEN, WOLFGANG. Historia de Rebus Transsylvanicis. Ed. Benkö. Cibinii, 1782–93.
*BONER, CHARLES. Transylvania: its Products and its Peoples. London, 1865.
Briefe Kossuths an Bem. Ed. Aladar Makray. Pest, 1870.
BROTE, EUGEN. Die rumänische Frage in Siebenbürgen und Ungarn. Berlin, 1895.
BUNEA, AUGUSTIN. Episcopul Ioan Inocenţiu Klein. Blaj, 1900.
—— Episcopii P.P. Aron şi Novacovici. Blaj, 1902.
Compilatae et Approbatae Constitutiones Transilvaniae et Partium Hungariae eidem annexarum. Claudiopoli, 1671–7.
Corpus Juris Hungarici. 7 vols. Budapest.
CZETZ, J. Bems Feldzug in Siebenbürgen. Leipzig, 1850.
DENSUŞIANU, N. Revoluţiunea lŭi Hora. Bucarest, 1884.
DRAGOMIR, SILVIU. Istoria Desrobirei Religoase a Românilor din Ardeal. Sibiu, 1920.
—— Avram Iancu. Sibiu, 1925.
FIEDLER, JOSEF. Die Union der Walachen in Siebenbürgen. Vienna, 1858.
FRIEDENFELS, EUGEN VON. Joseph Bedeus von Scharberg: Beiträge zur Zeitgesch. Siebenbürgens. 2 vols. Hermannstadt, 1877–85.
GERANDO, A. DE. La Transylvanie. 2 vols. Paris.
HERRMANN, G. M. G. VON. Das alte and neue Kronstadt.
HINTZ, JOHANN. Gesch. des Bisthums der griech.-nichtunierten Glaubensgenossen in Siebenbürgen. Hermannstadt, 1850.
HUBER, ALFONS. Die Erwerbung Siebenbürgens.
Hundert Jahre sächsische Kampfe. Hermannstadt, 1896.
*JANCSÓ, BENEDEK. A Román nemzetiségi törekvések törţénete. 2 vols. Budapest, 1896.

JARAY, GABRIEL. La question sociale en Hongrie. Paris, 1909.

KEMÉNY, ZSIGMOND. Forradalom után. Pest, 1850.

KURZ, ANTON. Magazin für siebenbürgische Landeskunde. 3 vols. Hermannstadt, 1844–52.

Kurze Geschichte der Rebellion in Siebenbürgen. Strasburg, 1785.

LÖHER, FRANZ VON. Die Magyaren und andere Ungarn. Leipzig, 1874.

*LUPAŞ, IOAN. Istoria Bisericeasca a Românilor Ardeleni. Sibiu, 1918.

—— Mitropolitul Andreiu Şaguna. Sibiu, 1911.

MOROIANU, G. Les luttes des Roumains Transylvains et l'opinion européenne. Paris, 1933.

OBERT, FRANZ. Stephan Ludwig Roth: sein Leben und seine Schriften. 2 vols. Vienna, 1896.

*PACAŢIAN, T. Cartea de Aur. 8 vols. Sibiu, 1902–15.

Sammlung der wichtigeren Staatsacten, Oesterreich, Ungarn und Siebenbürgen betreffend. Hermannstadt, 1861.

SCHAGUNA, ANDREAS. Gesch. der griechisch-orientalischen Kirche in Oesterreich. Hermannstadt, 1862.

SCHASER, J. G. Denkwürdigkeiten aus dem Leben des Freih. von Brukenthal. Hermannstadt, 1848.

SCHULER VON LIBLOY, F. Siebenbürgische Rechtsgeschichte. 3 vols. Hermannstadt, 1854.

SCHULLER, J. C. Beleuchtung der Klagschrift. Hermannstadt, 1844.

Der siebenbürgische Landtag. Hermannstadt, 1863.

SILBERNAGL, J. Verfassung und gegenwärtiger Bestand sämmtlicher Kirchen des Orients.

SLAVICI, J. Die Rumänen in Ungarn, Siebenbürgen und Bukowina. Vienna, 1881.

SZEMERE, B. Batthyány, Gorgei, Kossuth. Hamburg, 1853.

SZILÁGYI, F. Az Erdélyi Unió. Pest, 1861.

—— A Hora Világ. Budapest, 1871.

SZILÁGYI, SÁNDOR. Erdélyország története. 2 vols. Pest, 1866.

TELEKI, DOMINIK. A Hora támadás. Pest, 1865.

*TEUTSCH, G. D. and FRIEDRICH. Geschichte der siebenbürger Sachsen. 3 vols. Hermannstadt, 1899–1908.

VIROZSIL, ANTON VON. Das Staatsrecht des Königreichs Ungarn. 3 vols. Pest, 1865.

WATTENBACH, W. Die siebenbürger Sachsen. Heidelberg, 1882, 1843.

WESSELÉNYI, BARON M. Szózat a magyar és szláv ügyében. Leipzig, 1842.

Die Zertrümmerung des siebenbürgischen Sachsenlandes. 1876.

ZIEGLAUER, F. VON. Die politische Reformbewegung in Siebenbürgen. Vienna, 1885.

## 7. PAMPHLETS

Anon.

1858. Paris. Les Principautés Roumaines et l'Empire Ottoman.

Paris. L'Empereur Napoléon III et l'Angleterre.

Paris. Les Principautés devant le Second Congrès de Paris.

Paris. L'Empereur Napoléon III et les Principautés Roumaines.

Paris. L'Autriche et les Principautés Danubiennes.

1859. Paris. L'Autriche et le Prince Roumain.
1865. Paris. La Convention de Gastein.
BALCESCU, G. Questions Économiques des Principautés. Paris, 1850.
BIBESCU, G. Quelques Mots sur la Valachie. 1847.
BOERESCU, B. La Roumanie après le Traité de Paris. Paris, 1857.
BOERESCU, M. B. Étude sur la condition des Étrangers d'après la législation roumaine. Paris, 1899.
BRĂTIANU, D. Documents concerning the Danubian Principalities. London, 1849.
BRĂTIANU, D. and GOLESCU, N. The Danubian Principalities. London, 1858.
BRĂTIANU, D. and IRANYI, D. Lettres Hongro-Roumaines. Paris, 1851.
BRĂTIANU, G. Le Panslavisme et ses dangers pour l'Europe. Paris, 1877.
BRĂTIANU, I. C. Mémoire sur l'Empire d'Autriche dans la Question d'Orient. Paris, 1855.
—— Mémoire sur la situation de la Moldo-Valachie depuis le Traité de Paris. Paris, 1857.
CHAINOI (Ion GHICA). Dernière Occupation des Principautés Danubiennes par la Russie. Paris, 1851.
ELIADE-RADULESCU, I. P. Le Protectorat du Czar. Paris, 1850.
KOSSUTH, L. L'Europe, l'Autriche et la Hongrie. Brussels, 1859.
REGNAULT, E. Mouravieff et les Archives du Tzarisme. Paris, 1863.
—— Mystères diplomatiques aux bords du Danube. Paris, 1858.
Siebenbürgen und die österreichische Regierung in den letzten 4 Jahren. Leipzig, 1865.
UBICINI, M. La Question d'Orient devant l'Europe. Paris, 1854.
—— La Question des Principautés devant l'Europe. Paris, 1858.
—— L'Empereur Napoléon et les Principautés. Paris, 1858.

## 8. ROUMANIAN ORIGINS

BERTHA, A. DE. Magyars et Roumains devant l'Histoire. Paris, 1899.
BRIEBRECHER, R. Der gegenwärtige Stand der Frage über die Herkunft der Rumänen. Hermannstadt, 1897.
FISCHER, Dr E. Die Herkunft der Rumänen. Bamberg, 1904.
HUNFALVY, P. Ethnographie von Ungarn. Budapest, 1877.
—— Az Oláhok. 2 vols. Budapest, 1894.
JUNG, JULIUS. Römer und Rumänen in den Donauländern. Innsbruck, 1877.
MACARTNEY, C. A. The Magyars in the Ninth Century. Cambridge, 1930.
MIKLOSICH, F. Die slavischen Elemente im Rumänischen. Vienna, 1861.
MOLDOVAN, GERGELY. A Románság. 2 vols. Nagy Becskerek, 1895.
ROESLER, R. Rumänische Studien. 1871.
TAMM, T. Über den Ursprung der Rumänen. Bonn, 1891.
XENOPOL, A. D. Une énigme historique: les Roumains au Moyen Âge. Paris, 1885.

## 9. POLEMICS

Die Ausrottung des Deutschtums in Ungarn. Hermannstadt, 1881.
BÁNFFY, BARON D. A Magyar nemzetiségi Politika. Budapest, 1902.
DRAGOMIR, SILVIU. The Ethnical Minorities in Transylvania. Geneva, 1927.
HUNFALVY, PAL. Die Rumänen und ihre Ansprüche. Vienna, 1883.
—— Az Oláhok története. 2 vols. 1894.

HUNGARICUS. Das magyarische Ungarn und der Dreibund. Munich, 1899.
JONNESCO, THOMAS. La Question Roumaine. 2 vols. Paris, 1919.
KORODI, LUTZ. Ungarische Rhapsodien. Munich, 1905.
LAHOVARI, I. The Jewish Question in Roumania.
LÖHER, F. VON. Das Erwürgen der Deutschen Nationalität in Ungarn. Munich, 1874.
MERCATOR. Die Nationalitätenfrage und die ungarische Reichsidee. Budapest, 1908.
PAPIU ILARIANU, A. Die constitutionelle Unabhängigkeit Siebenbürgens. Breslau, 1862.
RUMÄNE, EIN. Die Sprachen- und Nationalitätenfrage in Oesterreich. Vienna, 1860.
STURDZA, D. A. Europa, Russland und Rümanien. Berlin, 1915.
SYDACOFF, BRESNITZ VON. Die Wahrheit über Ungarn. Berlin, 1903.
SZÁSZ, ZSOMBOR DE. The Minorities in Roumanian Transylvania. London, 1927.
VERAX. La Roumanie et les Juifs. Bucarest, 1903.
Programmes Politiques des Roumains de la Transylvanie. Bucarest, 1894.
"Reply." Die Ungarischen Rumänen und die Ungarische Nation: Antwort der Hochschuljugend Ungarns auf das Memorandum der Rumänischen Universitätsjugend. Budapest, 1891.
"Réplique." The Roumanian Question in Transylvania and Hungary: Reply of the Roumanian Students of Hungary. Vienna, 1892.

## 10. RECENT DIPLOMATIC HISTORY

*A.H.D.* = Oesterreich-Ungarns Aussenpolitik (1908–14). Ed. L. Bittner, A. F. Pribram, H. Srbik, H. Uebersberger. 8 vols. Vienna, 1930.
*B.D.* = British Documents on the Origins of the War. Ed. G. P. Gooch, H. W. V. Temperley, Lillian Penson. 10 vols. 1926–34.
*D.A.* = Diplomatische Aktenstücke zur Vorgeschichte des Krieges. 3 vols. Vienna, 1919.
*D.D.* = Die deutschen Dokumente zum Kriegsausbruch. Ed. Karl Kautsky, Graf Montgelas, W. Schücking. 4 vols. Charlottenburg, 1919.
*F.D.D.* = Documents Diplomatiques Français (1871–1914). 3rd Series. 14 vols. Paris, 1929–34.
*G.P.* = Die Grosse Politik der europäischen Kabinette (1871–1914). Ed. J. Lepsius, A. Mendelssohn-Bartholdy, F. Thimme. 51 vols. 1919–26.
*R.D.* = Internationale Beziehungen im Zeitalter des Imperialismus. Dokumente aus den russischen Archiven. Ed. O. Hoetzsch. Reihe I. 1914. 4 vols. Berlin, 1931–3.

BALCANICUS (STOJAN PROTIĆ). The Aspirations of Bulgaria. London, 1915.
BETHLEN, COUNT STEPHEN. Beszédei és Irásai. 2 vols. Budapest, 1933.
BOGIČEVIĆ, M. Kriegsursachen. Berlin, 1919.
BRANDENBURG, ERICH. Von Bismarck zum Weltkriege. Berlin, 1924.
BÜLOW, FÜRST BERNHARD VON. Denkwürdigkeiten. Vols. III and IV. Berlin, 1931.
CONRAD VON HÖTZENDORF, MARSCHALL. Aus meiner Dienstzeit. 4 vols. Vienna, 1919–22.
CZERNIN, COUNT OTTOKAR. In the World War. London, 1919.

Diplomatische Schriftwechsel Iswolskis (1911–14). 4 vols. Berlin, 1924.
GOOSS, RODERICH. Das Wiener Kabinett und die Entstehung des Weltkrieges. Vienna, 1919.
GUESCHOFF, IVAN. The Balkan League. London, 1915.
History of the Peace Conference. Ed. H. W. V. Temperley. Vol. IV. Oxford, 1921.
HORVÁTH, EUGENE. Magyar Diplomácia 1815–1918. Budapest, 1928.
Iswolski im Weltkriege: Diplomatische Schriftwechsel 1914–17. Ed. F. Stieve. Berlin, 1925.
JÄCKH, E. Kiderlen-Waechter: der Mann und der Staatsmann. 2 vols. Berlin. 1927.
L' Intervento dell' Italia nei Documenti Segreti dell' Intesa. Rome, 1923.
Un Livre Noir. Ed. René Marchand. 3 vols. Paris, 1922–3.
POINCARÉ, RAYMOND. Les Balkans en Feu. Paris, 1926.
PRIBRAM, A. F. Die Geheimverträge Oesterreich-Ungarns. Vienna, 1919.
—— Austrian Foreign Policy, 1908–18. London, 1923.
RADOSLAVOV, V. Bulgarien und die Weltkrise. Berlin, 1923.
RENOUVIN, P. Les Origines Immédiates de la Guerre. Paris, 1925.
SETON-WATSON, R. W. Sarajevo. London, 1926.
SIEBERT, B. Diplom. Aktenstücke zur Gesch. der Ententepolitik der Vorkriegsjahre. Berlin, 1921.
STIEVE, F. Isvolsky and the World War. London, 1926.
TISZA, ISTVÁN. Összes Munkai. 5 vols. Budapest, 1926–34.


## 11. ROUMANIAN ART AND CULTURE

### (A few selected works.)

Curtea Domneasca din Argeş (Buletinul Comisiunii Monumentelor Istorice). Bucarest, 1923. Illustrated.
GASTER, MOSES. Roumanian Literature (Encycl. Britannica, 11th ed.).
—— Chrestomathie Roumaine. 2 vols. Leipzig, 1891.
—— Geschichte der rumänischen Literatur (in Grober's Grundriss der romanischen Philologie, vol. II).
IORGA, N. and BALŞ, G. L'Art Roumain. Paris, 1922. Ill.
OPRESCU, GEORGE. Peasant Art in Roumania (The Studio). London, 1929. Ill.
PÂRVAN, V. Dacia. Cambridge, 1929. Ill.
PETRESCU, STELIAN. Calăuza Cailor Ferate Romane. Bucarest, 1930. Ill.
TZIGARA-SAMURCAS, AL. Arta în Romania. Bucarest, 1909. Ill.
VLAHUŢA, A. La Roumanie Pittoresque. Paris, 1908. Ill.
—— N. I. Grigoresco: sa Vie et son Œuvre. Bucarest, 1911.
Domnii Români dupa Portete şi Fresce Contemporane. Ed. N. Iorga. (Comisiunea Monumentelor Istorice.) Sibiu, 1929. Illustrations only.
Transilvania, Banatul, Crişana, Maramureşul 1918–28. 3 vols. Bucarest (Cultura Nationala), 1929. Ill.

# INDEX